Fire and Rain

Fire and Rain

Nixon, Kissinger, and the Wars in Southeast Asia

CAROLYN WOODS EISENBERG

OXFORD
UNIVERSITY PRESS

OXFORD
UNIVERSITY PRESS

Oxford University Press is a department of the University of Oxford. It furthers the University's objective of excellence in research, scholarship, and education by publishing worldwide. Oxford is a registered trade mark of Oxford University Press in the UK and certain other countries.

Published in the United States of America by Oxford University Press
198 Madison Avenue, New York, NY 10016, United States of America.

CIP data is on file at the Library of Congress

ISBN 978–0–19–763906–1

DOI: 10.1093/oso/9780197639061.001.0001

1 3 5 7 9 8 6 4 2

Printed by Sheridan Books, Inc., United States of America

Dedicated to my grandchildren:
Mia, Lucia, Sam, Cecilia Jane, Nina, and Eli
With love and hope

Contents

Acknowledgments

When I began this project I imagined a narrow, relatively brief study of Vietnam policy during the Nixon years. While there was considerable declassified material available at the time, I was unprepared for the avalanche of material about this presidency that has appeared over the previous fifteen years. The richness of these sources enables more insight into the foreign policy operations of an administration than we are likely to see again. In response, my conception of the topic widened considerably and has taken much longer and required more help from fellow historians, friends, and family than I ever anticipated.

Above all, this book reflects conversations with students. During decades of teaching, I realized the importance of integrating the study of high-level policy with an examination of its impact on people's lives. Absent that connection, then either subject loses its significance. Additionally, students' impatience with an exclusive focus on two or three men at the pinnacle of power (in this instance Richard Nixon and Henry Kissinger) compelled a wider inquiry: what were the societal and institutional forces that shaped their decision-making? And finally, how did the war in Vietnam, Cambodia, and Laos fit with broader trends in US foreign policy? Or more precisely, how to explain the paradox of an administration avidly seeking improved relations with Moscow and Beijing, while raining destruction on these smaller nations?

I hope this book will provide some answers to these questions. Without students' voices in my head, this work would not have been possible.

Among historians in related fields, I have received assistance of various kinds—from shared documents, insightful conversations, and close reading of individual chapters. I am especially grateful to: Chris Appy, Andrew Bacevich, Kai Bird, Bob Brigham, Gregory Daddis, the late Todd Gitlin, Jeffrey Kimball, Lien-Hang Nguyen, Arnold Offner, John Prados, David Schmitz, and the late Martin Sherwin. I am especially indebted to Elsa Dixler, an historian, friend and editor, who supported this work from beginning to end, bringing clarity out of fog.

I have been fortunate to have thoughtful, generous friends who were willing to read portions of the manuscript, offer pertinent advice, and reassure me that the content was truly significant. Among them were Fran Dreier, Barbara Epstein, Bill and Marlene Fried, Steve Leberstein, Judith Liben, Daniel and Barbara Pope, Margaret Power, Rosalind Pollak, Martha Saxton and Susan Yohn To concentrate on writing, I spent several summers in Amherst, where I received valuable advice from college friend Randy Ross, who had gone to Vietnam during the war and who was editing an English translation of Madame Binh's memoirs. Through Randy I was fortunate to meet with Lady Borton, who has lived in Vietnam for years and is a fountain of information and fresh insights.

Sadly, three people who played a vital role in this project are now deceased. Stanley Kutler believed in this work from the beginning, continually reminded me of its importance, readily shared his encyclopedic Nixon knowledge, and assisted me with archival access. A mellow Tom Hayden gave useful advice for my Vietnam trip, shared his insights about Congressional work past and present, and left ringing in my ears his admonition, "Hurry up!" And finally, Marilyn Young, who encouraged this book early on and for the last eighteen months of her life suggested, quipped, nagged, and argued with me—never losing her outrage at the destruction and suffering caused by the Vietnam War.

This book would not have seen the light of day without the support of two superb agents: Steve Wasserman, who helped me craft a proposal and to think carefully about "the arc of the story," and Katherine Flynn, who advised me through the vicissitudes of publication and whose confidence in this manuscript never wavered.

I remain especially indebted to freelance editor Beth Rashbaum, who entered this project at a critical time. Over an extended period, she helped me pare down a too cumbersome, detailed manuscript, while skillfully retaining the intertwined threads that kept this a coherent narrative. Beth's professionalism in the art of writing is matched by her profound attention to content. She was constantly alert to factual mistakes and did not hesitate to verify claims when they seemed unsupported or contradictory.

Historians rely on their archivists, and I was especially fortunate in having the assistance of John Powers at the Nixon Project in the National Archives, Donald Davis at the American Friends Service Committee Library, and Steve Maxner at the Texas Tech Vietnam Center and Sam Johnson Archive.

In Vietnam, the staff at the Vietnam-USA Friendship Society, headed by Bui Van Nghi, were efficient and gracious, facilitating travel for my husband and me, arranging for translators, meetings, and interviews with former officials, veterans, and other participants in the war. Especially helpful was To Ngoc Linh, who served as a guide and translator—and in his thoughtful way made the experience more meaningful.

Early in the trip, former Vice President Nguyen Thi Binh (Madame Binh) predicted that I would encounter a welcoming attitude by most Vietnamese. During the war, Ho Chi Minh had emphasized that the American people were not the enemy, only its government. In the postwar period, this perspective was reinforced by the numerous US veterans who had come back to Vietnam to work on humanitarian projects. Throughout our travels we were touched by the friendly response of young people, as well as the eagerness of those from the older generation to tell their stories.

Two Hofstra undergraduates, Ariel Flajnik and Carlos Gonzalez, did valuable research for this book. I am also indebted to Hofstra University for three Special Leaves and several Faculty Research Grants in support of this work. I benefitted as well from a Fellowship at the Cold War History Project, Tamiment Library, New York University, and a National Endowment for the Humanities (NEH) Summer Seminar Directorship. For the latter, an amazing gathering of high school teachers added depth to my inquiries.

During the last two years of this project, Susan Ferber, history editor at Oxford University Press, has assisted me with her confidence, superb judgement, and rapid ability to improve text. Working with her has been a privilege and pleasure.

My work on *Fire and Rain* has gone on for more years than I like to count—long enough to burden even my grandchildren. However, for sheer endurance and loving support special recognition goes to my husband Allan, who has sustained more life disruptions, carried more boxes, and heard more stories about Richard Nixon than any life partner should endure. In important ways, we have traversed this history together—from watching the 1968 carnage in Hue on our black-and-white television to visiting the Citadel four decades later, on a bright sunny day, as Vietnamese school children romped in a park.

During these last years of writing, my daughter Lizzy has served as my invaluable technology therapist, constantly reassuring me that "No, we haven't erased the whole book." For Lizzy and the others in my immediate family—Jenny, Annie, Miguel, and Jeremiah—I love you all and am constantly grateful for your joyful presence.

Map 1 Map of Southeast Asia

Fire and Rain

Introduction

"This Is Not Frivolous, Mr. Chairman"

It was viewed as an awesome responsibility. For members of the House Judiciary Committee, whatever they had said about Richard Nixon in the past, whether in anger or admiration, a decision to approve articles of impeachment weighed heavily. If approved, it would go to the full House of Representatives for a vote; and if the vote was in favor of impeachment, then the US Senate would decide whether the president was guilty of "high crimes and misdemeanors." While theirs was only the first step in the process, members of the Judiciary Committee had strong reasons to believe that what they collectively decided could determine the fate of the president of the United States. More than a century had passed since the last time Congress had entertained such a possibility. And it was no small thing to unseat a president—especially Richard Nixon, who in his re-election effort had carried every state in the union but one.

From May 9 through July 30, 1974, the Committee (consisting of 36 men and two women) pored over books of documents, questioned witnesses, weighed the arguments of counsel, and debated with one another. Its chairman, Democrat Peter Rodino, wanted to focus on the first three articles of impeachment; seeking to minimize party divisions, he believed those to be the most likely to find some measure of bipartisan support. Each of these three articles pertained to domestic crimes linked in some fashion to the Watergate break-in and subsequent investigations.

Since June of 1972, when seven men were arrested for illegally entering the headquarters of the Democratic National Committee in the Watergate Hotel, there had been a steady drip and then a flood of revelations about the administration's misuse of power. This break-in, which seemed inexplicable on the surface, had been executed by a "Plumbers" group connected to the White House and specifically to the Committee to Re-elect the President (CREEP). The "Plumbers," it emerged, had been responsible for illegal eavesdropping, burglaries, intimidation, and "dirty tricks."

Because the connection to the White House would be so damaging to Nixon if it came to light, there had been a wide-ranging cover-up designed to insulate him from the crime. During the 1972 election season, White House lawyer John Dean had successfully managed this task. However, since the inauguration the official story had steadily unraveled, and by the spring Dean himself had become a hostile witness. Over the course of the following year, more details had emerged about the administration's illegal efforts to suppress this and other scandals. By the time the House Judiciary Committee convened, key members of the president's team were facing felony charges, among them former Chief of Staff H. R. "Bob" Haldeman, Assistant to the President John Ehrlichman, Special Counsel Chuck Colson, and former Attorney General John Mitchell.

Given the weight of evidence, it was no surprise that a majority of the committee voted in favor of the first three articles: Article I, which accused the president of personally acting to obstruct justice in the Watergate case; Article II charging him with persistent misuse of his authority in upholding the country's laws; and Article III faulting him for defying subpoenas of his records and withholding other evidence pertinent to the impeachment process.[1] With their passage, it became unlikely that Richard Nixon would finish out his term of office.

Cast into oblivion were two other articles of impeachment, which were rejected by a majority on the committee. One of these had relatively narrow significance—the accusation that the president had underpaid federal income tax and accepted government financing of improvements to his personal homes. But Article IV had a much wider reach and sparked intense debate among committee members. Introduced by Representative John Conyers of Michigan, it charged the president with "the submission to the Congress of false and misleading statements concerning the existence, scope and nature of American bombing operations in Cambodia in derogation of the power of the Congress to declare war, to make appropriations and to raise and support armies."

For some Americans, any reference to Cambodia could evoke deep emotions. The uproar surrounding the president's decision to send troops in April 1970 had produced the largest antiwar protest of Nixon's first term, culminating in an explosion of dissent and some violence on college campuses, most memorably the shooting and deaths of four students at Kent State University.

The US invasion of Cambodia, which had been publicly announced, was not the primary focus of the proposed article. Instead, it was the fourteen months of covert bombing of Cambodia that Nixon had ordered prior to the ground invasion. During this period, B-52 bombers had launched 3,695 attacks on that country, despite the president's repeated insistence that the United States had never intervened there prior to the invasion.[2]

The dishonesty of that claim had only garnered attention in July 1973, when retired Major Hal Knight testified to the Senate Armed Services Committee that in his capacity as supervisor of radar crews in South Vietnam, he had helped falsify the flight records of at least two dozen missions by disguising American air strikes in Cambodia as attacks inside South Vietnam. In an elaborate arrangement, the real coordinates for the planes were hand-delivered to Knight by a courier from General Creighton Abrams' headquarters in Saigon, and then given to the pilots. Once the flights returned, there was a dual system of reporting in which fake information was entered into the Pentagon computers while Knight would gather and burn the incriminating documents. To signify a successful mission, he would place a call and report to an anonymous official in Saigon: "The ball game is over."[3]

The Senate Armed Services Committee quickly learned that Knight's experience was part of a larger pattern of falsifying records to hide the bombing of Cambodia from the American public and from Congress. So far-reaching was the secrecy surrounding this undeclared war that even the civilian Secretary of the Air Force, Robert Seaman, was not informed.[4]

Who had orchestrated the elaborate system of deception? In the aftermath of Knight's testimony, many wished to know. However, one thing was clear: President Nixon had ordered both the bombing and its concealment. By so doing, he had effectively denied members of Congress the opportunity to debate or vote on whether to authorize this military action in an officially "neutral" country.

Unlike the other charges the Judiciary Committee had considered, the veracity of the Cambodia charge was not disputed. Whatever the motive, the Nixon administration had clearly deceived Congress with the intent to sidestep its prerogative to declare war and appropriate funds for that purpose. Conyers wanted the Judiciary Committee to reaffirm that legislative responsibility:

> Many people don't know or have forgotten that the Congress constitutionally has that sole authority. And so, I would urge that we in an attempt to

> reassert those powers which we consider vital and precious, if the constitutional form of government is to prevail and continue and improve, that we give the gravest consideration to this article.[5]

He also contended that it was the desire to hide the bombing that had led to the "unparalleled" use of wiretaps and illegal surveillance of journalists and government officials.

The congressman was referring to events prompted by a May 1969 *New York Times* article in which Pentagon correspondent William Beecher reported that American B-52s had struck Vietcong and North Vietnamese supply dumps in Cambodia.[6] This story had gone nowhere, but had nonetheless infuriated Nixon and Kissinger. So eager were they to identify those who had "leaked" the story to Beecher that, at their behest, the FBI had placed warrantless wiretaps on thirteen government officials, several of whom were on Kissinger's staff, and on four members of the press. In Conyers' view, this was "the beginning of a policy of corruption" that had gone on for years.

While he had limited his proposed article of impeachment to the specific lies about Cambodia and the resulting wiretaps, John Conyers saw a direct link between the crimes of Watergate and the administration's lawless conduct of the Vietnam War. Two years earlier when the Nixon administration had resumed the bombing of North Vietnam and begun the mining of Haiphong Harbor, Conyers and several colleagues had taken out a two-page ad in the *New York Times* arguing that these were impeachable offenses.[7]

Partly for this reason, Chairman Rodino and some other Democrats on the Judiciary Committee were worried about Article IV. In their view, drawing too tight a connection between the process of impeachment and opposition to the Vietnam War would be needlessly divisive at a time when they were seeking consensus. Father Robert Drinan, antiwar congressman from Massachusetts and a Jesuit priest, objected to this reasoning. He did not believe "the process for picking articles of impeachment [should be influenced by] whether they will fly" rather than by the gravity of the infraction. The Founding Fathers had recognized that "the ultimate tyranny was war carried on illegally by the Executive without the knowledge or consent of Congress."[8]

Yet many on the committee did not agree. As Ohio's Republican Congressman Delbert Latta stated, "this was a time of war," when inevitably things happen "that you don't put on the front page of every newspaper."[9] Nixon's overriding concern had been to protect American troops and bring them home safely. To the extent that action in Cambodia had contributed to that result, this was a reason for gratitude. Few of Latta's Republican colleagues went that far, but several maintained that there was shared culpability for the constitutional violations that had occurred during the Vietnam War, and that it was unfair to single out President Nixon. Moreover, it was not only Republicans who had objected to Conyers' article. Representative Walter Flowers (D-Alabama) thought President Nixon was getting "a bad rap" on this matter. "We might as well resurrect President Lyndon Johnson and impeach him posthumously for Vietnam and Laos."[10]

For John Conyers and his newly elected colleague Elizabeth Holtzman (D-NY), getting Article IV on the agenda had been an uphill struggle. In allocating staff resources, opportunity for debate, even access to prime-time television, the committee chair had sought to marginalize their concern.[11] Up through the final day of the proceedings, Rodino had pressured the Detroit congressman to drop it. Yet Conyers stood by Article IV, maintaining, "This is not frivolous, Mr. Chairman."

Even those who understood the seriousness of the issue Conyers raised in Article IV did not necessarily want to proceed with it. John Seiberling, who represented the Ohio district of Kent State, acknowledged that "the issue is the falsification of information, the misleading of Congress, the failure to consult Congress on a matter as grave as an act of war." In his view four students had died because "the President of the United States again abused his power and again invaded Cambodia without consulting the Congress." Such behavior was reprehensible and must not be tolerated in the future, yet Seiberling contended, "we should not use our impeachment power to impeach" Nixon for "acts of the sort, other Presidents have taken with impunity . . . and for which the Congress bears a very deep measure of responsibility."[12]

Proposing to exonerate the president on the grounds that his predecessors had engaged in similar behavior and that past members of Congress had been indulgent was a curious line of argument.[13] For those who supported Article IV, however, it seemed clear that it was more important to establish a precedent for punishing any violation of Congress' constitutional right and responsibility to make decisions about going to war. Congressman Wayne Owens of Utah expressed his "hope we will set down a standard for Presidents and future wars, that something positive will come out of . . . the history of this sad war in Southeast Asia and the history of this sad proceeding." In subsequent years, perhaps the American people, acting through their elected representatives, would openly decide questions of war and peace "just like the Constitution requires."[14]

Conyers, Holtzman, and several others on the Judiciary Committee considered that secretly bombing a neutral country 3,600 times and lying to Congress about it was so egregious that Article IV article should be approved, so that the entire body of the House could vote on it. Nonetheless, when the roll was called every Republican voted against it, as did nine of their Democratic colleagues.

While members of the Judiciary Committee were casting their historic votes, the *New York Times* published a set of articles by Sydney Schanberg, who was reporting on the ground in Cambodia. Five years after President Nixon had ordered the bombing of that country, and four and a half years after the overthrow of its head of state, Prince Sihanouk, Cambodia was ravaged by the civil war that had resulted from those events. Writing from the town of Oudong, Schanberg described the aftermath of a battle between the government and the brutal insurgents known as the Khmer Rouge. "Forests have been mowed down, schools, pagodas, mosques and hospitals have been flattened."[15] The same was true of nearby towns Prek Kdam and Kompong Luong, and the villages in between.

Many of the 20,000 inhabitants of Oudang were captured by the rebels when they retreated into the jungle. The rest had escaped to the capital of Phnom Penh. Schanberg described the appalling conditions in this once beautiful capital city. Thousands of homeless children roamed its streets, begging for food. Five years earlier, Phnom Penh had a population of 600,000, but the mass arrival of refugees had swelled that number to more than two million, vastly exceeding the capacity of the residents to absorb them:

> Some have wood or plastic as lean-to covers to keep off the weather and some have straw mats to lie on. Others simply live in the open, sleeping in their dirty, tattered clothes on pieces of cardboard. Garbage is often piled nearby, and rats occasionally slither over sleepers.[16]

Illness was naturally on the increase. In addition to dysentery and tuberculosis, refugees had a common vitamin deficiency called speuk, which caused a progressive loss of sensation in feet and legs until the person could no longer walk.

With political events of such magnitude occurring in Washington, few people were focused on events in Oudang, Pred Kdam, Kompong Luong, or even Phnom Penh. Ignoring the life-altering consequences of America's war in Southeast Asia was not unusual for Americans. In voting down Article IV, the members of the Judiciary Committee effectively sanctioned that willful ignorance and denial and ensured that President Nixon would not face responsibility for the tragic events his invasion had set in motion. All the articles of impeachment that would be brought before the House were connected to the domestic crimes brought to light by Watergate. This meant that constitutional issues of the gravest importance would be overlooked in any impeachment proceeding.

During June 1974, one of America's foremost historians, Henry Steele Commager, had warned against obscuring the deeper constitutional issues that were raised by the administration's misconduct.[17] Nixon had already won a strategic victory, he wrote, "in the realm of public, and perhaps even of Congressional opinion" by successfully "concentrating attention on Watergate and its associated chicaneries." The minority on the Judiciary Committee who registered their dissent over the exclusion of Article IV expressed similar concerns:

> By failing to recommend the impeachment of President Nixon for the deception of Congress and the American public as to an issue as grave as the systematic bombing of a neutral county, we implicitly accept the argument that any ends even those a President believes are legitimate justify unconstitutional means.[18]

After the fact, one could reasonably argue that the particulars of the impeachment articles made no practical difference—what mattered was that the Judiciary Committee had found President Nixon guilty and unfit for office, and this finding had caused him to resign even before the House of Representatives could commence its deliberations. Yet by excluding foreign military activities from these articles, the committee framed how the events of that time have been remembered ever since. Although the illegal actions of Nixon's domestic officials were exposed the role of National Security Advisor Henry Kissinger was effectively spared congressional scrutiny or critique.

Shameful as the Watergate offenses were, they were hardly the most serious crimes. Yet they have largely determined the public's historical understanding. The resulting amnesia has left intact many of the ideas, practices, and institutions that over decades have damaged the United States while inflicting needless suffering on foreign nations and people.

* * *

Fire and Rain takes as its subject the Nixon administration's conduct of the war in Vietnam, Laos, and Cambodia, and the resulting diplomacy with the Soviet Union and China. This reverses more familiar accounts, which assume that US military actions in Southeast Asia were the consequence of Cold War fears of the communist "superpowers." While that description is arguably relevant to earlier decision-making, it is profoundly misleading when applied to the Nixon years. In fact, the administration's mounting difficulties in solving its Vietnam problem increasingly shaped interactions with Moscow and Beijing.

Inevitably, the actions and thoughts of President Nixon and his national security advisor Henry Kissinger occupy a central place in this narrative. Given the already large and impressive literature on their conduct of foreign policy, an obvious question is why produce another study?[19] The answer is paradoxical. On the one hand, the declassification of the extraordinary presidential tapes, along with the transcripts from thousands of Kissinger telephone calls, provides a close-up view of the two decision-makers that is without parallel in other administrations. On the other hand, the opportunity for this intense scrutiny has had the perverse effect of obscuring the role of other actors. To understand US policy during this period requires situating Nixon and Kissinger within the wider context of the people, the social and political institutions, the prevailing ideology, and the existing practices that framed their decision-making.

For all their distinctive qualities, both men were profoundly conventional in having reached their high positions by conforming to Cold War orthodoxy. Once in office, their management of the Vietnam War reflected the preferences of the national security bureaucracies—most formidably the Joint Chiefs of Staff in Washington and the headquarters of General Creighton Abrams in South Vietnam (Military Assistance Command Vietnam). Over time their close reliance on the career military would weaken, but in the beginning this was the expertise they trusted. Moreover, despite the sobering experience of the 1968 Tet offensive, at the outset of the administration there were no high-level voices within the executive branch pressing for a rapid end to the war. Within the State Department there was a lively interest in peace negotiations, but the advocates of diplomacy retained the hope that an independent. non-communist South Vietnam would emerge. Given that elusive objective, its members were held hostage to the imperatives of warfighting.

While illuminating the forces that propelled Nixon's and Kissinger's military measures forward, including an expansion of the US effort in Cambodia and Laos, *Fire and Rain* also examines the limitations imposed by public opinion and the organized peace movement. The narrowness of his 1968 electoral victory weighed heavily upon Richard Nixon, as did the political demise of his predecessor Lyndon Johnson. Throughout his first term, Nixon was plainly frustrated and angered by antiwar protest while at the time the impact of that protest on administration policy was ambiguous. However, decades of declassified records provide evidence that the waves of mass demonstrations, accompanied by growing resistance inside the military, ongoing electoral activity, and lobbying efforts on Capitol Hill imposed significant constraints on presidential decision-making.

The ensuing narrative pays considerable attention to the pivotal role played by Secretary of Defense Melvin Laird. To the outside world, he appeared to be another "hawk" in the administration's leadership circle, but behind the scenes he was a relentless advocate of US troop withdrawals. Unlike other national security colleagues, Laird was first and foremost a politician. A reluctant appointee, he had served in the Congress for sixteen years and was, at the time of his selection, chairing the House Republican Conference. Although conservative in outlook, he was also keenly attuned to the mood of the public and was convinced that without major steps to exit the war, the president and his party would pay a steep political price.

To tell this history from the hallways of power in Washington DC, as well as the battlefields of Southeast Asia and the streets of America, this book is divided into two parts reflecting the surprising redirection in US policy during the spring of 1971. Part One: The War is focused on the Nixon administration's approach to the fighting and the domestic ramifications of its conduct. While expanding the American effort in South Vietnam, Laos, and Cambodia, the administration also adopted a program of "Vietnamization," vigorously promoted by Secretary Laird. Under this rubric, tens of thousands of US troops were brought home in successive increments, accompanied by efforts to expand, equip, and train the South Vietnamese military so that it might function independently. For Henry Kissinger and top military officials this approach was folly, likely to undermine negotiations with North Vietnam and perhaps lead to defeat on the battlefield. From Nixon's perspective, these troop withdrawals were a political necessity no matter the pitfalls.

Part I concludes with Lam Son 719, the South Vietnamese incursion into Laos in the spring of 1971. This is a riveting and important story, too often overlooked. The plan was for South Vietnamese troops, aided by American airpower, to cross the border and proceed to the strategically located town of Tchepone, where they would remain for a minimum of two months. If successful, this would cut off the movement of men and supplies down the Ho Chi Minh Trail and prevent a major enemy offensive in the foreseeable future. The operation was regarded as a test case of Vietnamization, since for the first time the highly armed Army of the Republic of South Vietnam (ARVN) would be facing their North Vietnamese enemy without the support of US ground troops.

Despite high expectations, Lam Son 719 was a mortifying failure. Confronted by thousands of North Vietnamese soldiers, those from the South stayed briefly in Tchepone and then hurriedly fled Laos, some clinging to the skids of American helicopters. For administration officials it was an alarming demonstration of ARVN's inability to fight on the ground, at a time when American air power was still available. From a public relations standpoint, the pictures of the retreating South Vietnamese made a damaging impression on the American public.

The debacle in Laos was closely followed by previously planned antiwar activities, largely focused on Washington. As viewed from the White House, the most theatrical and dangerous development was the appearance of the Vietnam Veterans Against the War. During their week-long encampment, this disillusioned group brought their rebellion into the halls of Congress, punctuated by the eloquent address of Lieutenant John Kerry. Although votes were lacking in both the House and Senate to halt the war, it was evident that a continued policy of troop removals was necessary to prevent a majority from coalescing.

Part II: War and Diplomacy focuses on the period after Lam Son 719, when Nixon and Kissinger directed their attention to international diplomacy, and continues through the Paris Peace Agreement in January 1973. With their policy of Vietnamization imploding in Laos, the two went to extraordinary lengths to secure Chinese and Soviet assistance to extricate the United States from the war in a face-saving manner. During this entire time, Henry Kissinger's negotiations with the North Vietnamese were entangled with his complex dealings in Moscow and Beijing.

"If, when the chips are down, the world's most powerful nation, the United States of America, acts like a pitiful, helpless giant, the forces of totalitarianism and anarchy will threaten free nations and free institutions throughout the world," Nixon had famously warned.[20] Sharing that apprehension, millions of Americans continued to support his administration and its conduct of the Vietnam War. Yet from the beginning, both Nixon and Kissinger were looking to the Russians for help in the region. Their initial strategy was to delay negotiations on other disputed issues pending Moscow's cooperation on Vietnam. Yet this coercive approach had quickly proved fruitless. They had also hoped to open a relationship with the People's Republic of China, but after the US invasion of Cambodia this effort had stalled.

Fortunately for them, in April 1971 the Chinese reversed their position, commencing with an invitation to the US ping-pong team to visit their country. Following this and other overtures, the Soviet government also adopted a friendlier stance. Suddenly, the time seemed ripe for diplomatic breakthroughs. Thus began a series of historic visits, starting with Kissinger's clandestine trip to Beijing in July of 1971 and extending through two widely acclaimed summit conferences during the next ten months. For the country, these developments offered a welcome respite from the tensions of the Cold War and burnished Nixon and Kissinger's reputations as international statesmen and men of peace.

In their memoirs, the two convey the impression that, by resisting communist advances in Vietnam and elsewhere, they had established the "credibility" to deal effectively with the Soviets and the Chinese. This was untrue. What the declassified record reveals is the extent to which both men's positions on a range of issues, including nuclear arms control and the future of Taiwan, was driven by their need for assistance in obtaining a face-saving agreement to end the Vietnam War. Therefore, secrecy was of the utmost importance. On key occasions, Kissinger chose to exclude American translators from high-level meetings in order to effectively conceal their content from his colleagues. More remarkable was his solicitation of Chinese and Soviet cooperation in deceiving Secretary of State William Rogers and other administration officials.

These efforts notwithstanding, improved relations with Moscow and Beijing had obvious benefits—but they did not yield the desired results in Indochina. There is considerable evidence that diplomats from both countries encouraged the North Vietnamese to be more flexible in negotiations. Yet the Soviet and Chinese governments continued to provide substantial military and economic assistance to the North and failed to exert meaningful pressure on their ally.

This curious inversion of means and ends raises the broader question of whether US military and political intervention in Third World countries should be so readily described as a defensive response to an existential threat posed by the communist superpowers. In the specific case of the Vietnam War, the repeated alarms about US "national security" were increasingly at odds with reality. Even without declassified transcripts, the contradiction existed in plain sight: if Nixon and Kissinger were exchanging toasts with communist leaders in Moscow and Beijing, why did the killing in Southeast Asia continue?

Ultimately it was the killing and destruction that remain the heart of the story. During the Nixon period of the war, more than 20,000 American soldiers died, and between one and two million Asians, including Vietnamese North and South, Laotians, and Cambodians Fifty years later vast swaths of land remain poisonous; third and fourth generations of Vietnamese suffer grave birth defects from Agent Orange; and in Laos, the most heavily bombed country in the world, children continue to die from unexploded landmines.[21] Some of this damage was inflicted before Richard Nixon became president, but the fire and rain from continuous air strikes and toxic chemicals reached a peak between 1969 and 1973.

While one objective of this book has been to describe and explain the policy choices that were made, a second and equally important objective has been to consider the impact of these choices on the lives of particular people. As vast as it is, the literature on the Vietnam War is oddly bifurcated. Many valuable historical studies of US decision-making exist, as well as a wealth of books that describe the devastating personal experiences of American soldiers and of Vietnamese, Cambodian, and Laotian civilians. However, telling one story without the other can often obscure the significance of each. In the case of the Nixon years, the vast collection of documents and tapes can seal the historian in the claustrophobic rooms where high officials deliberated, thus replicating their disconnection from the human consequences of their choices.

Much of the critical writing on the Vietnam War emphasizes the intellectual errors and misunderstandings of the otherwise "best and brightest" American leaders.[22] However, in examining US policy during the Nixon period, this book argues that a key to the tragedy is less a failure of intellect than the selective vision of people in power. This not only included the president and his national security advisor, but also a host of subordinate officials whose jobs required a certain detachment from the places and people affected by US policy. Not seeing or learning about discomforting realities was often the prerequisite for career advancement.

This realization was brought home to me in an immediate way when traveling through Vietnam. The Cu Chi tunnels—dark labyrinths, three layers deep, extending at one time from their origin 40 miles northwest of Ho Chi Minh City (formerly Saigon) to the Cambodian border—have been turned into a tourist attraction. For decades thousands of Viet Cong moved in and out of these tunnels, launching military operations and retreating, exercising a mysterious political influence in the area that neither the South Vietnamese authorities nor the US military could thoroughly eradicate. How could anyone believe that these resourceful tunnel-dwellers would be intimidated by American military power?

Likewise, the Mekong Delta—with its thick foliage threaded by rivers, canals, and streams, populated by hundreds of thousands of farmers and fishermen whose families had been there for generations—offered a plethora of places for insurgents to hide. Could pacification work in such a place? And if it was temporarily accomplished, why would anyone expect it to remain permanent?

Of course, Nixon and Kissinger did not visit the stifling Cu Chi tunnels or paddle through the Mekong Delta, nor would either experience have changed their minds. Yet, in all the hours of their taped conversations and the thousands of transcripts and memoranda, there appears no sign of curiosity: What is it like there? What role is the Saigon regime playing in people's lives? How are the inhabitants experiencing the war? And for the American soldiers who found themselves in these unfamiliar, treacherous environments, what did counterinsurgency look like? As resistance and demoralization overtook the US Army, what experiences explained this?

In the Oval Office, an inability or unwillingness to imagine the experience of people directly affected by the violence of the war reached epic proportions during those years. It was clear that the bearers of bad news, whether coming from staff of the CIA or the State Department or from knowledgeable journalists, were unwelcome. Nor did Nixon or Kissinger wish to hear any negativity from the military, not even about the weather and its potential impact on bombing operations. Their reluctance to countenance bad news in any form made it nearly impossible for subordinates to provide reliable and urgently needed data. As an example of sheer willful blindness, it is difficult to equal the moment when, as millions of Americans were examining the horrifying photos of the My Lai Massacre, National Security Advisor Kissinger asked the secretary of defense *if* he should look at them.[23]

Unlike Kissinger, President Nixon was permanently attentive to the rumblings of the electorate, which was why he accepted Secretary Laird's formula of Vietnamization. Despite ARVN's dismal showing in Lam Son 719, the president continued to bring large increments of US troops home. To antiwar activists, it seemed incredible that the American public deemed Nixon a more reliable peacemaker than George McGovern. What many failed to appreciate was that by November 1972, more than half a million US soldiers had been withdrawn, with few combat troops remaining. The challenge for Nixon and his national security advisor was to forge a peace agreement that obscured the significance of the 140,000 North Vietnamese soldiers remaining in the South. As before, both men were prone to self-deception, so in the post-election phase their moods oscillated between acute anxiety and unjustified optimism. In the case of the president, his assessments were also affected by the darkening clouds of Watergate.

Their self-perceptions notwithstanding, the Nixon administration's conduct of the war—in Vietnam, Laos, and Cambodia—was a failure that yielded a tsunami of personal tragedies for both Americans and Asians. Yet nobody was ever held accountable. Apart from Nixon himself, those who devised and implemented the policy for these places continued in their public careers without significant disruption. One might have anticipated that certain lessons would be learned, such as the folly of invading a foreign country and seeking to impose a way of life and pattern of governance on the people who live there. Yet this never became a guide to decision-making in the decades following Nixon's presidency.

Herein lies the most challenging question in this book: How can leaders of a democracy conduct an extended war on behalf of a repressive, unpopular regime when the human costs are enormous and defeat seems likely? The answers are elusive and subject to debate. Hopefully the ensuing narrative will cast fresh light on the problem. But this troubling issue, unfortunately buried in the Nixon impeachment proceedings, remains now, as then, "not frivolous."

PART I
THE WAR

1
"Mired in Stalemate"

It was a year of crisis. By November 1968, when Richard Nixon was elected president of the United States, the public was bitterly split over issues of race, crime in the streets, sexual norms, cultural values, attitudes toward authority, and beliefs about the role of government in correcting social injustice. Yet with half a million Americans soldiers embattled in Vietnam, it was the war that cast the longest shadow over the nation.

American involvement in the affairs of Vietnam had begun decades earlier, when the Truman administration agreed to extend economic and military aid to France, which had been struggling against a communist-led independence movement that threatened colonial rule in Indochina. That commitment had been expanded by Presidents Dwight Eisenhower and John Kennedy to include the creation and subsequent protection of a separate anticommunist government in South Vietnam. As a civil war developed in the south, Kennedy had ratcheted up the number of US military on the ground from several hundred to 14,000. While he had carefully described them as "advisors," by the time of Kennedy's assassination in November 1963 many were engaged in fighting.

Under President Lyndon Johnson, the war rapidly became a massive, highly visible, and profoundly divisive affair. During his 1964 election campaign, Johnson had pledged to avoid a land war in Asia. "We are not about to send American boys nine or ten thousand miles away from home to do what Asian boys ought to be doing for themselves," he had pronounced. Yet in early 1965, he had initiated Rolling Thunder—dispatching hundreds of American planes to bomb North Vietnam in a vain effort to discourage it from supporting its allies in the south. Along with the planes had come ground troops—first to guard the American air bases, then to find and kill the enemy. Between March 1965, when the US marines first landed in Danang, and late 1968, the size of the American fighting force increased to 536,000 men, and draft calls skyrocketed to 40,000 men a month to meet the urgent need for more personnel.

The American peace movement, which had struck its deepest roots on college campuses, also expanded rapidly during this time. As it became increasingly evident that President Johnson was doing the exact opposite of what he had promised, many college boys didn't want to be taking up that burden of fighting. Nor did they see the point of it.

According to the official Washington story, the United States was fighting to preserve South Vietnamese freedom against aggression from the communist nation of North Vietnam. American involvement was viewed as a moral obligation and a vital national interest. This was a proxy struggle for the larger conflict with international communism spearheaded by the Soviet Union and China.

Yet news coverage during the mid-sixties had revealed a more complex picture. Each successive South Vietnamese government was an authoritarian regime, despised by many of its own citizens and fighting a rebellion from within. North Vietnam might be providing weapons and soldiers to topple it, but the impetus for resistance was coming from the National Liberation Front (NLF) and its military arm, the People's Liberation Armed Force (PLAF), also known as the Viet Cong. While the NLF was communist led, many of the groups supporting it were not communist but had joined forces with it because of their shared animosity toward the regime.

The United States was intervening in what was essentially a civil conflict. Because it was largely a guerilla war, all too often US soldiers were placed in the position of mistreating the Vietnamese population: clearing out villages, burning huts, shoving inhabitants into strategic hamlets, spraying chemicals to defoliate the jungle, dropping bombs in civilian areas. As these facts became known, they raised troubling questions for those who might be called: Is the preservation of a South Vietnamese dictatorship a cause worth dying for? And if I serve, will I be fulfilling my highest ideals or betraying them?

While colleges remained a hotbed of dissent, by late 1967 the antiwar movement was spreading. From Reverend Martin Luther King to pediatrician Benjamin Spock, Americans of many different ages, backgrounds, and beliefs were challenging not only the moral but also the practical justification for war. Increasingly, members of Congress from both parties were questioning the Johnson Administration's choices. Even if one believed concern about communist aggression was warranted, what was the prospect that victory in Vietnam could be achieved in a reasonable amount of time and at a reasonable cost?

Faced with this growing challenge, the Johnson Administration pursued a "success offensive" aimed at convincing people that the war was going well. In mid-November 1967, US Ambassador Ellsworth Bunker and General William Westmoreland, commander of the US Military Assistance Command, Vietnam (MACV), were summoned home to give the American people the good news. Speaking at Andrews Air Force Base, Westmoreland assured reporters, "I have never been more encouraged in the four years I have been in Vietnam. We are making good progress."[1] He was "absolutely certain that whereas in 1965 the enemy was winning, today he is certainly losing."

Events on the ground very soon challenged these perceptions. On January 31, 1968, the Viet Cong and their North Vietnamese comrades broke a holiday truce at Tet, the Vietnamese New Year. In what became known as the Tet Offensive, they attacked five of South Vietnam's six major cities, along with 36 provincial capitals, 64 district capitals, and approximately 50 hamlets. The most dramatic assault occurred in Saigon, where a platoon of Viet Cong sappers blew a three-foot hole in the protective wall of the American Embassy and climbed through the opening.

During the next six weeks, the American media saturated the public with news of the Tet offensive. The number of places penetrated by the enemy was shocking—from the Mekong Delta to the Central Highlands to the coastal provinces in the north. While the details might be murky, one fact seemed clear: these attacks had been carefully planned, with significant local support.

In most places the uprising was rapidly suppressed, although it was weeks before the enemy could be completely dislodged from Saigon. The most sustained and closely watched fighting occurred in the old imperial city of Hue, which had been attacked by 2,000 enemy soldiers on the first night of the offensive. Approximately 150 American reporters traveled there, some of whom chose to remain with the US troops inside the Citadel, the walled city within the city that contained the Imperial Palace and was one of the most historic sites in Vietnam. Sharing rations with the US troops and sleeping in the crowded, eerie quarter, reporters saw first-hand the ordeals of the marines and the disappointing performance of ARVN (the Army of the Republic of Vietnam). Others visited briefly, including CBS anchorman Walter Cronkite, who was enraged by the discrepancy between the official briefing he received in Saigon and what he actually saw in Hue. With 70% of the city's buildings in ruins and 100,000 displaced people, journalists filed story after story about the devastation they witnessed. For many Americans, it was the footage from Hue that formed their visual impression of the war.

Meanwhile, another deadly siege was claiming hundreds of American lives at the American base in Khe Sanh in northwestern South Vietnam near the border with Laos. General Westmoreland had poured large number of troops into the area in the mistaken belief that the major North Vietnamese attack would come there. Even so, between 20,000 and 40,000 enemy soldiers surrounded the base and maintained a steady barrage of rifle, rocket, and artillery fire. The situation was sufficiently alarming that President Johnson set up a model of the Khe Sanh plateau in the Situation Room, where he received daily reports on the siege.[2]

To reach the base in Khe Sanh journalists had to take extraordinary measures including a short but hair-raising flight, and landing at an airstrip regularly hit by enemy fire. Conditions were so dangerous that the military refused permission for Walter Cronkite to go there, not wanting America's most trusted news anchor to be killed in Vietnam. Meanwhile morale among the troops was dropping, as the men could discern no reason for their presence on these hills except as bait for North Vietnamese regulars. In one extraordinary news clip, filed from Khe Sanh, a CBS crew had filmed a group of young marines in one of the most exposed locations, mournfully singing:

> Where have all the flowers gone?
> Long time passing . . .
> Where have all the soldiers gone?
> Gone to graveyards everyone . . .
> When will they ever learn?
> When will they ever learn?[3]

The haunting lyrics, often featured at antiwar gatherings, were being sung by embattled American soldiers facing possible death.

While Cronkite never made it to Khe Sanh, he had seen enough to recognize the damage caused by Tet. In what would become his most famous broadcast, he declared, "To say that we are closer to victory today is to believe, in the face of the evidence, the optimists who have been wrong in the past. To suggest we are on the edge of failure is to yield to unreasonable pessimism. To say that we are mired in stalemate seems the only realistic, yet unsatisfactory conclusion."[4] Though President Johnson was reportedly disconcerted by Cronkite's commentary, his was just one of many voices lamenting the losses.

With his administration increasingly blamed for mismanaging the war and his poll numbers dropping precipitously, Johnson faced a difficult decision. He had on his desk a top secret request by the military for an additional 206,000 troops. To his great dismay, this recommendation was leaked to the *New York Times*, which on March 10 led with the headline: "Westmoreland Requests 206,000 More Men, Stirring Debate in Administration."

News of Westmoreland's request came as a bombshell to members of Congress, who were still reeling from the damage of the Tet offensive.[5] Nothing they had been told by the administration over the previous year had prepared them for the multiple uprisings across South Vietnam, let alone Westmoreland's reported wish to extend ground action into Laos and Cambodia in order to disrupt the enemy's infiltration routes.

Compounding Johnson's woes, Senator Eugene McCarthy of Minnesota was seeking to challenge him for the Democratic nomination for president. The previous year, peace activists had been on the hunt for a candidate who could credibly oppose Johnson. Senator Robert Kennedy was their preferred candidate, but he was unwilling to enter a race against such daunting odds, and McCarthy was willing. Early polls for the first presidential primary in New Hampshire had shown McCarthy at only 11% against Johnson.

However, the Tet offensive had changed the political calculus.[6] As it geared up for the March 12 primary contest the McCarthy campaign suddenly caught fire, with hundreds of young people flooding into New Hampshire to support the senator.[7] Galvanized by the bloodbath in South Vietnam—with the mantra of "Clean for Gene"—neatly dressed young men and women knocked on doors, engaged residents on the issues, and asked for their vote When the results were tallied, Johnson defeated McCarthy by just 47% to 42%, a humiliating result for a sitting president.

Seeing that the odds had changed dramatically, Robert Kennedy declared his own candidacy.[8] His entry into the race infuriated the president, since it was after all Kennedy's brother Jack who was responsible for the military commitment to Vietnam. Furthermore, it was the team of advisors he had inherited from the Kennedy administration—Dean Rusk, Robert McNamara, McGeorge Bundy, Max Taylor—who had driven the escalation. Yet somehow it was Johnson who was being made the villain.

Johnson faced the immediate question of how to handle the military's request for 206,000 additional troops. He handed the political hot potato to Clark Clifford, his newly designated Secretary of Defense. Johnson had picked Clifford because of his decades of experience and his reputation as a reliable "hawk." He would hopefully offer a contrast to his predecessor Robert McNamara who, more than any single official in the Kennedy and Johnson administrations, had become the public face of the war. But after years of claiming success even when he knew better, McNamara seemed close to a mental breakdown.

In the wake of Tet, however, Clifford's own views were rapidly shifting. Soon after he took over he had encountered a split between the professional military, which was eager to escalate, and civilian officials in both the Defense and the State Departments, who were becoming concerned that the ever-expanding Vietnam commitment was dangerously alienating public opinion and diverting attention from other crucial needs, including modernized nuclear weaponry. Proceeding cautiously, Clifford granted Westmoreland an additional 22,000 troops but stipulated that any future troop increments would require improved political and military performance by the South Vietnamese government.

The president, meanwhile, responded to the growing dissension by becoming more belligerent, yelling at his advisors that he was not going to stop the bombing even for the purpose of facilitating diplomacy."[9] Troubled by Johnson's stubbornness, Clifford unexpectedly convened a meeting of the "Wise Men"—an informal group of national security veterans who had moved in and out of high-level government positions since the early years of the Cold War. When they were last consulted in November 1967, these men had been enthusiastic supporters of the Vietnam effort. However, the losses in Tet and the perceived incompetence of ARVN had led many to conclude that any hope of military victory would require more time and resources than the American public was likely to accept.[10] It seemed clear that the administration needed a strategy of "disengagement," one that entailed a serious effort at diplomacy.

Upon hearing this revised opinion, the Johnson was stunned. "Somebody must have poisoned the well," he exclaimed. For years these sophisticated experts were among the very people who had been advocating for military escalation. He had followed their advice, but now they were turning away while he was left exposed to public wrath.[11] It was almost as if they had joined the antiwar movement.

They had certainly been influenced by it. For the past three years peace organizations had been building opposition to Johnson's policy, and they were even more energized by Tet. This could be seen in the spreading demonstrations, some militant and disruptive, others dignified and solemn.

Most recently it could be seen in young people who had flocked to New Hampshire to support Eugene McCarthy and who were now conducting a block-by-block canvas on behalf of their candidate in Wisconsin.[12]

The imminent Wisconsin primary exacerbated Johnson's misery. One week before Election Day, observers on the scene were telling the president he might receive as little as 35% of the vote, a mortifying prospect.[13]

An anguished Lyndon Johnson decided to deliver a major speech to explain his Vietnam policy. His inclination had been to hang tough, to emphasize the enemy losses during Tet and reaffirm the US commitment to South Vietnam. To his surprise, Secretary of Defense Clifford was insistent that the country wanted to hear about peace and diplomacy, not more war. On March 31, when Johnson went before the television cameras, he had altered the message, earnestly explaining that "peace in Vietnam and Southeast Asia" was the transcendent goal of US policy and that in order to de-escalate the conflict he was issuing new orders.[14]

There would be no further naval or aircraft attacks on North Vietnam except in the area immediately north of the Demilitarized Zone (DMZ), where an enemy build-up was threatening the safety of American troops. This ban would spare almost 90% of North Vietnam's population and most of its territory. If Hanoi was prepared to match American restraint, the US would stop its bombing of North Vietnam entirely.

The essential task, said Johnson, was to begin negotiations for a permanent peace. Toward this end, he was designating Averell Harriman as his personal representative to participate in future talks. Despite this change, he remained convinced that "what we are doing now in Vietnam is vital not only to the security of Southeast Asia, but it is vital to the security of every American."

He added one more announcement. At a time when America's sons were fighting on distant battlefields, and when the country's future was under siege at home, he would not spend any of his time on "personal partisan causes." Therefore, he said, "I shall not seek, and I will not accept, the nomination of my party for another term as your president."

It was a shocking statement—totally unexpected, even by Lady Bird Johnson. Television pundits were rendered temporarily speechless, while across official Washington there were expressions of amazement.[15] College campuses around the country erupted in joy. Two days later, Wisconsin's Democratic primary voters gave their verdict: 57% for McCarthy, 35.4% for the president.[16]

On the diplomatic front, it was unclear whether the offer of a partial bombing halt would incentivize the North Vietnamese to negotiate. But on April 3, Hanoi issued a statement saying it was "prepared to meet and to determine with the US representative the unconditional cessation of the bombing and all other acts of war against the Democratic Republic of North Vietnam (DRVN) so as to start the talks."[17] Read carefully, the North Vietnamese message was basically an agreement to start talking about talking, but there was still reason for hope.

It was uncertain how these developments might affect the American election. Johnson's sudden withdrawal had opened the field not just to the two avowedly antiwar candidates, Eugene McCarthy and Robert Kennedy, but also to Vice President Hubert Humphrey, whose stated position on the war resembled the president's. By contrast, the Republican race seemed to be coalescing around one man: Richard Nixon.

Six years earlier, following his defeat for the California governorship, Nixon's political career had seemed finished. At the time he had famously lashed out at the press: "You won't have Richard Nixon to kick around anymore, because gentlemen, this is my last press conference." From the time he entered politics in 1946 to run for the 12th district of the US Congress in Los Angeles there had always been an ugly, abrasive quality to Nixon's public persona, and his virulent anticommunism was an essential part of it. He defeated his opponent by slyly portraying him as a tool of a communist labor organization, and he similarly defeated Helen Gahagan Douglas in the 1950 Senate race, impugning her patriotism with a flood of "pink lady" flyers and whispered telephone attacks.

However, Nixon's anticommunist credentials had received their greatest burnishing from the pivotal role he played in the downfall of Alger Hiss, a well-respected State Department official who had accompanied President Roosevelt to Yalta and had done important work on the United Nations charter. In 1948, Hiss was head of the prestigious Carnegie Endowment for International Peace and had the support of mainstream foreign policy figures—including Republican John Foster Dulles and Under-Secretary of State Dean Acheson. Nixon, a junior congressman who was serving on the House Un-American Affairs Committee (HUAC) at the time, listened attentively when *Time* editor Whittaker Chambers testified before the committee that during the 1930s he had been part of a communist underground, in which capacity he had received information from government agents including Alger Hiss.

High-level figures from Harry Truman on down rallied to the defense of Hiss, and even HUAC was inclined to drop the matter. But Nixon found Chambers credible and doggedly pursued the case. Chambers lead a team of investigators into a field outside his home, where he reached inside a pumpkin and pulled out microfilms of State Department documents, some handwritten by Hiss, who was subsequently indicted and sent to jail for perjury. Hiss went to his grave protesting his innocence, but these events made Richard Nixon a rising star in the Republican galaxy. This arresting narrative of a brave crusader against America's enemy had until 1960 propelled his political ascent.

As the presidential race of 1968 loomed, many non-Republicans assumed the twice-defeated former vice president had been consigned to oblivion. But Richard Nixon was acutely aware that John Kennedy had defeated him in 1960 by no more than 100,000 votes. Millions of Americans had believed in him enough to support him for the presidency and, with a little prompting, might do so again.

Nixon was prescient enough to know that the road to the presidency would likely run through Vietnam, but as controversy mounted he was also shrewd enough to mute his opinions. Through the end of 1967 he remained quietly in the wings using the time to visit foreign leaders, read up on issues, and cultivate powerful backers. In the wake of Tet, silence was no longer an option. While Nixon had always been a Vietnam "hawk," he carefully adjusted his presentation. On March 4 he addressed a crowd in New Hampshire, announcing that if by November "this war is not over, I say that the American people will be justified in electing new leadership, and I pledge to you that new leadership will end the war and win the peace in the Pacific."[18] He did not reveal how he would accomplish this, but thereafter he would frame his commentary as a way of "winning the peace" rather than pursuing a victory.[19]

Such vagueness was a luxury that Nixon, with no announced opponents, could easily afford. Neither McCarthy nor Kennedy had that freedom.[20] On April 2, their candidacies became more complicated when Vice President Humphrey entered the race as the standard-bearer for the administration. Humphrey had disadvantages of his own, principally that it was his unhappy task to defend Johnson's handling of the war, and it was too late to enter any of the primaries. Fortunately for him, in most states the party organization chose the delegates to the national convention, and since party regulars were generally loyal to the administration, Humphrey became their logical choice.[21] Meanwhile, Kennedy and McCarthy were forced to compete against each other in primaries, squandering time and money that might otherwise be used against ideological opponents.

For his part, Richard Nixon was plugging along winning primaries, racking up fresh supporters, and talking mainly about "law and order," which he had shrewdly made the defining theme of his campaign. A useful phrase, it was code for an array of grievances that had become flashpoints in America's culture wars: crime in the streets, the militancy of black protestors, and the menace of antiwar demonstrators. By failing to take a "no-nonsense" stance toward people who did not observe the rules, the Democratic White House had allowed the country to drift into frightening instability, or so Nixon claimed.

On April 4, the domestic divisions became tragically apparent when an assassin murdered Dr. Martin Luther King on the balcony of a Memphis hotel. The civil rights leader was hardly a Nixon hero, but the Republican candidate was able to use the assassination and the riots that broke out in black communities across the country—Chicago, Boston, New York, Newark, Baltimore, Pittsburgh, and hundreds of other locations—to deplore a society in chaos.

In a different way Robert Kennedy sought to address the polarization, arguing that peace abroad and social justice at home were essential to any reconciliation.[22] At a rally in Indianapolis it had been his painful duty to inform a mostly African American crowd that the Reverend King had been assassinated. Speaking extemporaneously, he reminded the audience that Dr. King had "dedicated his life to love and justice for his fellow human beings." From his own experience of his brother's death, he knew how easy it was to feel "hatred and distrust," he said, but "we have to make an effort in the United States to understand" one another and to transcend these emotions.

Robert Kennedy had made the healing of divisions a major theme of his candidacy. Then on June 5 came a second shock: minutes after defeating Eugene McCarthy in a closely fought, winner-take-all California primary, Robert Kennedy was shot by a lone gunman standing in the kitchen of the Ambassador Hotel. Within 24 hours he was dead. For a country still reeling from the combined calamities of the Tet offensive, the slaying of Martin Luther King, and the ensuing riots, this second Kennedy assassination possessed a surreal, almost apocalyptic quality.

Until Kennedy's death it seemed possible that an antiwar candidate could win the Democratic nomination. But McCarthy had lost steam and credibility while Hubert Humphrey, with the support of the appointed state party delegates, was now poised to prevail. On the Republican side, Nixon's emergence as the nominee was virtually assured, leaving him and his party free to continue to equivocate on the war.[23]

When the Republicans gathered for their Miami convention, Nixon underlined his commitment to "law and order" by choosing as his running mate Maryland Governor Spiro Agnew—a man who had distinguished himself by his tough response to the riots in Baltimore.[24] Nixon's acceptance speech set the template for the upcoming campaign and for much of what would follow:

> As we look at America, we see cities enveloped in smoke and flame. We hear sirens in the night. We see Americans dying on distant battlefields abroad. We see Americans hating each other; fighting each other; killing each other at home. And as we see and hear these things, millions of Americans cry out in anguish. Did we come all this way for this?[25]

Fortunately, he said, there was a different voice, that of "the forgotten Americans—the non-shouters, the non-demonstrators," the majority of people who were "not guilty of the crimes that plague the land." Such people worked hard for a living, served in the military, and paid their taxes. Yet their essential decency had gone unrewarded while the government chose to coddle other constituencies. "For the past five years, we have been deluged by government programs for the unemployed; programs for the cities; programs for the poor," and the net result was "an ugly harvest of frustration violence and failure . . . ."

As if to prove his point, the Democratic conclave in Chicago erupted in an explosion of violence, thanks in large part to the choices of Mayor Richard Daley. In anticipation of the arrival of thousands of antiwar protestors, Daley had turned the city into an armed camp. He put his police force of 11,900 officers on 12-hour shifts for the duration, requested an additional 5,600 Illinois National Guardsmen for round-the-clock duty, and arranged for another 5,000 federal troops to be quartered nearby. The convention site was surrounded by a seven-foot chain link fence topped by barbed wire and riflemen standing guard on nearby roofs. The scene resembled what television viewers might have seen during the coverage of the Tet uprising at the American Embassy in Saigon.[26]

The protestors were a disparate lot. Many came to demonstrate lawfully, others intended to commit nonviolent civil disobedience. The most attention-grabbing were the "Yippies," who in the lead-up to the convention threatened to slip LSD into Chicago's water supply, set off smoke bombs in the convention hall, kidnap delegates in fake taxis, fornicate with their wives, and release greased pigs into the downtown. These were farcical suggestions, offered tongue-in-cheek, but they were also a willful provocation to an angry mayor and a police department ready for blood.[27]

Inside the convention hall, the mood was rancorous. During the preceding months it had become evident that millions of Democratic voters, possibly a majority, were opposed to the administration's conduct of the Vietnam War. Many had involved themselves in the McCarthy or Kennedy campaigns. Yet in the wake of Robert's assassination, they had little to show for that effort. Last-minute attempts to produce an alternative, perhaps Senator Ted Kennedy or Senator George McGovern, had fizzled.

Completing their rout was a bruising platform fight in which Lyndon Johnson, acting through Chairman Hale Boggs and a cowed Hubert Humphrey, defeated efforts to include modest antiwar language in the final Democratic Party platform document.[28] When the votes were announced, some delegates in the back of the hall began to boo, and then suddenly members of the New York delegation were standing on their chairs. After singing "We Shall Overcome," the New Yorkers began an impromptu walk through the aisles, passing out black crepe paper for armbands to fellow delegates from other states—New Hampshire, Oregon, California, and Virginia—who joined the unhappy procession.

However toxic the atmosphere inside the hall, the situation outside was far worse. Since the arrival of the antiwar demonstrators, tensions between them and the Chicago police had erupted in violent clashes and arrests.[29] While delegates debated the merits of the Vietnam War, thousands of demonstrators had gathered outside the Hilton Hotel in downtown Chicago, intending to march to the convention. Whether by pre-arrangement or spontaneous rage, the police suddenly charged into the crowd using mace and clubs, beating people mercilessly.[30]

Journalists' cameras were smashed, but enough members of the press managed to evade the police and to film the spectacle. "The whole world is watching! The whole world is watching!" the crowd chanted furiously. So uncontrolled were the Chicago police that they began attacking innocent bystanders, many of whom were huddled behind barricades against the windows of the Hilton. As described by Anthony Lukas of the *New York Times*, the policemen charged the barriers, "crushing the spectators against the windows of the hotel." Finally the windows gave way, "sending screaming middle-aged women and children backward through the broken shards of glass."[31] Then the police ran inside the building, beating some of the people who had fallen through the window and arresting others.

When they viewed the television footage later that night, many convention delegates were horrified. Speaking from the podium, the normally circumspect governor of Connecticut Abraham Ribicoff deplored "Gestapo tactics on the streets of Chicago." Mayor Daley leapt to his feet, red-faced and furious, shouting an obscenity at Ribicoff. Wisconsin delegate Donald Peterson shouted into a microphone, "Thousands of young people are being beaten on the streets of Chicago."

Later that night, against a chorus of hisses and jeers, Hubert Humphrey gained the Democratic nomination for president with 1761 3/4 votes compared to 601 for Eugene McCarthy and a smattering of votes for various other candidates.[32] It was a persuasive numerical victory under ominous conditions. Political operative Allard Lowenstein, who months earlier had conceived the extraordinary idea of challenging Lyndon Johnson's nomination, put it bluntly: "This convention elected Richard Nixon president of the United States tonight . . . I never thought it would happen."[33]

Coasting on his favorable numbers and a unified party, Nixon had the luxury of conducting a carefully controlled campaign.[34] He made relatively few appearances each day and, until the last week of the campaign, stayed away from television interviews, relying most on paid advertising spots on national television and scripted panel discussions created by a New York advertising firm. As he answered the questions of these handpicked panelists, Nixon projected an image of calm thoughtfulness, strengthening the impression of a "new Nixon," which some media pundits reinforced.[35] About Vietnam, he shrewdly claimed that with preliminary peace talks occurring in Paris, he would not play politics by injecting his personal opinions at this delicate moment.

By contrast, Lyndon Johnson's apron strings were strangling Humphrey. He had to face the wrath of the antiwar activists who showed up at his events, carrying insulting signs and sometimes jeering at his speeches. In early October, the Gallup poll showed him lagging badly behind Richard Nixon.

Finally convinced of the need to shift his position on Vietnam, Humphrey outlined his new stance in a one-hour paid television advertisement. Citing his long history of working for peace and disarmament, he affirmed that as president he "would stop the bombing of the North as an acceptable risk for peace."[36] It was a small change. Yet the speech was widely perceived as a move away from Johnson, thus enabling previously alienated liberals, including Eugene McCarthy, to endorse him.[37] Afterwards he enjoyed a notable increase in financial contributions and a decrease in the number of angry pickets at his campaign events. By late October, his candidacy seemed to be catching fire. In this final stretch, he also benefited from the waning support for George Wallace, who had been trading on his segregationist credentials to wage a third-party challenge. Encouraged by union leadership, many of Wallace's white working-class backers moved into Humphrey's camp.

As Nixon strategists grappled with these worrisome developments, there came a new bombshell. During a conference call on October 15 with all three presidential candidates, Lyndon Johnson revealed that there had been a breakthrough in Paris, which could result in a complete bombing halt and the commencement of official negotiations. The North Vietnamese had made several concessions: to accept South Vietnam as a participant in the upcoming negotiations, to respect the DMZ, and to halt the shelling of southern cities.

Although he expressed the requisite enthusiasm for Johnson's news, Nixon quickly recognized the potential for disaster. In a tightening race, a sudden movement toward peace might vault Hubert Humphrey into the White House. Harvard professor Henry Kissinger, who had served as a consultant to the Paris peace talks, had given the Nixon campaign an early warning of this possibility. That had enabled Nixon to make advance preparations for this contingency, which he did by holding a secret meeting with Bui Diem, the South Vietnamese Ambassador to the United States. Nixon and his campaign manager John Mitchell informed Bui that Anna Chennault, a Washington socialite, hardline anticommunist, and co-chair of the women's advisory committee to his campaign who had arranged the meeting, would henceforth serve as a liaison between the campaign and the embassy as events warranted.

John Mitchell began calling Mrs. Chennault every day, encouraging her to use Bui Diem to communicate a message to President Nguyen Van Thieu: if Thieu refused to participate in the peace talks now, he would get a better deal later if Richard Nixon was elected President.[38] Bui Diem readily complied, cabling President Thieu: "Many Republican friends have contacted me and encouraged us to stand firm. They are alarmed by press reports to the effect that you had already softened your position."

On October 31, Lyndon Johnson announced to the American people in a televised broadcast that he had decided to suspend all bombing of North Vietnam because of recent developments in the talks."[39] Hanoi had agreed that the Saigon government could participate in the negotiations, and the United States in turn had accepted the participation of the NLF in a four-way conversation to open shortly.

Suddenly prospects for a negotiated peace seemed bright. With only five days left until the election, polls showed overwhelming support for the bombing halt, and steady gains for Hubert Humphrey. Then on November 2, General Thieu threw the "monkey wrench" Nixon had been hoping for. Addressing the South Vietnamese parliament, Thieu declared that his government would not participate in the upcoming negations because the inclusion of the NLF had made this "impossible."[40]

Johnson was livid. The South Vietnamese had given their assurance they would take part, and Ambassador Bunker had confirmed it. Through illegal wiretaps and bugs on Thieu's office in Saigon and on the South Vietnamese Embassy in Washington, Johnson had known for a week about the behind-the-scenes Republican machinations but assumed they would have no practical effect.[41] Once Nixon's inducements had encouraged Thieu to balk, the president's hands were arguably tied, since the information had come to him through illegal methods.

However, he did alert Republican Senator Everett Dirksen to the skullduggery of the Nixon people. "Now that is treason," Johnson observed. Dirksen agreed and said he would speak to Nixon about it.[42] For Nixon, the peril was clear. Under the Logan Act of 1799, any interference by a private citizen to influence a foreign power in its negotiations with the federal government would constitute a felony. Prodded by Dirksen, Nixon called Johnson and vigorously denied any knowledge of this intervention. "My God, I would never do anything to encourage . . . Saigon not to come to the table, because basically that's what you got out of your bombing pause . . . good God, we want them over in Paris. We've got to get them to Paris, or you can't have peace."[43]

Though Johnson knew Nixon was lying, there was little he could do about it without going public about the wiretapping. His resentment of Humphrey's candidacy likely played a part.[44] Although the president belatedly informed the vice president of Nixon's treasonous role, he gave no indication of the source, depriving Humphrey of a credible basis for an accusation.[45]

Thus, 72 hours from the presidential election, a candidate who had disrupted the initial steps toward a possible peace accord was given a pass.[46] When the votes were counted on election night, Richard Nixon had won by the tiniest of margins, garnering 43.4% of the vote, while Hubert Humphrey took 42.7% and George Wallace 13.5%.

For Richard Nixon, there were many lessons to be learned—not just the effectiveness of "dirty tricks" that were his political staple, but the power of fake imagery. His final commercial, featuring a soundtrack of "A Hot Time in the Old Town Tonight," opened with a shot of the Democratic convention, moved swiftly to a newsreel of an inner city riot, then to footage of two grim GIs crouching behind a bunker under fire in South Vietnam, and finally to a photo of Hubert Humphrey, whose smiling face seemed to suggest that he was amused by these scenes of war and domestic violence.[47] In addition, Nixon had learned, the Vietnam War had destroyed the presidency of Lyndon Johnson. He would not let that happen to him.

2

"We Will Hit Them with No Warning"

At midnight January 20, 1969, in Tay Ninh province near the Cambodian border, an American patrol led by Sergeant Jose Olea of Buffalo, New York, was crossing a rice paddy when it came under attack by a large contingent of North Vietnamese soldiers. Olea quickly ordered his men out of the paddy and into a surrounding thicket. Besieged and outnumbered, the men hurled their grenades at the advancing enemy, exhausting their supply. By morning, when American choppers were able to land and rescue the frightened survivors, three of Olea's men were dead and seven were wounded.

Such encounters had become routine. Although described as "a lull," the war was being fought across South Vietnam in a series of deadly skirmishes such as that at Tay Ninh. Most often the communist forces were the initiators, but American soldiers were under orders from Washington to hunt the enemy. Despite the absence of large or dramatic battles, American soldiers were dying at the rate of 200 a week. The South Vietnamese casualties far exceeded this count, but nobody could say with certainty what proportion of these were actual combatants and what proportion were innocent villagers.

In Washington DC, January 20 was inauguration day for Richard Milhous Nixon, who stood with his wife Pat on the east portico of the Capitol, taking the oath of office as the nation's 37th president. Nixon was bringing to the White House decades of international experience, more than any of his recent predecessors, and a broad agenda for dealing with a host of foreign policy issues. But as he and the members of his administration well understood, how he handled the Vietnam War—which 52% of Americans considered a mistake—could eclipse everything else.

For most Americans, Nixon's inaugural address was their first indication of his intentions. In a conciliatory and high-minded speech, the new president observed that "the greatest honor history can bestow is that of peacemaker."[1] It was an honor "that now beckons America—the chance to help lead the world at last . . . onto that high ground of peace that man has dreamed of since the dawn of civilization." The period of confrontation was over, he proclaimed, and the United States was "entering an era of negotiation."

These were welcome words for a war-weary nation, but they obscured a more ominous reality: though Nixon was eager to negotiate an end to the war, he was also determined to maintain South Vietnam as a separate non-communist state, not part of the unified country, which his adversaries were demanding. If these goals were to prove incompatible—as there was every indication they would—then a tougher choice would surely lie ahead.

To help him on this and other issues, Nixon had surprised many observers by choosing Harvard professor Henry Kissinger, a German-born international relations scholar, as his national security advisor. With his thick accent and academic speech and writing, Kissinger was not the sort of person Nixon was known to favor. However, Kissinger had served as consultant to President Johnson and had demonstrated his usefulness by passing on confidential information about the sudden progress in the Paris peace talks that had helped Nixon to sabotage them. Kissinger maintained strong "establishment" connections and a reputation for Cold War orthodoxy. He had made his academic mark by writing about the prospects for a limited nuclear war, a sign that he was steely enough to accept mass casualties should the need arise.[2] As someone who had functioned outside the government, he lacked ties to any of the national security bureaucracies, which made him an attractive appointee for a president who intended to run foreign policy out of the White House.

From the moment of his selection to the post on December 2, 1968, Kissinger set to work centralizing authority.[3] He insisted that all national security decisions be routed through a series of committees directed by his office. By this simple mechanism, the Secretaries of State and Defense, as well as the director of the CIA, would come under his immediate scrutiny. National security advisors had been powerful figures before, but none possessed the far-reaching supervisory powers that Kissinger claimed for himself in the name of the president.

The first to raise a red flag was Melvin Laird, the newly designated Secretary of Defense. Laird had reluctantly accepted this post after serving 16 years in the House of Representatives, where he had amassed considerable expertise on defense issues during his time as a member of the House Appropriations Committee. He also understood the intricacies of turf warfare and quickly recognized that Kissinger's reorganization plan was a threat to his future effectiveness as a cabinet official.

Not yet in office, on January 9 Laird stated that he could not approve the proposal. If adopted, "it would create a closed loop in which all intelligence inputs would be channeled through a single source."[4] He objected to the idea that one individual would monopolize "the major tools that have always been intended to be utilized equally by all the president's top-level advisers." After some delay, however, Nixon supported Kissinger's plan, including a provision that the Joint Chiefs of Staff have a permanent liaison to the National Security Council (NSC) staff.[5] This meant that from day one, Kissinger had his own direct line to the professional military.

How the administration was organizing itself was of no interest to the public. The burning question continued to be the war in Vietnam: how and whether the new president would bring it to a rapid end. Kissinger's rather conventional views on the subject could be found in a January 1969 issue of *Foreign Affairs* magazine.[6] Although the article contained a familiar critique of the Johnson Administration's conduct of the war—too much emphasis on attrition, too little on pacification—it reaffirmed the necessity for continuing the military project. "The commitment of 500,000 Americans has settled the issue of the importance of Vietnam," Kissinger contended. "Those whose safety or national goals depend on America's commitments could only be dismayed" if the United States withdrew unilaterally from Vietnam. This would lead "to the erosion of restraints and to an even more dangerous international situation."

Kissinger recognized the need for a negotiated solution but resisted the idea of a coalition government for South Vietnam or anything resembling a military defeat. Viewing both the North Vietnamese and US troops as outsiders, he considered a slow mutual withdrawal of their troops to be a reasonable solution. In this regard, his perspective was not so different from many antiwar critics in the Democratic Party, who also regarded mutual troop withdrawal as a viable compromise.

Yet this took no account of how Hanoi and its South Vietnamese allies viewed the matter. Their foundational belief was that Vietnam was a single nation that had been artificially divided by outside powers at the 1954 Geneva Conference ending the French war in Indochina. As set forth in those accords, the division between North and South at the 17th parallel was a temporary arrangement, lasting for two years until a nationwide election could occur. That election had been scuttled by the South Vietnamese government, in coordination with the United States, thereby extending the unnatural division. But to Hanoi and the southern insurgents, the overriding imperative was to reunify the country.

If North Vietnam was unwilling to withdraw its troops, whether mutually or not, then a clear implication was that American combat troops would have to remain in South Vietnam for years, since there was no immediate prospect that the South Vietnamese government could survive on its own. But was there a limit to the price US soldiers or the Vietnamese people could be expected to pay? Writing as an outsider, Kissinger could safely ignore the question. But what clearly concerned a majority of Americans was the ordeal of the American troops. And for a vocal minority, the scenes of civilian suffering had become intolerable.

This matter of costs carried little weight for both Nixon and Kissinger, except insofar as the public's reaction to the casualty rate might undermine the war effort or prove politically damaging. Yet they initially imagined that the US military could inflict sufficient damage on the enemy, so this trial of wills might not be prolonged. Their thinking was hardly unique. On the fundamental question of whether the Nixon administration should continue the fight, a RAND Corporation survey of relevant government bureaucracies had found unanimous opposition to a unilateral American withdrawal.[7]

This early study, commissioned at Kissinger's behest, had identified significant cleavages on other matters. People in the professional military (including the Joint Chiefs of Staff and MACV) and the US Embassy in Saigon were relative optimists. They believed the enemy had sustained devastating, irreversible losses during Tet and that the South Vietnamese government was rapidly strengthening its political and military hold on the country. They further maintained that pacification of the villages was progressing rapidly, with three-quarters of the territory secure. From their perspective, an American victory was still possible, although they disagreed about how long this might take.

The more pessimistic officials were mainly the civilians in the office of the Secretary of Defense and top officials at the State Department and the CIA. They all agreed that the North Vietnamese troops had sustained significant blows during Tet, but they also believed the battered units had been reconstituted and were poised to return to battle. This group also saw no evidence of a fundamental improvement in either the government or the army of South Vietnam, and regarded the claims of 75% pacification as an illusion. Despite seeing no serious possibility of victory during the next four or five years, these pessimists were unwilling to say that the United States should cut its losses and leave. If there were people inside the national security bureaucracies who believed otherwise, they kept their silence.

The RAND survey had been conducted quickly, just prior to Nixon's inauguration. Once in office, Kissinger wanted a more thorough understanding of these diverse assessments. For this purpose he issued his first National Security Studies Memorandum (NSSM-1) requesting that all relevant agencies of government—the CIA, State Department, Office of the Secretary of Defense, the Joint Chiefs of Staff, MACV, the US Embassy in Saigon—respond to a list of key questions.

To formulate the questions, Kissinger had elicited the help of RAND analyst Daniel Ellsberg, who had worked on the preliminary survey. The national security advisor had known Ellsberg at Harvard as a zealous Cold Warrior, and during a 1965 visit to Vietnam had met with Ellsberg, who was there on a two-year mission attached to the embassy. During that period, the young man had begun to reevaluate his enthusiasm for the war, but this evolution was unknown to Kissinger. Ellsberg seemed a logical person at RAND to set up the review.

In designing the questions for NSSM-1, Ellsberg may have hoped that the answers themselves would stimulate a reappraisal.[8] Indeed, the queries were detailed and substantive: Why had the North Vietnamese agreed to the negotiations in Paris? What rate of enemy attrition would outrun their ability to replenish themselves? How adequate was the American information about the degree of support for the Saigon government? The questions covered a wide gamut of concerns. Noticeably missing were the issues at the heart of the antiwar critique: how many Americans would have to die to achieve an acceptable settlement in South Vietnam? What would be the impact on the people of South Vietnam if the fighting continued for an extended period? And was it really the case that, because the United States had committed half a million troops to the war, both national security and world peace required a successful outcome?

While government officials dutifully filled out their questionnaires, and Nixon and Kissinger figured out their overall strategy, the views of the military predominated. From the outset there was pressure from MACV to take out the enemy sanctuaries in Cambodia.[9] For years, military leaders had been complaining about the ability of the North Vietnamese to escape over the border into Laos or Cambodia and find safety there as they rebuilt their forces. In the aftermath of Tet, the enemy presence in both places had increased, and General Creighton Abrams, who had replaced General Westmoreland as commander of MACV, was pressing hard for action.

In the case of Laos, the Johnson administration had been bombing for years, claiming the tacit acquiescence of its leader, Prince Souvanna Phouma. Cambodia was more problematic, because its leader, Prince Norodom Sihanouk, had severed diplomatic relations with the United States in 1965, and bombing on its soil would constitute an attack on a sovereign nation. To the military's previous arguments, General Abrams claimed to have located COSVN (the enemy's central office for South Vietnam) inside Cambodia, which could be eliminated with a surgical strike. There was, however, reason for skepticism since it was not even clear that COSVN existed as a single entity in a fixed location. More convincing were military assertions that the Cambodian sanctuaries posed a direct threat to the safety and stability of the American project in South Vietnam.

To make his case for bombing Cambodia, on February 18 General Abrams dispatched a two-man briefing team to Washington to meet with high officials and describe his plans. In those discussions they gained a new White House ally in the person of Colonel Al Haig, a decorated Vietnam veteran who had become Kissinger's deputy for military affairs. In a sea of distinguished, Ivy League staff members on the NSC, Haig's military experience gave him a significant voice.

While Kissinger was positively disposed to General Abrams' recommendation, there was resistance from Secretary of State William Rogers and the specialists in his department. Their concern was about Cambodia's leader Prince Sihanouk, who was likely to resent this move. Despite a period of diplomatic estrangement, in recent months Sihanouk had seemed open to a rapprochement. Rather than worsening relations with unwanted air strikes, Department of State officials thought a wiser approach might be to resume diplomatic relations and to forge an agreement for joint action against the North Vietnamese intruders.

Secretary Rogers also had concerns about the likelihood of secrecy. If the administration openly attacked the sanctuaries, it would spark intense protest in the United States. But if, as the military suggested, it conducted these raids secretly and the information leaked, it would cause a serious public backlash. Secretary of Defense Laird shared some of Rogers' concerns and pressed to delay the decision about whether to bomb Cambodia pending the fact-finding trip he was about to make to South Vietnam.

Events were moving quickly, however. On February 23, in what some feared was a repetition of Tet 1968, the enemy launched 100 attacks across South Vietnam. For the first time since the November bombing halt, rockets hit Saigon and Danang, with additional strikes on 17 provincial and 26 district capitals. A prime target appeared to be US military installations, which resulted in a sudden spike in casualties: 435 Americans dead and 2,593 wounded in the first week of these attacks.

Convinced that the enemy was testing his mettle and that he needed to make a show of strength, Nixon agreed with the military that his administration should adopt a more aggressive strategy. From Saigon, both General Abrams and Admiral John McCain, commander of US naval forces in the Pacific, demanded immediate retaliation, calling for 96 hours of air strikes on North Vietnam in the area above the DMZ.

Secretary Laird opposed any bombing of the North, arguing that until this point Hanoi had honored its commitment to reduce their activity in the area of the DMZ, which had saved many American lives. A breach of the bombing halt would put that in jeopardy. And Nixon himself was concerned that an attack on North Vietnam—for even 96 hours—would lead Hanoi to cancel the Paris peace talks. This would be deeply disturbing to the American public. If anything, such considerations seemed to strengthen the case for hitting the Cambodian sanctuaries, since it would be a way to signal Hanoi that the new administration would react fiercely to any acceleration of the war while still avoiding the most provocative actions. By the end of February Nixon had made up his mind to go ahead, but wanted to get Laird's approval before doing so.

Until this point, Laird had managed to camouflage his true intentions with regard to Vietnam. Although generally hawkish on Cold War issues, his interaction with colleagues on the Hill and home constituents in Wisconsin had nurtured some pacific sentiments. For these House members, who faced the electorate every two years, the growing disaffection of the American people from the war was a continuing reality that slowly reshaped their attitudes. Unlike Nixon and Kissinger, Laird had quietly defined his mission as bringing the troops home.[10]

On March 5, the Secretary of Defense headed to Vietnam accompanied by his new military assistant Colonel Robert Pursley, and General "Bus" Wheeler, chairman of the Joint Chiefs of Staff.[11] In Saigon the generals were awaiting Laird's arrival with trepidation. General Phillip Davidson, chief intelligence officer, gave a briefing on what to expect, warning that Laird's "hidden theme" was almost certain to be "when can you start withdrawing troops?" Unfortunately, officials back in Washington were focusing on the human and material costs of the war, Davidson said—not on how to win it. Winning "means you're going to get men killed and hurt. The furthest thought from our minds is, how can you reduce casualties?"[12]

The military's apprehensions about Laird's visit were quickly realized. In six crammed days, Laird visited US installations across South Vietnam and met with General Abrams, Ambassador Bunker, and President Thieu. His message to each of them was blunt: the American people expected the new administration to bring the war to a conclusion.[13] That meant transferring the main responsibility for combat to the South Vietnamese. Toward that end, they must start planning for a draw-down of 50,000 to 70,000 US troops by the end of 1969.

While Laird was in South Vietnam talking about troop reductions, Nixon was sitting in Washington fuming about the continuing enemy attacks and once again entertaining the idea of secretly bombing Cambodia. On March 8, he authorized the bombing of Base 353 in the Fishhook section of Cambodia, across the border from Tay Ninh province, where US soldiers—including the late Sergeant Olea and his men—had been attacked. Once again Secretary Rogers interposed an objection, leading Nixon to briefly suspend the order. In conversation with Kissinger, Nixon expressed concern that "the little State boys will start squealing" and that the public would learn of Rogers' opposition.[14]

Nixon's preoccupation with secrecy reflected the changed political environment. Regardless of whether a measure made military sense, there was little disposition by the public to support any expansion of the war. If the administration was going to start bombing Cambodia, it seemed necessary to proceed by stealth. Meanwhile, the president's patience with Rogers was ebbing fast. While willing to delay a few days, he insisted that definitive action be taken.

He had already put the North Vietnamese on notice that there would be retaliation for their aggressive acts. "If they hit us again," he instructed Kissinger, "We will hit them with no warning." For Nixon, it was vitally important that the United States project power and resolve. "You only warn once," the president declared. Although CIA analysts were dubious about the military value of the Cambodian targets, "That doesn't bother me too much . . . we'll hit something," the president declaimed.

However, Nixon wanted to be sure that the Secretary of Defense would be in his camp. Bowing to White House pressure, Laird uneasily cabled his consent. Given his outlook, this was a significant concession. However, the Secretary's Vietnam trip had clarified for him the extreme disappointment of military officials over his plans to withdraw thousands of troops over the next nine months. Furthermore, General Abrams and Ambassador Bunker were still pushing hard for renewed attacks on North Vietnam. Needing to sign off on some military initiative, Laird agreed to the secret bombing of Cambodia as least likely to result in US casualties or a public furor.[15]

This fateful choice prefigured Laird's future political strategy in the years to come. While using his using his authority to reduce the American suffering in the war, he refrained from questioning the overall enterprise or expending political capital to cut the casualties of Vietnamese, Laotians, or Cambodians. During this Vietnam trip he gained a deeper appreciation of the weakness of the Saigon government and the obstacles to success. However, his primary objective was to bring the troops home as quickly as possible and, to achieve this, he was willing to compromise on other matters.

With Laird's consent, on March 18 Nixon gave the order for American B-52 bombers to strike enemy Base 352 inside Cambodia. In this raid, grotesquely titled Breakfast, American pilots flew 48 sorties on the first day. To conceal these air strikes, elaborate arrangements were made for the pilots to falsify their flight records so that it would appear they were bombing only on the South Vietnamese side of the border. This would ensure that officers all the way up the chain of command to the Secretary of the Air Force would be unaware of their activity.[16]

However, in the aftermath of Breakfast, a small team of US Special Forces was sent into the area to assess the damage and locate enemy stragglers. Although they had been assured that North Vietnamese soldiers in the vicinity were dead, wounded, or dispersed, they were hit with a barrage of bullets from several directions. Two American radiomen were killed instantly, along with two others. The stunned survivors were extracted by helicopter. When a second Special Forces unit was ordered into Cambodia, the men refused to go.[17]

By ordering the bombing of an officially neutral, sovereign country without notifying the relevant congressional committees or allowing for public discussion, Nixon and Kissinger had crossed a red line—the first of many. For both men, the only constraint that mattered was fear of possible disclosure and the ensuing criticism. Still lacking a larger strategy, they somehow assumed that by upping the level of violence they were more likely to gain concessions in negotiations. When two days after the Cambodia bombing Kissinger received word from Ambassador Henry Cabot Lodge in Paris that the North Vietnamese had agreed to hold private talks, he interpreted this as confirmation that Breakfast worked, although it was quite possible that news of the operation had not yet reached Hanoi.

Nixon and Kissinger had reached their Cambodia decision before reviewing the responses to NSSM-1. This detailed inquiry, with its 29 major questions and 50 subsidiary ones, had consumed a great deal of officials' time and energy. Although it underpinned the president's claim that he was reexamining Vietnam policy from top to bottom, this was unfortunately never the case. If read carefully, the results might have constituted a powerful argument for exiting Vietnam as quickly as possible lest the administration be bogged down in the war for its duration.[18]

As revealed in the previous RAND study, responses to the questionnaire verified a split between "optimists" and "pessimists," which roughly corresponded to the professional military on the one hand and civilian officials on the other. Yet the overall tone was notably bleaker, with surprising consensus on some distinctly bad news.[19] While acknowledging "improvements" in the South Vietnamese government and military, all parties agreed that ARVN "cannot now, or in the foreseeable future stand up to both the VC and sizeable North Vietnamese forces."[20] Even if North Vietnamese troops left, it would be several years before the South Vietnamese army could fight the Viet Cong on its own. Ongoing problems with corruption and ineptness had produced "severe motivation, leadership and desertion problems," which would have to be rectified.[21]

As for the enemy, it was recognized that the North Vietnamese and People's Liberation Armed Force had sustained significant casualties during the past year. However, the North's objectives were unchanged, and because of their large manpower pool they retained "sufficient strength to pursue them." Although large quantities of weapons and supplies had been captured and destroyed, the Soviets and Chinese were making up for losses. As matters stood at present, "the enemy basically controls both sides' casualty rates."

The grim implication of these and other points was that South Vietnam would need to rely on American combat troops and air power for years to come, perhaps indefinitely. With an authoritarian, unpopular South Vietnamese government in power, an unmotivated army still riddled with corruption and incompetence, a reviving enemy capable of striking blows throughout the South and willing to sacrifice its increasing manpower, the prospects for a positive outcome were dim. Yet once again none of the respondents to the survey advocated for a rapid withdrawal, at least not on paper. The virtual silence on this option reflected an unspoken consensus within the "national security" bureaucracies: their task was to find ways of achieving existing goals, not ways of abandoning them.

The position of the professional military was at least logical. It wanted to maintain existing troop numbers, or even increase them, and maximize the use of force. However, Nixon was already thinking about mid-term elections and his own political future. Keenly attuned to antiwar pressures, he believed "we are working against a time-clock" and that his administration had no more than six to eight months to find a solution. In escalating military action in Cambodia and Laos, he was meeting the military's concerns part way. But given the existing limits on such action and pressure to stop the war, there was no prospect that the military could achieve its aims.

Not the least of these pressures was the clamor to "bring the troops home." On his return from Vietnam, Secretary of Defense Laird was calling for a reduction of 50,000 to 70,000 soldiers by year's end and a more rapid transfer of responsibility to the South.[22] Such a recommendation appealed to Nixon's desire to create the perception that he was winding down the war, even as he continued it. At the March 25 meeting of the NSC, the president emphasized the need for a plan to begin handing responsibility for the fighting to the South Vietnamese military. As the United States removed some of its troops, it was of critical importance that ARVN be rapidly trained and equipped to replace them.[23]

Although Nixon did not specifically order the draw-down, his support of the concept was a relief to Laird, who encouraged his colleagues to use the term "Vietnamization" as a positive way to describe this new policy. For the moment, Kissinger was quietly furious, regarding the change as a dangerous mistake. In his view, the American military presence was his most powerful lever for obtaining North Vietnamese concessions once serious negotiations were underway. If it became clear that American troops were on their way out, Hanoi would lose its incentive to compromise. For all the talk about building up ARVN, the responses to his questionnaire had revealed major deficiencies in that army with little prospect for rapid improvement.

Indeed, as the administration's Vietnam policy was taking shape, there was a lack of coherence in the overall strategy. If half a million American soldiers had proved incapable of preventing the enemy's military challenge, there was no reason to think that the South Vietnamese army, which the United States had been unsuccessfully "building" for more than a decade, could rise to the occasion. Even if the American troop removals proceeded slowly, which was perhaps Nixon's intention, there was no obvious path to a positive outcome.

Intensified bombing of Cambodia and Laos might produce some short-term gains but could not force the North Vietnamese out of the South or prevent a revived insurgency.,

Yet, however unpromising the administration's approach, it reflected the conflicting pressures the president faced. On the one hand, a mobilized peace movement and a war-weary public. On the other, a sprawling military establishment and national security apparatus led by people for whom defeat was unthinkable. And then there was Richard Nixon himself, whose entire career had featured themes of crises overcome and enemies vanquished.

Meanwhile Nixon and Kissinger had one other card to play, which might have surprised many Americans: the Soviet Union. Even before taking office, the president was considering the possibility that if negotiations with Hanoi proved intractable, the Russians, who were the chief suppliers to North Vietnam, might proffer assistance. The idea was not as strange as it seemed. During the last months of the Johnson administration, Moscow had been helpful in getting Hanoi to the negotiating table in Paris and in settling the drawn-out quarrel over its shape. This suggested they might be reevaluating their overall approach to the war.

During the previous year, anti-Soviet upheavals in Eastern Europe and an increasingly open conflict with China had revealed Russian vulnerabilities. The Soviets now seemed eager to reach agreements with the United States in areas of common interest. On his first visit to Nixon's White House, Ambassador Anatoly Dobrynin brought with him a conciliatory letter from his government that spoke of creating "the widest opportunities for mutual agreement . . . and cooperation in solving the urgent international problems."[24] The road was open, it stated, for a collaborative approach to nuclear arms control, the structure of postwar Europe, conflict in the Middle East, and, most crucially, the Vietnam War.

Nixon responded by introducing the idea of "linkage." "It is incumbent upon us," he said, "when we begin strategic arms talks to do what we can in a parallel way to defuse critical situations such as the Middle East and Vietnam." The United States would welcome Moscow's assistance in getting the Paris talks "off dead-center."[25] To facilitate such cooperation, Nixon suggested that Henry Kissinger become a "confidential channel" through which they could communicate candidly on matters of grave importance—a role Kissinger was so eager to assume that he gave Dobrynin his personal phone number and expressed a willingness to meet "any time, any place."[26]

During their first working lunch on February 21, Kissinger outlined for Dobrynin the rudiments of a grand US–Soviet bargain. At the core of the Cold War were decades of friction over the division of Germany and the fracture of the European continent. For Americans, the goals of eventually reunifying East and West Germany and liberating Eastern Europe from the Soviets had always been presented as important, albeit something for the long term. According to Kissinger, President Nixon "agrees with the Soviet Government that the foundations of the postwar order in Europe should not be changed."[27] Alterations would only cause instability and upheaval. Going forward, "you will not hear any statements from us" about the importance of liberating this portion of the continent. If the Soviet Union were equally respectful of American interests in Western Europe, the post-1945 arrangements would remain in place.

By 1969, few expected US troops to be dispatched to Eastern Europe. The United States had not responded militarily when, less than a year before, 600,000 Warsaw Pact soldiers had marched into Prague, snuffing out its democratic stirrings. Nor had it rattled any swords when Soviet Leonid Brezhnev subsequently elevated such intervention into a "doctrine" proclaiming a right to use armed force in countries where socialist rule was being challenged.

Nevertheless, many Americans would have been shocked by Kissinger's words, since Soviet aggression against Eastern Europe had provided much of the moral content of the Cold War narrative. It was because the Soviets had erected the Berlin Wall and sent their tanks into Budapest and elsewhere that the United States needed to be vigilant and proactive against their Russian adversary and its allies. The threat of communist aggression was ostensibly why the United States had decided to build a huge military in peacetime, field thousands of nuclear weapons, plant bases around the globe, and send hundreds of thousands of soldiers to Vietnam.

The war in Vietnam, like the Cold War itself, was understood to be a life-and-death struggle between freedom and communist tyranny. From Truman on, American presidents had linked America's national security to fighting communism abroad. The fear that revolutionaries in other countries were harnessed to communist superpowers in Moscow and Beijing was the justification both Kennedy and Johnson had used to create domestic support for the Vietnam War.

However, with domestic support waning, Kissinger explained during his lunch with Dobrynin that Nixon felt an urgency about getting out of Vietnam. Still the United States could not accept "a settlement that would look to Americans and the rest of the world like an outright military defeat." During the peace talks in Paris, they would therefore insist on "a mutual withdrawal of troops" from the South and the preservation of the Saigon government, at least for the immediate future. But if, down the road, "events took their own 'purely Vietnamese' course," meaning a change of government, the United States would make no objection.

Dobrynin reported to his superiors that "Nixon is primarily concerned about his own political reputation and how the settlement in Vietnam might affect his political future. That will be the main yardstick he will use in his approach to matters of war and peace in Vietnam." This impression was strengthened during Dobrynin's own meeting with the president. There could be no doubt that "the Vietnam question and our role in the talks remain an important tool in our hands for influencing the new administration."[28] At a later meeting, Kissinger stressed that Nixon was interested in improving relations with the Soviet Union "as the only great power other than the U.S. which is capable of significantly influencing world events," and reducing the danger of nuclear war.[29] If he could achieve this end, "he will be assured of winning the next election."

During these early encounters with Dobrynin, Kissinger oscillated between intimations of an expanded US–Soviet friendship on the one hand, and more drastic military action in Indochina on the other. Yet with regard to Vietnam, the Soviet ambassador was remarkably consistent in his communications: the Soviet Union could not under any circumstances cut off aid to North Vietnam, their influence with Hanoi was limited in any case, the obstacle to meaningful negotiations was an obstinate Saigon clique that was determined to hold on to power, and meaningful change would only come when the Vietnamese people were freed from foreign intervention.

Meanwhile a new international crisis tested the Nixon administration's resolve to appear tough. On April 15, the North Koreans had shot down a US Navy EC-121 reconnaissance plane, killing all 31 crewmembers aboard. Nixon's immediate impulse was to retaliate in some dramatic way, perhaps with a blockade or a strike on a North Korean airfield. In a now familiar vein, secretaries Rogers and Laird recommended against these ideas. It was by no means clear that the North Korean government had authorized the downing of the plane, and the repercussions of an American attack could be grave. Kissinger, who had already learned that by taking the toughest line he could ingratiate himself with the president and further marginalize the two cabinet officers, encouraged Nixon to take a strong stand while simultaneously pointing out that "we have to be ready to go very, very far in case it led to ground action." He didn't anticipate that matters would come to this, but if it happened "we might have to go to tactical nuclear and clear it up."[30]

At this delicate juncture, Nixon flinched. Instead of retaliating against North Korea, the administration would show its mettle in Cambodia. The Joint Chiefs had been pressing for additional attacks since, despite their claims of success, the first round of bombing had not succeeded in hitting COSVN or pushing the North Vietnamese army out of the sanctuaries. The Chiefs wanted to strike additional targets in the tri-border area known as Fishhook, where South Vietnam, Cambodia, and Laos adjoined. On Kissinger's recommendation, Nixon yielded to their wishes. Under the rubric of Operation Menu, there would be a series of attacks: Operation Breakfast would be followed by Lunch, Snacks, Dessert, and Dinner, ultimately totaling 3,600 bombing raids over Cambodia. So long as B-52s were conflated with meals, they were easy to dispatch.

Inside Vietnam, little had changed. As of April 1969, the Vietnam conflict had become the third bloodiest war in casualties in American history. Since Nixon's inauguration more than 2,000 US soldiers had died—often in relatively small encounters, such as the ambush in Tay Ninh province during his first morning in office.

Struck by the numbers, *Newsweek* magazine posed the question: how did so many men die in a period of mild fighting? The article mentioned three young men: Sgt. Edward Lama, age 21 from Mundelein, Illinois, ambushed; Pvt. Raymond Geary, age 24 from Chicago, killed by a sniper; Cpl. and. James O' Shaughnessy, age 21 from Closter, New Jersey, struck by a machine gun, died in a hospital. There was nothing unusual in these personal tragedies. It could have been any day in Vietnam. The *Newsweek* reporter interviewed an army surgeon, Captain Richard Gayle, who had treated many dying soldiers. "The men don't understand why this war is being fought," he said. "They would like to know why they have to risk their lives."[31]

This demanded answers. Yet all the explanations that had been given—it was a fight for freedom, it was to prevent falling dominos, it was to preserve American security—had ceased to be convincing. If US soldiers had been privy to the many top secret conversations taking place in Washington, their perplexity might have grown.

3

"I See Death Coming Up the Hill"

Why were men still dying? It was an apt question. During the earliest months of the Nixon presidency, the number of American combat deaths was equivalent to the losses sustained during the Tet offensive. Yet in contrast to the previous year, the Vietnam War had ceased to dominate the news, with the result that significant military developments were unexplained or ignored.

One notable example was an article, appearing in the May 9 issue of the *New York Times,* "Raids in Cambodia by U.S. Unprotested."[1] Written by Pentagon correspondent William Beecher, the story accurately described a major change in US policy—the ongoing B-52 bombings on the Cambodian side of the border. It also contained the telling detail that "small teams of men are permitted to slip across both the Cambodian and Laotian borders to locate enemy concentrations of men and material." It was a huge scoop, but neither the *Times* nor any other news outlet investigated further.

If journalists paid this no attention, the same could not be said for Nixon and Kissinger, for whom the secrecy of the MENU bombings was of utmost importance. Kissinger suspected Beecher was getting his information from someone in Laird's office, where there were too many closet "doves." The president believed that the "leaks" might be coming from Kissinger's staff, which included several Jewish intellectual types whose loyalty was questionable. According to a memorandum by FBI Director J. Edgar Hoover, Kissinger explained that the White House "was determined to destroy whoever did this, if we can find him."[2] With Nixon's approval, Hoover was instructed to stomp out "leaks" by placing warrantless wiretaps on several government officials and prominent journalists. Though theoretically a short-term initiative, these illegal wiretaps were extended for another 18 months to an expanding list of "enemies."

In early spring the media were continuing to downplay major features of the US role—B-52 bombings inside South Vietnam and Laos, "the reconnaissance in force" missions of small American units, the battles inside hamlets, the enemy ambushes and sapper attacks, even the larger sweeps into the A Shau Valley. Nevertheless, across the United States the still-climbing

American casualties were being experienced as family and community tragedies.

Hardest hit were rural small towns like Beallsville, Ohio where, out of a population of 450, 15 of their young men had gone to Vietnam; five had already returned, and six had been killed there. When the body of the sixth man, Navy medic Robert Lucas, was brought home, the town undertaker Keith Harper and the county treasurer Clarence Miller asked their Republican congressman to intercede at the Pentagon and request that the four men remaining in Vietnam be withdrawn. The Defense Department turned them down. Mayor Ben Gramlich, whose oldest son was among those still there, was less angry about the war than about a draft system that favored the wealthy: "They got our boys because this is a poor town and the boys can't afford to go to college."[3] But others—like Mrs. Earl Pittman, whose son Jack had been killed years earlier and who had refused to have a military funeral for him—were furious at the government.

The spiking casualty rate was due in part to General Creighton Abrams, who as head of MACV was pursuing an aggressive combat strategy. When Johnson had replaced General Westmoreland with Abrams, there was palpable relief in Washington that this battle-tested, plain-speaking general would bring a new pragmatism to the job. His predecessor's eagerness for major engagements and high body counts had imploded during the Tet offensive when it became obvious that the enemy was everywhere, shrewdly positioned for attacks across the South. Abrams was determined to fight "a smarter war," to get into the enemy's system, to eliminate the Viet Cong infrastructure in the villages, disrupt their supply lines and infiltration routes, destroy their weapons caches, and kill as many fighters as possible while doing so.[4]

As different as Abrams' approach might sound, like Westmoreland he favored going on the offensive. To support his approach, he had done a study showing that "friendly" casualties were lower and the "kill ratio" more favorable when combat was initiated by the United States. According to his estimates, when offensive operations were undertaken the US–enemy kill ratio was somewhere between 22:1 and 15.5:1, as opposed to 1.4:1 and 2.8:1 when the enemy struck first—the decimals giving a bizarrely authoritative ring to a highly speculative enterprise.

However "favorable" the "kill ratios" might have been, the high American casualties were gaining increased attention in Washington. Many in the government were wondering why, with peace negotiations supposedly underway, the US military needed to be that aggressive. Among the skeptics was Secretary of Defense Laird, who was increasingly troubled by a military strategy that was so profligate in sacrificing American lives.

However, for the generals who were charged with conducting the war these complaints were undermining. Chairman of the Joint Chiefs of Staff General Wheeler cabled Abrams about the disturbing Washington atmosphere:

> The subject of US casualties is being thrown at me at every juncture: in the press, by the Secretary of Defense, at the White House and on the Hill. I am concerned that decisions could be made in response to strong pressures inside and on the administration to seek a settlement of the war, which could be detrimental to our objective, or to adopt a defensive strategy in South Vietnam.[5]

To counter this, Wheeler lined up his colleagues on the Joint Chiefs of Staff to make a case for Abrams' strategy to the Secretary of Defense and others. Their point was that the adoption of a defensive strategy would only lead to more American deaths by giving the enemy sitting targets, while forfeiting the key advantages of superior firepower and greater mobility.

Though Laird was unconvinced, Nixon and Kissinger were amenable to General Abrams' approach –both as a battlefield strategy and as the necessary underpinning for effective diplomacy. Indeed, since taking office Nixon had almost reflexively yielded to the pressure from the professional military. Yet as increasing numbers of people began questioning his policies, Nixon also recognized the political necessity of reassuring Americans that he was making progress in finding a realistic exit from Vietnam.

Indeed as spring arrived, antiwar stirrings were on the rise. In New York, Los Angeles, San Francisco, Atlanta, Chicago, and Seattle, there were large marches for peace. Beneath were countless local and even individual acts of dissent impacting the military: the 5,000 or more draft-dodgers and deserters who had fled the country, the organized refusals of draftees to accept induction into the military, the high-profile attacks on draft boards and associated destruction of files, the appearance of antiwar newsletters and flyers on or near military bases.[6]

In Paris, the four-sided negotiation was going nowhere. After several months had passed with no reduction in casualty rates, even Republicans were becoming restive.[7] On May 1 Senator George Aiken of Vermont, the ranking Republican on the Senate Foreign Relations Committee, called for the beginning of troop withdrawals.[8] It might take "some time" before all the troops came home, he argued, but the process "should be started without delay." A day later, Pennsylvania Senator Hugh Scott, who had never publicly voiced any reservations about the war, called for the removal of "a substantial number" of troops from Vietnam, a position quietly held by other GOP colleagues.[9]

In theory, the White House position overlapped that of the senators. In April, Laird had prevailed upon Nixon to issue NSSM-36, asking the Joint Chiefs to produce scenarios for four possible timetables for the withdrawal of American troops, with final withdrawal dates ranging from December 1970 to December 1972. Laird himself was pushing for the withdrawal of 50,000 soldiers by mid-year and at least 70,000 by December. But the Joint Chiefs were insisting that no matter what date was chosen, the United States would need to maintain a residual force of 306,000 men. Nixon and Kissinger were also reluctant to proceed with a unilateral withdrawal, which they feared would inspire the communists to be more unyielding at the bargaining table.

Nonetheless, with considerable fanfare the White House let it be known that the president was preparing a major Vietnam speech to explain how the administration was working assiduously toward peace. The absence of anything of real substance to announce was no deterrent to Nixon or his speechwriters. To underscore its significance, top officials were flown back to the United States, including Ambassador Henry Cabot Lodge from Paris and Ambassador Bunker and General Abrams from Saigon. While all three had been in regular communication with the White House, their arrival added necessary drama to the occasion.

On May 14, in a televised speech to the nation, Nixon assured the American people that since becoming president "nothing has taken so much of my time and energy as the search for a way to bring lasting peace to Vietnam."[10] His administration had recognized from the outset that "the popular thing to do" was to simply bring the troops home and end the war. To have embraced this course would have been irresponsible and would have been a betrayal of the Vietnamese people "who had placed their trust in us." The task at hand was to end the war permanently "so that the younger brothers of our soldiers in Vietnam will not have to fight in the future in another Vietnam someplace else in the world."

So how might progress come about? One answer was to bolster the military capacity of the Saigon government, which already showed great signs of improvement. Indeed he had been told by General Abrams, "the time was fast approaching when South Vietnamese forces will be able to take over some of the fighting fronts now being manned by Americans." The other was to pursue a fair and balanced negotiated settlement that would take proper account of the interests of all parties. His administration intended to do both.

By continuing to intervene in Vietnam, the United States was not acting selfishly. It sought no permanent bases, it would not seek a long-term military agreement, it would support the inclusion of all political groupings that renounced violence, and it would accept a "neutralist" government if this was preferred. The administration had only one immoveable goal: that the South Vietnamese had the right to freely determine their own destiny. For this to occur, all "foreign forces" must be removed from South Vietnam –meaning those from the North as well as the United States.

As he wound down, Nixon issued a veiled threat, warning that his "flexibility" should not be misinterpreted:

> No greater mistake could be made than to confuse flexibility with weakness, of being reasonable with a lack of resolution. I must also make it clear in all candor that if the needless suffering continues, this will affect other decisions. Nobody has anything to gain by delaying.

Returning to higher ground, the president expressed his personal sorrow at "the ugly face of war." He had "seen the wounded in field hospitals—American boys, South Vietnamese boys, North Vietnamese boys. They were different in many ways—the color of their skins, their religions, their races" —but those differences "were small compared with how they were alike." All were brave, all were young, and all had "their dreams for the future . . . shattered by a war over which they had no control." America could have "no greater and prouder role" than to end the conflict in a way that "will leave a world order in which people can live together in peace and friendship."

This was the first time since assuming the presidency that Nixon had needed to defuse mounting criticism. From that perspective, the speech was exquisitely done. It displayed the president as someone deeply attuned to the popular mood, sharing the common worries, and committed to constructive action. In making this case, Nixon had deftly pitched his words to the idealism of the American public.

However, the speech was also a work of obfuscation and in some respects outright dishonesty. It was not the case that the administration had carefully "challenged every assumption and every statistic" during an "intensive review of every aspect if the nation's Vietnam policy," as he had claimed. Indeed, it had ignored the more pessimistic findings of its' own experts to conclude that it was both desirable and realistic to continue fighting for a separate South Vietnam. Nor was it accurate to say that Nixon's only goal in Vietnam was to support the right of the South Vietnamese to determine their own destiny. The prospect of a communist government coming to power in South Vietnam, or of a reunification of North and South Vietnam, was anathema to Nixon.

In reality he was offering only two changes from previous American positions. One was a willingness to participate in discussions about the political as well as military points in dispute, thus overriding Saigon's previous objections to having non-Vietnamese "outsiders" involved in their internal matters. The other was a mutual and simultaneous withdrawal of American and North Vietnamese soldiers from the South. When Johnson had offered withdrawals, it was with the caveat that a residual force of US troops would remain until six months after the North Vietnamese had left—an untenable offer that the North would never have accepted. By framing mutual and simultaneous withdrawal as a major concession, Nixon was continuing to ignore the fact that neither Hanoi nor the National Liberation Front considered their fighters to be outsiders; rather they were patriots seeking the reunification of their country, which had been divided by outside fiat and was being ruled in the southern half by a corrupt dictatorship.

Initially members of Congress and the press responded to his presentation even more positively than Nixon might have hoped, treating it as a meaningful shift in America's position. Kissinger met immediately afterward with a group of senators who seemed enthusiastic. In his follow-up press briefing, the flurry of reporters' questions "suggested that everyone thought it was a very meaty speech."[11]

Nixon was especially delighted that his daughter Tricia was moved by his address. What had gotten to her "was when I was talking about the hospitals in Vietnam . . . the emotional thing."[12] In earlier drafts by his speechwriters, Nixon had been bothered by the absence of "schmaltz," so it was good to know this was effective. Even the critics, among them Ambassador Averell Harriman and Senators Mansfield, Dodd, and Percy, seemed satisfied. Nixon was curious about the reaction of Ted Kennedy, who was widely expected to challenge Nixon for the presidency in 1972, but there was silence from that quarter.

In the cold light of day, some journalists had second thoughts, wondering whether much had changed in the US negotiating position or whether these modifications would be sufficient to break the military stalemate on the ground. However, mainstream columnists and editorial writers were still unwilling to acknowledge that the United States could not prevail, or to face the possibility that the only genuine alternative to the ongoing devastation might be a full-scale, unilateral American withdrawal from the country.

After his initial euphoria, Nixon decided that the media were not adequately crediting his performance, a curious reaction since he had recognized the lack of substance from the outset. As would regularly occur, he turned to his most trusted confidant, Chief of Staff H. R. "Bob" Haldeman for validation. A former advertising executive, Haldeman had begun working for Nixon during his 1960 presidential campaign and had remained on his political team through the 1968 election. With his signature crew-cut, military bearing and curt way of communicating, he was widely regarded as a cold, authoritarian gatekeeper in the White House. Yet for Nixon, he was an intensely loyal, uncritical presence available to ruminate any time, day or night.

He complained to Haldeman that if John Kennedy had made the speech "they would have all been ecstatic."[13] This outcome reflected poor staff work, which had failed to properly burnish his image with the public. "The accurate story of how hard he works," the fact that he wrote the speech himself "is not getting out," Nixon lamented. This PR deficit was something that Haldeman, Kissinger, and his chief domestic advisor John Ehrlichman needed to address, since they were "the only people on the staff smart and strong enough to do it."

Nixon's problem, however, ran deeper than weak public relations. As with Johnson, his political vulnerability was rooted in the vicissitudes of the war itself. In mid-May, just days after his address to the nation, an American offensive in the A Shau valley launched shortly before his speech had started to go horribly, tragically wrong.

The offensive was part of General Abrams' effort to strike preemptively at enemy formations in order to disrupt their capacity for attack. It was aimed at I Corps, which encompassed the five northernmost provinces in South Vietnam, where thousands of enemy troops were continuing to operate despite repeated allied attempts to drive them out. Abrams wanted to hit them in the west near the Laotian border, blocking their advance toward the cities on the coast. For that purpose, the A Shau valley, a 30-mile stretch of land surrounded by heavily forested hills, was an obvious target. The scuttlebutt among soldiers, based on several disastrous missions that had been previously conducted, was that the A Shau Valley was a perilous place where grunts could be easily killed. Abrams' offensive, known as Apache Snow, was intended to be the largest air-mobile operation of the entire war, with a total of nine battalions (five American, four South Vietnamese) to be airlifted into the valley with the goal of capturing or destroying enemy supplies, disrupting the trails, locating and smashing the bases, and most importantly, killing as many enemy soldiers as possible.

On May 10, the first five battalions were airlifted into their different locations in the valley. It fell to the Third Battalion of the 187th Regiment to secure Dong Ap Bia Mountain, smack up against the Laotian border. Intelligence reports had revealed the presence of enemy forces on Ap Bia, but it was not known if they were there in large numbers, since the mountain was covered with a thick canopy of jungle making it virtually impossible to see clearly. On the ground tall elephant grass, bamboo shoots, and thick vines were certain to impede foot soldiers. The incline was quite steep in places, and deep ravines might have to be traversed—making this exceptionally difficult terrain.

The battalion commander was Lt. Col. Weldon Honeycutt, a career military man who had a reputation as something of a hothead. On assuming command of the battalion in January, he had reportedly told the men, "From now on this battalion is gonna fight, this battalion is gonna go out and find the enemy and kill him. This bullshit of running around and hiding is over."[14]

On Ap Bia, Honeycutt's men would indeed find the enemy, but with unexpected results. After being deposited by the helicopters, two of his companies advanced up a ridge on the northwest side of the mountain where they detected ominous signs of enemy activity-—lookout towers high in the canopied jungle, freshly-cut sections of bamboo, spider holes, and punji pits. Helicopters flying overhead could see trails, enemy bunkers, and supply dumps.[15] Within hours, shots coming out of the trees forced two companies to pull back for the night.

Before dawn, American aircraft struck the ridge, removing more of the vegetation and increasing visibility. Honeycutt ordered Bravo Company to resume their trek up the hill, with the hope that they could establish a command post near the pinnacle of the mountain. As they moved forward they saw suspicious signs and, sensing a trap, slowed their advance to a crawl.

Back at the command post, Honeycutt was furious at their cautious pace and began yelling commands at Captain Charles Littman over the radio. Littman made a snap decision to put a new platoon in the lead, one commanded by Lieutenant Chuck Denholm. His "point man" Bill Stevens had recently started panicking during engagements, but Denholm nonetheless put the terrified young man out in front. Stevens had only advanced a few meters when the platoon was hit by sniper fire. Everyone dashed for cover—at which juncture Stevens became paralyzed by fright and refused to leave the tree where he was huddled.[16] One of Denholm's closest friends, Aaron Rosensteich, offered himself in Stevens' place, while another friend, John McCarell, held up the rear. McCarell was known as the platoon "hippie" whose opposition to the war had landed him in frequent trouble, but under Denholm he had become a reliable soldier.

Back at the command post, documents had been found on the bodies of dead enemy troops and were rapidly translated into English, telling Colonel Honeycutt what his men were up against. An entire North Vietnamese regiment was operating on the mountain. The 29th NVA (North Vietnamese Army) was known to be especially dangerous and appeared to have 1,200 to 1,800 men on Ap Bia. A more cautious commander than Honeycutt might have feared such an encounter on unfamiliar, treacherous terrain. However, this was the battle he had been waiting for, and the danger was all the more reason to spur his men on.

As Rosenstreich resumed the slow climb up the mountain, the same sniper resumed shooting at them and, when Rosenstreich returned fire, another North Vietnamese soldier came out of a spider-hole and shot him in the chest. At the same time a different soldier hurled a rocket grenade at McCarell, setting off a claymore mine that he had been carrying in his backpack. The explosion tore his body into pieces and threw Lieutenant Denholm into the air. With bullets and grenades flying off the hill, shrapnel lodged in his skin, and two of his friends dead, Denholm was disoriented and stunned.[17] Nevertheless his men continued trying to move up the trail until they were overcome by fire from concealed attackers. Soon the bodies of dead and wounded Americans were everywhere, and Bravo Company was forced to retreat.

It was not only Bravo Company that was in trouble.[18] When it retreated, its forward observer had called in artillery and Cobra gunships to strike the area. The Cobra pilots became confused and, instead of hitting Ap Bia started firing rockets into Honeycutt's command post down below. The colonel began screaming into the radio, "You're shooting friendlies!" But before the pilots realized their mistake, they had killed two of their own men and wounded 35 others, including Honeycutt himself. With his command post in complete disarray and shrapnel in his back, he was in a rage.

Yet still he persisted, pulling in Alpha, Charlie, and Delta companies to join Bravo for an assault on Hill 937, close to the peak of Dong Ap Bia. Over the next 36 hours American planes struck it repeatedly, pouring gallons of napalm and dropping bombs designed for deep penetration—to no avail. When Honeycutt sent Bravo and Alpha companies moving up the trail again, they were overwhelmed by sniper fire and rocket-propelled grenades. Again, air power proved a mixed blessing when a fighter-bomber sent to relieve the pressure on Charlie accidentally killed and wounded some of the men from Bravo. A piece of shrapnel took off part of Specialist Myles Westman's head. As he lay dying and the men from his platoon were sobbing, the out-of-control Honeycutt was screaming, "You are killing my fucking people!"

But this was not the only error of the day. Delta Company had been ordered to approach the ridge from a different angle by going into a ravine and across a small river. In places the ravine became so steep the men had to cling to vines and tree branches to avoid a sheer drop. The first platoon had just crossed the river and was starting up the other side when an unseen enemy began flinging grenades at the column, seriously wounding three men. Other men lay on the ground suffering from heat prostration.

A Medevac was called in but was ordered to stay back until the enemy had been pushed away from the closest landing zone. Fearing that the delay was too dangerous for the wounded, the pilot decided not to wait. With the helicopter hovering one hundred feet off the ground, his crew lowered a basket to pick up the first man. An NVA soldier took aim and threw a grenade directly at the helicopter, which sent it crashing through the trees where it landed on the man they had tried to rescue, along with two others.[19] The most gravely injured of the survivors was the pilot, who would die from second- and third-degree burns before they could make it back to the command post. Before dying, he blamed himself.

Undaunted by the carnage, Honeycutt was more determined than ever to take the hill. Over the following days he intensified the air and artillery assault, using more napalm and greater numbers of heavy bombs. The men, however, were becoming more reluctant to keep assaulting the hill, and of those officers who were still functioning, many were coming unraveled and in some cases insubordinate.

The day after Delta Company's ordeal, Honeycutt put Charlie Company out in front. Following orders, they walked right into an ambush as squads of North Vietnamese soldiers bearing AK-47 rifles jumped out of their holes and began shooting. As the men pulled back, Honeycutt sent in Alpha Company to cover their retreat. However, once again "friendly" helicopter gunships aimed in the wrong direction, taking the life of 20-year-old Specialist Edward Brooks.

Honeycutt was furious over the incompetence of the airmen, despite the accumulating evidence that such errors were inherent in a situation where visibility was poor and the enemy's precise location difficult to determine. By the time Charlie Company had withdrawn to safer ground, 12 of their men were dead and 80 wounded. Their leader, Captain Dean Johnson, was overcome with grief and temporarily unable to continue his duties.

By May 16 the situation on Dong Ap Bia was generating concern among military higher-ups. Division commander Major General Melvin Zais was being questioned about why the men of the 187th were being repeatedly thrown up against the same well-fortified hill. What was to be gained by such an operation, and why couldn't B-52 bombs be used to drive out the enemy? Jay Sharbutt, a reporter from the Associated Press who had observed the demoralization and anger of the men on the mountain, was among those asking the questions. To Zais the answer seemed obvious: Hill 937 was the place where they had found the enemy in large numbers, and it remained the military's mission to kill as many as possible.

On May 18, Honeycutt ordered Alpha and Delta companies to head up the hill once more. By now the men's resistance to going back was extreme. Over the previous days, the constant bombardment from the air and from artillery had stripped even more of the mountain of its jungle canopy, giving North Vietnamese troops an open range to fire at Americans. As Alpha and Delta companies began their reluctant advance, they encountered a field of fire and a shower of grenades from the top.

Flying low overhead in his helicopter, Colonel Honeycutt continued to urge them forward even as men at the front of the columns were successively picked off. Slowly the depleted ranks proceeded. Within hours they were short of ammunition. Honeycutt then ordered Charlie Company, still traumatized from previous combat, to move quickly up the hill with supplies of ammunition. But as they emerged from the jungle and into the open space, they were hit from all sides. When Captain Johnson asked to retreat, Honeycutt screamed:

"Spread those men out and get them moving. You can't just sit there. Delta's running out of ammunition, and you've got to get up there to them right now . . . "

"We still can't move. The fire is just too heavy . . . "

"Dammit, you get these men moving up the mountain! Are you listening to me?

"You're being paid to fight the war, not discuss it on the radio!"[20]

As the men prepared for their final lunge to the top, lightning flashed across Dong Ap Bia and sheets of rain came pouring down the mountainside. Within minutes there were flash floods, and the ground was transformed into slippery mud, leaving no possibility of a further climb. Bowing to the inevitable, Honeycutt brought the men back down to the command post.

There the men found reporters waiting for them. Too exhausted, grief-stricken, and angry to be discreet, they told the press that the men were referring to Hill 937 as "Hamburger Hill," a place where they were being chopped up like fresh meat. By then the 187th Third Battalion had been sent up the hill on 10 separate occasions, losing more troops with each effort. Some of the soldiers spoke openly of their hostility toward Honeycutt, who was obsessed with taking the peak. Since the battle for "Hamburger Hill" had begun, Alpha and Bravo had lost nearly 50% of their original rosters and Charlie and Delta companies 80%.[21]

AP reporter Jay Sharbutt was among the journalists at the command post when the traumatized troops returned. One paragraph from the story he filed on May 19, which appeared in newspapers across the United States, conveyed the misery:

> Paratroopers came down from the mountain, their shirts dark green with sweat, their weapons gone, their bandages stained brown and red from mud and blood. Many cursed their hard-nosed Battalion commander, LTC Honeycutt, who sent three companies Sunday to take the 3000 foot mountain. . . . They failed and suffered. "That damn blackjack won't stop until he kills every one of us," said one.

Back in Washington, the news from Dong Ap Bia created a stir. On the floor of the Senate, Edward Kennedy of Massachusetts angrily demanded an explanation for this sacrifice of lives. Referring to Nixon's speech the previous week, Kennedy said that the president had made a great point of claiming that the United States was no longer seeking military victory and was asking for peace. If that was the case, "then how can we justify sending our boys against a hill, a dozen times or more until soldiers themselves question the madness of the action?"

Senator Kennedy made his remarks on May 20, the very day that the 187th was making its eleventh try up the hill. From Honeycutt's perspective, the troops were too close to victory to warrant retreat. Reinforced this time by the 1st Battalion of the 506th Infantry, they once again began their almost ritualized approach: more bombings near the summit, the dropping of napalm and artillery fire, then the slow crawl of individual platoons, watching for ambush.

This time there was less resistance. During the night the North Vietnamese had pulled back hundreds of troops into Laos, leaving an estimated 200 fighters on the hill. Charlie Company, which had been on the verge of mutiny, reached the summit at 11:20. In places the enemy was still holding out, shooting their rifles and throwing rocket-propelled grenades in what had become almost hand-to-hand combat. By 3:00 PM it was all over. Across the top of Ap Bia lay corpses of North Vietnamese soldiers, weapons, bandages, and backpacks. Near a cluster of trees, eight enemy survivors stared blankly into space. In their fury, the men from Alpha Company killed them all.[22]

As the US soldiers ransacked the area, climbing into tunnels and checking the spider holes, it became clear that the enemy had invested considerable resources in the defense of the peak. Underground there was a hospital, vast stores of weapons, and tons of rice. What was the purpose of all this effort? Was the goal to establish a base that could be used to launch an attack on Hue or Danang, as was subsequently suggested by the Pentagon? Or was the real goal to lay a great trap for gullible Americans, who could not resist a major opportunity to kill the enemy?[23]

To division commander Major General Melvin Zais, such speculation was irrelevant. In his view, expressed immediately thereafter and never altered, "It was a great victory by a gutsy bunch of guys." Some of the troops clearly disagreed. In a gesture that would be immortalized, one of them took a piece of cardboard from a C-ration box, wrote on it "Hamburger Hill," and nailed it to a tree trunk. Somebody else walked by and added: "Was it worth it?"

Back home the question on the cardboard was being asked by the press and in Congress. Barely a week after Nixon's well-received speech, articles in *Newsweek* ("Woe to the Victors")[24] and *Time* questioned the value of Hamburger Hill.[25] Referring to the Army's claim that victory there had been achieved with a "favorable" body count of 60 Americans versus 600 North Vietnamese, the *New York Times* wrote that if the Nixon administration was no longer pursuing military victory in Vietnam, as the president had claimed, "it is difficult to understand how it is showing it by this type of action. . . . Measuring success by the estimated number of dead bodies on the other side is a highly dubious proposition—morally and practically."

Though irritated by the press criticism, Nixon was especially disturbed by Ted Kennedy's attack.[26] Until recently, Kennedy, unlike his assassinated brothers, had seemed to be a conventional politician content to play by the rules of the Senate and to assert moderate public views. But he was rapidly staking out positions on a wide range of issues, domestic as well as international, that went well beyond the Democratic mainstream. His blast at the Nixon administration for its "irresponsible" sacrifice of US soldiers was his most radical move yet and augured serious trouble ahead.

The president lost no time striking back. Leading Republican senators were summoned to the White House and given their talking points. Even Hugh Scott, who had weeks before launched his own critique of administration policy, obediently sprang to the defense of the military. He urged Kennedy not to "second guess" the president, claiming that he possessed special knowledge that Nixon was "trying new initiatives to end the war." Senate Minority Leader Everett Dirksen affirmed his "affection" for Kennedy but also noted that Hanoi radio had already picked up his statements, and this would have an adverse effect on the morale of US troops.[27]

Yet Kennedy was unwilling to be silenced. In a commencement speech at Fordham University he intensified his critique, telling thousands of graduates and their families that military power was eclipsing other American values:

> As our nation is threatened from without, so it is threatened from within . . . We know our country is troubled. We know that part of the problem is that our domestic programs are starved for funds. Yet when we ask for justifications of our defense budget, we get slogans, not logic; we get scare, not reason.[28]

He was not the only voice warning about the outsized power of the military. Forty-five members of Congress had signed a statement warning that the United States was in danger of becoming "a national security state" and calling for Congress "to reassert control over the military bureaucracy and the policy decisions it has preempted."[29] While President Nixon was setting the broad framework of policy, it was clear that the generals, with their determination to win, were calling the shots. Deploring the "militarization" of American society and governance, it stressed the necessity for Congress "to resist this interwoven bureaucracy, so large and entrenched, so zealous and parochial, so unrestrained by an effective counterbalancing force in our society."

Although these were serious claims, worthy of sustained attention, Kennedy and the other signatories were a distinct minority.[30] Most senators and House members preferred to remain silent in the face of the tragic debacle on Dong Ap Bia, no matter how damning the information. In the days that followed, the estimates of US casualties climbed upward, reaching 84 deaths and 480 wounded. Lest there be any lingering doubt about the absurdity of the entire enterprise, as of June 5 all American troops had been removed from the mountain—and shortly thereafter, enemy forces had reclaimed it, resuming their habit of shooting at American airplanes that came too close.

The North Vietnamese had their own assessment of these events: the Americans had blundered into their trap. In a Hanoi newspaper article published in late May, the author crowed, "the arguments presented by the U.S. commanders are absurd and stupid."[31] From a military perspective:

> There is no reason to justify an operation by US commanders into such a disadvantageous battlefield as Ap Bia. Ap Bia belongs to the mountain forest battlefield, a type of battlefield very familiar to and the specialty of the Liberation Army. Ap Bia is in the liberated area, a location in which the revolutionary armed forces have full conditions favorable to them.

With its own hyper-inflated version of "the body count," the article claimed 1,700 American deaths, insisting that US military leaders "had turned their soldiers into targets of flesh." But having stumbled into a disaster, they were trying to cover their errors by presenting the "thrilling news" that they had seized a large command post at the top of the mountain. Anyone with "a shred of military knowledge" would realize that this was no place for a command post.

In the United States few Americans were following the details of "Hamburger Hill." The poll numbers on Nixon's handling of the Vietnam War were hovering slightly below 50% approval—not a terrible showing under the circumstances. But these figures did not register the rage and anguish coursing through specific sectors of American society and increasingly directed at the military and its associated institutions. Elite campuses that hosted ROTC programs had become the sites of tumultuous protests. In the spring, Harvard University and Dartmouth College experienced building takeovers culminating in arrests.

At the Yale graduation, valedictorian William McIlwaine Thompson Jr., who had been a page at the 1968 Republican convention, addressed the crowd of students and parents, citing the "frustration and despair" his classmates felt over the continuation of the Vietnam War. "We are told that the pride of the nation is at stake," Thompson observed. "But pride is expendable; lives are not. Within the next year some of us will die, others will be maimed in a war which has been declared a mistake."[32]

The valedictorian was not simply speaking for himself. Of a graduating class of 731 seniors, 77% had signed a petition requesting that their commencement speaker express opposition to the war; 143 seniors had signed a statement declaring that, if drafted by the military, they would refuse induction; and a majority of their classmates had pledged contributions to a legal defense fund for those facing charges.

Hostility to the military had become increasingly evident at local draft boards, the targets of escalating protest. On May 25 a small group of Chicago activists broke into the largest draft board in the city, dumped tar and red paint on some files, and threw others into a gasoline-drenched bonfire. Among those arrested in this startling display of civil disobedience were two Catholic clergymen.[33]

Already in progress was the trial of the "Milwaukee 14," who included five Catholic priests, for breaking into a Selective Service office the previous September and seizing thousands of 1-A files, burning them with homemade napalm in a nearby park. During the weeks of the trial, the courtroom was packed with supporters wearing red "Milwaukee 14" armbands. On several occasions Circuit Judge Charles Larson had to warn the audience to observe decorum. It was no surprise that the jury found the defendants guilty on charges of burglary, arson, and theft. More surprising was when stern Judge Larson, who, while sentencing one of the priests, took out his handkerchief and wept.

For those Americans who were paying attention to the Vietnam War, the month of June was a time to weep. *Life* magazine ran a special –the photos of the 241 US soldiers who had died in one week of combat.[34]They also printed the last line of a letter written by one of these soldiers to his parents: "You may not be able to read this . . . I am writing in a hurry. I see death coming up the hill." He was referring to Hill 937, where he perished.

From Nixon's perspective, even the survivors could pose problems. In a CBS television interview with a wounded soldier, the young man characterized the assault on Ap Bia as "a turkey shoot . . . and we were the turkeys." He also related that he and his buddies had cried all night because so many of their friends had been shot up in "a seemingly senseless exercise." Irked by the story, Nixon sent a message to Kissinger and Laird citing the interview as "a sad commentary on our public relations effort."[35]

4

"It Makes Our Position Murder"

The administration's problem ran deeper than public relations. To antiwar critics, the pointless sacrifice of young Americans on Ap Bia Mountain exemplified the irrationality of the entire project. As the list of casualties grew, support for this perspective was again on the rise. Secretary of Defense Melvin Laird remained a camouflaged ally. In public, Laird had defended US military action in the A Shau Valley. In private he was more determined than ever to minimize US casualties regardless of its impact on the overall war effort.[1]

The secretary was an unlikely "dove." Within the House of Representatives he had been a reliable proponent of advanced weaponry and large military budgets, as well as favoring tough policies toward the USSR and other communist states. Even his physical appearance contributed to an impression of bellicosity. With his large brow and balding head, piercing eyes and frequently stern demeanor, he seemed to personify the Nixon hardliners. Yet inside the government, he was fast becoming Henry Kissinger's most formidable adversary.

As a member of Congress Laird had been a canny infighter, who had spent years figuring out what the traffic would bear on any given issue, elbowing opponents, making deals, and when necessary biding his time. Regarding Vietnam, his sense of personal morality led him to focus on achievable ends. Since the United States was squandering the lives of its young people, he would do what he could to lower the numbers. But he was not one to wring his hands over the men whom he could not save, or the civilians in foreign lands.

It was for this purpose that he had persuaded President Nixon to approve NSSM-36, requiring the Joint Chiefs of Staff to produce four possible timetables for the withdrawal of American troops from Vietnam. However, the Chiefs were plainly skeptical about the whole concept of "Vietnamization"—the idea that a strengthened South Vietnamese military could safely replace American soldiers.[2] In their view, the Army of South Vietnam would never be able to fulfill the vacuum created by the departure of all US combat troops unless the enemy threat had been substantially reduced. For this reason, they wanted to restrict troop removals for 1969 to a maximum of 50,000 men, to be carried out in two increments: 25,000 in July, and an additional 25,000 later in the year, assuming conditions on the ground remained stable. No matter which "completion date" they selected, they still insisted on maintaining a "residual force" of 306,000 U.S. troops inside South Vietnam.

While Laird disliked the numbers the Joint Chiefs had proposed, he was most concerned with starting the process on the theory that once troop withdrawals began it would be difficult to reverse the momentum. What lent urgency to the decisions about the number and timing of the initial troop withdrawals was an upcoming June 8 meeting on Midway Island scheduled between President Nixon and General Thieu, the South Vietnamese leader.

The White House considered this first-time meeting of exceptional importance. During the closing months of Johnson's presidency, relations between Washington and Saigon had become increasingly hostile. At Nixon's behest, Ambassador Bunker had been busily patching up the alliance. Yet tensions remained. General Thieu was concerned about the constant rumors of US troop withdrawals, and both he and his colleagues were disturbed by Nixon's pronouncement that the United States would accept any form of government freely chosen by the South Vietnamese.[3] Did this mean that Nixon might be open to Hanoi's proposal for an interim coalition government in the South, and might this openness extend to including the communists in such a regime?

Nixon and Kissinger knew that reassuring Thieu of their intentions had to be a priority, while also using the meeting to convince the American public that administration policy was truly changing. To achieve the latter, they needed Thieu to sound cooperative on both the Paris negotiations and on troop withdrawals. To ensure that Thieu played his assigned role, everything about the conference was elaborately scripted in advance—including the news of the troop withdrawals, which Nixon had decided to announce at Midway. Although the press had already reported this, the White House had not yet made it official. Everything depended on how the story was packaged. It must not sound like an American retreat. Which in fact it was. If the enemy concluded that the United States was quitting the battlefields out of exhaustion or because of domestic dissent, it would have every incentive to fight on. Instead, the narrative must convey that the South Vietnamese army was so improved that there was no longer a need for 550,000 American troops.

To the president's annoyance, members of the press weren't buying this version of events. *Newsweek*, for example, said in early June that despite troop increases and a great infusion of new weaponry, the morale of the South Vietnamese soldiers was dismal, and US commanders lacked confidence in them. Such negativity about the early failures of Vietnamization, on top of the horrific news about "Hamburger Hill," made it even more urgent that the Midway conference succeed.

The administration had picked a curiously isolated setting for the conference. Thieu had wanted to meet Nixon in Honolulu,[4] but since peace demonstrators might show up, the decision was to meet at the site of a famed World War II battle, now a United States military base. In their initial meeting, Nixon hastened to blame the American press for any difficulties that might have cropped up between their two nations.[5] Any speculation that the United States was pushing for a coalition government was completely "unfounded," he asserted. However, he wanted General Thieu to understand the domestic pressures in the United States and the importance of the 1970 congressional elections. Thieu dutifully acknowledged the political challenges that the president faced. He emphasized that his government was open to a reasonable compromise settlement in Paris and was prepared to assume a greater burden of the fighting.

To avoid possible slip-ups, the press conference that followed the meeting was as tightly scripted as the official meeting had been.[6] Each man issued a formal statement, with no opportunity for reporters to ask questions. A compliant Thieu stated his government's willingness to hold fair and inclusive elections if all "foreign troops" were removed from the South. And as he had been instructed to do, he presented the American decision to make an initial cut of 25,000 soldiers as his own idea. For his part, Nixon reaffirmed US support for the Saigon government and its commitment to maintaining a military force large enough to ward off communist "aggression."

Together the two presidents "reiterated their common resolve to reject any attempt to impose upon the Republic of Vietnam any system or program or any particular form of government, such as a coalition, without regard to the will of the people of South Vietnam." Speaking in English, Thieu expressed the gratitude of the Vietnamese people for the sacrifice of Americans and their willingness "to join us in defense of freedom . . . and to defend the common cause of the free world."

Back in Saigon, it was unclear whose freedom was being defended. Although top US officials from Nixon on down preferred to ignore the matter, the awkward truth was that South Vietnam remained a dictatorship and the freedoms of its citizens were severely limited. Just prior to Midway, Thieu's government had suspended publication of three daily newspapers in the capital for undermining the war effort.[7] This brought to 30 the number of papers suspended since the regime had officially ended censorship the previous year. Whether in print or speech, it was against the law for anyone even to refer publicly to a "coalition government," and that did not change after Midway. Broadcasting live from Independence Palace, Thieu stated that President Nixon would never accept a coalition government and reiterated that anyone "who spread rumors that there will be a coalition government in this country . . . will be severely punished on charges of collusion with the enemy and demoralizing the army and the people."

Despite its reputation for having an antiwar bias, the American media ran few stories about the internal practices of the South Vietnamese government. In the very week that Nixon was heading to Midway, a private blue-ribbon U.S. Study Team on Religious and Political Freedom in Vietnam released a highly critical report that attracted little attention from the press or anyone in government.[8] The eight-person team included Congressman John Conyers from Michigan, John Pemberton, executive director of the American Civil Liberties Union, a retired admiral, and several prominent clergy. The group had made a week-long trip to South Vietnam where they interviewed a wide range of people: President Thieu and other government officials, national religious leaders, political prisoners, students, intellectuals, and journalists. On their week-long itinerary were three of the four largest national prisons for civilians. Some of the most damning sections of their report dealt with the detention, interrogation, and treatment of those prisoners. According to data provided by the Director of Correctional Institutions, there were 85,000 people in the national prison system, 64% of whom were classified as "communists." This did not include another 10,000 people in the provincial interrogation centers or the many thousands of enemy fighters in the custody of the South Vietnamese military. Thousands of people had been arrested in South Vietnam by a variety of government entities and incarcerated without trial, often with no knowledge of the charges against them. While the condition of some of the prisoners they visited "appeared to reflect modern notions of penal administration," the sheer weight of witness testimony concerning physical abuse seemed "overwhelmingly conclusive."

It was also apparent that government officials were using words like *communism* and *neutralism* "to silence dissent and weaken political and religious opposition." According to Article 4 of the South Vietnamese constitution, "Every activity designed to publicize or carry out Communism is prohibited." When the group met with General Thieu, he had cited Article 4 to explain why he had incarcerated his political opponent Truong Dinh Zhu, who had advocated the formation of a coalition government in which the NLF might participate. Students, opposition politicians, peace activists, Buddhist monks who advocated nonviolence, and defenders of freedom of the press had all been "systematically suppressed by an insecure government that relies more on police state tactics and American support than on true representation and popular support."

One of the facilities the team visited was the "showcase prison" of Chi Hoa, which the United States had been funding and advising since 1963. Upon arrival, they were given glossy brochures with pictures of prisoners in classes, at worship, or in recreational activities. As they walked around, they saw that the halls and cells appeared clean, and they watched prisoners engaged in a range of harmless activities. However, they were horrified to learn from the warden that 200 children between the ages of 10 and 14 years of age and another 200 between the ages of 15 and 18 were in Chi Hoa awaiting sentences. When they asked to see the children's section, they discovered another 47 youngsters under the age of eight:

> One child 4 years old said he was in prison because he had been caught stealing a necklace. The children were squatting in one end of the room eating when the Team members entered. They live in a bare room, with sanitary facilities at one end. No materials for play or study were in evidence. The food was rice with vegetables and fish. It looked inadequate. The children seemed to be well physically. When the Team entered, the children left their bowls of food and assembled in lines. All, even the 4-year-old, stood at attention and did not move or speak.

There were of course sections of the prison that could not be viewed, including disciplinary cells for men held in solitary confinement.

The most unsettling place they saw was Con Son Island prison, located about 50 miles off the coast and populated by more than 7,000 inmates. The adult occupants of this facility had been tried by military field courts and found guilty of political crimes. Before their arrival at Con Son, the Study Team had heard stories about "tiger cages" in which prisoners were chained to the floor and forced into a prone position. For obvious reasons, the South

Vietnamese authorities imposed tight restrictions on what the American visitors were permitted to see, but assured the group that the "tiger cages" no longer existed. However, one prisoner they met surreptitiously informed them that the "cages" were still in operation, but there was no simple way to verify this.

From their conversations with South Vietnamese functionaries, US advisors, and former prisoners, it became abundantly clear that the gravest physical abuse was not occurring in the long-term facilities they visited but in the interrogation centers, where people could be held for months on end without clear charges or even a right to counsel. One common practice was to place a soaked cloth over the nose and mouth of the prisoner, who was tied to a bench. Just before the victim choked to death, the cloth was removed and then the sequence was repeated. A variant of this procedure was to pump water into the person's nose. Another frequently used technique was to elevate the victim "on a rope bound to his hands which are crossed behind his back." Witnesses provided gruesome accounts of the sexual abuse of both men and women, and related incidents where children were tortured in order to elicit information from their parents.

The team's cover letter to President Nixon recounted that "religious and political suppression is widespread. Speaking for peace or in any way opposing the government easily brings the charge of Communist sympathy and subsequent arrest." There should be "no illusion that this climate of political and religious suppression is compatible with either a representative or stable government."

Though concerned to describe the humanitarian and moral issues that were at stake, the Study Team also made it clear that political repression was undermining the war effort and compromising the legitimacy of the government the United States was fighting to defend. Yet no one in the administration, from Nixon on down, including even Melvin Laird, showed any interest in following up on this report. As in the Johnson years, such obliviousness to the harshness of the South Vietnamese regime impeded sensible decision-making.

In the aftermath of Midway, Laird and Kissinger intensified their quiet duel over the direction of US policy.[9] On the surface, relations were amicable enough, the tension smoothed over by their private quips about the failings of Secretary of State Rogers. But both understood that with respect to Vietnam, they were each other's most dangerous opponent. They did, however, agree on one crucial point: for the immediate future there was no possibility of defeating the enemy on the battlefield. To Laird, this strengthened the case for a major reduction of US troops and the transfer of military responsibility to the South Vietnamese, who could then fight on indefinitely or, at some future point, simply crumble. For Kissinger it meant that the United States would have to achieve a favorable settlement at the negotiating table, which could only happen if the US continued to deploy significant military force. Absent that pressure, Hanoi would have little incentive to make concessions, He was extremely concerned about what would happen if Laird was able to convince Nixon to implement troop withdrawals in excess of 25,000 to 30,000.

From a tactical standpoint Laird had played a shrewd hand, recognizing that beginning the process of withdrawals would create a momentum for further removals. Indeed, Nixon's Midway announcement of the 25,000-man reduction was quickly followed by demands for an accelerated process from many quarters. In the July issue of *Foreign Affairs*, former Secretary of Defense Clark Clifford recommended removing 100,000 troops by the end of 1969 and withdrawing all of them by the end of 1970.[10] Other veterans of the Johnson administration—Ambassador Averell Harriman and Cyrus Vance, former US representative to the Paris peace talks—were also weighing in. Harriman privately warned that if more Americans were killed in Vietnam, it would be Nixon and Kissinger's "personal responsibility," while Vance was publicly advocating a "standstill cease-fire."[11] At the very moment that the president was hoping that the removal of 25,000 men would give him more room to maneuver, these recent insiders were undermining his approach. The doves were "vicious," Nixon complained. Kissinger called the LBJ ranch to protest: "it is hard to negotiate when Secretary of Defense of previous Administration does this—it makes our position murder, when he says the war is lost."[12]

During a White House press conference, Nixon was asked for his reaction to Clifford's article, to which he replied, "I would hope that we could beat Mr. Clifford's timetable."[13] As for the level of combat operations, he claimed that General Abrams had been instructed "to conduct this war with a minimum of American casualties."

Both claims were misleading. There was no administration plan afoot to surpass Clifford's timetable, and despite an admonition to minimize casualties in the aftermath of Hamburger Hill, General Abrams was still under orders to apply "maximum pressure" to the enemy. So long as the United States defined its mission as "the defeat" of the communists and preservation of an independent, non-communist South, it was inevitable that many would be killed or wounded.

After hearing the press conference, Kissinger was wracked with concern that Laird and Rogers were somehow twisting the president's mind and that there had been a secret decision "to reverse the Vietnam plan."[14] Turning to Haldeman, he speculated that Nixon had lost confidence in him and implored the Chief of Staff "to tell him if this ever happens." With no progress thus far in the Paris peace talks and nothing to show from his continued attempts to get the Soviets to exercise their influence on Hanoi, Kissinger was growing panicky.

Ignoring Nixon's instruction to be firm, throughout the spring Kissinger had gone out of his way to dangle diplomatic rewards in his conversations with Dobrynin. He assured the Russian ambassador of Nixon's willingness to allow Eastern Europe and East Germany to stay within the Soviet bloc. Whatever critical words the president might publicly utter on the subject could be safely disregarded, because they were "only a tribute to the mood of certain sub-strata of the American population, which plays a role in American elections."[15] The unification of Germany might be official US policy, but this was a topic for "the very, very distant future."

With Dobrynin heading back to Russia in June, Kissinger continued to press for Soviet assistance. The Paris peace talks were stalled, he complained, because the men in Hanoi assessed the entire international situation from their "own, specific, narrow viewpoint." To this silly complaint about a country at war, Dobrynin replied that no agreement was possible unless the "legitimate" aspirations of the Vietnamese people were considered. Kissinger emphasized the US willingness to compromise, but if Hanoi was inflexible, the administration would have no choice but to pursue "other alternatives." Dobrynin replied wryly that there was "no alternative" to a peaceful solution unless the US government "wants to repeat the previous administration's mistakes."

Meanwhile, the Kissinger was giving surprisingly little attention to a major development taking place in South Vietnam that would have a direct bearing on his diplomatic prospects. On June 6–8, while Nixon and Thieu were meeting at Midway, the South Vietnamese insurgents had assembled in a makeshift palace near the Cambodian border to establish a Provisional Revolutionary Government (PRG). The gathering consisted of 88 delegates and 72 guests, representing groups ranging from the National Liberation Front to the Vietnam Alliance of National, Democratic and Peace Forces (a non-communist group of urban intellectuals and professionals), the People's Revolutionary Party (the South Vietnamese communist party), and other non-Marxist nationalist groupings. Though they were far from united in their vision for the future, they had joined together to fight the war to overthrow the Thieu government and reunify their country. By so doing they hoped to become a major force at the Paris peace negotiations.[16]

At the entrance to the hall of the palace was a large painting depicting the progress of the Southern fighters; inside were banners and flags with inspirational slogans.[17] All the attendees joined together in singing their anthem, "Let's Liberate the South," and a round of speakers summoned them to sacrifice and fight harder toward that end. Attorney Nguyen Huu Tho traced the history of the people's struggle for independence and invoked their "gallant and successful resistance," which had provided a stirring example for progressive people everywhere:

> A nation with no large territory and population, an unshakeable identity of mind, an unflinching determination to fight, a judicious political and military line, which manages to rely mainly on its own strength, and at the same time to enlist outside support from the world's progressive people, is in a position to confront victoriously any imperialist aggression.

This had been the "most atrocious war in human history," but together they had "written an heroic epic" that should make them "boundlessly proud of our people, our seventeen million kindred northerners, our fine traditions, our glorious national history."

As for the United States government, Tho maintained that it was at "a serious strategic impasse," politically isolated at home, contending with the "sagging morale of its own troops," and beset by protests against US imperialism across the globe. This was the time, Tho said, to deal "hard stinging blows at US troops, destroying as much of the enemy's manpower and war materiel as possible."

The creation of the PRG reflected a strategic judgment that, from a domestic and international perspective, an alternative government would be far more effective than an insurgent organization. Among its benefits, it could participate in the Paris peace talks as the equivalent of Saigon's representatives, and in that capacity could generate fresh support from foreign governments and political sympathizers.[18]

Washington's failure to grasp the significance of the founding of the PRG was partly a matter of ignorance. There were no American officials or reporters on the ground to hear the songs, see the banners, listen to the speeches, or absorb the spirit of this insurgent conclave. And there was no one to follow the PRG ministries into their jungle hideaway, where they would take up residence under primitive conditions, living near starvation levels and hunting wild animals for food, remaining constantly alert to discovery.[19]

Even had this information been readily available to them, it was not the kind of data that interested the National Security Advisor or other high administration officials. The internal dynamics of guerilla armies and such intangibles as dedication to a cause and moral outrage mattered much less to them then the calculus of military power—kill ratios, quantities of supplies and weapons, location and percentages of pacified villages.

While Kissinger continued to spin his diplomatic webs with Dobrynin, he was oblivious to the fact that the Soviets had not only encouraged the formation of the PRG, but as of June 13 had formally recognized it. In the ensuing weeks, other eastern bloc and non-aligned nations had followed suit, in some cases opening embassies for PRG representatives.[20] The significance of the Russian decision was not lost on Hanoi, however. The official party newspaper *Nhan Duan* editorialized that Soviet recognition of the PRG was "the greatest embarrassment and setback" in Washington's plans to create a wedge between Vietnamese insurgents and the USSR.

Negotiators from the PRG soon replaced those from the NLF as the fourth participant—along with North Vietnam, South Vietnam, and the United States—in the Paris talks. At the same time, the leadership of the delegation passed to the PRG's Foreign Minister Nguyen Thi Binh. Within Vietnam she was known as the granddaughter of the revolutionary patriot Phan Chu Trin and for her work as roving ambassador for the NLF. A young, attractive, and razor-sharp diplomat, she eschewed Marxist rhetoric and presented herself to Western visitors as a pragmatic, approachable person.

Meanwhile, Thieu was wrestling with the results from Midway. Under US pressure he had committed himself to "free elections" under international supervision. He had also promised Ambassador Bunker that he would issue a public statement amplifying his commitment to a fair contest. This was no small challenge, given Thieu's private opposition to such an election any time in the near future. Nevertheless, his officials collaborated with Bunker's staff to produce an acceptable draft.[21]

With his feet to the fire, President Thieu delivered a television address in July to the South Vietnamese people in which he offered what he described as "a major initiative," a readiness to hold free elections at any time the two sides agreed upon. All political parties, including the NLF, would be allowed to participate assuming they renounced violence. To assure fairness, an international body could oversee the balloting. To untutored ears this might sound like an important change, but as Thieu had privately made clear to Bunker, these elections would not be held so long as any North Vietnamese troops remained in the South."[22]

On cue, President Nixon hastened to applaud this initiative, praising Thieu for his "comprehensive, statesman-like and eminently fair proposal." Leaders in North Vietnam were predictably contemptuous. In a blistering commentary, Radio Hanoi blasted the election proposal.[23] Noting the rapidity with which Nixon and Bunker had embraced it, they sarcastically observed, "This is like a mother praising her daughter's singing talent." How could there be free elections "while some 500,000 US expeditionary troops and satellite troops remain in South Vietnam" and when the "freedom and democratic rights of all strata of people are being trampled on?"

In fact, the speech was little more than a publicity stunt designed to assuage the restless American public, the fault-finding journalists, and an impatient Congress. Kissinger and Nixon hoped that if they could just buy time by mollifying the domestic front, they would be in a stronger position to wrest concessions from Hanoi going forward.

Unfortunately, while they marked time the destruction continued. American troops conducted their "search-and-destroy" missions, rechristened "secure and hold." B-52 bombers and tactical aircraft struck targets across South Vietnam, and during the first week of July another 772 Americans were wounded, 153 killed in action.[24] The terrible toll taken by these initiatives continued to fuel opposition within Congress. Members were hearing from grieving constituents, especially from places like Bealsville, Ohio, that were suffering disproportionate losses.

Among the congressional critics, perhaps the boldest was Senator George McGovern of South Dakota, who took it upon himself to fly to Paris in July so that he could learn first-hand from negotiators for North Vietnam and the PRG their actual position on the peace talks. On this visit, Senator McGovern discovered no new facts, but he gained a deeper appreciation of the enemy's negotiating position, an understanding that had thus far eluded Kissinger. North Vietnamese and PRG insistence on the complete withdrawal of American troops and removal of the Thieu government as a prerequisite for free elections posed a formidable challenge. But it was clear to the senator that "there will be no negotiations in Paris worthy of the name until we stop our offensive operations and begin the systematic withdrawal of our forces."[25]

Upon his return from the Senate floor, McGovern made an impassioned plea:

> If we truly seek for ourselves and for others "life, liberty and the pursuit of happiness " let us in the name of God and our own history end the slaughter and devastation that at once drain the blood of both Vietnam and America. If we cannot hear the anguished cries of Vietnam, let us at least look to what we are doing to our own beloved land.

Though by no means united on this stance, other Democrats, including Senators William Fulbright of Arkansas, Frank Church of Idaho, and Harold Hughes of Iowa, speaking in less emotional terms, echoed McGovern's sentiments, urging an immediate reduction of combat operations and an accelerated withdrawal of troops. Even hitherto "hawkish" Democrats were drifting into opposition. Among them was Thomas Eagleton of Missouri, who deplored the burden on American troops:

> Mr. President, if you had a boy 17 or 18 years of age, who was about to be drafted and . . . said, "I'm going into the Army and I will probably be sent to Vietnam." I guess if he asked you, you would have to tell him the truth: "Well young man, you are going to a war that we are not going to win . . . and you and maybe thousands of others will die. . . . I hope you will get back. I hope your picture will not appear in a future issue of *Life* magazine."[26]

Like some of his colleagues, Eagleton was hesitant to make specific demands of the White House, but dissatisfaction was mounting.

It was perhaps no coincidence that Secretary Laird, with his strong ties on Capitol Hill, was the one high-level official in the Nixon administration pushing for major troop withdrawals. In early July he had quietly instructed the Joint Chiefs of Staff "to reassess thoroughly our military strategy" in light of improved conditions on the ground and the president's recent statements about cutting casualties and shifting the burden of combat to the South Vietnamese. In conjunction with that request, he also ordered them to develop plans for additional troop withdrawals that could bring the number up to 100,000 by the end of the year.

At Abrams' headquarters there was strong resistance to both requests. While the level of fighting had gone down, this was viewed as temporary. In the general's opinion, enemy troops were merely regrouping in order to launch an offensive thrust. If people were naive enough to discern a change, they would wake up one morning and find the enemy taking over Quang Tri province.[27]

As for depending more on ARVN, Abrams knew this to be an illusion. The South Vietnamese troops might have new equipment and airborne training, but that wouldn't help with the kinds of activities that would really make a difference. In his view, they needed to get into the villages "and cream the VCI [Viet Cong Infrastructure], get out there in little units muckering around at night, helping the goddamn villagers, seeing that the goddamn rice stays in the warehouse and so on." Such actions the South Vietnamese army was reluctant to perform. And if the army of North Vietnam ever attacked them frontally, General Abrams expected the communists to "clean their clocks."[28]

In fending off Laird, Abrams had a strong ally in Henry Kissinger, who was also skeptical about any progress that the South Vietnamese forces had made, a skepticism he thought the enemy would share. As he reminded the president, "the communists probably cannot be fooled as to the rate of progress which the GVN (Government of South Vietnam) is achieving." Kissinger convinced Nixon to delay any decision about removing further troops until later in August. The timing was important to Kissinger because he was trying to arrange a secret meeting with Le Duc Tho, a member of Hanoi's politburo and special advisor to the Paris peace talks. For his first encounter with a top North Vietnamese official, someone who might have the clout to strike a deal, Kissinger was going behind the backs of the State Department and the Paris negotiating team. It was his intention to open a confidential, exclusive channel for future discussion with the enemy.

For Nixon, there was a balancing act. As of August his poll numbers were up again, but he also recognized that the promise of troop withdrawals was an important factor.[29] With this in mind, he overrode the objections of the Joint Chiefs of Staff, accepting instead Laird's reformulation of their mission statement, which emphasized "substantial changes in both the character of the war and the RVNAF ability to assume greater responsibility."[30] Therefore, it was the task of the US military to help the South Vietnamese troops "take over an increasing share of combat operations." In a nod to General Abrams, the document also included two other responsibilities: to carry out operations that would "reduce the flow of material and manpower support for the enemy," and to "maintain plans for a comprehensive air and naval campaign in SVN."

As a practical matter, this new language did not alter Nixon's and Kissinger's ongoing interest in some dramatic escalation of American military activity to impress the enemy. That preference was augmented when Kissinger's planned negotiation with the North Vietnamese proved fruitless. Not only did Le Duc Tho fail to appear, but when Kissinger met Xuan Thuy, the head of the North Vietnamese delegation in Paris, the latter offered no significant concessions. Instead, their three-and-a-half-hour colloquy made it clear to Kissinger, as it had to George McGovern, how firm and unshakeable were the North Vietnamese in upholding their core demands. Unlike Senator McGovern, however, Kissinger concluded that Hanoi's stand could be changed if the United States delivered a series of punishing military blows that conveyed unshakeable resolve.

By now nobody in the administration, including the president, was using the language of "victory." However, in substance this remained Nixon and Kissinger's objective: to preserve South Vietnam as a separate non-communist entity. This goal, after years of effort and sacrifice, was also important to the Joint Chiefs of Staff and MACV. Yet the fact remained that after six months of effort, the Nixon administration had nothing positive to show for its efforts despite more than 3,000 US soldiers dying.

While few high-level officials or politicians were willing to say flatly "this war is lost, bring everyone home," as during Tet the sense of futility was on the rise. This feeling was particularly acute for young people, given the reality of the draft. For both men and women of a certain age, the idea that American leaders might compel young men to risk their lives on behalf of a foreign dictator in a losing cause exemplified the amoral callousness and stupidity of those in authority.

In mid-August this amalgam of fury and outrage, idealism and rebellion, was on vivid display at the Woodstock "Summer of Love" Festival, billed as "Three Days of Peace and Music." A commercial venture designed to attract some 200,000 ticketholders, it unexpectedly drew a crowd of close to half a million young people, who flocked to the concert site on Max Yasgur's farm in Bethel, New York. A remarkable line-up of performers included Jimi Hendrix, the Jefferson Airplane, The Who, Janis Joplin, The Grateful Dead, and Ravi Shankar. When the size of the audience resulted in a drastic shortage of food, shelter, medical services, and sanitary facilities, with their misery compounded by pouring rain, the mud-streaked participants freely shared food and water—and drugs and sex—with each other.

Here in microcosm was an opportunity to show the world that "love" and "peace" could enable people to solve problems more effectively than war and anger. The result was a rapid formation of community and generational bonding.[31] In one richly symbolic moment, an Army helicopter dispatched from a nearby base flew overhead and dropped food for the audience. The gesture was warmly received, with "V" signs all around. Surely feeding people was a better use for an Army helicopter than flying over villages in South Vietnam and killing them.

One of the festival highlights came on day two, August 17—just as Richard Nixon was secretly deciding to delay more troop withdrawals. "Country Joe" of Country Joe and the Fish took up his guitar and began singing the "I-Feel-Like-I'm- Fixin'-to-Die Rag." In a powerful display of feeling, the 500,000 temporary inhabitants of Max Yasgur's farm stood up and joined the chorus:

> And it's one, two, three,
> What are we fighting for?
> Don't ask me I don't give a damn.
> Next stop is Vietnam.
> And it's five, six, seven, eight, open up the pearly gates.
> Well there ain't no time to wonder why,
> Whoopee! We're all gonna die.[32]

It was not only young concertgoers and hippies who had become cynical. For the soldiers still fighting in Vietnam, the removal of the first 25,000 troops had underscored how dim the prospects were for victory. The military's contempt for the ARVN was widespread, reaching all the way from the lowliest grunt to the headquarters of General Abrams. If the South Vietnamese army would never become capable of fighting on its own, how could the war be won? And if unwinnable, many soldiers wondered, then why should they be risking their lives?

By the fall of 1969, signs of soldiers' demoralization appeared—long hair, peace signs painted on helmets or dangling from neck-chains, the pervasive use of marijuana and other drugs, the subtle evasion of orders. Even some of the contingent of 25,000 soldiers who had been brought home in July were visibly hostile. A military order forbade them to wear peace medallions that had hung openly on many necks, but their words and actions once they returned home could not be as tightly controlled. As reporters gathered around the returnees at McChord Air Force base near Tacoma, Washington, a group of black soldiers gave a clenched-fist salute to passersby. Some of the soldiers were proud of their contribution, but others questioned its value when speaking to the press. In the words of Gary Doess, "I can truthfully say that I can't see any good reason for 36,000 Americans to have died."

Every so often more dramatic acts of direct insubordination were covered by journalists who were fortuitously on the scene. Thus it happened that Associated Press photographer Horst Fass was visiting the headquarters of Col. Robert Bacon's Third Battalion in late August, when a message arrived: "I'm sorry sir, but my men refused to go out. We cannot move out."[33] The six men in question were from Alpha Company a unit that had already lost two-thirds of its members fighting in Song Chang River valley 30 miles north of Danang. The men had been engaged in heavy combat for five days. Exhausted, hungry, and caked with mud, they refused an order to move toward enemy bunkers so that they could retrieve the bodies of two GIs. "Have you told them what it means to disobey orders under fire?" Bacon asked their lieutenant, Eugene Shurt. "I think they understand, but . . . they are broken," he replied. "There are boys here who have only 90 days. They want to go home in one piece." In the end, another officer was dispatched to the unit and the men agreed to proceed.

It was a small incident, but it raised questions about why US soldiers were being sent into battle in a seemingly futile effort. *New York Times* columnist James Reston had been vacillating over US policy for the past eight months. A Kissinger confidante, he had been generally optimistic about the Nixon administration's sincere efforts to end the war. Yet the story of Alpha Company bothered him. At some point the president must recognize that there is "a fundamental difference between his policy of ending the war gracefully and ending the war," he reflected.

It was a conundrum:

> He wants out on the installment plan, but the weekly installments are the lives of one or two hundred American soldiers. And he cannot get away from the incessant question: Why? To what purpose? The breaking point comes in politics as it came to Company A and it is not far off. What will be gained by this incessant killing? And how will the President or anybody else explain or excuse it?[34]

Reston's questions were hardly new. Ever since the Tet offensive, if not earlier, many Americans had been raising them. Yet paradoxically, the president's promise to "Vietnamize" the war lent them greater urgency. If the United States was going to exit Vietnam before an actual settlement, then why delay their withdrawal? By dint of his patience, tact, and bureaucratic acumen, Secretary Laird had managed the removal of a relatively small increment of troops, a process he was trying to make irreversible. But change was coming at a glacial pace, and meanwhile the suffering and devastation continued.

5

"Blow Their Candles Out"

What would happen in the fall? For months, Nixon and Kissinger had threatened North Vietnamese leaders with grave consequences if, by November 1969 (the one-year anniversary of the US bombing halt Lyndon Johnson had initiated), they did not modify their demands at the Paris negotiating table. In case they resisted, Kissinger's staff was working out the details of DUCK HOOK, which included several possible punitive actions including aerial mining of Haiphong harbor and the use of B-52s over North Vietnam. During this same period, the Joint Chiefs of Staff were working on their own plans under the rubric PRUNING KNIFE.[1]

While there was considerable overlap between the two approaches, Kissinger's staff put the emphasis on quick, devastating blows designed to convince Hanoi that failure to make diplomatic concessions would produce "unacceptable damage to their society." By contrast, the Joint Chiefs' plan was focused on military objectives—a series of escalating moves designed to fortify the combat position of the South Vietnamese troops. Excluded from this early planning were Secretary of State Rogers and Secretary of Defense Laird.[2]

When they finally learned of these proposals both men reacted negatively, fearing the domestic firestorm such actions might ignite. With a big national protest already pending, even Nixon was prepared to postpone.[3] An immediate worry was the emergence of a new group, the Vietnam Moratorium Committee.[4] The leadership and energy for this mainstream organization had come from young people, some of them student government presidents and college newspaper editors, who still believed change could be achieved by "working within the system," as many of them had done the previous year by volunteering for the Eugene McCarthy and Robert Kennedy campaigns. So long as the war continued, they intended to hold monthly protests across the country to encourage Americans to stop doing "business as usual" and engage in some kind of peaceful protest activity. This could take many different forms—a vigil, a tree-planting, an interfaith service, a seminar, an artistic display, a petition campaign, a rally—so long as it was peaceful and inclusive.

The group had scheduled its first one-day event for October 15. Successive monthly Moratoriums would increase in length: two days for the second, three for the third, and so forth. Eventually they would run out of days, but hopefully the war would have ended before then.

Taking a purposefully mainstream approach, the Moratorium Committee was distinguishing itself from the virtually defunct Students for a Democratic Society (SDS), the group that had provided much of the energy for antiwar activity on college campuses from 1965 to 1968.[5] At its peak, SDS had hundreds of chapters across the county and an estimated membership of 80,000 to 100,000 members. However, in the last two years the organization had been ripped apart by sectarian quarrels when much of its leadership concluded that peaceful, legal methods of protest were ineffective and that violent revolutionary activity was necessary.

For Nixon, the militancy of protesters like those in SDS made them useful opponents. By their actions they marginalized themselves and created enemies, even among people who might have been allies. The obvious danger of the Vietnam Moratorium Committee was its earnest respectability, which gave it potential to reach a larger audience than SDS ever had. And by early October, it gave every indication of doing so. Money was pouring in, enabling it to grow from one small Washington office with a handful of volunteers to 10 offices with a paid staff of 35. It was originally assumed that the October 15 events would take place mainly on campuses. But adults "over 30" began planning for a much wider range of protests. Each passing day brought fresh news of scheduled events in major cities, as well as in many smaller towns where nobody had ever protested before. Remarkably, many city councils, mayors, and state legislators were giving support.

The momentum building around Moratorium Day enlivened congressional opposition to the war.[6] Several prominent legislators were supporting the effort, among them Republican Senators Charles Goodell, Jacob Javits, Mark Hatfield, and George Aiken; and from the Democratic side, Senators McGovern, Ed Muskie, and Frank Church. Some even offered to speak at one of the Moratorium events, as did various luminaries from the entertainment field, from business and the professions, and from former public officials. Organizers became increasingly excited and hopeful. With so many people coming together, perhaps this would finally force a real change in policy.

Nixon inadvertently stoked the flames. When asked for his thoughts on the Moratorium at his September 26 press conference, he testily replied, "Under no circumstances will I be affected by it."

Nothing could have been further from the truth. Nixon and Kissinger were consumed with the question of how to undermine the antiwar movement. Since it was widely believed, both within and outside the administration, that the draft was a major source of campus dissent, and that without it the extraordinary politicization of college students would not have occurred, Nixon had pondered ending the draft.[7] Yet so long as the Army needed more men, there was no obvious way to eliminate it. As a long-term solution, he was convinced that an "all-volunteer" Army, offering higher pay and improved benefits, would enable future administrations to avoid the student rebellion that had plagued Lyndon Johnson's presidency and now his own.

As a short-term fix, on September 20 Nixon had announced that he was reducing draft calls for the coming year by 50,000 men. He also urged Congress to amend the draft law so that in the future he could implement a lottery system that would apply only to 19-year-olds or to those out of college who had not yet participated in a lottery. The great advantage of this system was that it would limit to one year, rather than seven, the time a young man was subject to the draft.[8]

However, these developments were too little and too late to slow the momentum of the upcoming protests or to quell widespread opposition to the war. A recent Gallup poll had showed that 47% of Americans were in favor of removing all troops by the end of 1970.

During this period, the White House was particularly concerned about a resolution introduced by Senator Goodell of New York that would cut all funding for the Vietnam War after December 1970. Until this point, congressional dissenters had made fiery speeches but had not attempted to use the "power of the purse" to stop the war. Goodell's resolution raised the stakes. As Nixon observed, "If Congress cuts the appropriation, then we are finished."[9] Seething over Goodell's perfidy, Kissinger claimed that his action "is almost treason," and Nixon warned the Republican leadership that "dovish" members of the House and Senate were creating new barriers to peace.[10] Should the United States provide a definite date for troop withdrawal, as Goodell and others were proposing, the practical result would be the collapse of the peace negotiations.

Some congressional critics, including Republican Senator George Aiken, were still susceptible to Nixon's arguments. It was one thing to oppose the war, another to force the removal of American troops. In a speech at Norwich University, Senator Aiken warned that if legislators compelled the withdrawal of US troops, it could lead to the "wholesale slaughter of those who . . . put their faith in the United States government."[11] Other colleagues shared his hesitation, among them Senate Majority Leader Mike Mansfield and chairman of the Foreign Relations Committee William Fulbright. Although convinced that the Vietnam War was a mistake, they were nevertheless reluctant to take responsibility for the possibility of an American defeat. Their reluctance was only reinforced by a letter sent by North Vietnamese premier Pham Van Dong to the Moratorium Committee praising their dissent:

> Your drive eloquently reflects the legitimate and pressing demand of your people to save the honor of the United States and to avoid for their boys a useless death in Vietnam. . . . We are firmly confident that with the solidarity and courage of our two peoples, with the sympathy and support of the peace-loving peoples in the world, the struggle of the Vietnamese people and the progressive people in the United States will end in total victory.[12]

Pham's letter was consistent with a strategic direction long espoused by Ho Chi Minh—namely the belief that their nation's bid for independence and unification would be significantly strengthened by support from ordinary citizens in the West, especially Americans.[13] With the establishment of the Provisional Revolutionary Government as the fourth participant in the Paris peace talks, cultivating the American antiwar movement was a definite goal.

However, there was also a boomerang effect. Pham's letter played directly into the hands of the White House, validating the claim that the protesters were aiding and abetting the enemy. Seizing the opportunity, Kissinger enlisted Haldeman to organize the response to the letter. It was rapidly decided to let Vice President Agnew lead the charge. In a White House press conference, he denounced the letter as a "shocking intrusion into the affairs of the American people" by an enemy power, and demanded that Moratorium leaders and the "public officials" associated with them "openly repudiate the support of the totalitarian government which has on its hands the blood of 40,000 Americans."

Yet, this last-minute effort to discredit the Moratorium was ineffective. As of midnight October 14, hundreds of demonstrators were on the steps of the Capitol reading out the names of the American soldiers who had died in the war. By early morning, reports from around the county made it clear that the

Moratorium would be a stunning success. In big cities and small, in every region of the country, perhaps as many as two million Americans halted "business as usual" at least briefly to express their opposition to the war.

The protests included recitations of the names of the dead, marches, silent vigils, teach-ins, and rallies. In Washington DC, Coretta Scott King led a silent parade of 30,000 people holding their placards past the White House. Throughout Manhattan there were scores of events. At the Old Trinity Church near Wall Street, the bells tolled as prominent businessmen, whose disillusionment with the war had grown exponentially, participated in an all-day service.[14] Art galleries, museums, publishing houses, and many Broadway theaters closed for the day or created activities devoted to peace. In the early evening, crowds of protesters tied up traffic in midtown Manhattan as they headed to Bryant Park for a rally that attracted 50,000 people. They came to hear a long list of speakers, including three leading politicians—Mayor John Lindsay and Republican Senators Jacob Javits and Charles Goodell.

In smaller cities where peace demonstration had been less common—Salt Lake City, Pittsburgh, Minneapolis, Atlanta, Little Rock, and Austin –people turned out in droves. In Lexington, Kentucky, 2,700 people stood quietly in front of the federal courthouse listening to the names of the state's war dead.[15] As they came to the end, a middle-aged woman approached the microphone and mentioned one name: "This is my son. . . . He was killed last week." In Cicero, Illinois, a conservative suburb of Chicago, 800 students from Morton Junior College participated in an antiwar assembly while 300 housewives from nearby River Forest marched to the local post office, where they mailed letters to President Nixon asking him to stop the war. At Whittier College, the president's alma mater, the wife of the school's acting president lit an Olympic-style lamp designed to burn until all the American troops came home.

The size and scope of the protests caused editors and station managers to treat the Moratorium as major news, while many of the reporters covering events were palpably moved by the experience. Consequently, the Moratorium received extended coverage on the nightly news broadcasts, with NBC and CBS running hour-long specials. It was front-page news in most newspapers, including the *Washington Post* and the *New York Times,* while the weeklies, *Time, Newsweek,* and *Life,* devoted large sections to photos and analyses of the gatherings. Much of the coverage highlighted the conventional nature of the protesters and the patriotic spirit and idealism they displayed.

However, the Moratorium also attracted serious opposition, especially in the white South, in small-town America, and among white working-class voters in the metropolitan areas, including New York City. In New York, the dissension exposed a deep social cleavage. When Mayor John Lindsay proclaimed October 15 a "day of mourning" and ordered that the flag be flown at half-mast, the Policemen's Benevolent Society, which loathed the protesters and the mayor in equal measure, called on all precinct houses to fly their flags at full staff.[16] The Uniformed Firemen's Benevolent Association dubbed the occasion "a day of national disgrace," as did the American Legion, which denounced Lindsay's action as "indefensible, reprehensible and outrageous." Not even the World Series was above the conflict. At Shea Stadium, where the fourth game of the World Series was commencing, the military color guard and 225 wounded war vets refused to parade onto the field unless the flag, flying at half-mast, was fully raised.

Such conflicts notwithstanding, the inclusiveness of the Moratorium was without precedent—so inclusive that two Ehrlichman children, Susan Haldeman's boyfriend, and John Laird, son of the Secretary of Defense, all participated.[17] *Life* magazine portrayed it as "the largest expression of public dissent ever seen in this country." *Newsweek* proclaimed it "a day destined to go down in history."[18] *Time* commented on the widespread participation of many people new to protests, people who had "never thought to grow hair, don a hippie headband or burn a draft-card." After the Moratorium, it warned, the president "cannot escape the effects of the antiwar movement."

Though neither Nixon nor Kissinger had any intention of being pressured into abandoning the war, it was at this juncture that their priorities diverged. Kissinger was desperate to inflict a harsh blow on North Vietnam, believing that such escalation had become essential to effective diplomacy. However Nixon, unlike his national security advisor, was not free to ignore the political environment—not if he wanted to be reelected. In the aftermath of the Moratorium, the president concluded that plans for DUCK HOOK would have to be indefinitely shelved.[19]

Both men took some comfort in the fact that the bombing of Cambodia was proceeding apace, with the American public unaware of its occurrence. With Nixon's approval, Kissinger had instructed Laird to schedule more MENU bombings to occur every day during the first week of October and to continue thereafter.[20] He also requested the Air Force "to hit them in the DMZ, so they know we are getting trigger happy."

Though cathartic, these maneuvers offered no solution to the president's fundamental problem of how to achieve a successful end to the war when faced with an implacable enemy and mounting opposition on the home front. Hope lingered that the Soviet Union might offer some assistance. Kissinger had held out various "carrots" to the Russians—acceptance of the post–World War II European settlement, a possible arms control deal, compromise in the Middle East, increased trade and economic benefits, even a personal friendship with the Russian ambassador. While this had improved the atmosphere, there had been no payoff with regard to the Vietnam War.

But if carrots did not work, then perhaps "sticks" would be more effective? Unlike DUCK HOOK, an effort to intimidate the Russians could be done under the radar—without the American public becoming aware of its occurrence. On October 13, the US tactical and strategic air forces began a stand-down of training and surveillance flights, indicating an increase in operational readiness.[21] For the first time since the Cuban missile crisis, the Strategic Air Command placed nuclear-armed B-52s on combat status—sitting on runways, fueled, and ready to fly attack missions. Meanwhile, secret orders went out to air bases around the world to ground American military planes.

Nixon and Kissinger viewed the nuclear alert as a subtle bit of strategy. It would remind the Russians of American capabilities and willingness to use extraordinary measures if necessary. Yet if anything, these moves had backfired. On his next visit to the White House, Ambassador Dobrynin complained about the lack of progress on substantive issues, including Vietnam, where the administration's rigidity in the negotiations and preference for military threats was making any compromise unachievable.[22]

Nixon was furious. After Dobrynin delivered his message, the president handed him a yellow pad and instructed him to take notes. "You have been candid," he observed "and I will be equally so."[23] He too was disappointed in the state of US–Soviet relations, but with regard to Vietnam, only the United States had made concessions. The Soviet government might think the American domestic situation was unmanageable or that the cost of war was too high. But the Russians should understand that they would "be stuck with the president for the next three years and three months," and under no circumstance would the United States accept "the humiliation of a defeat."

On a more positive note, Nixon suggested that if Moscow "found it possible to do something in Vietnam and the Vietnam War ended, the United

States might do something dramatic to improve Soviet–US relations; indeed something more dramatic than they could now imagine." In Dobrynin's reports the Soviet government, he reflected on how strange it was that they were being blamed "for the fact that the United States invaded Vietnam and now finds itself in the current serious predicament."[24]

With the Soviets unhelpful, the Paris peace talks stalled, and the military situation ambiguous, Nixon turned his attention back to winning over the American public. In advance of the first Moratorium, the White House had announced that the president would be giving a major policy address on Vietnam on November 3. In fact, Nixon had already made up his mind to continue on the present course: building up the military capability of the Saigon government, slowly removing US troops, limiting concessions at the negotiating table, using air power to lower American casualties, and, most significantly, continuing to fight. His particular challenge in this instance was how to generate public enthusiasm for a speech that was billed as a departure but in fact contained nothing new.

That daunting task was entrusted to a member of Bob Haldeman's staff, Alexander Butterfield. However, Nixon had his own ideas about what should be done. He wanted a "strike force" for each major television network, the *New York Times*, the *Washington Post* and the two major news magazines. The aim was to monitor the coverage, "hitting them hard on the positive side of the speech and taking them on if they take a negative view." He also wanted his team to line up prominent political figures to give a strong endorsement immediately afterward. On the congressional side, he was looking for a petition or letter to him, signed by as many people as possible, proffering their support.

These ideas were incorporated into Butterfield's 17-page "Game Plan for the President's November 3rd Speech on Vietnam."[25] This carefully laid out an elaborate six-stage process (Recruit, Organize, Prepare, Inform, Initiate, Follow-on) and divvied up specific responsibilities among 14 staff members. Before the speech was given, they would prepare the text of a congressional letter and line up at least 250 members of the House and 50 members of the Senate whom they could recruit as signatories. They would also alert their "wires and letters to the editor apparatus" to begin churning out letters about the speech beginning on November 4 and extending for two weeks. Leaving little room for spontaneity, the letter writers "should be well briefed as to theme and addressees." There would also be a plan "for how we get continual follow-up stories out to the press, telling of the 'fantastic loads of mail' pouring into the WH every hour . . . ' all letters and wires enthusiastically supporting the President."

The "game plan" also included a host of lesser schemes: producing "Tell It To Hanoi" buttons; American flag lapels and red, white, and blue bumper stickers; setting up a private telephone poll to quickly demonstrate the positive response to Nixon's speech; designing ads that could be placed in the key newspapers of congressional opponents "casting each in the role of a dissenter, one who by failure to support and work with . . . the President is aiding and abetting the enemy and prolonging the war." Butterfield's group also had plans for the upcoming November 15 Moratorium Day, when they intended to dispatch two private television crews and four still photographers to photograph and record on television film "the worst, rattiest, most disgraceful, despicable and seamy side of what transpires."

Kissinger featured prominently in the "game plan." His special mission was to brief key members of Congress and other national figures on the underlying rationale for the speech and to encourage their enthusiastic response.[26] According to his briefing, the White House had gotten word "to the other side that we would have to review the entire situation around the first of November. Within three weeks of that warning the level of activity declined sharply." To force the enemy to give up, he said, only one element was missing: the clear support of the American people. If that were present, Hanoi would be profoundly shaken. Nothing less than "the future of our society" was at stake.

The description of North Vietnamese behavior was false, which Kissinger well knew, but his supposedly inside news was sufficient to cow the Democratic leadership in both the House and Senate. Before the president had uttered a single word, they had hoisted up the white flag. "There is nothing to say," observed House Majority Leader Carl Albert, "except that we must support the President." Speaker John McCormack was equally compliant. "The President has called for unity behind his leadership," and in unity "there is strength, and this can lead to peace with justice." Kissinger urged them to incorporate these sentiments into a public statement to be delivered once Nixon had concluded his remarks.

In drafting his speech, Nixon was convinced that, while members of the press and other "elite" figures were unalterably hostile, most ordinary Americans were on his side and not prepared to accept defeat in Vietnam. The challenge he faced was to speak over the heads of the pundits and to tighten his bond with the public. Toward that end, he was careful to strike a conciliatory tone. "Let us all understand," he explained, "that the question before us is not whether some Americans are for peace and some Americans are against peace." The real question was: "How can we win America's peace?" In his speech, Nixon described how hard his administration had worked to reach a peaceful compromise and how Hanoi had "refused to even discuss our proposals."

Since diplomacy was presently stalled, his administration was simultaneously pursuing an additional path, which was showing early signs of success: Vietnamization. Beginning in March, the equipment and training of the South Vietnamese military had been increased, so they were able to take over more of the burden of fighting Moreover, he had personally changed the orders to General Abrams: "The primary mission of our troops is to enable the South Vietnamese forces to assume the full responsibility for the security of South Vietnam."

The change in the mission statement was already bearing fruit, he claimed. Over 60,000 soldiers had been brought home, the American casualty rate was at its lowest level, and enemy infiltration into the South was at a fraction of its former levels.[27] Regarding the future, "we have adopted a plan . . . for the complete withdrawal of American troops . . . on any orderly scheduled timetable." However, the timing could not be rushed.

In Nixon's estimation, the United States had only two choices—to withdraw in a precipitous fashion or to pursue "a just peace." He had chosen the second course. As president, he would be "untrue to his oath of office if he allowed a minority to impose their views on the rest of the country by conducting street demonstrations." But to the young people of America, who were concerned about the war, he had a message:

> I respect your idealism. I share your concern for peace. I want peace as much as you do. . . . I want to end the war to save the lives of those brave young men in Vietnam. But I want to end it in a way which will increase the chance their younger brothers and their sons will not have to fight in some future Vietnam someplace in the world.

He was therefore calling upon "the great silent majority of my fellow Americans" for help. The more domestic support they gave him, the faster peace would come. So long as the country was divided at home, the enemy would resist any accommodation in Paris. Then came the stiletto: "let us understand . . . North Vietnam cannot defeat or humiliate the United States. Only Americans can do that."

This was by far the most brilliantly executed speech that Nixon had ever given. Judicious in tone, carefully paced to communicate resolve and deep reflection, it struck many resonant notes: high moral purpose; a definite, albeit secret, plan to end the war; empathy with idealistic youth; and a quick but pointed jab at those people who would defeat their country.

Lest it not receive the hoped-for response, the White House staff's "game plan" went into action as soon as Nixon completed his remarks. Back in the residence, the president phoned Haldeman 15 to 20 times over three hours that night, peppering him with questions and demands.[28] What were people saying? Not just "big-shots but ordinary Americans"? What about the newspaper editors and the television commentators? And what were Haldeman's people doing by way of counterattack? Were they set to go with the news story about how all the wires and letters were pouring into the White House? Had Haldeman made sure that Laird and Rogers would support him? They needed "to hit network management for biased reports," and especially the *New York Times* and the *Washington Post.* If they only did one thing, they should get supporters to make "100 vicious, dirty calls" to the two papers slamming their editorials (although as Haldeman wryly noted in his diary, this was before they had any idea what the editorials would say).

Henry Kissinger, who had been given the task of eliciting the responses of influential people, was still phoning the president with the rave reviews at 11:30 PM. Conservative journalist William Buckley believed that Nixon had taken "the Churchillian stand not the comfortable Chamberlain stand," while labor operative Jay Lovestone declared that the president had "restored dignity to the American people."[29] Kissinger called again at midnight with some touching news from General Haig.[30] The parents of a boy who had been killed in Vietnam had contacted him to say the speech was "wonderful," "marvelous," what their son had died for.

The media's reaction was more mixed. ABC's Howard Smith, who was perhaps the most positive, was pleased that "the President is not going to allow himself to be hustled by the end-the-war-at-any-price Senators," and NBC's commentators were "fair to favorable," according to the report prepared by the White House staff. Yet some news anchors expressed disappointment at Nixon's failure to offer any substantive change in policy. Prior to his speech, there had been widespread speculation that the president would offer some new initiative—an altered negotiating position, some encouraging figures about troop withdrawals, perhaps a cease-fire. Yet there was nothing.

On Capitol Hill, Democratic Senator Al Gore lamented, "American hopes have been raised and cruelly dashed."[31] Republican Senator Jacob Javits was equally blunt: the speech was "a disappointment for those of us who had hoped he would give leadership to . . . the overwhelming desire of the American people" for a rapid disengagement.

Those planning for the upcoming Moratorium initially believed that this speech would build their movement by angering potential participants. "Clearly the word has not gotten through to the President," observed spokesman Sam Brown. Yet realistically, it was the critics who were out of touch, for they had drastically underestimated the ability of Richard Nixon and his staff to mobilize, exaggerate, or even fabricate public support.

As prearranged, immediately following the president's speech, thousands of wires and letters from the Republican National Committee, state and local officials, the AFL-CIO, Veterans of Foreign Wars, and a host of other groups began pouring into the White House. By mid-morning on November 4, the press was invited to view the pile-up of wires on the president's desk and to watch as Nixon cheerfully rifled through them. Of course, there was no way to determine how many were spontaneous and how many had come from people specifically recruited for this purpose.

One thing that was not manufactured, however, were the polls, which told an important story. According to Gallup, 80% of those Americans who were listening said they supported the president's plan, 77% claimed they were satisfied with his plan for troop withdrawals, and 72% believed that the upcoming Moratorium Day protests would be harmful to the attainment of peace.[32] Whatever sophisticated critics might say, millions of Americans had appreciated what they saw as the president's moral gravity and his calm assurance that there really was a plan to get the country out of the war.

As public support for Nixon seemed to mount, much of Congress fell into line too, and members who had intended to oppose him lost their nerve. Within a day, 100 sponsors from both political parties in the House agreed to support him, and with the help of Democrats Carl Albert and John McCormack that number quickly ballooned to 300. On the Senate side, there was some initial pushback, but that was short-lived, and even William Fulbright, chairman of the Senate Foreign Relations Committee, caved. For years Fulbright had been expressing regret for the failure to do due diligence before backing the August 1967 Gulf of Tonkin Resolution, which had given President Johnson sweeping powers to conduct the war in Vietnam. Five years later, he was once again displaying the same deference to the White House. Having already agreed to delay until November 3 the Senate hearings on Senator Goodell's bill to end funding for the war, Fulbright once again put them off, explaining that his committee "did not want to do anything . . . that might be interpreted as antagonistic. We want to be responsible and careful."[33]

The collapse of will on Capitol Hill was so pronounced that the president felt confident enough to schedule an appearance before the House of Representatives, where he received a standing ovation. He graciously thanked the 300 of its members of the House for signing on to the resolution for "a just peace" along the lines of his proposals.[34] Of one thing he was sure: "when the security of America and the world is involved and the lives of our young men are involved, we are not Democrats, we are not Republicans, we are Americans."

While reveling in the praise for what was already being called his "Silent Majority" speech, the president knew that its effect might be fleeting. In advance of the second Moratorium, which was scheduled to take place on November 15, he was prepared to mount a preemptive assault on the press. If the second Moratorium received the same kind of overwhelmingly favorable press as the first, this could pose a very serious threat to his administration.

Nixon had been furious at the media long before he was elected president, convinced it had treated him unfairly throughout his political life. Enraged by what he saw as the failure of the networks to pay him the homage he thought his speech warranted, he authorized Federal Communications Commission (FCC) chairman Dean Burch to ask the networks for transcripts of their coverage.[35] Even without specific threats, this was a chilling move because the FCC had the ability to grant or revoke the networks' licenses.

Nixon also gave the green light for Agnew to resume his attacks on both media and protesters. Agnew had delivered a speech a few days after the previous Moratorium in which he had said that its purpose was an "emotional purgative" for people without solutions. He went on to predict that the November 15 Moratorium would be "wilder, more violent and equally barren of constructive result."[36] The truly memorable phrase he uttered that day was his assertion that "a spirit of masochism prevails encouraged by an effete corps of impudent snobs, who characterize themselves as intellectual." This had produced front-page headlines, catapulting him into the spotlight.

Two days before the second national demonstration, Agnew assailed the television networks for their one-sided, negative commentary on Nixon's November 3 speech, proclaiming that the president "has a right to communicate directly with the people who elected him and the people of this country have the right to make up their own minds . . . without having a President's words and thoughts characterized through the prejudice of hostile critics." Who were these television commentators? "A tiny, enclosed fraternity of privileged men, elected by no one and enjoying a monopoly sanctioned and licensed by government." They all lived in or near New York City and Washington, communities "which bask in their own provincialism."

According to the vice president, it was these television personalities who had made the dissenters so effective by giving them a showcase for their activities. "How many marches and demonstrations would we have if the marchers did not know that the ever-faithful TV cameras would be there to record their antics for the next news show?" Agnew urged patriotic Americans to demand more responsible coverage. "The people can let the networks know that they want their news straight and objective" by sending letters to the national networks and making calls to local stations. In fact, people were already doing so at the behest of the White House. Feeling the pressure to be "fair-minded," the three major networks had agreed to broadcast Agnew's speech live, which predictably increased the flow of complaints to the stations.

Nixon was delighted by these developments, instructing the White House staff that the vice president had become "a really good property" that they should build up and use.[37] As on earlier occasions, Nixon viewed Agnew as an asset for wooing a particular demographic: non-wealthy, less educated white people, especially those from the Midwest and South, whose sons were more likely to be in the military than in college.

The network presidents were predictably outraged by Agnew's charges. Julian Goodman of NBC thought it "regrettable that the Vice President of the United States would deny to television freedom of the press." Frank Stanton of CBS claimed that Agnew had "made an unprecedented attempt to intimidate a timid news medium." Leonard Goldenson of ABC emphasized that "We will continue to report the news accurately and fully, confident in the ultimate judgment of the American people."[38]

Nonetheless, the networks approached the second Moratorium Day with great caution. There were indications that it might be a more confrontational event. Thanks to an agreement forged among the organizers over the summer, another entity, the New Mobilization to End the War in Vietnam, which was a more radical and overtly countercultural group than the mainstream Moratorium Committee, would be taking the lead on the November 15 plans. Unlike the earlier organizers who were eager to build relationships with establishment figures, the "Mobe" distrusted such people, holding them responsible for causing and prolonging the war.

Until recent weeks, Moratorium leaders had been reluctant to endorse the event, concerned that the possibility of violence in Washington could discredit their own organization. But powerful pressures were pushing them together. Once it became apparent that large numbers of people from across the country would be coming to Washington, they feared being marginalized if they remained aloof. After Nixon threw down the gauntlet to the peace movement on November 3, there was no choice but to join forces. With some trepidation, Moratorium leaders Sam Brown, David Mixner, David Hawke, and Marge Skelncar brought the substantial resources of their organization to help with the Washington march, while also providing backup for a major demonstration in San Francisco and hundreds of smaller events around the country.

While the Moratorium Committee feared violence, the White House was hoping for it—and even doing what it could to enable it. As reported by Haldeman, the president "wants to be sure we don't use too tight a rein, better to let the nation see what these people really are and let them do their own thing." Thus, although it had taken weeks for the organizers of November 15 to get a permit for their peaceful march, when a group known as "The Conspiracy" (denoting their support for the defendants in the Chicago conspiracy trial) had requested a permit to demonstrate at the Justice Department, they had no difficulty obtaining it.[39] One ace in the hole, of which Nixon may not have been fully aware, was the presence of government agents from the FBI and CIA who could act as provocateurs.

An additional development bore the mark of White House vindictiveness toward its enemies. David Mixner, one of the chief organizers of the Moratorium Committee, was a closeted homosexual. As the planning for November 15 proceeded, he had been approached in a bar by a strikingly handsome man who introduced himself as Frank and invited him back to his apartment, which was lined with shelves of books and records. Finding many areas of common interest, Mixner began a passionate affair with Frank, which was his first real experience of intimacy.

Then one day Frank arranged to meet Mixner at the Statler-Hilton coffee shop in Washington. When Mixner showed up, there was no Frank but instead two apparent agents who flashed their identity cards. They also held out an envelope filled with compromising pictures of Mixner and his lover. Their message was simple: they wanted Mixner to become an informant on the peace movement. If he refused, they planned to send the photos to his family and to the press. They gave him three days to decide. After taking to his bed in shame and panic, Mixner decided he would not comply, guessing that the agents would not follow through on their threat. However, the encounter sent him into an emotional spiral from which he did not easily recover and which briefly diminished his taste for political protest.[40]

By Thursday November 13, Washington DC was an armed camp. On the streets were tanks, trucks, and thousands of rifle-bearing soldiers. Rows of buses were lined up on all sides of the White House to ensure that the protesters could not break through, while hundreds of heavily armed soldiers were stationed in its basement. On a night of freezing temperatures and intermittent rain, a "March Against Death" commenced, scheduled to last for 40 hours and to culminate in the Saturday rally at the Washington Monument. This was to be a peaceful, solemn, silent, and law-abiding procession, with each marcher assigned the name of one of the Americans who had been killed in Vietnam.[41]

Starting from the gates of Arlington National Cemetery, the line of marchers with their candles and placards began the four-mile walk. They crossed Memorial Bridge, passed the White House, and went on to Capitol Hill, where they dropped their cards into one of the dozens of coffins that had been placed there. At the front of the line were six drummers, followed by Mrs. Judy Droz of Missouri, a 23-year-old widow whose husband Lt. Donald Droz had died in Vietnam. "There is no light at the end of the tunnel," she explained, "only the darkness that came over my husband." Behind her walked a dozen relatives of other American servicemen who had perished in Vietnam, and the two co-chairs of the upcoming rally: Reverend Sloane Coffin, a peace activist who was the chaplain at Yale, and Benjamin Spock, pediatrician whose popular books on childrearing had guided millions of families.

The most affecting moment for many of the marchers was the pause in front of the White House when they said aloud the name on their placard. Even the organizers, who had been focused to the last moment on logistics, were caught up in the emotion of the moment. Sidney Peck, one of the guiding spirits of the Mobe, recounted that "when I shouted out the name . . . it was as though my body was a medium, the Yiddish expression for it is *dybbuk*. You just opened your mouth and it was not your voice; it was a very haunting sound that came out."[42]

The March Against Death was a more elaborate and large-scale reprise of what had become a familiar practice around the country. Often led by a member of the clergy or a relative of a deceased soldier, such readings took place during local vigils and in parks, churches, and colleges. While the White House found it useful to imply that people who took part in such events were expressing enmity to the troops and their families, this was hardly the case. Indeed, the saying of the names was a way of forging an imaginative link to the suffering of those who had died.

By 1969, a growing number of families were motivated to join the antiwar movement by the drafting of a son, husband, or brother. Among the troops themselves, opinion was increasingly divided. Scattered news report suggested that many resented the protesters and considered their actions hostile. But support for the war was dropping precipitously inside the Army, with more shaggy-haired soldiers wearing peace insignia and expressing their discontent. In Vietnam and at military bases in the United States, some endorsed the Moratorium. Among them was Captain Alvin Goldstein, an Army dentist stationed in Long Binh just outside Saigon.[43] A petition he circulated among his fellow soldiers in support of the Moratorium was signed by 125 of them, including 30 officers. As he explained to a *New York Times* reporter, Americans who backed the war liked to exclaim, "Support the troops," but "you could count the soldiers in favor of this war on your hands and toes." As participants in the March Against Death were gathering in Washington, Captain Goldstein woke up and quickly pinned a black armband on his sleeve.

From Thursday night to Saturday morning, the single file of people moved steadily along the White House perimeter, as the list of the dead grew longer. Still exultant from his November 3rd triumph, the president pronounced himself not bothered, underscoring the point by going bowling.[44] On Friday night, he chatted with Haldeman and Ehrlichman as they worked the phones. He had a funny idea: how about "using the helicopters to blow their candles out?"

On Saturday morning the March of Death ended, and the rally began soon afterwards. To mark the occasion, hundreds of white doves were set loose, a striking sight against a sky that had finally turned blue. Estimates of the number of participants ranged from 250,000 to 500,000, perhaps the largest protest gathering that had ever been held in Washington. On the podium in front of the Washington Monument were Senators Charles Goodell and George McGovern, plus dozens of other speakers, whose words could scarcely be heard above the din of the crowd.

More audible were the musicians, an extraordinary mix of performers: folksinger Pete Seeger, John Denver, Peter, Paul, and Mary, the Mitch Miller band, the Cleveland String Quartet, and the cast from the Broadway musical *Hair.* It was Pete Seeger who brought the crowd to life with a song he had written:

> If you love your Uncle Sam,
> Bring them home, bring them home.
> Support our boys in Vietnam,
> Bring them home, bring them home . . .

By the end of the 10-verse song, the audience had joined Seeger in the refrain, "Bring them home." Seeger then asked the crowd to join him in singing "Give Peace a Chance." As described by Thomas Meehan, a father who had chaperoned his daughter's high school class to the march, "slowly in the fading late afternoon sunlight, everyone across the acres and acres of lawn, all quarter of a million began singing with him . . . repeating the words, "All we are saying is give peace a chance." Over the music came the voice of Dr. Benjamin Spock: "Are you listening Nixon? Are you listening Agnew?"

While all the official events jointly sponsored by the Moratorium Committee and the Mobe were peaceful, some independent protests took a more violent turn.[45] On Friday night, less than 1,000 demonstrators gathered at DuPont Circle and began their own march to the South Vietnamese Embassy. Stopped by the police, they threw rocks and were turned back with tear gas. More serious was a larger and more aggressive demonstration in front of the Justice Department the following day. While the rally was still under way, they split off from the main demonstration and lined up for a march down Constitution Avenue to the Justice Department. At the head of their formation, someone carried a papier-maché face of Attorney General John Mitchell, while others raised the flag of the National Liberation Front. Even here, most had a peaceful intent. But when they arrived at the Justice Department, splinter groups of Weathermen, as well as self-described Crazies and Mad Dogs, hauled down the American flag and hoisted up the Viet Cong flag. Someone threw a red paint bomb against the façade of the building, while others hurled firecrackers and bottles at the police.

Despite network claims that they would not be threatened by the administration, the somber, moving March Against Death received no live coverage, although there was a 40-hour opportunity to get the footage. Nor was there live coverage of the nonviolent demonstration involving hundreds of thousands of people on Saturday, despite its massive size. What they did run was film of the hooliganism at the Justice Department. The Butterfield "game plan" had counted on some protesters to discredit the antiwar movement through their disruptive behavior, and they did.

"I think we're in pretty good shape now," Nixon assured members of his national security team. After a rocky beginning in September, when antiwar forces seemed poised to achieve a significant victory, he and Kissinger had managed to neutralize them. Their not so subliminal message that ordinary Americans had the courage to defend their country while the liberal elites, in the press and elsewhere, shirked their responsibility, seemed to be resonating. The two did not achieve this by themselves. They were assisted by a military that still believed in winning, a Secretary of State and Secretary of Defense willing to conceal their own profound misgivings from the people, a fearful Congress unwilling to assert independence on matters of war and peace, a frightened media, and an all too gullible public still inclined to trust their leaders and unwilling to accept military defeat.

6

"You Shouldn't Kill That Many"

On November 13, 1969, while protestors were gathering in Washington DC for their March Against Death," an article appeared in the *St. Louis Post-Dispatch* and elsewhere about an alleged "mass murder" of South Vietnamese civilians by an American soldier. According to the writer, freelance journalist Seymour Hersh, the Army had revealed that it was investigating Sergeant William Calley of Charlie Company, 23rd Americal Division, on charges that he had deliberately murdered 109 "Oriental human beings, whose names and sex are unknown, by shooting them with a rifle." The killings had occurred in March 1968, during a search-and-destroy mission in a place known to the American troops as "Pinkville," and to the Vietnamese as Song My.[1]

Located in Quang Ngai province, south of Danang Air Force Base and in the northern part of South Vietnam, the area had long been a Viet Cong stronghold. In the immediate aftermath of the Tet offensive the previous month, there had been several failed attempts to flush out enemy fighters, but Calley's company claimed success, saying it had killed 128 armed insurgents. However, it subsequently appeared that many civilians, including children, had also died.

Several of Calley's fellow officers were outraged that these deaths were being investigated; collateral damage was the inevitable cost of waging war, and Calley should not be held accountable. "Killing becomes nothing in Vietnam," one of them observed. "He knew there were civilians there, but he also knew there were VC among them."

But were "VC" really there on the morning Calley and his men entered the village? For a follow-up article published on November 20, Hersh interviewed some of those soldiers and learned that, contrary to the official report, the Viet Cong had left the area. Charlie Company had found only unarmed women, children, and old men, who offered no resistance to the American soldiers. According to one of the men, Sergeant Michael Bernhardt, "It was point-blank murder and I was standing there watching it."[2] He described the different ways in which the troops had killed the villagers. They rounded up some of the villagers and then mowed them down with machine guns, set fire to the huts and shot people as they ran out, or else entered the "hooches" and shot their victims inside. "You're surprised?" he asked Hersh. "I wouldn't be surprised by anything these dudes did."[3]

It was obvious from Bernhardt's account that the killings were not committed by Calley alone. He had personally seen the lieutenant shooting people, but in his estimation as much as 90% of the Charlie Company had participated. Furthermore, Bernhardt doubted that it was Calley who had made the decision to murder everyone. Calley was, after all, "just a small fry." Some higher-ranking officer must have given the order, he believed.

While Bernhardt had not joined in the carnage, Hersh was able to find others who did and were also willing to talk. Private Michael Terry described how at one point they lined up 20 villagers in front of a ditch and shot them. It was "a Nazi-type thing . . . One officer ordered a kid to machine-gun everybody down, but the kid couldn't do it. He threw the gun down and the officer picked it up." Terry remembered that all the bodies in the ditch were women and children. During a lunch break, he and some other soldiers noticed that a few were still breathing. "They weren't going to get any medical help and so we shot them. . . . Shot maybe five of them."

When Hersh first tried to place his article about the massacre in various newspapers, he couldn't find any major publication willing to take it. He eventually enlisted the help of *Dispatch News*, a radical outfit that sold the article to five newspapers for $100 apiece. It almost instantly became major news, and reporters fanned out across the country in search of other veterans from Charlie Company willing to talk.

Correspondents also searched for survivors of the massacre to get their version of events. Even though the survivors had to talk to newsmen in the presence of US soldiers, they managed to tell a horrific story about the cold-blooded murder of 567 people from their village.[4] They described how the Americans had burned or dynamited all the homes, then placed all the people they could find, including babies and children of all ages, into three groups, which they systematically executed. One man, a 40-year-old rice farmer, recounted how he and his wife had survived because they hid beneath the dead bodies until the Americans left. His mother, brother, and three children had all perished in the massacre.

Another stunning development in the breaking of the story was the publication of a series of color photos taken by Army photographer Ron Haeberle. He had left the military without revealing their existence, but once it became known that he possessed them, he was warned by Army lawyers that they were still the property of the Department of Defense and that he had no right to circulate them. Haeberle gambled there would be no retribution once the photos had been seen by millions of people. On November 20, they were splashed across the pages of the *Cleveland Plain Dealer*, then reproduced for CBS television news, and finally published in *Life* magazine. Their appearance shut down arguments about whether a massacre had taken place, whether there were just a few people who had died after being caught in the crossfire or many more. Here for anyone to see were the piles of bodies on the road, the small children crawling about, the terrified faces of people about to be shot.

The Army tried in vain to keep a lid on the scandal. After the articles came out, the Pentagon announced that, in addition to Lieutenant Calley, they were charging Sergeant David Mitchell with "intent to commit murder" but had not yet decided whether there was sufficient evidence to warrant a court-martial. While these legal proceedings were underway, they said, it would be prejudicial to the rights of the accused to provide additional details. However, the details kept pouring out, from anonymous men still in uniform and from others who had returned to civil life.

Although the massacre had occurred during his predecessor's administration, President Nixon knew that the sensational accounts about it in the press could ignite a new round of protests. For him the story was simply a public relations problem that had to be managed, not a horrific tragedy that needed to be addressed. Once again, the press was seizing an opportunity to make trouble. "It is those dirty rotten Jews from New York, who are behind it," he complained bitterly. Eager to discredit the messengers, he entrusted White House Counsel John Ehrlichman with the task of obtaining damaging information about those responsible for the coverage.[5]

At Nixon's request, Kissinger phoned Laird.[6] The president "wants to make sure" that Laird was getting "on top" of the atrocity story. Did he have "a game plan"? This was "going to be a terrible mess," and they needed to have "a unified line." Laird did not have much to offer. He expected there would be a trial, that Calley would plead insanity, and that he would probably get off. As for the "game plan," Laird would prefer "to sweep the whole thing under the rug," but he didn't see how that was possible given the content of the photos. Would you "like to look at them?" the secretary queried. "Should I?" Kissinger asked. Laird said they were "pretty terrible" and he might as well not.

Secretary Laird recognized that "the boys" in Charlie Company "had suffered terribly," having lost one of their own just 24 hours before. You could "certainly understand a little bit of this, but you shouldn't kill that many . . . so many kids just lying there." Though bothered by the imbalance between one dead American soldier and hundreds of murdered civilians, Laird could recognize no connection between these face-to-face killings and the thousands of American air strikes that since inauguration day had been striking targets in Vietnam, Laos, and most recently Cambodia.

Meanwhile the coverage of the massacre in what was now identified as the village of My Lai was escalating, as participants were speaking to the press. In a devastating interview with CBS newsman Mike Wallace, Army veteran Paul Meadlo described how they had rounded up 40-45 people in the center of the village.[7] What kind of people, Wallace asked. Were they men, women, or children? And were there babies? Meadlo acknowledged that there were babies along with the men, women, and children. "We made them squat down, and Lieutenant Calley came over and said, 'you know what to do with them, don't you?' And I said Yes." Initially, Meadlo thought this meant guarding them. But 10 to 15 minutes later, Calley returned and said, "How come you ain't killed them yet . . . I want them dead." To underscore the point the lieutenant started shooting. Meadlo followed his lead, pouring four clips into the group, about 67 shots in all.

Did Meadlo know how many people he had killed? Wallace asked. The soldier was unsure. He was spraying the entire area, so "you can't know how many you killed 'cause they were going so fast." After finishing off the first group, they needed to deal with another 70 to 80 people, who had been herded to the edge of a ravine. Calley yelled out "Meadlo we got another job to do." In response Meadlo and his fellow soldiers "pushed them all off and just started using automatics on them." Again, Wallace wished to be clear. They were killing men, women, and children. Did this include babies? "And babies," the soldier confirmed. But why? Wallace pressed. Because "I felt like I was ordered to do it and it seemed like I was doing the right thing, because like I said I lost buddies."

Some of the other men who had described the massacre had been visibly distraught at the memory. Not Meadlo. He showed more emotion when he described his own injury the next day when he stepped on a land mine. He felt "cheated" by the VA, which had cut his disability benefits, falsely claiming that the injured foot was "well padded, without tenderness."

Back in New Goshen, Indiana, Meadlo's parents were watching their son tell a national audience something he had never shared with them. Asked by reporters for her thoughts, Mrs. Meadlo observed that, "I raised him up to be a good boy and I did everything I could. They come along and took him into the service. He fought for his country and look what they done to him, made a murderer out of him." People in Meadlo's hometown sprang to his defense. "How can you blame Paul David? He was under orders. He had to do what his officers told him," said one.[8] "Things like that always happen in war. They always have and they always will," reflected another.

These sympathetic responses were echoed at the national level, where there was a similar outpouring of support for Calley after the Army announced that it was going to court-martial him. Hundreds of letters began flooding in complaining that Calley was being made the scapegoat for higher authority, that he too was just following orders, that the killing of civilians was an inevitable feature of any war, and that his aggressive behavior in a Viet Cong village was understandable.[9]

Like Nixon, some blamed the media for rushing to print such a negative story. In fact, the media had all but ignored it for the better part of a year, and it was only Seymour Hersh's persistence that enabled it to be published. The Army had first announced the charges against Calley in September. Military officials braced for an onslaught of questions about the case, but except for Hersh, no one in the press ever asked them. The press (and members of the US government) had also failed to follow up on earlier reports about the massacre that came from Vietnam veteran Ron Ridenhour, who had made repeated efforts to bring the story to light.[10]

Ridenhour was friends with several men in Charlie Company, who told him about the massacre. Naming his sources, the veteran wrote a 1500-word letter describing what he had learned about the events and pressing for an investigation. He sent it by registered mail to President Nixon, Secretary Laird, Senator Edward Kennedy, Senator Fulbright, and 20 other members of Congress, including his own congressman, Mo Udall (D-AZ), who served on the House Armed Services Committee.[11] When no action was forthcoming, Ridenhour's agent contacted major newspapers in Boston and New York, several national magazines, and at least one television network with no response.

Members of Congress and the press were not the only ones to have ignored the story. From the very beginning, the officers to whom Charlie Company reported did their best to quash it. Air Force pilot Hugh Thompson, who together with two members of his crew had tried to stop the carnage that day, had sent a desperate report to headquarters while the killing was still going on. Lt. Colonel Frank Barker finally ordered the captain of the company, Ernest Medina, to halt the killing.

Afterwards Thompson took his allegations about the atrocity to his superiors, including Major General Samuel W. Koster, Commander of the Americal Division. Under proper military procedure, such charges ought to have been referred to the Inspector General's office. Instead, Koster put Colonel Oran Henderson in charge of an investigation. As the commanding officer of the 11th Infantry Brigade, of which Charlie Company was a part, Henderson was not a neutral party. He had gone along with the company's claim that it had successfully killed 128 insurgents at Song My, and he had no desire to undermine that conclusion. After some cursory questioning of a handful of soldiers, Henderson abandoned the quest for information.[12]

The official story only began to unravel when, in response to Ridenhour's letter, Congressman Udall raised the alarm among his colleagues. Inquiries were sent to Chairman of the Joint Chiefs of Staff Earle Wheeler and to General Westmoreland, the Army chief of staff.[13] Once Westmoreland heard that a possible massacre had been committed, he told the Inspector General's office to look into the matter, as should have happened in the first place. When the man assigned to the investigation, Colonel William V. Wilson, began to interview the men from Charlie Company, it became apparent that a major atrocity had taken place and that leaders of the Americal Division had participated in a cover-up.

Even so, it was not until the furor ignited by the Hersh story and the accompanying photographs that the Army began to deal more actively with the questions that had been raised.[14] On November 27, Army Secretary Stanley Resor acknowledged the grave concerns about the Army's initial investigation and announced that they had assigned a separate high-level team under Lieutenant General William Peers to review the matter.[15] Resor was at pains to emphasize that he and his fellow officers had reached the judgment "that what apparently occurred at My Lai is wholly unrepresentative of the manner in which our forces conduct military operations in Vietnam." President Nixon expanded on this theme. My Lai was clearly "a massacre," for which there was no justification, he said at a press conference.

Unfortunately, what had happened was not an isolated case. Spurred by the confessions of Charlie Company, other witnesses came forward with fresh atrocity stories. These included reports that Bravo Company, which had also participated in the Song My operation, had entered the nearby hamlet of My Khe and, finding no resistance, had proceeded to kill all 90 civilians in the area including local children who had rushed up to see their first US helicopter.[16]

There were also allegations about tortured prisoners, rape, and captured Viet Cong soldiers suspended from helicopters to extract information from them. The *Chicago Sun-Times* ran two photos that appeared to show a man being dropped from a plane. A GI had written on the back, "Nguyen takes a look at the world from 5000 feet . . . . I would imagine he's a little upset about this now—but not as upset as he'll be in a few minutes . . . "[17]

Although it was members of Congress who had alerted the generals to the massacre, they showed little inclination to probe the matter more deeply, even after members of the House and Senate Armed Services committees held a private session in which they viewed the Haeberle slides on a large screen. The spectacle of dead women and children, severed limbs and bloody organs was so affecting that one Republican congressman, Leslie Arends, abruptly left the room. "The pictures were pretty gruesome," he explained. "My stomach can't take it."[18] Congress had been intimidated by the outpouring of letters and telegrams supporting Nixon after his November 3 speech, and most members were reluctant to raise questions about the prosecution of the war.[19]

But what about the millions of Americans who leafed through the colored pages of *Life* magazine and encountered a scene that was so wildly at variance with their view of their country's role in the war? How did they react? Although it had initially s appeared as though news of the My Lai massacre would abet the antiwar cause, it seemed almost to backfire. The unspeakable behavior of apparently normal young Americans was not easily processed. The very horror of what they had done became a stimulus to denial. Three months after the My Lai story surfaced in the press, *Time* published the results of a Lou Harris poll that suggested that more Americans were disturbed by the publicity given to the My Lai massacre than by the actual killings. By a margin of 55% to 23%, most felt that Lieutenant Calley was being made a scapegoat, and 67% believed that the press and television had unfairly publicized the statements of other GIs before he went to trial.

Of course, the massacre had taken place a year and a half before it became news. Perhaps many Americans told themselves that what Nixon had said in his November 3 speech about changing the "mission" of the US armed forces was true, and that under General Abrams, American forces were now engaged not so much in making war but in "pacification" of the countryside as a prelude to their eventual departure. What the term exactly meant was not clear. As historian Greg Daddis has observed, it was used interchangeably with "nation building, civic action and revolutionary development."[20] The connotation in any case was of peaceful, humanitarian action. Under General Abrams' philosophy of "clear and hold," the measure of success would not be the enemy "body count" but the number of South Vietnamese people and hamlets rendered "secure" from enemy influence.

The US pacification activities were being coordinated and monitored by CORDS (Civil Operations and Revolutionary Development), which was under General Abrams' command. To determine the success of these programs, CORDS had devised an elaborate questionnaire entitled the Hamlet Evaluation Survey, filled out by American advisors in the field. On the basis of their answers, a computer tabulated the results and sorted hamlets into Categories A to F depending on their degree of "security" from enemy intrusion. By the end of 1969, CORDS was cheerfully claiming that fully 70% of the population of South Vietnam was living in areas under secure control.[21]

At MACV headquarters, there was growing frustration about the failure of Washington officials to appreciate American achievements on the ground. A few months earlier, captured enemy documents describing plans for upcoming military operations revealed Hanoi's recognition that until they rebuilt their military apparatus, there would be no possibility of a quick military victory. To Abrams, this was proof that his strategy was working, that they had Hanoi on the defensive.[22] In late December, the general returned to the capital brimming with this good news. To Nixon and Kissinger's surprise, he indicated that despite his revised orders and the upcoming round of troop withdrawals, he believed a military victory was in sight.[23]

As he mulled over this report with Kissinger, the president could scarcely contain his delight:

> Abrams told me that he hadn't changed a damn thing. We may finally have a military commander that is beating those bastards. I think he is going to beat hell out of them. I said take the casualties—they can go to 500 a week. Now the thing we ought to do is win the war.

Yet there was ample evidence that this success was illusory. Even Quang Ngai province, the scene of Charlie Company's rampage, was still fiercely contested. The Saigon government had never succeeded in bringing it under control, and local inhabitants were blamed for assisting Viet Cong and North Vietnamese main force units with food, shelter, and information. Since this meant that the troops often faced the possibility of an ambush or random sniper fire, the toxic brew of fear, anxiety, and contempt for "gooks" that had boiled over into the My Lai tragedy fueled other episodes of violence against unarmed civilians.

For medical personnel on both sides of the war, the continued killing was exacting a fearsome toll. Among them was Anne Auger, a young woman who had signed up as an Army nurse anticipating an adventure. Although her prior nursing experience consisted of work with newborns, she was placed in an ICU unit in the 91st Evacuation Hospital in Chu Lai.[24]These severely injured soldiers were her contemporaries. She was especially jolted by the suffering of an 18-year-old boy brought out of surgery after his armored personnel carrier had run over a mine:

> He was just a young kid. I don't even think he had hair on his face yet. And he came out of the anesthesia, crying for his mother. I felt so helpless. I was barely older than he was and he's crying 'Mommy! Mommy!! Mommy!' . . . I just held him., and I think that's all I did . . . It got me to realize how young and how innocent and how naive these poor kids were . . .

After six months working in intensive care, Augur was overwhelmed by what she saw of the life-altering injuries of men who had barely begun their lives. Every day there were so many "bodies lying in those beds minus arms and legs, genitals and faces, and things that can't be put back together again" that she almost wrote her mother to ask "if she could find one whole 18-year-old." It was hard for her to believe there were any left.

Because it was close to the fighting, the Chu Lai hospital was often subject to shelling and sapper attack. On the same day that Anne Augur's sister was getting married back in the United States, mortars were flying into the ward in Chu Lai and the young nurse found herself hiding under a mattress, as were 60 patients she and others had pulled to safety. "My God they're partying and here I am," she thought, overwhelmed by the contrast between her life and her sister's.[25] After a year, Anne went home a changed person—proud of her contribution, but also depressed, angry, hypersensitive to noise, and guilty about her own limitations as a healer.

Only a few miles south of where Augur worked, an "enemy" physician, 26-year-old Dang Thuy Tram, was running a makeshift clinic for Viet Cong and North Vietnamese soldiers as well as wounded civilians. Thuy was the daughter of a professional family in Hanoi and a recent medical school graduate. Moved by her love for a soldier and inspired by the idea of helping her country, she had volunteered to make the long trek down the Ho Chi Minh trail and into Quang Ngai province. Like Augur, she had no conception of the hardships that would lie ahead.[26]

Also, like Augur, Thuy found it hard to bear some of the injuries she was seeing. One summer morning, a wounded soldier was brought to her. He had been burned by a phosphorus bomb which had accidentally gone off. An hour later, his whole body was still smoking:[27]

> Nobody recognizes him as the cheerful, handsome man he once was. Today his smiling, joyful black eyes have been reduced to two holes—the yellowish eyelids have been cooked. The reeking burn of phosphorus smoke still rises from his body. He looks as if he has been roasted in an oven.

His young lover sat by his side, stricken with sorrow. "Looking at her," Thuy wrote, "I want to write a poem about the crimes of war, the crimes that have strangled to death millions of bright young loves, strangled to death the happiness of millions of people, but I cannot write it."

As she continued her work, the young doctor was deeply homesick. She missed her parents and sister, their comfortable home, the familiar holidays, and occasions she had taken for granted. On November 23, 1969, she remembered it was her sister's birthday, just three days before her own.[28] Like Augur, she was dumbstruck by the chasm that had opened up between her life and her sister's. "What is my sister doing to commemorate our birthdays?" she wondered. "You cannot imagine what I am doing these days. Today in the morning I went to work with a machete in hand; at noon, with a medical satchel on my shoulders."

Despite the sacrifice and her fear that she would probably not survive the war, her sense of mission remained strong. "The dreams now are of the American bandits' defeat, and independence and freedom for the nation." It was for these dreams that she and so many from her generation had endured "the explosions of bombs, the sounds of bullets." Thuy's fears for her own future were not misplaced. In June 1970, American troops attacked her temporary clinic in Nai Sang Mountain, killing her and the five remaining patients.

The brutal war in Quang Ngai province was fought by young people on both sides, who had more in common than they knew. Yet there were also profound differences, which were expressed in the disparate reactions of Anne Augur and Dang Thuy Tram to the suffering they encountered. For Thuy there was never any doubt about why she was fighting for "independence and freedom for the nation," or the importance of the sacrifice she was making. For Augur, her sense of the war as a noble cause had quickly dissipated. As she continued in her dangerous, at times devastating work, she was motivated to help the young Americans who came under her care, but she could not discern any larger purpose.

As horrific as the battles in Quang Ngai province were, the operations in the Mekong Delta were perhaps more brutal. Lying south and west of Saigon, home to more than six million people, the Delta was the most fertile area in Vietnam. Its flat landscape was laced with jungles, rice paddies, and thousands of rivers and canals. Before the war, it had supplied rice as well as fish to the rest of the country. But for years the US Air Force had been spraying the Delta with millions of gallons of Agent Orange, a chemical that had stripped much of the area of its foliage, leaving vast swaths of wide open space where once there had been lush forests and farms.

The local population had conflicting and ever-changing political attitudes. While many peasants were indifferent or even hostile to the Saigon government, the coercive tactics of the revolutionaries had also alienated many.[29] Peasants who had benefited initially from their land reform policies were forced to pay taxes, to perform compulsory labor, and to surrender their sons to a military draft. By the time of Tet, the revolutionary leadership had backed away from these counterproductive tactics, but it was unclear whether they had regained the loyalty of the peasants. As it turned out, to the surprise of the Americans and South Vietnamese, trust was regained, and large numbers of young men and women from the countryside had participated in the Tet offensive.[30]

For the US military leadership, the uprising in the Delta during Tet dramatized the need for a more vigorous pacification program. Retired Lt. Colonel John Paul Vann, widely regarded as an unsung genius in this field, was brought in to handle the political side of things, while the military effort in the Delta was handled by the Ninth Infantry Division under the leadership of Lt. General Julian Ewell.

Ewell's assignment had actually begun during the final months of the Johnson administration and was expanded during Richard Nixon's first year. Code-named "Speedy Express," its main thrust was to depopulate the areas where insurgents had established roots and relocate the locals into places that were more tightly controlled by the Saigon government. To achieve this result, Ewell utilized the kind of harsh military tactics that even Westmoreland had declined to use, pushing his troops into contested areas in an effort to achieve a high "body count."[31] Units that reported many "kills" could expect to be rewarded in a variety of ways, including more air support for their missions, three-day passes for "R and R" (rest and relaxation), and recommendations for awards and promotion.

Ewell, whose relentless pressure for more enemy deaths earned him a reputation as the "butcher of the Delta," boasted that within a period of six months the Ninth Infantry Division had slain more than 10,000 soldiers, and that its "kill ratio" was the highest in the war theater. Some of these deaths were the result of ground operations. But most were the consequence of indiscriminate artillery fire and air strikes—a total of 3,381 strikes by fighter-bombers, many concentrated on the single province of Kien Hoa.[32] "Death is our business and business is good," was a slogan painted on one helicopter unit's quarters. One curious feature of "Speedy Express" was that although thousands of people were reported dead, only 700 weapons were ever recovered, which strongly suggested that many of the victims were unarmed civilians.

For the inhabitants, this was the cruelest period of the war. When *Newsweek* reporter Kevin Buckley traveled to Kien Hoa two years later, every person he met had experienced losses. "There were 5,000 people in our village before 1969, but there were none in 1970," one old man told him. "The Americans destroyed every house . . . About 100 people were killed by bombing, others were wounded, and others became refugees. Many children were killed by concussion from bombs, which their small bodies could not withstand, even if they were hiding underground."[33]

Several of Ewell's subordinates had grave reservations about his approach, as did others, including John Paul Vann. Vann complained to Lt. Col. David Hackworth, who was commanding an infantry battalion in the Delta, that too many civilians were being killed.[34] "You guys have been the VC's biggest recruiter. You kill a boy's mama, which side do you reckon he'll join?" Hackworth, a highly decorated officer, agreed with Vann that it had been a major mistake to send the Ninth Army into the Mekong Delta. Because of Ewell's desire to demonstrate the highest body count in the theater, "a lot of innocent Vietnamese civilians got slaughtered." Yet nobody intervened to halt "Speedy Express," and by the spring of 1970 the Mekong Delta had become the symbol of successful Vietnamization. Having drained the most worrisome villages of their people and chased the NLF into remote areas, for the time being Ewell's infantry units had seriously disrupted enemy operations.

In recognition of this accomplishment, Ewell received a promotion to the largest combat command in South Vietnam.[35] Yet the danger of "backsliding" was ever present. In fact, no sooner had the Ninth Infantry Division left the Delta claiming victory than news arrived of North Vietnamese regiments crossing the border from Cambodia and returning to the western provinces, most likely assisted by surviving members of the Viet Cong.

Because of experiences like this, the leadership of CORDS, including its new director William Colby, a career CIA officer, had been focused for several years on undermining the Viet Cong "infrastructure" or "VCI." To tackle the VCI, which was believed to control many of the hamlets and villages of South Vietnam, and to be responsible for much of the local support for both the North Vietnamese and the Viet Cong forces, a program known as Phoenix had been put into operation across South Vietnam. With strong support from the CIA, Phoenix sought to identify and "neutralize" the leadership of the Front's infrastructure. If anything, Phoenix was even more toxic and more likely to alienate the South Vietnamese populace than Operation Speedy Express.

At the heart of the Phoenix strategy were the Intelligence and Operations Coordinating Centers for the 242 districts (DIOCC) and 44 provinces (PIOCC) of South Vietnam, assisted by similar offices for the four military regions and the country as a whole. Staff at each of these centers would compile dossiers on individuals suspected of being VCI and were expected to meet monthly quotas for the number of enemy cadres to be "neutralized," whether by getting them to switch sides or by capturing or killing them. Those taken prisoner could be held for extended periods of time, during which they could be subjected to intensive questioning at the interrogation facilities attached to each of these centers.

William Colby was the driving force behind the program. He had been the CIA station chief in Saigon until 1962, then worked in Washington, but at the height of Tet he returned to Saigon as assistant chief of staff in CORDS. In November 1968 he became its head, with ambassadorial rank. The third-highest ranking US official in South Vietnam, Colby was a fervent believer in the importance of political warfare. He had helped produce the original directive for Phoenix and fervently believed in its fundamental premise: that it was acceptable to round up, imprison, and possibly kill Vietnamese civilians who were suspected of loyalty to the Provisional Revolutionary Government.

Even on paper, the safeguards against abuse of the system were few. There were no clear criteria for who might be included on the target lists. Assuming the person was not killed during capture, he or she was interrogated by the Special Branch of the South Vietnamese National Police and hauled before a provincial or district security committee, which would make the final decision about that person's fate. This was not a judicial procedure. The security committees were composed of military officers and police officials, advised by an American who might be from the CIA or military intelligence. The accused were not entitled to counsel, nor were they informed of the specific charges or the evidence that had led to their arrest. Based on the available data, the person could be released, given an option of "rallying" to the government side, or, when a serious crime was alleged, referred to a military commission.

The Phoenix system therefore had great potential for corruption and abuse of power. South Vietnamese officials at both the provincial and district levels were expected to produce a fixed number of VCI members every month. However, often these goals could not be easily met. A relatively benign solution was to arrest and release the same individual multiple times. Another was to retroactively identify individuals who had been killed in firefights as political cadres. The more lethal and perhaps the most common stratagem was to accuse innocent people or people who seemed vaguely suspicious to bulk up the numbers.

"Nighttime house calls" and ambushes were the typical methods for scooping up suspected VCI members, which gave Phoenix its reputation as "an assassination program."[36] While many South Vietnamese were killed during these actions, the preferred result was actually capture, because political cadres who could be hauled in for questioning were potentially valuable sources of information.

The questioning that occurred in the CIA-built "interrogation centers" often involved torture, a reality that the Americans chose to ignore or even condone. Officially the interrogations fell under the purview of the Special Branch of the South Vietnamese National Police, though there was usually someone from Central Intelligence or US Military Intelligence on the scene. Captain Michael Uhl, who was in charge of one military intelligence unit, described what he saw when he arrived at the interrogation center in Quang Ngai province. There was a huge cage, broken down into smaller cages, in which South Vietnamese officials were questioning civilians:

> When I walked in, there were approximately seven or eight interrogations going on. Each interrogator was brutalizing in some way one of the Vietnamese, slapping him around, kicking him, hitting him over the head with a pencil, banging his fist down on the man's hand.[37]

Uhl also observed a young woman, suspected of being part of the VCI infrastructure, taken to a special room where she was wired up to an electrical field telephone. Whenever she gave a negative response or claimed ignorance, "the crank was turned and she was given an electric shock." Eventually "she was shocked so severely that she began to menstruate profusely," causing the officer to stop the interrogation.

By early 1970, the stench surrounding Phoenix was unmistakable. Among journalists, US military officials and even some CIA operatives, it had developed a reputation for incompetence, corruption, and cruelty. It had even aroused opposition in MACV headquarters, where there were mounting objections to military personnel operating outside the normal chain of command.

In February the Senate Foreign Relations Committee opened its long-postponed hearings on the Vietnam War, following the year's grace period chairman William Fulbright had given the Nixon administration. The committee was set to probe the effectiveness of the "pacification effort" and to gain a better understanding of the role played by the Phoenix program in that effort. CORDS director William Colby and John Paul Vann were called back from Vietnam to testify.

The senators had in hand a critical report, produced by three members of their staff, who had gone on a fact-finding tour of Vietnam.[38] The writers reported that the Phoenix program had failed to neutralize a significant number of Viet Cong officials but had caused serious problems because of the pressure to meet quotas, the difficulty of identifying cadres, and the tendency of local officials to target personal enemies.

Yet William Colby delivered a relentlessly upbeat message, telling the committee that while the enemy's prospects had once seemed bright, the United States and its South Vietnamese allies had developed new tools to defeat them, and that the Phoenix program was a vital part of this endeavor. The most exciting thing, Colby wanted the committee to understand, was that

Vietnamese people themselves were running the show. Across the South, one could see the resulting improvements—"the sparkling roofs," the open roads, the functioning markets, the returning families tilling their long-abandoned farms.

Members of the Fulbright Committee were naturally curious about how many members of the VCI had been killed. Colby replied that during 1969, a total of 6,187 had perished, approximately one-third of the number of the VCI who had been "neutralized." But if there were no assassinations, how did all these people die? According to Colby, many were slain during military firefights. This was peculiar, since the Phoenix program was supposed to target individuals who were part of the civilian infrastructure, not soldiers. Why then were people dying in firefights, and not just a handful of people but thousands?

As he probed this and other matters, Fulbright was scathing.

THE CHAIRMAN: Has this program any precedent that you know of in our history? Have we done this before?

MR. COLBY: The identification and arrest of subversives?

THE CHAIRMAN: No, a program for the assassination of civilian leaders.

MR. COLBY: I question whether that is an appropriate title for it, Mr. Chairman.

THE CHAIRMAN: Neutralization is the word. I couldn't think of it for a moment—the neutralization of civilian leaders.

MR. COLBY: No sir, my title for it and actually the Vietnamese government's title . . . is a program to protect the people against terrorism.

Fulbright wondered if some of those captured were then "legally executed" in South Vietnamese jails. Taking refuge behind the word "legally," Colby maintained that they were not "legally executed," although he "would not want to say here that none has ever actually been executed."

Frustrated by the exchange, the senator shifted gears. He had in hand two articles by Peter Kann of the *Wall Street Journal,* published during the previous year.[39] The reporter had observed a Phoenix sweep into the village of Vinh Hoa in the Mekong Delta. This involved a "largely fruitless interrogation of fearful tight-lipped villagers, calculated brutality applied to suspected Viet Cong, the execution of one suspect, the looting of homes by Vietnamese troops, systematic destruction of village installations and a largely unproductive hunt for Viet Cong officials who apparently had fled by sampan." After six hours in Vinh Hoa, the net result was eight people killed, seven arrested, one war memorial blown up, and a hospital burned—with no obvious gain in intelligence or political control. Despite the stated preference for capturing people alive, targets were being assassinated, "sometimes brutally as an object lesson for others."

Had Colby read these articles, Fulbright wanted to know? Was Mr. Kann just inventing things? The CORDS director acknowledged that Kann had told an accurate story. This was why he had stated that "while the policy of the government is definite, I would not want to testify that nobody was killed wrongly or executed." In the intervening time, the US government had tightened its procedures, but "unfortunate things" sometimes happened in Vietnam.

This provoked a soliloquy from Fulbright. Some of these "unfortunate things" were upsetting to the American people who do not wish to be implicated in "such inhumanity" regardless of the objective. He was not suggesting that Colby or anyone had "a declared policy" for the sort of things reported. But somehow these shocking events kept happening. As in My Lai—nobody ordered that massacre to take place either, but it did. And this was obviously not a unique case. Such cruelties had become common, so what was the explanation?

Hanging over these proceedings was the specter of My Lai. According to Colby and the others, it was no easy matter to distinguish enemy civilians from the fighters, which explained why more than 6,000 Vietnamese political cadres had been killed during 1969. But if the lines were that "fuzzy," Fulbright asked, wouldn't this account for situations like My Lai, where "you cannot tell the difference, so you resolve all doubts in favor of the fact that they are all VCI?"

John Paul Vann heatedly denied that there was any connection between Phoenix and this documented massacre. Yet in reality, both stemmed from similar causes and produced at least some results that were similar. Whether a Vietnamese farmer was killed by a B-52 bomber, a helicopter gunship, a rifle, or a knife, he left aggrieved survivors who would be hungry for revenge.

In Washington, Nixon and Kissinger might comfort themselves with the reams of information provided by MACV: the Viet Cong was dispersed, the North Vietnamese supply lines were disrupted, the South Vietnamese militias were patrolling more districts, the attacks on "friendly" forces had been reduced. But ignored in this data was the war's impact on those Vietnamese who had been driven from their homes, who were gravely injured, or who had lost family and friends. It also obscured the impact on tens of thousands of American troops who sometimes found themselves fighting old ladies and children and could not understand why nobody from the village warned them about the booby-traps.

7

"The Idealists Are the Builders"

In early 1970 Kissinger had his staff complete a document for Congress and the public that illuminated the "conceptual outline" of the Administration's foreign policy. The 68-page report, "US Foreign Policy for the 1970s: A New Strategy of Peace," was written in the president's voice and struck an inspirational note:

> A nation needs many qualities; but it needs faith and confidence above all. Skeptics do not build societies; the idealists are the builders. Only societies that believe in themselves can rise to their challenges."[1]

Since taking office the president had thought deeply about the meaning of peace and had concluded that it "must be far more than the absence of war." To be truly lasting, there must be "a durable structure of international relationships, which inhibits or removes the causes of war." For the sake of this "durable structure" the United States needed to maintain its military strength, and the Vietnam War must be continued. The American people must understand that "because of its strength, its history and its concern for human dignity, this nation occupies a special place in the world." A too-rapid exit from Vietnam could produce a bigger war down the road.

The document surveyed a range of international problems, advocating for an improved relationship with the Soviet Union and China, since the rivalry between them was manifest. A flowery conclusion was addressed to the nation's youth, admonishing them that there was "no greater idealism, no higher adventure than taking a realistic road for peace . . . a peace responsive to the human spirit, respectful of the divinely inspired dignity of man, one that lifts the eyes of all to what man in brotherhood can accomplish." For these lofty goals to be achieved, it was necessary for the American people and for Congress to give their support to the White House.

Although produced by his own NSC staff, the language of the report might have left Kissinger chuckling. A self-proclaimed "realist," he viewed relations between nations as based on careful calculations about national interest, not long-term visions about "the divinely inspired dignity of man." Yet he understood that his boss had a taste for soaring rhetoric, and during a period when the United States was under fierce criticism for perpetuating atrocities in Southeast Asia he understood its usefulness in maintaining consensus.

In early 1970 Nixon and Kissinger were on one of their periodic highs about prospects for settling the war. Encouraged by signs from Moscow of eagerness for an improved relationship with the United States and by evidence that the Chinese were possibly moving in a friendly direction, they entertained the hope, however remote, that the USSR and the People's Republic might pressure Hanoi into a more tractable stance in the Paris peace talks.

On the domestic front, however, they were worried, fearing that a disgruntled public, acting through Congress, would prevent them from using the necessary force to succeed in Vietnam. The president's November 3 speech had made a positive impression, leading 82% of Americans to believe that Nixon was doing everything possible to end the Vietnam War.[2] However, the same poll also reported, "Americans are less interested in fighting the war than ending it and will support their president's efforts to wind it down but not continue it indefinitely."

For Nixon, the message seemed clear enough. So long as he was drawing down troops, he had a reasonable prospect of holding on to his public support. In December he had overridden the wishes of both General Abrams and the Joint Chiefs of Staff and announced the redeployment of 50,000 soldiers by mid-April, the third withdrawal in less than a year, a decision he attributed to improvements on the ground. Yet it was unclear when, if ever, the United States could finally turn over the fighting to South Vietnamese forces. Under White House pressure for good news, MACV reported that enemy troop numbers were down, with resultant losses of territory during the winter months, while Saigon was moving ahead with its pacification effort, increasing the size of regional (RPF) and popular militias (PF), thereby enhancing security in the countryside.

Despite their preference for such optimistic accounts, Nixon and Kissinger were canny enough to know that internal reporting from MACV was unreliable. To get a more realistic picture of the progress of Vietnamization, in late January they had dispatched Kissinger's military deputy Al Haig to South Vietnam.[3] Echoing the message from MACV headquarters, Haig confirmed that although "tremendous progress" had been made in the ARVN units, most South Vietnamese divisions were not ready to function independently. While the first two American troop reductions had done no harm, any additional cuts "would seriously risk the gains made thus far." Despite a temporary decrease in enemy action, the infiltration of men and supplies was increasing quickly, creating the possibility of a dangerous spring offensive.

By dispatching Haig, Nixon and Kissinger were purposefully giving themselves an alternative pipeline to General Abrams as a hedge against Secretary Laird, whose bi-monthly visits to the South and reports they had come to thoroughly distrust. This was clearly the attitude in MACV, which looked upon Laird's impending visits with increased trepidation.[4] Indeed, upon his arrival in February 1970 Laird bluntly informed the generals that in the upcoming budget there would be less money for the war—which meant decreased manpower and reduced air sorties. Abrams strenuously objected: pacification might be going well, but ARVN still had serious problems, and its divisions were still untested. People in Washington should understand that they were not dealing with "a bunch of real tigers." What they had on their hands were "hothouse plants," which, with careful cultivation, could become "rugged trees."[5] It was an arresting metaphor, but Laird was unwilling to wait as Americans died for Saigon's houseplants to become rugged trees.

In reporting to Nixon, Laird chose to minimize the concerns in MACV about the fighting capacity of ARVN.[6] He acknowledged there were differences of opinion about the rate and size of future American withdrawals. But he professed to find this puzzling in light of General Abrams' apparent confidence that for the foreseeable future the enemy would be unable "to mount any wide, sustained or decisive military moves."

When President Nixon appeared to credit Laird's report, Haig fired off a blistering memo to Kissinger, contending that the secretary's account was "naïve, misinformed and indicative of his failure to understand . . . the existing military situation in Vietnam."[7] He thought it incredible that the president was accepting this "serious whitewash job." In light of his own observations in South Vietnam, Haig was unwilling to "sanction a steamrolled, optimistically glossed propaganda ploy by a Secretary of Defense who has every intention of getting out of Vietnam as quickly as possible."

Of course, nobody in the administration had asked Haig for his "sanction" and, as a subordinate on Kissinger's staff it was hardly his place to be giving or withholding a stamp of approval on a report by the Secretary of Defense. Yet Kissinger was willing to tolerate this presumption because of his own animus toward Laird and his growing awareness of Haig's potential usefulness as a private conduit to the professional military.

If Laird was purposely exaggerating, he was by no means the lone dissimulator. At Abrams' headquarters, there was a reluctance to state the obvious: true pacification might well require years of American and South Vietnamese effort, and for the foreseeable future hundreds of thousands of US troops would still be needed. Instead, they continued to affirm publicly that progress was being made, thus averting the challenging question: why continue with a strategy you expect to fail? For Henry Kissinger, this was a non-issue because in his view the unhampered use of military power was a prerequisite for diplomatic success. For that reason, he had opposed Vietnamization from the outset, and at each turn of events had tried to argue for some dramatic military action. In its absence the peace negotiations seemed stalled.

The secret talks had been in abeyance for several months. In the wake of Nixon's November 3 speech, the North Vietnamese had declined to meet again. Since the United States was still bent on military victory, another meeting between Kissinger and Xuan Thuy would be "futile," they maintained.[8] But early in the new year they changed course, agreeing to another secret meeting between Kissinger, Xuan Thuy, and Le Duc Tho, the high-ranking member of the politburo who had failed to appear last time.

To maintain secrecy Kissinger created complex travel arrangements that involved slipping out of Washington, arriving at the apartment of the military attaché in Paris in the dead of night, and crouching in the back seat of a car as it headed toward a North Vietnamese residence. As Bob Haldeman observed, the "intrigue around all these preparations got the National Security Advisor all cranked up."[9]

Despite the elaborate preparations, the meeting came to nothing, for neither side had altered its position. In his remarks Kissinger chose to emphasize the vulnerability of North Vietnam, including an unsubtle allusion to international developments that could render Vietnam "no longer the undivided concern of other countries," presumably the USSR and China.

While acknowledging that his nation had suffered many hardships, Le Duc maintained, "We have won the war. You have failed." Nixon's Vietnamization strategy made no sense, he continued. "Before, there were over a million U.S. and puppet troops and you failed." How did the United States expect to succeed after they withdrew their troops and only the "puppet troops" were left to do all the fighting? And if the military approach could not work, why did Kissinger think they could force Hanoi into accepting their conditions in negotiations?[10]

The Americans might persist in their effort, Le Duc Tho continued. But they should understand what was coming. "Our people will not step back before military pressure. We have been fighting for tens of years with weapons in our hands." And if need be, the struggle would continue into the next generation, for their sons and nephews would take up the fight. "We will sacrifice everything," he declared, but they would not be enslaved to foreigners. Both France and the United States mistakenly thought they could "quench our spirit with bombs and shells," but they would never get the Vietnamese to submit.

While a coerced solution was impossible, the North Vietnamese spokesman emphasized that if the Americans were willing to accept the removal of the Saigon leadership, then perhaps some progress could be made. For Kissinger this was a nonstarter. To remove the Thieu government would signal defeat. Although nothing had been accomplished, Kissinger reported to Nixon this was "an important meeting, certainly the most important since the beginning of your administration." The conversation had been "frank and free of trivia."

Understanding that much of his value to Nixon lay in his role as negotiator, Kissinger was apt to inflate diplomatic prospects. Following yet another fruitless meeting in March, he assured Haldeman that the enemy was bending. Inflating his diplomatic prospects, he claimed to have played "a tough, uneager role and they keep going for the next step."[11] If the president could just hold the country, Kissinger anticipated there would be a peace agreement within the next two to four months.

For Kissinger, "holding the country" meant thwarting the Secretary of Defense. In his department's budget for 1971, Laird had craftily reduced the funding for Southeast Asia from $14.7 billion in fiscal year 1970 to $10.5 billion. By so doing he was virtually insuring a more rapid removal of troops, along with greater restrictions on B-52 and tactical air strikes in Vietnam and its environs. Kissinger was strongly opposed, writing Nixon that these reductions were being proposed with no evidence that the South Vietnamese main force units were capable of conducting a greater share of the war. The budgetary cuts Laird was proposing would make it impossible for Nixon to deliver on his threat of draconian military action should negotiations fail.

For the president this raised a question: "Why is it that those forces trained by the communists seem to have a will to fight whereas those that are trained by the United States are pretty sad?" It was difficult for Nixon and other top officials to recognize that people fighting at the behest of a foreign power on behalf of a government many viewed as corrupt had less motivation than those who were fighting for their homeland. This inability to recognize the nationalist character of the enemy was one reason why, after a year in office, the Nixon administration was no closer to a solution to the war than its predecessor.

During that year 11,000 American soldiers had died, along with larger numbers of Asian fighters and civilians. Yet so long as success seemed remotely possible—whether on the battlefield or at the negotiating table—Nixon and Kissinger were determined to continue the war. Given the reduction in American ground troops, they were looking for alternative ways of expanding the military effort. Particularly appealing were places where the enemy was vulnerable, American losses minimized, and the impact on civilians easily ignored. Such a place was Laos, a small country bordering on North and South Vietnam with a population of 2.7 million people.

To understand the ongoing tragedy in Laos, the worldview of the Nixon Administration and its predecessors had continuing significance. Kissinger's staff may have exaggerated the rhetoric, but the "conceptual outline" they had drafted was reflective of how the administration viewed international relations. A peaceful world was one in which American military supremacy was unchallenged and where most countries were governed by regimes friendly to Washington. If this was established, more amicable relations with the Soviet Union and China would prove possible.

Such ideas were not simply a way of soothing the public but were unquestioned assumptions that rendered the experiences of people caught in the crossfire as practically invisible and thus irrelevant. By the time Richard Nixon assumed the presidency, the ordeal of Laos was well underway. It required no further intellectual effort to continue the devastation. And so long as the veil of secrecy remained in place, the suffering of its people would have little impact on the American debate.

From the time Laos had gained its independence from France in 1954, it was torn by civil war and foreign interference. There was a brief hiatus in 1962 when, under the terms of an agreement negotiated by the Kennedy administration, a "neutralist" government was put in place and foreign troops barred from the country. These arrangements had quickly unraveled as the ostensibly "neutralist" government led by Prince Souvanna Phouma drifted to the right, while the communist-controlled Pathet Lao moved into armed opposition.

During the mid-1960s as civil war inside Laos intensified, both Hanoi and Washington saw Laotian territory as vital to their own projects. For the North Vietnamese, southern Laos was an essential link in the Ho Chi Minh Trail, along which they were able to move men, vehicles, weapons, and supplies into the South. It was also a convenient base for their soldiers when they needed time to regroup and rebuild, as in the aftermath of the Tet offensive. To bolster their position they provided ongoing military and economic assistance to the Pathet Lao.

Conversely, the United States was determined to cut off North Vietnamese access to the Ho Chi Minh Trail, and under Johnson it had conducted a covert bombing campaign in southeast Laos—Operation Steel Tiger. The Johnson administration also instituted a bombing campaign in the north, Operation Barrel Roll, to support an anticommunist army of Meo tribesmen under the leadership of General Vang Po. Thirty thousand strong, the army was a secret project of the CIA. Its primary goals were to defeat the Pathet Lao and to strengthen the government of Souvanna Phouma.

In November 1968 the American effort escalated when the Johnson administration agreed to halt the bombing of North Vietnam. Instead of reducing the overall level of violence, its officials redirected the planes to Laos. When Richard Nixon assumed the presidency, the rate of bombing was approximately 15 to 20 sorties a day.[12] Yet by early 1970, American planes were striking Laos roughly 300 times a day, making it the most heavily bombed country in history relative to its population.

The Plain of Jars in northeastern Laos, 100 miles north of the capital Vientiane, was especially hard hit. Control of this diamond-shaped plateau, populated by 50,000 people, had passed back and forth between pro-government forces and communist insurgents for years. However, with the intensification of American bombing on the Plain of Jars, Vang Pao's CIA-directed army had made unprecedented gains. From Udorn air base in Thailand and carriers in the South China Sea, a fleet of propeller-driven bombers and fighter jets swept the area in an effort to destroy its usefulness if enemy troops returned.

By early February 1970, this beautiful mountain plateau had lost three-quarters of its population. Many of those who remained had become homeless. As the *New York Times* reported, the only visible structures were newly created refugee centers.[13] "Bomb craters pockmark the valleys, knolls and ridges of the plain as densely as the most embattled regions of South Vietnam."

For the Laotian peasants, squeezed between the demands of the Pathet Lao and the American bombing, life was unbearable. The greatest threat was from the air, as US bombs eradicated whole villages and prevented farmers from tilling the soil except at night.[14] In order to protect themselves, the inhabitants dug large holes in which entire families burrowed for months on end.[15] As described by *New York Times* reporter Henry Kamm, who interviewed some Plain of Jars refugees living outside Vientiane:

> They were frightened and unhappy in their holes, they said. Most were deep slip trenches in zigzag patterns, shored up by planks and covered with corrugated iron roofing and dirt. They spent their days there for six months, afraid to come out because of the planes.

The rhythms of life on the Plain were thus reversed, with people sleeping during the day and waiting until dark to obtain their food, empty the buckets they were using as toilets, and allow the children a chance to play.

According to one Laotian living in a refugee camp, his entire village had been wiped out and the people had fled into the forest. And still "the planes came almost every day. It was as if we were in jail. We couldn't go anywhere. All we could do was sit in the mouths of the holes." Another young man, whose house had been destroyed the previous year, lived with his family in a mountain tunnel:

> During that time I thought of my house and belongings and everyone in the house had to wash away their tears. We didn't even have a little happiness. Difficulty and deprivation came every day. The rice was nearly gone in less than a year because of the fires from the bombs. These difficulties enveloped my heart.[16]

The suffering of the people who lived in northern Laos was neither heard nor seen in the United States.

This facet of the war had been shrouded in secrecy for an array of reasons, including the absence of congressional authorization. The Gulf of Tonkin resolution had provided a legal basis for military action in Vietnam and could arguably be stretched to cover air strikes on the Ho Chi Minh Trail, through which North Vietnamese soldiers and supplies were moving. . However, in northern Laos the United States was clearly intervening in a civil war between different groups of Laotians, a mission for which there was no constitutional basis. And not only was the United States conducting air strikes, but US advisors were on the ground guiding Vang Pao's army in the field and helping transport fresh troops, weapons, and supplies to the combat zone.

An additional reason for secrecy was the pivotal role of the CIA in building up General Vang Pao's army as a counterweight to the Pathet Lao. Associated with this project was a good deal of dirty linen, including the general's habit of withholding food as a means of inducing villagers to make their sons (many under age 16) available to his army. Also sensitive was the Laotian leader's use of CIA-owned *Air America* planes to ship locally produced opium out of the country as a way to generate income for himself and his cronies.[17]

By contrast, Vang Pa's success in driving the communists out of the Plain of Jars in September had elicited greater media attention. Ordinarily there were few regular journalists in Vientiane, but more arrived to cover this apparent victory. Although physically removed from the fighting, they were allowed to visit the refugee camps springing up around the capital. During these visits, Henry Kamm of the *New York Times* and other reporters availed themselves of the translation services of Fred Branfman, a young American who had just finished a two-year stint of duty under the auspices of the International Voluntary Service. A critic of US policy in Vietnam, Branfman had been unaware of the sustained American bombing occurring in northern Laos. But in the refugee camps he met people who told him horrific stories about "a beloved grandmother burnt alive by napalm before their eyes, a child buried alive or wife blown to bits by 500 pound bombs, a husband shredded by antipersonnel bombs."[18]

Branfman could see the evidence for himself. "There in front of my eyes was a young boy missing a leg, a beautiful young 6-year-old girl with napalm wounds on her breast, stomach and vagina." He had taken a picture of that girl, but when he came back a few days later to give the photo to the mother, she appeared "tired and miserable." The daughter had died, she explained.[19] Until this experience of the refugee camp, Branfman had been an apolitical person, eager to avoid the war but not inclined to activism. However, his encounter with these refugees was shattering:

> At the age of 27, a moral abyss suddenly opened . , . I was shocked to the core of my being as I found myself interviewing Laotian peasants, among the most decent, human and kind people on earth, who described living underground for years on end, while they saw countless fellow villagers and

> family members burned live by napalm, suffocated by 500 pound bombs and shredded by anti-personnel bombs by my country.

What he saw of these refugees transformed him. Determined to get the story out, he began photographing and taping interviews with the refugees so that he could use them to launch a personal campaign to engage members of Congress in the plight of the Laotian peasantry.

On Capitol Hill, there was already a growing curiosity about the extent of US involvement in Laos. In the Senate there had been several calls for hearings on the subject.[20] As chairman of the Senate Foreign Relations Subcommittee on Foreign Commitments, Senator Stuart Symington agreed to probe the matter. "We have been at war in Laos for years and it is time the American people knew the facts," he proclaimed. Yet the chances this could occur in a timely way were slim, since he had acceded to the administration's request that their testimony be taken in a closed executive session.

Determined to conceal its actions in Laos, the administration was even reluctant to extend appropriate benefits to American servicemen who were operating there. Early in Nixon's presidency, the Department of Defense had recommended that Laos and Thailand be officially designated as "combat zones" so that US military personnel serving in those places could be afforded the same tax benefits as those in Vietnam. However, the State Department was opposed to this move because it would entail an acknowledgment that the United States was acting in direct contravention of the 1962 Geneva agreement prohibiting the introduction of foreign troops into Laos.[21] Kissinger agreed: "[I]t would be inadvisable on political grounds to indicate in any way that we consider Thailand and Laos to be a combat zone."

Yet, once the enemy had been driven from the Plain of Jars, American involvement in Laotian combat was an open secret. Members of the administration might insist there were no US ground troops in Laos and that US planes were simply flying reconnaissance in the northern region, but these falsehoods were being exposed. Even *Time,* which was normally sympathetic to the administration's perspective, had punctured its claims:

> Towns Flattened: . . . besides bombing the Ho Chi Minh Trail, Thai-based American planes provide considerable tactical air support for the Royal Laotian Army, flattening whole towns in the Communist Pathet Lao zone. In the last eleven months the bombing of Laos has increased fivefold.

> "We've creamed that place," allowed a US Air Force pilot recently, "some places even worse than Vietnam."[22]

In the face of such stories, President Nixon recognized that his administration had placed itself in an "indefensible position." He and Kissinger toyed with the idea of having Prince Souvanna Phouma, who was visiting Washington, announce to the press that he had requested American military assistance. But this would entail an official acknowledgment that the United States was indeed bombing Laos in locations far removed from Vietnam. While members of the administration testified at the Symington hearings, their statements remained confidential.

Frustrated by the secrecy, Senator Fulbright complained to CIA director Helms that the US government was engaged in a full-fledged clandestine war without notifying Congress or seeking its assent. This was precisely the kind of unconstitutional expansion of executive power that had created the mess in Vietnam. For the White House, a major concern was whether Congress would try to limit its options in Laos by writing restrictions into the defense appropriations bill. In December, Republican Senator Cooper introduced an amendment to the 1970 defense appropriations bill that would not only prohibit US military activity on the ground in Laos, but would also restrict Air Force sorties.[23] However, by the time the amendment was brought to a vote, Cooper had been persuaded to drop the restriction on air strikes.

It was a significant congressional retreat, just as the administration was moving toward another escalation. Fearing an enemy counteroffensive on the Plain of Jars, the new US ambassador to Laos, McMurtie Godley, warned that if they succeeded in driving out Vang Pao's army, the combined North Vietnamese and Pathet Lao forces could threaten the CIA base in Long Tieng and possibly Vientiane. He urgently endorsed a request from Prince Souvanna Phouma to add B-52s to the mix of planes that were already showering the area with bombs.[24]

The deployment of B-52s in Laos was nothing new. Since the bombing halt in 1968, the Americans had conducted thousands of B-52 sorties over southern Laos directed at the winding pathways of the Ho Chi Minh Trail. But to use these draconian weapons in the north would constitute a change in policy and might generate unwanted attention to American activity there. Nevertheless, both Nixon and Kissinger were instinctively drawn to Godley's proposal as a further demonstration of American resolve. They were supported in this decision by the Joint Chiefs of Staff, who perceived an opportunity to inflict significant damage on North Vietnamese troops.

By this point, all remaining civilians had been evacuated from the area. In addition to losing their homes and livelihood, many had seen friends and relatives die or had themselves been injured by anti-personnel weapons, bombs, or napalm. In the burgeoning refugee camps the CIA was airlifting generous quantities of rice, but medical assistance was meager and the materials for shelter limited.

Following Nixon's authorization, the B-52s struck —too late to prevent the return of enemy soldiers to the Plain of Jars. However, the attack caught the attention of several senators, who were quick to express their alarm at what they regarded as an unwarranted intervention in another country's civil war. Yet, by failing to prohibit the use of air power in the 1970 defense appropriations bill, they had left the door open to such activity. With fresh zeal, several pressed the White House to permit the declassification of administration testimony that had been given to the Symington subcommittee two months earlier.

Such efforts were fruitless, despite new revelations. On February 24, T. D. Allman, a stringer for the *New York Times,* published an article detailing what he, John Saar of *Life*, and Max Coffait from France had found when they breached security and entered the CIA base in Long Tieng. Until then, curious journalists had been steered to the nearby location of Sam Thong, a supply and medical center where they could observe the dispensing of American aid to newly arrived refugees. Knowing that Long Tieng was also the headquarters of General Vang Pao, the three reporters had hiked the 15 miles into the base.[25] For two hours they walked around asking questions until troops from the Laotian army had them arrested.

In their meanderings, the three made no further discoveries about the B-52 campaign, but what they did glean was an appreciation of the scope and scale of the CIA-directed project, including its ground component.[26] Some 40,000 Laotian soldiers and civilians were living there, although the site appeared on no maps. The Meo tribesmen were clad in their native attire, while young American men wearing civilian clothes drove around in open jeeps, carrying M-16 rifles and pistols. Allman surmised that they were ex–Green Berets, working on contract for the CIA. Their private status made it possible for the Nixon administration to claim that it had no soldiers fighting in Laos. Working in new, windowless buildings were a team of CIA agents "who supply, plan, finance, direct and sometimes even participate in the fighting against the Pathet Lao and North Vietnamese." A new all-weather landing strip appeared to be heavily utilized, with planes taking off and landing once a minute. These included T-28 single-engine propeller bombers, which were being flown by Laotians but serviced by Americans who were "loading bombs and rockets, instructing Laotian pilots and taxiing the planes up and down the runway."

In response to Allman's revelations, Ambassador Godley issued an angry statement announcing, "[T]he American mission has lost any interest in helping out the press whatsoever because of what happened this afternoon." Given the tight secrecy that had successfully kept the press at bay until then, Godley's warning was almost comical. The degree of suffering warranted more, rather than less, attention. As Henry Kamm of the *New York Times* observed, "the present level of hostilities is enough to have killed, maimed . . . or made homeless as much as a third of a population, estimated at three million people."

On Capitol Hill tempers were growing short—less because of the suffering of the Laotians than because of the administration's flouting of the congressional prerogative to declare war. A host of politicians from both parties, among them Senators Fulbright, Gore, Mansfield, Symington, Cooper, and Mathias, demanded to know whether their country was fighting a new war in Laos and, if so, insisted on their right to convey information to the public.[27] How many Americans had died in Laos? they asked. And would US ground troops become necessary if conditions continued to deteriorate? Senators were especially curious about the number of sorties being flown in northern Laos, which in one year had increased from a monthly total of 908 sorties to 3,400. Wasn't this a sign of a larger commitment?

To address the outcry, Nixon finally issued a 3,000-word statement on March 6, explaining that in recent months there had been an increase in North Vietnamese troops in Laos, from an estimated 50,000 North Vietnamese troops to 67,000.[28] Hanoi was deploying these troops to protect the vast quantities of weapons and supplies that travelled along the Ho Chi Minh Trail and "to weaken and subvert the Royal Lao Government" in order to pave the way for the establishment of a government "more amenable to Communist control." Faced with a situation that threatened the lives of Americans and their allies, his administration was conducting bombing campaigns aimed at disrupting the movement of supplies along the Ho Chi Minh Trail and at supporting "the independence and neutrality of Laos" as requested by Prince Souvanna Phouma.

Given the "grossly inaccurate" speculation about an alleged escalation on the American side, Nixon was offering "a precise description" of the American role. These were the facts:

> There are no American ground combat troops in Laos. We have no plans for introducing ground combat forces into Laos.
>
> The total number of Americans directly employed by the US government is 616. In addition, there are 424 Americans employed on contract to the Government or to Government contractors.
>
> No American stationed in Laos has ever been killed in ground combat operations

Nixon's statement failed to allay congressional concerns. Within a day, serious question about its veracity cropped up in a variety of places. The most obvious inaccuracy was the president's claim that "No American stationed in Laos has ever been killed in ground combat operations." By slipping in the words "stationed in Laos," Nixon avoided mentioning US deaths in "Prairie Fire," a series of cross-border operations by Americans and Vietnamese soldiers between 1966 and 1970 to gather intelligence and harass the enemy on the Ho Chi Minh Trail. This formulation also neatly excluded 200 American pilots who had been shot down over Laos, but whose flights had taken off from sites in Thailand and Guam.

Even with this sleight of hand the accounting was false, for other US soldiers had died in Laos as well as several CIA agents disguised as civilians.[29] Secretary Laird had immediately recognized the inaccuracy and had twice removed this exact line from Nixon's statement, but Kissinger had put it back, contending that US soldiers whose mission had its source in South Vietnam should not be counted. The result of Kissinger's zeal was to needlessly expose Nixon to charges of deception. Realizing his mistake, according to Haldeman, Kissinger was "all shook up," fearing that he had forfeited his influence with the president.[30] The psychological situation would recur many times: the tough-minded national security advisor could calmly advocate for thousands of bombing raids but panicked at the possible loss of presidential approval.

While journalists and members of Congress criticized the administration for its dissembling about Laos, the bombing continued at an accelerated pace. Despite their indignation, senators backed away from the plan to ban air strikes. Meanwhile, a deteriorating situation around the CIA base at

Long Tieng was creating renewed presidential interest in using B-52s. Apart from nuclear weapons, these were the single most terrifying and destructive weapons in the American arsenal, and as such, they held continuing appeal for Nixon.[31]

From a strictly military standpoint, it was far from clear that the use of these particular planes would alleviate the situation in Long Tieng. The Air Force was already saturating the area with tactical aircraft and, in a cable to the Joint Chiefs of Staff, General Abrams had written, "[T]here is no adequate intelligence on which to select B-52 targets."[32] Even if targets were developed, there was no assurance that Ambassador Godley could clear them, because knowledge of friendly troop dispositions was inadequate. Beneath this bland communication, Abrams was seething. From his perspective, the entire project in northern Laos had been conducted in a wasteful, incompetent fashion: "just a bunch of guys playing soldier." In his opinion, the B-52s were an invaluable tool for the fighting inside South Vietnam, and he feared their misuse in Laos would backfire.

On March 19, the Washington Special Action group chaired by Kissinger and including representatives from the CIA, Defense, and State Departments, discussed the issue.[33] Thomas Karamessines, the CIA's Deputy Director of Plans, argued strenuously for dramatic action to help Vang Pao, namely the use of B-52s as well as the immediate transport of two Thai battalions to supplement his forces. When confronted by the discomfiting fact that MACV was unable to identify any worthwhile targets, Karamessines pressed for a policy decision that once such targets had been identified, the Air Force would be permitted to go ahead.

Marshall Green, the Assistant Secretary of State for East Asian Affairs, demurred. It was unwise, he said, to ignore Congress, where impatience with the escalating American involvement in Laos was mushrooming. Kissinger disagreed. The lesson he had learned from the president's November 3 speech was that Congress could be managed effectively when the White House took a tough line. After several hours of dispute, General Wheeler identified two potential sites north and east of Long Tieng, although nothing in the immediate vicinity of the base.[34] Kissinger recommended that they "give authority to Ambassador Godley and MACV to order B-52s if they identified useful targets" and if there were ground rules "that would exclude attacks on populated areas."

It was clear to everyone that an important barrier had been crossed—and that B-52 bombers would be part of a long-term strategy to hold the line in Laos. While this might not solve the immediate problem of protecting the CIA base, Kissinger reminded everyone that, once again, the North Vietnamese were testing their mettle, and until the United States "stopped backing away" from the challenge, a reasonable settlement would prove elusive.

In accord with this decision, Laird was instructed to dispatch reconnaissance planes to pick out targets for the B-52s. Within hours the Air Force had come up with its recommendations. Laird was still skeptical about the idea but chose not to pursue the matter. The last holdout was Secretary of State Rogers, who just three days before had assured Senate Majority Leader Mike Mansfield that the president had no further plans to use these planes in northern Laos.[35] However, when Kissinger told him that targets had been selected and planes ordered to strike, Laird refrained from further protest. His one request was that the Kissinger break the news to Mansfield, who was apt to feel "double-crossed."

Within 24 hours, Kissinger reported to Nixon that "twelve B-52 Arc Light sorties struck two targets in northern Laos."[36] In a related move, the president overruled the views of the State Department and the Secretary of Defense, opting to send a Thai battalion, also in secret.[37] If anyone asked, the administration would take the position that "reports of movement of Thai troops are exaggerated" and that further inquiry should be directed to the Laotian or Thai governments, which would be encouraged to respond "no comment."

With the principals all focused on the tactical situation, there was little discussion of a fundamental question: what was the rationale for greater American involvement in the internal affairs of Laos? Most observers, including the analysts on Kissinger's staff, believed that the North Vietnamese had no immediate interest in taking control of the entire country. Their overriding priority was to keep the Ho Chi Minh Trail functioning. Even the advance on Long Thien could be interpreted as a reaction to the prior CIA decision to have General Pao seize the Plain of Jars. The surface justification for US operations in northern Laos was that if anti-government forces became too strong in that area, then Souvanna Phouma might choose to eliminate US bombing in the South as the price of an accommodation with the Pathet Lao. Yet this was sheer speculation, built on tenuous observations.

Driving the policy was Nixon's and Kissinger's predilection for raising the level of violence in order to intimidate Hanoi and impress its superpower backers. But the responsibility was not theirs alone. There was also a disposition inside the national security bureaucracies to protect their own projects regardless of larger consequences. In this instance, it was no coincidence that the CIA was pushing the hardest for B-52 bombers and the use of Thai troops. The agency had spent years building up Vang Pao's secret army and developing the base at Long Tieng, and was simply unwilling to accept its loss.

There was little need to scrutinize this logic so long as the costs of US intervention were primarily paid by people of a different race in a faraway land. Even Laird and Rogers, who were eager for an end to the war, gave little attention to the plight of the Laotians. The Laotians' invisibility made it psychologically possible to accept thousands of airstrikes on the basis of tenuous reasoning. It was enough to know that on paper, if not in practice, populated areas were to be exempt from attack. Such collective complacency was at odds with reports from the refugee camps, which made it clear that civilians were victims. Yet nobody in the administration chose to investigate.

For Fred Branfman, the encounter with the victims from the Plain of Jars was a shattering experience, opening for him a "moral abyss." But what of officials who had ordered, implemented, or simply ignored the wholesale displacement of another people—how did this comport with stated ideals?

Also unanswered were more practical queries. Nixon's and Kissinger's expectation that an American display of air power in Laos would gain them a satisfactory peace in Vietnam was belied by past experience. No matter how much force American officials had utilized, in this and previous administrations the enemy had not been cowed. If anything, its determination and ferocity had increased with each US escalation. Yet, for those outsiders in search of a logical explanation for the Laotian carnage, the task was about to become even more challenging. On April 30, Nixon took a bold step that few had expected: he dispatched thousands of American troops into Cambodia.

8

"Hit 'Em in the Gut"

For years American generals and the Joint Chiefs of Staff had complained about the sanctuaries in Cambodia, where enemy soldiers could escape the rigors of battle by fleeing across the border. Even more infuriating, the base camps in Cambodia allowed the enemy to regroup and rebuild, and to funnel men and supplies down the Ho Chi Minh Trail into the Mekong Delta and other nearby areas of South Vietnam. In the aftermath of Tet, as the numbers of North Vietnamese and National Liberation Front fighters on the Cambodian side of the line had multiplied, the problem had become more serious than ever.

It was this state of affairs that had led Richard Nixon to appease the military by authorizing secret cross-border B-52 attacks on Cambodia in March 1969. By spring 1970, overall enemy activity in South Vietnam was markedly lower than the previous year. How much of this was attributable to the bombing of the sanctuaries, as opposed to Hanoi's decision to conduct "protracted war" and avoid large-scale scale operations, was unclear.

Prince Sihanouk had tried vainly to limit the damage to his country by allowing the North Vietnamese to maintain their bases in Cambodia while also keeping silent about the B-52 bombers that were pounding the eastern border. But as some enemy troops fled deeper into Cambodia to escape the bombing, tensions between them and the local populace grew, and in the summer of 1969 a fed-up Sihanouk had shut down the flow of Chinese supplies that were being passed through the port city of Sihanoukville and overland to the sanctuaries. By early 1970 he was pressing the North Vietnamese, without success, to curtail their activities in the borderlands.

Sihanouk's actions were too little, too late, as anger at the foreign presence, coupled with a severe economic downturn, fueled dissatisfaction with his leadership, most notably in the nation's capital of Phnom Penh. On March 18 while he was receiving medical treatment at a clinic on the French Riviera, his prime minister Lon Nol and deputy Sirik Matak engineered a coup. The overthrow of the prince was accompanied by an upsurge of nationalist sentiment, much of it directed at the Vietnamese. In Phnom Penh there were riots outside the embassies of North Vietnam and the Provisional Revolutionary Government (PRG).[1]

It was assumed in many quarters that the long arm of the United States had been behind the coup. But at the upper levels of the administration, the reaction was one of genuine surprise.[2] Initially Nixon and Kissinger lacked confidence that the coup would work to the advantage of the United States. It was by no means obvious that Lon Nol would be an improvement over Sihanouk. Since it was known that he had personally profited from black market dealings with the North Vietnamese army, his anticommunist credentials were suspect.

Over the following weeks, however, it became apparent that Lon Nol and his colleagues were serious about getting rid of the Vietnamese interlopers. They demanded that Hanoi's soldiers leave Cambodia immediately, a demand given weight by their rapid efforts to increase their own 35,000-man army. This insistence on a quick exit was a grave challenge to Hanoi, which regarded the bases as indispensable to its war plans. As tensions mounted, Prince Sihanouk exacerbated the situation from his new home in Beijing. On March 23, he set aside years of animosity toward the Cambodian communists, known as the Khmer Rouge, by announcing the formation of the United Front of Kampuchea, which was committed to the liberation of "our motherland." In short order, the Khmer Rouge as well as the North Vietnamese, the PRG of South Vietnam, and the Pathet Lao all declared their support for this effort.

To the Nixon administration these developments seemed both a challenge and an opportunity. For the State Department, Lon Nol's sudden ascendancy in Cambodia was another bit of dismal news. Here was a volatile, corrupt, and untested leader courting trouble. What chance would his inexperienced, untrained, poorly equipped troops have against the tens of thousands of North Vietnamese and communist guerillas entrenched along the border and inside the country? The likely endgame would be a military debacle or irresistible pressure on the United States to come to Cambodia's rescue.

In the aftermath of the coup, Marshall Green, the Assistant Secretary of State for East Asian and Pacific Affairs, and other area specialists searched for diplomatic alternatives.[3] They briefly flirted with the idea of bringing Sihanouk back, a thought that became moot after he aligned himself with the communists. If not Sihanouk himself, was there a way to retain his policies? However problematic, they had resulted in a certain degree of stability and maintained at least the veneer of neutrality. On balance it might be less damaging to American interests to tolerate the sanctuaries than to have a full-blown war between Cambodia and North Vietnam.

President Nixon saw this regime change as a new opportunity to satisfy the generals by doing something about the sanctuaries. Sihanouk's overthrow came at a moment when his war policy was again in trouble. The Nixon administration was taking a beating over Laos in the press, in Congress, and in the court of public opinion. While troop withdrawals were a key to domestic consent, the Joint Chiefs of Staff were adamantly opposed to cuts beyond the three that had already taken place and the reduction in air strikes that Secretary Laird had proposed.[4] The next four months would be "critical," they contended, in determining the success or failure of the administration's strategy throughout Indochina. While the South Vietnamese army had shown signs of improvement, the gains were still "fragile." The Chiefs acknowledged that the public would be disappointed if the expected troop withdrawal was delayed, but maintained that the response would be far worse if the US strategy failed.

Despite their vigorous objections and that of General Abrams, Laird dug in his heels. Ignoring the weakness of ARVN, he dispatched another optimistic memo reminding the president of the "rich dividends" already yielded by the Vietnamization program.[5] The South Vietnamese government had taken greater steps toward self-sufficiency; American combat deaths had dropped from a high of 400 a week to an average of 100; war costs had been cut by one-third; and "popular opposition to our conduct of the war has diminished." To make a show of good faith to the Chiefs, Laird said he was willing to cut the next increment of troop withdrawals, which was planned for August, from the 50,000 that he preferred to 40,000. However, he considered it both politically and practically imperative to maintain the momentum.

As a politician, Nixon recognized the potency of Laird's arguments. However, he was inclined to credit the military's pessimistic view of South Vietnam's capabilities. The fact that Kissinger and Haig shared these doubts carried considerable weight. For his part, Haig was in a white-hot fury at Laird's maneuvering, believing that he was suppressing information from the field and lying to the president. If the secretary's advice was taken, the result would be "a disaster" somewhere in South Vietnam.[6]

As a military novice, Kissinger was more dependent on the opinions of General Haig than he liked to admit. But apart from purely military considerations, there was a psychological factor: the retention of a large ground force was would aid diplomacy, which for the moment was stymied.

When he met Le Duc Tho and Xuan Thuy in early April, they remained immoveable on the core issues of mutual withdrawal and the formation of a new South Vietnamese government.

Because these secret discussions were taking place against the backdrop of new fighting in Laos and shortly after the overthrow of Sihanouk in Cambodia, the North Vietnamese were disdainful. In their view, the Americans had engineered the overthrow of Sihanouk. The Vietnamese have a saying, Le Duc Tho observed: "You can't use a basket to cover a lion or an elephant."[7] American actions in both places represented "a prolongation and extension of the war." They were part of a strategy to put overwhelming military pressure on the Vietnamese resistance forces in order to obtain a favorable agreement. Again, he tried to impress upon Kissinger how delusional this strategy was:

> It is a fact that in South Vietnam our forces consist only of infantry. No planes, no helicopters, no tanks, no high speed machines. What is the cause of our success? It is precisely the union of our people, the political force of our people, which helps us enhance our weapons, which are only infantry weapons.

The Americans should learn from their experience, Le Duc Tho suggested. After fighting for so long and "suffering defeat in Laos and Vietnam, how can you fight in Cambodia?" The United States had "sowed the wind and you must reap the whirlwind."

About the only thing the two sides seemed able to agree on was that until there was something new to say, there was no reason to meet again. For Kissinger, these meetings had become a punishing ordeal. In this most recent exchange, his interlocutors were barely polite, lashing out contemptuously. Even his urbane jokes seemed to fall on deaf ears. While substantive positions had not changed, the tone of this April meeting was harsher. However, in his report to Nixon, he emphasized that he had taken "a strong line, as you instructed," and while the tenor of things was "harder than in the past two," he had discerned some hopeful signs.[8]

The problem, ventured Kissinger, was that the North Vietnamese were so obsessed with the Cambodian situation that they would not make any moves until they could get a sense of what their prospects were there. As for what had been accomplished in these talks, the United States had gained some "significant concessions" and also "established a good public record because their concessions are subtler than ours." The president was unimpressed. As he reviewed the transcript, Nixon sniped to Haldeman, "It's obvious he can't negotiate, he makes debating points instead."[9]

The net effect of these developments was to convince both Nixon and Kissinger of the need to strengthen Lon Nol's government. One priority was the continuation of the secret B-52 bombing, which had been ongoing since March 1969. Fearing that Laird might be sabotaging this effort, the president urged Kissinger to speak directly with General Wheeler. Sure enough, the Office of the Secretary of Defense had ordered a suspension of these sorties, pending a clarification of the political situation. Did the president's instruction supersede this, Wheeler asked? "It damn well better," Kissinger replied.[10] He had no reason to worry. The MENU bombings were popular with the Joint Chiefs of Staff and General Abrams.[11]

To clean out the sanctuaries once and for all, however, the military believed it was necessary to send in ground troops. Some even saw this as a key to ending the war.[12] In this they had an important ally in the president, who was restlessly hunting for a game-changing move. Within one day of the coup, Nixon had ordered the CIA to produce a plan for "maximum assistance" to Lon Nol.[13] He had also charged the Joint Chiefs of Staff with the task of planning for a range of possible cross-border operations, some deploying only the army of South Vietnam, others that would be joint efforts with US forces.

There was, however, one serious impediment to South Vietnam's willingness to assist the new Cambodian government in its effort to expel the North Vietnamese soldiers from the sanctuaries: the Cambodian regime's effort to whip up anti-Vietnamese sentiment.[14] Unfortunately, its targets were not limited to Vietnamese associated with Hanoi. An estimated 400,000 ethnic Vietnamese lived in Cambodia, many of whom were Catholic and most anticommunist, yet supporters of the coup had marked them as potential traitors and agents of the Viet Cong. By early April, the Cambodian police were indiscriminately rounding up Vietnamese residents and detaining them in schoolyards, churches, and open fields.

On April 10, Western reporters came upon scores of civilian bodies, many of them women and children, on the grounds of an agricultural cooperative in the border village of Prasaut. The Cambodian authorities claimed that the victims had been caught in the crossfire when Viet Cong soldiers had unexpectedly attacked.[15] However, the wounded survivors told a very different story, claiming that when the Viet Cong came near, the authorities told the people to run and then mowed them down with machine guns. As described in *Time*, "the bullets literally shredded bodies. Half of the head of a young boy was blown away; children fell at their mothers' sides; old men collapsed in crumpled heaps"[16]

With each passing day tensions inside the country were mounting, as was the animus toward its Vietnamese inhabitants. Rumors circulated about the burning of villages, the seizure of hostages, and mass detentions, but most journalists were unable to investigate because they were banned from areas where the Vietnamese were being held. However, two American reporters did manage to get through. Robert Anson of *Time* and T. D. Allman, having moved to the *Washington Post* after his experiences in Laos. They arrived in the town of Takeo, hoping to interview a Cambodian captain they called "Killer," who was thought to be responsible for the massacre in Prasaut, and to check up on the 200 Vietnamese men and boys reportedly being held in a school.[17]

As Anson and Allman neared the building, they could see walls covered with blood, but there were no more than 50 people. What happened to the others, they asked an elderly Vietnamese man. "They killed them all last night. They will kill us all tonight. They say we are Vietcong. But we are just shop-keepers." The bodies had been carted away in the middle of the night. "Can you save my brother?" someone pleaded, pointing to a man on a blood-soaked mat with multiple bullet wounds. Next to him was a boy of about ten, with two bullet holes in his leg. Robert Anson appealed to the Cambodian guard to let them take the boy for medical treatment. "Stay with us or they will kill us too," the old man pleaded. Promising to return before dark, the Americans took the boy to a French hospital in Phnom Penh.

When he went back to the school, Allman asked one of the young Cambodian soldiers: "Was there an attack here? Is that why you killed them?" The soldier conceded that there had been no attack, but they had been ordered to carry out the killings anyway: "The Viet Cong are our enemies and all Vietnamese are Viet Cong."

After dark, the two Americans were able to rescue four little boys and three wounded men, whom they crammed into a car. On the outskirts of Phnom Penh the reporters were repeatedly pulled over by police, but managed each time to bluff their way through, aided by their white faces and press credentials. After depositing their injured passengers at the hospital, they rounded up some additional colleagues and made their way to the villa of Prince Sirik Matak, hoping to appeal to him to save the lives of those who remained at the school. They got no further than his bodyguard, who urged them to attend Matak's press conference in three days. By then the people would be dead, Allman argued. "The men in Takeo killed no one. This will hurt you in America," the journalist said. The guard was not so sure: "Prince Sirik Matak talked for an hour yesterday with your charge d'affaires, Monsieur Rives. He was very sympathetic."

Having witnessed the horrors of Laos, Allman was furious about this latest atrocity. For Anson the experience was devastating. In an unusually emotional piece that appeared in *Time* he graphically described his own feeling of helplessness as he encountered the misery around him.[18]

> Next to the suffering, the most horrible thing in Takeo was the hope that our presence created. We naively assumed that other people would be carrying these victims out. We could not have been more wrong. Nobody gave a damn.

Unable to interest Cambodian officials or Western diplomats in the fate of these 50 people, Anson could only hope his article would survive the editorial chopping block and readers would care.

"It will hurt you in America," Tim Allman had warned Matak's bodyguard. But it wasn't hurting them in America, or at least not inside the Nixon administration. By mid-April Allman's two-part story, published by the *Washington Post,* was available on every newsstand in the capitol. But in the offices where American policy was being made, neither the massacre at Prasaut nor the one in Takeo, nor the thousand rope-bound corpses that mysteriously appeared on the Mekong River one week later, seemed to matter to anyone.

With North Vietnamese soldiers advancing into new areas of Cambodia, Lon Nol had publicly called upon the nations of the world to provide his "salvation government" with weapons. His grandiose plan was to quickly create an army of 400,000—a scheme so unrealistic that it alarmed the American officials. While publicly proclaiming their "hands off" approach, CIA operatives, several ambassadors, and Lloyd "Mike" Rives, the top US diplomat in Phnom Penh, were all busy behind the scenes trying to arrange for covert assistance to the new regime.[19] They asked the South Vietnamese to fly in thousands of captured AK-47 rifles and urged a reluctant Indonesian government to supply arms with the understanding that the United States would quietly "replenish" the items sent. In addition, US officials sent two battalions of Cambodian mercenaries (Khmer Serai), who had been fighting under US Special Forces in South Vietnam, back to their homes. The president's press secretary Ron Ziegler wondered how they should handle these developments with the media.[20] Tell them, "We are in favor of neutrality," Kissinger said. "Waffle. . . ."

The escalating commitment to the new Cambodian regime was directly at odds with the administration's efforts to convince the American public that the war in Southeast Asia was winding down. Of course, the central feature of this winding down was the withdrawal of US troops, which in light of ongoing military pressures Nixon and Kissinger were hesitant to authorize. To handle their public relations problem, the two hit upon a clever trick. While Secretary Laird had been pushing for another cut of 40,000 troops in the next four months, Nixon would go on television with the announcement that over the next year, he planned to bring home 150,000 soldiers. Hopefully this unexpected news would obscure the fact that the withdrawals would be backloaded: in the immediate future, no troops were coming home.

Hours before the president's television appearance, Kissinger called Laird to tell him of his ostensible victory.[21] "We can get to your ceiling," he explained. But when Laird wanted to know more, Kissinger acknowledged that Nixon would authorize no further cuts until July 15. After that, the rate might be as many as 10,000 a month but he did not want to be pinned down. He falsely suggested that he had pressed for Laird's figure but had been unable to persuade the president.

To Secretary Laird's dismay, Kissinger also let him know that Nixon wanted the Air Force to be more proactive in knocking out air defenses and therefore needed him to lift the budgetary ceiling on tactical aircraft and B-52s. Laird wondered how they would pay for this: "I need $3 billion dollars for Laos, and I have been having trouble hiding that. We increased Laos by more than double." With these orders, he would need to ask Congress for a supplemental, which was impossible because most of their bombing was secret, and "we are flying very little in SVN."

On April 20 the president addressed the nation with a carefully crafted "Progress Toward Peace" speech.[22] The purpose of his remarks was twofold: to highlight the success of Vietnamization and the fact that additional US troops would be coming home, and to lay the groundwork for his still secret plan to expand the war into Cambodia. He gravely explained that Hanoi had sent "thousands more of their soldiers to launch new offensives in neutral Laos," and that more than 40,000 communist troops "are now conducting overt aggression against Cambodia." Men and supplies were continuing to pour down the Ho Chi Minh Trail, and "in the past two weeks, the Communists have stepped up their attacks . . . in South Vietnam."

The good news was that American casualty rates were at their lowest level in five years, and the army of South Vietnam was taking on increased responsibilities. So, over the next year, the United States would be able to remove another 150,000 of its troops. However, the enemy should understand that they will be taking "grave risks" if they used this opportunity "to jeopardize the security of our forces" by increasing their military activity in South Vietnam, Laos, and Cambodia. Under that circumstance, he would "not hesitate to take strong and effective measures" to stop them.

As president, he could say "with confidence" that the end was in sight. This was attributable to the bravery of hundreds of thousands of Americans who had served in Vietnam, and the perseverance of millions of Americans at home:

> When men write the history of this Nation, they will record that no people in the annals of time made greater sacrifices in a more selfless cause than the American people sacrificed for the right of 18 million people in a faraway land to avoid the imposition of Communist rule against their will and for the right of these people to determine their own future.

Part of the greatness of the United States was that its people could debate, sometimes with great intensity. But no enemy should confuse this free exchange as "weakness." The United States had never been defeated in war and "we shall not be defeated in Vietnam."

It was another masterful Nixon speech, designed to reinforce the feel-good bromides that Americans had always been taught about their country—that the United States is a distinctively moral nation; that countries everywhere look to it for leadership and count on American idealism to keep them safe; that brave soldiers were dying for a reason; and. most important of all, that the United States could still win because it always does. It was also disingenuous, since it in no way acknowledged that far from having an end in sight, the administration was actually moving toward an expansion of its military activities in Southeast Asia, contemplating a possible invasion of Cambodia.

From Nixon and Kissinger's point of view, such a step might serve several purposes. It would grant General Abrams' longstanding wish to eliminate the enemy sanctuaries in Cambodia,[23] give Hanoi a "jolt" that would make its leaders more pliable, and simultaneously curtail the effectiveness of its troops. Nixon's views had crystallized during a brief trip to Honolulu the previous week, where he greeted the Apollo 13 astronauts. On this occasion, he met with Admiral John McCain, the commander-in-chief of US forces in the Pacific (CINCPAC), who warned him that the North Vietnamese were trying to take over the entire country of Cambodia. If successful, this would send the entire program of Vietnamization down the drain. On the positive side, McCain seemed confident that a cross-border operation by the army of South Vietnam could be effective even if no US troops were used.[24]

Impressed by McCain's presentation, Nixon decided it was crucial to act swiftly to support Lon Nol's government and also to impose greater discipline on the relevant bureaucracies in his own government. "We need a bold move in Cambodia . . . to show that we stand with Lon Nol," he instructed Kissinger.[25] Because they had hesitated far too long, the communists were "romping into" Cambodia and "the only . . . government in the last 25 years to take a pro-western and pro-American stand is ready to fall." They also needed to deal "with some of the lily-livered ambassadors from our so-called friends in the world," among them their very own State Department.

According to General Westmoreland, the acting chairman of the Joint Chiefs of Staff while General Wheeler was in the hospital, this was the time to "rescind some of the current restraint on US forces," allowing them to come up to the border of Cambodia to provide logistical and artillery support to the army of South Vietnam.[26] This would not only relieve the pressure on the Cambodian army, but would allow the United States "to exploit the situation to our overall advantage without any substantial involvement of US forces on the ground."

An ongoing worry for both Nixon and Kissinger was the potential opposition of Secretaries Laird and Roger. However, during the April 22 meeting of the National Security Council, Kissinger described a cross-border operation that would involve two division-sized South Vietnamese units totaling 10,000 men with artillery support from the Americans.[27] Proposed in this limited way, the two cabinet officers seemed willing to go along. For his part, Rogers expressed appreciation for a decision-making process in which "the president gets all our views." In return, Kissinger offered his own high praise: "Anyone who thinks you are soft is nuts." Explaining his support for the plan, Rogers stated, "I just want to be smart about how we do it."[28]

While conflict with the cabinet officers had been averted, Kissinger was unexpectedly faced with a brewing rebellion among his own staff. Several of the expert, highly credentialed young men Kissinger had brought to Washington were rapidly losing faith in the administration they served. Disappointed in its failure to end the war expeditiously, they viewed the growing US involvement in Cambodia with great trepidation. In written memoranda, Roger Morris, Anthony Lake, and Winston Lord emphasized that the Cambodian military was too weak and incompetent to succeed on its own.[29] However, it was an illusion to think its deficits could be remedied by South Vietnamese or American divisions. In the case of ARVN, the Cambodians might not welcome them. But if US soldiers were dispatched, they could become bogged down in another foreign misadventure, which would invite massive opposition in the United States. Similar to the State Department specialists, Kissinger staffers considered the best option to be "a neutral, Cambodian government under current or other non-Sihanouk leadership which has reached a private understanding with the Communists that they may use the border areas in the same fashion as earlier."

The erudite young men on Kissinger's staff had identified some of the major flaws in the military approach and had advanced a solution designed to minimize bloodshed. Yet there was no possibility that their ideas would be accepted. How could anyone in the Nixon administration advise Lon Nol to let the North Vietnamese stay? Or ask him to accept a situation in which the North Vietnamese would remain, and the United States would continue to bomb? This odd arrangement had been possible because Prince Sihanouk had permitted it, but with him gone, no successor was likely to adopt it. And would the US military tolerate a resumption of a situation in which enemy soldiers could simply cross a border and escape?

While these arguments were simmering, neither the American public nor the Congress were aware that another large-scale military operation was pending. What counted as major news in the media was that the administration had arranged for thousands of rifles to go to Cambodia, and even that news was enough to stir the waters. With Secretary Rogers slated to testify on Capitol Hill within the next few days, the question of what to tell Congress arose. Rogers' own preference was to be candid and to enlist members of Congress as partners in the president's decisions. However, candor was the last thing Kissinger wanted.[30] Faced with his resistance, the Secretary of State suggested that they could "make a virtue out of necessity" by telling them that the Cambodian government had asked for "massive military assistance" and a cross-border operation by American troops. Then what the administration was planning would seem small.

Kissinger agreed "this was a clever way to do it," so clever that he used it in a telephone chat with Senate Majority Leader Mike Mansfield.[31] The president wants you to know his thinking, Kissinger explained. They had received "a large request for military assistance to the Cambodian government." But the administration was not going to grant that. "We are trying to keep our involvement to a minimum." They had agreed only to send the Cambodians some small arms that had been captured in Vietnam. That was good news, the senator replied. But they would have to be careful. Meanwhile he would keep his fingers crossed.

These fingers might have been quickly uncrossed had Mansfield gotten a peek at Kissinger's top-secret memo to Nixon describing their options in Cambodia, which went far beyond "small arms." In the section entitled "What We Are Doing," the national security advisor presented a list of actions, some already accomplished, others underway. It included the shipment of AK-47 rifles and 1,000 man-packs of US arms and equipment, the airlift of four battalions of ethnic Cambodians into Phnom Penh, B-52 strikes against communist base camps, and, under the rubric of Operation Patio, air strikes covering "an area 20 miles deep into Cambodia" to be conducted by tactical aircraft. The army of South Vietnam had already launched several ground operations into Cambodian territory. From Saigon, General Abrams was working with South Vietnamese military officials on plans for a larger, multi-division effort directed toward the Parrot's Beak, a portion of Cambodian land that jutted into Vietnam just 40 miles from Saigon.

For Kissinger, there was nothing extraordinary about deceiving Mansfield. The United States had been bombing Cambodia for over a year while keeping it a secret from Congress, most of the federal bureaucracy, and of course the public—despite the appearance of William Beecher's early *New York Times* article, which had been somehow overlooked. The ramifications of this deception were wide-ranging. It interfered with the ability of anyone outside the White House to analyze the reasons for certain events, including the destabilization of Sihanouk or the movement of North Vietnamese troops into greater swathes of Cambodian territory. It also impaired the ability of the president and his national security advisor to get relevant advice outside of a very narrow circle. For Nixon and Kissinger, this was no loss. When it came to Cambodia, the only opinions they valued were those of the military and the CIA.

The two were also dismissive of Rogers and Laird, although both had approved the "cross-border" operation Kissinger described, with the clear understanding that no US troops would be involved. However, even this commitment quickly began to unravel. As General Abrams hammered out the plan for Parrot's Beak, he included the immediate use of American tactical aircraft, which in turn created a necessity for US advisors to identify targets—a task that might be better accomplished if the advisors were on the ground. There was even greater difficulty when it came to Fishhook, the area where South Vietnam, Cambodia, and Laos shared a common border and where COSVN, the enemy headquarters for operations in South Vietnam, was supposedly located. Perhaps because the enemy was expected to put up a stiff resistance in that area, South Vietnamese military officials said they were reluctant to conduct an offensive there without American troops.

Back in Washington, President Nixon was also beginning to think that US ground troops would have to be involved. The last thing he needed was an ARVN offensive that failed. His anxiety was inflamed by Al Haig, who was familiar with the area and who claimed that because COSVN was located in Fishhook, the South Vietnamese soldiers lacked the ability to successfully attack it by themselves.[32] With thousands of enemy troops in this location, Haig thought the more promising course was a joint operation by American and South Vietnamese ground troops, to be accompanied by artillery and air power. After Kissinger discussed this idea with CIA Director Helms and Admiral Moorer (the new acting director of the Joint Chiefs of Staff), both of whom offered support, Nixon agreed to it.[33]

Yet that decision was kept under wraps when, later that morning, Kissinger chaired a meeting of the White House Special Action Group, which included representatives from the State and Defense departments along with the CIA and the Joint Chiefs of Staff.[34] During the April 24 discussion of plans for Cambodia, he gave no indication that Nixon was contemplating the use of American ground troops in Fishhook.[35] In fact, when Marshall Green asked whether there would be any US involvement in the plans for COSVN, Kissinger assured him: "No Americans go into Cambodia." With that lie, an operation involving thousands of men, planes, and equipment was propelled forward, with minimal scrutiny outside the professional military.

That evening Kissinger met with the dissenters on his staff—Morris, Lake, Lord, and Larry Lynn. Noticing that William Watts was hovering near the door, Kissinger asked if he was "another bleeding heart." Since Watts nodded, Kissinger suggested he might as well join the group.[36] By now these staffers were personally sick of the war. When they ventured outside the White House bubble, even to their own dinner tables, they met with widespread disapproval of the administration's actions. The most obvious costs—the deaths of American soldiers and foreign civilians, the horrific injuries, the psychological wounds, the wholesale destruction in the countryside, the rending of the social fabric at home and abroad—had settled the issue in their minds: the war was a nightmare that must be rapidly ended. From that vantage point, they argued, the expansion of military operations in Laos and Cambodia was truly absurd.

When he later recalled the scene, Roger Morris reflected:

> In this encounter, as others, there was for the staff members—certainly for me—the pernicious problem of discussing outrageous, irrational official actions in the cool, bloodless language of cost effectiveness and manliness the culture of government seemed to demand. Not for the first or last time, a policy in Indochina that warranted screaming was too gently opposed.[37]

In the end the staffers got nowhere with Kissinger because he and Nixon were entirely focused on the prospect of damaging the enemy and bringing about a favorable peace agreement.

As planning for the operation continued, Kissinger was concerned about how John Stennis, chairman of the Senate Armed Services Committee, would react if they didn't give him an advance heads-up. While he didn't mind deceiving Marshall Green—the Assistant Secretary of State for East Asian and Pacific Affairs, for whom he had little use—Kissinger was more concerned about alienating Senator Stennis, one of the administration's most reliable supporters in Congress. At Kissinger's suggestion, the president phoned Stennis to assure him that US aid to Cambodia was so far limited.[38] "However, going forward, they might continue the B-52 bombings," adding, "*Only* you and Senator Russell know about it. It's the best kept secret of the war." Any ground action would be limited to the South Vietnamese, but there was a remote possibility American troops might be called upon to assist, if this would reduce casualties in the long run. "I will be with you on the nail-head," Stennis asserted. This misleading conversation represented the limit of Nixon and Kissinger's willingness to consult members of Congress about the planned deployment of American troops in Cambodia.

As the prospect of dramatic action loomed, the president became more and more excited. "This is one hell of a big thing. It's a small version of the Bulge and Calais," Nixon observed to Kissinger.[39] Perhaps he even compared himself to General Patton at the Battle of the Bulge, after multiple viewings of the film *Patton* in the lead-up to the planned invasion. Yet while this movie-watching might have expressed the president's grandiosity and view of himself as a besieged, lonely hero, the actual situation was different. In handling the Cambodia situation, as on many previous occasions, Nixon was adhering to the preferences of a military leadership that could not accept defeat in this long-running war.

Up to this point, the president still had not issued a formal order for US ground troops in Fishhook. As of Saturday, April 25, Kissinger thought Nixon might lose his nerve and back away from the plan. But then word arrived from General Abrams that the South Vietnamese were refusing to attack the well-defended base area without American troops.[40] Whether real or exaggerated, this information strengthened Nixon's conviction that American soldiers were indispensable for the operation. It also meant that Rogers and Laird would have to be told. This was going to be awkward: once they realized the military had already made specific plans for this attack, they would be rightfully furious at being excluded from such a high-risk and critical decision. If once the invasion was underway word leaked to the press that both the Secretary of State and the Secretary of Defense opposed it, the political results could be dire.

Time was now at a premium. One key factor was the weather. With the monsoon rains coming in mid-May, an invasion involving US troops would have to start no later than May 1–3. The president scheduled a high-level meeting for Sunday morning, April 26, with an ad hoc group that included both secretaries, Helms, and General Wheeler, chairman of the Joint Chiefs of Staff. The need to obfuscate the already-existing plans for Fishhook left the purpose of the gathering so unclear that Rogers and Laird failed to register the anticipated objections.[41] Immediately thereafter, Nixon issued an order authorizing "ground operations by US forces or by US/GVN forces into identified North Vietnamese/Viet Cong sanctuaries in Cambodia up to a depth of 30 kilometers." He included approval for US tactical air/helicopter and artillery attacks up to the same depth.[42]

Once they fully realized what had occurred, Laird and Rogers were incensed. On reflection, it was obvious that the president and the national security advisor had gone around them to engage the military in a plan they would not have approved. While both men had accepted, perhaps too readily, the idea of a South Vietnamese attack on Parrot's Beak and Fishhook, the use of American ground troops there was something else entirely. In a subsequent call to Kissinger, Laird urged him to consider the likely casualties. "Just so you know . . . that regardless of what Wheeler tells you the casualties will run at least as high as the iron triangle."[43] Laird hoped Nixon appreciated what might be coming, "because when it gets up to 800 he will blame me." Kissinger encouraged him to put his concerns in a note.

Laird's objections were not so easily compressed. Producing instead a detailed memorandum, he listed the numerous ways in which the United States was already intervening in the Cambodian situation, which he considered more than sufficient. This included the secret MENU bombings which, in this one week alone, had dropped 3,000 tons of ordinance, and in the past year 100,000. In short, the United States was already making a massive effort, and while the dispatch of ground troops might result in some short-term gains, the enemy "has shown the requisite flexibility . . . to adjust his base areas in South Vietnam, Laos, and Cambodia against strikes by our side." Meanwhile the costs would be significant. There would be new strains on an already tight military budget; the number of US combat deaths would be substantially increased; and the American public would be seriously disturbed.

Although Laird's arguments were laid out in a closely argued document, they ultimately boiled down to a simple point: the president was running a high political risk by sacrificing American lives for uncertain military gains. However, Nixon was energized by this risk and was unwilling to reverse course—unless, as Laird was insisting, General Abrams was having fresh doubts about the wisdom of using US troops in Cambodia.[44] Seeking clarification, the president put a one-day hold on further action until they could get confirmation from Abrams that he still favored the plan.

By nighttime they had a "back-channel" cable from Ambassador Ellsworth Bunker containing Abrams' message: "It is my independent view that these attacks into the enemy's sanctuaries in Cambodia are the military move to make at this time in support of our mission in South Vietnam both in terms of the security of our own forces and for advancement of the Vietnamization program."[45] That settled matters. In a brief meeting the next day, Nixon called in Rogers and Laird to confirm his authorization.

Once the dissenters on Kissinger's staff got word of the decision they were appalled. When Kissinger handed William Watts the task of coordinating the White House effort, he refused. "When I came to work for you, my sense of loyalty was first to the American people, secondly to you and finally to Richard Nixon. I'm against this action on every count and I'm resigning."[46] Six months earlier, Watts discovered his wife and daughter on a picket line protesting the war; now he was free to join them. Kissinger was disgusted.

"Your views represent the cowardice of the Eastern establishment," he observed. To Alexander Haig this was insubordination. "You've just had an order from your commander-in-chief, and you can't refuse." "Fuck you, Al," Watts retorted, "I just have and I've resigned." One day later Anthony Lake and Roger Morris submitted their joint letter of resignation: "We believe the costs and consequences of such an action far exceed any gains one can reasonably expect."[47]

Meanwhile, even as thousands of American and South Vietnamese soldiers were massing for a march toward the Cambodian border, the American press was reporting on alleged splits within the administration about something smaller: whether or not to provide rifles, ammunition, and other equipment to this besieged nation coping with North Vietnamese aggression. A handful of journalists sensed or knew that something bigger was in the works. Veteran correspondent Stanley Karnow wrote in the *Washington Post*: "Current trends suggest that President Nixon . . . is edging toward a commitment to Cambodia. . . . The prospect is a wider Indochina war that a measure of restraint could have prevented."[48] The telltale sign in his view was that administration spokesmen had "suddenly discovered that the Communists are invading Cambodia—even though North Vietnamese and Vietcong troops have occupied large parts of that country for years."

Yet prescient as he was, even Karnow had not imagined a massive cross-border invasion. At worst, he thought the administration might be planning to use B-52 bombers in the sanctuaries, which would in turn generate requests for more advisors, Special Forces, and CIA operatives. Neither he nor his colleagues were aware that all these steps had already been taken, primarily because the government had systematically concealed all past and impending decisions concerning Cambodia. Still, over the past year there had been some indication of the shift—including William Beecher's front-page article about US bombing in the sanctuaries. A more vigilant press corps might have pursued the matter. Still unknown was the wide-ranging wiretapping program that this one article had precipitated.

During the last two days of frantic preparations, Nixon and Kissinger looked for ways to limit media access and control the message. Lon Nol had been purposely kept out of the loop until this point. Mike Rives was instructed to inform him of the impending attack and make it clear that Washington "wanted no sensationalized publicity."[49] The attaché should further inform the Cambodian leader that "an attempt will be made to prevent public media representatives from accompanying the forces" and suggest that "Cambodia do what it can to prevent or discourage correspondents . . . from entering the area." Lon Nol seemed happy to oblige.[50]

In Saigon, US officials carefully monitored the text of General Thieu's announcement so that it would minimize the American role. After announcing that his own troops were going into the Parrot's Beak, he was to say the Americans had agreed to provide support in the form of advisors, tactical air coordinators, medical evacuation, and some logistics assistance.[51] General Abrams would duplicate this account. The goal was to establish the impression that it was South Vietnamese soldiers heading into the sanctuaries, with the United States acting only as back-up. And Nixon himself would address the nation to this effect once the invasion got underway.

It was not only the press that was being tricked. The Nixon administration had done what it could to blindside Congress—not to mention its own Secretaries of Defense and State. On April 26, Rogers was scheduled to testify in a closed hearing of the Senate Foreign Relations Committee, and he was wondering how he could square his obligation to testify truthfully to Congress with the strict instructions he was given from the White House to keep their plans under wraps.[52] What saved him from outright lying was that members of the committee failed to ask pointed questions, so he had no need to tell them that thousands of American soldiers were poised to enter Cambodia. They would not get this news until the very last minute, just prior to a presidential address to the nation on April 30.

As Nixon prepared the final draft of his speech, Kissinger began calling influential individuals to rally them. For him personally this was an exhilarating moment in which his own toughness had tightened his bond with the president. In speaking with Governor Rockefeller, his enthusiasm was palpable: "We are going tonight into the headquarters of the North Vietnamese operation along the Cambodian border . . . the nerve center."[53] Rockefeller promised to issue a statement of support shortly after Nixon's speech was delivered. "I'm just thrilled," he responded, "take care now and don't let him slip." Not to worry, replied Kissinger, "We're over the Rubicon now."

At the other end of the Republican spectrum, Kissinger sought the backing of California Governor Ronald Reagan.[54] Once Nixon gave his speech, "the peaceniks and student radicals are going to try to break us," he said, but if this endeavor failed, "the world is going to be turned over to the communists." Reagan was more than happy to support the president.

In the final hour before the speech, Kissinger met with the Washington press corps for a briefing. Since the Cambodian government had not requested US soldiers on their soil, one reporter asked, on what grounds were they conducting this operation? Nixon was proceeding on the basis that as the commander-in-chief he was responsible for the security of American troops, in effect negating concerns about sovereignty. US troop movement into Cambodia should not be regarded as "an invasion," he maintained, because the presence of 60,000 North Vietnamese troops and their advance beyond the sanctuaries had defined the situation. The reporters continued to ask tough questions, but they were no match for Kissinger's outright lies, including his insistence that "we made no efforts during the first fifteen months of this administration to move against the sanctuaries."

Perhaps the most telling exchange involved a small factual matter concerning the location of the communist headquarters: "What is the name of the province in Cambodia in which the COSVN headquarters is located?" Kissinger acknowledged, "I frankly don't know the name of the province . . . . The South Vietnamese province to which it extends is Tay Ninh."

This minor lapse was indicative of a major blind spot. What did Kissinger, Nixon, or their colleagues know about conditions in Cambodia? Since the overthrow of Prince Sihanouk, they had repeatedly told themselves and each other that whatever steps they were contemplating in Cambodia were pertinent only to Vietnam. They seemed to think it was a mere "technicality" that their actions would be taking place on Cambodian soil. Yet the people of that country would be profoundly affected by what the United States did there. And the United States, in turn, would find its prospects for success shaped by events there.

The previous week, Madame Binh, the chief negotiator for the PRG in Paris, had offered her own reflections on what might happen if the Americans expanded their military presence in Cambodia.[55] She readily conceded that "the spilling of the war into that country poses problems for the PRG/National Liberation Front." However, time would play in their favor. "Cambodian resistance is now being organized, as there are peasants, intellectuals and members of the middle class who will oppose Lon Nol." This would require some work, but it would be done. "The United States miscalculated in Cambodia as it did in Laos and Vietnam," and would now have to cope with an even wider opposition.

Top US officials were not in the habit of heeding Madame Binh's prognostications. They were more inclined to credit the National Intelligence Estimates (NIE) that were routed through the CIA. Oddly enough, the findings of the NIE that were most pertinent to the prospective Cambodian operation ran parallel to the thinking of the Vietnamese diplomat:

> One conclusion is that current developments in Cambodia will bring at least temporary advantage to the non-Communist cause but over the long run the Communists will probably cope with the degradation of their sanctuary by reorganizing their supply lines, relocating their bases, and adjusting their combat tactics. In the meantime, Cambodia will have suffered a debilitating internal struggle with large areas lost to communists and the seeds of eventual communist control spread widely across the country.[56]

The report contained one other prediction with which Madame Binh would also probably have concurred, but that was in direct opposition to Nixon's and Kissinger's expectations about the results of the invasion: "It is unlikely that Hanoi will move toward early negotiations."

However, the time for second thoughts was over. In Nixon's words: "The big game is to pull this off. It's a bold move, imaginative, and it's no more screwing around. Hit 'em in the gut! No defensiveness!"

9

"The Great Mystery of Life"

The president's game plan for rallying the country behind the invasion of Cambodia was to make a direct appeal to that "silent majority" he had invoked so successfully in his November 3 speech. Some might think that themes of patriotism, loyalty, strength, and national honor had become obsolete, but he was confident they would continue to resonate if linked to a credible promise to end the war.

As Nixon stepped before the television cameras on the night of April 30, 1970, pointer in hand and a map of the area behind him, Jeffrey Miller, Sandy Scheuer, Allison Krause, and William Schroeder, students in Kent, Ohio, were going about their familiar college activities. In the Cambodian town of Snoul, six miles from the border with South Vietnam, men and women were starting their workday, which for many involved tapping rubber on the nearby trees. One week later, the students would all be dead and the Cambodian town in ruins.[1]

The fundamental idea Nixon wanted to convey to the public was that through his attack on Cambodia he was saving lives, not squandering them, bringing the nation closer to ending the war rather than expanding it. The problem, he explained, was that North Vietnam "had increased its military aggression" in Cambodia, Laos, and South Vietnam, thus jeopardizing his plan to bring 150,000 troops home.[2] Regarding Cambodia, since signing the Geneva Agreement in 1954, the United States had scrupulously respected the neutrality of its people. The North Vietnamese, however, had been building sanctuaries on both sides of the border from which they could launch "hit-and-run attacks" on American and South Vietnamese troops. Pointing to the sprawling red areas on the map, Nixon claimed these "contain major base camps, training sites, logistics facilities, weapons and ammunition factories, airstrips and prisoner of war compounds." Yet for five years, he falsely asserted, "neither the United States nor South Vietnam has moved against these enemy sanctuaries because we did not wish to violate the territory of a neutral nation." However, the enemy had taken advantage of this restraint and, in the last four weeks, in addition to the "massive attacks" they were gearing up to launch, they were encircling the Cambodian capital of Phnom Penh.

Cambodia's leaders had asked the United States for help in their fight against these communists, and, after "full consultation" with his national security team, he had concluded that to protect American troops and guarantee the success of Vietnamization it was time to clean out the sanctuaries. The major responsibility for this enterprise would be borne by the army of South Vietnam, supported by American advisors and air power. But there was one place known as Fishhook, located only 33 miles from Saigon, where American ground troops would be fighting alongside the army of South Vietnam. This was no ordinary locale, because it contained "the headquarters for the entire Communist military operation in South Vietnam."

He was putting Hanoi on notice. The United States "will not be humiliated" and it "will not be defeated." The stakes were high. Across the globe, small nations were under attack both from within and without. All were reliant on the credibility of the United States. "If when the chips are down, the world's most powerful nation . . . acts like a pitiful, helpless giant, the forces of totalitarianism and anarchy will threaten free nations and free institutions throughout the world." In conclusion, he asked his audience to give their support, not for him but "for our brave men fighting tonight halfway around the world . . . so that their younger brothers and their sons . . . can have a chance to grow up in a world of peace and freedom and justice."

Nixon's speech conveyed the impression that both American and South Vietnamese troops were in immediate danger because of fresh acts of enemy aggression from across the border. However, the events Nixon was describing—including the surrounding of Phnom Penh—presumed an enemy movement *away* from the South Vietnamese border. His listeners also had no way of knowing about the US bombing that had been going on for more than a year, or about the increase in American and South Vietnamese military activity in the wake of Sihanouk's overthrow. The president's ability to conceal these items was aided by the silence of knowledgeable subordinates, who objected to the policy decisions but for whom loyalty to the nation's chief executive was continuing to trump their responsibility to the public.

The speech seemed to work exactly as Nixon intended. The internal White House poll showed a 3 to 1 margin in favor of the president's policy.[3] Less overwhelmingly favorable but still very positive, an early CBS tally produced a 2 to 1 ratio, and the Gallup poll registered a 7 to 5 ratio.[4] According to

Gallup, however, there was one contradictory finding. When people were asked: "Do you think we should send U.S. troops to help Cambodia?" 58% said "No."

While much of the public seemed willing to give the policy a chance, there was fury on Capitol Hill, where members of the Senate Foreign Relations Committee had recently been told by Secretary of State Rogers that the United States was reluctant to provide any support to the Lon Nol government. Had Rogers deliberately deceived Congress, or was he simply out of the loop? Either way, the administration's actions in Cambodia and Laos raised a serious constitutional question. If the president of the United States was free to send thousands of troops to any place in the world without consulting Congress, any notion of "separation of powers" went out the window.

The ranks of the Senate "doves" suddenly swelled. One convert was Majority Leader Mike Mansfield from Montana, who argued that "the U.S.–South Vietnamese thrust into Cambodia . . . can be regarded in no other light than as a widening of the war and an escalation of the conflict."[5] He rejected Nixon's warning that America was in danger of losing prestige." "What confronts this nation is not a question of saving face. It is a question of saving lives." There was nothing in past experiences in Indochina to suggest that the way to reduce casualties was to expand the area of operations.

The editorial reaction of the major newspapers was also predictable. According to the *Washington Post,* "the President has confronted us with a fait accompli, carefully concealed in advance by suspect evidence, specious argument, and excessive rhetoric."[6] Two weeks ago Americans had been told that Vietnamization was going so well that 150,000 troops could be coming home. All of a sudden, the situation had become so "intolerable" that the invasion of another country had become imperative. To the *Post* editors, this reversal illustrated the absence of a coherent strategy. The *New York Times* editorial, "Military Hallucination Again," was equally harsh, scoffing at the *suggestion* that sending troops into the Cambodian sanctuaries would save lives and shorten the war:

> This is the same kind of rhetoric Americans have heard from their leaders at every stage of this country's long, misguided plunge into the Southeast Asian morass. Time and bitter experience have exhausted the credulity of the American people and Congress.[7]

While the *Washington Post* and the *New York Times* played a vital role in shaping the opinions of a certain sector of the population, there were millions of people outside their sphere of influence whose credulity remained intact. They were Nixon's audience.

But would even his "silent majority" support him if the incursion into Cambodia was not successful? For all their bravado, both Nixon and Kissinger were worried about what the troops would find. During the first four days, the 10,000 American and South Vietnamese soldiers advancing rapidly through Fishhook found neither enemy fighters nor anything resembling a headquarters.[8] Laird had warned them they would not find COSVN, and while the soldiers located some tunnels and bunkers, it was unclear what they signified.

Nixon was edgy, wondering if the Americans and South Vietnamese troops were being sufficiently proactive.[9] The Joint Chiefs of Staff were "not thinking fast enough." Perhaps General Abrams did not appreciate the time pressure they were under. "They have to take risks and jump in. Bomb whatever is necessary."

Meanwhile, the flames of outrage were being fanned by a new revelation: the United States had just launched a series of bombing raids over North Vietnam. This constituted the first sustained break with the 1968 bombing halt agreement between Hanoi and the Johnson administration. Like the operations in Fishhook and Parrot's Beak, its purpose was to break Hanoi's will with a fresh demonstration of America's power. Although intended to be kept secret from the American public, the airstrikes were described with remarkable accuracy a day after they occurred by *New York Times* reporter William Beecher.[10] According to his account, 128 American planes had attacked supply dumps and other targets north of the DMZ. Hanoi claimed that many civilians had been killed, including 20 children.

Members of the Senate were stunned by this latest news. Majority Leader Mike Mansfield observed, "Events are piling upon events in a way which indicates that there is without question . . . an escalation of the war." The most tangible expression of congressional anger was a new bipartisan amendment, introduced by Senators Goodell (R-NY), Hatfield (R-OR), McGovern (D-SD), and Hughes (D-IA) that would cut off funds for military activities in Vietnam, Laos, and Cambodia unless there was a formal declaration of war. Another amendment, introduced by Sherman Cooper (R-KY) and Frank Church (D-ID) would prohibit the use of any defense funds for military assistance or future military activities in Cambodia.

While anger simmered on Capitol Hill, it threatened to boil over on college campuses. In the run-up to Nixon's speech, both Laird and Rogers had been apprehensive about its impact on young people. "It will make the students puke," Rogers predicted.[11] In Washington, the normally moderate National Students Association called upon the House of Representatives to start impeachment proceedings against Nixon on the grounds that the invasion of Cambodia showed "an obvious disregard of the Constitution of the United States." As feared, the reaction on campuses was furious and fast. Within a day, student groups had launched impromptu demonstrations and strikes. All across the country, in public universities, local colleges, and small religious institutions, as well as many high schools, students sprang into action.

Shock, despair, and a sense of impotence fueled the demonstrations, most of which were law-abiding. But some institutions were home to ROTC buildings or other military-related facilities. These proved tempting targets for attack and, when law enforcement personnel came on campuses to quell disorders, some students fought back. Within a day there were violent confrontations at the University of Maryland, Michigan State, Ohio State, and Stanford University.

Nixon's response, on a spontaneous visit to the Pentagon—one place he could be assured of a warm welcome—was to draw an invidious comparison between the brave American troops fighting in Vietnam and "those bums . . . blowing up the campuses."[12] These students, he complained, "are the luckiest people in the world, going to the greatest universities and here they are burning up the books, storming around about this issue."

Kent State University in Ohio did not fit Nixon's narrative of elite institutions catering to the alienated sons and daughters of wealthy Americans.[13] A former teachers' college, most of its 21,000-plus student body was from inside the state, with parents from lower middle-class or blue-collar backgrounds. Although the majority of students were politically inactive, there was a growing strain of antiwar sentiment on the campus. The previous fall, 3,000 students had marched through the city of Kent as part of the Moratorium Day, and an estimated 5,000 had boycotted classes.

There was also a smaller group of radicals who had been associated with a chapter of Students for a Democratic Society that was banned from campus. The chapter had been founded in the fall of 1968, at precisely the moment when national SDS had turned decisively in the direction of provoking confrontation.[14] With its embrace of disruption, Kent State SDS was an easy target for university administrators. A sequence of protests during the 1968–69 academic year, directed at the ROTC program and the Liquid Crystals Institute (which was conducting research for the Defense Department), had led to the suspension of SDS leaders and the banning of their organization from the campus. By the time of the Cambodia invasion, however, there were a small number of students, some of them former SDS members, who still embraced militant resistance as the only way to challenge US policy in Vietnam.

However, the initial response to President Nixon's April 30 speech was a more peaceful form of political activism. On Friday at noon, 300 young people gathered on the university Commons to witness the mock burial of the Constitution—because if the president could dispatch American troops into a foreign country without a congressional declaration of war, then the constitutionally mandated separation of powers was plainly dead.[15]Among the speakers was Jim Geary, a highly decorated Vietnam veteran, who expressed his disgust and alienation by burning his discharge papers as did fellow veteran Tim Butz. The presence of the two men at the rally signified a new phenomenon on college campuses: soldiers returning from Vietnam, who added their own anger and disillusionment with the war to the volatile atmosphere.

By Friday night events took a more ominous turn. As students gathered in the downtown bars for a typical weekend night, a fistfight erupted and spilled out into the streets. What began as a minor skirmish spread, as small groups of angry students shouting "One-two-three-four, we don't want your war," marched through town, flinging rocks and bottles as they went. In response, the mayor declared a "state of emergency," ordered an immediate curfew, shut down the bars, and ordered local police to clear the streets.[16]

The following night a small, restless crowd heeded a spontaneous call to march on the ROTC building. After circling the site, some participants began throwing rocks, while a handful of people aimed flares at the wooden building and two young men lit gasoline-soaked rags. As flames shot up into the night sky, local firemen were hampered in their attempt to put out the fire by angry protesters who cut their hoses. By 10:00 PM the National Guard, which had been summoned by the mayor, had arrived at the scene and was able to restore order. At that point, the ROTC building had been damaged but was still standing. On Sunday morning this structure had mysteriously burned to the ground.

By then, the university resembled a war zone, with thousands of National Guardsmen wearing white helmets and carrying bayonets walking the grounds.[17] Armored vehicles were parked on the surrounding streets, and occasional helicopters could be seen flying overhead. Throughout the day, there were isolated confrontations between students and the Guard. By evening the announcement of an early curfew inspired another sit-in just outside the campus, culminating in a furious clash as Guardsmen used bayonets and tear gas to herd the students into a dorm.

As tensions grew, Republican governor James Rhodes held an inflammatory press conference in which he described the demonstrators as "the worst type of people we harbor in America, worse than the brown shirts and the communist element."[18] Indeed, for many of the townspeople in Kent this was a face-off between upstanding military youth and the privileged college "bums" Nixon described.

Yet this stereotyped distinction did not really fit the protest movement on campus. One activist, former SDS member Alan Canfora, shared an off-campus apartment with six other students, two of them Vietnam veterans. A few days earlier the entire group had attended the memorial service for Sergeant William Miles Caldwell, age 20, from their hometown of Barberton, Ohio. Caldwell had been accidentally run over by an American tank in Vietnam.[19] The seven young men, including William's brother George, stood by the gravesite and promised to take some action to address this senseless death. To these grieving roommates, the invasion of Cambodia was salt in an open wound.

Although Alan Canfora had a history of antiwar activism, the swelling crowd of demonstrators included many young people who had only recently become political. Among them was Jeff Miller, who had recently transferred there to be with old friends from Plainview, Long Island. Miller was troubled by the war in Vietnam and had attended Moratorium Day events the preceding October. However, he had been disappointed in the lack of results and had refocused his attention on private concerns—until he heard about the invasion of Cambodia. He believed Nixon's decision demonstrated that "he will never listen" and, although he had previously opposed the use of violence, he thought that more extreme forms of campus protest might be the only way to get his attention. Miller was furious about the behavior of the National Guard, telling a friend, "Those fucking pigs lied to us . . . we have a right to have rallies and be on the street. It's our campus."[20]

Another distraught student was Allison Krause, from suburban Maryland. At a professor's suggestion, she had attended the Friday rally where the US Constitution was symbolically buried.[21] Like Jeff Miller, Allison and her boyfriend Barry Levine had participated in Moratorium Day activities in Washington but had been turned off by militant demonstrators carrying NLF flags. On Sunday, Alison had come upon a Guardsman and had stuck a lilac in the barrel of his gun. Stopping to chat, she was dismayed when a nearby officer rebuked the man, ordering him to remove the flower and "start acting like a soldier and forget all this peace stuff." As the officer turned away, Allison called after him, "What's the matter with peace? Flowers are better than bullets."

By Monday morning, May 4, many of the Kent State students were exhausted by sleeplessness and rage. Anger over Cambodia had become fused in their minds with the encroachment of the National Guard at their school. Chants of "one-two-three-four, we don't want your fucking war!" alternated with cries of "pigs off campus."[22] By then all demonstrations had been banned from the university, but another antiwar rally was nevertheless scheduled for the Commons at noon.

With news of the disturbances at Kent being broadcast around the country, some worried parents encouraged their children to come home, or to stay away from potential trouble spots. Among them was Jeff Miller's mother, Elaine. At 10:00 AM they spoke briefly on the phone. Jeff said he would be going to the noon protest, but he promised to be careful.

Yet, events were already spiraling out of control. Governor Rhodes had made it clear that the Guard was free to use whatever force was necessary to halt the protests. And after 36 hours on the ground at Kent, surrounded by angry students, these men were on a short fuse.

At noon protesters on the Commons rang the Victory Bell, normally used to celebrate the school's football wins. One thousand students gathered in the immediate vicinity; another 2,000 milled around and watched. The observers ran the gamut of opinion. Many like Sandy Scheuer, a friend of Jeff Miller's, were sympathetic with the goals of the protest but not the tactics. Described as an outgoing, optimistic person, Sandy was a speech-and-hearing therapy major, who told friends, "Maybe I'm not going to set the world on fire through speech therapy. But if I can help a few people that's good enough." On Sunday night, she had briefly considered joining the next day's demonstration but chose instead to study for a test and to attend class. However, when protesters gathered at noon, she paused to observe.

Another ambivalent onlooker was Bill Schroeder, a basketball player on a ROTC scholarship, from Lorain, Ohio[23]. On the morning of May 4 he was wearing gold-orange bellbottom trousers, a striped tee-shirt, and a denim jacket. Except for his short hair, he could easily have been mistaken for one of the angry protesters. But he had come to campus to take an ROTC test, and after he finished, he and a friend had drifted toward the Commons to watch the action.

On the surface, Schroeder seemed the prototype of the all-American soldier whom Nixon and others counterposed to the longhaired "bums" running wild at colleges. From elementary school onward, he had been a leader in mainstream activities—Eagle Scout and captain of his high school basketball team. At Kent, he managed to maintain a high academic average while playing sports, fulfilling his ROTC obligations, and working part-time in a succession of jobs. Yet Schroeder was having serious second thoughts about his affiliation with the ROTC. He had originally thought the scholarship was a good deal, but he told friends," l just can't justify our being in Vietnam. I don't think I could ever fight there."[24] In his ROTC classes he had no problem learning the military history part, but "when they start telling us about the best way to kill peasants, I really hate it."

Just as the clock struck 12:00, two jeeps with National Guardsmen drove up to the Commons. Using bullhorns, the officers ordered the students to disperse. Shouting angrily at the troops, the students stood their ground. The jeeps pulled back slightly, and members of the Guard started hurling canisters of tear gas in their direction. As the students spread out, some threw rocks and shouted angry epithets.

The Guardsmen pursued them, but being unfamiliar with the campus ended up backed against the fence that surrounded the football field. Outnumbered and unsure what to do, since they had used the last of their tear gas grenades, the men retreated to the top of a hill. Then with no warning of any kind, a row of them knelt down and fired their M-1 rifles and pistols into the crowd. In the span of 13 seconds, they aimed between 60–67 shots at a cluster of students standing in a parking lot.

The popping of the guns was bewildering at first, as the young people were slow to recognize the sound of live bullets. The first person to go down was Jeff Miller, shot in the mouth. The bullet shattered his skull, killing him instantly. With his blood dripping onto the ground, a 14-year-old runaway, subsequently identified as Mary Ann Vecchio, stood over his body screaming for help—a moment of anguish captured on film by campus photographer John Filo.

Among those who were shot, a few were students whose involvement in the day's protest had made them conspicuous. Jeff Miller had become increasingly enraged by the actions of the National Guard and, just prior to his death, could be seen shouting "Pigs off campus." Another such victim was Allison Krause, who the previous Friday was a hesitant, peace-loving demonstrator but by Monday afternoon was reportedly yelling obscenities at the Guard. When the shooting started, Allison and her boyfriend hid behind a car in the parking lot. Mistakenly thinking the attack had ended, she moved into the open and was mowed down by a bullet in the chest. Activist Alan Canfora was shot in the wrist while carrying his black flag in memory of Bill Caldwell.

It was not only protesters that the Guard hit. Sandy Scheuer was walking with a friend to the Music and Speech building on her way to class when shots came from behind. The two young women both dropped to the ground, but not quickly enough to save Sandy from a fatal bullet in the neck. ROTC cadet Bill Schroeder, who had moved to the parking lot in order to observe the situation, was struck by a bullet that penetrated his lungs. An hour later he was dead. Another curious onlooker, freshman Dean Kahler from an Ohio farm family, also hit the ground when the shooting started but sustained a back wound that fractured his vertebrae, leaving him paralyzed from the chest down.

None of the students had imagined that the National Guard would fire live ammunition. Many were frozen to the spot, unable to believe what they had just seen. Others were shrieking and weeping. Some tried to assist the wounded, who were lying in pools of blood. The Guardsmen moved back toward the Commons and were quickly confronted with an even larger crowd of students. Suddenly the deadly sequence seemed about to be repeated. The commander of the National Guard, General Canterbury, ordered the students to disperse immediately or be fired upon again. At that point a few faculty members intervened, pressing the Guard to hold their fire, as biology professor Glen Frank urged the frightened but enraged young people to move back: "I'm begging you right now, they're going to move in, and it can only be a slaughter."[25] Heeding his warning, the students withdrew. By mid-afternoon the National Guard had left the campus, and shortly afterward the university closed.

Within hours the events at Kent State became national news. It came as a shock to Nixon. As described by Haldeman, "He's very disturbed. Afraid his decision set it off, and that is the ostensible cause of the demonstrations there. Issued a condolence statement then kept after me all the rest of the day for more facts." The president hoped that the rioters had provoked the shooting, but there was little evidence of this. He also "talked a lot about how we can get through to the students, turn this stuff off."[26]

As the Kent State story spread, it seemed to eclipse the controversy that had sparked it: the American invasion of Cambodia. But for the Cambodians, unlike Americans, the invasion remained only too real. As the devastated Kent State parents arranged for the remains of their children to be shipped home, it was already morning in Cambodia. On May 5 in the small town of Snoul, units from the US 11th Army Calvary Regiment came in with their tanks and guns. Encountering enemy fire along the road, they blasted sections of the community with their cannon and called in airplanes, which dumped flaming napalm and 500-pound bombs into the village center.[27]

At the sound of gunfire, most of the 2,000 inhabitants fled into the forest or to nearby villages. But not everyone escaped. When Associated Press reporter Peter Arnett entered Snoul, he came upon "the remains of a woman and a young child and two men, their bodies fused together by the fire of an explosion, probably napalm." There were huge craters and smashed up stores. American soldiers were openly looting the shops that were still standing. While they did so, their commanding officer, Lt. Col. Grail Brookshire, who would later laughingly refer to himself as "the butcher of Snoul," stood by watching. When asked how the townspeople might be affected by the destruction, Brookshire dismissed the question, explaining that, "We can't get involved in administering civil government." *New York Times* reporter Gloria Emerson arrived a few days later and found a few hundred Cambodians sorting hopelessly through their ruined homes and stores.

The fate of Snoul and other small villages in Cambodia was the last thing on Nixon's mind. But the deaths at Kent State did weigh heavily on him. Even before he knew the full extent of the bad news, he knew he was in deep trouble.

Pictures of National Guardsmen in combat gear and rifles, down on one knee, shooting at students, were plastered across the country. Literally millions of high school and college students were profoundly affected by Kent State. More than any other event of the period, the killings there, in combination with the Nixon's reference to "bums blowing up the campuses," consolidated a sense of outrage and victimization among students. The photo of the young woman shrieking over the body of Jeffrey Miller may have been even more real and devastating to them than recent images of the women and children lying in a ditch in My Lai.

The senseless murder of the Ohio students was also horrifying to millions of older people—a painful reminder of those who had already perished in Vietnam or whose lives were at risk in Cambodia. The funeral of Jeff Miller at the Riverside Memorial Chapel in Manhattan saw an outpouring of grief. Mayor John Lindsay had ordered government flags to be flown at half-mast and designated May 8 as a "day of reflection" in memory of the deceased. Thousands of sympathetic onlookers lined the streets around the chapel[28] while hundreds of people crowded inside. The mayor attended, and eulogies were given by New York Senator Charles Goodell and Dr. Benjamin Spock. Praising the idealism of youth, the physician ventured the thought that the death of the four students "may do more to end the war in Vietnam than we will have been able to do in five years."

When the Miller family exited the chapel, thousands of young people in the streets opened a corridor and silently held up their hands in the V-sign that had come to signify peace in the context of the Vietnam War. One reason for the large turnout was that the New York City Board of Education had closed the 900 public schools as a "memorial to the four students who were tragically killed at Kent State University."[29]

Meanwhile protests on campus—most of them nonviolent but many of them highly confrontational—were spreading far beyond the usual locations.[30] At normally conservative Finch College in New York, Tricia Nixon's alma mater, students voted to strike. At the University of Nebraska students were occupying the ROTC building. There were clashes between National Guardsmen and protesters at the University of South Carolina.[31] From affluent Amherst College, where the president's son-in-law David Eisenhower was enrolled, to small religious institutions in the Midwest, to the previously silent white colleges in the South, young people were springing into action. Indeed, the sense of embattlement deepened when, on May 15 at the historically black Jackson State College in Mississippi, police opened fire on a women's dorm killing two students and wounding another 12.

The circle of dissent kept widening. In the aftermath of the Kent State deaths, some college athletes were refusing to compete in scheduled events.[32] Business school students from Harvard and elsewhere were reaching out to the corporate community to express their opposition to the war. Less visible, but consequential, were returning veterans on college campuses who were embracing the antiwar cause.[33]At Hofstra University on Long Island, Ron Kovic, a Marine from Massapequa who had returned only months earlier after a gunshot wound that left him paralyzed, reached a turning point:

> I was sitting alone in my apartment listening to the radio when I first heard the news about Kent State. . . . For the moment there was a shock through my body. I felt like crying. I remember saying to myself the whole thing is coming down now. I didn't know where I was going but I had to find other people who felt the way I did. . . . Students were congregating in small groups all over the place. The campus looked as if it was going to explode. Banners were going up and monitors with red armbands were walking up and down handing out leaflets . . . I thought carefully for a moment or two, and then decided to participate.[34]

In response to the roiling protests, university administrators began to change their approach. Until recently most of these officials had taken a hands-off approach to their students' antiwar activities. Whatever their private views, they insisted that educational institutions should remain politically neutral. But this stance was increasingly untenable. When students at Princeton identified antiwar candidates whom they pledged to support in the midterm elections, the university agreed to suspend classes for the two weeks prior to the election so that students and faculty could campaign for their chosen candidates. At Yale, President Kingman Brewster led a group of 1,000 students to Washington to lobby Yale alumni in the House and Senate for legislation that would speed the war's end. Thirty-seven college and university presidents signed a letter to President Nixon citing "the severe and widespread apprehensions on our campuses."[35] "We implore you," they wrote, "to demonstrate unequivocally your determination to end the war quickly."

With his finely honed political instincts, Nixon realized he had to recalibrate. Moving quickly into damage control, he invited to a private session at the White House six Kent State students who had come to Washington to speak with members of Congress.[36] He also agreed to meet with a delegation of college and university presidents, consisting of eight prominent educators who had notably not signed the antiwar letter. The approved topic of the meeting was the management of student dissent, rather than US policy in Southeast Asia.[37] Speaking for the group, Dr. Nathan Pusey of Harvard emphasized the gravity of the campus crisis. They were no longer dealing with "a small group of radicals" but with "a broad base of students and faculty, who are upset." Alexander Heard, the chancellor of Vanderbilt University, observed that at his school there were "many moderate students trying to work inside the system," but they found themselves being derided by Vice President Agnew, Attorney General Mitchell, and others. It was essential that they "sense a warmth and receptivity from the administration" or they would "join the other side."

At a news conference shortly afterward, the group described the president as an "attentive listener" and claimed that he had agreed to halt hostile comments from members of his administration toward the students.[38] The one tangible result of the meeting was that Nixon agreed to appoint Alexander Heard to serve a two-month term in Washington as liaison between the academic community and the president.[39] Yet, Nixon had no real interest in this communication, suggesting to Haldeman, "we'll give Heard a nice little office . . . a Coca Cola, and put him away."[40] Sensing his irrelevance, the chancellor ultimately resigned before the completion of his term.

While Nixon was publicly conciliatory toward student protesters, he was privately seething at the landslide of criticism he was receiving from journalists and other "liberals." In apocalyptic fashion, Kissinger reassured him that "they will be the first to be destroyed," but the president was blunt: "I have no use for them. I hate these bastards."[41]

An immediate challenge was a forthcoming march and rally planned for Washington DC on May 9, 1970. Hurriedly put together by unpaid volunteers in New York City, it was supported by student organizations across the country as a way of expressing their collective outrage over the events at Kent State and Cambodia. Despite the stated intention of the organizers to keep the gathering peaceful, nobody could say for sure how the crowds would react once in the Capitol. To avert the possibility of violence or serious disruption, hundreds of Third Army combat-ready troops had taken up positions inside the Executive Office Building, with an additional 5,000 soldiers in the nearby streets. The White House itself was surrounded by a phalanx of buses.

As these military formations moved into place, Nixon's unease seemed to grow. For almost two weeks he had been performing in the mode most comfortable for him: making the high-risk move, plotting the sequence of steps, choreographing his staff, managing media, packaging the necessary falsehoods. These were activities that he had engaged in throughout his political life, and they had insulated him from many painful realities. But as he waited for the tens of thousands of wrathful youths to descend on Washington he was unable to sleep. By 4:30 AM he was still awake. Summoning his valet, Manolo Sanchez, and a Secret Service man, he instructed the driver of his limousine to head over to the Lincoln Memorial where hundreds of protesters were already gathering.[42]

On the steps, he approached a group of students: "I know that most of you probably think I'm an SOB but I want you to know I understand just how you feel." The young people were mostly silent, perhaps out of uncertainty about how to address the president of the United States, whom many of them viewed as something far worse than an SOB. But there he was chatting about the value of foreign travel, reflecting on the plight of the American Indian ("What we have done with the American Indian is in its way just as bad as what we imposed on the Negroes"), pointing out his administration's work on the environment, speaking to a group of coeds from Syracuse about their university football team.

Above them all loomed the marble sculpture of Abraham Lincoln, whom Nixon greatly admired, a man who had experienced the deaths of America's soldiers during the Civil War with a moral agony that made his language resonate through time. Nixon himself could be quite eloquent in his prepared speeches, but as he struggled to connect with the students the necessary words were elusive. Finally, one young man brought up the reason they had come to Washington: "I hope you realize that we are willing to die for what we believe in." The same was true of his own generation, Nixon countered. His goal, he assured the students, was "to build a world in which you will not have to die for what you believe in."[43]

Presidential aides Ron Ziegler and Egil Krogh appeared on the scene just as Nixon was moving the conversation to a higher philosophical plane. People thought too much about material things, he suggested. "What we must all think about is why we are here, what are those elements of the spirit that really matter?" He knew they were searching for the answers to these questions just as he had done as a young man. He wanted them to realize "that ending the war and cleaning up the streets and air and water is not going to solve the spiritual hunger that all of us have—which has been the great mystery of life from the beginning of time." Of course, to most of the students at the Lincoln Memorial "the great mystery of life" was the never-ending, futile Vietnam War, a subject Nixon seemed to avoid.[44]

To Haldeman this predawn visit was an indication of the president's overwrought frame of mind. In his May 9 diary entry, Haldeman recorded his worry:

> I am concerned about his condition. The decision, the speech, the aftermath killings, riots, press etc.; the press conference, the student confrontation

> have all taken their toll and he has had very little sleep for a long time and his judgment, temper and mood suffer badly as a result.[45]

Nixon's mood could not have been improved by the negative reaction of his staff. On Monday morning as the press reports of his impromptu appearance rolled in, John Ehrlichman told the president bluntly that his words made him seem tired and ineffective to the students.[46] In response, Nixon dictated a 10-page memorandum for his staff, emphasizing "even when I am tired I do not talk about nonsensical things."[47] The team was so focused on "material things and what we accomplish in our record," they had lost "the ability to communicate on these matters that are infinitely more important—qualities of spirit, emotion, of the depth and mystery of life, which this whole visit was really about." He did not mean to knock the staff, but none seemed able to "really understand or appreciate what it is . . . a President should mean to the people."

Inside the administration there were deeper problems. Both Nixon and Kissinger were worried about the allegiance of the Cabinet and the federal bureaucracies. As reporters had quickly learned, Secretaries Laird and Rogers had opposed the Cambodia foray from the outset. The State Department was a problem because its regional specialists disapproved of the broad direction of US policy in Cambodia. In their view, American interests had been most effectively protected by Prince Sihanouk, despite his official stance as neutral. It was a serious mistake to have so quickly endorsed and armed Lon Nol, an error compounded by the decision to send ground troops. In an unprecedented move, 250 State Department and foreign aid employees signed a letter to Rogers expressing "concern and apprehension over the enlargement of hostilities in Southeast Asia" and urging him to challenge the direction of US policy.

During the first two weeks of May, instances of administration insubordination seemed to proliferate. One unlikely dissenter was Secretary of the Interior Walter Hickel, who in a public letter chastised the president:

> About 200 years ago there was emerging a great nation in the British Empire, and it found itself with a colony in violent protest by its youth—men such as Patrick Henry, Thomas Jefferson, Madison and Monroe to name a few. Their protests fell on deaf ears and finally led to war. . . . My point is, if we read history, it clearly shows that youth in its protest must be heard.[48]

This was a remarkably insulting letter for a cabinet member to write to the president., but it reflected the profound sense of urgency that led some officials to cross the normal boundaries.[49] Nixon intended to fire him when the controversy died down, but to the amazement of Haldeman he instead ordered the closing of the White House tennis court as punishment for fickle cabinet members.

The most serious challenge was from Congress, where antiwar legislation had gained traction. Congressional offices were being inundated with calls, telegrams, letters, and petitions urging them to stop the war. As reported by Western Union officials, this was "the greatest volume of single-subject telegrams we've ever handled," even exceeding Pearl Harbor. Congress was also the target of intense student lobbying. On the Monday following the huge Washington demonstration, large numbers of students surged onto Capitol Hill to express support for a new Hatfield–McGovern amendment, which set a fixed deadline (July 1971) for cutting all funding for the Vietnam War.[50]

A narrower initiative, which seemed likely to pass the Senate, was the bipartisan Cooper–Church amendment, which required the administration to adhere to its stated deadline of June 30 for withdrawing troops from Cambodia and stipulated that any future US military activity there must be approved by Congress. The White House lobbied furiously against the measure, arguing that the proposed restrictions on the Executive's use of military power would inevitably serve the enemy. But this argument was wearing thin for many senators.

Adding to outrage over the administration's expansion of the war was mounting concern over the alienation of young people. This was hardly a new theme, nor was it confined to Congress. For years, "the generation gap" had been a staple of mainstream conversation, involving a tangled weave of cultural, political, and moral divergences. Somewhere near the center of these strands was always Vietnam. The faraway conflict kept students on elite campuses in a perpetual state of antagonism toward their own government. By May 1970, the balance seemed to have tipped from it being a minority concern to mainstream. Millions of students across the country were striking, campuses were shutting down everywhere, and the antiwar movement was gaining recruits. The passion and pervasiveness of the response struck fear into the hearts of many members of the elite, who worried that the so-called gap was becoming a gulf, and even their own children might be passing irretrievably into opposition.

In New York City, 1,000 "establishment" lawyers formed an ad hoc group with the aim of lobbying Congress.[51] As explained by Francis T. P. Plimpton, president of the New York Bar Association, they were speaking out because "those of us who are older are determined there shall be no generation gap and no communication gap" on matters of peace and war. On the eve of their departure for Washington, former Supreme Court Chief Justice Earl Warren addressed the group: "So long as youth carries the burden of the war, while their elders seem in no hurry to end it . . . we may expect to have a generation gap that widens every day."

Within the business community, opposition to the Vietnam War was mounting. Normally complacent executives were asking themselves if the defeat of communism in Southeast Asia was truly worth the instability at home. They were also worried about the precarious state of the nation's economy, which had been sliding into a recession. Many attributed the high rate of inflation to war spending. The Dow Jones industrial average had been falling for over a year and, in the immediate aftermath of Kent State, experienced the most startling drop since Pearl Harbor. According to a recent Lou Harris poll, 78% of corporate executives attributed the fall in the stock market to Nixon's policies, notably his apparent inability to end the war.[52,53]

Even Kissinger's old friend David Rockefeller, the President of Chase Manhattan Bank, seemed to be moving away from his unqualified support for the administration's policies. "I am terribly disturbed by what one hears on every hand. It is distressing," he told Kissinger.[54] Rockefeller had recently met with 40 students at the Columbia School of International Affairs, and there was "no question that the more moderate ones are terribly upset," he said. Kissinger appealed to his sense of loyalty. "The cohesion of our society depends on the leaders sticking together no matter what their reservations are." Then "deal with this as quickly as possible," the banker replied. If the war continued to drag on for months, it would be "very difficult" to defend.

David's brother Nelson was also beginning to shift. The New York governor spoke regularly with Kissinger and clearly enjoyed his insider relationship. Nelson routinely cheered on his old friend with effusive praise and had told him he was "thrilled" by the advance news of the Cambodian invasion. However, after the slayings at Kent State the governor visited Elaine Miller, the school secretary whose 20-year-old son Jeffrey had just been killed.[55] On Sunday afternoon May 10—an unimaginably bleak Mother's Day—a limousine pulled into the driveway of her Long Island home. Rockefeller and the state's attorney general, Louis Lefkowitz, joined Jeff's mother and grandmother in the small living room. Still reeling from the shock, she was unexpectedly touched by the governor's warmth and concern. He too had lost a son, Rockefeller explained, and he understood how devastating this experience could be. Rockefeller was sitting quietly on the couch, with his arm around Mrs. Miller, when Jeff's older brother Russ burst in after returning from Washington, where he had addressed his first protest rally –100,000 upset, angry young people. Yet somehow Nelson Rockefeller made a personal connection with Russ that day, which lasted beyond the visit.

The Miller family's grief may have weighed on Rockefeller when a few days later he attended a meeting of the nation's governors, who were given a confidential briefing by Nixon about the situation in Cambodia. Subsequently his office released a critical statement emphasizing that the prolonged war in Indochina had caused "devastating repercussions," including "the polarization of the American people . . . the diversion of $100 billion in national resources" and "the worst inflation since World War II." Furthermore, Americans had also "suffered a major blow to their morale." The governor thought the goal must be to get the troops out of Cambodia "as rapidly as possible," negotiate a deal with the enemy and bring the boys home.[56]

10

"The Greatest Success"

The Rockefeller brothers and other elite figures might be wavering in their support for Nixon's war policy. However, the president and Kissinger were still counting on the "silent majority"—the millions of less affluent white citizens across the country whose hostility to protestors could be siphoned into support for the war. In Kent, Ohio, even after the massacre the townspeople were furious at the students—for trashing the local stores, for wearing long hair, for shouting obscene words, for dishonoring the flag, for protesting the war, and for bringing unwanted publicity to their community.

When Allison Krause's father arrived at her apartment to retrieve her possessions, the landlord greeted him with praise for the National Guard and a demand that he pay the remainder of his daughter's rent. For weeks the local papers ran extra pages with the rage-filled letters of the citizenry: "How dare they," wrote one housewife. "I stand behind the action of the National Guard! I want my property defended." "Hooray," she concluded. "I shout for God and Country, recourse to justice under law, fifes, drums, martial music, parades, ice cream cones, America, support it or leave it."[1]

To some, it was an economic issue. "We are paying our hard-earned money to support and educate these young people," wrote one. "For what? To let them burn and destroy property that more of our tax money has paid for?" But the rage went far beyond money.

The parents of Bill Schroeder, the slain ROTC member, received anonymous hate mail: "Dear Mr. and Mrs. Schroeder, There's nothing better than a *dead* destructive, riot making *communist*," read one such letter, "and that's what your son was, if not he would have stayed away like a good *American* would do. They should all be shot, then we'd have a better USA . . . "[2] To his mother someone wrote: "I saw you on T.V. and if I were a policeman I would kill a lot more of these kids."

While these letters represented an extreme element, others reflected the much more common belief that the National Guardsmen were compelled to defend themselves against violent student demonstrators. Indeed, the first reports were that a sniper had opened fire on the Guard, triggering the volley of shots. That story was quickly disavowed, but soon replaced by the claim that a barrage of rocks and other flying objects had put the Guard in danger. One week after the events at Kent State, a *Newsweek* poll revealed that 58% of Americans blamed the students for the deaths, while only 11% blamed the Guard. Meanwhile support for the White House was holding steady. After ten days of mainly negative publicity, a Gallup poll found that 57% of Americans approved of the way Nixon was handling his job, as opposed to the 31% who disapproved.[3]

These polls confirmed Nixon's belief in the dependability of that constituency which, from the time of his Checkers speech in 1952, had been the bedrock of his personal political success. Few people in politics understood as well as Nixon the potency of class resentment. Nelson Rockefeller might regard Jeff Miller as just another longhaired kid who, like some of his own nieces and nephews, had gotten swept up in the misguided but basically idealistic aspirations of youth. But to people for whom college remained an elusive privilege, or whose family members were drafted to go to Vietnam, the behavior of the students was deeply offensive.

The class divide became most dramatically apparent in the events that unfolded in Lower Manhattan in the heart of the financial district. For years Manhattan had been the site of huge antiwar demonstrations, and in the week following Nixon's announcement, antiwar protestors had been gathering in the Wall Street area, making speeches and passing out flyers. Nearby construction workers who were building the World Trade Center were repelled—by the demonstrations and by Mayor Lindsay himself, who seemed to embody patrician indifference to their lives and concerns.

In what was clearly a planned attack, several hundred of these construction workers put on their own violent demonstration. Wearing their brown overalls and orange and yellow hard hats, some of them carrying iron pipes and crowbars, they came marching into a nearby antiwar demonstration from all directions.[4] Singing "God Bless America" and other patriotic favorites, they waded into the crowd, beating up students.[5] Several used their hard hats as weapons to strike the protestors. When passersby on their way to lunch tried to help the battered young people, they were assaulted as well.

As the protestors fled, the construction workers turned their attention to City Hall, where the American flag was flying at half-mast in honor of the Kent State students. With cries of "Kill the Commie bastards," "Lindsay's A Red," and "Love It or Leave It," they stormed past a handful of policemen and forced inside staff to raise the flag. Then, spotting an antiwar banner flying from Pace University a few blocks away, they raced over to the building, smashed the lobby windows, attacked students with their clubs and crowbars, and downed the offending banner. Within two short hours these few hundred hard hats had committed more acts of violence than the thousands of protesting students on the Kent State campus.

Oddly enough, organized labor appeared to be the White House's greatest ace in the hole. From early in his administration, Nixon had recognized its potential support and had assigned his special counsel Chuck Colson to serve as liaison to the unions. Colson's particular function in the White House was to advance Nixon's political fortunes. Regarding the war, some unions, notably the United Auto Workers and the State, County and Municipal Employees Union, were long opposed. However, the AFL-CIO Federation of Unions, the umbrella organization for most national unions, had provided strong institutional backing.[6] In mid-May the executive committee of the AFL-CIO voted overwhelmingly to endorse the invasion into Cambodia.[7] .

After the hardhat "riot," Colson encouraged union leaders to keep on demonstrating. And on May 20, the Building and Construction Trades Council of Greater New York hosted what was intended to be the largest pro-war march and rally in the city's history. The event attracted crowds variously estimated at between 60,000 and 150,000 from across a broad spectrum: mainly blue-collar workers but also secretaries, clerical workers, businessmen, and housewives. The marchers expressed a familiar array of motives. Marcher Robert Geary explained, "I'm very proud to be an American, and I know my boy that was killed in Vietnam would be here today, marching with us. . . . I know he died for the right cause."[8] According to Brooklyn housewife Allison Greaker, who had brought her two children, "We're part of the silent majority that's finally speaking and in answer to the creeps and the bums that have been hollering and marching against the president."

The huge turnout buoyed Nixon's spirits. But he and Kissinger continued to resent what they perceived as the betrayal by the elite, with a special animus reserved for the architects of the Vietnam War—McGeorge Bundy, Averell Harriman, Cyrus Vance, Clark Clifford—who had suddenly been reincarnated as "doves" clamoring for a too-rapid exit from Indochina.[9] One of the most troubling manifestations of "establishment" collapse was the crisis in the elite colleges and universities, where future leaders of the country were being educated. In Kissinger's opinion the real culprits were not the students but their directionless parents, professors, and school administrators, who lacked proper values.[10] The resulting disturbances had "very deep and . . . maybe even metaphysical causes" resulting from the "seeming purposelessness of the modern bureaucratic state."

Kissinger felt increasingly estranged from his former colleagues at Harvard. While distaste for Richard Nixon was endemic at the university, the national security advisor had managed to remain on positive terms with its leading lights, meeting informally with a small group—Thomas Schelling, George Kistiakowsky, Richard Neustadt, Adam Yarmolinsky, and others.[11] But during the week following the Kent State deaths, this contingent arrived in Washington declaring they had lost all confidence in the ability of the White House to conduct foreign policy wisely. Therefore, "we are no longer at your disposal as personal advisors."

Kissinger would later claim that this meeting was a turning point for him—the moment when he realized that the worldview of these academics was light years away from the world of practical affairs.[12] This was also the period during which both Kissinger and Nixon concluded that their most reliable constituents would never be people of privilege, but rather ordinary working men and women whose patriotism could be translated into support for the administration. "The only hope for this country is the blue-collar guys,"[13] Nixon observed.

Nixon and Kissinger also knew that with this demographic, support was conditional upon their belief that the administration was taking effective steps to wind down the war. Consequently they had to position the Cambodian operation as a stepping-stone to that end, and then to convince their followers that the operation there had been a success. But was it? In most places the combined North Vietnamese/Viet Cong forces were indeed pulling away from the border, often abandoning weapons and supplies. Inside Fishhook, US soldiers were advancing rapidly and taking a minimum of casualties. However, there was so far no sign of their having found COSVN, the "headquarters for the entire communist military operation in South Vietnam" that Nixon had publicly stated was a major reason for sending in American troops.

In its absence Kissinger quickly began to rewrite history, instructing General Wheeler to claim that they had never wanted to seize COSVN headquarters itself, only the supplies that supported the headquarters.[14] To make this credible, Nixon needed the Army to produce some evidence of those supplies—and quickly. But to do so, it would have "to get off its fat butt," Nixon complained to Kissinger.[15] Fortunately for both men, the Army was able to retrieve some large hauls of material the enemy troops had left behind in their race to escape the bombing: vast quantities of weapons, rice, supplies of various kinds, even important records. Reporters were invited to inspect the caches, and in meetings with the Washington press corps Nixon and Kissinger emphasized that these seizures were going to save hundreds if not thousands of American soldiers' lives.[16]

For his part, General Abrams was privately skeptical that these material losses were so meaningful,[17] reminding his staff, "the war is about the control of people." He had personally gone to inspect some of the captured weapons and found that they were "a lot of junk."[18] Meanwhile, the retreating enemy was penetrating into new areas of Cambodia as they fled the border regions.

Since the coup in early March, Lon Nol's eagerness to expel the communists had far exceeded his military capabilities. He had foolishly picked a fight with the North Vietnamese that he had no ability to win without massive outside assistance. As enemy soldiers moved deeper into his territory, Lon Nol became frantic. Surely the Americans would come to his rescue. Yet apart from their activities in the sanctuaries, they seemed reluctant to help.

Under these emergency conditions, the Cambodian leader turned to the South Vietnamese. It was an unnatural alliance. Historically, relations between the Khmer people and the Vietnamese had been hostile, and in recent weeks they had grown exponentially worse as Cambodians—some inflamed by the violent, nationalist rhetoric of the new regime—lashed out at the ethnic Vietnamese who were long-term residents of their country. Nevertheless, Lon Nol saw no alternative to enlisting Saigon's help. In a meeting with South Vietnamese vice president Nguyen Cao Ky, the two men agreed that South Vietnam's soldiers would remain in Cambodia for "at least six months."[19,20]

Ironically, the South Vietnamese army was demonstrating a zeal for fighting in Cambodia that was not previously evident on its own side of the border.[21] But as they chased the enemy deeper into the countryside, the traditional animosity between the Khmers and the South Vietnamese flared. In some locations the ARVN was a greater menace to the local population than the communists. The town of Neak Leung had been briefly occupied by the Viet Cong, until the South Vietnamese army drove them out. But as one inhabitant related, these troops "have been taking radios, chickens, duck and rice from the homes here. They have raped young girls in our villages." By contrast the Viet Cong "had forced people to work but they left our homes and our women alone."

Yet, brutality was not the monopoly of any one group. Once Lon Nol had asked the ARVN to come in to support his government, he warned his people against mistreating Vietnamese residents. However, the warning came too late. In addition to the April massacres in Prasaut and elsewhere, local law enforcement agencies had rounded up tens of thousands of Vietnamese residents and imprisoned them under suspicion of collaborating with the communists. An even greater number were fired from their jobs and deprived of their shops, their homes, and their land.[22]

Few in Washington knew—or cared—about the way in which the expansion of the war into Cambodia disrupted the lives of its people. And during the first weeks of the invasion, the lack of reporters on the ground would have made it impossible for anyone to find out. However, three American reporters—Richard Dudman of the *St. Louis Post Dispatch*, Elizabeth Pond of the *Christian Science Monitor*, and Michael Morrow of the *Dispatch News Service*—had extraordinary access to what was happening when they were taken prisoner by the North Vietnamese.

Curious about conditions in Cambodia, on May 7 the three abandoned the obligatory viewing of the captured caches, jumped into a car, and headed across the border into Parrot's Beak. They were immediately picked up by Cambodian rebels and turned over to North Vietnamese troops. Under suspicion of being CIA agents, they were interrogated and treated roughly during their first days of captivity. However, the North Vietnamese quickly decided that, pending further clarification of their identity, they needed to insure the reporters' safety.[23]

This was no simple matter, because many Cambodian villagers were furious at Americans, holding them responsible for the removal of Sihanouk, the destabilization of their country, and the massive destruction inflicted by the rain of bombs and artillery. Moreover, because they were in a so-called "enemy area," the three were at risk from the same US attacks as the local people.

For 40 days Dudman, Morrow, and Pond were guarded by a group of five men: two Viet Cong, one North Vietnamese officer, and two Cambodians who had joined Sihanouk's newly formed United National Front of Cambodia. For much of the time they were on the move—taking flight from helicopters, tactical aircraft, and B-52s. Fortunately Mike Morrow spoke Vietnamese and was able to communicate with three of the guards. Confronting a common peril, the Americans and their captors became tightly bonded. On several occasions the Vietnamese risked their own lives to save their prisoners. The need to keep moving from place to place had the incidental effect of allowing the reporters to form a far more complex picture of developments in the border regions than was available to other members of the press.

From the outset of the invasion, Washington officials had framed the attacks on the "sanctuaries" as taking place in locations controlled by the enemy, where there were very few local residents, North Vietnamese soldiers would suffer, not Cambodians. However, the three American reporters saw that large numbers of Cambodians were in fact living there and were being cruelly affected by the attack. They watched as Cambodian families took to the road to escape the bombing, often accompanied by North Vietnamese or Viet Cong fighters. During their 40 days of captivity, it also became clear that hatred of the United States was on the rise as the Cambodians grappled with the after-effects of the bombs and artillery.

Insofar as US officials acknowledged the presence of Cambodians in Cambodia, they persistently conveyed the impression that the locals needed protection from the Vietnamese communists. But what Dudman, Pond, and Morrow observed was that the Cambodians and the communists were beginning to come together in common cause against the US forces and the ARVN. Previously apolitical farmers were affiliating with the United National Front of Cambodia and aligning themselves with the Viet Cong and the North Vietnamese army. Dudman reflected that "two weeks after the US and Saigon forces crossed the border into Cambodia, it appears evident from this vantage point that the results will be the exact opposite of what was intended."

The areas where the enemies could take sanctuary were not being wiped out, as was claimed, but were spreading into the heartland of the country. Meanwhile, the bombing and shooting were "radicalizing" the inhabitants of rural Cambodia. "American shells and bombs are proving to the Cambodians beyond any doubt that the United States is waging unprovoked colonialist war" against them.

White House officials knew as little as the public did about political developments in the rural areas of Cambodia and had little interest in finding out. They preferred to dwell on their success in driving the enemy soldiers out of the sanctuaries and forcing them to abandon their caches of supplies, thus reducing the pressure on American soldiers in South Vietnam. Yet there were certain disquieting facts that Nixon and Kissinger could not ignore. Because they had retreated so quickly, few of the enemy soldiers had been killed, and those who survived were operating in small but intact units across an ever-expanding terrain. Combined NVA-Viet Cong units moved into the northeastern part of the country, consolidating control along the Laotian border and opening the possibility of a new supply route into South Vietnam. Others moved south and west, entering the city of Kompong Som (formerly Sihanoukville) and coming closer to Phnom Penh. Most ominous of all, they were demonstrating on a daily basis how easily they could attack the inept Cambodian army.

Despite these troubling signs, by the third week in May Nixon's mood had shifted once again. No longer the beleaguered chief executive managing the aftershocks of the Kent State disaster, he reassumed the mantle of the bold leader of the "free world," with a viable plan to achieve peace with honor. His burst of confidence had less to do with events on the ground than with the shifting domestic tides. The dreaded Washington DC march had come and gone, with far less impact than anticipated. The crowds of mainly young people had been enormous, but the lack of coordinated leadership posed a problem for any immediate follow-up.

Nixon also took great solace in the May 20 labor demonstration in Lower Manhattan, where tens of thousands of marching workers had proudly displayed their love of country and loyalty to their president. Moreover, the polls were great. The latest Gallup survey showed that 59% of Americans approved of his job performance, while only 29% expressed disapproval.[24] It was also helpful that Secretaries Rogers and Laird were maintaining a solid public front. News of their dissent had leaked to the press, but to the dismay of many of their subordinates, Rogers insisted that it was the duty of all cabinet members to support the president's "courageous decision, now that it had been made."[25]

Laird's role was more complicated.[26] As always, his overriding agenda was to reduce the number of American combatants as quickly as possible. In the service of this goal, he had repeatedly made a devil's bargain to back administration decisions with which he disagreed, so long as he could continue to press for troop withdrawals. This strategy had so far yielded the safe return of 90,000 American soldiers to their families. Thus, when asked by reporters at a press conference if it was true that he and Rogers had been circumvented, Laird denied it. He insisted that the administration hadn't consulted Congress about Cambodia because they hadn't done anything new there. "You invaded another country," someone called out. "I do not believe that for one minute," Laird retorted, echoing the White House line. "The following day, the Secretary presented his familiar trade-off to the president: if the Cambodian incursion was as successful as MACV was now claiming, it should be possible to bring home another 150,000 soldiers by Christmas.[27]

Despite his optimistic effusions, the president was aware that the situation inside Cambodia was precarious. Concerned about Lon Nol's survival, by late May he had decided to extend American bombing beyond the 21-mile limit and to encourage ARVN to remain in Cambodia past the June 30 deadline.[28] In making these changes, Nixon feared his instructions would be sabotaged down the line by either the State Department or the Defense Department. To insure they would be implemented and to obtain reliable intelligence, General Haig was dispatched to Phnom Penh and Saigon.

In the wake of the resignations of Kissinger's staff, Haig's influence in the White House was continuing to grow. Among his immediate responsibilities, he was to make clear to General Abrams the White House desire for a more aggressive use of air power. Presidential orders had already been transmitted to MACV, authorizing tactical and B-52 bombing beyond the previously prescribed 21-mile range inside Cambodia. But so far General Abrams had made no use of this authority, which according to Laird was because he had not identified any suitable targets.[29] In his meeting at MACV, Haig pursued the matter. Were there targets his planes could strike, "which you are reasonably sure are not going to result in civilian casualties and will be remunerative?"[30] The answer was yes. The bottleneck was apparently in the Defense Department, which was not approving their recommendations. Haig furiously emphasized that the president had issued orders a week ago "that he wanted these targets hit." Regardless of Laird's directives, they needed to go ahead and bomb.

Haig met privately with Lon Nol in Phnom Penh, sidelining Mike Rives, the *charge d'affaires* in the embassy. Rives had been generally negative about extending military assistance to the regime.[31] However, Haig was limited in what he could offer. Lon Nol requested that US troops be sent to northeastern Cambodia, where the enemy was growing ever stronger, but this was not possible. The good news, Haig suggested, was that the South Vietnamese military would be available past the June 30 deadline.

Given the serious complaints of the local populace about ARVN abuses, this was of little comfort to Lon Nol. He and his colleagues were doing their best, he said, but their troops were no match for the strong, experienced VC/NVA army. "We feel the ground trembling under us." Haig reiterated that "American hearts and sympathies were with the Cambodians, and we will do all we can." Hearts and sympathy were not what Lon Nol had in mind. Upon hearing those noncommittal words, he broke down and sobbed.

From this and other conversations, Haig was beginning to appreciate the extreme weakness of Cambodia's government and the real danger of an enemy takeover. His chief conclusion was that the United States needed to do more to help Lon Nol.[32] Returning to Washington he recommended that the United States provide thousands of light weapons to the Cambodian army and that Thailand be asked to loan their T-28 planes. He also urged that permission be given for MACV to commence tactical and B-52 bombing raids on northeast Cambodia for the officially proscribed purpose of aiding Cambodian ground troops.[33]

On May 31, Nixon convened a meeting at his western White House to hear a progress report from General Abrams. At this gathering, which also included Laird, General Wheeler, and Admiral McCain, Abrams highlighted the positive achievements in Cambodia.[34] The army of South Vietnam was performing more effectively than anticipated, absorbing twice as many casualties as the American forces. With this information Nixon could reassure the American people that his plan was working splendidly.

However, the destabilization of Cambodia was a significant problem. Nixon had already concluded that South Vietnamese troops should remain there after June 30 to assist the regime. He added that if these soldiers ran into trouble, they were to receive US air support. However, great discretion was needed in communicating this to the public. Going forward, these actions were to be framed not as support for Lon Nol, but as a defense of US troops:

> U.S. airpower will be used for the purpose of defending U.S. forces in South Vietnam. That is what we say publicly. But now let's talk about what we will actually do. . . . We may find that the South Vietnamese in Cambodia need our help and we can actually deal with that. In other words, publicly we say one thing. Actually, we do another."[35]

Furthermore, General Abrams should know that he had the authority to respond affirmatively to ARVN's requests for help and did not require permission from Washington to do so.

As Nixon intended, the news leaking out of San Clemente was that he had met with his chief military advisors and had learned that the gains in Cambodia were even greater than anticipated.[36] To reinforce this message, on June 3 Nixon provided a televised progress report to the nation. Citing his meeting with General Abrams, he could give the American public the good news that the Cambodian initiative "has been the most successful operation of this long and difficult war."[37] Every one of their major military aims had been achieved. Using film clips as evidence, Nixon pointed to the stacks of rifles and ammunition that had been captured in Cambodia, items that "will never be used against American boys." As promised, American troops would be leaving that country on June 30. Following the deceptive approach he had outlined, he declared that after this deadline the only remaining military activity would be "air missions to interdict the movement of enemy troops and material where . . . it is necessary to protect the lives and security of our men in South Vietnam."

From Nixon's words, there was no way his audience could discern that his original goal had shifted from cleaning out the sanctuaries to keeping the Cambodian government in power. Yet it was likely that Nixon himself did not appreciate the degree of American effort that would be required to achieve this objective. In this as on other matters, there was a degree of willed ignorance. Over the past 15 months, certain topics were consistently downplayed or ignored: from the ordeal of US soldiers fighting on the ground, to the shortcomings of the South Vietnamese army, and the devastation the war had inflicted on Vietnamese and Laotian civilians and their homelands. In the case of Cambodia, both Nixon and Kissinger were inclined to dismiss the warnings from US Charge Mike Rives in Phnom Penh and to regard negative news articles as maliciously inspired.

Had he pressed General Abrams for honest answers, the president might have learned that the general was indeed baffled and worried about the resilience of the North Vietnamese soldiers and the National Liberation Front. He could not explain their ability to keep operating under such seemingly adverse conditions. At a MACV briefing following his trip to San Clemente, Abrams expressed amazement at the performance of the 275th North Vietnamese Regiment, which was operating so far away from its original base.[38] As far as he could tell, they had made no prior arrangements. Abrams saw no obvious way to account for this:

> What kind of a system is there to refuel the trucks? What do they do with their wounded, or their sick? Where do they get their ammunition? Assume that they pick up food from the peasantry and live that way, live off the country. There aren't any guerillas out there. . . . It's just a hell of a lot

different than anything those fellows have been accustomed to. Does this mean they are just super-adaptable?

Washington had just authorized MACV to carry out an air interdiction program against the enemy for the period after June 30. But for that "to be worth a goddamn we ought to have some idea of what the hell he's doing." At least Abrams, unlike Nixon, knew what he didn't know.

Nonetheless Abrams failed to appreciate the damage that US firepower was inflicting on the country they were supposedly helping, and the terrible harm ARVN was doing to Cambodian civilians. Nor did he consider how these actions were intensifying loyalty to Sihanouk in the rural areas, or residents' increased willingness to assist the communists. From his exile in China, Sihanouk had invited North Vietnamese troops and the Viet Cong to operate freely inside his country in support of his newly created National United Front of Kampuchea.[39]

Such cooperation was a recent development. The North Vietnamese had never embraced the Khmer Rouge, which until the coup and the American bombing had been a small left-wing movement of approximately 4,000 people that was carrying out isolated acts of antigovernment terrorism. But to defeat the Americans and South Vietnamese soldiers who had invaded the country, Hanoi quickly recalibrated.[40] Its defense minister General Vo Nguyen Giap announced in mid-June that North Vietnam would "fight shoulder to shoulder with the fraternal peoples of Laos and Cambodia." Toward that end, North Vietnamese leadership reassigned units that had recently fled the sanctuaries to form "action teams" that could advance peacefully into the countryside and help establish local administrations loyal to Sihanouk.

By mid-June enemy fighters were popping up across Cambodia, consolidating control over all territory east of the Mekong River and interfering with traffic on every major route.[41] They were also attacking Siem Reap in the northwest, close to the famed temples of Angkor Wat. There appeared to be as many as 91,000 North Vietnamese soldiers inside Cambodia,[42] and there were reports that Laotians from the Pathet Lao were fighting alongside the insurgents in the Siem Reap area. Sydney Schanberg of the *New York Times* viewed this as evidence that the Vietnamese communists had turned their campaign in Indochina into one single theater of war instead of three separate fronts.[43]

On the morning of June 16, Nixon woke up to the news that enemy soldiers had just taken over the town of Kompong Speu, 30 miles southwest of Phnom Penh. By seizing the town these soldiers were effectively cutting off the one road that connected the Cambodian capital to Sihanoukville, the only deepwater port in the country and the source of all the oil needed in Phnom Penh. Enraged by this development, Nixon ordered Kissinger to get the road opened immediately, which meant driving the enemy out of Kompong Speu. "Tell them to get in the whole South Vietnamese army, bomb them, everything. Tell them to get off their butts and get going and I want a report in two hours," he snapped.[44]

Kissinger quickly conveyed the president's sense of urgency to Admiral Moorer. The *New York Times* was reporting that the enemy had 1,500 troops inside Kompong Speu and 5,000 outside. Nixon "doesn't want to hear what can't be done; he wants to hear what can be done." When Kissinger followed up with the Undersecretary of Defense, Packard explained that the problem was that "they're holed up in the middle of the town . . . we could bomb it but it would destroy the town."[45]

A potential confrontation with Nixon was averted when word came from General Abrams that, under cover of Cambodian fighter-bombers and South Vietnamese artillery, a joint force had retaken Kompong Speu. When they arrived, they discovered that the enemy had vanished.[46] This was good news for the White House but less so for the people who lived there. According to the Associated Press, when the South Vietnamese troops reached the central market they broke into stores by shooting off the locks: "Everything of value was taken . . . from flashlight batteries to sewing machines and motorcycles." Many of the townspeople had fled the area when the fighting began. When they returned to their homes, "they were stopped and ordered to empty their pockets and hand over jewelry and watches." A Cambodian commander lamented that the "population now has more to fear from the South Vietnamese than the Viet Cong."[47]

Despite administration efforts to restrict news coverage, stories about the advance of enemy forces and the weakness of the Cambodian troops were getting more prominent attention.[48] Although Nixon and Kissinger were reluctant to acknowledge it, even to themselves, these reports pointed to the fact that a mission that had been undertaken for a limited purpose had backfired, creating a fresh imperative for expanded action. After weeks of projecting optimism, the White House staff was slow to realize the change.

On June 24 Kissinger provided a more realistic update. As recorded in Haldeman's diary, many were shocked and disappointed to learn that even if the American troops left Cambodia on schedule, the administration would have ongoing responsibility for the survival of Lon Nol.

There was less surprise in the Senate, where a group of critics had warned from the outset that the invasion of Cambodia would widen the war. Back in May, the Senate Foreign Relations Committee had dispatched two of its staff members, James Lowenstein and Richard Moose, to South Vietnam and Cambodia for a fact-finding trip.[49] Their June 7 report offered a narrative of events that was in direct opposition to the White House version. Lowenstein and Moose found no evidence of "an increased enemy threat to US forces in Vietnam from the sanctuaries"—a key element in Nixon's rationale for the invasion. Instead, the administration had simply used the overthrow of Sihanouk as the opportunity to accomplish the military's long-standing desire to drive the enemy out.

While the administration might insist that there were no Cambodians living in Fishhook or the Parrot's Beak, Lowenstein and Moose had seen with their own eyes that this was not true. They encountered a crowd of approximately 80 people in a village near Fishhook. An American Army doctor had told them that he had treated several wounded civilians from the village that morning and had seen the bodies of others who had been killed.

It was also clear to the Senate staffers that the army of South Vietnam would choose to remain in Cambodia because Saigon could not run the risk of losing large swaths of that country to the communists. They could observe for themselves that the ARVN was moving well beyond the 21-mile limit that Nixon had originally set, a sign of how expansive the project had become.

By June, an increasing number of senators were moving into the peace camp, and it seemed more urgent than ever to get legislation on the books that would block any further US military activity in Cambodia past June 30. Senate opponents were coalescing around the Cooper–Church amendment, which would prohibit the use of funds for "retaining" US ground forces in Cambodia, for providing military advisors or mercenaries to the Cambodian government, or for air operations over Cambodia except those required for interdicting communist troops and supplies moving into South Vietnam.

Both Nixon and Kissinger considered it a priority to defeat this legislation lest it establish an ominous precedent of limiting presidential war-making power. To counteract the unfavorable findings contained in the Moose-Lowenstein report, the White House dispatched its own delegation on a lightning four-day visit to Vietnam and Cambodia. Herb Klein, the White House communications director, and Bruce Harlow, counselor to the president, headed up the group, which also included three governors, four senators, and three congressmen. Except for Senator Thomas McIntyre of New Hampshire, all the elected officials were known supporters of the war.

Not only had he handpicked the delegation, but Kissinger insisted that it be kept out of Phnom Penh. Once there, they might be exposed to a cacophony of skeptics, as Moose and Lowenstein had been. Instead, their visit was to consist of official briefings by Ambassador Bunker and General Abrams, meetings with General Thieu and other South Vietnamese generals, a drop-in at a defectors center (Chieu Hoi) in the Mekong Delta, and the obligatory viewing of a captured weapons cache in Cambodia.[50] Everyone in the group received a rifle and "Chicom" belt and holster as souvenirs.

One sour note in this stage-managed expedition was a *New York Times* article that described the delegation's foray into Cambodia. Headlined "Firebase Spruced Up For Visit," it recounted how the men at Firebase Sharkey, who had been manning a muddy base high on a mountain, were suddenly given haircuts and shaves, and, in some cases, issued new fatigues.[51] A few were set to work building new latrines. Although they had all been living on C-rations, when the visitors arrived a table was set up with layer cake and freshly baked cookies. While there, the delegation was treated "to a spectacular air strike against a neighboring hillside." This came as a surprise to the soldiers, since there had been no indication of an enemy presence at that location. In a staged display the F-100s swooped low, dropped their bombs and napalm, and then, in an apparent salute to the visitors, passed twice over the base. Even Nixon was disgusted when he read the article, wanting to know "who in the name of Christ gave everybody a haircut, built new latrines and flew in tablecloths. That's just stupid."[52]

The delegation came back with a predictably glowing report.[53] According to Herb Klein, the morale of US troops was "fantastic," and the people of Cambodia were rallying behind Lon Nol—"a quiet, tough, self-confident-person" who knows what he is doing.[54] With the exception of Senator McIntyre, everyone affirmed that the invasion was a success and that US troops would be able to withdraw from South Vietnam on schedule or even faster.[55]

Although Nixon and Kissinger may have hoped that the report would undermine congressional determination to proceed, those on Capitol Hill were under intense pressure from antiwar groups. Since early May, mail had been pouring into both houses of Congress and was running in heavy opposition to the invasion. They were hearing not just from dissident students but some of the new organizations created by establishment-minded adults: Corporate Executives for Peace, the Pillsbury Committee to End the War (formed by 26 food company executives in Minneapolis), Concerned Military Academy Graduates, Academic and Professional Alliance for a Responsible Congress, Publishers for Peace, and others.[56]

Believing that the vast majority of Americans still supported the president, White House political operative Chuck Colson was stoking up conservative sentiment with the message that congressional dissent constituted a "stab in the back" to the remaining troops. Spiro Agnew lent his voice to this accusation, faulting "the Cassandras of the Senate" for "trying to hobble the Commander in Chief of the armed forces when 400,000 of his men remain vulnerable in the field."[57]

These were the powerful crosscurrents shaping the Senate debate on Cambodia. How personal this could be was reflected in the experience of Republican senator William Saxbe from Ohio. Saxbe was under strong pressure from the White House to stand with the president. However his son, Lieutenant Charles Saxbe, stationed at Camp Lejeune in South Carolina, leaned on him to make a different choice. "I'm going to have to risk my life in Southeast Asia within the next year; risking my life in a war that hasn't been declared, can't be fought and can't be won; a war that is contrary to everything I've been taught to believe about America."[58] Over the past 10 years the voters had been electing people who claimed they had a solution to the conflict. "You were one of those men," the lieutenant observed pointedly to his father.

When the vote was finally taken, Cooper–Church passed by a surprisingly wide margin of 58–37, with 16 Republicans including Senator Saxbe voting in favor. However, during the seven weeks of deliberation, its language on air power had been weakened. In its final form, the amendment clearly prohibited the use of funds for retaining US troops in Cambodia and barred "any combat activity in the air above Cambodia in support of Cambodian forces." But this language did not exclude US bombing in aid of South Vietnamese troops, nor did it prevent the administration from describing airstrikes in support of Lon Nol's government as animated by a different purpose.

On the day of its passage, the last American troops left Cambodia, although 25,000 South Vietnamese troops remained. The White House claimed, as it had all along, that the mission had been a great success. Some goals were accomplished. Together the American and South Vietnamese armies had driven enemy forces out of the sanctuaries, forced them to abandon large quantities of material, disrupted their supply lines, and scattered their soldiers over a wide geographical area.

Yet by undertaking this mission, Nixon and Kissinger entertained the hope that their boldness would intimidate North Vietnam and make their representatives more tractable in negotiations. Unfortunately, the opposite had occurred. Concluding there was nothing to discuss, Xuan Thuy left Paris for Hanoi along with Madame Binh, the spokesperson for the Provisional Revolutionary Government.

As for the dynamics on the ground, there was much to be learned from Richard Dudman, Elizabeth Pond, and Michael Morrow's imprisonment in Cambodia. On June 18 when their captors finally received confirmation from Hanoi that they were indeed reporters and not agents of the CIA, they were released on Route 1 near the border of South Vietnam, and traveled this road back to Saigon. In a press conference and subsequent articles, they described their experience constantly moving as American bombs rained down on different areas. According to Richard Dudman:

> We felt that we were watching the terrorization of the peasants of Cambodia. We felt we were observing the welding together of the local population with the guerillas. The peasants were turning to the fighters as their best friends. We felt that this held the most serious significance for American policy.[59]

These three had a uniquely close-up view of conditions in the countryside, but other reporters had discovered similarly negative results. Arriving in the village of Prey Koth, 12 miles north of Phnom Penh, Sydney Schanberg was told by inhabitants that "the South Vietnamese soldiers came into their thatch houses late on Sunday afternoon and [held] all protestors at gunpoint, stole gold, money and rice and undressed some of the women to get at the jewelry they had hastily hidden inside their clothes."[60] According to Schanberg, 23 of the 33 houses in Prey Koth had been sacked by the ARVN.

The fighting had also brought Cambodia's economy to a virtual standstill—which was further cause for the local population to turn against the Americans and the South Vietnamese. Tourism was of course dead. The rubber industry, source of one of Cambodia's major exports, was ruined.[61] Farmers who grew rice, another of its major exports, were also facing ruin because it was increasingly difficult for them to either sell their goods or buy the equipment they needed for their farms. Since the economy was failing to generate any money, the government was facing possible bankruptcy at precisely the moment when it was rapidly expanding its armed forces.

The communists also bore some responsibility for these ills, because shutting down the roads, which made transporting goods so difficult, was mainly the result of their offensives. Moreover, in key cities and towns held by Cambodian forces, it was not uncommon for the North Vietnamese and their Viet Cong allies to lay siege, resulting in the death of civilians caught in the crossfire.[62]

However, if for no other reason than its overwhelming advantage in air power, the Americans were inflicting a level of damage far greater than the North Vietnamese.[63] As described by Richard Dudman, the members of Sihanouk's National United Front "clearly have a relationship of friendship and solidarity with the Cambodian people," whereas "America and Richard Nixon . . . are hated with a fervor rarely seen anywhere because of the American intervention in Cambodia and the American bombing and strafing of Cambodian civilians."[64] Perhaps the most telling fact was that after two months of American activity, the North Vietnamese and Viet Cong fighters held somewhere between 30% and 50% of the Cambodian countryside—far more than they had occupied at the beginning of the invasion.[65]

Despite the many protests and discouraging news, most Americans were not paying close attention to the events there. That circumstance allowed the president, with his brilliantly crafted speeches, to control the narrative. According to a CBS poll taken in the last week of June, 60% of Americans agreed that the Cambodian mission had been the "the most successful operation of this long and difficult war."[66] With that domestic support the war would continue, as would the carnage in Cambodia, Laos, and Vietnam, in the name of "American national security."

11
"Enjoy the Breeze"

While Cambodia disintegrated, Nixon and Kissinger sought assistance from the Soviets. In early June 1970 Kissinger invited Soviet Ambassador Anatoly Dobrynin for an evening cruise down the Potomac on the presidential yacht *Sequoia.* When he arrived at the White House, Dobrynin was unexpectedly summoned for a brief chat with Nixon, who expressed delight that the two men would be conducting their conversation onboard the ship."[1] The president emphasized that Kissinger had his complete confidence, and that "this was the channel in which he wished things to be settled." To this point, Nixon acknowledged, there had been little progress in US–Soviet relations, but it was his intention to "let bygones be bygones," and he hoped the Russians would do the same.

If one imagined that the battles engulfing the small villages of Cambodia had no connection to American–Soviet relations, then this leisurely boat trip for their two diplomats was unremarkable. But why were American soldiers fighting and dying in Cambodia if not to stave off a totalitarian threat to the free world? And why were US planes relentlessly bombing ever deeper into that country if not to demonstrate American power to their most dangerous adversary? From the very beginning this was what the American public had been led to believe about the overall project in Southeast Asia. There was never any possibility that Vietnamese communists could threaten the American homeland, but if they were allowed to win, this would embolden the men in the Kremlin, and perhaps Beijing, to challenge the United States in new and dangerous ways. Or so it was said or implied.

Unlike his predecessors, Nixon used coded language to refer to these adversaries, but in his many efforts to explain to the American people why he was continuing the Vietnam War, he subtly invoked the Cold War paradigm. His speech on the eve of the US–South Vietnamese invasion of Cambodia had continued the pattern: "If, when the chips are down, the world's most powerful nation, the United States of America, acts like a pitiful, helpless giant, the forces of totalitarianism and anarchy will threaten free nations and free institutions throughout the world."

There was an important reason for the coded language, since even though public consent for the war was predicated on fear of the Soviets, Nixon was privately seeking Moscow's cooperation on Vietnam and other contested matters. During the first year of his administration, he and Kissinger had made this aspiration clear to the Soviets but with no success. However, by early summer of 1970 they hoped the right combination of "carrots and sticks" would cause the USSR to lean on Hanoi and persuade it to be more pliable at the Paris peace talks.

Regarding Cambodia, Nixon was keenly aware that while the Chinese had offered sanctuary to Prince Sihanouk and were overtly supporting the resistance to Lon Nol's government, the Soviets had proceeded with greater caution. They were still maintaining their embassy in Phnom Penh and were continuing to recognize the regime there. Quite apart from these particulars, Nixon was also thinking ahead to the November elections. US troops would be out of Cambodia by June 30, but regardless of the results, the domestic divisiveness and anger that had been unleashed by the invasion would cast a long shadow over the voting. If by that time he could showcase a forthcoming summit with the Soviets, it could burnish his reputation as a peacemaker.

With Nixon's support, Kissinger planned to use the time on the *Sequoia* to review all the key issues upon which the two sides seemed stalemated. If points of agreement emerged, this could provide the basis for a successful summit.[2] With regard to the Vietnam War, Kissinger planned "to project a very calm and confident attitude as a result of our actions in Cambodia" and let Dobrynin know that the time seemed right for genuine progress on Southeast Asia. He hoped the Soviet Union could help the United States and North Vietnam arrive at a compromise that was consistent with the interests of all parties.

The Russian ambassador disagreed, arguing that the US foray into Cambodia had complicated the prospects for a peaceful settlement.[3] Whatever military gains they had made, the practical effect was "to give the Chinese a tremendous shot in the arm," so that Beijing's influence in Hanoi was ascendant. This was of great concern to his country's leadership, whose enthusiasm for a summit had diminished.

Whatever Kissinger might think, the Soviet Union had no desire to install a communist regime in Cambodia. But while US troops were operating there, Dobrynin did not foresee any progress at the negotiating table. Moreover, according to the North Vietnamese, the Americans at the peace talks showed no willingness to alter the political arrangements in the South, and thus precluded any chance for an early agreement.

Dobrynin managed to leave the door slightly ajar by implying that once the US operation in Cambodia was ended, the situation might change.[4] However, if Kissinger harbored any illusion that by their dramatic move into that country they had somehow jolted the Soviets into a more compliant attitude, it was quickly dissipated. As the two men reviewed other areas of dispute—on arms control and the Middle East in particular—an amicable resolution seemed elusive.

In response, Kissinger offered his familiar pitch—the United States and the Soviet Union stood on the cusp of a possibly transformed relationship. They could either "proceed along tactical lines," as they had been doing since the end of the Second World War, or they "could make an effort at a fundamental improvement."[5] As the president had indicated, he hoped his administration could "be the one in which the basic turning point toward peace had been made."

By dangling this incentive, both Kissinger and Nixon were as sincere as they knew how to be. They were earnestly desirous of ending the war in Vietnam and of entering a new period of great power relations. But while both men prided themselves on their realism, they were profoundly ideological in their view of the conflicts they faced. Like their predecessors, they took it for granted that the United States and its allies should have a permanent military advantage. And they considered Soviet support for factions and governments around the world as illegitimate "interventions,"[6] while they viewed US involvement in foreign places, no matter how coercive, as reinforcing the popular will. This double standard, which they routinely and myopically applied to various disputes, was one reason their diplomacy had yielded scant results.

This intellectual rigidity proved especially crippling when it came to arms control—a vital issue which, if resolved, could potentially unlock other disputes. Unlike Vietnam, which posed no threat to American security, the nuclear arms race threatened the very existence of the United States. Even assuming the most benign intentions on both sides, the ability of the two nations to destroy each other within a period of days vastly increased the possibility of a catastrophic accident. As the Cuban missile crisis had revealed, when both countries were using the implicit threat of nuclear weapons to advance geopolitical goals they could find themselves on a precipice from which retreat might be difficult. In the case of Cuba cooler heads had prevailed, but with different leadership the results might have been calamitous.

American and Soviet policymakers broadly agreed that arms control was too important a project to be dropped. However, while administration officials did genuinely desire to make nuclear weapons a less prominent feature of US–Soviet rivalry and therefore less likely to be used, they also wished to maximize American security by ensuring that the nuclear balance would always favor the United States.

By the time Nixon took office a new complicating factor had entered the equation. In the years since the Cuban missile crisis, the Soviet Union had embarked on a rapid-fire buildup of long-range land- and sea-based strategic missiles. The Soviets were rapidly closing the gap between the two countries and in fact seemed likely to surpass the United States in the number of such missiles within a few years. The Pentagon, not normally a booster of arms control agreements, was beginning to realize that a deal with the Soviets on strategic missiles might be the only way to freeze an American advantage.

Yet Nixon and Kissinger were so convinced that the Russians wanted an agreement on nuclear weapons even more than they did that they had deliberately delayed the opening of the arms control negotiations. They hoped to gain Moscow's help with Hanoi by making the negotiations a reward for such efforts.[7] It was evident after several months that this foot-dragging was getting them nowhere, while enabling the Russians to keep turning out new missiles at a rapid clip.[8] By 1970 Kissinger was leaning the opposite way, wondering if concessions on arms control might prompt the Soviets to lean on Hanoi.

The official US–Soviet Strategic Arms Limitation Talks (SALT) had begun in Helsinki in November 1969 with a preliminary exchange of views. However, the real work of defining the American negotiating position did not begin until the spring of 1970, and was complicated by the diverging perspectives among members of the American delegation and their respective agencies.[9] The US delegation chief Gerard Smith, director of the Arms Control and Disarmament Agency (ACDA) and State Department representative Raymond Garthoff were most concerned about stabilizing the nuclear arms race and reducing the prospects of a nuclear war. By contrast Paul Nitze, representing the Secretary of Defense, and General Royall Allison, representing the Joint Chiefs of Staff, were mainly interested in slowing down the Soviet deployment of long-range missiles so as to preserve the American advantage. Ultimately the positions to be taken by the arms control delegation were subject to the recommendations of a White House "Verification Panel," a committee of the National Security Council headed by Kissinger to review the technical aspects of arms control proposals.

One urgent item to be considered was the future of MIRV (multiple independently targeted reentry vehicles), a topic with life-and-death implications for both countries. MIRVs were missiles deploying multiple warheads, each targeted at a different location. A single MIRV could obliterate eight to ten different cities at once. The United States was well ahead of the Soviet Union in the development of this new technology and had already tested the weapon the preceding summer. If MIRVs worked, they would be a relatively cheap way to counter the growing Soviet arsenal of long-range missiles. Even if the Soviets took the lead in numbers of long-range missiles, the United States could trump this with many more warheads per missile.

Despite the likely advantage of the MIRV arsenal, Gerard Smith and his colleagues from the ACDA argued for a negotiated MIRV ban, or at the very least a freeze on testing. They considered MIRV missiles to be potentially destabilizing weapons, especially if two adversaries possessed them. In that instance, during a time of international tension, either party might feel forced to strike preemptively, fearing an imminent attack from the other side. However, the Pentagon was determined to acquire MIRVs and thereby vastly increase its nuclear capability. On this matter both Nixon and Kissinger were inclined to acquiesce.[10]

That put the American chief negotiator, Gerard Smith, at odds with the White House over a key issue. However, he could be relied upon to follow instructions. Kissinger disdained Smith but thought it wise to retain him as American representative on the SALT talks. By keeping him in this prominent role, it would reassure members of Congress that the administration was sincerely pursuing an arms control agreement with the Soviets. Meanwhile, Kissinger was expecting to handle the real arms control negotiations in his backchannel with Dobrynin. One purpose of the pleasant *Sequoia* cruise was to underline this arrangement.

By June 1970, the official SALT talks were already deadlocked. During the opening round in Vienna, which had commenced in mid-April, the US delegation was hamstrung by exceptionally rigid negotiating instructions. The Russians had argued for a ban or restriction on antiballistic missile systems (ABMs) —weapons in which the Americans had a technical advantage—as well as a ban on MIRVs. By contrast, the American delegation had attached so many conditions to a MIRV ban as to make it unacceptable.[11] And they had linked ABM restrictions to a freeze on the construction of offensive weapons, thereby insuring American nuclear superiority in perpetuity. As opening positions in a negotiation this might be plausible, but the SALT team had no ability to go beyond these guidelines.[12]

On their *Sequoia* voyage Dobrynin expressed curiosity about the real American position. Kissinger was vague, suggesting something along the lines of restricting ABM sites to the two capitals, and an undetermined ceiling on offensive weapons. The unmistakable signal was that the Russians might get a better deal in the backchannel with him than from the official SALT delegation. The most important thing, Kissinger emphasized, was that the two delegations meeting in Vienna not be informed about his confidential discussions with Dobrynin.[13]

Thus, unbeknown to Smith and his colleagues, as of June 10, 1970, they had been quietly marginalized by the White House. However, what they did understand was that the instructions they had been given had left them with no ability to make a deal. Returning to Washington later that month, Smith pressed for more flexibility. Secretary of State Rogers urged Kissinger to accede to this reasonable request. The latter demurred, claiming that Nixon did not want the delegation "running wild."[14] This was not a matter of people running wild, said Rogers, but of being able to accomplish the job they were assigned to do.

That inability did not disturb Kissinger, but what did bother him was news from Smith that given the lack of progress, his Russian counterparts were proposing a recess of the talks until year's end. If the Soviets were abandoning hope for a rapid arms control deal, did that mean as well that they were closing the door to a summit any time soon? Of concern to Kissinger was the situation in the Senate, where a huge fight was brewing over funding for the ABM system. A prolonged delay in the SALT talks could easily provide ammunition for the administration's critics.

Shortly after their evening cruise, Kissinger sought an explanation from Dobrynin of this rumored postponement. Perhaps amused, the ambassador wondered why Kissinger was getting "so worked up." After all, "the president and you yourself suggested thinking over the situation." Nevertheless, as a sop to the White House the Russians agreed to keep their delegation in Vienna, where they were simply marking time. However, unlike the clueless Gerard Smith, the Soviets' chief negotiator Vladimir Semenov was apprised of the secret channel and the more complex situation behind the scenes.

In his report to Moscow, Dobrynin stressed that electoral factors were weighing heavily on the White House. It was apparent that Nixon "attaches considerable importance to the time factor, when . . . some kind of strategic arms agreement, even the most limited agreement, can be reached, and most importantly when it can be made public."[15] Until this point, the president had been clearly opposed to an ABM-only agreement, but given the political circumstances that position might be changing.[16] Also relevant was Kissinger's personal agenda. "He is a very ambitious individual," the ambassador observed, "and highly values the fact that some issues are handled only through him."[17] It was obvious that Kissinger enjoyed circumventing the Secretary of State, a predilection that the Russians could occasionally use "in our own interests."

Meanwhile the two diplomats were becoming fine friends. In late July Dobrynin was returning to Moscow for vacation. Before he left, Kissinger phoned in a jocular mood: "I am sitting on my back patio thinking about coexistence." The ambassador responded with similar good humor: "Good for you Henry . . . . I will be in Moscow thinking in the same way."[18] In his absence, Kissinger would be working on the budget. "You are building so many SS-9s, you are upsetting the balance," he quipped. In reply Dobrynin hoped the United States. would not be spoiling his vacation with any surprises, as had happened the last time he returned to Moscow—an allusion to the Cambodian incursion. Unless the Russians' "friends in Hanoi" acted up, Kissinger said, he did not foresee any dramatic American moves.

Within minutes of hanging up the phone, Kissinger reported the conversation to the president.[19] The conversation had gone well. Dobrynin "was slobbering all over me," he bragged, and had even said "I would have a lot of business when he returns." He concluded the Soviets wanted a summit "as much as we do."

Yet, differences with the Russians were not confined to Vietnam and arms control. During this period there were tensions over Middle East policy and misplaced fears of a new Soviet submarine base on Cuba. In both instances there were exaggerated alarms by Kissinger, stimulated in part by his concern that Rogers was gaining too much influence over US foreign policy.

On the Middle East, Nixon had deliberately bypassed Kissinger, believing that an American Jew should not be handling issues related to Israel. Responsibility for this area went to Rogers, who was vigorously seeking a way to defuse the conflict between Israel and its neighbors. However, his effort to achieve cooperation with the Russians sent Kissinger into an emotional tailspin. Back in the spring when he learned that the Secretary of State had met with Dobrynin, he made the insulting demand that all contacts with the Russian ambassador must be cleared ahead of time, with all talking points pre-approved by the White House.[20]

Ignoring his complaints, Nixon had allowed Rogers to proceed with his diplomatic initiative. This entailed further conversations with Dobrynin and the possibility that apart from the Middle East, the two might discuss prospects for peace in Vietnam. Such exchanges were hardly unusual for a Secretary of State, but when Kissinger got wind of this he had another meltdown. As recorded by Haldeman:

> K in to see me for his periodic depression about Rogers. This time he's found Rogers is meeting with Dobrynin tomorrow, and K is absolutely convinced that he's going to try to make his own Vietnam settlement, plus get a summit meeting and take full credit for it. K's temptation is to confront Bill [Rogers] and insist they have it out with the President, or else one will have to leave. Thinks he can scare him.[21]

As far as Kissinger was concerned, this was all part of an invidious plan "to do him in and to take over foreign policy by State from the White House."

In his own plan to discredit the Secretary of State, Kissinger sounded the alarm about Russian ambitions in the Middle East and alerted friendly journalists about Rogers' alleged inability to resist their behavior. Echoing his message, *New York Times* columnist Max Frankel lamented that Rogers had "showed himself less alarmed strategically than the White House about the possibility of a permanent Soviet presence" in the region.

In actuality, Kissinger was indignant, despite American assistance to the government of Israel, about the Russian provision of military aid to the Egyptians. Yet his greater fear was that through his Middle East diplomacy, Rogers was beginning to impress the president. On most occasions Kissinger was content to badger Haldeman with his fears and complaints; however, Nixon was mindful of these histrionics and concerned about his reliability. As Haldeman noted in his diary, "P realizes that K's basically jealous of any idea not his own, and he just can't swallow the apparent success of the Middle East plan because it is Rogers'. In fact, he's probably trying to make it fail for just this reason."

By late summer Nixon was beginning to wonder if Kissinger had outlived his usefulness. Haldeman demurred, maintaining that his hyper-emotionality was "the price we pay for his enormous assets." Yet as a practical matter, these "enormous assets" had yielded nothing of value. Kissinger and his staff had produced mountains of sophisticated memoranda and reports, but so far there was no sign from Moscow of any eagerness for an imminent summit; the Chinese were unresponsive to the subtle American overtures; and the Paris negotiations seemed to be stalled.

However, on August 28 Kissinger was delighted to learn that the North Vietnamese would be sending a representative to meet with him. In high excitement he reported to Haldeman "their big guys would be there." This led him to speculate that perhaps the invasion of Cambodia had done the trick, convincing "the other side" that they could not prevail on the battlefield.

There were warnings to the contrary. According to the CIA, the Cambodian invasion had made the North Vietnamese more stubborn than ever. At a meeting of the National Security Council, CIA Director Richard Helms had reported:

> There is a new consensus in the Hanoi leadership. They look to the long haul, but they are confident they eventually will win. They see their difficulties as great, but they are willing . . . to accept the privation and the manpower losses. To keep their economy afloat they need Soviet and Chinese help. The rivalry for leadership between the USSR and China makes it difficult for either one to reduce its aid to Hanoi. Their manpower losses are actually not overwhelming.[22]

Indeed, the CIA Director saw little prospect that they would alter their negotiating position any time soon.

Whatever Kissinger's expectations, once in Paris he found Xuan Thuy to be immoveable. Many of the administration's proposals relied on good faith between former adversaries. But recent American actions had clearly undermined this. As explained by Xuan Thuy:

> The US thought it could intimidate the Vietnamese people by extending the war to Laos and Cambodia. As a result, the U.S. has sunk deeper and has met with more difficulties, and it will be difficult for the U.S. to get out of the war now. . . . You may think that by your operations in Cambodia you have gained an advantage. As for us, we understand that the more the U.S. extends the war, the more difficulties the US meets with.[23]

This response was especially disappointing because Kissinger had purposefully omitted the long-standing American requirement that there be *mutual* withdrawal of troops.

Toward the end of the session, Kissinger asked Xuan Thuy what he should say to the president in reporting on their meeting. "Does there exist the theoretical possibility that after studying my remarks the Minister might discover something new and make changes? Or do we have to make all the modifications?" Xuan Thuy was blunt: "For the time being, I tell you what I have been saying is reasonable and what you point out is unreasonable."

While such an exchange might have seemed disheartening, in reporting to the president Kissinger managed to feign enthusiasm. He had expected vituperation in the wake of Cambodia, but "the atmosphere was the friendliest of any of these sessions."[24] He found it noteworthy that the North Vietnamese had dropped their demand for a six-month unconditional withdrawal of American troops and seemed open to reconsidering their political proposal. Kissinger discerned great significance in their apparent eagerness "to continue this channel, coming back repeatedly with proposals to meet again."

The exaggeration of North Vietnamese flexibility was designed to please a president who liked to hear that adversaries were impressed by American power. But it reflected, as well, Kissinger's personal desire to continue the negotiations. Xuan Thuy was not clamoring for secret talks with Kissinger any more than Dobrynin had been "slobbering all over" him. While the mood in Paris was perhaps friendlier than before, the major change was on the American side, not Hanoi's, when Kissinger for the first time omitted the familiar reference to the mutual withdrawal of troops.

Since 1968, mutual withdrawal had been a cornerstone of US policy—a prerequisite for any peace agreement. However, by fall 1970 there had been a significant alteration in the disposition of North Vietnamese troops, with the majority outside South Vietnam in Cambodia, Laos, and across the DMZ on their side of the demarcation line. While this change had vast implications, it had crept in quietly. If those troops remained in place, the United States might safely withdraw a significant number of soldiers.[25]

This apparent alteration in the American stance elicited no sign from Hanoi of any greater willingness to settle the war. Meanwhile, Kissinger was facing unrelenting domestic pressure. Secretary Laird was writing a defense budget that would force the removal of large increments of troops, even without a satisfactory peace agreement. To this point, approximately 200,000 soldiers had been brought home without unduly handicapping the military effort. But the Kissinger anticipated "a crunch time" when they would be "caught between an ally that cannot withstand any further withdrawals and a public that will not stand for any further American involvement."

Congressional dissent remained a challenge. On September 1, the Senate voted on the Hatfield-McGovern amendment to a military procurement bill. The clearest antiwar measure to reach the Senate floor, this would cut off funds for American troops in Vietnam after December 1971 in the absence of an accord.

The Senate debate was unusually emotional, as the normally mild-mannered McGovern addressed his colleagues:

> Every Senator in this chamber is partly responsible for sending 50,000 young Americans to an early grave, and in one sense this chamber literally reeks of blood. Every Senator here is partly responsible for that human wreckage at Walter Reed and all across this land—young boys without legs, without arms, or genitals, or faces, or hopes. . . . If we don't end this damnable war those young men will curse us for our pitiful willingness to let the Executive carry the burden that the Constitution places on us."[26]

The McGovern-Hatfield amendment was ultimately defeated by a margin of 55–39. Despite the 16-vote spread on the measure, the results for the administration were worse than appeared. Among those who had voted against were several Republican senators known to be in the antiwar camp, among them George Aiken of Vermont and John Sherman Cooper of Kentucky. Both expressed willingness to give the president time to get a deal, but made it clear there were limits to their patience. And with no discernible progress, their votes would likely change.[27]

For the president there was the additional pressure of the mid-term elections. Whatever gains he might be making in other areas, it was clear that for the American public the critical issue remained Vietnam. With the Cambodian ground incursion over and the massive protests diminished, signs of progress had yet to materialize. There were just so many times the administration could show off caches of rice or weapons. People still wanted to know how and when this war might end.

Recognizing that something more was needed, the president thought the time was right for another major speech. For this purpose he entrusted speechwriter William Safire with the task of producing a short, punchy draft that would incorporate previous plans but make them sound new. Safire was personally bothered by the fact that there was no expectation that the content would be acceptable to the enemy but was merely designed to convince the public that the administration was embracing peace. As Kissinger subsequently explained to his journalist friend Joseph Alsop, while they did not expect the proposal to be accepted, they hoped "it might shut up some in this country."[28]

As on previous occasions the Nixon team whipped up advance excitement with the information that a "major" development would be coming from the White House.[29] By now, these performances had assumed a ritual character: foreign dignitaries called in for a last-minute briefing, the huddle with the cabinet, the updates to the congressional leadership, and then Nixon himself leaning earnestly into the lectern, sharing his hopes and aspirations with the American people.

And so, he began: When he authorized operations against the enemy sanctuaries in Cambodia back in April, he had also promised "an intensive effort . . . to develop new choices for peace."[30] Fortunately, he had something to present. At the heart of his proposal was the call for an immediate "cease-fire-in-place" throughout Southeast Asia. This would halt the killing, while the affected parties negotiated the shape of a final settlement.

On the surface, this was a new and appealing idea: calling an immediate halt to the fighting. Yet there were few Americans who understood that while 300,000 American troops remained in South Vietnam, most of the North Vietnamese soldiers were somewhere else. Thus, a ceasefire would preserve an American advantage and would have no chance of being accepted.

In his skillful fashion, Nixon carefully invoked the wider context. "Since the end of World War II, there's always been a war going on somewhere in the world," he lamented. "The guns have never stopped firing." But if they could achieve a ceasefire in Indochina and maintain the ceasefire in the Middle East, they could hear the sound of peace across the globe. "Let us give our children," he implored in closing, "what we have not had in this century: a chance to enjoy a generation of peace."[31]

Knowing his boss, Kissinger hastened to call and congratulate him on another exceptional performance.[32] The two men assured each other that it was Cambodia that had made this possible. As others were finally acknowledging, without it they would have been dead. "Listen Henry, Cambodia won the war," Nixon said, but what did he think about that "generation of peace" line? Kissinger thought it was terrible, an opinion he had shared with Safire.[33] He would have preferred a more "manly" closing. You cannot have the president of the United States "being a pacifist," he had grumbled. But in speaking with Nixon, he assured him it was a fine phrase—another "major step forward again."

Of concern was the response in the Senate. Within a day, Kissinger was able to inform the president that senators were flocking to their side.[34] Long-standing Republican critics like Chuck Percy, Charles Mathias, and Clifford Case were registering their support. Margaret Chase Smith of Maine was lauding Nixon for his "statesmanship and foresight." In the House as well as the Senate, legislators on both sides of the aisle were putting together resolutions backing the White House. "It was wild," Kissinger told Nixon. "They were clapping and getting to TV cameras to endorse you."

One discordant note, which barely registered through the din of enthusiasts, was a scathing report from Senator Kennedy's Subcommittee on Refugees. This documented the pervasive human suffering throughout the region.[35] With the spread of war into Cambodia, "fear now gripped almost the entire population of Indochina, vastly increasing human misery, the flow of refugees and the occurrence of civilian war casualties." The report attested to the crisis of people, millions displaced within their country or fleeing across international boundaries. In many cases American military activities, especially the heavy toll taken by the bombing, had caused this flight. In Laos alone there were 300,000 refugees, most of them people who had been forced to flee during the past eight months.

In Cambodia at least one million Khmers had been displaced, and the population of Phnom Penh had grown from 700,000 to well over a million in recent months. Other cities and towns were also swollen with refugees:

> Provincial capitals and district towns throughout the country are bulging with new arrivals from the countryside. Thousands now live in squalor and filth in overcrowded refugee centers. Hospitals and dispensaries are overburdened with hundreds and thousands of civilian war casualties. The situation is growing so critical . . . that the international relief agencies in Geneva are now preparing for a possibility of famine next year, since many Cambodian peasants are not planting this year's rice crop due to the insecurity of the countryside.[36]

In South Vietnam, the government had reclassified whole categories of displaced people to make it appear that the problem had disappeared although it had actually grown, as did the number of injured civilians showing up in hospitals. In his introduction to the study, Senator Kennedy reflected that the United States was "a great and powerful" country that had used its power and influence in Indochina for many purposes. And yet, the "power to heal, to salvage and rehabilitate the hapless victims of the conflict" had never been exercised in commensurate fashion.

Fortunately for Nixon, the media gave the report almost no coverage—a small article in the *New York Times,* little mention elsewhere. It was one of the ironies of the period that while the president and his circle were convinced of the media's bias against them, there was remarkably little reporting on the human costs of the war, either to US soldiers or the people in the region. Most of that information was limited to the antiwar subculture where these pitiful stories abounded, building frustration and anger.

In the mainstream media, the focus was on Nixon's "major new initiative," from which valuable results were eagerly anticipated. The deceptiveness of his offer, given the existing distribution of troops, escaped scrutiny.[37] Indeed, the haste with which members of Congress, news commentators, and other establishment figures uncritically embraced the presentation reflected their desperation for good news. It also expressed a long-standing failure to recognize that Hanoi was unwilling to stop fighting if the Saigon regime remained in place.

This matter of peace plans could be the occasion for cynicism on both sides. By mid-September the North Vietnamese government was rallying behind an "Eight Point" plan recently introduced by PRG foreign minister Madame Binh. Under its provisions, American troops would depart from the South, military prisoners would be released, and a temporary administration would replace the existing government pending the removal of President Thieu, Vice President Ky, and Prime Minister Khiem.

Yet this proposal was also disingenuous. On a visit to Beijing, Premier Pham Van Dong described how his government was using the peace talks to create support for their side:

> First, we have to win the sympathy of the people in South Vietnam, especially the ones in urban areas. Furthermore, we must influence the antiwar public opinion in the United States that includes not only the people at large, but also the political, business, academic and clerical circles to ensure a stronger support by them.[38]

As for Madame Binh's "Eight Points," the North Vietnamese leader readily admitted they were not so new but explained that the goal was "to corner Nixon." There was not "any illusion that they will bring about any results."[39]

While the peace talks had degenerated into a series of maneuvers designed to confuse domestic and international audiences, on the American side there remained the need to end the war in some favorable way. For that purpose, Nixon and Kissinger were ready with a new move, publicly calling upon the Soviet Union to use its "considerable influence" with North Vietnam's leadership to cooperate. In the past, such probes had been made privately. What made this appeal to Moscow unusual was that it was occurring after several months in which American criticism of the USSR for its interventions in the Middle East and elsewhere had been especially sharp.

Yet behind the scenes that relationship was on the upswing. On his return from Moscow, Dobrynin brought a note from his government affirming its interest in a summit during the spring of 1971.[40] While not the timetable that Nixon and Kissinger had originally wanted, if this could be announced before the November elections it would still be helpful, as would a summit conference in the spring. Nixon had been reading the polls and noted that when people were asked whether they desired a summit, 75% said yes, while only 18% said no.[41]

As Kissinger and Dobrynin resumed their cordial relationship, they each went through an obligatory recitation of their leaders' grievances over recent events in the Middle East and Cuba. But after airing them, they let their grievances drop. For Kissinger the priority was to get moving on the summit and to make sure the Secretary of State was kept in the dark. Thus Rogers was not informed that the president had asked to meet Soviet Foreign Minister Gromyko later that month when he came to New York for the opening of the United Nations General Assembly, or that Gromyko had accepted.

When the Russian foreign minister arrived at the United Nations, he would inevitably encounter Rogers. Therefore, Kissinger had one little favor to ask of Dobrynin. He hoped, when they met, Gromyko would not say anything about a possible summit meeting, since Secretary of State Rogers was unaware that it was being discussed.[42] Dobrynin had become familiar with these curious power grabs by Kissinger, but was truly surprised that something as simple as prospects for a summit would be concealed from the State Department.

Gromyko's United Nations speech on October 22 bristled with criticisms of American foreign policy. However, weeks earlier Dobrynin had alerted

Kissinger that this barrage was coming and encouraged him to pay it no mind. It was the private exchange with Nixon that would matter more. However, when that meeting occurred, Gromyko expressed genuine puzzlement at the hostility the administration had directed toward his country over the past two months.[43] He was at pains to stress the peaceful aspirations of his government and its desire to see a significant improvement in their relationship. Nixon seemed to agree. The recent "cooling" of their connection had been troubling, so it was of consummate importance "to give a signal to the world that the United States and the Soviet Union were not looking for areas to confront each other" but for areas such as arms control and trade where they could find new forms of cooperation. His reward was Gromyko's assurance that his government was anticipating a summit, although it was premature to make a public announcement.

Moving away from these generalities, the two officials reviewed the recent points of controversy—the Middle East especially, Cuba, Berlin, arms control, and the Vietnam War. About Vietnam, Nixon was still euphoric about the domestic response to his speech and was less direct about soliciting assistance from the USSR. However, Gromyko reiterated a point that Dobrynin had made repeatedly: If America was really seeking a diplomatic solution, it would have to accept the idea of a coalition government in South Vietnam and the need for a schedule for unilateral troop withdrawals. On these core issues, the USSR lacked the ability to change Hanoi's approach.

Nixon's reply might have surprised the millions of Americans who had just recently applauded his speech and shared his concern that if the United States lost the war, "the forces of totalitarianism and anarchy will threaten free nations and free institutions around the world." Addressing the foreign minister of the world's most formidable "totalitarian" state, Nixon explained that the problem of Vietnam, of course, involved the United States to a far greater degree than the Soviet Union, for the simple reason that so many US soldiers had been killed there. "If in the future, we should have to undertake forceful measures to protect the interests of our men . . ." he hoped that Mr.Gromyko "would understand our position, by putting [himself] in our place."[44]

Missing from this formulation was any reference to the self-determination of the Vietnamese people or protection from external aggression. Nor was it clear how this explanation enhanced American "credibility" with the Soviet Union. If anything, the message signaled weakness by asking the Soviet Union to tolerate a bloody US war for the lame reason that so many US soldiers were already dead. This might sound absurd, yet perhaps in the rush of conversation the president had spoken more truthfully to Gromyko, his authoritarian adversary, than to the American people. We are continuing in Vietnam "for the simple reason that so many U.S. soldiers [have] been killed there."

However, for those soldiers who were alive, whether back home or still "in country," the purpose of their sacrifice had become increasingly obscure. And while diplomats fenced and the politicians deliberated, some were finding their voice.

12

"We Might Have Burned Your House"

Why was the United States continuing the Vietnam War? It was a question that left growing numbers of soldiers perplexed and discontented.

On Labor Day weekend 1970 a new organization few Americans had ever heard of—Vietnam Veterans Against the War (VVAW)—mounted a four-day "search and destroy" mission from Morristown, New Jersey, to Valley Forge, Pennsylvania. Many of the men in this group of approximately 100 GIs were highly decorated, honored with Bronze and Silver stars, Purple Hearts, and combat infantrymen badges. Dressed in Army fatigues and carrying military backpacks, they marched along the historic route once taken by George Washington and the Continental Army during the Revolutionary War. Along the way, they attempted to replicate the activities they had conducted in "pacifying" South Vietnam. They called this endeavor Operation RAW ("Rapid American Withdrawal"), which not incidentally was "WAR" spelled backwards.

The event was the culmination of months of discussion among a small group of antiwar veterans who had been struggling with the question of how to make the Vietnam experience real to Americans at home. Few of their fellow citizens had any idea of what it had meant to be a soldier in an often hostile, unwelcoming land. To convey that reality, they conceived the idea of reenacting the behavior of American soldiers in South Vietnamese villages as a way of shocking people into greater understanding.[1]

VVAW had enlisted for this purpose a Philadelphia guerilla theater troop whose members agreed to be cast as Vietnamese villagers. As the scruffy troops made their way through New Jersey and Pennsylvania towns, they stopped in many localities to interrogate these characters and detain those they deemed suspicious. In a series of dramatic scenes, they surrounded a private house and terrorized the inhabitants, dragged a woman from a downtown street as she kicked and screamed for help, and demonstrated the use of physical force to compel uncooperative people to provide information.[2]

The antiwar leaflets the veterans passed out captured the brutality which some of these men had experienced:

An infantry company just came through here! If you had been Vietnamese,
We might have burned your house
We might have shot your dog
We might have shot you . . .
We might have raped your wife and daughter
We might have turned you over to your government for torture
We might have taken souvenirs from your property. . . .
We might have done all these things to you and to your whole TOWN!
If it doesn't bother you that American soldiers
Do these things every day to the Vietnamese
Simply because they are "Gooks," then picture YOURSELF
As one of the silent VICTIMS.
HELP US TO END THE WAR BEFORE THEY TURN YOUR SON INTO
A BUTCHER or a corpse.[3]

One of the major themes of the VVAW's protest movement was that abuse and atrocities against the Vietnamese people were commonplace and being carried out by young Americans who in ordinary circumstances were upstanding, ethical people. They wanted the public to understand that US soldiers had done terrible things to their victims but were suffering the psychological harm which resulted from being in situations where immoral behavior was almost a requirement. Since the typical American soldier was 19 years old, there was for some a feeling of betrayal by their irresponsible elders.

Another stinging flyer was accusatory: "Many of you have known that Vietnam is a trap and ambush for American GIs and have done nothing to prevent our buddies (your sons) from going into it." On an average day in the war "about 32 of our buddies . . . will be killed" and another 140 seriously wounded. Noting that when local villagers failed to warn troops of an ambush the soldiers might respond by killing them, the leaflet asked: "WHAT SHOULD WE DO ABOUT YOU?" Such angry rhetoric was perhaps counterproductive as a way of persuading the public, but it expressed the simmering rage of the marchers.[4]

At Valley Forge, the culminating event consisted of the veterans forming a skirmish line with toy rifles held aloft and sweeping across the Grand Parade Grounds shouting, "Peace Now" as they merged with a crowd of more than 1,000 people who had gathered there to greet them. Among them was a group of disabled vets in wheelchairs who had been unable to join the march.

Although officials at the nearby VA hospital where they were being treated had discouraged their attendance, the men had wheeled themselves to the protest.

Speakers at the event included antiwar politicians, civil rights leader Rev. James Bevel, members of the clergy, and actors Jane Fonda and Donald Sutherland.[5] The presence of the two Hollywood stars was the outgrowth of months of effort on their part to raise money for Operation RAW and to whip up interest in the first national event organized by antiwar veterans. The main spokesman for the men was John Forbes Kerry, a much-decorated patrician war hero who had commanded a Swift Boat in the Mekong Delta.

As Kerry mounted the platform, he appeared against a backdrop of black zippered canvas bags that resembled the body bags coming back from Vietnam. On each one was stenciled a question: "Your son?" With an eloquence that galvanized the crowd, he struck a resonant note:

> We are here because we above all others have earned the right to criticize the war in Southeast Asia. We are here to say that it is not patriotism to ask Americans to die for a mistake, and that it is not patriotic for the president to talk about not being the first president to lose a war and then using us as pawns . . . .[6]

Despite the torrents of material pouring out of the media and the many orations on the floor of Congress, almost no one until Kerry had managed to so eloquently focus on the cynicism of leaders who were willing to forfeit young lives to preserve their reputations.

Although the proceedings at Valley Forge had received financial and moral support from many sources, including presidential aspirants George McGovern and Ed Muskie, the size of the crowd, which numbered between 1,000 and 2,000 onlookers, was disappointingly small. Yet the four-day protest had been personally cathartic for the participants. Many of these men had felt isolated upon their return from Vietnam, unable to talk about their experiences with their families and friends. The opportunity to join together with those who shared those experiences had come as an immense relief. During their nights on the road, the men had sat around lanterns, eating pork and beans and sharing war stories. As expressed by William Crandell, an Army second lieutenant who had led a rifle platoon in Vietnam, there was "a terrific need to get together and a terrific need to talk."[7]

Until this point, Vietnam Veterans Against the War had been a marginal entity. It had come into existence almost by accident in April 1967, when six returning veterans decided to join a New York City antiwar march. Somebody had made a sign reading "Vietnam Veterans Against the War," which parade organizers had shrewdly placed at the front of the demonstration hoping to attract additional soldiers.

In the group was 24-year-old Jan Barry Crumb, who had served in Vietnam in 1963 when the US presence there was still "advisory."[8] After the demonstration he had invited a small group of veterans to his apartment, where they created the framework for a wider organization. Over the next 12 months new members came in through word of mouth or in response to advertisements placed in the *New Republic* magazine and other publications. However, the presidential election of 1968 had demoralized this small group of activists, leaving the organization moribund.

During the 1969 Moratorium Days, however, the VVAW's activity picked up, and in the aftermath of the Cambodian invasion and the killings at Kent State the membership grew rapidly. On some campuses, returning veterans joined the ranks of the student protesters. One unnoticed byproduct of the war was that young veterans who might never have attended college had the economic resources to enroll. This was true at Kent State, where 300 students had cheered as veteran Jim Geary burned his discharge papers on the very first day of the demonstrations,[9] and where Tim Butz, an Air Force crew chief who had returned from Vietnam in 1968, joined Vietnam Veterans Against the War after watching the National Guard fire into the crowd of students. Butz had intended to finish college and put the war behind him, but the carnage at the university made that impossible.

Veterans on other college campuses were also reacting with strong emotions. To some it seemed though the war had chased them back to America, shattering civilian tranquility. At Swarthmore W. D. Erhart, a combat Marine, found himself weeping uncontrollably after hearing the news of Kent State:

> The war was a horrible mistake and my beloved country was dying because of it. America was bleeding to death in the rice fields and jungles of America, and now the blood flowed in the streets. I did not want my country to die. I had to do something. It was time to stop the war. And I would have to do it."[10]

For Ron Kovic, the 23-year-old paraplegic Marine enrolled at Hofstra University, the shock he felt when he heard about Kent State was a turning point. Until then, Kovic had been frozen and isolated, overwhelmed by unprocessed feelings of rage and guilt. Although reluctant to admit it, even to himself, his most significant actions during his two years in Vietnam were the accidental slaying of a US soldier during a firefight and an assault on a village where his unit had unwittingly shot up a houseful of children.[11] Becoming reckless in battle and despairing, Kovic had gotten himself shot.

When he was shipped home and sent to the Bronx Veterans Administration Hospital for treatment, Kovic was stunned to find himself in a filthy institution where the staff was overworked and hostile, and rats had the run of the place. The hospital marked "the end of whatever belief I'd still had in what I've done in Vietnam." It left him wanting to know "what I'd lost my legs for, and why I and the others had gone at all."

Despite this feeling he had found it difficult to ally himself with the antiwar movement, "to think of joining those I'd once called traitors." Yet as hundreds of Hofstra students marched and rallied in opposition to the invasion of Cambodia, Kovic followed along in his car, cheering privately. A week later, he and his cousin Skip drove to Washington to participate in the giant demonstration there. Kovic was moved by the camaraderie he felt that day, beginning a journey that would lead to his emergence as a spokesman for Vietnam Veterans Against the War and the subsequent author of a classic antiwar memoir.

Kovic's evolution from war veteran to antiwar protester was hardly unique. There were others whose traumatic experiences in the veterans' hospitals had accelerated their disillusionment. The Bronx VA was one of the worst of them—so disgraceful that it featured prominently in a May 1970 *Life Magazine* article, "Our Forgotten Wounded." Its black and white cover photo featured a young man slumped over in a wheelchair with other inert bodies in shadowed beds behind him.[12] "Staff shortages, overcrowding, dirt and leaky roofs in a medical slum," summarized the article. Facilities for long-term treatment and rehabilitation, essential for those who had become paralyzed, lacked trained personnel, which partly explained Ron Kovic's neglect.

The article focused on the ordeal of Private Mark Dumpert, who had volunteered for an extra assignment at Khe Sanh and had his neck broken when the truck on which he was traveling was hit by a rocket and flipped over on top of him. At the Bronx VA he found himself in a ward with six other men who could not wash themselves or even reach a glass of water.

> "We're all hooked up to urine bags, and without enough attendants to empty them, they spill over the floor. It smells and cakes something awful. The aides don't commit themselves wholeheartedly, but with what they earn, why should they? I've laid in bed on one side from 6 a.m. to 4 p.m., without getting moved or washed . . . . It's like you've been put in jail or you've been punished for something."[13]

He also spoke of rats that climbed on patient's beds, especially terrifying for men who were immobilized by their injuries. "I have nothing but disgust for my country," Dumpert told the *Life* reporter. Because of horrific conditions such as these, the military hospitals were fast becoming recruiting grounds for VVAW.

Such veteran rumblings were making scant impression in the Nixon White House, where attention was focused on the upcoming midterm elections. In Nixon's view, the winning issue for his side was "the war at home," which counterpoised dirty young hippies against clean-cut, patriotic young soldiers. This theme had served him well in 1968 and seemed even more promising in the aftermath of Kent State. Incredibly, the polls indicated that many Americans believed he had been insufficiently tough on student protesters.[14] "Campus disorder" might seem like a minor problem when set against larger international and national challenges, but it seemed to resonate deeply among the millions of Americans who saw them as an expression of class privilege and elitism. Moreover, concerns about unruly students were closely related to other widespread fears about crime, racial conflict, and changing cultural values.

The challenge was to somehow tie Democratic candidates to the violent protesters. Nixon assigned Agnew to spearhead the effort to convince normally Democratic voters, like the white ethnic blue-color workers they had appealed to successfully in 1968, that their former party had been taken over by extremists who did not share their values.[15] Toward this end, Agnew's job was to wring maximum advantage from the scruffy demonstrators who regularly showed up for his appearances. Nixon recommended that, in the presence of cameras, Agnew plant himself near an obscene sign or directly confront his angry adversaries.[16] Should Mrs. Agnew be pushed, however gently, it would be helpful if she fell to the ground.

As he campaigned across the country the vice president embraced his assigned role, flaying even moderate Democrats for tolerating student "bomb-throwers." At a $100-a-plate dinner in Grand Rapids he acknowledged that some Democrats were truly patriotic, but radical liberals had successfully infiltrated the party. Fortunately, there was "a man in the White House, who has his roots in Middle America and is proud of it."[17] With Nixon as president, "We remember who pays the taxes. We remember who has had to fight the wars. We remember who makes the automobiles, builds the plants, and makes this country run."

Despite Agnew's volubility the October polls were alarming, suggesting that Republicans could lose as many as 30 seats in the House and all but one of the seriously contested Senate seats.[18] If Republicans did poorly, it would create a negative momentum going into the 1972 presidential race and could well undermine Nixon's Vietnam policy. Having lost a Senate fight over the Cooper–Church Amendment, the last thing Nixon needed was more "troublemakers" on the Hill who might support an amendment like the one Hatfield and McGovern had proposed, with its end date for the war.

To forestall any renewed public agitation over the issue, Nixon announced in mid-October that because of how well things were going he planned to bring home an additional 40,000 US troops before Christmas. There was somewhat less here than met the eye, because the 40,000 would be subtracted from the 100,000 figure already promised for the spring of 1971.[19] In combination with the peace plan he had announced in his early October speech, the president conveyed the impression that the Vietnam War was truly winding down.

But there was no winding down of the domestic battle. As election day neared, Nixon surprised his staff by choosing to embark on a cross- country campaign tour. The president loved political campaigning: the excited crowds, the challenge of tailoring just the right message for a particular audience, the satisfaction of besting complacent opponents. Agnew had faithfully carried out his strategy of saddling the Democrats with the responsibility for youthful disorder and violence, but Nixon believed his own skills were superior.

As the president raced across the country he repeatedly denounced the "people shouting obscenities about America and what we stand for."[20] By the time he arrived in San Jose on October 30, Nixon was exhausted but also pumped from the experience of the cheering crowds. So far the protesters had played directly into his hands, providing just enough disruption to illustrate his points Anticipating a large indoor rally, the Secret Service, at his behest, ordered buses and trucks placed in such a way that Nixon's limousine would be able to drive right through a line of antiwar demonstrators.[21] Inside the hall there were few hecklers, but according to Haldeman, "we wanted some confrontation," so they delayed Nixon's departure in order to allow the crowd outside to gather.[22] To heighten the drama, the president unexpectedly climbed on top of his limousine, giving the V-sign to his adversaries. A few responded by hurling eggs, rocks, and candles in his direction, providing footage for the national media.[23]

Nixon immediately sensed that, if properly handled, this incident could be a public relations windfall. As frazzled staff members regained their composure, he urged them to crank up the media operation and make this a really major story about how he had faced down "a mob of about a thousand haters." In an emotional speech in Phoenix the next day, he deplored the "viciousness" of the protesters. They were "not romantic revolutionaries but the same thugs and hoodlums that always plagued good people." Then the inevitable link: these dangerous individuals had gotten the upper hand because of "appeasement."[24] However, Nixon wanted everyone to understand that he would not be intimidated or kept a prisoner in the White House. "As long I am President, no band of violent thugs is going to keep me from going out and speaking with the American people, whenever they want to hear me." It was the most personally combative speech the president had given on the campaign trail and the one he most preferred. The staff was instructed to edit the tape and to run it as an advertisement on all three major networks the night before the election.

Despite Nixon's efforts—20 states in seven days--the election results were dismal. Most of the candidates he campaigned for were defeated. The Republicans lost nine seats in the House and gained only two seats in the Senate. This outcome virtually guaranteed future congressional challenges to his war policy. While the president loved to excoriate the "violent" protesters, who shirked their military responsibilities, there was a growing problem from "non-bums" in uniform, whose discontent was growing exponentially. Some of this had to do with their experiences in the war and at home, some of it with a generational divide that was cutting across class and race and ripping apart the armed forces.

By 1970 any new soldier going over to Vietnam was keenly aware of the domestic dissension surrounding the war, as well as the youthful counterculture. The precise social meaning of its signifying features—long hair, Afros, drugs, rock'n'roll, sexual permissiveness—might not always be clear, but the overall thrust was that young people were challenging their parents' values. Such a disdain for authority was certainly at odds with the whole concept of military hierarchy.

There was also a racial dimension to these tensions. Any black soldier from an urban area would likely have imbibed some of the racial militancy and anger that was bubbling through his community. Thrown into the cauldron of Vietnam, black soldiers were if anything even more alienated than their white counterparts. When polled, 60% of African American soldiers in the Mekong Delta saw no justification for being there.[25] While the majority followed orders, there was enough angry resistance to alarm their white officers.

Sensing that the time was right for reaching out to men in the military, antiwar activists had begun establishing a presence near military bases.[26] They joined forces with GIs to create a network of coffeehouses throughout the country, including Fort Bragg in North Carolina, Fort Lewis-McChord in Washington State, Fort Dix in New Jersey, and Fort Hood in Texas These were places for soldiers to relax, listen to music, become more educated about the Vietnam War, and sometimes organize resistance to it.[27] Not surprisingly, military authorities and local officials were usually hostile and found a variety of excuses to shut them down.[28] Yet they somehow sprang back up.

The coffeehouses often provided a base for people who were involved in the creation of an underground press. By the end of 1970, perhaps as many as 100 of these underground papers were circulating on or near domestic military bases. A few had been in existence for a number of years, including *The Fatigue Press* near Fort Hood, *FTA* (short for "Fuck the Army") near Fort Knox, and *Gigline* in the environs of Fort Bliss. Others were short-lived and insubstantial, a few mimeographed pages stapled together by a handful of people. Taken together, these antiwar publications gave soldiers valuable exposure to a range of critical voices from the time of their arrival on base until their departure for Vietnam.

As military leaders correctly feared, all of this ferment—the barbed entertainment in the coffeehouses, the counseling and legal services that were often offered there, the informal discussion groups, the underground press—paved the way for active duty personnel to organize into antiwar groups. Among them were several national organizations, including the American Servicemen's Union, the Movement for a Democratic Military, and perhaps most remarkably, the Concerned Officers Movement (COM). In September, the COM had directly challenged military norms by holding a Washington DC press conference in which they publicly deplored "the military mentality that promotes absurd measures like the body count that leads to the indiscriminate slaughter of innocent civilians."[29]

More alarming to the authorities was the willingness of rank-and-file soldiers to join civilians in demonstrations near the bases. During the tumultuous month of May, commanding officers at 25 facilities had chosen to cancel the traditional Armed Forces Day celebrations for fear of disruption in reaction to the Kent State killings.[30] There were nevertheless protests in numerous places, from Fort Bragg, where a rally of several thousand people heard speeches by "Chicago conspirator" Rennie Davis, actress Jane Fonda, and left-wing lawyer Mark Lane, to the "People's Armed Forces Day" outside Fort Bliss, where soldiers gathered for a rock and folk music festival.

There were still many soldiers on the domestic military bases who remained apolitical. While showing no interest in protesting the war itself, they were engaged in another kind of rebellion, having absorbed some of the countercultural attitudes of their generation. By 1970 white and black soldiers in Vietnam were letting their hair grow, putting peace beads around their necks, or wearing Black Panther bracelets on their wrists.[31] At Fort Bliss in Texas the number of activists remained small, but according to antiwar veteran David Cortright, there was an insubordinate atmosphere. The black GIs were particularly bold, "wearing their army caps perched atop oversize Afros, sneakers rather than combat boots, and shirts untucked and unbuttoned." There were also the "heads," white soldiers who spent their free time smoking weed and listening to rock music, which they blasted from their sound systems. Yet with the stockade at the base already overflowing, the commanders had become reluctant to take disciplinary action.

When the movie *Woodstock* was shown on the base theater, Cortwright was struck by the "raucous" response of his fellow soldiers. "The place went wild" when they reached the segment with Country Joe and the Fish performing their original signature song "Vietnam Rag." As the smell of marijuana wafted through the air, the men in the audience added their voices:

And it's one, two, three, what are we fighting for?
Don't ask me I don't give a damn
Next stop is Vietnam
And it's five, six, seven,
Open up the pearly gates
Well there ain't no time to wonder why
Whoopee! We're all gonna die . . .

Come on mothers throughout the land
Pack your boys off to Vietnam
Come on fathers, and don't hesitate
To send your sons off before it's too late
And you can be the first ones in your block
To have your boy come home in a box...

Embodied in these lyrics was a biting cynicism more shocking at Fort Bliss than in Max Yasgur's farm in Bethel, New York. But whereas the 100,000 long-haired flower children at the Woodstock concert had been front page news, the mainstream media was paying scant attention to the cultural disaffection emerging on the domestic military bases. As a consequence, millions of Americans had no idea that many of the clean-cut soldiers the White House liked to invoke as exemplars of patriotism were coming to resemble the alienated students who were supposedly their antithesis. The signs carried by protesters had a counterpart in military helmets that doubled as blackboards for antiwar messages— "Give Peace a Chance!"... "War is unhealthy for children and other living things," or just "UUUU" (grunt shorthand for "the unwilling, led by the unqualified, doing the unnecessary for the ungrateful").[32]

In Vietnam itself, the currents of disillusion were becoming a torrent. Ironically one critical factor undermining morale was the administration's policy of troop withdrawals.[33] From a public relations standpoint, each new increment of returned soldiers was craftily orchestrated so as to reduce domestic dissent. What no one anticipated was how this would impact the soldiers who remained in Vietnam. For those in the field, who typically regarded the army of South Vietnam as cowardly and incompetent, the obvious conclusion was that if American withdrawals continued, then sooner or later the enemy would win.[34] Given that likelihood, why should they continue to fight?

Throughout 1969–70, there were reports of units refusing to follow orders, sometimes with the connivance of their own officers.

[35]A *Newsweek* article entitled "The Troubled U.S. Army in Vietnam" quoted 22-year-old Sergeant Ralph Mitchell as saying, "If I think a mission will be too costly, I weigh the value of it and my men come first." It also cited a "hard-nosed" lieutenant colonel, who observed that "the idea of another Hamburger Hill is definitely out.... The most important part of our job now is to get as many men as possible back to the U.S. alive." Moreover, it was no longer possible to just give an order and assume it would be obeyed. Soldiers

would "ask why, and you have to tell them." Although direct insubordination was still uncommon, the more pervasive phenomenon was a practice GIs called "search and avoid" or alternately, "search and evade."

Another sign of how far military discipline had eroded was the drastic increase in the use of marijuana and hard drugs by American troops in Vietnam. The *Newsweek* story included Pentagon estimates that 50%–60% of soldiers were using drugs. Both marijuana and heroin were easily available in Vietnam at bargain-basement prices and with a degree of purity—and deadliness—not found in the United States. During the summer and fall of 1970, at least 75 soldiers had died of an overdose over a two-month period, according to government figures.[36]

Writing in the *Armed Forces Journal*, Marine Colonel Robert D. Heinl described the gravity of the problem.[37] "The morale, discipline and battleworthiness of the U.S. Armed Forces are, with a few salient exceptions, lower and worse than at any time in this century and possibly in the history of the United States," he warned. "By every conceivable indicator, our Army that now remains in Vietnam is in a state approaching collapse with individual units avoiding or having refused combat, murdering their officers and non-commissioned officers, drug-ridden and dispirited where not near-mutinous."

Colonel Heinl was not writing from an antiwar perspective. His dissatisfaction, echoing that of many other career officers, was over the fact that the civilians in Washington had given them an impossible mission:

> Intolerably clobbered and buffeted from without and within by social turbulence, pandemic drug addiction, race war, sedition, civilian scapegoating, draftee recalcitrance and malevolence . . . unsupported in their travail by the general government, in Congress as well as the executive branch . . . the uniformed services today are places of agony . . . .

The bitterness of "the lifers" was plain to see. After so much blood and sacrifice, their government was in obvious retreat, imposing upon them the thankless task of managing young soldiers who saw no point in dying.[38]

The morale problems Heinl described could become lethal, as was apparent from mounting reports of "fragging," when angry soldiers killed or wounded officers they deemed too harsh or too zealous in combat. Accurate statistics on this were inherently difficult to obtain. If an officer was killed by "friendly fire" on the battlefield, it could be difficult to discern whether this was a bona fide accident occurring in the heat of combat, a premeditated murder, or something in between. According to Army records, during 1969–70 there were 563 incidents of fragging, a figure that likely understated the phenomenon.[39] More consequential than the actual numbers was the widespread perception by officers that it was dangerous to push reluctant men into combat or even to report infractions.

Regarding military morale, there was a much darker problem, which the mainstream media tended to ignore but which VVAW decided to spotlight: participation in "war crimes." What happened to the nation's young men, many still teenagers, when placed in situations where atrocities had become commonplace?

The issue of "war crimes" had come to the fore in the fall of 1969 with the My Lai story.[40] However, the White House had managed to position this as an aberrant and isolated incident. While politicians from both parties and mainstream journalists were content to leave the matter there, for some soldiers who had been privy to war crimes, the experience was part of their trauma. For this group, the need to acknowledge their participation in these acts, to expose the reasons for it, and to try to prevent other soldiers from being placed in such moral jeopardy was the only route to redemption.

This was one impetus for Project RAW—the street theater the vets enacted on their way from Morristown to Valley Forge. As they departed George Washington's winter encampment, the organizers of this operation had determined that looking ahead, they must continue to focus on the matter of US war crimes.

In planning for a public forum, leaders of VVAW intended to coordinate with a Citizens Commission of Inquiry led by lawyer Tod Ensign and journalist Jeremy Rifkin, which had been holding hearings around the country on this subject. Yet, differences of approach quickly emerged, and the two groups went their separate ways. The veterans decided to hold their inquest in Detroit—a working-class city, where military deserters in Canada might have media access.

Ahead of the event, there was detailed planning to verify that those who had offered to testify were in fact from the units and the locations they described. On January 31, 1971, hundreds of veterans, family members, and supporters gathered at a Howard Johnson Motor Inn. Approximately 150 men had volunteered to testify to military crimes they had personally witnessed or participated in. Over the next three days, they related horrifying stories that posed challenging moral issues for the men themselves, a society that seemed oblivious, and a government that had placed them in these compromised positions.

As explained in their advance publicity:

> We have come home to acquaint America with its policy. My Lai was not an "isolated incident," and those responsible for it are not a few aberrant individuals. Those responsible do not live in the hootches of the Mekong Delta; they reside in Washington D.C., where the policies that comprise attempted genocide are originated.[41]

Reflecting this purpose, veteran Bill Crandell opened the proceedings with an eloquent statement. "Like the winter soldiers of 1776 who stayed after they had served their time, we veterans of Vietnam know that America is in grave danger," he explained. "What threatens our country is not Redcoats or even Reds, it is our crimes that are destroying our national unity by separating those of our countrymen who deplore these acts from those of our countrymen who refuse to examine what is being done in America's name."[42] He and the others had gone to Vietnam to fight for freedom, but their testimony would show that "we have turned Vietnam into a series of concentration camps." They had believed they were defending self-determination for the South Vietnamese, but "our testimony will show that we are forcing a corrupt and dictatorial government upon them."

The opening panel consisted of 12 members from the First Marine Division, whose collective service spanned the period 1964–1970. Among the most electrifying speakers was Scott Camil, a decorated 24-year-old sergeant who had returned from Vietnam still a committed "hawk." However, by the time of these 1971 "Winter Soldier" hearings, Camil had reconsidered and had come to regret his military zealotry.

In rapid-fire delivery, Camil described a host of chilling practices, including an artillery game in which observers would identify a house in a "friendly village'" and call in artillery. Once it was destroyed, they would call for a mortar attack on a second house and so forth. The object of the game was to see who could use the least amount of artillery, and whoever earned that distinction would be rewarded with a free beer or some other prize. There was also the practice of burning down Vietnamese homes. Camil testified that "before we went out on the operation, we were told not to waste our heat tablets on food but to save them for the villages." When this happened, they "didn't give people any time to get out." They just "went in and burned them and if people were in the villages yelling and screaming, we didn't help them." The moderator of the panel wondered why they had used heat tabs rather than simply matches. "We'd throw the heat tabs in," Camil explained, "because it was quicker and you couldn't put the heat tabs out."

The former sergeant had also witnessed torture. In one instance, two prisoners were handled together. The first one "was staked on the ground and he was cut open while he was alive and part of his insides were cut out and they told the other prisoner if he didn't tell them what they wanted to know they would kill him." Since he did not understand Vietnamese, Camil wasn't sure what the second man said, but they killed him anyway.

The sergeant provided gruesome descriptions of the mistreatment of women, including rapes described as "searches" and a sadistic dismemberment and murder. These acts had been witnessed by the company commander. For the soldiers, such behavior was widely accepted because they had been conditioned to see the Vietnamese as less than human. Whatever was being done was for "the good of the nation, the good of our country. . . . And when you shot someone you did not think you were shooting at a human. They were a gook or a Commie . . . and they'd do it to you if they had the chance."

Camil's stories might have been written off as wild exaggerations or the product of an earlier period of the war were it not for the testimony of others from the First Marine Division. Sergeant Ted Eckert, who had joined the Marines out of high school, described a game he had witnessed in Quang Tri.[43] At about 5:00 AM he was out with a group in a small jeep that was patrolling the perimeter, when they spotted a woman running through the trees. Although this was not a free-fire zone, "from the hours from dusk to dawn, there's not supposed to be anybody out there." The soldiers decided to have some fun:

> . . . they let her run about fifty yards and they'd fire in front of her so she'd have to turn around, and then they'd let her run another direction and then they'd cut her off. This went on about a half hour until the time the sun started to come up. So then they decided it best to eliminate her as soon as possible, so they just ripped her off. . . . Her only crime was being out probably tending to her buffalo before the time she should have been. These guys just decided to waste her.

In attempting to explain this murder, Eckert also cited the common belief that the Vietnamese were inferior beings and that "the only good one was a dead one."

The Vietnamese were also being killed by chemicals the Americans used, including Agent Orange, which was sprayed to defoliate forests where it was believed the enemy might be hiding. Sergeant Joe Bangert stated that he had seen approximately 20 deformed babies during his tour of duty,[44] which he later concluded was the result of the routine spraying of Agent Orange. According to Sergeant Fred Nienke, US soldiers were also using white phosphorus, colloquially referred to as Willie Peter, to clear bunkers and sometimes houses.[45] When fearful that a particular location might be sheltering Viet Cong, "We'd send in Willie Peter mortars, 60 millimeters and this would burn up the hootches and sometimes the people." This was one of the worst sights he had ever seen, because when Willie Peter started to burn a person it didn't stop. "It just burns all completely through your body."[46]

The recital of crimes kept coming; contests between soldiers to see how high they could throw a bound prisoner,[47] the mutilation of corpses and desecration of graves, the group rape of girls in front of their families, the tossing of prisoners out of helicopters in an effort to intimidate the survivors,[48] the denial of medical treatment to enemy captives[49] and sometimes ARVN allies.[50] Some of the testifiers spoke in angry tones, others with flat affect. Several seemed almost bewildered, as if they could not believe these things had happened or that they had really been there. Many wept, as did people in the audience.

Quite a few of the speakers were barely out of their teens, and the majority had only high school educations. The overwhelming theme was the murder and abuse of civilians. The military's unrelenting pressure for a high body count was placing a premium on corpses, regardless of their identity. In some places it was enough to know that the person was dead in order to qualify them as VC. However, many veterans reported on the confiscation of ID cards and the planting of weapons as the means to establish that the person was an enemy.

Some of the most heartrending stories concerned the cruelty to hungry children.[51] When they approached vehicles transporting food, this sometimes gave rise to a nasty game in which US soldiers threw cans of spaghetti, meat balls, ham, and lima beans at their heads and, if they managed to duck at the right moment, they might obtain a meal. According to Corporal Robert

Clark and other witnesses, there were many skirmishes over garbage.[52] Clark had frequent responsibility for garbage runs and was under instructions that, if anyone jumped on the back of the truck in order to find scraps of food, "they were fair game for anything." As a trick, a bunch of soldiers hid, and when a group of women and children climbed in, "they'd just beat 'em with their rifle clubs until they were either knocked senseless and then they'd knock them on the ground and just kick their ass all the way across the garbage dump . . ."

As the tumultuous hearings wound down, Master Sergeant Donald Duncan, a former Green Beret, offered a summary of the proceedings. The aim of their endeavor had been "to bring some reality as to what the war in Vietnam really means to people who must fight it, to the people that must suffer in it, to the Vietnamese, to the Americans, to all the mothers, fathers, sisters, wives, brothers."[53] The American public needed to grasp the enormity of what was being done in its name. No president could have continued with this war "had there not been some sort of cooperation or concurrence . . . on the part of a large segment of this country," which was why it was so important to remove "the blinders" from their eyes.

If the main purpose of the hearings in Detroit was to remove blinders from the eyes of their fellow citizens, they could not be counted a success. Although organizers of the event had attempted to interest the media, there was an absence of press coverage outside the Detroit newspapers. As a result, few people outside the antiwar circuit heard anything about the horrors they had described. And yet, for those who were there, the experience was deeply important. Thousands of Vietnam War veterans had come home and refused to speak about their experience. Those in Detroit had the opportunity to come to terms with what had happened in Vietnam and their personal role. Some might say it was self-serving for men struggling with guilt over atrocities they had committed in a war zone to blame them on their superiors and on the society that had sent them to Vietnam. Yet, final responsibility went higher.

For Washington policymakers, the personal tragedies exposed in these Detroit Winter Soldier hearings had little reality. Nobody in the upper echelons had ever sat down to "systematically kill whatever number of people are necessary" to achieve American ends. As described in the policy papers, the military objectives were antiseptic: to create "free-fire zones," to "neutralize" enemy cadres, to "defoliate" forests, to "relocate populations," or to conduct "saturation" bombing. Each of these bland terms provided a mindset in which resulting acts of criminality were obscured. Along with lesser perpetrators, both Nixon and Kissinger were disconnected from the suffering described in Detroit. Instead, they were preparing for yet another expansion of the war—this time into Laos.

13

"Something Like a Moron . . ."

As promised, on June 30, 1970, US troops were withdrawn from Cambodia. However, Nixon and Kissinger were left with an ongoing problem: how to prevent the enemy from conducting a large-scale offensive during the interval before the presidential election in 1972. In the service of that goal they had undertaken the controversial Cambodian operation. While nobody in the administration would acknowledge this, the overthrow of Sihanouk and the subsequent invasion by US and South Vietnamese troops had created a new set of daunting military and political problems.

It was clear that Lon Nol's army of neophytes was no match for the North Vietnamese troops which, having been expelled from the sanctuaries, were pushed deeper into Cambodian territory. By summer's end, some 30% to 50% of the country's territory had come under the control of Lon Nol's enemies. In varying combinations these included North Vietnamese soldiers, main-force NLF units, members of the indigenous Khmer Rouge, and local groups still loyal to Prince Sihanouk. Left unchecked, their activities could bring about the collapse of the Cambodian government.

To avert that threat, the Nixon administration was continuing to funnel weapons and supplies to Phnom Penh, while pressuring Thailand and Indonesia to offer economic and military assistance to their neighbor. At the administration's behest, the South Vietnamese government was keeping its troops in Cambodia past the June 30 deadline. Despite committing to Congress that it would limit air strikes there to situations in which the movement of men and materials directly threatened American troops,[1] the US Air Force was providing round-the-clock bombing in support of the Cambodian and South Vietnamese ground operations.[2]

Such measures notwithstanding, by October 1970 General Abrams was increasingly fearful about a new enemy offensive—a concern made more acute by unexpected news from Secretary Laird that another 40,000 American troops would be withdrawn from South Vietnam during the last quarter of the year. After two years on the job, the general was exhausted and eager for reassignment. Unlike the "spinners" in the Nixon White House, whose message was that the Cambodian operation had devastated the enemy, Abrams had come to appreciate the resilience of the North Vietnamese and feared that cultural prejudice was leading Washington officials to underestimate these troops.[3]

A further impediment to gaining Nixon's attention was the latter's fierce insistence that Cambodia was an unqualified success. Having weathered the storm of domestic critics, the president preferred the advice of Army Chief of Staff Westmoreland and British counter-insurgency expert Sir Robert Thompson, both of whom highlighted the military gains. By forcing the North Vietnamese to keep fighting in Cambodia, the president had reduced the threat to South Vietnam—or so they claimed. Abrams was unconvinced.

However, in the disappointing aftermath of the midterm elections, the president was becoming agitated. On the public relations front, he faulted his staff for failing to amplify his accomplishments. He became infuriated when a girl who was receiving a "bravery" award at a White House ceremony informed him that she would not be convinced of his sincerity until he ended the war in Vietnam.[4] Why hadn't she been property vetted? he complained. And more to the point, why wasn't the staff doing a better job of conveying his special qualities—"the courage, the independence, the boldness, standing alone, overruling advisors," and so forth?

The midterm losses had left the administration more vulnerable to congressional obstruction, especially since the conflict in Cambodia had depleted Defense Department resources far beyond expectations.[5] In order to keep the fragile government of Lon Nol afloat by equipping his "officially" numbered 100,000-man army, Nixon needed Congress to pass a supplemental spending bill of $285 million. But there was serious resistance to doing so, despite the president's claim that the American and South Vietnamese invasion of Cambodia had been a brilliant stroke. Members of Congress need only pick up a newspaper to understand that in its wake, that country was unraveling.

Despite the dismay of many Democrats and Republicans, nobody suggested that negotiations aimed at returning Cambodia to its previous neutral status might be a more effective way of restoring stability than spending more money on its army. To overcome congressional hesitation, Nixon and Kissinger settled on the cynical ploy of wrapping their Cambodian request into a supplemental spending bill that also included $500 million for Israel. If the aid to Southeast Asia was not forthcoming, the president remarked, it would be "cold turkey" for Tel Aviv."[6]

Such maneuvers might yield temporary gains, but the larger picture was worrisome, with a rebellious Congress on the one hand and deadlocked negotiations with Hanoi on the other. As for the battlefield, by December Nixon was belatedly paying attention to Laos, where the enemy was actively rebuilding its logistical system. Having been driven from their sanctuaries near the Cambodian border, the North Vietnamese had become more dependent on their ability to send men and material down the Ho Chi Minh Trail through the Laotian panhandle and into South Vietnam. They had also achieved a presence in northeastern Cambodia, which provided them with a brand new route for men and supplies to enter the South.

Compounding the danger, on December 9 Nixon and Kissinger learned that the enemy had isolated the eastern Cambodian town of Kompong Cham and could potentially move back into the sanctuaries—thereby nullifying the one obvious gain from the 1970 invasion.[7] Nixon was furious, demanding to know why nobody had alerted him to the gravity of the situation and ignoring the fact that subordinates were afraid to give him bad news. While under congressional strictures, the president was not free to use American ground troops, so he demanded that General Abrams relieve Kompong Cham at once by striking enemy soldiers from the air.

Yet this was easier said than done. Admiral Moorer, chairman of the Joint Chiefs of Staff, explained the Cambodian military was in charge there, and with poor weather conditions it was impossible to identify good targets from above.[8] This alarmed Nixon, as he contemplated the possibility that his much-touted foray into Cambodia could be publicly exposed as a failure. He ordered Kissinger to get hold of Moorer immediately and demand a plan "where every goddamn thing that can fly goes into Cambodia and hits every target that is open." He was sick of an Air Force that had gotten into the habit of "running these goddamn milk runs in order to get the air medal."[9]

"They are not imaginative," Kissinger allowed. Not just that, Nixon opined. They had to stop bombing jungles and hit some real targets:

> They have to go in there and I mean really go in. I don't want the gun-ships. I want the helicopter ships. I want everything that can fly to go in there and crack the hell out of them. There is no limitation on mileage and there is no limitation on budget. Is that clear?

As for the specific problem of Kompong Cham, he wanted Saigon to rush in some troops by airlift. American planes could be used to deliver them. Since this was a violation of congressional restrictions on the use of air power in Cambodia, the ostensible reason for the flights would be that the planes were delivering supplies to the town. If it happened that a lot of South Vietnamese soldiers were on board to help with the equipment, nobody in Congress need know. Kissinger thought the approach "ingenious," although it was essential that there be no leaks lest it jeopardize the passage of their "damn supplemental."

Having made these decisions, Nixon could not let the matter rest. Why had this mess in Kompong Cham been allowed to develop? The real problem was the "whole goddam Air Force over there farting around doing nothing." What had they really accomplished? They hit "one or two trucks a day, fly 800 sorties and get 1,500 air medals. It's awful." Kissinger assured his angry boss that he was going to get on Moorer right away and make sure there was a bombing plan by morning. Still steaming, Nixon directed: "I want them to hit everything. I want them to use the big planes, the small planes, everything they can . . . and let's start giving them a little shock."

The threat to Kompong Cham crystallized Nixon's thinking about the need to extend the ground war into Laos. During the previous weeks, the infiltration rate of North Vietnamese troops moving down the Ho Chi Minh Trail in Laos had accelerated, increasing the possibility of a major spring offensive, whether in Cambodia or the northern provinces of South Vietnam.[10] Kissinger's Washington Special Actions Group and a MACV planning group in Saigon were favoring a preemptive move: dispatching thousands of South Vietnamese troops into the Laotian panhandle and back to the border area of Cambodia.[11]

Once he decided on a Laotian move, Nixon urged Kissinger to initiate the necessary steps immediately. It was a problem, the president reflected, that in the White House they had let themselves become preoccupied with minor things. So they worried about the Chilean elections and whether or not there would be a vote in Guinea, "and all that bull, but the only thing that really matters" at this point, he said, was the war.[12] Let the State Department handle these other matters: "I don't give a damn what happens in those other places now. There is nothing we can do about it anyway." Going forward, he didn't want to see anything about Chile, or Biafra, or Guinea, or "all this other crap." They had to concentrate instead on the things that "can make or break us and none of these things will."

Regarding Kompong Cham, which had occasioned Nixon's recent outburst, Admiral Moorer assured Kissinger that South Vietnamese troops were being airlifted in. Somewhat mollified, Kissinger asked Moorer if they could also please drop some bombs nearby "because the president is driving me out of my mind."[13] There was no need for concern, Moorer replied. Under their latest orders, the military had already doubled or tripled the sorties in the area, an assault that he expected to be ongoing.

The outrageousness of Nixon's demands was not lost on Kissinger, who privately mocked the president to Haig: "He wants a massive bombing campaign in Cambodia. He does not want to hear anything. It's an order. It's to be done. Anything that flies on anything that moves. You got that?" While recognizing the childishness of this response, Kissinger quietly indulged such fits.

There was, however, one item on which Kissinger stood firm. At year's end, Nixon was repeatedly drawn to an apocalyptic ending to US involvement in the war: a cancellation of the Paris peace talks, mining of Haiphong harbor, and massive bombing of North Vietnam as a prelude to pulling out all US troops and allowing ARVN to finish off a decimated enemy. Kissinger knew better.[14] If the American military left Vietnam in 1971, no matter how much damage they inflicted, the political consequences for the administration could be disastrous. In the absence of American soldiers there was good reason to fear the enemy would win, if not immediately then still in time for election day.

The more pragmatic plan was the one Nixon had already endorsed: a major offensive in Laos accompanied by some fresh initiatives in Cambodia to keep the enemy away from the sanctuaries. To obtain more accurate information and to convey the president's wishes to MACV, Kissinger again relied on his deputy Al Haig.

Stopping first in Phnom Penh, Haig quickly realized that accurate information about conditions outside the capital was unavailable. From what little he could discern, the situation seemed bleak. The North Vietnamese enemy was rebuilding quickly, while the Cambodian military was suffering from weak leadership and poor tactics. In South Vietnam, things looked brighter. Haig toured III Corps and found "irrefutable evidence" that because of their Cambodian operation, this section had "enjoyed almost a complete respite from enemy activities" since the summer.[15]

In Saigon Haig had a lengthy meeting with President Thieu, who was eager to hear of his appraisal of the political and military situation in Cambodia.[16] Not wishing to deprecate their new ally, Haig disingenuously claimed that Lon Nol had become more realistic about his goals and understood that it was not feasible to sweep the communists out of the country. But he also acknowledged that Lon Nol's military lacked experience, adequate firepower, reliable intelligence, and competent leadership. In order to survive, his regime would need substantial assistance from the United States and South Vietnam.

On a sour note, Haig observed that one impediment to cooperation between Saigon and Phnom Penh was the "misbehavior and thoughtless performance" of the South Vietnamese soldiers who were there. During Haig's visit to the Cambodian capital, he and his staff heard repeated complaints about their mistreatment of the population, and he strongly advised Thieu that the Saigon government needed to address this unruliness for the collaboration to work.

The irony of being given this advice by an American was surely not lost on Thieu. For years the recklessness and cruelty of the American troops toward civilians in South Vietnam had enraged the people, turning many of them against Thieu's government and providing some with an incentive to join the Viet Cong. While Haig was in Saigon, a mini-crisis had erupted in the provincial capital of Quinhon over this very issue. For no apparent reason, an American soldier shot and killed a 12-year-old student, Nguyen Van Minh, who was sitting on the fence outside his school.[17] The soldier's superiors claimed the shooting was an accident, some warning shots gone astray. The killing triggered two days of demonstrations and riots, as young people from the town hauled the bloody body through the streets, burned an Army jeep, and sacked an American bar.

The outbreak was sufficiently newsworthy that it received front-page coverage in the *New York Times.* The article quoted Buddhist Monk Thich Tam Hoang: "The people have been suffering in silence. The people were backed against the wall. We are like worms that have been stepped on." Cyclo driver Tran Quang Phouc mentioned other animals:

> The Americans used to have fun by pulling our hats as they drove past. We stopped wearing our hat. I was also stoned by them from time to time, but that did not hurt much. We are like mice and the Americans are like cats. We are their playthings.

Despite being pressed about his Army's misdeeds in another country, which like those of the Americans in Vietnam had compromised the effectiveness of the military, Thieu skipped the opportunity for invidious comparisons.

Instead, he chose to focus on something he found much more disturbing: the precipitous rate at which American troops were being withdrawn from South Vietnam. How could Washington expect South Vietnam to send its troops into Cambodia if it meant leaving their own territory undefended? This made no sense. If the Americans wanted their help in Cambodia, it would have to slow the withdrawals.

Sidestepping his complaint, Haig was fulsome in his praise of the ARVN and emphasized the need for a joint strategy to get them through the dry season. In the White House, there was a strong sense that "preemptive offensive operations" had become necessary in order to disrupt the enemy's agenda. Toward that end, they were looking to the South Vietnamese military to implement a three-pronged effort: a move into southern and central Cambodia to prevent the enemy from reentering the sanctuaries, a covert raid program into North Vietnam, and most importantly a ground campaign into southern Laos. Haig was delighted to see that General Abrams and General Cau Van Vien, the chairman of the South Vietnamese Joint General Staff, had already made substantial progress formulating the kind of "imaginative" plans Nixon had been seeking.

One undecided question was the prime location for the Laotian offensive. After talking with the two generals, Haig had concluded that the town of Tchepone should be the focus since it was viewed as the nerve center of the enemy's supply effort and of infiltration of personnel into both Cambodia and South Vietnam.[18] President Thieu was amenable toward all Haig's suggestions but continued to insist that if his troops were being removed from South Vietnam to fight in Laos and Cambodia, then the planned withdrawal of American soldiers was unacceptable.

Haig returned to Washington more convinced than ever of the need for rapid and substantial preemptive action. Although they could not be openly acknowledged, he understood the range of new problems created by the incursion into Cambodia. Following the advice of General Abrams and Admiral McCain, he believed a vigorous South Vietnamese drive into southern Laos would increase security in Cambodia and South Vietnam by halting the flow of men and material into both places.[19]

Although joint military planning for that effort was already underway in Saigon, Secretary of Defense Laird was not in the loop.[20] As on previous occasions, Kissinger had circumvented the secretary's office by using Admiral Moorer and General Haig as the direct links to Abrams' headquarters. However, this deception was unsustainable since Laird would be going to Saigon in early January. Haig suggested that his own return to Washington could be the occasion for informing the secretary of the military plans, but Kissinger wanted delay.[21] On this matter, even the normally deferential Haig could recognize how preposterous it was to conceal this information from the Secretary of Defense, who was technically in charge of such operations.

In the end, Kissinger yielded on Laird but was insistent that Rogers and the State Department be kept in the dark for as long as possible. Their exclusion was remarkable, given the fact that Ambassador Bunker, who was technically under the authority of the Secretary of State, was fully cognizant of their plans. However, it was established procedure for Bunker to keep important information from his department superiors, while communicating more candidly with the White House.

During the past two years, these increasingly deceptive arrangements had the effect of eliminating any input on major issues from people with relevant expertise, and precluded informed debate. As on previous occasions, the dominant voice from within the government was that of the career military, using its access through Admiral Moorer and General Haig. Indeed, the early decisions to bomb Cambodia in the spring of 1969 and to invade the country in the spring of 1970 were both products of a truncated policy process in which military views prevailed. Each of these choices had engendered a cascade of unintended consequences that were propelling the massive Laotian operation.

On December 23, Nixon convened a meeting at which the administration's plans would finally be revealed to Laird. With Kissinger, Moorer, and Haig in attendance, Nixon explained that it was time to discuss their future strategy.[22] Beginning with the obligatory assertion that Vietnamization was on track, Nixon went on to say that the task before them was to "find a way for SVN to survive in the long term." Following the president, Haig highlighted the improvements in ARVN, including the great boost in confidence of its soldiers in the aftermath of the Cambodian incursion. These men were prepared to carry the entire burden of ground operations so long as they were assisted by American artillery and air power.

One target was the Chup rubber plantation in Cambodia, where South Vietnamese troops were already battling several North Vietnamese regiments in order to block their return to the sanctuaries.[23] On a grander scale, plans were being developed for thousands of ARVN troops to cross into Laos, fighting their way to Tchepone, a crossroads town through which the enemy was routing men and supplies into Cambodia and Laos. Nixon quickly endorsed the plan for the Chup plantation but waited to see how Laird would react to the plan for Laos. In this instance there was no reason for apprehension. While the secretary had been a consistent voice for moderation, he was usually more flexible about proposal that did not involve the use of American ground troops. As for Tchepone, it was fine with him "to take a crack at it." Nor did he object when Nixon added to the list air strikes on North Vietnam and selective raids on its territory. If all these initiatives were pursued, proclaimed the president, "We can break the back of the enemy."[24]

During his fact-finding trip to South Vietnam in early January, Secretary Laird wanted to be sure that General Abrams and his colleagues were truly in favor of the military actions that Haig and the president had outlined. Their enthusiasm eliminated whatever reservations he might have entertained. Indeed, the headquarters in Saigon had been advocating a ground operation into Laos for years, which, if successful, would sever the Ho Chi Minh Trail and exact high casualties from the North Vietnamese forces. Earlier proposals had entailed the participation of American soldiers, but with the South Vietnamese carrying out the ground campaign, the project had even greater appeal.

On his return to Washington, Laird followed his established pattern of filling his report to Nixon with flattery and good news.[25] When his administration took office, there was no plan in place to advance South Vietnamese self-sufficiency, but "under your guidance all of that was changed." Under his policy, American soldiers were being redeployed and South Vietnam was en route to genuine self-determination. Furthermore, the free nations of Southeast Asia were forging a growing partnership. In Cambodia and Laos, as in South Vietnam, "one senses a growing resolve by the leaders and the people to help themselves and to make the sacrifices for their own security."

A skeptic might wonder on what basis Laird had "sensed" this "growing resolve," but the secretary always found reasons for praising Nixon's decision. He even managed to praise the invasion of Cambodia, which he had initially opposed. "Nothing begets success like success," he dissembled. American, South Vietnamese, and Cambodian forces had all reaped "major dividends from your bold decision . . . to move against the enemy sanctuaries."

Of course, the increased infiltration down the Ho Chi Minh Trail had introduced an "element of uncertainty," but Laird maintained the new MACV proposals would address that challenge. Meanwhile, the war "is winding down" and the substitution of South Vietnamese soldiers for Americans was proceeding apace. All this was attributable to President Nixon. "Your pledge to have the US out of military operations in Southeast Asia by 1972 can and will be met," he affirmed. This approach continued the strategy that the Secretary of Defense had pursued from the beginning—designed to minimize American casualties. By this time, there were still more than 330,000 American young men in harm's way, with no definite timetable for their removal. To get them home, Laird was prepared to support various escalations without looking too closely at their practicality, if the main burden of fighting was shouldered by foreign troops.

Remarkably, military planning for the Laotian offensive was far advanced before Secretary of State Rogers and CIA Director Helms were officially notified on January 18, 1971.[26] By then they had surely learned about this through the Washington grapevine. As anticipated, both men expressed some reservations. Helms worried that ARVN "would run into a very tough fight in Laos" with potentially dangerous consequences, while Rogers feared a spike in US casualties because of expanded air operations.[27] Nixon replied that so long as casualties "remained at the 40/60/70 level, this should be acceptable."

What made these numbers "acceptable?" For antiwar critics and many demoralized soldiers, the continued sacrifice of American lives made no sense at all. But it was clear from the context of the president's remarks that he was making a familiar political assessment. If US deaths stayed below 100 a week, there would be little adverse publicity and most Americans, busy with their own affairs, would give the matter slight attention.

The Secretary of State voiced other concerns, too. Like Helms, he was worried about what would happen if ARVN failed in Laos, which "would be very costly to us." Nixon acknowledged that this could be a problem but thought they could manage public expectations by setting very limited goals for the operation. Even though the offensive would involve thousands of South Vietnamese troops and hundreds of American planes, it should be possible to lower expectations. Then if things worked out well, they could "crow about accomplishments."

CIA Director Helms had other worries, unexpressed in this initial discussion. In mid-December, the CIA had produced a study that highlighted the many risks of an ARVN operation in Laos.[28] The report described a large presence of North Vietnamese infantry, armor, and artillery formations near Tchepone, and warned that the enemy had also deployed formidable air defenses along the Ho Chi Minh Trail and in the immediate vicinity of Tchepone. Moreover, the surrounding terrain was mountainous and jungle-covered, with few clearings for helicopters to land. Even in the "dry season" the weather could be treacherous, with sudden rainfalls that could make it impossible for planes to fly—critical information given the importance of US air power to the viability of the entire Laotian operation. Indeed, American planes were needed for the airlift of South Vietnamese troops and supplies, for striking concentrations of enemy troops, and for the evacuation of wounded personnel.

Despite their well-warranted concerns about the stiff military challenge ARVN might encounter in Laos, neither Helms nor Rogers wished to quarrel with the president. Although this January meeting was perhaps the best opportunity for all the principals—Nixon, Kissinger, Laird, Rogers, Helms, and Moorer—to evaluate the wisdom of the Laotian offensive, the exchange of views was perfunctory. Midway through Nixon's first term, there was not even the illusion of a serious policymaking debate.

Under the schedule proposed by MACV, only two weeks remained before the offensive operations would commence.[29] For his part Kissinger concerned himself with the management questions: Who in Congress should be alerted and when? What should be said to the governments of Thailand and Indonesia? And when should they inform Laotian Prince Souvanna Phouma of the impending arrival of South Vietnamese troops into his country? Preoccupied with these issues and busily devising "game plans" and "scenarios for every step," it was easy for Kissinger to ignore the most difficult questions: Should they be doing this? Could these military operations work?

People in the State Department were continuing to raise objections. While Rogers had proved initially compliant, the few subordinates he was permitted to inform, notably Undersecretary of State Alexis Johnson and Assistant Secretary of State Marshall Green, expressed grave doubts. Some of their objections were rooted in their broad-based disgruntlement over the Cambodian incursion and reluctance to expand the conflict even farther. They also had quite specific concerns about the survival of Laotian Premier Souvanna Phouma. Under the 1962 Geneva Agreement, Laos was to be officially neutral and foreign powers were required to desist from any military activities on its soil. Although these provisions had been violated for years by North Vietnam and the United States, a fig-leaf of "neutrality" was still in place. This had enabled Phouma to remain in power by imposing some restraints on his domestic and international adversaries. If thousands of South Vietnamese soldiers came pouring over the border, State Department officials feared it would be the death-knell for the regime.

Pressed by Johnson and Green, Rogers wrote Nixon that it was crucial to obtain Souvanna's acquiescence before proceeding with the plans for Tchepone.[30] Although the president was instinctively inclined to keep the Laotian leader in the dark until the last minute, as he had done with Lon Nol, he grudgingly yielded to this request. When Ambassador Godley informed Souvanna of the plan, Souvanna was plainly alarmed.[31] He was especially concerned about the size of the South Vietnamese forces given press reports of their bad behavior in Cambodia. If the Americans went ahead, he would have no choice but to publicly protest the presence of South Vietnamese soldiers on his country's soil.

In Washington, Souvanna Phouma's objections resonated with Alexis Johnson and Marshall Green, who were still hoping to block the planned offensive. As on previous occasions, their dissent inflamed Kissinger's anxieties about being undercut by the bureaucracy and had the perverse effect of persuading him that the operation was not only prudent but "would in effect end the war because it would totally demolish the enemy's capability."[32] For this assessment, he was relying on Admiral Moorer, who emphasized the immense value of Tchepone, which was the "control center for the three exit points from North Vietnam" through which all supplies flowed to Laos, Cambodia, and South Vietnam.[33]

Moorer gave no credence to CIA warnings about the enemy's potential strength in Laos If the North Vietnamese stood and fought, which he anticipated, "U.S. air power and fire power should inflict heavy casualties, which will be difficult to replace." The communists "lack of mobility" would enable them "to isolate the battlefield and ensure a South Vietnamese victory." As chairman of the Joint Chiefs of Staff, he could assure everyone that this was a practical plan that could achieve "decisive results," or at the very least take them safely through 1972.

As the invasion approached, Nixon became belatedly concerned. Congress had finally passed the supplemental funding he had requested. Would legislators feel betrayed by this expansion of the war into Laos? And might they react by imposing new restrictions on the administration's activities? This might occur if Souvanna Phouma denounced the South Vietnamese offensive as an "invasion" of his nation. To alleviate Souvanna's objections, the State Department instructed Ambassador Godley to meet with him and provide answers to his questions. However, in line with the irregular and deceptive way administration policy was routinely handled, General Haig sent a back-channel message to Godley, circumventing the State Department, and telling him to say whatever was necessary to gain Souvanna's acquiescence—especially on the subject of how long the South Vietnamese troops were expected to remain inside his country, which in reality was several months.[34]

This matter of truthfulness had become an ongoing source of contention between the White House and the State Department. While it was sometimes the case that Henry Kissinger told the truth and the officials in the department were willing to lie, more often than not it was the other way around. Unlike the NSC staff, which was only accountable to the president, the State Department answered to Congress, and its members were expected to provide accurate information.

This difference emerged sharply in mid-January as Secretary of State Rogers was scheduled to appear before the Senate Foreign Relations Committee to give an update on the situation in Cambodia. Rogers was acutely aware that Nixon had violated a promise he had made to Congress that once US troops exited Cambodia on June 30, his administration would take no further military steps to defend that country from communist adversaries. Any US air strikes would be for the limited purpose of preventing the enemy from threatening its troops in South Vietnam. Based on that pledge, Senate leaders who were then working on the Cooper–Church amendment had agreed to strike the ban on US air activity from the legislation.[35] However, since that time the Americans had bombed a multitude of targets in Cambodia to prevent the collapse of Lon Nol's government.

Anticipating that the committee might ask about this, Rogers thought it best to admit that US policy had changed since the time Nixon made his promise.[36] Such candor seemed especially important considering the impending offensives in which American planes would be directly supporting South Vietnamese and Cambodian troops. Otherwise, he would be quickly perceived as a liar. However, Nixon demurred on the feeble ground that the use of American air power, whether in recent months or the future, was ultimately in the service of protecting US ground troops.[37] Even Kissinger knew this to be a stretch, and that in his June 30 speech the president had given Congress and the country a much narrower sense of when US air power would be employed.

Nixon acknowledged that regardless of what Rogers did or did not say on Capitol Hill, "Congress and the country would be up in arms" once the new offensives were known. But he argued that if his administration could just take the heat in early 1971, this would give them "insurance" for next year. And if South Vietnam was to have a "chance for survival" once US troops had left, these forthcoming operations would advance that goal. Left unstated was the political motive: success in Laos, even if short-term, might avert a disaster before the 1972 election day. Bolstered by skeptics in the State Department, Rogers was unconvinced. It was already clear that the enemy had been forewarned about the forthcoming operation in Laos. And along with Helms, he was worried about the tens of thousands heavily armed North Vietnamese soldiers clustered in the area. As had been true throughout the deliberations, the assurances of the professional military carried the day. Preparations on the ground were moving quickly. During the last weekend of January 1971, 25,000 South Vietnamese ground troops had massed near the Laotian border, while 9,000 US soldiers traversed Route 9, moving from Quang Tri on the coast westward toward Laos. On their way, the Americans were busily repairing the roads, establishing firebases, setting up artillery, and restoring the airport at Khe Sanh. In preparation for ARVN's advance into Laos, the number of B-52 sorties pummeling the Ho Chi Minh Trail was accelerated. Meanwhile, in Vientiane Ambassador Godley was leaning hard on Souvanna Phouma to mute his objections.[38] These were major developments, but MACV had imposed an embargo on news reports from the area, making it difficult for either Congress or the public at large to know what was going on.

In Washington, Henry Kissinger had been operating at a furious pace, sticking close to Nixon while trying to keep everyone in the administration in line on the eve of another high-risk military campaign. However, for this weekend he had a long-standing commitment to go to Boston to meet with an organization called Project Runnymede.[39] Conceived at MIT during a protest of the Cambodian invasion, its purpose was to bring together responsible academics, businessmen, and a sprinkling of moderate students to wrestle with the complexities of the Vietnam War. For this evening, the group was appropriately eminent, including among others Jeremy Wiesner, Provost of MIT; Cyrus Vance, former Deputy Secretary of Defense; Osborn Elliott, editor of *Newsweek;* and Jeremy Stone, Executive Director of the American Federation of Scientists. A less famous attendee was a man named Daniel Ellsberg—a consultant from the RAND Corporation who had known Kissinger for many years.

In 1969, when Kissinger was beginning his tenure as National Security Advisor and had recruited Ellsberg to help set assemble the initial "options" survey on Vietnam policy, Ellsberg had dispensed some entirely unasked-for advice. "Henry, there's something I would like to tell you for what it's worth.

You are about to receive a whole slew of special clearances, maybe fifteen or twenty of them, that are higher than Top Secret." Once you become a recipient of this secret information, he said, "you will feel like a fool" because of all the things you hadn't known. Without even noticing, you will tend to start trusting only those with the same clearances and become unable to learn from anyone who lacks them:

> The danger is, you'll become something like a moron. You'll become incapable of learning from most people in the world, no matter how much experience they may have in their particular areas that may be much greater than yours.

In the intervening years, Ellsberg's prediction had come true. Both Kissinger and Nixon had become largely dependent on information generated by MACV and the Joint Chiefs of Staff. Any views to the contrary, especially when presented by the media, academic specialists, or congressional staff reports, seemed to them either naïve or malevolent, and certainly nothing they could learn from.

Addressing the distinguished audience, Kissinger spoke of the "burdens" resting on the White House, the "crisis" atmosphere that had left so little time for deep reflection. He emphasized to the group that when Nixon came into office, he inherited a situation in Vietnam that left him "no good choices."[40] Unilateral withdrawal was not an option, because it would have provoked a huge right-wing reaction, in which the victors would have been the hardhats, not the liberals. In fact, the Nixon administration had been the "best protection of those who most loudly deplore our policy." Despite all the claims to the contrary, President Nixon was winding down the war and bringing it to an end.

Following these brief remarks were scattered questions from the audience, some friendly, others vague. But Daniel Ellsberg had a more specific question: had the administration prepared any estimates of the number of Indochinese dead and wounded, including civilians, that would result from another year of war? Could Kissinger provide them with some numbers?

Recognizing the speaker, Kissinger halted for a moment and then replied, "That is a very clever question . . . I answer even if I don't answer." Ellsberg interrupted to say that he was not intending to be clever, he was simply asking a basic question: Did Kissinger have such an estimate? Kissinger suggested that Ellsberg was accusing the White House of a racist policy. Race wasn't the issue, Ellsberg insisted; he just wanted to know "how many human beings we will kill under your policy."

This was indeed a "clever" question because the consultant already knew that the administration had no desire to know how many Indochinese people would be killed, especially if they were civilians. However, Kissinger could not simply say to this esteemed audience that they had no interest in gathering such data. He strategically deflected the issue, pressing Ellsberg to offer an alternative policy. The latter tartly replied, "I know the language of alternatives and options very well and it has nothing to do with the question. . . . Do you have an estimate or not?" Suddenly the genteel mood and amiable character of the gathering began to dissipate. The student moderator quickly proposed refreshments and ended the program.

Once back in Washington, Kissinger provided a detailed description of the event to Nixon. He especially noted "the bitter and vindictive questioning" of Daniel Ellsberg.

Unbeknownst to the luminaries at Runnymede and to the veterans gathered that same weekend in the Howard Johnson Motel in Detroit, Laotian Premier Souvanna Phouma had just granted Ambassador Godley his reluctant consent to the presence of South Vietnamese troops in his country.[41] With that acquiescence, a new operation was about to unfold. It was to be called Lam Son 719, and it would be one of the largest allied offensives of the entire war. Soon more Americans would be killed there, and of course many more South Vietnamese and Laotians, civilians as well as soldiers. The possible numbers of these deaths would not have been considered by the planners of the invasion, as Daniel Ellsberg well knew.

14
"Take a Stinking Hill"

Still traumatized by the domestic furor caused by the invasion of Cambodia, the White House was determined to avoid a similar response to the invasion of Laos. Though some criticism was unavoidable, Nixon and Kissinger intended to minimize its impact by exercising tighter control over the news media.[1] As Phase I of the operation was set in motion on January 29, with South Vietnamese and American troops closing in on Vietnam's border with Laos, US military headquarters in Saigon slapped an embargo on journalists. Reporters were prohibited from publishing their stories until the ban was lifted. The seriousness of this became clear the next day, when three news organizations, including the *Washington Post,* were informed they were in violation of the policy, and that future violations by them or others could result in a loss of their military accreditation. Taking the ban to preposterous lengths, the military also embargoed the embargo by forbidding news outlets from informing their readers that censorship had been imposed.

By the time the embargo was lifted one week later, thousands of South Vietnamese troops were 48 hours away from invading Laos. Although the news blackout was theoretically designed to save the lives of American soldiers, reporters were appropriately skeptical. There was nothing stealthy about these early troop movements. American and South Vietnamese soldiers were traveling along Route 9, a major road plainly visible to the local inhabitants, some of whom were affiliated with the National Liberation Front. Hanoi had no doubt where these troops might be going and was already protesting the imminent attack in Laos.[2]

The only people kept in the dark were the Americans back home. They could read speculation about the impending mission in the foreign press if they had access, but not in their own media. The most tangible effect of this censorship was the short-circuiting of public debate over the wisdom of invading Laos. By the time the invasion was open for discussion, it was already too late. After the embargo was finally lifted on February 5, a *Washington Post* editorial complained, "when the subject at hand is what the United States government is up to in Vietnam and the result is very nearly a total breakdown of the power to communicate . . . it begins to approach a crisis in the capacity to govern in a free society."[3]

Once the first increment of South Vietnamese troops crossed the border into Laos on February 8, the official briefings in Saigon—always a dubious enterprise—contained even less information than usual. Whereas in previous years reporters had been allowed to travel to battlefields, under instruction from the White House the military banned their presence on American planes flying into Laos. One intrepid NBC reporter managed to get a ride anyway, only to have his movie camera flung out the door by a crewman acting on orders. For its part, the Saigon government needed little urging from Washington to limit media access. On the very first day of the invasion, reporters expecting to follow ARVN were stopped at the border by armed military police, who forced them to turn around. In subsequent days a few prevailed upon South Vietnamese pilots to take them along, despite concerns about the pilots' inexperience.[4]

One of the angriest journalists was the normally staid columnist James Reston of the *New York Times.* For years Reston had defended the American commitment in South Vietnam. Even when many of his colleagues became disillusioned, Reston had vacillated, finding good reasons on both sides of the case. Until Cambodia, much of his ire was directed against student protestors, whose excesses he found offensive. Yet in the aftermath of that adventure, he saw the new restrictions on journalists as a dangerous assault on democracy. With deep divisions in the country, "it ought to be possible to agree on getting the facts." Unfortunately, "the Administration's record is a disgrace," he wrote in a column a few days after the launch of the Laotian campaign.[5] If the White House believed it necessary to bomb a path for the South Vietnamese in Laos, "why not let the reporters go along as before to record the facts as best they can?" The answer, he speculated, was that routing out the enemy through the saturation bombing of a small, pacific country was such a "ghastly business," so cruel in its effects that "they don't want the facts recorded any more than they can help."

From the outset, the South Vietnamese advance into Laos was mired in trouble. The name of the operation was Lam Son 719—a reference to the birthplace of one of Vietnam's great national heroes Le Loi, who had defeated a Chinese army in the 15th century. In the 20th century, the first increment of troops did not immediately receive the help they expected. Reinforcements on the ground were slow to arrive, and airplane traffic was erratic due to heavy fog and rain. Denied access to Laos, reporters who were pursuing the story just south of the DMZ were nonetheless able to see for themselves how muddy roads were inhibiting the movement of soldiers, and they heard from the pilots that many flights had to be canceled.

Disturbed by these accounts, Kissinger raised the topic with the chairman of the Joint Chiefs of Staff, who assured him there was no reason for concern.[6] Moorer stoutly insisted that it never rained in "the operational area" at this time of year. Perhaps there was some difficulty with visibility near Khe Sanh airport at sunrise and sunset, but planes were flying as usual. So was there really no rain, Kissinger pressed? Moorer conceded there was some rain, but not in the operations area. "Everything is on schedule."

By day three of Lam Son 719, the media was still reporting on military delays and poor weather.[7] Absurdly, the Washington Special Action Group could not obtain a straight answer about the rain. Fortunately, whatever obstacles of nature the South Vietnamese were encountering they had so far met little resistance from North Vietnamese troops in Laos. Yet there were 19,000 enemy soldiers in the area, with another 3,500 set to arrive. "This doesn't worry us?" Kissinger asked. General Abrams was confident, Moorer replied. Although there was the equivalent of a North Vietnamese division just north of Route 9, CIA Director Helms maintained this was good news because "we want to give them a good pasting." B-52s were already bombing the area and would continue to do so.

As was the case during the many weeks that Lam Son 719 was being planned, the atmosphere of these high-level meetings discouraged negative thinking. Throughout their advance deliberations, the chairman of the Joint Chiefs of Staff had consistently minimized concerns about the superior number of enemy troops that could be brought into action. While Moorer's reasons for optimism varied, they usually rested on some comforting news from Abrams. Yet Abrams himself was more of a skeptic than Moorer—more mindful of ARVN's limitations and the strength of their adversaries.

During the planning stage, CIA Director Helms was in possession of staff reports that emphasized how dangerous the North Vietnamese were likely to be in their well- entrenched Laotian bases.[8] But he had chosen to downplay these findings when faced with an obvious White House preference. Nevertheless, there were sufficient warning signs that would have become more visible had either Nixon or Kissinger been inclined to probe. As with previous initiatives, their joint desire for good news and exaggerated confidence in the military trumped their curiosity.

With Lam Son 719 underway, Nixon's determination to stifle negative publicity was contributing to the administration's mistakes. Moorer was still under orders from the president to keep correspondents off military helicopters:

> We should clamp down on it slowly so that it does not become too obvious. The President feels we cannot gain anything by having a bunch of reporters running loose in the battle zone, sending back all these gory pictures of people being wounded.[9]

By trying to limit the flow of information from the field, Nixon and Kissinger had effectively blindsided themselves. During these critical first weeks, with no journalists on the ground in Laos to offer independent assessments and a military hierarchy under great pressure to inflate positive developments, the White House had severely compromised its own ability to obtain reliable intelligence.

Of course, some worrisome information was getting through. Reporters were learning from American pilots, who were flying back and forth into Laos, that they were encountering unusually intense anti-aircraft firing. For many, these were the most dangerous flying conditions they had ever encountered, and they were arriving back at base dazed and frightened, having sustained multiple attacks. "Every time we've gone out, we've had our aircraft shot to hell," said one. "We've told the Vietnamese to stay out of there."[10] These were the survivors. But every day more planes went down with resulting casualties. The pilots also told the journalists how slowly ARVN was moving toward Tchepone, which was supposed to be their target destination.

On edge, Nixon and Kissinger sought a direct report from General Abrams. The general acknowledged that ARVN's advance was slower than expected.[11] This was due to the fact that before proceeding to Tchepone, Lt. General Hoang Xuan Lam, the commander of the ARVN forces, "considered it prudent to insure adequate flank security" and to secure his lines of communication "against the contingencies of prolonged bad weather and enemy interdiction." Abrams acknowledged that Lam was taking "a somewhat more deliberate approach to the attack . . . than was visualized in our initial concept." Still, he felt that to this point ARVN had been performing well. While the battles it had engaged in were relatively small, it had achieved a "kill ratio" of ten to one. Once the South Vietnamese occupied Tchepone, which might take another eight to ten days, they would be in a position to disrupt the enemy's "entire logistical structure."

Reading between the lines, Kissinger and Nixon might have discerned that "somewhat more deliberate" was a euphemism and that the American general was having difficulty with his South Vietnamese counterparts, who were being more cautious than promised. While perhaps not alarming in itself, this development was so reminiscent of the long of history of ARVN failing to deliver on its commitments that it might have signaled serious trouble ahead.

On February 16 Nixon convened a cabinet meeting at which he and Laird presented a blandly optimistic account. Regarding Lam Son 719, "all planned objectives are being accomplished on schedule," Laird assured the group. There would, however, be tough days ahead combatting the North Vietnamese, "The South Vietnamese will not win all of the battles, but they will win most." There was also good news from Cambodia, where the South Vietnamese offensive near the Chup plantation was accomplishing its goals. "From the U.S. standpoint . . . the war is winding down," he announced. Whether or not Laird really believed it, his conclusion was predictable: success in Laos was "making possible further withdrawals of U.S. troops and protecting the lives of the Americans who remain." There was also the "side benefit" that they were giving the Cambodians additional time to build up their own military.

An apparent convert was Rogers, who was fulsome in his praise of Lam Son 719 as "one of the best coordinated planned operations he had ever seen in Washington." How impressive was the president, he flattered, who had to be so involved "briefing the leaders, coordinating diplomacy, dealing with Congress." True, 25 helicopters had been lost, but they had been losing six every day before that. With a concrete goal in mind, if Lam Son 719 accomplished its purpose, "it will be a major blow." Nixon himself could not resist a little preening to the group. He understood that people had raised questions about Laos. After all, three-quarters of this cabinet had reservations about Cambodia—"another tough decision." But "if we hadn't done Cambodia, the South Vietnamese would not have been able to do Laos." All things considered, Lam Son 719 was "a spectacular success," and it had been done "with strong opposition politically, especially in the Senate and with almost no support from the establishment."

Regarding Vietnam, the president had long since abandoned any notion of candor with his cabinet. These sessions were more performance than discussion, conducted with the hope that some good news would leak. Yet Nixon was more worried than he was willing to admit. He knew that Laird was getting "jumpy." For the moment, he and Kissinger were in a charitable mood, appreciating Laird's willingness to go to bat for them on Laos. Kissinger reflected, "when the chips are really down, he's amazing and he's also loyal to you." Laird was a "rascal" replied Nixon, "but by golly he's our rascal." And on Lam Son 719, "thank God we're not going to lose it." They could lose an election, "but we're not going to lose this war, Henry. . . . Do you agree?"

It was a peculiar question this late in the game, but it was expressive of the uncertainty behind Nixon's bravado. With so much bombing, it would be difficult for the North Vietnamese to carry on, Kissinger predicted. There would certainly be some rough days ahead for their own side, even "panicky moments," but if they could remain in Laos until the end of the dry season they could "chew up" the enemy. This would prevent the North Vietnamese from launching any major offensive through the spring of 1972, and might even yield that ever elusive peace agreement.

But what might happen afterward? Nixon hoped they would "fight well" in Cambodia and Laos because he expected that there to be fighting in South Vietnam for many years to come. "If they fight well, North Vietnam can never beat South Vietnam." But what if they didn't? Nixon could not stop returning to the question of what would happen "if we get knocked out of Laos."

KISSINGER: But we won't get knocked out of Laos . . .

NIXON: . . . The South Vietnamese are going to fight. They're going to stand and fight. Aren't they?

KISSINGER: . . . So far they have. They are right now moving cautiously to reconnect, so that they can cover each other with artillery. That's fine. We don't care as long as they've got the roads cut. But I think we can win in '72. Those guys won't be able to stand 4 years in the wilderness.

"The important thing," said Nixon, "is to see this miserable thing through."

The warfare was "miserable," although perhaps not in the way that the president was thinking. Recent developments included the accidental bombing by American planes of the CIA base in northern Laos. For 10 years their installation at Long Tieng had been the home of General Vang Pao's army of Hmong tribesmen. The base had narrowly escaped capture by the Pathet Lao during the previous dry season but had been "rescued" by a combination of American bombs and Thai battalions. When it had come under attack again as the rains began to dry, American bombers tried to rescue it once more. But this time they had missed their target and accidentally hit the base itself.[12] The civilian death toll from the attack was pegged at 30, while more than 200 other civilians were wounded, many quite seriously.[13] Making matters even more "miserable," this error came only one week after US aircraft had mistakenly dropped cluster bombs on South Vietnamese troops gathered on the Laotian border.[14]

All of this was occurring in a context where American B-52s and tactical aircraft were carrying out thousands of bombing raids on Laos: in the Panhandle in the south, and the Plain of Jars in the north. Even from afar, some in the media knew enough about what was happening to be sickened by it. In a blistering editorial, the *New York Times* observed that Laotians, "like their neighbors in Vietnam have had long and bitter experience of American bombing." In recent years, hundreds of thousands had been "driven from their homes and untold numbers of civilians have been killed and maimed as a result of the extensive use of American airpower against the North Vietnamese in northeastern Laos." Now this was happening in the Panhandle, where "because of their scope, their power and their lack of precision, the air attacks inevitably do inflict harm and hardship on friend as well as foe."[15] In the White House none of this mattered. It was enough to know that in the long run everyone would benefit when the communists were defeated. But would this happen?

From the outset, an underlying weakness of their military plan was the unfavorable ratio that could rapidly exist between the soldiers of North Vietnam and those from the South. While the CIA had estimated a total of 11,000 North Vietnamese combat troops in the vicinity of Tchepone, they also claimed there were nine regiments of approximately 70,000 North Vietnamese soldiers in an adjacent area.[16] How could the 20,000 South Vietnamese prevail if Hanoi chose to dispatch those additional divisions to Tchepone? Whenever this topic had arisen during their planning sessions, Admiral Moorer had been quick to dismiss it. The North Vietnamese troops lacked mobility, he had claimed. And if large numbers were massed in one place, the United States could decimate them from the air.

Why was such wishful thinking so readily accepted? In microcosm, the planning for Lam Son 719 was recapitulating the tragic dynamics of the war itself: a restless military wanting to win, a civilian leadership too impressed by their expertise, and both entities compromised by the damage already done and needing vindication. By the winter of 1970–71 none of the principals—not Nixon, not the Joint Chiefs of Staff, not MACV—was capable of an objective evaluation of plans. Too many Americans had already died on their watch, too many assurances had already been given. The need to salvage something positive from the carnage disposed them to further risk-taking, especially when it was mainly Asians who would pay the price.

During the first two weeks of Lam Son 719 there was some reason for optimism, as ARVN had encountered surprisingly little opposition from the enemy. However, by February 19, North Vietnamese troops had surrounded the 39th Ranger Battalion, one of South Vietnam's elite fighting units, near the northern end of its military thrust.[17] The combination of poor weather and anti-aircraft fire turned deadly, making it impossible for supplies or reinforcements to come through by air. This attack on the Rangers opened a new phase in the fighting as North Vietnamese troops blasted the advancing formations with rockets and mortars. By February 20, it was apparent that the South Vietnamese advance had stalled and, more ominously, three North Vietnamese regiments were being moved into the area.[18]

On February 22, Abrams met with President Thieu and General Cao Van Vien to address the apparent stalemate. The original plan had called for South Vietnamese troops to march into Tchepone, while additional units would be flown in by air. Thieu was proposing to step up the arrival of the airborne units but was offering no clear date for when the infantry might arrive.

He was also intimating another significant change from their previous understanding that once in Tchepone, ARVN would need to stay there for an extended period. This site had been identified as the crossroads through which men and supplies were routed into three different South Vietnamese and Cambodian locations, making it the ideal place to maintain troops. However, in his conversation with Abrams, Thieu claimed the communists were planning a major attack in the northern provinces of South Vietnam, which meant that he might need to bring his troops back home. Therefore, once in Tchepone, his men would clean out the area and then withdraw.

For the moment, nobody shared this startling information with Nixon. Regardless, he was increasingly upset by what he was reading in the press, which differed so markedly from the bland twice-a-day updates from the Pentagon. To get a clearer picture he phoned Admiral Moorer, who was still upbeat.[19] The plan, said Moorer, "was to jump off into Tchepone" during the next two or three days, with two South Vietnamese brigades. Things had admittedly been slow, because it had taken awhile for ARVN to establish their logistics and support bases. However, once they arrived in Tchepone, "things will start to really move."

Nixon said he was counting on the South Vietnamese to remain in Laos for at least another month. Moorer predicted they would stay even longer. The South Vietnamese leadership was very determined, and "they recognized they are going to have more casualties and they are willing to take them." At Christmas time, they had indicated a willingness to lose over 1,000 men in this effort, and so far they were not even close to that number.

As he listened, Nixon swung back and forth between his anxiety that the military was concealing things by painting too rosy a picture and his belief that the media was up to its usual tricks of painting everything black. Not to worry, Moorer reassured him. The South Vietnamese had 10,000 additional troops they had not yet inserted into the battlefield. And he had observed for himself "their enthusiasm and drive." At this juncture, Nixon was finding inspiration in Carl Sandburg's biography of Abraham Lincoln as a wartime leader, perceiving a similarity between Abrams' situation and that of General Grant during the Wilderness campaign. In that blood-drenched effort, Grant had lost twice as many men as Lee but still managed to win the war. And that's what mattered for Lincoln's subsequent reputation.

Yet the news from Laos was getting steadily worse. Much of it centered on the fate of the 39th Ranger battalion, which had been flown in by helicopter to a blocking position just north of the advancing troops. After days of heavy fighting, they were driven off the hilltop base they were defending. Casualties from this encounter were horrific, with an estimated 298 men dead out of a total of 450 and another 100 or more wounded.[20] As helicopters brought out the injured fighters, newsmen were picking up the story and hearing as well about the intense anti-aircraft fire that was making these evacuations so dangerous.

Henry Kamm of the *New York Times* managed to get himself into Laos, where he was able to observe first-hand a well-kept road on the Ho Chi Minh Trail.[21] This confirmed what he had heard from American pilots in Danang, who had described "the speed and daring" of the North Vietnamese in keeping these roads in good repair despite repeated aerial attacks. Even more alarming, from the American perspective, was the report of a dramatic increase in the volume of supplies from North Vietnam getting through to the South since the inception of Lam Son 719. While ARVN had managed to cut off the trail in several places, the enemy had simply moved its operation westward and was accelerating the deliveries.

The White House demanded to know why all this negative information was getting into the media. And who was responsible for the leaks?

"The President is having conniptions about TV reports last night and this morning," Kisssinger admonished Laird in an 8:00 AM phone call.[22] The news outlets were claiming that it was the Defense and State Departments that had told them that "the operations are stalled, the roads aren't cut and the White House is putting an optimistic gloss on it all."

"We have got to make people shut up," Kissinger instructed Laird, who denied that the leaks were originating in the Pentagon and blamed the State Department. Laird also opined that the problem was that there were too many briefings—as many as six just in the past 24 hours, including one at his department, one in State, two in the White House, another in Saigon, and one in MR-1, and that they contradicted each other.[23] No wonder the press was having a field day.

However Laird, like Nixon and Kissinger, was sidestepping the real issue: the news from the field was bad because the campaign was going poorly. None of them appreciated the degree to which the administration's ham-fisted effort to control the press had antagonized the reporters. Kissinger got an earful from James Reston, who complained that here you had "an invasion of a sovereign country and not a word from the president on it."[24] There was nothing very new about this, the national security advisor insisted: "We are not doing a hell of a lot more than we have done before." If so, it was secret. It was simply "outrageous," Reston continued, that the White House was expecting US soldiers to fight while it was unwilling to clarify the mission for the public.

During the last week of February, the administration altered its approach to the news media.[25] The new instructions called for members of the press corps to be transported in US. military planes going into Laos. They would be allowed on helicopters "under controlled conditions" in order to view the positive achievements of Lam Son operations and would also be accommodated on AC-10 gunships, which were shooting up traffic on the Ho Chi Minh Trail. These experiences were intended to give them a greater appreciation of what was being accomplished.

However, what was not getting accomplished was the real news. By late February ARVN was effectively stalled at approximately 17 miles north of the Laotian border—halfway to Tchepone. The Ho Chi Minh Trail had been greatly expanded during the previous six months and consisted of hundreds of miles of looping roads and paths. Some of these had just been severed by the South Vietnamese troops, but Saigon's soldiers could not significantly reduce the flow of men and material into South Vietnam and Cambodia unless they advanced further north and west to Tchepone, and unless they remained there through the dry season, which had been the plan at the beginning. Yet the prospect of this occurring was diminished in the face of fierce enemy resistance.

On February 25, Nixon and Kissinger met with Admiral Moorer to review the overall situation in Laos. The original plan for Lam Son 719 was that once across the Laotian border, the South Vietnamese troops would take a maximum of five days to reach Tchepone. Yet already two weeks had elapsed, and Moorer thought the attack would take several additional days. Despite everything he was continuing to express optimism, while admitting that General Lam was a "cautious performer." As for the fate of the 39th Ranger battalion, although it had unfortunately attracted considerable press attention in the United States, what reporters had failed to appreciate was "the discipline with which the ARVN handled the operation and the fact that four observers had counted more than 600 enemy bodies."

The president assured Moorer that he was prepared for setbacks and that the most important thing was for ARVN to fight well. The chairman of the Joint Chiefs of Staff wanted Nixon to understand what these South Vietnamese troops were up against. At present there were at least 28,000 enemy forces in the immediate area, organized into 12 or 13 regiments. But the good news was that in order to insert so many of its soldiers into Laos, Hanoi had been compelled to strip its forces along the DMZ to approximately 8,000 men, leaving only three regiments to repel any incursion across the border into North Vietnam.

Unfortunately for the White House, the bad tidings kept rolling in. By February 27 the dreadful rout of the South Vietnamese 39th Ranger battalion had been replaced in the news by the siege of Hill 31, where an estimated 500 South Vietnamese paratroopers were fighting off enemy tanks and infantry.[26] American planes bombed the attackers but could not prevent the North Vietnamese troops from overrunning the firebase.

Meeting once more with Moorer, Nixon demanded an explanation. The admiral replied that fighting was still going on at Hill 31 and that the enemy had sustained large casualties, perhaps 450 soldiers dead.[27] He was also encouraged by the news that despite heavy losses, "the South Vietnamese are staying there and fighting." The president recognized they needed something more to impress the public. If only "the South Vietnamese could just win one cheap one, just a cheap one . . . . Take a stinking hill. Carefully bring back a prisoner or two," something they could brag about.[28]

For now, the Laotian adventure was a public relations disaster. At least 30 American planes had been shot down, and every day the bodies from Lam Son 719 were piling up. At Khe Sanh, which had become a hub for the operation, helicopters were regularly disgorging their supply of corpses and wounded men.[29] As described by reporter Gloria Emerson, there was a "small dismal scene" reenacted daily, as the orderlies removed the gruesome cargo from the choppers. Lacking adequate stretchers, they sometimes carried the wounded over their shoulders. At the makeshift field hospital, which was short on anesthesia and qualified medical staff, injured Vietnamese lay on cots unattended for hours.

A veteran reporter, Emerson preferred to focus on individual stories such as Pvt. Tran Van Gu, a Ranger with the 21st Battalion whose head was covered with bandages. In emotional detail, Tran related how the North Vietnamese, who had surrounded his hill, had sustained three waves of B-52 bombers but managed to hold on through the night and to keep attacking. These were terrifying fighters. They were people who "don't fear air strikes or artillery." There is no way we can fight them in Laos, he told the journalist. For confirmation of his experience, Emerson needed to look no further than the nearest cot. As she was learning, across the Laotian panhandle the South Vietnamese were facing the most frightening enemy force they had ever encountered, and they were discovering with each passing day there was "no cheap way to take a stinking hill," or even to hold the ones they occupied.

Back on Capitol Hill there was a growing perception that more than the usual dishonesty was emanating from the White House, as the realization dawned that Lam Son 719 was in fact a major operation. More to the point, it was heavily reliant on substantial assistance from American air power. Just as it had minimized the invasion when it was launched, the Nixon administration seemed bent on concealing its negative consequences. The provocation was sufficiently serious that some "middle of the road" senators began drafting new antiwar amendments.

James Reston, who was already furious with the White House over its manipulation of the press, was getting even angrier. For reporters assigned to Vietnam, fury was a familiar emotion, but Reston had always been a restrained "fence-sitter." Lam Son 719 struck a nerve. This had less to do with the long-suffering Vietnamese or Laotians than with his concern about American democracy and the erosion of its political institutions, embodied in this arguably illegal invasion.

So influential was James Reston that he had ready access to the White House and felt empowered to speak his mind. On the phone with Kissinger he deplored the absence of candor. The problem is, "We are being tricked. There is not an honest debate between you and the critics of your policy. Not at all."[30] Kissinger demurred. There was nobody who had spent more time meeting with students and other outside groups to discuss the administration's policy. That begged the "central question," Reston maintained, which was the issue of deceit. "This town is riddled with distrust," which even in Johnson's time was not so profound.

Yet the White House itself was being tricked—although arguably by invitation. For two years Nixon and Kissinger had relied on the words of Ambassador Bunker and the leadership of MACV, all but ignoring any other input. But the gap between their rosy assessments and reality was becoming ever greater and impossible to ignore. If Thieu's military was as strong and confident as they described, why had it been frozen in place for two weeks? The history of ARVN, willfully ignored, might have provided some clues.

On March 1 Kissinger sent an urgent personal message to Bunker on an "eyes only basis," listing questions he wanted the ambassador to discuss with General Abrams.[31] He reminded the Bunker that the cornerstone of the administration's policy in Vietnam was their expectation that as US troops withdrew, the army of South Vietnam could take over. The president's support for Lam Son 719 had been specifically premised on the belief that by going into Laos, the army of South Vietnam would be able to impede offensive operations by the North Vietnamese "during this dry season and the next as well." But he was "beginning to wonder what if anything has been achieved in this regard."

Citing the numerous modifications to the original plan, each accompanied by new promises, Kissinger noted that these were largely unfulfilled. In fact, it had become clear that South Vietnam was committing only a small fraction of its available manpower to what was intended to be a major thrust. If consequently these forces should be overrun, it would completely undercut domestic support in the United States for continuing the war. The national security advisor had complete confidence in General Abrams and was fully appreciative of his difficulties in prodding ARVN to undertake operations, which they might not wish to conduct:

> But we can accomplish nothing unless we face facts. You know what we are up against here. We have just seen the tip of the iceberg in this respect.

> We will do our best to hold the fort. But we must know what we are up against. There is no chance to keep panic from setting in if we are constantly outstripped by events.

In eliciting information from General Abrams to be relayed to Washington, Kissinger urged Bunker to bypass military channels. The unstated reason, which the ambassador would readily understand, was to keep Secretary of Defense Laird out of the loop.

Bunker's response, vetted by Abrams, was upbeat. Of course things were tough, because they were going after the enemy's jugular.[32] Yes, there had been some modifications of the original plan because of bad weather, poor roads, and problematic terrain. But the South Vietnamese were fighting well, while the North Vietnamese were sustaining painful losses of men and materiel. Roads were being cut, and more would be severed in the future. Things seemed worse than they were because members of the press had falsely assumed that Tchepone was the target. But steps were underway to correct that misimpression. For the moment, Kissinger and Nixon seemed to accept these assurances, despite some obvious falsehoods—including the suggestion that Tchepone was not the target of the South Vietnamese operation.[33]

Finally there was good news on March 6, when 2,000 troops from the South Vietnamese First Infantry Division came marching into Tchepone.[34] Most had been helicoptered into nearby locations by the Americans and had traveled by foot only a short distance. However, reinforcements were expected shortly, and Abrams anticipated being able to cut all the roads around Tchepone within the next few days.

In one of his characteristic mood swings, Kissinger concluded that Laos was going to be even more successful than Cambodia. He had just spoken with a briefer that very morning—"a tough combat type" cut from the same mold as Haig—who said there was "no way we can lose it." Also encouraging was the reawakening of General Abrams, who was "now going like the Abrams of Cambodia," whereas for a while "it looked like he was shell-shocked." Members of the press, who had eagerly lapped up every sign of failure, would need to reassess. The situation on the ground was so auspicious that he thought the North Vietnamese might seek a peace agreement during the summer. The exciting news in any case was that ARVN was finally on the move, with the prospect of dramatically reducing the fighting capacity of the enemy.

Except this was not exactly the case. Just as the White House was congratulating itself on the merits of Lam Son 719, its hopes were betrayed. While President Thieu was prepared to mollify his American allies with a symbolic entry of South Vietnamese troops into Tchepone, he was not willing for them to face the full wrath of the North Vietnamese adversary, whose numbers were steadily increasing in the hills around the town.[35] Back in Saigon there was mounting discontent with the lengthening list of casualties, including at least 70 soldiers who were killed or wounded when an American fighter-bomber accidentally dropped napalm on their firebase. There was concern as well that in order to carry on the fight in Laos and Cambodia, too many experienced South Vietnamese troops were being dispatched outside the country for too long a time.[36] Whether their rapid removal was his secret intention all along or something he belatedly decided, within three days of their arrival Thieu opted to remove the South Vietnamese troops from Tchepone and rapidly terminate the entire Laotian operation.

Kissinger was horrified by this unexpected reversal. Cabling Bunker, he instructed the ambassador to see Thieu immediately and put pressure on him to keep his troops in Laos until the arrival of the rainy season, well into April as the plans had called for.[37] From the White House perspective, "every week ARVN stays in Laos represents a serious blow to the enemy's offensive capability, not only for this dry season but more importantly for the next."

Until this point, General Abrams had stoutly defended both the competence and determination of the South Vietnamese. While Thieu's sudden shift was a personal embarrassment, he did not regard the decision as set in stone. With "a good kick in the ass," Thieu might be persuaded to hang on longer.[38] Kissinger was eager to oblige. "We haven't gone through all of this agony to have it end now," he observed. Anyway, "they can't get out without our airlift," he added maliciously.

But Thieu was not easily dissuaded from abandoning Tchepone and the surrounding area. In less than a week his troops were moving south.[39] As they struggled with their disappointment, Nixon and Kissinger were on the horns of a dilemma.[40] They believed this was the last opportunity ARVN would have to launch a full-scale offensive with significant support from the United States. So should they push Thieu harder? Clearly the South Vietnamese were pulling back out of a genuine fear of the North Vietnamese regiments concentrated in or around the Laotian panhandle. What if their apprehensions turned out to be justified, and pressure from Washington led to the troops staying and then being mowed down? This would mortally wound Thieu politically and perhaps fatally compromise the entire Vietnam project in the eyes of the world.

Since the Cambodian incursion, Nixon had allowed himself to believe that the years of American training and money had finally yielded a high-functioning ARVN. These events shook him. "We've got to get the hell out of there. That's for sure," he told Kissinger and Haldeman.[41] US troops would have to leave the country. No more draftees should have to fight. And as for "the poor bastards" who had volunteered for the military because they feared the draft, he hoped to limit their combat role.

Meanwhile, following their precipitous withdrawal from Tchepone, the South Vietnamese troops headed for firebases east and south of the town.[42] While some units fought tenaciously, others beat a hasty retreat, abandoning weapons and supplies. These developments did not prevent the Saigon propaganda machine from heaping praise on its army and insisting that all of the important aims of Lam Son 719 had been fulfilled.[43]

Incredibly, back in Washington, Moorer was still sugar-coating the news, assuring Kissinger that the Lam Son plan was "being handled all right."[44] He was confident that the South Vietnamese were going to remain in Laos "through the full extent of the dry season." Would they be "fighting or horsing around?" Kissinger inquired acidly. They would be fighting, Moorer assured him. There was a plan to head south into Base Area 611, where an intense battle would undoubtedly occur. "Everyone is itching to go."

This whitewashing of the truth was not unique to Moorer. Having swallowed the bitter pill of ARVN's retreat from Tchepone, General Abrams and Admiral McCain were again lauding the accomplishments of Lam Son 719 and reaffirming Saigon's determination to extend the battle. Abrams insisted that the South Vietnamese had inflicted massive damage on enemy soldiers and their logistical system, which would have a major impact on their strategic plans going forward.[45] Admiral McCain, who was perhaps the earliest and most gung-ho supporter of the operation, was even more enthusiastic, maintaining "enemy losses indicate that attainment of his objectives becomes increasingly remote, as success of the South Vietnamese forces is assured."

By mid-March there was so much contradictory information that Nixon and Kissinger were not sure whom to believe. The uncertainty was partly their own creation, the long-term effect of pressuring the military to emphasize success and bury problems. To get to the bottom of things, they decided to send Alexander Haig as their emissary to Saigon. Other than Kissinger himself, there was nobody whose views on the war carried so much weight. Yet quite often Haig was not simply speaking for himself, but was reflecting MACV on matters of policy.

Haig arrived in Saigon on March 16 against a backdrop of embarrassing stories about ARVN's loss of several firebases—none of which were reflected in the enthusiastic account he received from Ambassador Bunker about South Vietnam's stellar performance. Bunker further maintained that President Thieu was "determined to see the Laos operation through" and was expecting it to last until the end of April.

On the ground the situation was deteriorating hourly—or so it appeared to anyone watching American television or reading the major newspapers. This was beginning to look like the rout of the South Vietnamese Army. Kissinger and the president were alternately furious at the media for distorting events and angry at their South Vietnamese allies for cowardice. On March 17, Kissinger cabled General Haig:

> URGENTLY NEED YOUR ASSESSMENT OF LAMSON SITUATION . . .
> IN AS MUCH DETAIL AS POSSIBLE. NEWS REPORTS HERE ARE GLOOMY AND LOUD. RESULT IS PREDICTABLE WIDESPREAD NERVOUSNESS.[46]

While waiting to hear from Haig, it became clear that despite White House pressure on the Thieu, South Vietnamese soldiers, under orders from their officers, were abandoning the firebases near Tchepone in droves. American pilots were trying to conduct an orderly evacuation, as desperate men could be seen clinging to the skids of the helicopters. Photographs and films of the chaos were flashed around the world, conveying a sense of utter panic. A ludicrously inappropriate press release from the Defense Department explained that the South Vietnamese were engaged in "mobile maneuvering" and that the evacuation was "proceeding according to plan."[47]

For Kisssinger and Nixon, March 18 was "the moment of truth"—or as close to any "truth" as they could manage. Their own military was still producing bland assurances, not just to the press but to them. For once, Kissinger wasn't having it. In a phone call with Admiral Moorer, he complained bitterly about Thieu's duplicity, which was putting them in a terrible situation politically.[48] Thieu had claimed to be rotating his troops, with new units coming into Laos as others went out. There were no new units. South Vietnamese troops were also not going into Base Area 914 as had been promised.

If only the Saigon government had been candid. Had they "told us a week ago they were doing this," Kissinger lamented, "then we could have claimed a victory." Of course, he went on, "we control the helicopters," intimating they might strand the South Vietnamese in Laos. Taking this facetious threat seriously, Moorer panicked: "We can't just leave them in there." Kissinger had no such intent, but as news kept arriving about ARVN's retreat, he cabled Ambassador Bunker expressing his frustration: "It would be hard to exaggerate the mystification and confusion caused here by ARVN's latest scheme of maneuver which envisages a rapid pullout from Laos."[49] It was frankly "intolerable to have the President vulnerable to constant changes of plans which are unilaterally implemented."

March 18 was also the day Kissinger got definitive word from General Haig that the operation was a fiasco. During his visit Haig had realized "that ARVN's enthusiasm for continuation of Lam Son 719 is completely lacking."[50] The South Vietnamese troops were in grave danger, threatened as they were by no fewer than five North Vietnamese regiments. The problem was no longer to convince them to stay but to get them to pull out "in an orderly way." For all practical purposes, Lam Son 719 was over.

Over the course of three days, Haig had grasped the futility of further efforts to generate a more aggressive approach by the South Vietnamese. He realized that to put further pressure on Saigon "risks not only rupturing . . . the kind of intimate coordination needed to assure an orderly displacement," it could also cause a severe fracture of US–Saigon relations. He very much regretted having to transmit such discouraging news to Washington, but he was convinced "this frank appraisal is essential for you to have."

Haig had sent his assessment directly to the White House, bypassing MACV as well as the Joint Chiefs of Staff. Unaware of Haig's blunt message, Moorer was continuing to relay cheerful messages from Abrams, including the news that the Thieu government had "a solid plan" for Laos.[51] "They had solid plans for six weeks and not executed one," Kissinger replied acidly. By misrepresenting their intentions to the Nixon administration, "they have us babbling all the wrong things." To this point not a single one of their plans had stuck, not even for a week.

Despite his irritation, the national security advisor was still handling Moorer with kid gloves and remained protective of Ambassador Bunker. Throughout his tenure Bunker had functioned as an echo chamber for the views of the Thieu government, uncritically accepting its pronouncements. However, he had made himself invaluable to Kissinger by serving as a "back-channel" confidante who had no reservations about circumventing his superiors in the State Department, just as Moorer was equally willing to go around the Secretary of Defense.

By contrast both Kissinger and Nixon were furious at the Air Force for being insufficiently zealous in bombing the enemy, despite receiving authorization to strike North Vietnam.[52] "They blew it themselves," Kissinger claimed. "I just have no patience with an air force that in two and a half weeks, with a commander who is willing to take the heat for a massive bombing attack, can't get one damn strike off." Nixon found their excuses pitiful. The idea that bad weather was preventing them from targeting moving trucks was "Bullshit." To the president the task was obvious: "Cream the fuckers."

The hope for an orderly retreat seemed destined for failure. The South Vietnamese military was pulling out of Laos in ignominious fashion. For the next five days, American helicopters continued airlifting thousands of Saigon's soldiers from their firebases in Laos to the allied installation at Khe Sanh. In several locations there was heavy fire, making the airlift hazardous not just for the men on the ground but for the pilots. Meanwhile the press continued to describe in photos and film the horrifying sight of panic-stricken South Vietnamese combatants clinging to the skids of the choppers as they took off.[53] In Saigon, General Abrams was preparing to hold a press conference. "I hope he is not too honest," Nixon remarked to Kissinger. There was not much danger of that happening. In MACV headquarters, the general and his colleagues were still assuring each other that Lam Son 719 was going well.

During his press briefing in Saigon on March 23, General Abrams was confronted with a string of skeptical questions. In response he bobbed and weaved, refusing to acknowledge certain facts that seemed obvious to everyone. "Are we in the last stage of the operation?" someone asked. They were in a "withdrawal phase" but this did not necessarily mean it was the "last stage."[54] Was the timing of things what had been envisioned from the outset? There had never been any set time for withdrawal, the general replied, it was always weather-dependent. "No contradiction to the original plan."

If Abrams wanted to mislead the press, this was fine with Kissinger. But he was privately furious at the way the military had deceived the White House, telling press secretary Ron Ziegler, "the military screwed us."[55] They were "a selfish bunch of incompetents"—a characterization that included Abrams as well as Moorer. Both he and Nixon had briefly considered firing the general, but ultimately concluded that with the American role winding down, this was not worth the controversy that would inevitably ensue.

Kissinger had every incentive to heap the blame on others. As national security advisor, it was his responsibility to present and clarify alternative approaches so that the president could make an informed decision. And he had chosen to ignore the warnings from the CIA and the State Department. Meanwhile the South Vietnamese soldiers, who were seriously outnumbered on the ground, had paid in blood (for the White House refusal to face the facts) as had American pilots and some infantrymen.

On the plus side, North Vietnamese forces had sustained significant losses. According to administration "talking points," 13,000 enemy soldiers had been killed and an equivalent of 13 battalions put out of action.[56] These numbers appeared to exceed any losses by ARVN. Washington officials were claiming that because of the accomplishments in Laos, an enemy offensive that had been planned for 1971 had been happily averted. Yet there had never been any clear evidence that such an offensive was in the works.

Where Lam Son 719 clearly fell short was in the hope that by moving so decisively into Laos, it would be possible to forestall a major enemy offensive in 1972. That second year was of greater importance because by then the number of US combat troops would have been drastically reduced and a presidential election would be looming. Yet beyond this disappointment was something more damaging to the White House: the operation looked terrible. To see it on television was to observe a defeat, regardless of any kill-ratio statistics that could be offered in defense of it.

There was also the eerie reemergence of Khe Sanh, which had featured so prominently in the Tet Offensive of 1968. Although abandoned shortly thereafter because of its proximity to the Laotian border, it had been rebuilt as the center of allied operations for Lam Son 719. In its second incarnation, Khe Sanh became a bustling place with American and South Vietnamese military men moving briskly through the area and planes taking off every few seconds. But once combat had begun and it became host to Med B, an emergency medical facility for severely wounded American pilots and infantrymen and South Vietnamese soldiers, the images became much grimmer.[57]

The medical teams were desperately overworked, and they were forced to do without beds, sinks, X-ray machines, and hospital gowns. By the middle of March more than 100 soldiers had died at the makeshift hospital, and another 800 had been treated for wounds. Making matters worse, by then the enemy was shelling Khe Sanh, leaving Med B dangerously exposed. Gloria

Emerson of the *New York Times* had remained at the site, where she observed Dr. Robert Roth, a 29-year-old pediatrician from San Francisco, desperately trying to cope.[58] Wearing two flak jackets to protect his chest and back, Roth continued to work on the patients, profoundly upset as he watched so many young boys die. It horrified him to think that back in the United States parents were going about their daily lives while "here I am standing here, with their child dying."

As South Vietnamese soldiers continued to flee Laos, North Vietnamese troops became increasingly lethal in their attacks on Khe Sanh. On March 26, a demolition squad penetrated the perimeter of the base and attacked an American platoon of 33 men, killing five and wounding 13 others. Along the way they blew up a control tower overlooking the airstrip. Morale among the soldiers at the base was non-existent. "I don't just want to get out of here—I want to run for it," one told the reporter.[59] "We don't want to be relieved. We want to get the hell out of here." Captain Roth could not believe the carnage he was seeing. When an arriving soldier happened to mention Secretary Laird's claim that an invasion of Laos was going according to plan, he was simply livid. "Then the plan must be to get us all killed," he reflected.

Lam Son 719 would prove to be the turning point in the American war, signaling the end of the administration's optimism. Until then, the president and some officials could comfort themselves with the idea that while they continued withdrawing US troops, they could build up ARVN as a fighting force of comparable power. Yet many of the problems that had emerged in Laos reflected a South Vietnamese weakness that had been evident since the early 1960s and that years of American training and money had not corrected. For anyone who cared to look, Nixon's policy of "Vietnamization" was in tatters.

15

"Everyone Was Crying"

For a White House prone to self-deception, the debacle in Laos was a shock. For almost two years president Nixon had touted a strategy of "Vietnamization" as the route to an honorable American withdrawal from the war. He had firmly maintained that the ARVN was improving to the point where its troops would soon be able on their own to prevent a communist takeover. In the interim more than 16,000 Americans had died on Nixon's watch, and billions of dollars had been spent. And yet with Lam Son 719, the first major test of the success of Vietnamization, the South Vietnamese military had been definitively—and publicly—routed. However one tried to spin it, the pictures told the story: South Vietnamese soldiers fleeing Laos in droves, terrified men clambering aboard helicopters, and American pilots flying hundreds of missions to rescue them, often at great risk to themselves.[1]

It was in tough situations like this that Henry Kissinger proved his personal worth to Nixon and outshone his rivals. The national security advisor fully appreciated that Lam Son 719 had been a fiasco. But he knew that the president could not tolerate suggestions of error, and he therefore recast the invasion of Laos as largely a success—except for the embarrassing conclusion. And, he abetted Nixon's tendency to scapegoat. If only General Abrams and the Joint Chiefs had been more candid in their assessment, that would have enabled the White House to adjust its messaging and avoid much of the negative fallout. Of course, there was as always the press to blame—the reporters and editorial writers who seemed so determined to paint a grim picture of the events on the ground.

The news coverage was indeed damning. *Newsweek*'s report was typical:

> Throughout the bomb-blasted moonscape of the central Laotian panhandle, troops of the South Vietnamese Army (ARVN) and Communist forces waged some of the bloodiest ground battles of the war. And when the fighting died down, the ARVN troops seemed to be scurrying back to their own border. As the Pentagon described it, the South Vietnamese were

engaged in "mobile maneuvering." But in the eyes of many observers, it seemed more like an old-fashioned retreat.[2]

Time's assessment was very similar:

> Only hours after the latest Washington assurances that all was continuing "according to plan," the South Vietnamese began streaming back—on foot, aboard armored columns repeatedly raked by enemy fire, and by helicopter from shell-scarred hilltop firebases deep in Laos. The last group out, the 2000-man 1st Marine Brigade barely made it. After clinging to positions on firebases Delta and Hotel . . . the Marines abandoned their artillery and their dead and headed for the border . . . "[3]

As damaging as these overviews were, the many stories about the ARVN's mistakes and incompetence made it clear why the operation had ended so ignominiously. There was, for example, the tale of the Hueys, which *Newsweek* had tracked for several weeks. In February a Huey helicopter manned by the South Vietnamese Air Force had crashed just after takeoff, killing an ARVN commander, eight South Vietnamese soldiers, and *Newsweek's* veteran correspondent Francois Sully.[4] Two days before the crash, Sergeant John Keith, an American advisor to the 223rd Squadron, had found such shoddy maintenance on US helicopters that he had urgently requested the South Vietnamese general to ground all of these planes. That request had been denied. In the weeks following the crash, there was no attempt to correct the dangerous conditions that Keith and others had identified. In its report, *Newsweek* quoted another American advisor as saying: "The next time President Nixon talks about the South Vietnamese hacking it alone, I suggest that he spend the day here first."

In Saigon, President Thieu was so furious about this reporting that he temporarily banned several opposition newspapers along with *Time* and *Newsweek*. For Nixon and Kissinger, these bleak stories were evidence not a defective strategy but of media malevolence. Yet, as they struggled to contain the damage from Lam Son 719, a new problem appeared on the horizon: the conviction and sentencing of Lieutenant Calley for the murder of 22 Vietnamese civilians at My Lai.

The Calley trial had been going on for months. Certain facts were never in dispute. The lieutenant had murdered unarmed women, children, and elderly people and had demanded that his subordinates do the same. His main defense was that he had been following orders from his superior, Captain Ernest Medina. When the atrocities at My Lai were first exposed in the fall of 1969, it was widely assumed that numerous soldiers from Charlie Company would be called to account. However, in the 18 months since, it had become increasingly clear that almost everyone involved would be spared on various technicalities.

As a result, when the jury came back with its guilty verdict on March 29, it appeared as though Calley might be the only man held accountable for the vast crime that had been committed. When he was sentenced the next day to a lifetime of hard labor, protest erupted across the country. People were outraged at the injustice of his bearing the exclusive guilt for an action that had involved so many others. The White House, congressional offices, and the courthouse at Fort Benning where he was tried were all flooded with telegrams, letters, petitions, and phone calls.[5] Indeed the intensity of the reaction far exceeded any public outrage over the massacre itself.

Riding the wave of protest, Nixon waited only 24 hours before announcing that Calley would be removed from the stockade and kept under house arrest while his appeal was being processed.[6] He also announced that after Calley's appeal was heard, he would personally review the results and make the final decision on the lieutenant's fate. Such meddling infuriated Captain Daniel, the army prosecutor, who responded with a blistering letter: "I would expect that the President of the United States, a man whom I believed should and would provide moral leadership for this nation, would stand fully behind the law of this land on a moral issue which is so clear and about which there can be no compromise." For this country "to condone the acts of Lieutenant Calley makes us no better than our enemies . . . "

As the prosecutor in the case, Daniels' outrage was no surprise, although the tone of the letter was remarkably sharp. More problematic was the way people's anger over the verdict was fueling antiwar sentiment across the political spectrum, in some unpredictable directions.[7] Even for longtime "doves," there was something appalling about singling out a lowly lieutenant, no matter how vicious his actions, for harsh punishment, while high-ranking officers and officials straight up to the Pentagon and the White House, who were responsible for killing on a mass scale, remained exempt from blame.

For many "hawks" the lieutenant's experience highlighted the plight of America's soldiers: thrown into a conflict they had never sought, faced with terrifying challenges on the ground, and rejected by the country that sent them there and failed to honor their efforts. As one woman put it, "I think it is dangerous and a degradation to the United States . . . to take one of our boys, teach him to kill, put him into that kind of war where they tell you everybody's an enemy . . . and then prosecute them for doing what they're taught to do."[8]

For years there had been two basic lines of criticism of the American role in Vietnam: a practical assessment that the war was not winnable, and a moral objection to the suffering and death it caused both Vietnamese civilians and American soldiers. In the wake of the defeat in Laos, followed within days by the Calley verdict, these objections seemed to be converging. What possible justification could there be for asking US soldiers to fight and die for a cause that was futile, while putting them in situations that would corrupt their values and make them pariahs in their own society?[9]

Recognizing his public relations problem, Nixon was counting on the television speech he would be delivering to the nation on April 7. His confidence in the effectiveness of his own oratory was undiminished, although the surrounding conditions were less auspicious. His polls were at their lowest point since taking office, with less than half of the population trusting his communications about the war. Meanwhile inside Congress, a raft of new antiwar resolutions were pending.

During the first week of April, nine influential Republican senators had dined with Defense Secretary Melvin Laird at the spacious New York home of Jacob Javits.[10] Over roast beef they told the secretary that the president had run out of time. "You don't see any hawks around here," said Minority Leader Hugh Scott.[11] "The hawks are all ex-hawks." Everyone wanted the war to stop. The president could not simply throw out new numbers on troop withdrawals and expect people to calm down.

This clamor by Republicans infuriated Nixon, as did the growing anxiety of the White House staff. In preparing his remarks he emphasized to Kissinger that on matters of substance he would give no quarter. Any notion of conciliating "doves" was bull.[12] If we "start simpering around and catering to those bastards, they'll just eat us alive." He intended to slightly increase the monthly rate of troop withdrawals in order to demonstrate that Lam Son 719 was a success. But he was unwilling to go beyond that.

Indeed, for the days leading into his speech the president had been in a rage—aggravated by the growing list of people whom he saw as lacking the competence or character to meet the challenges of Vietnam. However, on the evening of April 7 as he went before the television cameras to address the nation, he managed to appear calm and amiable.[13] The final text of his remarks was the product of days of work by his speechwriter Patrick Buchanan and his closest advisors, but as he pored over the successive drafts he had kept at the forefront the attitudes of ordinary Americans, those he privately called "the folks."

The president adroitly opened with the announcement that he was now able "to increase the rate of American troop withdrawals." Between the beginning of May and December 1, he would be bringing home 100,000 troops from Vietnam. Together with previous reductions, this would shrink by two-thirds the number of American troops that were in Vietnam when he took office. Since that time US casualties had been cut dramatically, although even "one American dying in combat is one too many." His goal, he claimed, was to have "no American fighting man dying anyplace in the world." All of his decisions as president reflected that priority.

It was the recent successes in Laos and Cambodia that had made it possible to accelerate the rate of withdrawal, he claimed. Then after dismissing all those who had raised doubts about those operations, he described the achievements of Lam Son 719. The South Vietnamese "had demonstrated that without American advisors they could fight effectively, they had inflicted far more casualties upon the North Vietnamese than they had received and most importantly by disrupting enemy supply lines and destroying its equipment, they had limited its ability to launch a major offensive in the future." Because of these great strides, Nixon contended, "the American involvement in Vietnam is coming to an end." But the final US forces would not leave until North Vietnam negotiated a satisfactory end to the war, by which he meant a peace agreement that "gives the South Vietnamese a reasonable chance to survive as a free people."

The stakes were tremendous. The United States faced "the choice of ending our involvement in this war on a note of despair or on a note of hope." Like Thomas Jefferson, he believed that "Americans will always choose hope over despair." It was "in our power to close a difficult chapter in American history, not meanly but nobly so that each one of us can come out of this searing experience with a measure of pride in our nation."

It was his obligation, the president continued, "to speak up for the two and a half million fine young Americans" who had served in the armed forces. In an indirect reference to the Calley trial, he maintained, "the atrocity charges in individual cases should not and cannot be allowed to reflect on their courage and their self-sacrifice." Because "never in history have men fought for less selfish motives, the right of people to determine their own political destiny."

His overriding goal as president was to accomplish one thing: "to bring peace, peace abroad and peace at home for America." He was not motivated by his own political concerns or by his place in history, he claimed untruthfully. Instead, what weighed on him were the families of the soldiers who given their lives in the war. He recalled how a few weeks earlier he had awarded the Medal of Honor to the family of Marine Sergeant Karl Taylor, who had died taking out a machine gun that was firing on fellow Marines. Such ceremonies were the most difficult task he had to perform. When he shook hands with Mrs. Taylor and her two boys, eight-year-old Karl Jr. and four-year-old Kevin, the younger fellow "suddenly stood at attention and saluted." For him that moment had underscored the purpose of his administration's policy: to end the war in a fashion that was "worthy of Karl Taylor's sacrifice" and to make it possible "that Kevin and Karl, and all the children like them . . . could grow up in a world where none of them would have to die in a war."

This was Richard Nixon in another peak performance—crisp rhetoric, high ideals, clear reasoning, and respect for others. It also involved the usual spinning of the truth. While he was slightly increasing the monthly rate of troop withdrawals, he intended to backload the reductions so that during the next six months it would be lower than at present. He wished to insure that when the South Vietnamese went to the polls in October, there would still be 200,000 US soldiers on the ground to prevent an enemy upsurge and to help insure General Thieu's reelection. As for his suggestion that "without American advisors, [the South Vietnamese] could fight effectively against the very best troops that North Vietnam had to offer," it obscured the fact that American planes had pummeled the enemy with bombs, causing thousands of casualties. If Lam Son 719 had demonstrated anything, it was that the army of South Vietnam could not fight alone.

As always after delivering a major address, Nixon remained in the Oval Office where he could receive phone calls and track the responses to his performance. The usual tributes came in, including an early one from a euphoric Henry Kissinger who assured Nixon that this was the best speech he had given since taking office.[14] It brought "a lump to my throat," he said, and he had been impressed by Nixon's superb delivery, "dignified, strong and not ingratiating." Had he seen the television commentaries? "I don't care what these bastards say," the president replied. Whatever their view, he knew "the speech was a work of art. It was not an act because no actor in Hollywood could have done it." "Nor could any actor have written it," echoed Kissinger.

His own top people, Alexander Haig and Winston Lord, had been similarly "moved, overwhelmed."

While heartened by the praise, the president's thoughts reverted to the treachery of his fellow Republicans. He was still fretting over a recent White House meeting with GOP leaders from the House and Senate, who had besieged him with their worries about Laos and their requests for a final withdrawal plan. "These leaders were a miserable lot," he reflected, citing especially Senate Minority Leader Hugh Scott and Minority Whip Robert Griffin. But he had told them straight out that if Vietnam "goes down the drain," they would have to take responsibility. "You are saving the country," the national security advisor observed.

Nixon was also fed up with the members of his administration who had lost their nerve in the face of adversity. As Laos unfolded, many had remained conspicuously silent or had leaked their opposition to the press. This evening's speech would put them in their place. "Screw the Cabinet. I'm sick of the whole bunch," the president opined. "If they like it fine," but from now on there will be "no sucking around, from now on they come to me."

On a more cheerful note, Kissinger observed that some of their most persistent television critics, including Dan Rather from CBS and John Chancellor of NBC, had been generous in their praise. Nixon was unimpressed. In the weeks preceding his address, his vice president had launched a deliberate round of attacks on the news media, challenging its patriotism and the integrity of its reporting. Nixon speculated that these commentators might be "afraid that Agnew will jump on them." Kissinger replied, "Deep down they know you are right." Unfortunately, too many journalists were "cowards and publicity seekers."

But Kissinger's flattery was not having the desired effect. Off camera Nixon was reverting to the state of rage that kept him railing against the press, members of his own administration who had lost their nerve in the face of adversity, and the GOP leaders of Congress who were besieging him with their defeatist attitude. To this point all his efforts to overpower the enemy with military force had been to no avail. The failure of Lam Son 719—however he chose to describe it—had left North Vietnam as obdurate as ever. If this latest gambit did not work, he assured Kissinger, he was going to "bomb those bastards right off the goddamn earth."

Meanwhile, the president checked with his personal secretary Rosemary Woods to see if any members of his cabinet had called. Not so far, she indicated. "They're all running away," he bitterly observed. But just then,

Secretary of State Rogers came on the line to congratulate him on a "tremendous" speech that would surely have "one hell of an impact."[15] The best part was the little boy saluting. Nixon acknowledged that he "was practically crying myself when I delivered it."

Rogers predicted that this speech would "really turn the tables." Mindful that the Secretary of State had opposed the Laotian operation from the outset, Nixon was suspicious. "You wouldn't bullshit me?" he asked. Rogers reassured him. Indeed, if the measure of a man was his willingness to defend a disastrous campaign in which other men had fought and died, Rogers had earned his spurs. For weeks he had gone before congressional committees and the media defending the wisdom of Lam Son 719. Unlike Melvin Laird, who had privately distanced himself, Rogers had remained loyal.

By 10:30 PM, two hours after the speech, enthusiastic calls from aides and supporters were still coming through the switchboard.[16] The Reverend Billy Graham was "inspired." Bebe Rebozo, Nixon's closest friend, had found the story of the Taylors "beautiful." Press secretary Ron Ziegler had been monitoring the flow of news all evening and stated extravagantly that, "Every person in the country was on the edge of their seats." White House political operative Chuck Colson had been talking with George Meany, the president of the AFL-CIO, and other top union officials, who were all "very, very enthusiastic."

However, the silence from moderate Republicans was ominous. The one notable exception was Governor Nelson Rockefeller, who called to praise the president for doing "a tremendously able job" and for "having the courage to stick with your principles." The governor's call was hardly spontaneous. By this time, his brothers David and John had lost any enthusiasm for the war, and Nelson himself had been wobbling. But earlier that day Kissinger had leaned on Rockefeller to reach out to the president, invoking nothing less than the future of the republic.[17] "If we are destroyed it has to be known that some people stood." Rockefeller ought to phone Nixon after his speech because "he has been all alone again with no one with him." This was after all the president of the United States, whose leadership was needed. In a world of dangers, serious people could not let him be destroyed.

In the ensuing hours Nixon continued to brood about the people who had not bothered to phone or issue positive statements. Chewing this over with Haldeman, he found it curious that labor leaders were rallying to his side while members of the business community were holding back. None of the businessmen "are worth a shit," said the president.[18] These were the kind of people "who won't do a goddamn thing with their lives or their fortune except screw somebody else." And where were the members of his administration? Had anyone heard from Connelly? What about the fence-sitters Robert Finch and Donald Rumsfeld? This was the time when people showed their true colors.[19] They were in "a hell of a fight," and if these men couldn't speak up until reading the polls, then "screw 'em."

Nixon's behind-the-scenes wrath could easily be construed as a personality quirk. And he was surely somebody on a short fuse, with a ferocious temper. Yet in his present state he most resembled Lyndon Johnson during the latter years of his presidency and for similar reasons. To the extent that it was politically possible, he had mostly followed the guidance of the military, and in the more generalized sense the relevant bureaucracies, that South Vietnam must not be abandoned. Yet having done so for the past two years, he was personally exposed in a way these others were not. Like Johnson he had become the face of the war, the person most directly responsible for the deaths of thousands of Americans. Unlike these others he could be readily held accountable at election time if the policy proved a disaster.

In one crucial respect, Nixon's position diverged from Johnson's. When he assumed office, there was a mobilized antiwar movement and a skeptical public. It was that political reality that had compelled him to keep withdrawing troops under the mantra of Vietnamization. In theory, this might have worked out: holding critics at bay with a steady withdrawal of troops, while preparing ARVN to take over when US ground forces were finally removed.

But it was that theory that Lam Son 719 had just exploded. An immediate danger was that because of its failure, the enemy was still in shape to launch an offensive inside South Vietnam in 1972, jeopardizing Nixon's reelection prospects. But in a broader sense, it suggested that without American support into the future, ARVN could not defeat or even fend off a North Vietnamese/National Liberation Front attack. In that circumstance the enormous American commitment to Saigon—in money, lives, and arguably social cohesion—would have been for naught.

Against that backdrop Nixon's need for praise and reassurance about his speech was intense. Although the hour was late, he called Kissinger a second time to see if he had any word from Joe Alsop, the veteran columnist for the *Washington Post*.[20] For years this elderly pundit had been one of the most vigorous supporters of the Vietnam War, but there were rumors that Lam Son 719 had shaken his confidence. Had the speech made a difference?

Kissinger had not heard from Alsop, but he reiterated that the mood of all those he spoke to was one of "exaltation." Everyone was crying. The address had been remarkable and "the way you delivered it, Mr. President, was an absolute masterpiece."

As he pondered the evening's results, one fresh concern began to nag at the president. He realized that he had made the Taylor family the linchpin of his remarks. But what if Mrs. Taylor was against the war? Nixon had already seen that military spouses could be unpredictable. Some POW wives had been climbing off the patriotic bandwagon and demanding an immediate end to the war so that their husbands could be released from North Vietnamese prisons. Realizing it was likely that the press would be descending upon Mrs. Taylor by early morning, he called Kissinger to ask him to "get hold of [her] to be sure she stands firm."[21]

Kissinger acted swiftly, phoning the widow to say, "the president wished to apologize for using your name . . . and hoped you weren't hurt."[22] Mrs. Taylor acknowledged that she had been "rather shocked but very proud." Kissinger thanked her and explained that the president had been "very moved by what your husband did, and your sons and he just wanted me to tell you that it reflected great courage."

In advance of his April 7 speech, Nixon had expected to duplicate the success of his previous appearances, with letters and telegrams flooding in, newspapers commending his "statesmanship," and opponents in Congress cowed into silence. Despite all the fawning calls, by morning it was clear that this time the promise of another troop withdrawal was beginning to fall on deaf ears. The numbers he had offered would mean that by January 1, 1972, 184,000 American soldiers would still be in Vietnam. As Nixon's Republican advisors had warned: people were fed up with the war and needed to hear that it would end rapidly. This was evident from the response of both journalists and politicians who were lambasting the president for offering "more of the same."[23]

In its lead editorial, the *Washington Post* applauded the troop withdrawal but characterized the speech as "self-serving, defensive, mawkish, patronizing and needlessly partisan." It emphasized the "real anguish" of Americans who want to see a "terminal point" but are instead "being toyed with, tantalized with a momentary vision of total withdrawal and then told in the next breath that it is impossible." In similar fashion, *Time* noted that Nixon "changed virtually nothing" as he delivered "a foxhole speech digging in tenaciously in defense of his previous position." The reference to Karl

Taylor might be a useful reminder of the courage displayed by American soldiers, but it was appropriate to ask, "how many more Karl Taylor's need die, however nobly, for purposes that are no longer clear or perhaps even attainable."

Most of the critical commentary focused on the implications for Americans of the Nixon speech. But what did it augur for the Vietnamese themselves? Among the mainstream pundits, *New York Times* columnist Anthony Lewis was one of the few who noted that the president had "said not one word about the cost of the war to the civilians of Indochina, the people who happen to live there."[24] Since the United States had intervened in Vietnam, "there were more than 1.5 million casualties, most of them caused by American or allied action." Another four to five million people had become refugees. "No one could have learned from the President of the United States that this year right now, more civilians are being killed and wounded and made homeless in Indochina than ever before." To Nixon none of this had any weight, but hopefully "the American conscience will understand murder in Vietnam for what it is."

Most Republicans would not have shared Lewis' moral condemnation, but among their elected officials there was a widespread sense that the president had left them in the lurch. Oregon Senator Mark Hatfield wryly observed that they had "expected an elephant and we got a mouse."[25] The speech was "blah," said another. It was clearly unsuited to the sense of emergency produced by the Laotian operation. When Minority Leader Hugh Scott tried to put a positive face on things by saying that he knew from private conversation that Nixon had "a timetable" for complete troop withdrawal, press secretary Ron Ziegler immediately contradicted him.

Plus there was a new cause for concern, what Senator Robert Dole, on a visit to the White House, described as a "tinderbox about to explode." POW wives were becoming more and more upset about Nixon's failure to establish a clear end point for the war. He feared that they might reverse their support for the president and he therefore urged Nixon to take a major initiative on this matter, if only for "cosmetic purposes."

While Republicans squirmed, Democrats continued their attacks. Emboldened by the Laotian fiasco, they had a new sense of optimism about the possibility of defeating Nixon in the 1972 election. Many in the party believed that by temporizing on the war question in 1968, candidate Hubert Humphry had damaged himself in the polls. This was one mistake that was unlikely to be repeated if the war continued. Already Senator George

McGovern, a passionate advocate for peace, had thrown his hat in the ring, and other aspirants, including Maine's Senator Ed Muskie, were aligning themselves with an antiwar position. Previous Nixon speeches had temporarily intimidated his political opponents into silence, but not this time.

Clearly the speech had pacified some and reassured the faithful, but it had not worked the magic Nixon had been looking for. The antiwar legislators on Capitol Hill sounded more assertive than ever.[26] Chairman of the Senate Foreign Relations Committee Fulbright was intending to hold public hearings, and many Vietnam-related resolutions were in the offing. Moreover, the weather in Washington was getting warmer, bringing with it the prospect of mass protests. Vietnam Veterans Against the War had planned an encampment and march in the Capitol, and two national coalitions had called for large-scale demonstrations there.

Then quite suddenly, Nixon caught a break. Across the Pacific a story was developing in the Chinese capital of Beijing that startled the world. On April 7, in a departure from its long-standing policy, the Chinese government invited the American table-tennis team to visit their country. This was newsworthy since, with rare exceptions, American visitors had not been permitted to visit. Then on April 14, at a banquet for the team, the Chinese Premier Zhou Enlai greeted them with a stunning message: "You have opened a new chapter in the relations of American and Chinese people." The old revolutionary was confident that "this beginning again of our friendship will certainly meet with majority support of our two peoples."

To the American public and much of the press, Zhou's words came out of the blue. For decades the People's Republic of China had been portrayed in the United States as an unrelenting, indeed maniacal foe, more dangerous and aggressive than the Soviet Union. In large measure the American project in Vietnam had been understood as a response to the threat that "Red China" could ultimately seize control of all Asia. Yet suddenly, with the war raging, the Chinese leader was opening the door to a more cordial relationship and promising greater openness between the two peoples.

For Nixon and Kissinger this was a welcome but not entirely unexpected development—though the timing had certainly been a surprise. It was in fact the culmination of a series of careful initiatives the two governments had been making for the purpose of ending the years of estrangement. As early as 1967, Nixon had published an article in *Foreign Affairs* recommending a change in US China policy.[27] This placed him in agreement with the swelling number of foreign policy experts who considered it both absurd and counterproductive to deny the existence of the government of a country with 800 million people. The most compelling factor, however, was the growing appreciation in official circles of the deepening rift between China and the Soviet Union.[28] By the time Nixon took office that breach had assumed a military character, with clashes erupting along their shared border. As the Soviets shifted many of their troops from Europe to Asia, there was speculation in Washington that a full-scale war might erupt. This provided an opportunity for American diplomacy to exploit the bitter conflict.

At the inception of his first term, Nixon flashed a series of signals to Beijing indicating a desire for improved relations. That effort had appeared to be bearing fruit until the American incursion into Cambodia in May 1970, which led Beijing to suddenly freeze communication. However, the White House had continued its overtures, indicating through intermediaries that it was willing to discuss a whole range of mutual issues, including the problem of Taiwan and the US military presence in Asia.[29] In the March 1971 State of the World message, released by the White House, Beijing was referred to for the first time as the People's Republic of China, a clear sign that the American stance was changing. That same month, the State Department had lifted remaining visa restrictions on Americans wishing to travel there, a move that was quickly followed by Beijing's invitation to the U.S. ping-pong team.

Of course there were formidable obstacles still standing in the way of a new relationship. There was no doubt that improved ties with Beijing would come as a cruel blow to nationalist Chinese allies on Taiwan. As the two discussed the impending change, Kissinger acknowledged "the tragedy that this had to happen" to Taiwan's leader Chiang Kai-Shek "at the end of his life," but he thought they "had to be cold about it." Nixon agreed: "we have to do what's best for us," although he would try to protect Taiwanese interests.[30] And of course, the Beijing Chinese would be useful "for our game with the Soviets."

The White House responded to Zhou's overture with alacrity, announcing that it was lifting a 20-year embargo on trade with China and easing other impediments to travel and commerce.[31] Two days later, Nixon used an appearance at the convention of American Newspaper Editors to convey an even more astonishing suggestion. Alluding to the forthcoming marriage of his daughter Tricia to Edward Cox, he recounted his travel advice to them: "I hope that sometime in your life, sooner rather than later, you will be able to go to China to see the great cities." He then continued, "as a matter of fact, I hope sometime I do." The hint was unmistakable. Richard Nixon, a man who had built a political career on blasting opponents for softness on "Red China," was fishing for an invitation to the People's Republic.

In the United States, the administration's new approach to China was widely acclaimed. Television stations carried stories of the ping-pong team as it toured hitherto inaccessible sites in the Chinese capital. Journalists who had been deeply critical of Nixon's handling of Laos were quick to praise his courage in staking out a new direction. On both sides of the aisle, Democratic and Republican politicians expressed cautious optimism.

Nixon and Kissinger were convinced that they had finally scored a major coup. Perhaps news commentators would take more seriously the administration's claim to be seeking international peace. In his remarks to the American Society of Editors, the president had skillfully embedded his overtures to China within a moral framework. One audience member asked, what do you worry most about, when you find yourself awake in the middle of the night? Nixon replied, "[I]f there is any one subject that more often than not comes across my mind, it is what I can do the next day that will contribute toward the goal of a lasting peace for America and for the world."[32] And this was so important for young people who "by nature . . . tend to be idealistic, hopeful," wanting the world to be a better place. If they could see real progress toward peace, much of their present alienation would subside.

It was an inspiring answer, conjuring up a more hopeful future for a war-weary nation. But it masked a profound cynicism. When Kissinger commended the president for his skillful handling of the evening and the effective way he managed to turn the first question "into a little speech on peace," Nixon countered: "You mean I dream of peace all night and all that crap? . . . Better to have said, I think of going to the bathroom."[33] The important thing, Kissinger observed, was that the China move was taking Vietnam off the front pages.

Something even more exciting was potentially afoot. It was "conceivable and very possible" that the Chinese were anticipating that "Hanoi is going to make a peace move and they don't want to be left out." In fact, Kissinger was willing to predict that in the coming months there would be a break in the Paris negotiations. Whatever the complexities of Lam Son 719, the North Vietnamese had sustained huge losses and must now perceive the iron determination of the United States to block their victory. And this Chinese overture could be the sign that Hanoi was ready to cave.

Kissinger credited Nixon for these achievements, assuring him if "you had not stuck to your guns you couldn't have done it."[34] Nixon thought the

April speech was "the key to the whole thing." His national security advisor agreed: had the president acted "like a man on the verge of bugging out of Vietnam," Beijing leaders would not have regarded him as someone worth dealing with.

Yet Nixon was still skittish about public opinion. As he analyzed the political implications of the China opening with Chuck Colson, he wondered how much this would really help with "middle America." After all, the Chinese had been arming and advising the North Vietnamese for years and had been portrayed as a main culprit in the continuation of the war. Under these conditions, the "intellectual bastards" might be satisfied,[35] but ordinary Americans might wonder: "What the hell are you doing, they're killing our boys and you're trading with these people?"

Therein lay the rub: Americans were still dying in the war. Casualties might be down, but that very week more than 100 US soldiers had perished, raising the death toll above that of the Korean War. And there was trouble everywhere—in Laos and Cambodia, where both anticommunist governments were at risk, and in South Vietnam itself, where the North Vietnamese troops and the NLF retained the ability to strike in many locations.[36]

The greatest peril was to be found in the northern provinces of South Vietnam where the communists had never been dislodged. Thousands were still there in April 1971, but the fighting in Laos had so depleted the South Vietnamese divisions responsible for the area that the ratio of ARVN to communist forces had become dangerously low. There were also vulnerabilities elsewhere, as the NLF was re-emerging, especially in areas like the Mekong Delta where the departure of US troops and the diversion of South Vietnamese forces into Laos and Cambodia had left a vacuum.

Neither Nixon nor Kissinger had been fully cognizant of ARVN's many weaknesses, because military officials had withheld bad news. But they both understood that the failure of Lam Son 719 had increased the likelihood of a formidable enemy offensive in 1972. One indication of their jumpiness came in mid-April when General Abrams was quoted in the *Washington Post* suggesting that South Vietnamese soldiers fighting in the A Shau valley might renew their attacks on Laos. Perhaps the commander thought this idea would please the president, but if so he was wrong. Nixon hoped to push the Vietnam War "off the front pages" and for Laos to disappear from the news. Kissinger wondered if Abrams had been tricked into saying this. Regardless of the reason, Abrams should have known better, Nixon retorted: "I don't care if he goes and bombs the hell" out of the place, "just don't say it." Why does Abrams feel "so compelled to be so goddamn honest all the time?" His job was to "just shut up."[37]

Meanwhile, challenges from fellow Republicans on Capitol Hill were unabated. On the House side, Representative Pete McCloskey of California had visited Laos and South Vietnam and came back charging that American bombings and ground action had caused thousands of civilian casualties plus millions of refugees.[38] In the Senate, Howard Baker, Bob Dole, and other party colleagues who had previously supported the president made a trip to the White House to impress upon him the need to provide a specific date for ending US participation in the war. Nixon responded for perhaps the umpteenth time that leaving South Vietnam with the ability to survive was essential for American "credibility." Upon their departure he fired off a memorandum to Haldeman saying that he was unwilling to hold this sort of "crying towel session" in the future. He had agreed to the meeting hoping to garner support, but if these people were going to act like "a bunch of old farts . . . screw 'em."[39]

Despite this truculence, Nixon was beginning to rethink his strategy. "The American people are sick of this war," he reminded Kissinger, so "therefore our game here . . . must be to deal with it."[40] We have played our part "right to the hilt with no support," but Laos had hurt them badly: "goddamn poor execution on the part of the military." If they now stuck with their previous positions and as a consequence went down to defeat, the United States would be no better off. From now on, "everything has to be played in terms of how we survive."

As of fall 1970, Nixon had believed the Vietnam issue might be fading away. But Lam Son 719 had dropped them 10 points in the polls, and while his April 7 speech had gained them a little reprieve, they were not back to where they had been before the invasion. Hereafter "we have to ruthlessly play for the best news that we can" while attempting to convince Hanoi of American implacability. Toward that end, he wanted new air strikes on North Vietnam, which could be described in the usual way as "protective reaction."[41] Kissinger pronounced himself "thrilled."

Of course, these air strikes would not solve their public relations problem, which included the growing impatience of the POW wives. Nixon thought they needed to give David Bruce, the official US negotiator in Paris, a concession he could present to Hanoi, which would give the appearance of the president's concern. This could be a "cosmetic offer . . . which we can publish."

This could be anything Nixon explained, just some "gobbledygook" David Bruce could say in Paris, which the other side would turn down. It was, however, absolutely urgent that they get a proposal out there, because otherwise the wives might run off and join the protestors. These wives were their "Achilles heel." If they started criticizing the president before election time, the administration would be in "deep trouble." And in that event, "Congress would move so quickly to end the war, it'd make your head spin."[42]

While wrestling with these domestic woes and a still unmanageable war, on April 27 the two received another thrilling message from Zhou Enlai, this time brought by the Pakistani ambassador. While reaffirming Beijing's longstanding position that a normalization of relations with the United States would require the removal of all American military forces from Taiwan, it had ceased to be a precondition of talks. In a major shift, "the Chinese government affirms its willingness to receive publicly in Peking a special envoy of the President (for instance, Mr. Kissinger) or the U.S. Secretary of State, even the President of the U.S. himself for a direct meeting or discussions."[43] Here was the breakthrough Nixon and Kissinger had been hoping for.

While the original impetus for seeking a new relationship with the Chinese had been the desire to counterbalance the Russians, the exigencies of the Vietnam War had framed the matter differently. In the short term, the president needed some achievement to burnish his foreign policy credentials, which an opening to China would accomplish. There was also the tantalizing possibility that in their desire for improved relations with the United States, the Chinese could be helpful with their North Vietnamese allies.

Who should be the emissary? Fully aware that Kissinger would like to be that person, Nixon floated other options.[44] What about Governor Rockefeller? he asked maliciously. "Not disciplined enough," came the answer. George Bush? Definitely not him, "too soft and not sophisticated enough." Maybe Haig could accompany Rockefeller and keep him in check? That was too awkward, Kissinger observed. Nixon thought it unfortunate that former New York governor Thomas Dewey was dead, since he would be an excellent choice.

As they traded names back and forth, the two men could see on the horizon a hopeful international scenario unencumbered by the fortunes of ARVN. "We played a game and we got a little break," Nixon reflected. It was possible they could settle everything, added Kissinger. Within the next 12 months, they might get a summit with the Russians as well as a new relationship with China, and, if these things fell into place, "we will end Vietnam this year." Nixon thought it remarkable. Two months ago such developments would have been "inconceivable." After Laos, "the people over two to one thought it had failed and yet here comes the Chinese move, the Ping Pong team, and something more significant that it pales into nothing."

Yet there was no gainsaying the fact that in the aftermath of Lam Son 719, prospects for Vietnamization had surely dimmed. Much would depend on whether international diplomacy could somehow rescue the situation. But if it failed, President Nixon was sure of one thing: "We're not gonna go out whimpering; we're gonna blast the goddamn hell out of them."[45]

16

"Bring Our Brothers Home"

Despite the carnage in Laos and Cambodia, Nixon and Kissinger were dismissive of accusations of immorality. They considered themselves principled upholders of American power at a time when others in the elite had lost their nerve, and they had little patience with the people who were wringing their hands over needless deaths. Kissinger thought it remarkable that while "eighty-five percent of the bombing was in the uninhabited areas," critics kept talking "as if we're slaughtering civilians." What did anyone expect? Nixon mused. "This crap about morality, of course it's violent. War is immoral because people are immoral, they're aggressive all over the world." Anyway the North Vietnamese were "bastards," and if need be, he would "level that goddamn country."[1]

Beyond the White House walls, however, were millions of people for whom the morality of the Vietnam War was becoming an increasingly serious issue. In the wake of the Cambodian invasion and subsequent offensive into Laos, for the first time a Lou Harris poll revealed that a majority of Americans considered the conflict to be morally wrong. On the campuses and elsewhere, people were asking what justified the continued killing of soldiers and civilians in a palpably unsuccessful venture. If in fact one's own government was engaged in cruel acts of aggression against other nations, what was the responsibility of individual members of the society?

Among the critics the most haunted and driven were the Vietnam veterans, who had come together in Detroit during February to testify about war crimes. The impact of their witnessing was to deepen their own collective understanding of their experience and intensify their determination to end the war. Yet, as moving and cathartic as the "Winter Soldier" hearings had been for the participants, lack of media coverage meant the event was virtually unnoticed by the public.

By the end of that gathering the organizers had agreed to hold their next major event in Washington, where they hoped to get more attention from the press. The logical time was spring. But in selecting a date, the veterans chose to separate themselves from two national antiwar coalitions that were also planning Washington protests for this period. They felt their message was distinct. Americans needed to understand that being opposed to the Vietnam War did not mean being opposed to the troops who served there. Indeed, with each passing day, Vietnam Veterans Against the War (VVAW) was gaining additional members, while in Vietnam itself more and more of the soldiers were turning against the war they had been sent to fight.

The VVAW leaders settled on a week of events that would begin Sunday, April 18, before the two national coalitions came into town. But there was internal disagreement about the nature of the week's activities. A frequent spokesman for the group, John Kerry of Massachusetts, wanted the organization to focus on lobbying members of Congress to support end-the-war legislation. Others gravitated toward more emotionally expressive activities: marches, guerilla theater, musical performance, and a symbolic return of medals. One issue on which everyone agreed was that the protest must remain lawful. Toward that end, the organizers had reached out to the Capitol police with a flyer explaining that they were gathering for peaceful purposes and intended to comply with the law.

On their first day in the capital, however, a Federal District Court, responding to a petition from the Justice Department, barred the veterans from making camp on the Washington Monument Mall. As their lawyers swung into action in response, the veterans moved ahead with plans for a silent march to Arlington National Cemetery, where they intended to lay wreaths honoring American and Vietnamese dead. Dressed in their uniforms and displaying their many medals, the men were led by five Gold Star mothers and two soldiers in wheelchairs. To their astonishment they were halted at the gates and forbidden to enter. Marcella King, one of the Gold Star mothers, was distraught: "My boy was killed in Vietnam. I didn't speak out then. It's my fault." One of the veterans observed ruefully, "You've got to go back to Nam and die there, man," in order to enter Arlington.[2]

A day later the cemetery superintendent reversed himself, explaining that he had not realized the group's aim was to lay wreaths. Before entering the gates, more than a thousand veterans gathered around as former Army Chaplain Jackson H. Day, who had served with the Fourth Infantry Division in Vietnam, gave the invocation:[3] He supposed that most of those gathered there had tried to believe in the goodness of the Vietnam War and would like "to wave a flag for the dream of an America that brings medicine and candy." But now they come to Arlington "in the ruins of that dream," understanding that "no goal could be so laudable, or defense so necessary, as to justify what we have visited upon the people of Indochina."

It had taken only a day for the Vietnam veterans to gain access to Arlington. Their plan to camp on the mall required a more prolonged battle. Their legal team, headed by former Attorney General Ramsey Clarke, had gone into court to challenge the injunction barring their presence. Removing the men from the mall was a high priority for the White House because this high-profile location had become a magnet for press and sympathetic politicians. As the Supreme Court entered the fray, Clarke thought he had an agreement that would allow them to stay on the mall so long as they took down their tents and agreed not to cook or sleep there.

Yet, for vets who had slept in rice paddies, this legal hair-splitting was intolerable. In a furious outburst Mike Oliver, one of their leaders who had fought with the 101st Airborne Division in the Ia Drang Valley, objected: "Fuck that. We're gonna sleep on this mall tonight and we're gonna see what happens." When the matter was put to a vote, by a narrow margin the veterans who had come to DC as law-abiding protestors voted to defy an injunction.

Having taken this risk, the men gained immediate support from antiwar members of Congress, several of whom appeared at their illegal encampment over the night. At midnight Senator Edward Kennedy of Massachusetts sat with the group, telling them, "You have served your country well abroad and will serve it even better here in Washington. If your country can find a place for you to stay in Vietnam, they can find a place for you to stay here."[4]

To their surprise, law enforcement personnel were also sympathetic, with park policemen and members of the DC police, many of whom had served in Vietnam, assuring the demonstrators privately that they would not carry out arrests. Active duty soldiers, including some from the honor guard at Arlington, also arrived with messages of support. There were even a few visitors from Fort Bragg, who reportedly announced that men at the base who were on stand-by to clean out the encampment had "dropped sand in the gas tanks," vowing that "these trucks will never move." Perhaps apocryphal, such anecdotes fed the conviction of the veterans that by refusing to leave the mall, they were representing those still in uniform.

In the White House the president and his men were frustrated, but they realized that if the Washington police made arrests, many in the country would be horrified to see men who had served in Vietnam carted off to prison. Nixon's lawyer John Dean warned that this spectacle would be "politically devastating." Presidential speechwriter Patrick Buchanan concurred: "If we want a confrontation, let's have it with the crazies." To the annoyance of the federal court judge who had issued the initial injunction at the behest of the administration, on April 22 the White House requested that it be revoked.

The veterans were heartened by this retreat. Perhaps their message was finally getting across. However, Congress was less welcoming than they had hoped. Over the course of three days, many of the veterans had gone to Capitol Hill, bringing with them a list of 16 far-reaching demands.[5] The centerpiece was a call for Congress to pass legislation mandating "the immediate, unilateral, unconditional withdrawal of all United States Armed Forces and Central Intelligence personnel" from Southeast Asia. They were insisting as well that the US government grant amnesty for all men who refused to serve in the military, that Congress convene public hearings looking into American war crimes, and that it enact legislation "to provide proper care and services" for all patients in the VA hospitals. Although warmly greeted by the antiwar bloc on the Hill, they were surprised to find that a great many doors were shut to them, including those of representatives and senators from their home states.[6]

The veterans were also disappointed when it seemed that no one from their group would be given the opportunity to testify before Congress. However, a sudden invitation from the office of Senator Fulbright was delivered to John Kerry, inviting him to appear before the Senate Foreign Relations Committee the next day. Holder of bronze and silver medals, as well as three purple hearts, Kerry was also a Yale-educated, articulate officer likely to make a favorable impression on the committee.

As his fellow veterans packed the galleries of the Senate Foreign Relations Committee, Kerry opened his remarks by saying that he was speaking not as an individual but as a representative of the men encamped on the mall, and of the much larger group of veterans around the country. They wanted the country to understand that what was maddening to all of them most was not the dangers of the war or even the deaths of friends, but the pointlessness of the entire Vietnam enterprise, and the way fighting there had compromised their own values.

Kerry then described the Detroit Winter Soldier hearings, at which 150 honorably discharged veterans had relived "the absolute horror of what this country, in a sense, made them do." The participants had related harrowing stories of how they:

> had personally raped, cut off ears, cut off heads, taped wires from portable telephones to human genitals and turned up the power, cut off limbs, blown up bodies, randomly shot at civilians, razed villages . . . shot cattle and dogs for fun, poisoned food stocks and generally ravaged the countryside of Vietnam . . . in addition to the . . . very particular ravaging which is done by the applied bombing power of this country.

The Winter Soldier hearings had brought to light harsh facts that Americans needed to know, because these unacknowledged crimes were more dangerous to the well-being of the United States than to the communists of Vietnam.

Vice President Agnew liked to denounce the "criminal misfits" who were protesting the war and to contrast them with those "best men" who were risking their lives in rice paddies, Kerry said. It was a false dichotomy. Those whom Spiro Agnew was deriding as "misfits" were "standing up for us" in a way that others had not. And by calling for US withdrawal from Vietnam, they were speaking for the "best men," some of whom had become "quadriplegics and amputees" lying forgotten in Veteran's Administration hospitals.

Kerry also addressed the lies that had been used to recruit men to fight in the war. They had been told they were protecting the freedom of the people in South Vietnam. But when they arrived there, they found that "most people didn't even know the difference between communism and democracy. They only wanted to work in their rice paddies without helicopters strafing them and bombs with napalm burning their villages and tearing their country apart." He saw such activities as not just immoral but racist, because "we fought using weapons against those people, which I do not believe this country would dream of using were we fighting in the European theater."

And how dishonest was the intervention in Laos, under the pretext that the war was winding down? "We veterans can only look with amazement on the fact that this country is unable to see there is absolutely no difference between ground troops and a helicopter crew." Somehow the notion had taken hold that killing Laotians from the air is more acceptable than shooting them face-to-face. In reality, American "helicopter crews fill the same body bags and they wreak the same kind of damage on the Vietnamese and Laotian countryside as anybody else." In reality, the lives of American soldiers were being squandered on absurd projects:

> And so we watched while men charged up hills because a general said that hill has to be taken . . . . [W]e watched pride allow for the most unimportant battles to be blown into extravaganzas, because we couldn't lose and we couldn't retreat and it didn't matter how many American bodies were lost to prove that point.

In this latest phase, they had to sit back and "watch quietly while American lives are lost so that we can exercise the incredible arrogance of Vietnamizing the Vietnamese." No matter how rationalized, Kerry continued, this Nixon policy seemed to them more farcical than its precursors. Every day "someone has to give up his life so that the United States doesn't have to admit something that the entire world already knows, so that we can't say that we have made a mistake."

Apparently President Nixon was prepared to continue the war for many years, albeit in altered form. So the veterans were appealing to members of Congress to carry out the wishes of the American public and bring it to a halt. In undertaking this last mission as men in uniform, they sought "to search out and destroy the last vestige of this barbaric war, to pacify our own hearts, to conquer the hate and the fear that have driven this country these last 10 years and more."

Kerry's emotional plea stunned the room. During the days of hearings, nobody had spoken to the senators with anything like the eloquence and directness of John Kerry. Moreover, the presence of so many antiwar veterans seated in the chamber underlined his message.

In the White House, Nixon was fuming about the entire spectacle. Fortunately for him, Kerry's speech had not been carried on national television. But there were cameras and reporters all over the mall, amplifying the veterans' views. As usual, the president blamed the media for the negative publicity. The problem, as he saw it, was not that there were so many embittered, tortured veterans coming home from the war, but that reporters were writing about them.[7] And they were undermining his preferred narrative of hippies versus the troops, causing his poll numbers to drop.

For an entire week, from morning until night, there were marches across town, candlelight parades, a protest at the Pentagon, and a sit-in at the Supreme Court, all designed to capture media attention and signal the larger society that its soldiers had reached a breaking point. From the standpoint of public relations, the most damaging event was the culminating ceremony during which the Vietnam veterans threw away their medals. For many of these soldiers this was a painful act, since irrespective of their criticisms of the war, the medals constituted recognition of their sacrifice and individual acts of heroism. For this very reason the forfeit of these objects was the most dramatic step they could take to display their rejection of the military enterprise.

On Friday April 23, a large crowd gathered outside the Capitol building near a hastily erected wire fence. Men in fatigues lined up, along with a smattering of Gold Star parents clutching the medals, ribbons, and certificates awarded to their deceased sons. Marine Sergeant Jack Smith from West Hartford was the first to speak: "We now strip ourselves of . . . those citations for gallantry and exemplary service . . . we cast these away as symbols of dishonor, shame and inhumanity." Smith offered his apology to the people of Vietnam, whose hearts "had been broken, not won" by the damage American fighters had inflicted on their land.

Outside the Capitol, where for years senators and representatives had listened to the grim statistics of the Vietnam War but heard little about the people behind those numbers, it seemed to the veterans important to name the dead. Many of the more than 700 men tossing their awards over the Capitol fence did so in remembrance of friends who had died. Among them was Ron Ferrizzi, who had been flying on a reconnaissance mission when the lead helicopter was shot down. Racing from his own chopper, Ferrizzi rushed into the burning aircraft attempting to save the trapped men. For these efforts he had received a Silver Star and a Purple Heart, but those whom he had tried to save had died in his arms. Weeping openly, Ferrizzi stepped up to the microphone: "This is for Specialist 4 Bob Smeal and Sergeant Johns and Lieutenant Panamaroff, who were killed on behalf of their country." Nearby, a large burly Marine captain, Rusty Sachs, was crying as he prepared to honor his slain friends Roger Harell and Robert Cramer.

Neil Russell, World War II veteran, walked to the front of the line wearing the fatigue jacket of his dead son, Bill. Russell blew taps in memory of his boy, the 50,000 other American war dead, and the hundreds of thousands wounded. He had planned some remarks but could only blurt out, "I pray for peace."[8] By his side were two Gold Star mothers. "I am here to join all of these men," said one. "In each one of them I see my son."[9]

As hours passed and hundreds of men were still lined up to return their awards, the remarks became shorter, and people bunched up to fling them at the Capitol. These were a ragged group of people, half clad in military clothes and partly dressed like civilians. From the long hair, headbands, and beads donned by some, this might have been a gathering of young people at Woodstock. But there was a grimness and sorrow that resembled no rock concert, along with a steely determination to bring something positive out of tragedy.

Could Americans watching these demonstrators on television identify with them? The president and his men fervently hoped not. Indeed, political operative Chuck Colson was busy spreading the word that these were not real veterans but a disreputable crowd of marijuana smokers trying to pull the wool over the country's eyes.[10] In truth, throughout the week there had been enough angry outbursts and provocative demonstrations to alienate many mainstream observers, and the veterans' generally scruffy appearance had not helped either. But some combination of the Kerry speech and the visibly heartfelt anguish of the veterans had moved the legions of reporters who had been following them. It was not so easy to discount a crippled veteran camping on the mall who was fervently chanting, "Bring Our Brothers Home!"[11]

In an unusual step, the *New York Times* opened its editorial pages to Jan Barry, one of the founders of Vietnam Veterans Against the War.[12] To explain their purpose, Barry cited the recent conviction of Lieutenant Calley, which had brought home "the real dilemma of my generation." For men of a certain age, the only choices were "to kill on military orders and be a criminal, or to refuse to kill and be a criminal." Brought up on the lessons of Nuremburg and the importance of individual conscience, his generation was not prepared to work on behalf of "perhaps the world's most deadly efficient police state."

Nixon and Kissinger were deaf to all of this, viewing the dissenting soldiers as people out to destroy their own country. Kissinger thought it might be time to go on the offensive: "Instead of batting back the balls they throw," maybe the wiser thing would be "to accuse them of turning things over to the communists."[13] This suggestion surprised the president, who reminded him, "I have been on the offensive as much as I can be." There was no sense telling Richard Nixon he was too soft on opponents. Kissinger quickly retreated: "You can do no more. You can do no more." But this left the problem of the plummeting polls, which the China developments had not yet alleviated.

Meanwhile the new group of protestors, numbering between 200,000 and half a million people, had begun pouring into the capital.[14] By the spring of 1971 the peace movement had become more splintered than ever, divided over goals and tactics and hindered by limited resources. Yet so sharp was the reaction to Laos that a relatively new entity, the National Peace Action Coalition, had been able to pull together one of the largest demonstrations in Washington history. On April 24, protestors came by plane, train, bus, and car, tying up the Maryland Turnpike for more than 20 miles. The peaceful and diverse crowd included students, African Americans, trade unionists, middle-class professionals, and most remarkably, active duty soldiers and wounded veterans. More than one-third of those attending reported that this was their first protest.

Wending their way from the ellipse to the Capitol, the marchers were greeted by friendly politicians and luminaries.[15] The message of the day was clear: it was time for Congress to exercise its constitutional power and end the Vietnam War. There was no hope for a White House that was spinning wildly out of public control.

At times, the peace movement activists underestimated the impact of their organizing and of antiwar sentiment in general. In fact, the debacle in Laos and the associated protests had convinced the president that he had to move swiftly to assuage public impatience.[16] As he explained to Kissinger:

> The war presents a very serious problem. The people are sick of it, and so therefore our game here, must be to deal with it. And we've played it right to the hilt with no support and got as far as the Laotian thing, goddamn poor execution of it on the part of the military.

Going forward, "everything has to be played, now, in terms of how we survive." Mindful of the calendar, Kissinger reminded him of the South Vietnamese elections coming up in October. It would be unwise to do anything that might undermine President Thieu before that time. "Don't worry so goddamn much about the Vietnamese election," Nixon replied irritably. "You'd better worry about our own."

Such presidential rethinking was unknown to the protestors, many of whom were certain that Nixon would continue to fight "down to the last Asian," or so it was said. Had they been cognizant of Nixon's evolving strategy, they would likely have disapproved. No matter what plan was being hatched in the White House, if it included additional years or even months of senseless killing, this was unacceptable. It was this acute awareness of wasted lives that had been fragmenting the peace movement for years. Among antiwar activists, the perception of people dying every day intensified the desire for an effective strategy. But what approach would work best? Was it better to stick with "tried and true" democratic practices—electoral politics, congressional pressure, and large, peaceful demonstrations? Or did the urgency of the crisis require a willingness to shatter mainstream norms and engage in disruptive, possibly violent and illegal actions?

In an effort to sidestep these ideological rifts, organizations agreed that April 24 would be set aside for a dignified, restrained event that could attract a broad spectrum of participants.[17] On subsequent days, leadership would be yielded to the People's Coalition for Peace and Justice (PCPJ), a multi-issue coalition focused on both domestic and international policy. Over the next week, Washington was treated to the appearance of "guerilla theater" in diverse locations, mimicking the crude experiences of war.[18]

From Nixon's perspective these hijinks were something of a blessing, hopefully erasing the positive impression made by the veterans' protests. But there was greater apprehension in the White House about the possible antics of the Mayday Tribe, a faction of the PCPJ led by Rennie Davis, formerly of the Chicago Eight. The Mayday Tribe had announced its plan to shut down the capital and was calling upon people to organize themselves into "affinity groups," with the idea of closing all the major bridges and roads into downtown DC.

Over the weekend their people could camp out in West Potomac Park, ready to swing into action bright and early Monday morning, May 3. Arriving demonstrators were handed neatly printed instruction sheets containing a map of the downtown area, with circles and arrows indicating the places most suitable for blocking. They also received a statement of purpose: "The aim of the Mayday actions is to raise the social cost of the war to a level unacceptable to America's rulers. To do this we seek to create the specter of social chaos, while maintaining the support or at least toleration of the broad masses of American people."[19]

In unconscious parody of American GIs gearing up for a "search and destroy" mission, the protestors were up before dawn and on the move. Many wore boots and army jackets, with handkerchiefs around their necks for protection from teargas. Since the Mayday map of downtown DC with its colorful circles and arrows was as available to law enforcement personnel as to demonstrators, the police were able to place themselves in the target areas and, using nightsticks and teargas, easily disperse or arrest the demonstrators.[20] It was no surprise that police would pick up demonstrators who were obstructing the streets and bridges or being otherwise disruptive.

But they did not limit themselves to demonstrators, having absurdly decided to carry out mass arrests downtown.

In practice this meant hauling off large numbers of people unaware that they were near the designated "choke points," with the ironic result that people who had nothing to do with the protests were arrested more easily than the fleeing protestors. By mid-day more than 7,000 people were under arrest, and the DC courts and jails were overwhelmed. Instead of processing the arrestees in normal fashion, the police brought them to a football field near RFK Stadium, surrounded by a wire fence.

For hours they were held without sanitary facilities, food, or protection from the wind. Toward nighttime black residents from the surrounding neighborhood arrived with beans, soup, and sandwiches for the prisoners, who were yet to be identified or charged with any crime. Chuck Colson saw a chance to score a quick political point, sending crates of oranges to the prisoners in the makeshift holding area courtesy of Ed Muskie, perhaps the strongest presidential candidate in the Democratic field. Linking him to lawbreakers seemed clever. Colson was amazing, Nixon reflected, "I don't know how the hell he does this stuff . . . but it was good, so long as he didn't get caught.[21]

When domestic advisor John Ehrlichman drove past the football field, he realized that it resembled "a concentration camp." At his urging, the prisoners were moved to the coliseum, where they were held under equally adverse conditions but out of the public eye. Meanwhile the number of those arrested continued to grow over the course of the week, eventually numbering 12,000, making this the largest mass arrest in the nation's history.[22]

As an avid consumer of polls, Nixon was delighted to see that the public was overwhelmingly critical of the Mayday actions, with 18% saying they approved and a whopping 81% expressing opposition. Yet the events that had preceded Mayday, the veterans' demonstrations and the April 24 demonstration sponsored by the PJCP—not to mention demonstrations held at the same time in other places, including the largest demonstration ever in San Francisco, big rallies in Boston and New York, and numerous marches in other cities—made clear that there was a large and ever-growing peace movement that was attracting mainstream Americans.[23] Of particular concern were the antiwar actions at 19 military bases in the United States, including Fort Bragg, Fort Bliss, Fort Hood, and Fort Lewis.[24]

One of the Mayday demonstrators was Daniel Ellsberg.[25] By this time the 40-year-old RAND analyst and former strategist for the Kennedy and

Johnson administrations had become so disillusioned about the war that he had gone with a Boston "affinity group" to be part of the protests. Ellsberg's emergence as an antiwar activist reflected a dramatic about-face. He had once been such a Cold War zealot that a year after graduating near the top of his class at Harvard, he had enlisted in the Marines. In subsequent years he had worked for Secretary of Defense McNamara, and in late 1965 had gone to Vietnam, where he was assigned to Major General Edward Landsdale, who was working on pacification. His experiences there had convinced him that the war was being conducted unwisely, although he had continued to believe in its necessity.[26]

In 1967 Ellsberg had returned to the RAND Corporation where he had previously worked.[27] Still a believer, he was one of a cadre of several dozen writers and researchers, six of them from RAND, who were recruited to work on a top secret project initiated by McNamara. The distraught McNamara had reluctantly concluded that the Vietnam War had veered seriously off course, and he was determined to find out why. When the study—which bore the prosaic title "U.S. Decision-making in Vietnam, 1945–68" (later known as "the Pentagon Papers")—was finally complete, one copy of it, totaling 7,000 pages, was deposited in a safe in the Washington offices of RAND, where Ellsberg used his insider status to obtain access to it all.

As he pored over the complete text, doubts that had developed during his Vietnam sojourn continued to grow.[28] Especially dismaying was the extent of the lying, and his realization that despite their awareness that success in Vietnam was unlikely, high-level policymakers had cynically plowed ahead, more fearful of losing a war on their watch than of forfeiting thousands of American lives. Ellsberg had briefly hoped that with the advent of Henry Kissinger as Nixon's national security advisor, wiser heads might prevail, and a graceful exit from Vietnam could be arranged. But while troop levels were coming down, he had been warned by friends on the NSC staff that new plans were afoot to pressure Hanoi with even greater levels of violence.[29]

By fall 1969, Ellsberg had started to attend antiwar events where he met young activists who shared his sense of urgency and moral outrage. And he began to ask himself, what risks was he willing to take? Having read through all of McNamara's secret study, he believed that its contents were explosive. What if the American public could see this work? Perhaps people could more readily grasp the disastrous path on which the Nixon administration was now embarked and demand an end?

To make that happen, Ellsberg knew he would have to break the law. But there were 7,000 pages that had to be photocopied. For assistance he turned to Anthony Russo, a friend who had previously worked at RAND. Russo had gone through his own conversion experience after completing a study of "VC Prisoners and Defectors," which revealed to him qualities of dedication and patriotism among the communists that were notably absent on the South Vietnamese side. When Ellsberg suggested they work together, Russo readily accepted, though he also understood that if discovered, they could both be sent to jail.

The photocopying stretched over many months and was not completed until early 1970. Ellsberg had entertained the hope that he could give the study to Senator Fulbright, who would reveal its findings to the Foreign Relations Committee. But, after numerous expressions of interest, the senator backed off, claiming that the material was of historical significance only. More than likely Fulbright, as well as other colleagues approached by Ellsberg, was reluctant to take classified materials from a private citizen and make them publicly available on his own authority.[30]

By early 1971 Ellsberg was in a quandary. If nobody in Congress was willing to step up and publicize the study, who else would have the standing or the ability to summarize for the public the meaning of 7,000 pages of complex, dense material? Yet the price of silence weighed heavily on him. Then in February 1971 came the very escalation he had feared. With thousands of South Vietnamese troops pouring into Laos, Ellsberg wrote a blistering article for the *New York Review of Books* in which he reiterated the question he had posed at MIT:

> How many will die in Laos? What is Richard Nixon's best estimate of the number of Laotian people, "enemy" and "non-enemy" that US firepower will kill in the next twelve months. *He does not have an estimate.* He has not asked Henry Kissinger for one, and Kissinger has not asked the Pentagon; and none of these officials has ever seen an answer to this or any comparable question on the expected impact of war policy on human life.[31]

In the shadow of Lam Son 719, a public airing of the papers assumed a new urgency. Following a suggestion from Senator George McGovern, Ellsberg turned to Neil Sheehan of the *New York Times*, with whom he had become acquainted in Vietnam. They shared a desire to escape the Saigon bubble and had ventured beyond the usual places to see for themselves what the war had wrought.

As he examined the papers in early March, Sheehan readily grasped their significance. But would the editors of the *New York Times* be willing to publish classified documents? At an earlier point, they might have turned this down. But relations with the Nixon administration had deteriorated badly, and censorship of the Laotian operation had made things worse. Realizing they had a major story on their hands, the editors ignored legal advice and decided that the public's need to know outweighed other considerations.

On June 13, the first of what was to become a multipart series appeared in the paper. Among the revelations, the published material showed that the Johnson administration had misrepresented events in the Gulf of Tonkin, falsely claiming that American destroyers on routine patrol in international waters had twice been unlawfully fired on by North Vietnamese torpedo boats. This dishonest claim had provided the justification for the Gulf of Tonkin Resolution, passed by both houses of Congress on August 7, 1964, which had given the president virtually unlimited authority to wage war in Vietnam.[32]

With this opener, it was clear that many damaging revelations were in the offing. But did any of this pose a threat to the Nixon administration's handling of the war? The president's initial reaction was that it did not. After all, the chief impact of the Pentagon Papers, which covered a period before he took office, would be to cast an unfavorable light on the Kennedy and Johnson administrations. Kissinger seemed to concur.[33]

However, their complacency soon evaporated. For a major newspaper to be brazenly printing classified documents set an alarming precedent. Attorney General John Mitchell warned that if they wished to challenge the paper, they would have to do so immediately.[34] In light of their dependence on keeping information secret from the public, they could hardly do otherwise. On June 14 the Justice Department instructed the newspaper to cease publication of the papers, lest it face prosecution under the Espionage Act. When it continued to do so, Mitchell obtained a temporary restraining order, enjoining the newspaper from publishing further articles pending a court ruling.

Within three days the source of the leak became known. When Kissinger heard it was Daniel Ellsberg, he was both infuriated and frightened. Given Ellsberg's ties to former members of Kissinger's staff, several of whom had resigned from the NSC in the wake of the Cambodian invasion, there was no telling how much dirt they all had in their possession.[35] The president had always doubted the loyalty of these highly credentialed Jewish intellectuals on Kissinger's staff. Here was another Harvard traitor whom Kissinger had recruited. If he was not careful, Nixon would be blaming him.

Kissinger vigorously denounced Ellsberg as a psycho, a drug user, a sexual pervert—somebody who had to be stopped at all costs. He was also "a genius, the brightest student I ever had,"[36] and once such "a hardliner" that he had volunteered to go to Vietnam, where he drove around shooting at peasants. But he had become "an intransigent radical" and "totally wild." Their personal connection was long gone, except for a recent encounter at an MIT conference, where the man "heckled me and called me a murderer."

It was clear to Nixon and Kissinger that their enemies were on the rampage, with even veteran Cold Warriors like Ellsberg turning traitor and papers across the country publishing the Pentagon Papers. Faced with an injunction, the *New York Times* had ceased publishing, but within 24 hours the *Washington Post* was featuring the story. When the Justice Department got an injunction against the *Post*, the *Boston Globe*, the *Chicago Sun-Times*, the *St. Louis Post Dispatch*, and others picked it up (since in anticipation of these legal challenges Ellsberg had circulated copies to multiple news outlets). It was a virtual mini-revolt by the media. Lest the Supreme Court successfully rule against the press, Senator Mike Gravel of Alaska was reading the Pentagon Papers, page by page, into the Congressional Record. "The story is a terrible one," he maintained.[37] "It is replete with duplicity, connivance against the public. People are being killed as I speak to you."

The administration's legal strategy was having a perverse effect. By obtaining injunctions against the *New York Times* and the *Washington Post*, it had inadvertently elevated the significance of the Pentagon Papers and thrust them into the headlines, adding drama to what might otherwise have seemed a too-dense and technical set of revelations. As the stories kept popping up in other papers the details may have eluded many readers, but the overall message was clear: successive administrations had deceived Congress and the American public for decades. Within a week, the political ground seemed to be shifting. By the time the Supreme Court ruled 6–3 on behalf of the newspapers' right to publish the Pentagon Papers without fear of prosecution under the Espionage Act, their content had been widely disseminated.

There was also new difficulty on the legislative front. For almost two years, antiwar senators had been pushing "end-the-war" amendments to defense appropriations and other bills, which would have cut off Vietnam funding by various deadlines. While support for these had increased over time, they had never passed. Sensing a new mood in the country, Majority Leader Mike Mansfield put forward an alternate amendment to a Selective Service bill that would establish as official policy "the prompt and orderly withdrawal" of all American forces from Indochina in "not later than nine months" provided Hanoi released all American prisoners of war.[38] Unlike previous measures, this one passed the Senate by a margin of 57–42. The House subsequently voted it down, but with a closer vote than before (219–176).[39]

Nixon took the congressional challenge very seriously.[40] Not only were the votes tightening with a growing number of Republican defectors, but whatever support he retained was tied to the promise of ongoing troop withdrawals and hopes for a diplomatic solution. Yet unlike Kissinger, Nixon was dubious about the chances of a negotiated settlement. The leaders in Hanoi could obviously observe that the United States was getting out of Vietnam. Therefore, what incentive would they have to accept a compromise? As for troop withdrawals, Lam Son 719 had made it clear that ARVN was woefully unprepared to fight alone. This left a serious question about how low US troop levels could safely go without opening the door to a communist victory.

Beyond these strategic concerns, the administration was facing a legitimacy crisis of major proportions. Could the American people believe their government? As articulated by the antiwar veterans and plainly revealed by the Pentagon Papers, American leaders had abused the trust of their own citizens for years, with tragic consequences for many at home and abroad. This generalization applied to Richard Nixon as well as to his predecessors. But unlike the others, Nixon was facing reelection in 18 months. Before things got worse, he was determined to crack down on dissent—especially dissent from government "insiders."

Nixon had special anxiety about Morton Halperin and Leslie Gelb, two former White House officials who had access to top secret documents.[41] By 1971 both men were senior fellows at the Brookings Institution. The president feared that they had removed classified material and stored it in the Brookings safe. It was possible that Gelb, who had directed the McNamara study later published as the Pentagon Papers, might have taken files pertinent to the 1968 bombing halt. If so, there could be evidence of Nixon's illegal sabotage of Johnson's peace negotiations. On June 17, 1971, Nixon ordered Haldeman to arrange a break-in. "Hell, they do that. You're to break into the place, rifle the files, and bring them out."[42] If necessary, to divert attention, the president thought they could "firebomb" the building.

In fact this was easier said than done and, despite various schemes, Nixon's order was never carried out. More proactive was the administration's campaign against Ellsberg himself. On June 28, after two weeks in hiding, Ellsberg turned himself in to federal court in Boston and was charged with espionage, theft, and conspiracy. Yet the combination of Ellsberg's actions, plus a broader White House apprehension about the loyalty of people in other government agencies, spurred a new initiative. At Nixon's behest, a special investigative unit (SIU) was tasked with preventing and ferreting out "leakers" of government secrets. For all presidents the disclosure of classified information was an affliction; in this instance, Nixon had a larger problem because over the previous two years, so many agencies involved with "national security" had been marginalized that the administration was rife with discontent. But the first important job of SIU –dubbed the "the plumbers"—was to discredit Daniel Ellsberg.

June 1971 proved to be the lowest point of Nixon's tenure in office. In the aftermath of Lam Son 719, the administration's Vietnam policy was going nowhere. Neither its costly build-up of ARVN nor its diplomacy had yielded any discernible success. Antiwar protest was rising, while the demoralization in the military was cutting deep. Meanwhile, its effort to bludgeon the news media into suppressing the Pentagon Papers had not only failed but also had contributed to the public's sense of dishonesty in the highest places.

Yet as grim as the situation might appear, Nixon and Kissinger were pinning their hopes on something new and remarkable: a burgeoning relationship with the People's Republic of China. Since receiving word in late April that Chinese Premier Zhou Enlai would welcome a visit from an envoy of the president, or even the president himself, to discuss relations between their two countries, the two were eagerly embracing the idea. Top secret arrangements were underway for Kissinger to go to Beijing for meetings with Zhou on July 9–11. If these talks went well, Nixon would make a public announcement that was sure to cause a sensation in the United States and rattle the communist world: in 1972 he would be traveling to China. This exciting prospect appealed to Nixon despite his dark mood. It was the kind of bold, dramatic move that only the great leaders in history make. It was thrilling on every count: diverting people's attention from Vietnam, and paving the way for a dramatic turnabout in superpower relations.

PART II
WAR AND DIPLOMACY

17

"You've Only Got One Card"

Given their Vietnam woes and the furor surrounding the Pentagon Papers, diplomacy with Beijing assumed particular importance. As of July 1971, both Nixon and Kissinger were hoping that success in this venture could boost Nixon's political standing at home and perhaps facilitate a diplomatic breakthrough with Hanoi. In discussions with his national security advisor, the president emphasized the stakes: "You've only got really one card. That's the card with meeting in Peking with Zhou; but that's a pretty good card too."[1] Both men were determined that the card be played well—and secretly. It was first high-level negotiation with the Chinese government since 1949, and they limited the news of it to a handful of people, purposefully excluding Secretary Rogers and the Asian specialists in the State Department.

Nixon coached Kissinger about what posture to strike. Communists appreciated straight talk, he explained. Over the years, his own effectiveness with leaders like Romania's Ceausescu was because "I don't fart around." He tried to be nice, but then "I come right in with cold steel."[2] They were dealing with "bastards" who only understood blunt language.

Kissinger should play on their fears. Remind them of Nixon's toughness, emphasize "this is the man who did Cambodia; this is the man who did Laos; this is the man who will . . . protect our interests without regard for political considerations." As for Vietnam, the Chinese should be clear that if the Paris talks failed, Nixon was prepared "to go hard." Kissinger was to hint at some additional dangers—of a US–Soviet agreement on nuclear arms control, or a revived militaristic Japan. "These things are going to move them a hell of lot more than all the gobbledygook about . . . our being civilized."[3] He recognized that Zhou would want to discuss the status of Taiwan. On this sensitive subject, Kissinger should not indicate "a willingness to abandon much of our support for Taiwan until it was necessary to do so."

This posture notwithstanding, the Americans were the supplicants going into the July negotiation. From the beginning of his administration, Nixon had been seeking an opening to China for several reasons, of which the desire to pressure the Soviet Union was perhaps most salient. However by the time of Kissinger's trip, Nixon's political weakness had lent new urgency to the effort. Despite the reference to "cold steel," Kissinger understood how desperately Nixon wanted to go to Beijing. An invitation to China would add luster to a foreign policy record that was thus far devoid of achievement. As for Kissinger's personal fortunes, a successful encounter with Zhou Enlai was no less necessary. Much of his power within the administration turned on his alleged skills as a negotiator, but his accomplishments were few.

To facilitate this adventure, Nixon and Kissinger were relying on the government of Pakistan, then under martial law. The situation in that country was appalling.[4] To quell an independence movement in West Pakistan, the Pakistani army had killed, tortured, or raped hundreds of thousands of people, with the result that millions of mostly Hindu refugees were fleeing across the border into India. From Dacca, American consul Archie Blood had plaintively written, "we are mute and horrified witnesses to a reign of terror by the Pak military." Sooner or later "the full horror of Pak military atrocities will come to light," but there was no reason to accept the government's lies. "We should be expressing our shock at least privately . . . at this wave of terror directed against their own countrymen."

For Nixon and Kissinger, however, there was every incentive to withhold criticism. Pakistan's president Yahya Khan was an important US ally, who had the right to handle his recalcitrant people as he chose. The moral arguments of US diplomats carried no weight, nor did the warnings from the US Embassy in India that the refugee situation was unsustainable and might lead to a full-scale war with Pakistan. For Kissinger in particular, the emotional cables from Dacca and New Delhi were further grist for his never-ending effort to discredit the State Department in Nixon's eyes.

The important consideration was that Yahya Khan, a friend of China, had proved a discreet carrier of messages between Washington and Beijing. To facilitate Kissinger's secret journey to China, the plan was for him to go on a "fact-finding" trip to Islamabad, where he would feign a stomachache and drop out of sight. While ostensibly recovering he would be surreptitiously whisked away on a Pakistani plane to Beijing.

For Kissinger, such maneuvers had become commonplace. For 18 months he had enjoyed slipping in and out of Paris for clandestine meetings with Le Duc Tho, The ruse for his China trip added drama to an historic venture.

Upon meeting the Chinese prime minister Zhou Enlai for the first time, Kissinger opened on an idealistic note:

> We have come to the People's Republic of China with an open mind and an open heart. We hope that when we leave, we may have contributed to sowing seeds from which will grow peace between our countries, peace in this region, and peace in this world.

Of course, there were "deep ideological differences between us." But they should let history decide which point of view should prevail. Meanwhile, the two nations should cooperate on matters of joint concern "on the basis of mutual respect and equality and for the benefit of all mankind."[5]

Such friendly rhetoric might seem an unexceptional beginning to this dramatic new relationship. But what Kissinger went on to say was more remarkable: "It is the conviction of President Nixon that a strong and developing People's Republic of China poses no threat to any essential U.S. interest." In the light of this confidence, he was authorized to promise Zhou that the United States would take "no major steps affecting your interests" without prior discussion with the Chinese government. Such a statement might have surprised the millions of Americans who had been led to believe that the nation's soldiers were fighting and dying in Vietnam in order to stave off both a Chinese and Soviet menace.

Zhou Enlai was gracious in response but turned quickly to the question of Taiwan, about which "we cannot but blame your government." Taiwan had been a part of China for 1,000 years, "a longer period than Long Island has been part of the United States." In recognizing China the United States "must do so unreservedly," accepting that Taiwan was an "inalienable part of Chinese territory." Furthermore, there was no justification for an American military presence on Taiwan or in the surrounding waters. This was a reference to the approximately 10,000 American troops who were on the island as part of a mutual defense treaty. Within a short period all US armed forces in Taiwan should withdraw, and all military installations should be dismantled.

Nixon's instructions to Kissinger had specified that "we not appear to be dumping on our friends" and should be "somewhat mysterious about our overall willingness to make concessions" on Taiwan. However, in replying to Zhou Enlai, Kissinger went further. Two-thirds of the US military presence in Taiwan was related to the war in Vietnam, he said. Once that conflict had ended, these soldiers would be removed. As for the remaining third, those numbers could also go down "as our relations improved." Kissinger emphasized that such assurances must be kept confidential. These were "personal ideas of President Nixon" that had not been shared with "our bureaucracy or with Congress."

As for the political future of Taiwan, the United States did not support a "two-China" or "one China, one Taiwan" policy. Over time he thought relations might evolve in the direction Zhou had described. During the next year and a half, there was no possibility of US recognition of the People's Republic of China "as the sole government of China," but during Nixon's second term this might change.

According to Kissinger, the settlement of the Taiwan question was linked to the resolution of the Vietnam War. While the American government was determined to make peace, it was also seeking a settlement "consistent with our honor and self-respect." If this proved elusive, then the war would continue and the United States would be compelled to take actions which, while not directed at China, "will have unfortunate consequence for our relations."

Kissinger disclosed his secret negotiations with Le Duc Tho, emphasizing that the United States was prepared to set a date for complete withdrawal from South Vietnam. However, the North Vietnamese were stubbornly insisting on the removal of the Thieu government and were refusing to implement a ceasefire before all the Americans soldiers had left. To be clear, the United States government would not engineer the overthrow of the Thieu government, Kissinger stated. But it would guarantee the right of the South Vietnamese people to determine their own political future without interference. Once US troops left Vietnam, "we will not reenter . . . and will abide by the political process." The important thing was to separate the political solution from the military settlement.[6]

Was this Kissinger's subtle way of signaling to the Chinese leader that the United States was reconciled to the triumph of the communists, so long as there was a face-saving "interval" between the departure of its troops and the success of its enemy? Or was this a false promise designed to lull Zhou into support for the American approach? Whatever the intent, the Chinese prime minister was unimpressed. Nor did he seem moved by Kissinger's suggestion that "the end of the war in Indochina will accelerate the improvement in our relations."

The "most honorable and glorious" way to solve the problem, Zhou observed, was for the United States to pull all of its troops out of Vietnam, Cambodia, and Laos, and let the local people decide their own fate. An "overwhelming majority of people around the world" favored this course. It was perfectly clear that without American propping up the "puppet" government of South Vietnam, that entity would have collapsed years ago. The Vietnamese were a fiercely independent people who had already been "hoodwinked" once when they accepted the Geneva Accords of 1954. They would not be tricked again.

The Vietnamese might be heroic, Kissinger countered, "but the same qualities which make them such great fighters make it hard for them to make peace." And that's why it would be so valuable "if some of their friends . . . can help with their perspective so that they understand that . . . political evolution is necessary."

Overnight, Zhou reviewed the most recent North Vietnamese peace plan submitted by the PRG negotiator Madame Binh. This proposal seemed eminently reasonable and was more conciliatory than Kissinger had indicated. It offered the release of all American POWs in exchange for a complete withdrawal of American troops. It also provided for a ceasefire if the United States withheld its backing of General Thieu, thus enabling an interim Saigon regime to be formed that could negotiate a political settlement with the PRG.

As Zhou understood the American position, the roadblock was its desire to leave the Thieu government in power after a ceasefire had gone into effect. This insistence ignored the North Vietnamese view of the Saigon regime as a foreign construct, and their determination to rid their country of foreign control. "There have been 25 years since the Vietnamese people began their resistance against the French," plus another 10 years fighting US "aggression." These were tough people, Zhou emphasized, who would be willing to sacrifice another million men in order to get the Americans out. The Nixon administration would be wise to withdraw its troops, but if "the situation does not relax in Indochina, we must continue to give aid."

It was clear from Zhou Enlai's remarks that he was not inclined to pressure Hanoi into a peace agreement anytime soon. But Kissinger's other major objective was to create favorable conditions for a presidential visit. If this was achieved it could tip the scales domestically, begin to reshape the Cold War, and, as a minimum, inject fear into the Hanoi leadership.

Yet on their last day, Zhou was still looking to clarify Kissinger's ideas on "normalization" of relations with his government. He said he did not understand why, if the Nixon administration really did intend to downsize its military on Taiwan, it needed to postpone announcing changes in the political relationship until some future time. It was not Zhou's intention to set "preconditions" for the president's trip, but if Nixon were to come to China without any plan to make public some kind of resolution of the political questions regarding Taiwan, "what impression would this give the world?"

Kissinger temporized. Since the United States was not supporting a "two-China" approach, this clearly implied its acknowledgment that Taiwan was not an independent entity. Formal recognition of the People's Republic as the sole legitimate government of China would require more time, he maintained, but when Nixon came to China they could discuss an actual date.

Zhou pointed out that United Nations delegates would soon be deciding the status of China, and American ambiguity would surely complicate matters. Kissinger replied that the United States was willing to allow a simple majority of the General Assembly rather than two-thirds to decide on admission, a procedural shift that would virtually ensure China would be accepted and be given a seat on the Security Council. The Nixon administration would also call for a two-thirds requirement for expulsion—which might enable Taiwan to hang on a bit longer. When voting occurred, he expected that the United States would vote in favor of admitting the People's Republic and against the expulsion of Taiwan.

In his effort to cement a friendship with Zhou, Kissinger also dangled an anti-Soviet concession, promising to share "any proposal made by any other large country which could affect your interests" and to take Beijing's views on the matter very seriously. Testing this promise of transparency, Zhou wondered if there were plans for President Nixon to visit the Soviet Union any time soon. While an invitation had been extended, Kissinger acknowledged, the details were unresolved. He expected that a meeting would occur within the next six months, with the purpose of addressing specific problems—notably arms control and the future of Berlin.

By contrast, the goal of a Beijing meeting, apart from its symbolic significance, was to establish an overall framework for ongoing relations—a task best handled by President Nixon and Chairman Mao. Zhou concurred. The announcement of such an event would indeed "shake the world." Following the two and a half days of intense conversation, the meetings ended on a hopeful note. Kissinger professed himself to be "moved . . . by the idealism and spiritual qualities" of Zhou and his colleagues. He looked forward to a brand-new "relationship of friendship and cooperation." Zhou was less euphoric. "We have taken a first step," he observed.

Ignoring Zhou's caution, Kissinger was ecstatic about the talks. He was bringing home the prize the president coveted: a summit meeting in Beijing during an election year. Compared to this accomplishment, other issues seemed minor. Kissinger was confident that his extraordinary journey would open the door to other benefits. In Zhou Enlai he had found an intellectual peer to whom he could relate.

Heading home from China, Kissinger cabled Nixon that his talks in Beijing were "the most searching, sweeping, and significant discussions I have ever had in government." Apart from the particulars was the extraordinary atmosphere:

> I am frank to say that this visit was a very moving experience. The historic aspects of the occasion; the warmth and dignity of the Chinese; the splendor of the Forbidden City; Chinese history and culture; the heroic stature of Zhou Enlai; and the intensity and sweep of our talks combined to make an indelible impression on me and my colleagues.

As he summed up the visit, Kissinger assured Nixon that he had dealt with the Chinese prime minister in a firm way. In fact, he had made secret promises to betray a long-standing ally and offered the possibility of other tempting concessions on key issues.[7] But he rightly assumed that Chinese agreement to a Nixon visit would eclipse other presidential concerns.

Indeed, as news of Kissinger's success reached San Clemente, the vacationing president was jubilant. In a rare display of excitement, he was standing by the helipad in California as Kissinger exited the plane at 7:00 AM on July 13. For more than two hours they met privately, reviewing the details of the trip and the character of the negotiations. Kissinger conceded that it was doubtful that the Chinese government would give them any immediate assistance with Hanoi.[8] But he thought that once news of their meeting surfaced, it would create enormous anxiety for the North Vietnamese. Moreover, it would highlight the administration's willingness to make bold moves for peace.

It was finally time to inform the Secretary of State.[9] Nixon instructed Kissinger to present a "sanitized" version of his meeting with Zhou Enlai. Before Kissinger left on his trip, Rogers had been told that he was going to Islamabad to meet a Chinese emissary who had important news to discuss. Once Kissinger was in Beijing, Rogers was informed that at the last minute he had been invited to the Chinese capital. For Nixon, the duplicity seemed advisable because it was a safe assumption that State Department personnel would have been concerned about how such a meeting would impact relations with Japan and Taiwan. Had they known the content of Kissinger's conversations they would likely have been furious. To make "the big play," Nixon thought it necessary to disregard traditional lines of communication, even if it meant forfeiting access to expert opinion within the government.

When Rogers arrived for the meeting, Kissinger showered him with details and flattered him with the suggestion that the mission was the realization of the Rogers' own ideas. For the moment, the Secretary of State seemed satisfied. In an effusive follow-up phone call, Nixon congratulated Kissinger on his deft handling of Rogers. Yet both men were aware that once Nixon announced the news of the Beijing talks, they would face a much tougher response from Republican conservatives in Congress and elsewhere, who would be appalled by this betrayal of Taiwan.

Over the next 24 hours the China news was kept shrouded in secrecy as arrangements were put into place for what Nixon intended to be a dramatic television appearance. On the night of July 15, Nixon informed a surprised nationwide audience that he had sent Henry Kissinger to China to begin the process of normalizing relations between the two countries. China's prime minister Zhou Enlai had responded to this gesture by extending an invitation to the president to visit China before May 1972, which he had accepted with pleasure.

The president was quick to emphasize that this action would not come "at the expense of our old friends," nor was it directed against any other nation. He had taken this step out of a conviction that a reduction of tension between the United States and the People's Republic of China was to the advantage of all countries. It was in this spirit "that I will undertake what I deeply hope will become a journey for peace, peace not for our generation but for future generations on this earth we share together."

The presentation was vintage Nixon, a high-toned articulation of idealistic goals that cast him as a man of peace. And they had the desired effect. Journalists and politicians who had been lambasting his administration for months over its mishandling of the Vietnam War were rushing to praise him.[10] Kissinger himself became an overnight celebrity, with media outlets clamoring for interviews.

For Kissinger it was a moment of unmitigated triumph. As was often the case, Governor Rockefeller was among his biggest fans.[11] "You did it! Fabulous! Isn't this the most exciting thing?" Kissinger enjoyed telling Rockefeller about all the ruses that had been employed to get him to Beijing. "It was real James Bond." Rockefeller thought the Pakistanis must have enjoyed their role in the elaborate subterfuge. "They haven't had as much fun since the last Hindu massacre," Kissinger quipped, inadvertently revealing his detachment from the ongoing tragedy in East Pakistan and along the Indian border. "Only you" could manage something this remarkable, Rockefeller marveled.

The president saw matters differently. While appreciative of Kissinger's formidable skills as a diplomat, he thought it was his own creativity and bravery that had produced the dramatic breakthrough. While there was plenty of spontaneous praise flowing into the White House, he wanted his PR team to crank it up. Lest they overlook any of his exemplary qualities, he made a list:

1. Strong convictions.
2. Came up through adversity.
3. At his best in a crisis. Cool. Unflappable.
4. A tough bold strong leader . . .
5. A man who takes the long view, never concerned about tomorrow's headlines.
6. A man with a philosophical turn of mind.
7. A man who works without notes . . .
8. A man who knows Asia.
9. A man, who in personal style is very strong and very tough . . .

These were traits he shared with Prime Minister Zhou Enlai, a similarity that might be usefully emphasized. It was a curious thought—this suggestion that he be identified with one of the leading communist revolutionaries of the twentieth century even as he continued to rain bombs on three small nations because of a communist presence.

Naturally there were some discordant notes. The government of Taiwan was predictably furious about the secrecy of Kissinger's mission as well as the substance. Terming this "a shabby deal," their Washington ambassador, James Shen, lodged a formal protest with the State Department. In a meeting with Assistant Secretary of State Marshall Green, he demanded to know what had transpired during Kissinger's meeting with Zhou Enlai.[12] Green, who had not even seen the un-sanitized transcripts, reassured him that nothing had been said that would undercut the long-standing friendship between the United States and the Republic of China or affect America's commitment to Taiwan's defense.

In a subsequent meeting with Ambassador Shen, Kissinger apologized profusely for the secrecy of his trip.[13] This occurred because of "general necessities" that had nothing to do with their commitment to Taiwan. Nor was he under any illusion about the character of the Beijing regime. As he had told the president, "we were dealing with fanatical maniacs." Ambassador Shen wanted to know more about the specific items discussed—including the question of "two Chinas" and his government's seat on the UN Security Council. Kissinger assured him that "we took the position which we had always taken" on these matters and that the subject of the Security Council had not come up at all.

What then did the People's Republic of China hope to gain from a Nixon trip? Shen wondered. Kissinger couldn't say for certain, but he could assure the ambassador that whenever it took place, the president would make no concessions on Taiwan—despite the fact that he had already done so. Among other things he had informed Zhou that the United States would cease blocking the PRC's admission to the United Nations, had disavowed the policy of "two Chinas," and had intimated that American recognition of Beijing would likely come in Nixon's second term. He had also specifically stated that once the Vietnam War was over, two-thirds of the American military presence on Taiwan would be removed.

The non-recognition of "Red China" had long been a conservative touchstone in American politics. Hence the dismay was predictable in right-wing circles when they heard the news of the diplomatic initiatives with China. Faced with objections from a handful of senators, notably John Tower of Texas and James Buckley of New York, Kissinger was dispatched to assure them the United States had no intention of selling out their old ally.[14]

Apart from the right-wing complaints, Nixon's China move was causing his poll numbers, which had been dropping since Laos, to bounce up.[15] Nixon was convinced that to win the presidential election he needed to make peace his own issue.[16] For this purpose, the overture to China was of key importance.

To promote this image, Kissinger was an ideal spokesman. In his briefings to the media and other groups he provided riveting detail about his dramatic trip, the character of Chinese officialdom, and the rich diplomatic possibilities that lay before them. In recounting these exchanges to Nixon, he liked to emphasize how attendees seemed to lap it up. He especially mentioned Hugh Sidey of *Time*, who was "beside himself" with excitement over the prospect of the presidential visit.

Throughout his tenure as national security advisor, Kissinger had cultivated the friendship of favored journalists. In the aftermath of his Beijing trip this network of connections grew exponentially. It was fully apparent that he was the man to see in the administration. The State Department might hold sway over secondary issues but on the major decisions, power was in Kissinger's hands.

Hugh Sidey's enthusiasm paid immediate dividends for *Time* when Kissinger agreed to a two-hour off-the-record interview with him and others from the magazine.[17] During the session he was asked to compare the Russians and Chinese, to which he responded with some locker-room talk: "The Russians are tough you know. They grab you by the balls first and then ask if it hurts." They acted this way because they were suffering from "an inferiority complex" and quite often their positions were not well thought-out. They compared unfavorably to the Chinese, who were more business-like, capable of real discussion, and able to acknowledge past mistakes.

Turning to Vietnam, the reporters wondered if Beijing would be able to exert leverage over Hanoi. Kissinger sounded dubious. It was not clear that the North Vietnamese would abide by the outside judgment of anyone. However, the developing relationship with China was keeping the Vietnam War off the front pages. This was in itself a positive development because Hanoi was reliant on publicity in the United States to advance its goals. His purpose in going to China was to "open up new vistas" and to mentally consign Vietnam to "the periphery of the Asian problem as a whole," where it belonged.

The journalists wanted to know what the Chinese were hoping to gain from these diplomatic initiatives. Kissinger thought they wished to return "to the community of nations." Since the United States appeared to the Chinese as "the least dangerous world power that threatens it," their effort to heal the breach made sense. Although at odds with the decades-old charge that "Red China" was a dangerously expansive power, he thought its purposes were in fact defensive. "Is it now your view that we are dealing with a non-expansionist China?" one asked. As far as he could discern, "the Chinese don't think of themselves as expansionist," Kissinger replied. The Korean War was an outlier, a situation where Chinese leaders perceived a "plausible threat." But at the present time there "wasn't much military activity" going on there.

These jaw-dropping claims flew in the face of Cold War orthodoxy. Yet the journalists did not pursue the matter, choosing to lob softball questions at Kissinger instead. Did people in China read *Time?* they wondered. Kissinger couldn't say, but observed the Chinese seemed extraordinarily "well informed," more so than many Europeans. And what about their culture? Was there talk of music, poetry, and art? Kissinger said he had seen "interesting calligraphy, poetry in the guest house." In fact when he mentioned it to his hosts, it turned out to be Mao's poetry adorning the walls. Could it be said that the Chinese have "a deep feeling about their country?" Kissinger wasn't certain, but "when you meet the Chinese, you sense a spiritual quality—a monkish cult that I could understand."

"Then it's one, two, three, what are we fightin' for?" Two summers before, this was the angry refrain that Country Joe and the Fish had sung at Woodstock. In the quiet Washington office of *Time-Life* in July 1971, the same question might have been asked, but wasn't: If Chinese leaders were such reasonable, spiritual, non-expansionist people, what was the rationale for continuing the Vietnam War? For years, leading officials had been warning of "Red China's" ambitions and need to oppose the Vietnamese communists to block their aggression. But if this was all illusory, what was the point of the war?

Although the reporters did not ask the question, Kissinger answered it preemptively. It was still important to end the war on the right terms, he maintained:

> We must control events. Even if we goofed our way into the Vietnam War . . . we must end the war in a competent way. We must reveal a national purpose. We must get the young to understand that purpose requires suffering and can't be had for nothing.

By the summer of 1971, America's young were certainly aware of the suffering; perhaps as many as 40,000 of them had died in the service of this "goof." Hundreds of thousands more were coping with severe wounds in body and mind. What then was this "national purpose" Kissinger had in mind? And how would the continuation of a failing war in three small countries advance it? Nobody asked. The *Time* reporters had come to this interview for the inside story of a secret, historic trip to a mysterious and until now forbidden country, not to pose adversarial questions.

Nixon and Kissinger were eager to nail down specific arrangements for their China initiative. At the end of the Kissinger's departure from Beijing, it had been agreed that he would return in the fall to begin steps toward the normalization of relations and to prepare for Nixon's visit in early 1972. However, in advance of this second trip a complicating factor was the impending fight in the UN General Assembly over the seating of the People's Republic.

The dispute about Chinese representation was practically an annual ritual, but over the years, opinion within that body had been shifting with a clear majority in fall 1971 favoring the seating of the People's Republic.[18] All that prevented its admission was a rule requiring two-thirds approval for seating a new member. In response, the US State Department was prepared to abandon this rule, while pressing a "dual representation" formula that would allow Taiwan to remain in the organization.

Within the administration this approach was not disputed, but the question was how to vigorously fight for Taiwan. Simmering beneath the surface of this dispute was the bitter rivalry between Kissinger and Rogers, exacerbated by the secrecy surrounding the China trip. This was not simply a conflict of personalities, but a difference over policy. Though not opposed in principle to the overtures toward Beijing, the State Department was less willing to take steps that would jeopardize long-standing alliances with Taiwan and Japan.[19]

For Kissinger, the overriding priority was to maintain the momentum of his diplomacy with the PRC. Nixon's position was more complicated, since Taiwan's President Chiang Kai-Shek remained an icon to the right. It therefore served both men's purposes to allow the State Department, acting through UN Ambassador George Bush, to carry on the quest for votes in New York.[20]

Yet the contradiction in US policy was apparent. While Bush and his colleagues were in the trenches meeting with as many of the 126 delegations to the UN as they could convince to support Taiwan, the administration's overture to Beijing had plainly damaged their case.[21] It was one thing to claim, as Americans had done for decades, that the communists had illegally seized power on the Chinese mainland and had no right to representation in the international body. But once the United States began diplomatic dealings with the government of the People's Republic, there was less rationale for providing legitimacy to a second government claiming to represent the Chinese populace.

Despite weeks of hard work, the prospects for preserving Taiwan's United Nations seat were increasingly dim. On the most optimistic projection, the vote would be very tight. To bolster the American case, Rogers set his sights on Kissinger's upcoming mission, which by an unfortunate accident of timing seemed likely to coincide with the General Assembly vote on Chinese representation. If that occurred, it would become impossible to gain the support of the majority. Kissinger's trip must be delayed, Rogers informed the White House.

Kissinger was undeterred. The Chinese had settled on an October 20th date in consultation with the United States and, given the delicacy of this new relationship, it seemed imprudent to upset those arrangements. And to what end? In Kissinger's view, the United States was going to lose the battle for Taiwan regardless of how it was handled.[22] A higher priority was to move forward with Nixon's visit to China.

This final consideration held sway.[23] Nixon understood that if Kissinger went to China and Taiwan ended up being expelled from the UN, the conservatives might blame him. But believing that his reelection might depend on his ability to seem a "peacemaker," the Beijing opening mattered more. Already the president's public relations men were drawing up plans for massive media coverage of his arrival there, with live television feeds to the United States.

Furthermore, as of October, Nixon had obtained an agreement from the Russians for a Moscow summit in the spring. In his view, the two commitments reinforced each other. Already his plan to go to China had sped up Soviet agreement for a summit. With the Russian visit on the horizon, the Chinese had a powerful incentive to make the Beijing meeting a success. Best of all, the fact that the United States was still at war—in Cambodia, Laos, and Vietnam—was fast receding from national attention. As editorialized by *Newsweek* there was "no doubt that, politically, summits have positioned Presidents beautifully."[24] And the timing for these meetings was "little short of perfection."

There was to be no disruption of Kissinger's plans. However, when he arrived in China in late October there were some discordant visuals. Anti-American signs were posted along the route to his hotel, and once he and the members of his party got to their rooms they found English-language propaganda bulletins summoning the people of the world "to overthrow American imperialists and their running dogs."[25] The "atmospherics" quickly improved once Zhou Enlai took command. As in July, he proved a solicitous host. this time escorting the American diplomat and his entourage to places where they would be observed by both party cadres and ordinary citizens. Between negotiating sessions there were also sumptuous banquets and warm-hearted toasts.

Although Kissinger's primary purpose in coming to China was to iron out arrangements for Nixon's visit, he also had substantive matters to discuss.

One priority was the text of a Communiqué to be issued at the conclusion of Nixon and Mao's meeting. Zhou thought it strange to be working on a statement to describe conversations that had not yet occurred, and he was clearly reluctant to put lines into Mao's mouth before he had even met with Nixon. Why not wait until the actual meeting before hammering out a Communiqué? Kissinger argued that under the intense press scrutiny of this historic occasion, it would be difficult to resolve complex issues and it would be helpful to agree in advance on some general points they could both accept.

Furthermore, having an agreed-upon text would preempt any meddling by Secretary of State Rogers, who would be accompanying the president. "My secret dream," he explained to Zhou, "is to do to the State Department what the Prime Minister did to his office—reduce it to three." As would become his habit, Henry Kissinger freely disparaged Secretary Rogers and his State Department colleagues to the Chinese leadership.

By speaking in this revealing manner, Kissinger was attempting to strengthen a personal bond with Zhou while actively seeking the Chinese government's cooperation in marginalizing the State Department during Nixon's visit. He had a particular request: "If those people who will not be meeting with Chairman Mao and the President could be separated from them in the most delicate way possible, it will help me tremendously." In addition, "we may want to rely on your interpreters, in order to guarantee security" because "we have not yet found an interpreter whom we can completely trust."[26] By using a Chinese translator it would be possible to keep the content of any conversation secret from members of his own government.

In these preliminary talks, Kissinger and Zhou quickly turned to the status of Taiwan. Both were acutely aware of the intense battle underway at the United Nations over Chinese representation. To explain the American position, Kissinger told Zhou that there remained "many elements in our bureaucracy . . . who are pursuing traditional policies and since we have not told them the details of our discussions in July, it has not been possible to instill in them the discipline that will be the case as the years go by." In other words, Zhou and his colleagues should pay little mind to the official US position; this was merely some backward thinking by people out of the loop.[27]

Zhou appeared to sympathize, observing that UN representation was not that urgent for his government, but also stating that his government was bothered by the formula for "dual representation" at the UN, which conveyed the impression that Taiwan was a separate country.[28] If relations between the United States and China were to move toward "normalcy," the United States needed to explicitly acknowledge the unity of China and make a clear commitment to withdraw its troops from Taiwan.

Kissinger assured Zhou that they were moving in the same direction and reminded him of his previous statement that his government would not support an independent Taiwan, and planned to remove two-thirds of its military forces once the Vietnam War was concluded. It would also strongly oppose any Japanese efforts to replace the American political or military presence in Taiwan, a concern Beijing had previously expressed. For the present, the Nixon administration had to be cautious in its public statements, but fortunately it was "possible to do more than we can say."[29] Zhou must recognize that for the United States, redefining its relationship to Taiwan was a "painful process." It was not easy to set aside old friends.

Regarding Vietnam, Zhou wondered why the United States had not set a firm date for withdrawing its troops. And why was it ignoring the constructive seven-point program introduced by Madame Binh on behalf of the Provisional Revolutionary Government, a proposal that "the whole world" viewed as reasonable?[30] During his July visit, Zhou recalled, Kissinger had said that "you really did wish to withdraw from Vietnam, that you didn't want to continue to be bogged down in that quagmire." So why wasn't that underway? Or at the very least, why had there been no reply to the PRG proposal?

Kissinger insisted that they had replied. Since his last trip to China, he had met with North Vietnamese negotiators twice and offered them an eight-point response, which included a fixed date for withdrawal, new elections six months after the peace agreement was signed, the withdrawal of all US troops one month before that election, and the resignation of both the South Vietnamese president and vice president in that same month. None of these concessions seemed to register with Hanoi, whose leaders were "so suspicious, so convinced that we are trying to trick them" that they were incapable of recognizing a fair proposal. "They believe we have nothing else on our mind than how we can out-maneuver them." It was an interesting question "whether one little country obsessed with its suffering and obsessed with the war should be permitted to thwart every progress because its suspicion is so great that it will not make a negotiated settlement." If North Vietnamese leaders "ever spoke to us with anything approaching the largeness of spirit that has been shown by you . . . we could settle the war in a matter of days."[31]

Zhou speculated that there must be "some knots" in the American proposal that were producing Hanoi's skepticism. After all, these people had been betrayed before. Accepting Western assurances, in 1954 an "anguished" Ho Chi Minh had persuaded his southern compatriots to leave their families and move north in the expectation of national elections. But John Foster Dulles had played "false, dirty" and those elections were never held.

The Nixon administration had "a completely different outlook from the Dulles policy," Kissinger insisted. However, the North Vietnamese persisted in their stubborn ways. Their people "are in a state of war," Zhou reminded him. One should not rebuke people "who are suffering in extreme misery at the present, for not accepting anything they do not feel is safe." Two hundred years ago George Washington had been in their position and made a similar choice, said Zhou. With this "pioneer spirit" the Americans had defied the British Empire.[32]

Perhaps the Chinese could make a difference, Kissinger suggested. Should "an opportunity present itself you could perhaps offer your opinion as to the degree of our sincerity" to your friends. It was a remarkable suggestion, as if a character reference from the Chinese government would ameliorate Hanoi's doubts. Such an abject request would have amazed members of the State Department, not to mention the right-wing stalwarts such as Governor Reagan and other media pundits, who still regarded China as a major perpetrator of revolution. Zhou Enlai could hardly miss the fact that the American was needing help extricating from Vietnam, but he was unequivocal in stating that so long as US troops remained there, his government would continue to aid the Vietnamese resistance.

During the final days of Kissinger's visit, the two men returned the subject of a Communiqué. Zhou Enlai had consulted with Mao, who preferred specific statements rather than meaningless generalities. Given the sharp differences, Zhou proposed that they prepare a Communiqué in which each side stated its position separately. This sounded plausible, but once Kissinger saw the harsh criticisms in the Chinese draft, he balked. How could Nixon allow the Chinese to describe themselves as "the reliable rear area of a just war," when American boys were still dying in Vietnam? And what of the statement that the United States must withdraw all forces from Taiwan, Indochina, Korea, and Japan, while also giving up a major military base on Okinawa? "People will ask themselves why the President had to go 12,000 miles to be told all these things."

The alternative was to go line by line over the prospective draft—cutting out the words that were offensive to each. This proved to be grueling work, despite Kissinger's appreciation of Zhou's erudition and wit. The two were ultimately unable to find satisfactory language on the future of Taiwan. Meanwhile the news from home was disappointing. As conveyed by Haig, President Nixon had decided that during his Beijing sojourn he wanted to meet one-on-one with Mao and Zhou—which would leave the national security advisor out.[33]

More enraging was the White House instruction that Kissinger delay his return home by making an extended stopover in Anchorage, Alaska. The official reason was that Nixon wished to be on hand when Kissinger arrived in Washington. According to Haig, the real reason was Rogers' insistence that Kissinger's arrival just before the UN vote on Chinese representation "would seriously jeopardize its outcome and . . . would be the subject of harsh criticism should the vote go against us."[34]

Bothersome as they were, these distractions did not derail Kissinger from his main tasks, which were to create a friendly environment for Nixon's visit and to produce a positive-sounding Communiqué. After seven drafts he achieved success, although leaving unsettled the provisions concerning Taiwan.[35] Exhausted by the effort, Kissinger was returning home in a triumphant spirit. He had strengthened his personal rapport with Zhou, advanced the arrangements for the president's historic trip, produced a document that could demonstrate its success, and managed all of this without the participation of the State Department. As he was driven to the Beijing airport, he noticed the anti-American signs had been taken down.

By contrast, the US delegation to the United Nations was facing defeat. On October 26, despite months of effort by Ambassador Bush and Secretary Rogers, the General Assembly voted by a margin of 76–35 to seat the People's Republic of China and to accord it a permanent spot on the Security Council. In a narrower contest, it also voted 59–54 with 17 abstaining to expel the delegation from Taiwan.

This ended the many years of conflict over the legitimacy of Taiwan's claim to represent the real China. Some jubilant delegates danced in the aisles. To Nixon, who had anticipated this outcome, the most distressing thing was the display: "The problem is not Taiwan. The problem is . . . the United States getting kicked around by a bunch of goddamn Africans and cannibals," he lamented. On the far right, there was a backlash against the vote, with some well-known conservatives using the occasion to bash the United Nations and threaten to withhold funds.

None of this dimmed the president's excitement over the upcoming China trip and a possible rapprochement with its government. Kissinger had returned bubbling with enthusiasm and obviously smitten with Zhou Enlai and other Chinese officials. Throughout the visit, the Americans had experienced "a remarkable display of courtesy and warmth," which ranged from "the detailed and meticulous way we were housed, fed and transported, to the cordiality of our social conversations and tours, to the beautiful gifts and collections of photographs with which we were plied prior to departure." It was apparent to him that the Chinese government shared his eagerness for a new relationship.

Although diplomacy with the People's Republic of China was already a net political gain for the Nixon administration, Kissinger was viewing his conversations with Zhou through rose-colored glasses and exaggerating the practical outcome. Discussions about the Vietnam War were a case in point. He expected, without any evidence from his exchanges with Zhoa, that his assurances about removing US military forces from Taiwan once the Vietnam War had ended would lead the Chinese to pressure their ally. Should negotiations with Hanoi fail, and without taking into account intelligence reports of a July agreement between China and North Vietnam for a substantial increase in weapons deliveries, Kissinger was hopeful that both Beijing and Moscow would discourage the North Vietnamese from launching a spring offensive.[36] His two trips to China had been intoxicating. The "high wire" act of maneuvering between great nations, the sense of moving pieces on a large chess board, the long travels into the night, the multiple deceptions, and dramatic revelations—this all created a heady brew. No matter what else happened, it was practically certain that Richard Nixon would be going to Beijing in the all-important election year.

18

"Man of Peace"

For all his grandiosity, the president could be coldly realistic about his own public standing, and during the spring of 1971 his internal political meter was signaling that the Laotian operation had shattered trust. "Trust is like a thin thread, once you break it, it's very hard to splice together," he had admonished Kissinger. That was what Lam Son 719 had done: "[I]t has broken our thin thread with the American people as to the winding down of the war."[1] More than ever, Nixon needed a clear path out of Vietnam. For this purpose, improved relations with the Soviet Union were critically important.

From the earliest days of his administration, Nixon had been interested in tamping down US–Soviet rivalry, both for its own sake and to obtain their help in pressuring Hanoi. However, during his first two years not much had been accomplished. The failure was partly the result of institutional and ideological inertia; neither Nixon nor the people in the national security bureaucracies could readily abandon long-standing Cold War attitudes and policies. Moreover, his belief that he could induce the Soviets to help with Vietnam by delaying progress in vital areas of mutual interest had proved to be mistaken.

In parallel with Kissinger's unfolding diplomacy with the Chinese, fresh efforts were made to place relations with the USSR on a more amicable path. Of particular importance as the presidential election grew nearer was the desire to put together a Moscow summit, which could brighten the president's image as a man of peace. For that to materialize, however, progress on an arms control treaty was essential.

The official Strategic Arms Limitation Talks (SALT) had been underway since late 1969, alternating between Helsinki and Vienna. Though technically under State Department authority, the US delegation was being tightly controlled by the White House through an intradepartmental verification panel chaired by Kissinger.[2] Their instructions had left little room for compromise, with the result that after a year and a half of negotiations, the SALT talks had produced a stalemate.

However, with a summit conference in mind, Nixon and Kissinger had become increasingly desirous of a breakthrough. To make that happen Kissinger secretly took over the talks, using the "back channel" with Ambassador Dobrynin to explore a deal. Apart from the sheer dishonesty of going behind the backs of their own representatives, this end run denied Kissinger the advice of experts in the field, although he considered himself sufficiently knowledgeable to negotiate on his own.

In these exchanges the highest priority for the Soviets was to set a limit on the deployment of antiballistic missiles (ABMs)—on the theory that a power that possessed such weapons might be tempted into a preemptive first strike. Since the United States was ahead in this technology, Nixon had accepted the military's desire to use this as a bargaining chip to constrain the rapid growth of the Soviet arsenal of long-range offensive nuclear missiles. Yet as of April 1971, nothing that the United States offered had made this attractive to Moscow. To break the stalemate, Kissinger raised the question with Dobrynin: if, instead of insisting on a comprehensive treaty that included both defensive and offensive weapons, what if they limited themselves to an ABM treaty, with an "understanding" that the ICBMs (intercontinental ballistic missiles) would be curtailed in some unspecified way?

After consulting with his Moscow superiors, Dobrynin was receptive to this approach.[3] Yet this formulation left many items unresolved: What specific steps should their two nations take toward the limitation of land-based offensive weapons? Would remaining ABM systems be limited to the defense of capital cities (what the Soviets wanted), or could they also protect missile sites (which the Americans preferred)? Would this new understanding require that negotiations on offensive missiles be concluded at the same time as an ABM treaty (the American view), or could the agreement on offensive weapons be left indeterminate for the time being (the Soviet preference)? And most important from Nixon and Kissinger's standpoint—would this new understanding be made public, or would it remain confidential?

By mid-May, the Soviet government had agreed there was enough progress to warrant a joint announcement. By this point, delegation chief Gerard Smith had returned to Washington, where he became belatedly aware that Kissinger had been wheeling and dealing on nuclear issues without letting the US SALT team know.[4] To Smith, who had spent months abroad trying to reach a deal under impossibly rigid guidelines, such duplicity was appalling. When Kissinger finally showed him portions of the negotiating record, he was also struck by the stupidity of the deal in surrendering an important national interest. And for what end?

Smith communicated his outrage to the Secretary of State, who had final responsibility for the Arms Control and Disarmament Agency of which he was the director. As on other occasions, Rogers was angry and humiliated by this exclusion, asking Haldeman, "Why didn't you tell me that you were doing this? There's no need for me to be involved but I do have to be informed."[5] Was this Nixon's signal that it was time for him to resign? If that were the message, he would go. But as Secretary of State he could not do his job if the White House did not trust him on crucial matters.

On the surface, Kissinger's one-upping of Rogers was nothing more than a battle for personal turf. However, in the case of arms control, as on other subjects, there were substantive differences over policy. In approaching their mission, State Department professionals were interested in reducing the danger of a nuclear conflagration. For that reason they had initially favored a ban on ABMs and MIRVs (multiple independently targeted reentry vehicles), both of which were perceived as destabilizing because of their first-strike potential. A similar concern animated their focus on Soviet long-range missiles, given the Russians' ever-increasing numerical advantage. This set them at odds with Kissinger, who had chosen to pacify the military in the first instance and who seemed unaccountably blasé about the second.[6]

In setting the stage for a public announcement, Kissinger gave the impression that he had wrested major concessions from Dobrynin.[7] This fit nicely with Nixon's eagerness for some dramatic achievement on the peace front. With his PR team cranking up the excitement, on May 20 Nixon summoned the cabinet and congressional leaders to hear his great news.[8] There had been "a major step forward" on arms control, he told the assembled group, the happy result of special negotiating efforts occurring in Washington and Helsinki and involving the highest levels of government in both countries. While much hard work lay ahead, there was also reason for optimism. Thus informed, the crowd gave the president a standing ovation. And lest there be lingering resentment, Nixon had shrewdly invited Secretary Rogers and Gerard Smith to say a few words, as if this were their accomplishment.[9]

One hour later, Nixon was on national television reading the statement that had been so tortuously hammered out with the Soviets. "The two sides . . . have agreed to concentrate this year on working out an agreement for the limitation of . . . antiballistic missile systems."[10] Together with concluding an agreement to limit ABMs, "they will also agree on certain measures with respect to the limitation of offensive strategic missiles." Now using his own words, Nixon gravely explained this was "a major step in breaking the stalemate on nuclear arms." It expressed the genuine commitment of both the American and Russian governments to achieve this essential goal. If they succeeded, this day would be remembered as "the beginning of a new era" in which all nations might devote their energies and resources to the pursuit of peace, instead of war.

Cleverly obscured by the speech was the lack of specificity in the accord. When the SALT team got back to work in Helsinki, they hoped to begin negotiations on offensive strategic weapons as well as ABM systems.[11] However, the chief Russian negotiator Vladimir Semenov insisted on settling the ABM part of the agreement first, claiming that Gerard Smith's call for parallel negotiations on both offensive and defensive weapons contradicted the bargain that Kissinger had recently announced.

Unfortunately for Smith, the Soviet representative was on firm ground for his contention. The private exchange of letters between Nixon and Brezhnev that were part of the May 20 agreement had been handled in an irregular way. Ordinarily a State Department translator would have reviewed the Russian-language version of Brezhnev's text to make sure that it was identical with the English version. However, Kissinger had short-circuited this procedure, so the match was undetermined. Gerard Smith could read Russian and, once the dispute arose, he irritably requested that Kissinger make the Soviet letter available.[12] When he finally reviewed the document he was forced to concede the legitimacy of Semenov's position.

This was not the only error. To the extent that Kissinger and Dobrynin had discussed offensive weapons, the national security advisor had focused on the land-based ICBMs, while indicating a lack of interest in sea-based weapons (SLBM). Yet on a rare point of agreement, the Joint Chiefs of Staff and the Arms Control and Disarmament Agency considered it critically important to address this latter category because with their active construction program, the Soviets were obtaining a growing advantage.

While Kissinger's flawed machinations were demoralizing for the SALT delegation, they were largely invisible to others. For most journalists, who had neither expertise in this area nor access to the relevant documents, the account of the president and his national security advisor was their exclusive source of information. Following their lead, television and newspapers billed the agreement as an exciting development. *New York Times* columnist James Reston exemplified the response. Six weeks earlier, Reston had been livid about the incursion into Laos, but he seemed willing to believe that Nixon was "taking risks for peace" that went beyond partisan considerations. "Aside from politics," he opined, "Mr. Nixon would obviously like to preside over the creation of a new world order and believes he sees an opportunity to do so in the last twenty months of his first term."[13]

For Richard Nixon, in this most dangerous period of his presidency there was no "aside from politics." Both he and Kissinger imagined themselves as contributors to a more peaceful world. But his day-to-day decision-making was propelled by his political vulnerability. Years later, some might wonder about Kissinger's flawed handling of the arms control negotiations and his disregard of relevant experts. But apart from his propensity to monopolize policymaking wherever possible, he was driven by the president's urgent need for rapid accomplishments.

As summer approached, the president was eagerly awaiting Kissinger's diplomacy with China, which would hopefully result in his own trip to Beijing. However, a Moscow summit was of comparable importance. In an election year, if he could showcase two dramatic visits to these enemy capitals, this might reframe the narrative of his administration. And there was the additional benefit that journeying to both places within a matter of months would intensify their rivalry and increase his leverage with each.

To snare a Russian summit, there was one significant obstacle to be overcome. Inside the Soviet government, Foreign Minister Gromyko was insisting that such a meeting could not occur until there was a signed four-power agreement on Berlin.[14] Unlike his younger colleagues, the Soviet diplomat had been wrestling with this conflict for decades and, to him, it was rich in symbolic and practical significance.

At the end of World War II, Stalin had agreed to let the United States, England, and France occupy their own sectors of Berlin, although the entire city was inside the Russian zone.[15] This was a large concession, because the Red Army had paid for the conquest of the German capital with an estimated 80,000 deaths. It was premised, however, on the understanding that all four powers would be collectively responsible for overseeing an eventually unified Germany.

In the summer of 1948, the three Western powers had decided to create a separate West German government, blaming the Russians for repressive policies in their zone of occupation. In response Stalin had cut off the roads and rail lines from western Germany into the western sectors of Berlin. This provocation and the Americans' emotionally charged airlift of food, coal, and medical supplies into the city had become the iconic confrontation of the early Cold War. In the intervening years, the status of the city and its access routes had been an ongoing source of potentially explosive conflict.

Undergirding the tensions over Berlin was a deeper argument over the division of the country and of Europe. However, during the period 1970–71, West German Chancellor Willi Brandt's *Ostpolitik* signified his acceptance of the geographical status quo, paving the way for a Moscow–Bonn Treaty.[16] Despite its broadly favorable provisions, the West German Bundestag was unwilling to ratify it until a four-power Berlin agreement had also been completed. For these latter negotiations, the Russians seemed resigned to the fact that West Berlin would retain its autonomous status, which would include guaranteed access for the people of West Germany, but the detailed arrangements would require further negotiation.

The process was being slowed by the need to make decisions with all four occupying powers. In this forum, the United States was represented by Ambassador Kenneth Rush, who was under the authority of the State Department. The Russians were increasingly concerned that the group was proceeding too slowly and legalistically. To meet their complaints and accelerate the move toward a summit, Kissinger agreed to another secret "second track."

While the quadripartite group continued its deliberations in Bonn, the real decisions were being made in Berlin by Russian ambassador Valentin Falin, West Germany's state secretary Egon Bahr, and American ambassador Kenneth Rush. Major points of contention were referred to Kissinger and Dobrynin. For these clandestine deliberations to succeed, Kenneth Rush needed to conceal his activities from the Bonn group and from his superiors in the State Department. Fortunately for Kissinger, Rush was a friend of Attorney General John Mitchell, and his loyalty to the White House trumped whatever commitments he felt to the State Department.

By mid-1971, Kissinger and Nixon had become habituated to sidelining government specialists and trampling on established norms of behavior. In their handling of arms control, relations with China, the future of Berlin, and the conduct of the Vietnam War, deception of their own administration had become commonplace. Any remaining deference was toward the professional military, but even these bonds had begun to fray. All this trickery came at a psychological price: overconfidence in their own powers, and chronic suspicion (not without merit) that there were many adversaries in their ranks.

While the troika of Falin, Bahr, and Rush continued their work on the Berlin accord, the Russian government dragged its feet on the summit. Dobrynin considered this unwise. Following a three-hour dinner with Kissinger, the ambassador sent an urgent cable back to Moscow, emphasizing that with the presidential election pending, a summit conference was a top priority for Nixon.[17] He was therefore "prepared to pay our price by agreeing to resolve issues that are primarily of interest to us, particularly the agreement on West Berlin, a possible all-European security conference and negotiations on troop reduction." Dobrynin acknowledged that such a meeting would likely help Nixon get elected, but among the potential Democratic nominees, "there are no great friends of ours among them." Moreover, in the aftermath of a summit, "Nixon himself will not conduct his election campaign in an anti-Soviet tone, but rather advocate an improvement of relations with us."

Dobrynin's advice notwithstanding, as of July 5 the Soviet government had not responded. As the days ticked by without any positive news, Nixon and Kissinger looked forward to the nasty surprise the Russians would receive once they learned of the China visit:

KISSINGER: I think Mr. President that in their brutal, cheap third-rate way, they're a miserable bunch of bastards, I mean if you look at—

NIXON: It's terrible.

KISSINGER: —the way the Chinese have done business with us and the way they (the Russians) do business. You just don't treat the United States this way. Here is Gromyko sitting in here, inviting you to Moscow and now, they've been stringing you along, dancing around.

NIXON: Boy if they only knew what the hell was coming up, they'd be in here panting.[18]

The news was not long in coming. Just after Kissinger's triumphant return from Beijing on July 15, with only an hour to spare before President Nixon went on the air to announce the China "breakthrough," Kissinger phoned Dobrynin with a heads-up. "Knowing of President Nixon's expressed desire to visit the People's Republic of China, Premier Chou Enlai . . . has extended an invitation for him to come." He added that the president had "accepted this invitation with pleasure."[19]

Although unpleasantly surprised by the news, the Russian government moved slowly. It was almost a month before Dobrynin could assure Kissinger that a Moscow summit would take place. Yet during this intervening period,

US–Soviet relations were steadily improving across a spectrum of issues. The Berlin agreement was virtually complete, including American acceptance of a Soviet consulate in the western portion of the city. The German accords had been activated by Brandt, but more profoundly they represented the Nixon administration's acceptance of the division of Europe.

On the economic front, Nixon approved a series of machine purchases from the United States that had been held up for review, a relaxation of controls on the export of nonstrategic goods, and a promise to lift an embargo on American grain sales to the Soviet Union.[20] Each of these actions served multiple purposes, but in aggregate they were creating momentum for a Nixon–Brezhnev meeting.

Less clear was their helpfulness for resolving the Vietnam War, which remained a core objective. In late July, the Elmo Roper organization found that 64% of Americans thought the country was on the wrong track, with 40% identifying that conflict as the most important problem facing the country.[21] It was noteworthy that these numbers were appearing three months after the failed Laotian operation and during a period of reduced fighting. If another North Vietnamese offensive materialized in the upcoming dry season, the numbers might skyrocket.

Of particular concern were the POW wives, whom Nixon had typically invoked to justify continuing warfare. However, in the most recent seven-point proposal offered by Madame Binh, the enemy appeared to be offering the release of all US prisoners in exchange for a complete withdrawal of American troops from Vietnam.[22] The plan had other problematic features, including a stipulation that the US "cease backing" Thieu, but its publication conveyed the clear impression that the most reliable way to get the prisoners home was to stop the fighting.

During these months, Kissinger continued to hope that his diplomatic engagement with the Chinese and the Soviets would make the North Vietnamese more flexible. Yet when he met Le Duc Tho on July 26, the diplomat was scornful:

> Over the past few years, you have gone here and there to seek a way out. I wonder whether you have drawn from your experience. In fact, your efforts are futile, and they make things more complicated. There is no miraculous way to settle the Vietnam problem other than seriously negotiating with us at the Paris Conference on the basis of our proposals and yours. In a chess match, the winner and the loser must be the players

themselves, there is no other way . . . We are independent in solving our problem.[23]

If anything, this maneuvering might have backfired. Hanoi's leaders first learned about Kissinger's China visit from Zhou Enlai, who arrived in their capital with this unwelcome news. Zhou assured them that he had strongly supported Madame Binh's "seven points" in these discussions. However, in describing the exchange, he also revealed Kissinger's assurance that once the Vietnam War was settled, the United States intended to remove their troops from Taiwan. This set off alarm bells for the North Vietnamese. If Kissinger was serious about linking the conclusion of the war to American military withdrawal from Taiwan, this might tempt the Chinese to abandon their cause at some early date.[24]

Thus, Zhou's news had the paradoxical effect of strengthening Hanoi's resolve. Their leaders were already contemplating a major offensive in 1972. The possibility of Beijing's betrayal increased the attractiveness of a military solution, especially since they had reviewed the results of the Lam Son operation and concluded that their side had scored a major victory. They regarded this as uniquely significant because they had met and defeated South Vietnam's most "elite" forces, including its paratroopers and marines. Another campaign might prove decisive.

Meanwhile negotiations with the Americans were stalled on one crucial point: the survival of the Thieu government in South Vietnam. The North Vietnamese were simply unwilling to accept a ceasefire if this regime remained in place. Their preferred solution, which they had repeatedly put forward, was for an interim coalition government to be installed that could run South Vietnam pending negotiations with the PRG for a new administration. However, with October elections scheduled in the South, Madame Binh and Le Du Tho had suggested that perhaps the United States could simply withdraw its support from Thieu, or even back some alternative candidate. This might be more palatable than removing him from power.[25] To Kissinger these ideas were still unwelcome because the survival of Thieu was viewed as necessary for the stability of the South Vietnamese government.

Unfortunately for the Americans, this October election quickly proved to be an embarrassment. Although President Thieu wielded dictatorial powers, the Nixon administration had maintained the polite fiction that South Vietnam was a democracy. For this reason the upcoming presidential contest, in which Thieu would be facing at least two opponents—Vice President

General Ky and ARVN General Duong Van Minh (sometimes known to Americans as "Big Minh")—would hopefully provide confirmation that there was popular support for his leadership.

To their chagrin, Thieu was determined not just to win but to win by a significant margin. And to ensure that result, he had pushed through an election law that required any candidate for president who wished to get on the ballot to obtain the written endorsement of either 100 provincial and city counselors or 40 national legislators. He then quickly swept up the bulk of these supporters for himself, leaving General Ky without sufficient backers. After the South Vietnamese supreme court had barred his candidacy, Ky furiously denounced the process, charging that Thieu had rigged the election. This left only General Minh as an opponent. While Ambassador Bunker wanted him to remain on the ballot so that the election might have a shred of legitimacy, Minh would not play along.[26]

Instead, Minh announced that he could not "lend a hand to a dirty farce which would only make the people more desperate and disillusioned with a democratic system." It briefly appeared as if the crisis might blow over when the supreme court in Saigon reversed its decision on Ky's candidacy and agreed to place him on the ballot. If he returned to the contest, perhaps General Minh would also reconsider? Despite Bunker's offer to pay his campaign expenses, Minh remained adamant, telling a press conference that unless Thieu was willing to step down and enable an interim government to supervise the election, he would not participate.[27] Under current leadership, he said, there was no possibility of an "honest election."

As it wrestled with the challenge of making the South Vietnamese elections appear valid, the Nixon administration's unyielding support for the Thieu government was unchanged. However, this unfolding electoral mess was all grist for the North Vietnamese mill. On September 13 when Kissinger returned to Paris, Xuan Thuy was belligerent.[28] The United States was supporting "the fascist and dictatorial acts" of General Thieu, he asserted, and was engaged in the charade of "persuading other people to run in the election so as to give it a democratic façade." These developments highlighted the importance of removing Thieu from power as a prerequisite for a viable peace settlement. The South Vietnamese people would have no possibility of a free political choice so long as the Thieu government "controls nearly a million-man army equipped by the United States, with American advisors, a large police force, numerous pacification teams," plus "a heavy net of CIA agents and thousands of American troops."

In what proved to be the shortest session on record, the secret meeting adjourned without any plan to reconvene. Unfortunately for Nixon, the fake South Vietnamese election was strengthening domestic dissenters in the United States. Especially worrying were the activities of George McGovern, a presidential aspirant and long-time opponent of the Vietnam War.[29] In September he had gone to Paris and, after meeting with the North Vietnamese and the PRG negotiators, had come away with the mistaken belief that if all US troops were withdrawn from Vietnam by December 31, Hanoi would release the POWs. It was therefore his intention to re-introduce the amendment he had co-authored with Republican Senator Hatfield, cutting off funds for the war by a fixed date.

For now, the North Vietnamese were unwilling to grant a ceasefire and the return of the POWS in exchange for the withdrawal of American troops. They were also insisting on the removal of the Thieu government. However, Kissinger warned the president that at some future point, they might say "flatly" that "we will let the prisoners go, if you will go out by December 31." Should this occur the POW wives might become unmanageable and the White House political position possibly untenable.[30]

As they were wont to do, Nixon and Kissinger blamed their troubles on others. One culprit was Thieu himself. The man was "a dope," said Kissinger.[31] He would have won the election anyway but his actions "made it possible for the vultures to slam him.". And once again disloyal subordinates within their own administration were creating a poor impression. Nixon was particularly incensed to learn that General Abrams had discussed plans for troop withdrawal with Senator McGovern.[32]

Abrams had been in the presidential "dog house" since Lam Son 719. Maybe it was time "to get rid of the son-of-a-bitch," Nixon suggested. The general was a "meritorious person," replied Kissinger, but he was no longer on top of things as he once was. Perhaps a younger man would do better in the job? The danger was that in dismissing Abrams, they would resurrect unpleasant memories of the Tet offensive and Johnson's removal of Westmoreland. Perhaps the wiser move, Nixon reflected, was to install someone as second in command who could prevent Abrams from "drinking too much and talking too much." Nobody can stop the drinking, Kissinger asserted, but he had "raised hell" with Admiral Moorer and Secretary Laird about the need for military people to shut up.

With no apparent progress in the war or in the peace negotiations, Nixon chose to bomb the North. Originally intended as a one-day affair, it would be a warning of his willingness to escalate the level of violence if continually thwarted. Admiral Moorer was instructed to draw up a target list—"good ones so that he can go in there and send a hundred planes and bomb the shit out of them." This attack was scheduled for September 19, but as happened during Lam Son 719 the weather interfered, with cloud cover as low as 500 feet. Kissinger was disgusted. What kind of Air Force was this, which seemed capable "of only bombing in the desert in July in clear weather if there's no sandstorm," he complained to Secretary Laird.[33] Although visibility remained problematic, the next day more than 200 American planes struck North Vietnamese targets, the largest air attack on North Vietnam since the 1968 bombing halt. However, Kissinger was still fuming over Air Force "incompetence." For all he knew, they were only hitting cows.

In the absence of good news, Nixon asked Kissinger to draw up a memorandum analyzing their present impasse and evaluating their future options.[34]As outlined in the document, from its earliest days the administration had been pursuing two parallel lines: transfer of responsibility to the South Vietnamese military, and the pursuit of a diplomatic solution. There was always a question of whether the strengthening of ARVN would occur quickly enough before domestic opposition forced a complete American withdrawal. For that reason, a negotiated settlement had been their "preferred choice." Unfortunately, the incentives for the North Vietnamese to engage in constructive diplomacy had weakened. The threat of US military action "has all but withered away" because domestic pressure in the United States had insured a rapid departure of the remaining troops. The "botched election" in South Vietnam had destabilized the Thieu government, giving the enemy every incentive to stall until the "combination of unrest in South Vietnam and the American domestic squeeze" would allow them to topple Thieu and pave the way for their victory.

The situation was "unmistakably complex," Kissinger asserted pedantically. Yet arguably this was because he and the president had chosen to ignore some obvious factors: the high-handed despotism of General Thieu and resulting political weakness, the willingness of the enemy to sacrifice and sustain immense losses, and the moral revulsion of millions of Americans, including some government officials, at the senseless waste of human life. Each of these elements had been present from the beginning of their administration, yet it had suited their purpose and that of the career military to ignore them. In turn, these strands fed into the central contradiction of the

White House policy: that it could somehow wrest a victory on the battlefield or at the negotiating table with ever-decreasing numbers of American troops.

Under such conditions there were few realistic options for the White House. Diplomacy remained their most promising approach, but this would require a more attractive negotiating package. By itself, Kissinger recognized that this was unlikely to produce a positive response. To tip the balance, he thought they would need an "influential and motivated" third party to play an "active role" in shaping Hanoi's response. The obvious candidates for this role were the USSR and China. However, as of September Zhou Enlai had shown no interest in being embroiled. Then perhaps the Russians could take on this role and push Hanoi into a reasonable settlement? It was an idea he and Nixon had entertained since the beginning of their administration, but this prospect had become more urgent and perhaps more likely.

In Moscow, First Secretary Leonid Brezhnev had consolidated his control of the politburo and seemed clearly bent on improving relations with the United States. In a cordial letter to Nixon, he indicated a broad spectrum of issues on which compromise seemed possible. Although his letter indicated an alignment with Hanoi's position on a peace deal, Kissinger was hopeful this would change. Feeding this expectation, Ambassador Dobrynin let him know that Nikoai Podgorny, chairman of the Presidium of the Supreme Soviet, would soon be flying to Hanoi at the request of the North Vietnamese. If the Americans had any new ideas for narrowing the differences between the two sides, the USSR was prepared to be helpful.[35]

So exciting was this news that Kissinger thought he might go to Moscow in November for a clandestine meeting with North Vietnamese President Pham Van Dong. In that event, there could be a signed peace agreement by the end of the year. This was no casual idea. Kissinger's staff had already sketched out an elaborate scenario for a Russian-brokered meeting with the North Vietnamese leader.

In late September 1971, Soviet foreign minister Gromyko flew to the United States for the opening of the UN General Assembly. As in previous years, he also used the occasion to visit Nixon, Rogers, and Kissinger in Washington. These exchanges were among the most positive in recent memory, reflecting the completion of the German agreements along with Moscow's approval of a public announcement of a Nixon–Brezhnev meeting in the spring.

The president had left it to Kissinger to discuss Vietnam with Gromyko. In their meeting of September 30, the national security advisor complained that the heroic North Vietnamese found it easier to make war than to effect a peace.[36] The remainder of the year would be a time of testing. The United States was preparing a new "generous" peace proposal, but if this was rejected the administration would be forced "to go unilaterally." Neither Saigon nor Hanoi had seen this draft proposal, but he willingly shared its main outlines with Gromyko. Among its features: complete withdrawal of US troops by a specific date, early elections following the peace agreement, an interim government to oversee preparation for elections, and full participation by the PRG in whatever mechanism was established for electoral purposes. It contained familiar elements from previous offers. It was, however, notably vague on the most contested item. Was the interim body he had mentioned an actual government, or merely an oversight board for the election? This was a critical distinction on which prospects for a settlement would likely rise or fall.

In connection with Podgorny's upcoming trip to Hanoi, Kissinger claimed that Nixon wished him "to inform the DRV of the current direction of White House thinking, and if it deems possible, facilitate an agreement." Indeed, the Soviets could play an even bigger role, he told Gromyko:

> It might be that Hanoi would feel easier if one of its friends helped to assure the good faith of the participants. I was therefore prepared to go secretly to Moscow to meet for three days with a suitable personality from Hanoi if this had a high probability of leading to a solution.[37]

Whether acting as character reference or midwife, the Russian government could bring this American-driven peace agreement to completion, for whatever benefits they might garner.

"If when the chips are down, the world's most powerful nation, the United States of America, acts like a pitiful, helpless giant, the forces of totalitarianism and anarchy will threaten free nations," Nixon had uttered on the eve of the Cambodian invasion. To avoid that imagined danger, three Asian nations had been ravaged and thousands had died. But was there something "pitiful" about asking the USSR to facilitate a face-saving exit for what had clearly become a disastrous war for the United States?

Over the years, American leaders had invoked the term "credibility" to justify their pursuit of the Vietnam War. Although vague in its application, for the public this clearly meant impressing the country's adversaries with the superior power of the United States. Yet to this point, the Vietnam project had demonstrated the opposite: namely the inability of US government to defeat "third world" revolutionaries despite a massive military effort, nor to maintain the consent of their own people for such an effort. The weakness of this position was exemplified by Kissinger's secret pleas to Zhou Enlai and Andrei Gromyko to vouch for the "good faith" of the United States.

While the news from Vietnam and Paris was discouraging, as of October Nixon and Kissinger were on a fresh high. With Russian permission they were free to announce that a Moscow summit would occur in the spring. Meanwhile, Kissinger was on track with plans for a Nixon trip to Beijing in early 1972, giving then "a terrific double play."

These two meetings alone would elicit an enthusiastic response from the American people. This was not all. With both Russia and China establishing closer ties to the United States, Nixon did not see how Hanoi could hold out much longer. This "high-wire diplomacy was changing everything." Buoyed by these achievements, Nixon thought that a "good touch" might be to establish a Whittier Institute of World Peace at his Quaker alma mater to reflect his new identity as peacemaker.

His instructions to Haldeman were firm. From now on, "We should really go to work playing the 'Man of Peace' issue all the time, move all the other issues to a lower level and really build this one up because it's our issue and we have to use it."

"Our issue." It was a comforting thought. In the euphoria of the moment, it was possible to ignore the tens of thousands of North Vietnamese troops remaining in Laos, Cambodia, and just north of the DMZ, preparing for a possible spring offensive. And to imagine, as Henry Kissinger did, that officials in Moscow and perhaps Beijing would rein them in.

19

"Knock the Shit Out of Them"

If Nixon were to be reincarnated as a "Man of Peace," he recognized the necessity for settling the Vietnam War prior to the 1972 presidential election. So far that goal had proved frustratingly elusive. It was more than a year since Kissinger had quietly dropped the American demand for mutual withdrawal of North Vietnamese and American troops. Beneath a blizzard of details, the remaining point of contention was the continuation of the Thieu government as part of a ceasefire. To assuage North Vietnamese objections, Kissinger had tweaked and re-tweaked American proposals, but as of November 1971 none of these formulations had proved successful.

For Kissinger this enemy stance seemed perverse. Surely the North Vietnamese ought to recognize that once the United States withdrew all its troops, there would be sufficient opportunity to change the regime. Why should they insist that the Americans be responsible for removing the Thieu government? He continued to ascribe their stubbornness on this point to their inability to recognize a favorable peace offer when it came their way. As always, he failed to consider that from the enemy's perspective the Saigon government was an American creation, which remained a direct threat so long as its repressive apparatus was in place.

Whatever the explanation, both Kissinger and Nixon were increasingly reliant on their improved relations with the Soviet Union and China for help with this impasse. In recent talks with Kissinger, Ambassador Dobrynin fanned these hopes.[1] He acknowledged that in the early years of the Nixon administration, his government had been content to sit back and let the Americans deal with their own "mess." But their attitude had changed. They recognized that it was necessary to end the Vietnam War, certainly by the time of the Moscow summit. With the encouraging news from Hanoi that Xuan Thuy and Le Duc Tho would return to Paris on November 20 to resume their "confidential" negotiations with Kissinger, the national security advisor believed that his complex strategy was beginning to pay off.

Once again, disappointment followed. On November 17, just three days before Kissinger was scheduled to fly to Paris, came a message from the

North Vietnamese. Regrettably, Special Advisor Le Duc Tho had "suddenly become ill" and would not be able to participate in the meeting.[2] While Minister Xuan Thuy was prepared to attend, this was a thinly disguised reversal—a clear sign that the officials in Hanoi had changed their minds. Understanding that Xuan Thuy had no authority to reach a deal, Kissinger cancelled the session.

Why had this initiative fizzled? Confident of the effectiveness of his superpower machinations, Kissinger had exaggerated the willingness of the Soviet Union to undercut a long-term ally, as well as its ability to do so. It was fine to transmit messages from Washington, as President Podgorny had agreed to do, or to encourage Hanoi to compromise on the matter of Thieu's removal, but these limited interventions did not ensure Hanoi's compliance on a matter of extreme importance. To make a difference, the Soviets would need to use their real leverage—namely the massive arms shipments and economic assistance they had been providing for years. Although not immediately known to the Americans, during Podgorny's October visit to Hanoi, he had signed the largest military aid package his government had ever granted to North Vietnam, thus enabling another year of war. The Chinese had also promised the North Vietnamese an increase in weapons deliveries back in July, a fact that Kissinger had chosen to ignore.

Although unclear at the time, the leadership in Hanoi was furious about the two pending summit meetings as well as the attempted interference with their negotiating position.[3] This outside advice reawakened old grievances over past sell-outs of Vietnamese interests by the USSR and China. Fearful that their situation was likely to become worse in the coming years, with possibly diminished support from the communist superpowers, they became more determined than ever to launch another large-scale offensive in the coming dry season. Having made that decision, they gave Le Duc Tho "a political illness" and broke off negotiations. Until the situation on the South Vietnamese battlefield was more favorable to their side, they believed that diplomacy would not serve their purpose.

Nixon was also blindsided by North Vietnam's reversal. Like Kissinger, he still did not appreciate the extent to which North Vietnam was an independent actor powered by a fierce nationalism and unwilling to genuflect to any outside power. Nor did he and Kissinger recognize how the ARVN's disastrous performance during Lam Son 719 had strengthened Hanoi's confidence that with one more massive effort, they could inflict a decisive blow on the South Vietnamese military.

Stung by Hanoi's rejection, Kissinger appealed immediately to both the Soviets and Chinese. The administration was reaching the end of its "patience," he warned Dobrynin. If this stubbornness persisted, the United States would take whatever action was necessary to effect a remedy. His government would not tolerate "the humiliation of the president."[4] And if there was no progress on the release of American prisoners, the United States reserved the right to escalate its military effort. The normally affable Dobrynin did not hide his annoyance. On what basis did the United States claim the right to respond violently because the North Vietnamese had halted negotiations?

In a less threatening manner, Kissinger sought help from Zhou Enlai. In their October meeting he had assured Zhou that, in the interest of US–China amity, his government was prepared "to treat North Vietnamese concerns with generosity." But as a great country, the Chinese must recognize that "we cannot permit ourselves to be humiliated no matter what the possible consequences for other policies."[5] Though he had "no specific request," knowing that Pham van Dong was coming to Beijing, Kissinger was hoping that Zhou would put pressure on the North Vietnamese prime minister to be more flexible.

His choice of words was instructive. The relevant concern was "humiliation," he explained. This was something he expected the Soviets and Chinese to readily understand. In connection with Vietnam it was a familiar theme—the original emphasis on American "credibility" which had morphed into the bedrock principle that no American president should be perceived as a loser. Yet it was telling that for all their public preening about superpower diplomacy, Nixon and Kissinger were pressing their ostensible enemies to salvage their domestic and international reputation.

This pattern had been developing over the past eight months and required a certain degree of public and even self-deception. The preoccupation with personal reputation was present at many levels for both these men. Kissinger needed a deal with North Vietnam to prove his worth to the president and to permanently marginalize his critics in the State Department. And Nixon needed the war to end in some impressive fashion so that he could run for reelection without having to worry about POW wives, critics in the press, marchers in the streets, and an obstructionist Congress.

Regardless of advice from their Chinese and Soviet patrons, the North Vietnamese had thumbed their nose at the president and his national security advisor, whose personal disappointments gave way to rage. Nixon was determined to make them pay for this mistake. For the present, he envisioned a three-pronged attack: several days of bombing, South Vietnamese patrol boat operations in the Panhandle, and "massive CIA harassment" behind enemy lines.[6] However, both men agreed that this effort must be limited so as not to jeopardize the upcoming visit to Beijing or to arouse the American public's opposition.

In mulling over the situation with Kissinger, Nixon was also thinking ahead. Suppose the war continued beyond the presidential election? Whether he won or lost, Hanoi should understand there would be no mercy.[7] Do they realize "that they have to deal here with a man who if he wins the election will kick the shit out of them, and if he loses will do it even more?"[8]

Nixon had been thinking about all of this when he woke up that morning—the time when "the best ideas come in." He had just realized that no matter what, Hanoi would lose. If the American Air Force was not up to the job, would pull in the Navy and say, "Boys here's your chance to be heroes. I want you to knock out everything. Those bastards have got your buddies up there and they haven't turned them loose. Now punish them." And he wouldn't worry if there was "a little slop over" and they knocked out a few villages and hamlets.

As he reflected on the past three years, he thought their great error was not to have followed through on their ultimatums. He instructed Kissinger that when next he saw the North Vietnamese, who would inevitably return to the negotiating table, he was to alert them to Nixon's attitude:

N: And just say, "Now gentlemen regardless of how this election comes out . . . this man is going to be president, and I have never seen a man more determined. He's made the decision. We're going to finish it off." And I mean, I really would. I'd finish off the goddamn place.

K: And they'll . . .

N: Bomb Haiphong. You know the whole thing. I would put a crippling blow on it. Go on for 60 days of bombing. Just knock the shit out of them—

K: That's right!

N: And then everybody would say, "Oh horrible, horrible, horrible" (*laughs*). That's all right. You agree or not?

K: Absolutely! Absolutely!

It was a brutal vision, light years removed from the "generation of peace" that the president offered publicly. But before the administration could "knock the shit" out of Vietnam, a new crisis exploded on their watch. In early December 1971, India and Pakistan went to war.

This ought to have been no surprise, since there had been multiple warnings, which Kissinger had discounted. Since the summer, Indian prime minister Indira Gandhi had been warning that the situation inside her country—with literally millions of East Pakistan refugees camped inside its borders—was unsustainable: "What was claimed to be an internal problem of Pakistan, has also become an internal problem for India," Gandhi explained. Her demand that West Pakistan cease its attacks on the East so that the refugees could return home under safe conditions was echoed by governments and human rights advocates around the world.

US ambassador to New Delhi Kenneth Keating, along with regional experts in the State Department, had advocated a cut-off of American military aid to Karachi, and for serious pressure on its government to cease its repressive behavior.[9] However, they were repeatedly overruled by Nixon and Kissinger, for whom humanitarian arguments were anathema. Pakistan was a loyal ally, and its leader Yahya had performed an important favor by getting Kissinger to China. How he behaved in his own country was not a US concern. Indeed, it was their policy "to tilt" toward Pakistan.

Yet in this instance, as so often throughout the Vietnam War, moral indifference in the White House morphed into strategic blindness. Ambassador Keaton and the others were not exclusively concerned about matters of principle. They feared that violence in East Pakistan and the unstoppable flow of refugees would lead Prime Minister Gandhi to take provocative measures leading to war. Indeed, by the fall of 1971 she was openly assisting the independence movement for East Pakistan on the basis that its success was a prerequisite for the safe return of the refugees.

For Nixon and Kissinger, such warnings fell on deaf ears. After three years in office, they were tired of alarms from State Department bureaucrats, congressional handwringers, and media bleeding hearts. Nor did it improve their attitude that the suffering of the Bengalis was becoming a liberal issue, as exemplified by the vivid reports Senator Edward Kennedy brought back from the refugee camps he had visited along the border of India and Pakistan. As chairman of the Senate Sub-committee on Refugees, Kennedy felt it his duty to convey to his countrymen the atrocities their government was supporting. In a scathing presentation at the National Press Club, he described what he had seen:

> "The look on the face of a child paralyzed from the waist down, never to walk again: or a child quivering in fear on a mat in a small tent still in shock from seeing his parents, his brothers and his sisters executed before his eyes; or the anxiety of a two-year-old girl out foraging for something to cover the body of her baby brother who had died of cholera a few moments before our arrival."[10]

To Kennedy, this was too reminiscent of the tragedies he had observed in Vietnam: "Unfortunately, the face of America today in South Asia is not much different from its image over the past years in Southeast Asia. It is the image of an America that supports military repression and fuels military violence. It is the image of an America comfortably consorting with an authoritarian regime."

Nixon and Kissinger had no intention of allowing the specter of dying children to shape the course of American foreign policy. They were seeking a "generation of peace" that would eventually be good for everyone's children. For the moment, they would demonstrate "credibility" by standing firmly behind their friends even if they were strongmen, unafraid to use brutal methods in the interests of order.

An additional factor was their personal dislike of Indira Gandhi, only confirmed by her November visit to the White House.[11] By the time of her arrival there were an estimated 10 million Pakistani refugees inside her country, with profoundly destabilizing effects on the surrounding area. Her sense of urgency was reflected during a welcome banquet, when she unceremoniously asked her fellow guests to "imagine the entire population of Michigan State suddenly converging onto New York State," thereby offending Nixon, who had given a more gracious toast.

The official talks did not go well. For Nixon, the overriding concern was the recent massing of Indian and Pakistani troops along the border. He wanted the prime minister to pull back her troops, stop aiding the insurgency, and commit to a peaceful solution. Gandhi denied any intention to go to war but reminded the president of the atrocities committed by the Pakistani army and the resulting emergency this had created inside her country. She specifically asked that the United States stop providing military and moral support to the Pakistan government, a request that Nixon and Kissinger were unwilling to fulfill. The president acknowledged the need for political change there, but this could occur over time.

Though civility was maintained, the leaders parted company with no plan in place to arrest the impending conflagration. Afterwards, as they reviewed the meeting with Haldeman, Kissinger congratulated the president on his restraint. The woman was "a bitch," but Nixon had skillfully deprived her of the ability to go home and complain about American intransigence. "We really slobbered over the old witch," Nixon observed. But "only over the things that didn't matter," Kissinger offered.[12]

Their personal loathing for the Indian prime minister handicapped both men's ability to think strategically. Gandhi was not asking for special favors from the United States. Her essential point was that US support for Pakistan—both psychological and material—had facilitated its rigidity and ruthlessness over the past eight months. Nor did they grasp the magnitude of the problem created by the refugees, including their unwillingness to return if West Pakistan still held the reins of government.

The previous summer, Kissinger had stopped off in India before proceeding to Pakistan and then secretly to China. At the time, Indian officials encouraged him to visit the refugee camps, which he declined to do. Unlike Senator Kennedy, he had no interest in unpleasant scenes. But had he viewed the human catastrophe for himself, he might have recognized the acute pressures on the Indian government and thus the likelihood of war.

Throughout the unfolding regional crisis, Kissinger had consistently erred in his assessment of its gravity. However, by November 22 the denouement was clear, as the Pakistani government conveyed the news that 12 Indian divisions had crossed the border into East Pakistan, signaling the onset of a full-scale invasion. This proved to be a premature assessment, as the troops quickly withdrew. But Prime Minister Gandhi had made her decision: once their military was ready, they would enter in force.

Faced with this impending calamity, the White House signaled its continuing support of Pakistan, assuring its ambassador to the United States that the administration was on its side. Then, utilizing his newest secret channel, Kissinger and UN ambassador George Bush met with the recently arrived Chinese ambassador Huang Hoa in New York. Kissinger wanted him to know that whatever critical views of Pakistan were appearing in the American press did not reflect the opinion of the administration. As a demonstration of their sympathies, Kissinger shared classified information about the disposition of Indian troops along the Chinese border, with the suggestion that more intelligence data might be forthcoming.

For future communication, Kissinger explained that Ambassador Bush was working directly for the White House and that "no one in the government except for the people in this room knew about this channel." This was accurate, because Bush was under strict instructions to conceal the meeting from his State Department superiors. It was nevertheless "head-spinning" for the ambassador, who only weeks before had been fervently lobbying for a dual admission policy for China and Taiwan at the UN, and here was Kissinger offering up secret intelligence to Beijing's ambassador.

Yet this initiative was less of a reversal than Bush might imagine. Since the summer, a China priority was subtly influencing the administration's response to the crisis. Yahya's role in facilitating Kissinger's secret trip was a factor. But it was also important that the Pakistani government was a friend of both the United States and the People's Republic. Neither Nixon nor Kissinger was inclined to abandon an ally on account of a human rights crisis. Oddly enough, there was also a desire to impress Beijing with their firmness of purpose.

On December 3, the Pakistani government launched a preemptive attack on India, blowing up several of its air bases and seizing territory in Kashmir. They had beaten, by only one day, the plans of the Indian military to begin their invasion of East Pakistan. With events spinning out of control, Bush introduced a resolution in the UN calling for an immediate ceasefire and a withdrawal of both party's troops to within their own borders.[13] Yet having now dispatched India's troops. Indira Gandhi was aiming for the independence of East Pakistan. To the dismay of the White House, the Soviet Union vetoed the US resolution.

Having underestimated for months the gravity of the situation in East Pakistan, Kissinger swung in the opposite direction: with Russian backing, the million-man Indian army was going to destroy all of Pakistan, he warned.[14] With Nixon's acquiescence, there ensued two frantic weeks of activity by the national security advisor based on exaggerated fears that the entire structure of his diplomacy might collapse, with a valued ally destroyed, the Soviet Union unleashed, and their new Chinese friends disillusioned by American weakness.

As he maneuvered back and forth, fielding messages to Moscow, Beijing, and Karachi, to some observers Kissinger appeared emotionally unstable.[15] In previous months he and Nixon had been treading a high wire—alternating between feelings of immense excitement and imminent disaster. Three years into this presidency, their record of foreign policy achievement was less than stellar. Everything rested on future accomplishments: a "face-saving" peace in Vietnam, major agreements with the USSR and China, enhanced stability in the global system. In early November these achievements seemed within reach, but suddenly the war in South Asia had thrown everything into question.

Inside the State Department it was widely believed that Kissinger had served the president poorly. By doggedly standing by the Pakistani government through months of horrific crimes and ongoing repression, closing his ears to the desperation of millions of refugees and their beleaguered Indian hosts, he had set the stage for the present conflict. Many also believed he misunderstood the role of India and overstated its designs on West Pakistan. Mindful of this second-guessing, Kissinger was angry and demanding, lashing out at colleagues and insisting upon his authority. After one stormy meeting, Joseph Sisco, the Assistant Secretary of State for Near Eastern Affairs, reminded him that his colleagues were trying to do their jobs. There was no need "to threaten or intimidate us . . . You will scare the hell out of so many people in this building that no one will give you the information you should hear."[16]

On December 7, with the crisis still accelerating, Kissinger complained to Haldeman that his position had become untenable.[17] He intended to announce his retirement within the next few weeks, accompany the president to China in the spring, and leave during the summer. Sick of this egotistical nonsense, the chief of staff advised Nixon to resist this threat. With his concurrence, Haldeman drew the line: if Kissinger was determined to resign, he should do so immediately. Nixon would not take him to China if he had become a lame duck. This effectively quashed Kissinger's threats. The last thing he wanted was to be left behind on the China trip.

During the next 10 days, the situation became even more nerve-wracking, with Kissinger determined to prove American toughness to the Chinese.[18] Toward this end, he shared information on Indian troop disposition along their common border and let them know that if China "took measures to protect its security, the U.S. would oppose any effort by others to interfere." The message was hardly subtle. If the Soviet Union resisted Chinese moves on India, the United States would have their back.[19] In reality these machinations were quite unnecessary, since the Chinese had no intention of going to war with India, and Indira Gandhi had no plan to attack West Pakistan.

On December 16 the apparent emergency came to a halt, when the Pakistani army surrendered in Dacca—thereby settling the independent status of Bangladesh. One day later, just as the Russians had assured the Americans, India Gandhi honored her promise to implement a ceasefire and withdraw her troops.[20]

The outbreak of war between India and Pakistan was the largest, most complex international crisis the Nixon administration had faced since taking office, involving as it did convoluted machinations with multiple foreign actors, domestic critics, and a fragmented national security bureaucracy. Because both Nixon and Kissinger had the habit of prevaricating, it was sometimes difficult for anyone to discern their true motives. Their default story throughout the crisis was the need to check the "naked aggression" of a Soviet-backed client state and, by so doing, preserve the international "balance of power."[21]

In its bare outlines, this resembled their case for continued war in Vietnam, namely limiting the expansion of the communist superpowers. Yet as familiar as such talk might be, it obscured the underlying dynamics in both situations, including the link between them. The histrionic Cold War rhetoric in which these matters were transacted implied a threat, whether immediate or indirect, to the safety of the American nation. Yet in neither instance was the security of the United States ever at risk, nor was there an act of aggression by a communist superpower. Instead, the real concerns were less tangible or important: the imagined prestige of the United States and the personal reputations of Nixon and Kissinger. Also present was the desire, with the Beijing visit on the horizon, to impress the Chinese.

As the South Asian situation calmed down, Kissinger faced a related challenge. Syndicated columnist Jack Anderson began a series of articles, based on top secret government documents, which cast a harsh light on the administration's decision-making. Anderson's columns, which appeared in 700 newspapers, especially focused on Kissinger's role in lying to the public, ignoring humanitarian concerns, and disrespecting his own government's regional experts.

Commenting on the portrait of the administration that emerged from these articles, *New York Times* columnist Anthony Lewis observed: "The flavor is of some ancient oriental court. Deep in the inner recesses of the palace, the unapproachable potentate draws up his edicts. A grand vizier emerges periodically and proclaims them to other courtiers. If anyone asks a question, the grand vizier warns him to be less curious or he may lose his head."[22] This raised procedural questions: Why did this one person, Henry Kissinger, enjoy such exclusive access to the president? And why was he allowed to shut down dissenting voices in advance of decisions? The mishandling of the India–Pakistan conflict seemed the direct consequence of this high-handed approach.

Jack Anderson readily acknowledged that he was "trying to force a showdown with the administration over their classification system." Everything "Kissinger does—even the toilet paper he uses—is being stamped secret. That's not in the public interest in a democracy." Of course, Nixon had no interest in reassessing his administration's secrecy, only in protecting it against any further breaches. For him the operative question was, how had Jack Anderson obtained access to a cache of top secret documents? To find out who was responsible, he brought in the White House "plumbers." Supervised by John Ehrlichman and including former CIA agent Howard Hunt and former FBI man Gordon Liddy, the Special Investigations Unit's mission was to carry out politically sensitive investigations for the president.

In looking into the Anderson leaks, their work was simplified by the fact that only a tiny circle of people had access to the documents. They were able to quickly determine that the culprit was Yeoman Charles Radford, a Navy stenographer assigned to the National Security Council. After a grueling round of interrogations managed by Ehrlichman, Radford broke down and confessed that he had been regularly copying and distributing top secret documents under orders from his immediate superior Admiral Robert Welander, the Joint Chiefs of Staff liaison to the NSC.[23] His transgression might have gone undetected had he not passed material to Jack Anderson—a decision prompted by his personal sympathy for India and his disgust with Kissinger's tyrannical ways.

Radford's thievery had begun in September 1970 when Welander's predecessor, Captain Rembrandt Robinson, directed him to observe Kissinger's operations closely and to pass along any significant documents. This material was then routed to Admiral Moorer, the chairman of the Joint Chiefs of Staff. Over a 16-month period, Radford acted with increasing boldness—returning to the office at night to rifle through Kissinger's personal briefcase, the NSC "burn bags," and other classified items placed on nearby desks. Moreover, as a highly trusted, seemingly innocuous presence in the office, he was frequently asked by secretaries to fill in during coffee breaks and to run the copying machine. It was easy enough to make an additional set for his military superiors, a practice that continued when Admiral Welander replaced Robinson during the summer of 1971. By the time he became ensnared in the

Anderson inquiry, the stenographer had managed to dispatch thousands of White House documents to Admiral Moorer.

Ehrlichman and his fellow investigators were stunned by the scope of this internal espionage. It seemed obvious that in addition to Moorer, the other service chiefs were also receiving the purloined material. Based on Welander's subsequent confession, it was even possible that Deputy National Security Advisor Al Haig had been aware of the spying.

Could Radford and his fellow conspirators be charged with a felony? To advise him on this critical matter, Nixon pulled in Attorney General John Mitchell. The lawyer's advice was clear: no prosecutions and no firing. If Nixon went after Moorer or his colleagues, "You would have the Joint Chiefs . . . directly against you." After all, the damage was done. The important thing was "to paper this over" while being sure to close the military liaison office in the NSC.

Kissinger thought otherwise. To him the appropriate response was a "no-brainer." Admiral Moorer and the others should be fired immediately.[24] The president's decision was to him incomprehensible. Venting to Haldeman, he exclaimed, "They can spy on him and spy on me and betray us and he won't fire them. I assure you all this tolerance will lead to a very serious consequence for this administration."[25]

Nixon's reluctance was hardly a case of tolerance. One restraining factor was his appreciation of Moorer's previous willingness to bypass the Secretary of Defense in carrying out instructions from the White House. If faced with dismissal or prosecution, he might choose to go public with this information, which would be more than embarrassing. It was safer to let the admiral know that his espionage had been uncovered and to do nothing—which would insure his cooperation in the rocky months ahead.

In addressing this security breach, Nixon adopted the stance that such bureaucratic shenanigans were to be expected—that the military would naturally wish to know what the civilian authorities were up to. This was palpably false. The ransacking of presidential materials on the scale of Radford's effort was a stunning breach of security. The unexplored question was what would motivate the Joint Chiefs of Staff to conduct such a massive and risky intrusion into White House affairs?

A major factor was the extent to which Nixon and Kissinger had strayed from White House norms in their handling of high-level policy. There was nothing new about lying to the American public, but such consistent dishonesty in dealing with government principals was extraordinary. Whether the issue was conduct of the Vietnam War, arms control, the future of Berlin, relations with the Soviet Union, diplomacy with China—there was a willful effort to deceive other high-level officials whenever there was a potential for disagreement. Much of the time, the two men made their policy decisions based on the recommendations of the Joint Chiefs or MACV. However, this was not always the case, especially as large numbers of American troops were being removed from Vietnam against military advice. Lacking a reliable way to know what the White House had in mind, the Chiefs had turned to espionage.

While Radford's revelations outraged Nixon, he was acutely aware that within the government, professional military men were still his closest allies—and he was not eager to antagonize them. Ironically it was Kissinger, his comrade in duplicity, who bothered him more.[26] Nixon was appalled by Kissinger's mood swings and unceasing complaints about the Secretary of State. Yoked together during the India–Pakistan crisis, he had wearied of his advisor's exaggerated fears and jealous tantrums. No sooner had India declared its ceasefire than he took a break from their private meetings. This did not deter Kissinger from arriving in the Oval Office on Christmas Eve, demanding that he fire Moorer. To Nixon, this was another sign that his tempestuous assistant was in need of psychiatric attention, a suggestion he passed along to Ehrlichman.[27]

More than once during this period, Nixon wondered if he should get rid of Kissinger. But the national security assistant had made himself indispensable. Apart from his intellectual agility, Kissinger had demonstrated a willingness to break rules and to screen out sentimental worries about death and destruction that was as thoroughgoing as Nixon's own. Like the president, Kissinger had the capacity for drowning out unpleasant truths in a torrent of words. Ignoring a sea of corpses—whether in South Vietnam or Bangladesh—he could speak with conviction of a "generation of peace." More emotionally balanced men like Bill Rogers or Mel Laird were easier company, but both lacked the grit or ingenuity to dispense so completely with moral or institutional norms.

Heading into 1972, Nixon faced a complex set of problems. The South Asian crisis had deflected attention from the still-dangerous situation in Vietnam. With a presidential election getting closer, he had to extricate himself from this failing war in some successful fashion. Yet three years out, he had fewer combat troops on the ground and less public support than at any time in his presidency. Moreover, the news from MACV was truly ominous.

On January 20, General Abrams cabled the White House: "[T]he enemy is preparing and positioning his forces for a major offensive. It is apparent that the high-level decisions and planning for such an effort have already been made." Although unsure "of his precise plan of attack, it is apparent that he is going to face us with the most difficult situations of which he is capable."[28]

Receiving this alarming news, Kissinger mentioned how fortunate it was that he and Dobrynin would be having dinner the following night, when he could update him on the situation and perhaps renew their previous dialogue.

This was a surprise to Nixon. During the high drama of India–Pakistan, Dobrynin had been in Moscow. Yet in his absence, American–Soviet relations had been rubbed raw, with uncertain implications for the future. Now the Soviet ambassador was back in town and, according to Kissinger, was in fine spirits and eager for a long conversation. "I made some jokes about India–Pakistan," he said. And Dobrynin's response was, "Let's put it behind us. Let's work positively for the future."[29] To which he had replied, "You know Anatoly, every time you leave town, I know you're doing something mischievous because every time you're out of town things are in a crisis."

India–Pakistan was one of the great humanitarian tragedies of the Cold War era, but as Kissinger would later write: "And then suddenly it was all over . . . the basic structure of our foreign policy was intact. Planning for both summits could resume."[30]

20

"Seize the Hour! Seize the Day!"

The China summit would come first. Throughout the South Asia crisis Kissinger had kept the calendar in mind, fearful of any disruption. As planning proceeded, he was determined to exclude the State Department from any significant discussions. Underlying his personal rivalry with Secretary of State Rogers was the awareness, intensified by recent events, that experienced members of the State Department would disapprove of his transactions with Beijing.

To wrap up the final details for Nixon's forthcoming visit in February, Kissinger chose his deputy Alexander Haig, whose repeated visits to South Vietnam and Cambodia had demonstrated his reliability and willingness to keep secrets. Before leaving Washington he was handed a lengthy script, which he used during his first meeting with Zhou Enlai on January 3.[1] Invoking the recent crisis, Haig claimed "strong confirmation" that American intervention had been "effective in convincing the Soviet Union to influence the Indians to accept a cease fire" instead of proceeding with attacks on West Pakistan, which had been their original goal.

After a "careful assessment" of the total situation, the White House had concluded that the Russians were changing their strategy.[2] Whereas previously their aim had been to divide the Asian subcontinent, they appeared bent on the "encirclement" of China by ringing its territory with unfriendly states. In past months the Russians had tried various stratagems to lure the United States away from its rapprochement with the People's Republic. But Washington had rejected these seductive offers. This partly reflected their principled commitment to Pakistan, but also a new awareness that "the future viability of the PRC was of the greatest interest to us." If the Russians were permitted to neutralize China, they would inevitably turn on the United States.

On the topic of Vietnam, Haig responded to Beijing's concerns about recent American bombing of the North. During a five-day period at the end of December, the United States had launched more than 1,000 bombing raids there, with reports of widespread civilian deaths and the destruction of a hospital.[3] This controversial decision to bomb, the general explained, had been taken with the "greatest reluctance." Despite the Nixon administration's sincere efforts to find a diplomatic solution, Hanoi had cut off negotiations and was intensifying its military campaign, developments which connected to the alleged Soviet menace. "We feel strongly that Moscow is urging Hanoi in the direction of continued military action," thus forging "another link in the chain . . . designed to constrain the People's Republic."

In a policy change, the United States had become "dedicated to the proposition that the viability of the People's Republic should be maintained." Just as Stalin and Churchill had bridged their ideological differences in the face of a common foe, their two nations faced a similar challenge. As emerged during the India–Pakistan crisis, the Nixon administration was prepared to deploy its resources on behalf of China. As one example of this new orientation, during his next visit Kissinger would be prepared "to discuss the modalities" for sending along fresh intelligence information about the Soviet military deployments.

In effecting this policy change, President Nixon had a serious domestic problem: an odd merger of a pro-Soviet left and a pro-Taiwan right, both "dedicated to preventing the President's visit . . . or to contributing to its failure." There was also a governmental bureaucracy stuck in its old ways. It was therefore important that President Nixon's visit be successful not merely in fact but in appearance. Unfortunately, American journalists were a bunch of "shallow idiots" incapable of long-range analysis, so there must be no embarrassment of the president while he was in China.

This brought Haig to the delicate subject of the Communiqué, which was nearly complete. It could be strengthened by including increased trade, scientific collaboration, and cultural exchange among the goals. More problematic was the wording pertaining to Taiwan, which Kissinger and Zhou Enlai had been unable to resolve. Having clarified the political background, he hoped the Chinese would agree to language on Taiwan that was "somewhat less truthful and somewhat less precise" than the formulations that had been discussed previously.

Haig's presentation was rich in invention, including his suggestion that the administration had recently uncovered some new and diabolical Soviet strategy directed against China. This could hardly fool Zhou Enlai, who surely knew better. However, he deferred comment pending consultation with Mao. Upon hearing Zhou's report, the old revolutionary expressed amusement. So the Americans were worried about China? "Its concerns for us are like a cat feeling sad for a mouse."[4]

Nevertheless, Mao had made the decision to pursue "normalization" with the United States, and accordingly Zhou assured Haig at their next meeting that his government was eager for improved relations. As for the alleged change in Soviet strategy, he greatly doubted its reality. There was nothing new about the Soviet antipathy or their backing of India. As before, China would continue to assist the government of Pakistan, but there was no cause for excessive concern by the Americans.

On the other hand, the US bombing of North Vietnam had stirred deep opposition in Beijing and around the world, and Haig's justification for it was completely "untenable." After all, the Vietnamese people "have the right to take every necessary action in self-defense." US officials might claim that they were seeking to avoid the "humiliation" of their country, but this made no sense. If there was an insulted party, it was the Vietnamese. "By what logic may a big country willfully commit aggression against a small country" and claim victimhood?

As for the newly discovered desire by the United States to preserve Chinese "viability"—China might not yet be a "great power," but it was entirely capable of acting on its own behalf. "Facts have already proved that all schemes to isolate, encircle, contain and subvert China will only end up in ignominious defeat."

Haig's script had him making the dubious case that a new Soviet menace gave China a stake in building up Richard Nixon as an international statesman. Zhou tactfully but firmly set this aside. Such a strategy was difficult to understand: "The image of a man depends on his own deeds," he asserted. He also saw no gain in obfuscating the Taiwan issue in order to quiet the president's domestic foes. The future of the island was of central importance to his government and should be addressed candidly when the two leaders met. As for Vietnam—as he had told Kissinger previously, the Nixon administration should draw a lesson from Charles DeGaulle's actions in Algeria by withdrawing in one strike, "wholly and cleanly."

Up to this point, General Haig had adhered closely to his "talking points." Yet he felt so impelled to defend the American project in Vietnam that he strayed briefly from them. "From our perspective it is not United States forces that are in Laos . . . or Cambodia, but North Vietnamese forces." Washington had repeatedly offered to withdraw its troops and had made conscientious offers for a settlement, but Hanoi had not responded.

There was no ambiguity about the Vietnam War, Zhou replied. The United States was "in the wrong." By "bringing up excuses to drag on in a messy way," they were creating more complications for themselves. They might wish for "an honorable and glorious withdrawal," but this was no longer possible. The complaint that it was the North Vietnamese who had gone into Laos and Cambodia first was beside the point. The real issue was that American troops "should not have gone to Vietnam in the first place." The same held true for Cambodia and Laos. The president and the Pentagon were calling these operations "successes," but "this kind of fighting will not bring victory."

In the mouth of anyone but Zhou Enlai, such a lecture would have aroused Haig's wrath. The Chinese prime minister's points had been a staple of American antiwar rallies for years. But Haig was not in Beijing to engage in ideological debate.[5] He was there to advance the summit and iron out some procedural matters of particular importance to Kissinger. Chief among them was the requirement that Kissinger be present for "all conversations between the President and yourself and whatever meetings might occur between the President and Chairman Mao," while excluding the Secretary of State. To achieve the latter, Haig proposed that the Chinese schedule meetings between their foreign ministry and the people from State that would coincide with the times when Nixon was conferring with China's leaders.[6]

Despite disagreements on key issues, it was clear that the Chinese were eager for President Nixon's visit and willing to take the necessary steps to make it a success. While Haig was in Beijing, staff from both sides worked through the many technical complexities of the trip, which involved among other things the Americans' need for a large entourage to include both members of their delegation and representatives of the media. Of particular importance to the White House was the desire to have live television coverage of major ceremonial events. Although unaccustomed to such requests, the Chinese went out of their way to accommodate them.[7]

While plans for the Beijing summit went forward, Nixon remained worried about an enemy offensive overturning these brightening prospects. At home he was facing unremitting pressure to end the war in Vietnam and bring the POWs home. To buy some breathing space, he planned a speech in which he would unveil Kissinger's multiple missions to Paris.[8]

On the evening of January 25, the president went on national television with another lofty speech, reminding his audience of everything he had done to obtain an honorable exit from the war. In addition to the publicly known peace talks in Paris, there were also 30 months of secret negotiations by his personal representative Henry Kissinger. Contrary to what his critics were claiming, the United States had repeatedly offered to set a six-month deadline for the withdrawal of all its troops to facilitate the "speedy return" of all POWs.[9] The American proposal also called for a ceasefire throughout all of Indochina, along with an international commission that would supervise new elections in South Vietnam, with the understanding that one month before the balloting General Thieu would step down. Despite the obvious fairness of this approach, the enemy had repeatedly turned it down, always insisting that the overthrow of the Thieu government was the true price of peace.

Nixon acknowledged that "some of our citizens have become accustomed to thinking that whatever our government says must be false, and whatever our enemies say must be true, as far as this war is concerned." But by disclosing this hitherto secret record, "We can now demonstrate publicly what we have long been demonstrating privately—that America has taken the initiative not only to end our participation in this war, but to end the war itself for all concerned."

While Nixon-haters might gnash their teeth at these performances, or furiously shut off their television sets, these presidential speeches had wide appeal. For millions of Americans the revelation of Kissinger's secret trips evoked some of the excitement of his original China adventure and suggested a sincere determination to end the war. Congressional and journalistic response to Nixon's speech was mixed, but some critics saw reason for optimism. Public opinion polls, which had shown the president trailing behind Democratic candidate Ed Muskie, revealed an immediate bump.[10]

In his lawyerly presentation, Nixon had rushed over one crucial item of major importance to the North Vietnamese: the need to pair a ceasefire with an interim government in the South. The president's willingness to have Thieu step down one month before an election might be symbolically significant but was unresponsive to their concern. The issue for Hanoi and for the PRG was the danger of halting the fight while the entire leadership and administrative machinery of the South Vietnamese government remained in place.

Nixon had no expectation that North Vietnam would accept his proposed bargain. A more immediate goal was to "steal the thunder" of his presidential rivals and to inoculate the American public against the military battles he knew were coming. In the aftermath of his speech, Governor

Rockefeller phoned Kissinger with a question: Why had they blown the secret channel?[11] Because the North Vietnamese would be "launching a big offensive in February," Kissinger replied bluntly. The United States might have to strike back. If they did, this speech would put us in "a better position" to do so.

At General Abrams' headquarters in Saigon, there were deep concerns about ARVN's readiness and motivation for battle when faced with a large-scale enemy assault. Thieu seemed asleep at the wheel, while the decision-makers in Hanoi appeared prepared to go for broke.[12] "This battle—it will last at least 45 days, and . . . We're going to have to take losses to do it, but that's what's going to have to be done," Abrams exhorted.[13]

In Washington, policymakers struggled with the requests for money and support coming from MACV. A particular concern was the possibility that Hanoi would launch its attack while the president and his entourage were in Beijing, creating embarrassment and disrupting the proceedings. To address the likely offensive, Nixon scheduled a rare strategy session with all his key people: Ambassador Bunker, Secretaries Laird and Rogers, CIA Director Helms, Admiral Moorer, Vice President Agnew. Also in attendance were Attorney General John Mitchell and Secretary of the Treasury John Connally, both invited for their "tough-minded" attitude.

For over two hours the group kicked around narrow issues with which they were all most comfortable: in particular, what kind of firepower should General Abrams have at his disposal? Rogers took the opportunity to showcase his hawk-like proclivities by urging the president to "seriously consider giving the military any authority that it wants—within reason, of course, not nuclear authority, but anything else."[14] After all, this might be "the key play . . . the turning point of the whole battle for South Vietnam," he announced. Agnew thought Haiphong Harbor might make a good bombing target.

Nixon was looking for something more intense and dramatic they could do. In considering the whole history of the Vietnam War, he thought the major mistake was the slow drip of gradual escalation. That had to change. You know when "the other guy gives you . . . a slap on the wrist," the only thing to do was "kick him in the groin . . . that's what we've got to do here."[15]

> I would just double the number of '52s . . . whatever is necessary, so there's one hell of a show. . . . We've got four hundred . . . get them the hell over there, right now. Let's have an awesome show of strength. . . .

> Between now and the time we return from China, we cannot hit the North . . . On the other hand, we can dump everything we've got on the South.

Laird introduced a cautionary note about problems with war- funding. Despite the temporary lull in criticism, nobody should make the mistake of thinking that Congress was going to assent. "Maybe others think the atmosphere has changed and that we get . . . this money through easily, but it hasn't changed as far as the damn gut questions in those committees." Furthermore, they had to look down the road and protect their ability to get military and economic assistance for South Vietnam over a period of years, or Vietnamization would eventually go down the drain.

For Nixon, the year that mattered was 1972—election year. He agreed with Laird that "we don't want to do anything stupid" by "exacerbating the public" or arousing "the ugly youth."[16] But in his judgment they had a 60- to 90-day period to get in a strong position for beating the enemy. He was personally determined that "we're not going to lose out there." They were going to do whatever was necessary to defeat the enemy offensive and would not be constrained by "pusillanimous planning."

For the next few weeks, the American effort must focus on South Vietnam. As part of dumping "everything we've got," Nixon ordered a fourth aircraft carrier, the *Kitty Hawk,* into the South China Sea, and an increase of B-52 airplanes and fighter bombers in the immediate area to enable a sortie rate of 1,500 a month.[17] This would facilitate "saturation bombing" near the Central Highlands with additional targets in Laos and Cambodia. Nixon hoped this demonstration of American power would "frighten the hell out of them."

The approach was hardly new. For the past three years the administration had been trying to "frighten the hell" out of the enemy, with little to show for the effort. Their adversaries continued to fight on, while many previously indifferent people had become bitter foes of the United States. This was certainly the situation in Cambodia, where thousands of peasants who might have been content to ignore politics and cultivate their rice farms were being turned into fighters for the Khmer Rouge.

Yet Nixon was somehow convinced that the Air Force was holding back, using poor weather as an excuse for diminished attacks. If they really struck with full force, the outcome would be different. This obsession with massive bombing was as quixotic in its way as Kissinger's perpetual expectation that the North Vietnamese were about to cave at the conference table. Back in

October, the national security advisor had been especially optimistic about the prospects for a peace agreement but was unpleasantly surprised when Le Duc Tho developed an "illness" at the last minute. Since then Hanoi had made no move to reschedule.

Then quite suddenly there was news from the North Vietnamese. On February 14, the leadership sent word of their willingness to reopen the secret negotiations with the United States. Kissinger was ebullient.[18] "Well, you remember Mr. President . . . that I figured that they would make the move between the Beijing and the Moscow summit?"[19] None of this, he claimed. would have happened if Nixon had not been so strong: revealing the secret negotiations, standing up to domestic opponents, deploying additional military power. This was the first time in two administrations that Hanoi had actually asked for a meeting or proposed lunch. Even if not ready to settle, the invitation to meet Le Duc was a clear indication there would be no offensive before the summit.

Nixon was as always less sanguine than Kissinger about possible results. But this lent even greater importance to the benefits that might accrue from the China visit. In preparation for his heroic journey, the president was avidly reading up on the Chinese leadership. He was especially impressed by French writer André Malraux, whose *Anti-Memoirs* contained fascinating portraits of Mao and Zhao Enlai. As a young leftist in the 1920s, Malraux had met the two revolutionaries in China, and then decades later as Charles De Gaulle's Minister of Culture he had returned there to interview Mao, whom he regarded as one of the towering figures of the twentieth century.

In the week before his departure for Beijing, Nixon invited Malraux to appear at a White House dinner in his honor.[20] In a private conversation beforehand, the French writer described Mao as a "colossus facing death." The main thing he cared about was what could benefit his country. Indeed, the Chinese had "never helped anyone, neither Vietnam, nor Pakistan. They only cared about their own country." Everything else was "a brilliant lie." In this was a powerful hint that communist internationalism would be of slight significance.

At dinner, Nixon urged Malraux to share his assessment of Mao with the assembled guests.[21] Although his revolutionary years were behind him, Nixon would be meeting a man who "had a fantastic destiny and who believed that he was acting out his last act in his lifetime." His unstated aim for the summit would be to gain US assistance in the economic development of his still agricultural country.

"What comes after Mao?" Nixon inquired. This was a difficult question, Malraux replied. Years before, Mao had told him, "I have no successor," by which he meant, "Great leaders, Churchill, Gandhi, DeGaulle had been created by traumatic historical events which would occur no more." This got Nixon reflecting on the "mystique" of great men, a favorite topic of his. He related an anecdote about Abraham Lincoln who, before his death, dreamed of steering a ship "through treacherous shoals."

Picking up the theme, Malraux compared Nixon's impending visit to China with the voyages of the famed sixteenth-century explorers. Nixon was attempting "one of the most important things of our century." If Charles De Gaulle were alive, he would put his hands on the American's shoulders and say, "All men who understand what you are embarking upon salute you." Such extravagant praise was music to Nixon's and Kissinger's ears. For both, it was a magical evening, highlighting the bravery of the journey upon which they were about to embark.

On the eve of the trip, Kissinger drafted a memo for the president, "Mao, Zhou and the Chinese Litmus Test," to prepare him for the intellectual challenge to come.[22] Echoing Malraux, he emphasized Mao's tactical genius, "his unique capacity to judge when to press, when to retreat and adopt a humble posture, how to build a strong coalition of support." That said, Mao's true greatness "derives from his visionary side."

On the other hand, it was Zhou who was truly running the country. Nixon would find the prime minister to be "charming, articulate and tough." And the president would surely enjoy "the give-and-take . . . on several planes, on all of which he is equally at home—historical discussion, philosophic dissertation, tactical jousting." All in all, this would be an irresistible battle of wits for Nixon, who prided himself on his intellectual breadth and larger-than-life statesmanship.

As Kissinger explained, the Chinese were still making up their minds about the United States. At the summit they would be evaluating whether Washington was a friend worth cultivating or a feckless foe they should seek to undermine. Therefore:

> Our essential requirement is to demonstrate that we are serious enough to understand the basic forces at work in the world and reliable enough to deliver on the commitments we make. If in our formal and informal talks we can impress the Chinese with these intangibles, we will have truly made your visit an historic success.

Flattery hit its mark. In the wake of the brief India–Pakistan War, Nixon had wearied of Henry Kissinger—his mood swings, his histrionics, the constant griping about Rogers and other government colleagues. There were also ample grounds for believing that his recent advice had been poor—both in handling Indira Gandhi and exaggerating Beijing's willingness to intervene in Pakistan. Yet any thoughts of replacing him had dissipated as the China trip approached, for nobody but Kissinger seemed as awestruck by the prospect or as familiar with current Chinese thinking.

From reviewing the unsanitized transcripts and other documents, Nixon could also discern that in his conversations with the Chinese prime minister, Kissinger had made commitments that would be poorly received by State Department specialists. Yet, by denying them access to the relevant materials Secretary Rogers and Marshall Green, the Assistant Secretary of State for Far Eastern and Asian Affairs, were effectively marginalized even before their plane left Washington.[23]

The long trip to Shanghai was punctuated by stopovers in Hawaii and Guam, where the president offered brief remarks to excited crowds about his aspirations for the visit. Although adept at feigning enthusiasm when needs be, on this occasion Nixon was undeniably in high spirits. He had always yearned to take heroic action, which was perhaps why he referred so often to the great men of history. Here he was, on a trip of epic proportions, journeying into the heartland of a country long considered a pariah by the people of the United States. Lending drama to the occasion were the years of ostracism and the wall of fear that had been erected against the diabolical aims of "Red China," a wall that a younger Richard Nixon had helped to fortify. Yet time and events had changed him.

As Nixon headed west, Anthony Lewis of the *New York Times* was reflecting on the paradoxical nature of his trip.[24] There were the "four million pounds of bombs still being dropped daily, the forests destroyed by chemical agents . . . the 100,000 casualties and refugees caused by American bombing every month," all of which had been justified by the need "to contain China." But with that objective disappearing, what rationale was there for the continued killing in Indochina?

Though carefully scripted, Nixon's arrival in Beijing was low-key.[25] Zhou Enlai greeted him at the airport, but there were no crowds, and the streets leading into the capital were devoid of spectators. However, shortly after he was installed in a government guest house, Zhou Enlai brought the welcome news that Chairman Mao would like to see him. Kissinger inquired if he could bring along his assistant, Winston Lord. "Won't the Secretary (Rogers) be mad?" Zhou speculated. "We won't tell him," Kissinger replied.[26] Excited by this sudden opportunity, the president hastily got dressed and the three Americans rushed out the door. They did not bring a translator or any member of Nixon's security team.

It scarcely mattered to the Americans that Mao was less impressive than advertised. He was clearly ailing and spoke with obvious difficulty. The Chinese leader struck a modest note. He had read in the newspaper that the president planned to discuss philosophy.[27] This was because of the Chairman's reputation and important writings, the Americans explained.[28] Kissinger hastened to add that he had previously assigned Mao's collective works to students at Harvard. "Those writings of mine aren't anything," Mao observed. "There is nothing instructive in what I wrote." Nixon demurred. "The Chairman's writing has moved a nation and has changed the world."

Mao was at pains to puncture old stereotypes. If the Democrats came into office, he would have to deal with them. But he had supported Nixon in the last election. "I like rightists," he announced. Latching on to this news, the president reflected that sometimes "politicians on the right could take steps that those on the left can only talk about." This inspired Kissinger to bring up a false notion he had been purveying for months—namely the alleged existence of a pro-Soviet left in the United States, which was imperiling their new relationship.

To amplify the point, Nixon turned immediately to the India–Pakistan war where, he claimed, these pro-Soviet "leftists" had been part of the problem. However, as a matter of principle, his administration had been unwilling to see a big country "gobble up its neighbor." He had paid a political price for his firm stance, but he was confident that he had done the right thing. He looked forward to confidential discussions with the Chairman and the Prime Minister about a range of international issues: Taiwan, Korea, Vietnam, the future of Japan, and the nature of US–Soviet relations. Mao agreed these were "troublesome problems," but he would rather not "get into them very much." These items could be discussed with Zhou. His own preference was to talk about "philosophy."

Ignoring the hint, Nixon continued as if he and Mao were old friends. "We . . . must ask ourselves . . . why the Soviets have more forces facing you than on the border of Western Europe?" Mao thought it "strange" that for 22 years their two nations "had never met in talks," although neither country had aggressive designs against the other. Alluding to his earlier views, Nixon said that he and Kissinger understood that the important thing was "not a nation's internal political philosophy" but its attitude toward the world and "toward us." When the president gravely declared that the United States was not a threat to any other country, Mao chose to keep his silence.

Though a bit disjointed, the conversation fulfilled Nixon's expectations.[29] Plainly Mao was a down-to-earth person with whom one could do business. This was the high-level, candid exchange that Nixon had been hoping for when he pursued the China opening. Fortunately, there were photographers on hand to snap the historic photos and quickly flash them around the world. The one snafu was that Winston Lord had been included in the group shots, which would surely offend the Secretary of State.[30] However, it was a simple matter to crop the picture, a Soviet practice sometimes ridiculed in the United States.

Shortly after his session with Mao, Nixon joined the US delegation at a magnificent banquet in his honor at the Great Hall of the People.[31] It was morning in America as millions watched Zhou and Nixon raise their glasses to toast one another and their new beginning. Zhou was warm, though restrained. The Chinese and the Americans were both "great people" he said, with a long history of friendly relations. Alas, "owing to reasons known to all," lines of communication had broken down. But it was his hope that "through a frank exchange of views . . . a new start can be made."

In contrast to Zhou, President Nixon spoke with eloquence and passion. At this very moment, "more people are seeing and hearing what we say than . . . in the history of the world."[32] Their words might be forgotten but "what we do here can change the world." There were of course differences, which would not disappear overnight. But together, they must begin "the long march" toward "building a world structure of peace and justice" in which every nation, whether large or small, "has a right to determine its own form of government, free of outside interference or domination."

"What legacy shall we leave our children?" Nixon continued. Were they destined to fight and die "for the hatreds that plagued the old world," or "to live because we had the vision to build a new world?" In an emotional peroration, he quoted Chairman Mao: "So many deeds cry out to be done and always urgent. The world rolls on. Time passes. Ten thousand years are too long. Seize the day!" It was a stellar performance. This was Richard Nixon at a peak moment of his political career, standing in Beijing, summoning his audience to noble deeds.

Behind the scenes much of the detail work was left to Kissinger. In the interval between the session with Mao and the banquet, he huddled with Zhou Enlai to review the agenda. As previously planned, only a Chinese interpreter was present.[33] Kissinger took the opportunity to remind Zhou of America's "complicated system of government" and to review who in the US delegation "knows what" in order to ensure that no one on the Chinese team would inadvertently reveal anything in their private meetings with the State Department people.

As previously agreed, Rogers and his team would be kept busy discussing matters of cultural exchange and trade, while Nixon and Kissinger engaged the more important issues with Zhou Enlai. As for the Communiqué, Kissinger was prepared to hammer out the uncompleted sections with whomever the Chinese designated. He was also willing to share without reciprocity an update on American negotiations with the USSR and detailed information about the state of its military.

Throughout the five days of talks, both Nixon and Kissinger brought up India–Pakistan as a shining example of the kind of assistance the US government could provide China in international disputes. Yet there was reason to wonder if the Chinese government ever believed their own interests were seriously threatened by that conflict or if American pressure on the Soviet Union had been at all helpful.

Of more obvious value was Kissinger's offer to pass along classified intelligence of a military and political nature about the Soviet Union. For this purpose, the national security advisor met for three hours with top military officials from the People's Republic, carefully explaining that he was providing this information with no request for reciprocity—only for "complete discretion." In this session he described in detail the Soviet ground forces, tactical aircraft and missiles, strategic air defense, and strategic attack forces deployed near the Chinese border and elsewhere. He also provided specific numbers for each Soviet division and descriptions of each category of aircraft and missiles, along with data on its nuclear capability.

General Yeh Chien-ying commended Kissinger for providing this valuable report, which was "an important indication of the sincere desire of the United States government to improve our relations." The latter assured him that, other than the NSC staff seated in the room and the president, "none of our colleagues here" or other government officials back in Washington "know that we have given you this information." Indeed, nobody from the State Department, the Department of Defense, the CIA, or Congress had any idea of the classified data he was passing along. The extent to which the White House had been currying favor with the government of China had been concealed for many months. And while there was perhaps a fine line between opening a cordial relationship and making dangerous concessions, this transmission of top secret military information had surely crossed it.

As for US concessions, the most difficult issue between the Chinese and the Americans remained the future of Taiwan. In previous meetings with Zhou, Kissinger had already agreed to five key points: there was only one China, of which Taiwan was a part; the United States would not support a Taiwanese independence movement; it would discourage Japan from moving into the area as the American presence decreased; it would support any peaceful resolution of the issue that the two Chinese parties mutually accepted; and it would oppose any military attempt by the Taiwanese government to return to the mainland.

But this did not resolve the controversy. From Beijing's perspective, a major bone of contention was the presence of approximately 10,000 American troops on the island, whose presence was underpinned by a Mutual Defense Treaty. Recognizing the "emotional content" of the Taiwan question, President Nixon had addressed the matter during his first working meeting with Zhou. "In all candor," he wanted the prime minister to appreciate the "political" problem he faced at home, the alleged coalition of pro-Soviet leftists, pro-Taiwan rightists, and pro-India advocates that was deeply opposed to a US–China détente.

For this reason, they needed to be clever enough to find language for the Communiqué that will "meet the prime minister's need" but "not stir up the animals so much that they gang up on Taiwan and thereby torpedo our initiative." Presumably the "animals" in question included those millions of Americans who had been assured for decades that US treaty commitments to Taiwan were of vital national interest as well as a matter of national honor.

In a follow-up meeting with Nixon and Kissinger on February 24, Zhou said he was sure they could find wording for a Communiqué that would meet the domestic needs of both sides. But the fundamental issues concerning Taiwan remained to be resolved. Was there a commonality of direction? While there was an American commitment to remove two-thirds of its soldiers after Vietnam was settled, there was no specificity about the removal of the remaining third or the political future of the island.

In response, Nixon sought again to differentiate between words and deeds, If the language of the Communiqué allowed political opponents to charge that the president of the United States came "16,000 miles" to repudiate a commitment to the government of Taiwan, he would be in deep trouble. This was not a matter of personal political fortune but of the future of their new relationship. Zhou could surely understand that when Nixon returned to Washington, he must be able to say, "No secret deals have been made between the prime minister and myself on Taiwan."

Having clarified the matter, Nixon proceeded to make a secret offer. To this point, Kissinger had hinged the removal of the final third of US troops on the peaceful evolution of relations between Taiwan and Mainland China. But Nixon was now willing to say that if elected for a second term, his "goal" would be to remove all US troops from Taiwan before he left office, with no conditions mentioned. This was a handshake commitment, not something that could be made public. It would require some work on his part to bring Congress around, but it could be done so long as discretion was maintained.

Indeed, the cloak of secrecy hung so heavily over the Beijing visit that there were no announcements or real news of any kind. The journalists who were accompanying the president (most of them television personalities) were among the most luminous in the industry—notably Walter Cronkite, John Chancellor, Barbara Walters, Max Frankel, Bernard Kalb. But while there was rich material for the camera, there was nothing specific to report.[34]

Americans back home could see dramatic scenes of Nixon's orchestrated arrival in Beijing with hand outstretched to greet Chinese prime minister Zhou Enlai, and an avuncular looking Mao, sitting cheerfully in his armchair, together with Nixon and Kissinger. More elaborate was the footage of the long banquets in vast dining halls, the president's toasts to the Chinese people, the welcoming greetings from the hosts, the trips to the Great Wall, the Tombs of the Ming Dynasty, and the Forbidden City, and elsewhere.

More absurdly, there were Richard Nixon and his wife Pat at the ballet watching *The Red Detachment of Women*—a Cultural Revolution special produced by Mao's wife Chiang Ch'ing, in which a despotic landlord beats a peasant woman, who runs off to join the communist revolution. Then, having won battle after battle, she returns with her comrades to slay the landlord. At the end everyone marches off "into the red sun with swords flashing, machine guns chattering, grenades exploding and, certainly blood all over."[35]

For news-starved print journalists, who had not been provided with translators, there were scant opportunities to have any significant exchange with ordinary Chinese people, as few of them spoke English. Nor did the Chinese government seem eager to promote conversation. Consequently, their main activity was following Mrs. Nixon and, when available, the president, as they toured various sites.

The desperation of the underemployed reporters was reflected in a *New York Times* article, "Mrs. Nixon's Shopping Day: Pajamas, China."[36] In addition to buying silk pajamas for her husband, she also purchased a set of china in a blue and white pattern for her daughter Julie. Trivial perhaps, but riveting compared to another feature, "Nixon and Chou Stroll and Go Boating in Hangchow."[37] On this walk the president, accompanied by his wife and Zhou Enlai, had stopped to feed some goldfish—some of them more than a foot long—from a stone bridge. "Look at the size of these fish," Nixon exclaimed, "I never saw goldfish that large."

What the leaders were saying to each other was anyone's guess. NBC anchor John Chancellor spoke for many in the press when he complained: "Never before had an American president traveled abroad in peacetime under such a cloak of secrecy."[38] But this was precisely the point. Nixon was not visiting China "in peacetime." There was a war going on.

From the moment Nixon arrived in China, Vietnam was the "elephant in the room" and Taiwan the big sticking point in their negotiations. In a February 8 memorandum to Nixon, Kissinger had pointed out, "from July onward the two key issues in our dialogue have been Taiwan and Indochina, and they contain an inherent quid pro quo. Only we can help them concerning Taiwan and they can help us in Indochina. Accordingly, I have indirectly, but consistently, linked these two in my talks with Chou."[39]

Yet going into the Beijing summit, Kissinger knew they had to tread lightly. Haig had forewarned him about Zhou's fierceness on the topic of Vietnam. This was not the moment to ask for help in the Paris negotiations. However, it was Zhou Enlai who brought up Vietnam on the second day of the visit, letting Nixon know that the Chinese government believed in the right of each nation to determine its own destiny free of military intervention.[40] Therefore, "so long as you are continuing your Vietnamization, Laoization, and Cambodianization policy, and they continue fighting, we can do nothing but continue to support them."

Nixon maintained that the United States was fully prepared to let the people of Indochina settle their own affairs. Toward that end, he had offered a simple peace plan: a withdrawal of all American troops accompanied by a ceasefire and a return of the POWs. But the North Vietnamese had stubbornly insisted that the United States government overthrow General Thieu on its way out, which was the deal-breaker. If a nation like the United States, which so many countries around the world depended upon for their defense, were to abandon its allies, it "would cease to be a nation to have as a friend."[41] There was a certain irony in making this point when in Beijing—the capital of "Red China"—as he and Kissinger betrayed promises made to Taiwan decades earlier, offering concessions so controversial that their own State Department was being misled.

Despite Zhou's refusal to help with the Paris negotiation, Nixon and Kissinger did not walk back these new commitments." Midway through the visit they were still wrestling with the text of the Communiqué. Their problem was how to find wording that would satisfy their hosts without setting off a firestorm back home. For the Chinese, a critical point was their wish for an unequivocal American statement about withdrawing all of their troops from Taiwan. In presenting the American point of view, Kissinger was almost abject, conceding to Zhou that he had made "the bigger moves" during the past few days:

> We cannot complain about anything you have done. We recognize that you consider this your own country. You might take the position that you should not talk to us at all. I am sorry we have so many domestic difficulties, but our actions will be more impressive than our words.[42]

The Chinese prime minister seemed to understand. After all, "your president said, you can do more than you can say."

By the fourth day of the summit the press was getting impatient with their steady diet of no news. They had been promised a rapid announcement of a Communiqué that would illuminate the discussions going on behind closed doors. However, it was not until the morning of February 26 that Kissinger and Ch'iao Kuan-hua, his Chinese interlocutor, were able to settle on language acceptable to both sides. Only then was the Secretary of State provided with a complete draft. On first sight Rogers was noncommittal, but when he showed the text to his staff they were furious.

Since their arrival in Beijing, the State Department team had been steadily humiliated. Rogers's exclusion from the historic meeting with Mao was a slap in the face. Obviously the secretary and his subordinates were being cut out of the important policy discussions and consigned to relatively minor matters. Suddenly, with only hours to go before the Communiqué was made public, the team was confronted with a fait accompli.

For Marshall Green, the most egregious mistake was a sentence confirming the American commitment to its treaties with Korea and Japan while not mentioning the Mutual Defense Treaty with Taiwan—a clear indication that the United States intended to bail on its obligation. Green insisted that the Communiqué could not be issued in its present form.

While enraged by Rogers' and Green's opposition to the Communiqué, Nixon realized that he could not afford an open revolt by the State Department. There were already rumblings in the media and on Capitol Hill about the exclusion of the State Department from key negotiations.[43] This was hardly a new problem, but, as Senator Fulbright explained in an appearance on the *Today Show*, the "downgrading" of the Secretary of State had the effect of preventing appropriate congressional oversight. If Henry Kissinger, who was under no legal obligation to inform Congress of his activities, was setting American foreign policy, it was surely the president's intent to evade congressional scrutiny and to silence the government's experts, impunities that had been amply demonstrated during the previous three years.

Recognizing the political fallout from the sidelining of the State Department, Nixon could also acknowledge the strategic mistake of omitting Taiwan from the list of countries with which the United States had a defense treaty. At his behest, Kissinger was obliged to return to the Chinese with the proposed revisions. Since the Politburo had already signed off on the document, their negotiator Ch'iao Kuan-hua was understandably annoyed.[44]

This was a spat Kissinger fervently wished to avoid. However, as the two men reviewed the State Department objections, the necessary changes proved less difficult than had initially appeared. The problem of omitting the US defense treaty with Taiwan was readily solved by dropping the reference to the treaties with Japan and South Korea.

Though Marshall Green had saved the Nixon administration from what would have been a political firestorm, there were no thanks for his intervention. To the contrary, he and Rogers were sharply criticized for causing needless trouble. "Since when was the Secretary of State offering constructive criticisms defined as poor-mouthing?" Green demanded.[45] It was a fair question, but Nixon and Kissinger were so deep into their own machinations that they failed to recognize how far they had drifted from the normal operations of government. They had no qualms about concealing from Rogers and Green the national commitments they had made in secret, or refusing to allow anybody at State to view the transcripts of their actual negotiations. In so doing they were actively overturning some of the chief safeguards of democratic governance without so much as a backward glance.

With the announcement of the Communiqué on February 27, the hitherto intense negotiations slowed down. The two countries had committed themselves to a process or "normalization," but in the absence of official recognition with accredited ambassadors, there remained a question of how they would communicate. Even here, Kissinger preferred deception. With Nixon's approval, he proposed that the US Embassy in Paris serve as the "open channel" for ordinary business, while the Chinese ambassador to the United Nations would function as the "secret channel" through which the more important messages would pass.[46]

From the very beginning of the summit, Zhou seemed to assume his government held the upper hand, and he was not disappointed. Behind the scenes the Americans had handed over a trove of intelligence data on the USSR, and they had promised to deliver a variety of diplomatic benefits during Nixon's second term. Perhaps some of these promises would prove empty. Even so, the Chinese would be coming out ahead, for they had conceded nothing. Their contribution was to carefully accommodate the White House desire for a televised pageant featuring Richard Nixon in an historic quest for peace—a priceless benefit in an election year.

Nixon was genuinely captivated by the experience. Since taking office he had been eager for original statesmanlike acts, which the Vietnam War did not afford him. He had gone to China and met two of the most powerful revolutionaries of the twentieth century, with more people listening to their words than "in the history of the world." It was an intoxicating brew, which the Chinese had cleverly laced with heavy doses of flattery. Chairman Mao had claimed to favor "rightists," said he would have voted for Nixon, and even told him he found his book *Six Crises* compelling. Zhou also seemed impressed: "Zhou said I had a poetic turn of mind like Mao," Nixon later remembered.[47]

As long as he remained in China, Nixon could indulge the feeling that he was contributing to international peace. Much of the public thought so, too. When his plane landed at Andrews Air Force Base, 15,000 people were there to welcome him home. Exhausted as he was, he went on national television that evening to share the results of the trip.

The purpose was peace, he explained:

> In the last 30 years Americans have in three different wars gone off in the
> hundreds of thousands to fight and some to die in Asia and the Pacific. One of the central motives behind my journey to China was to prevent that happening a fourth time to another generation of Americans.[48]

As a result of his visit, they had demonstrated that even nations with different philosophical systems and goals could work together on the foundation of their common interest, he said. In regard to Taiwan, he had reiterated "our established policy that our forces overseas will be reduced gradually as tensions ease, and that our ultimate objective is to withdraw our forces as a peaceful settlement is achieved." He and China's leaders both recognized that "a bridge of understanding that spans almost 12,000 miles and 22 years of hostility can't be built in one week," and their Communiqué was "unique in honestly acknowledging their differences" and not attempting to cover them up.

This was less than accurate. From reading the Communiqué, it would be difficult for anyone to discern that President Nixon had promised to pull out all US troops from Taiwan during his second term without clearly stated conditions. Nor could a reader know that the United States had just turned over vast quantities of intelligence data on the Soviets and pledged to assist China if confronted with a prospective threat from the USSR.

Nevertheless, the vague language of the Communiqué fueled the suspicions of some American conservatives. A *Washington Post* article, "Nixon Pledges Pullout of Forces in Taiwan," gave credence to the idea that Nixon and Kissinger had made greater concessions on Taiwan than they were admitting. *National Review* editor William Buckley, who had been present on the trip, was advancing the same idea. To silence this line of criticism, Kissinger contacted leading conservatives Senator Barry Goldwater and Governor Ronald Reagan. Senator Goldwater was skeptical: If the administration was still committed to Chiang Kai-Shek, then why not say so directly?[49] By contrast, Reagan seemed willing to accept Kissinger's assurances.[50] "He was just bubbling" with appreciation, Kissinger reported. Even Nancy, "who's got a hell of a lot more brains than he," was impressed.

Still, Nixon was nervous that Reagan would turn against him, which would certainly have happened if he had viewed the transcript of the negotiations. For precisely this reason they were restricting access to four or five people on the NSC staff. In the absence of the relevant information, Reagan trusted the White House. In fact, he thought of the visit as a great "television pilot," which they should now "run as a television series."

It was certainly a great "television pilot" for a president running for reelection. Once the North Vietnamese started marching, he would have major problems on his hands. But for the short term the trip was a public relations windfall exceeding all expectations. Yet, in implementing this initiative Nixon and Kissinger had exhibited the worst tendencies of their administration. For years, the two had been going behind the backs of their own ambassadors and of the State Department as a whole. But their behavior in Beijing, where they had undermined their own government colleagues in front of the Chinese, was truly bizarre. How extraordinary to bring top US officials thousands of miles to the capital of an adversary and connive with that adversary to trick them.[51]

But these departures from simple etiquette, as well as democratic norms, had paid off for both men personally. A few arrows from the political right notwithstanding, the two were widely acclaimed for their dedication, their skill, even their courage in traveling those many miles to dramatically alter the international landscape. For Nixon and Kissinger, the China visit would become a psychological watershed—feeding their grandiose tendencies and self-deceptions, nurturing the conviction that anything they did was in the service of humanity and that nobody in Washington held a candle to their own brilliance.

The president was still pumped up when he met with congressional leaders the next morning to give his report.[52] While invoking confidentiality as to the substance of his conversation with Mao, Nixon waxed on about the Chairman's directness, sense of humor, and ability to talk and think "big picture," and about Zhou Enlai's understanding and knowledge of world affairs, which surpassed that of many foreign leaders. He carefully assured members of Congress that he had held the line on Taiwan and that no Machiavellian bargains had been struck.

Following his presentation, Nixon gave the floor to Secretary of State Rogers for his reflections on the trip. Still smarting from the week-long humiliation, Secretary Rogers quickly went off message. It was his impression that China "was a spiritless society, completely controlled by its leaders . . . everything was controlled—controlled TV, controlled radio, controlled summaries of world news." Invoking the familiar images of docile "blue ants" scampering around the People's Republic, Rogers described how an editor of the *People's*

Daily came up to Zhou Enlai during a reception asking for his approval of the dummies and layout for the next day's front page.

Nixon quickly interrupted to say that Zhou was "meticulous" with details. One morning of their visit, the prime minister was up at 2:30 AM because "he heard the weather report and wanted to make sure the highways and streets were safe for the President the next day and he practically supervised the snow cleaning operation."

The Secretary of State did not take the hint. The Chinese authorities were not simply meticulous, they were despots, he continued. And their people were cowed. In Taiwan, one saw an energetic, "on the go" population. But in the PRC, the inhabitants seemed "aimless and hapless." It reminded him "of walking through the Bronx Zoo."

Following the congressional briefing, Nixon met with his enthusiastic cabinet, each of whom received small souvenirs from the meeting that "has changed the world."[53] After prolonged applause, he described his 20 hours of intense negotiations with Zhou Enlai, which he said had involved "tough, straight talk" on the issues but was conducted in a tone that was "totally elegant, and courteous—on my part and on his part." It was an experience that "will probably not be exceeded in my lifetime."

The president took this opportunity to address the question that the *Times*' Anthony Lewis and many Americans were surely asking at that time: If relations between the United States and the People's Republic were taking this new affirmative turn, what was the reason for continuing the fight in the smaller peasant nations of Vietnam, Laos, and Cambodia? If fear of Chinese expansion was no longer a significant factor, then why not stop the war?

Nixon's answer was that in assessing other countries, what mattered to the Chinese was strength of character. "The willingness to sacrifice, faith, belief—these factors are enormously important to them." While they would no doubt keep saying publicly that the United States should get out of Vietnam, if the United States failed to meet its "responsibilities in the world," the Chinese would conclude that we are "weak." During his time in Beijing, he discovered how much the Chinese admired the American Revolution. But now after 200 years, they were wondering "are we too fat, too rich, too educated, too far from the soil to have the guts, the discipline, the steel to lead?"

Here in a nutshell was an updated version of the old "credibility" argument—except that instead of fighting in Vietnam to deter the communist "superpowers" from acts of aggression, the new goal was to make a favorable impression on them and solidify a new friendship.

While implying that the Chinese government's support for Hanoi was superficial, neither Nixon nor Kissinger gave an honest accounting of what Zhou Enlai and the others had said about the foolishness of the American effort. Yet, however one interpreted Chinese aims, there was no ambiguity about the intentions of Hanoi. Tens of thousands of North Vietnamese and Viet Cong soldiers were massing along the DMZ and at the borders of Laos and Cambodia. They were freshly armed and equipped with modern anti-aircraft missiles, planes, trucks, and tanks—paid for in part by the Chinese government. For reasons unknown, Hanoi had delayed their departure, but General Abrams' headquarters had no doubt that this enemy was coming.

21

"The Whole Ground Shakes"

It would be another month before thousands of North Vietnamese troops began pouring into the South. In the intervening weeks, General Abrams sent a steady stream of warnings to the White House. By March 8, he forecast five distinct but possibly simultaneous threats that would have to be countered. Most alarming was the situation near the DMZ, where the enemy was building up troops and rapidly improving its air defense capacity. If these units crossed into the northern tier of South Vietnam, American planes flying to the rescue would be at grave risk. North Vietnamese troops were also massing at the Cambodian border in the Chup / Mimot / Snoul area, from which they had supposedly been expelled years before, and in Laos despite years of American bombing.

According to Abrams, if North Vietnam launched these multiple attacks it could result in heavy and competing demands for American airpower support. Washington officials needed to grasp the complex, intertwined nature of the enemy effort. "It is a system integrating MiG's, SAM's, heavy anti-aircraft artillery, long-range artillery, tanks and other ground forces," he explained. Given the threat, the general had urgently requested authority to strike the enemy north of the DMZ up to the 18th parallel. The one-time approvals that had been granted in the past were no longer adequate for the job. He needed the flexibility to hit the North whenever weather conditions permitted.[1] Both Admiral Moorer of the Joint Chiefs and Admiral McCain of CINCPAC strongly endorsed his request.

However, Nixon and Kissinger were resistant.[2] The dispersal of the North Vietnamese troops inside South Vietnam, Laos, and Cambodia argued for intensified bombing of those areas rather than strikes inside North Vietnam itself, which would immediately ignite domestic criticism. While the two had feared the enemy attack for months, once it was approaching they told themselves and each other that ARVN would stand. After all, Kissinger reasoned, the enemy was "a lot weaker than they used to be," and they would probably exhaust all their supplies within a short time.[3] He was inclined to see this coming offensive as an act of desperation, and predicted that by

April 24, when he expected to meet Le Duc Tho, Hanoi would be ready to settle.

Nixon and Kissinger were still reveling in the glowing reviews following the Beijing visit, with enhanced expectations for the Moscow summit. They were therefore in an uncharacteristically complacent mood when on March 30, the eve of Easter weekend, thousands of North Vietnamese and Viet Cong fighters came marching across the DMZ as Abrams had warned. The next two days brought a rude awakening. If the enemy was short of weapons, they gave no sign of it. Their fighters were equipped with newly supplied armored vehicles, artillery, and rockets, which they used to drive ARVN from the northernmost tier of military bases.[4]

In a development reminiscent of Lam Son 719, many of the ARVN units seemed reluctant to fight, with one entire regiment deserting to the other side. By April 3, the South Vietnamese forces had abandoned the northern half of Quang Tri province, opening the possibility of an enemy advance into Quang Tri City itself and possibly on to Hue.[5] Yet unlike the year before, some units of ARVN's Third Infantry Division were digging in, while the Saigon government was quick to send reinforcements. For civilians the situation was immediately perilous, with an estimated 100,000 people evacuating their homes and taking to the road.

There were ominous developments elsewhere. Simultaneous with the attack over the DMZ, enemy units were moving across the Cambodian border and had commenced fighting in adjacent Tay Ninh province, where they had many sympathizers. An expected attack in the Central Highlands had not yet materialized but appeared imminent. Over the span of 48 hours, the possibility arose that, faced with these multiple threats, South Vietnam could collapse suddenly.

Nixon was beside himself. After so many years of careful planning and billions of dollars spent, how could this be happening? He had always ignored the naysayers, domestic and foreign, who had argued that pacifying South Vietnam was a doomed project because the local insurgents and their North Vietnamese allies would never give up, no matter how intense the American firepower. Under pressure, he reverted to his longstanding habit of blaming incompetent or treacherous subordinates. This time it was the professional military that had failed him.

Conferring with Kissinger on the morning of April 3, Nixon complained that Abrams or someone in MACV was insisting that the South Vietnamese had been caught by surprise. The idea that this was a surprise was inexcusable:—"For Christ's sake, we're in charge of the goddamned intelligence out there"—and this was their responsibility.[6] The real problem, Kissinger added, was that the military had suppressed "disquieting information." They must have known about the buildup right near the DMZ. Why hadn't they said so?

But they had said so, repeatedly.[7] General Abrams had been giving this warning since January. And in his most recent communication with the White House, he had expressed specific alarm about the enemy buildup just north of the DMZ. Yet instead of taking responsibility for their own inattention, Nixon and Kissinger went back to blaming Secretary of Defense Laird, who must have intercepted intelligence reports before they reached the White House. In line with this self-serving theory, Kissinger raised an additional concern about Abrams, who was hoping to succeed General Westmoreland as Army Chief of Staff. Maybe he was following the defense secretary's lead to insure his promotion. "Goddamn Laird," Nixon exclaimed, "we should throw him out of there as fast as we can."

There was no way they could "throw out" Laird, who was their indispensable link to Capitol Hill. Nor could they fire Abrams without a storm of criticism from inside the military. Their attention shifted to the Air Force, which was once again complaining about poor flying weather. Kissinger promised to lean on Laird. American planes will "be attacking by tonight," he asserted. If US aircraft could fly through blizzards during the Battle of the Bulge, they could surely do their work now.

Perhaps they should engage the Russians? Kissinger planned to call Dobrynin and lay it on the line: if this offensive continued, the German treaty would not be ratified. This would threaten the summit, which would surely disturb them. Nixon wondered if anyone had contacted the Chinese. A message would be going out tonight, Kissinger assured him. With superpower diplomacy he was optimistic that everything would come together, and they could parlay this into an end to the war.

However, if "ARVN collapses, we've done everything we can Mr. President," he ventured. There must be no collapse, Nixon replied. "Don't even think of it," because if the South Vietnamese army collapsed, "a lot of other things will collapse around here."[8] Kissinger backpedaled: "That's why we've got to blast the living bejeezus out of them." Nixon wanted Kissinger to be clear: In his interactions with the military, there must be no discussion of a potential collapse. That might be fine if all that mattered was Vietnam, "but we're playing a much bigger game . . . a Russian game, an election game . . . " so losing was not an option.

To tighten his grip on the military, Nixon called in Admiral Moorer for a rare personal dressing-down.[9] There had been too much listening to Laird. "I am the Commander-in-Chief and not the Secretary of Defense. Is that clear? Do you understand that?" In recent days, he had ordered the use of airstrikes above the DMZ. While it was possible to carry out 500 sorties in a day, they had done only 125, using weather as their "excuse." In the future, the pilots had to take some risks. And he wanted that number to rise to 500 within the next few days.

He also emphasized his dissatisfaction with Abrams. Why wasn't the general moving more quickly to stop the offensive? This was the job he was sent out there to do. As for the rumors that Abrams would be replacing Westmoreland as the Army Chief of Staff, because of his poor performance that wasn't going to happen. "He shows no imagination. He's drinking too much." He better start coming up with some practical plans, "rather than sitting back on his ass waiting for things to happen." One year ago Abrams had "screwed up Laos," but he's not going "to screw this one up." Meanwhile Nixon wanted to be briefed on military developments twice a day, with the information coming directly from MACV rather than whitewashed by the Secretary of Defense.

Over the next few days, as bad news continued to flood in, Nixon and Kissinger agreed that B-52 planes should be used up to the 20th parallel inside North Vietnam. These were known to be the most terrifying and potent weapons inside the American arsenal. A formation of six B-52s, flying at 30,000 feet, could take out an area approximately two miles long and five-eighths of a mile wide. The expanded use of these planes is "music to my ears," said Nixon. But nothing good would happen if Secretary Laird and General Abrams continued to drag their feet. Kissinger heartily agreed.

When it came to bombing North Vietnam, Defense Secretary Laird was in fact reluctant, fearing that more pilots would be shot down and imprisoned for dubious gains.[10] Another complication was that Abrams and his MACV colleagues had reversed their previous request for using B-52 planes against North Vietnam. This made sense before the offensive started, but once it was underway, the greater need was in the South.

With each passing day, the North Vietnamese troops seemed to be making gains. In addition to Quang Tri province, Tay Ninh, and the Central

Highlands, there was growing concern about the developing contest in Binh Long province, near the Cambodian border. On April 7, enemy troops had taken over the town of Loc Ninh and were threatening An Loc, the provincial capital. The fear in MACV and in the presidential palace was that if the enemy was successful in An Loc, they would be positioned to attack Saigon a mere 60 miles away.

As the White House groped for solutions, Kissinger turned to the Russians. Three years of getting nowhere with his imagined diplomatic scenarios had not dampened his hopes, despite the clear evidence that it was primarily their tanks, planes, and artillery that had enabled the North Vietnamese onslaught. During an April 3 meeting with Ambassador Dobynin, he emphasized that his government regarded this "large-scale invasion of South Vietnam" as an aggressive act designed to not only defeat ARVN but "to put President Nixon personally in a difficult position" during an election year.[11]

Because Hanoi's leadership had chosen "to publicly humiliate the U.S. and to humiliate President Nixon," there would be retaliation by the United States. Hopefully, the Russian government would appreciate the necessity for this response. Meanwhile, the president "leaves entirely to the discretion of the Soviet government, which views or recommendations it could or would convey to Hanoi in the present situation." Since they were allies, he would not presume to make any specific suggestion, though the demand for help was implicit.

Unimpressed, Dobrynin reminded Kissinger of his government's consistent view that the only realistic solution to the Vietnam problem was the complete, unconditional withdrawal of US troops. Furthermore, in his most recent letter, Brezhnev had warned that American bombing of North Vietnam would "complicate" the atmosphere leading up to the convening of the summit. Despite the Ambassador's discouraging words, Kissinger assured Nixon that "the Russians will do something." There was too much at stake—the summit, Berlin, arms control—to allow the North Vietnamese to sabotage these potential achievements.[12]

In the absence of a response, Kissinger pushed harder during the ensuing days. Since it was the Russian government that had provided North Vietnam with all the implements of war, it did bear some responsibility for the "invasion," he observed. But did the White House seriously believe that Russia had arranged for this to happen? Dobrynin asked. Kissinger replied that Moscow had either planned or facilitated the offensive through its "negligence." In either case it was "an unpleasant eventuality" they had to cope with on the eve of their historic summit.

While both the American and Soviet governments issued contrasting statements about the unfolding situation in Vietnam, reactions behind the scenes were more tempered. Kissinger and Dobrynin maintained a dialogue on issues related to the summit. Even Nixon was privately restrained. Encountering the Soviet ambassador at an official event, he urged him to keep in close touch with Kissinger so their two governments would not lose control of events.[13]

These conversations notwithstanding, it remained a question whether a summit conference could occur if the Vietnamese situation remained so precarious. While a final determination could be postponed, an immediate item was whether Kissinger would go to Moscow, as previously planned, to work on preparations for the meeting. Nixon's views kept shifting, but on April 12 he authorized Kissinger to make the trip, with a clear instruction: go to Russia, talk first about Vietnam and, if Soviet assistance was not forthcoming, then leave.

Having already invested time and effort on plans for the summit, both Kissinger and Dobrynin were relieved by the president's decision. So eager was Kissinger to share the news, he had Dobrynin tracked down to a Maryland gas station.[14] This was the most "cheerful" news he had received all day, said Dobrynin. "It lifts my spirits."

In reporting the exchange to Nixon, Kissinger described the Russian as "slobbering" over this assurance.[15] The national security advisor believed that the president liked to hear how their stratagems were throwing enemies into a state of anxious desperation. But, in this and other instances, the characterization was often exaggerated. And in important respects, Ambassador Dobrynin had ceased to be an adversary.

Meanwhile the North Vietnamese soldiers were still on the move, leading Kissinger and Nixon to the conclusion that despite the intensive bombing, the United States had not yet demonstrated sufficient "ferocity." Kissinger's remedy was to bomb the North Vietnamese port of Haiphong for at least 24 hours—"just level the goddamn docks"—as a sign of the destruction they could wreak if not conciliated. Yet if they were going to take that controversial step, it made sense to do more. Accordingly, Nixon decided on two days of intense bombing raids on Hanoi and Haiphong, to be implemented before Kissinger's arrival in Moscow.

As a major port that regularly received shipments of supplies from China, Russia, and other Eastern Bloc countries, Haiphong was a natural target. It was less clear what there was to hit in Hanoi apart from civilians and government offices. Kissinger suggested that Nixon was looking for something "lucrative." But as Defense Secretary Laird pointed out, "the most lucrative" targets were in the battlefield area, meaning South Vietnam. Both General Abrams and Admiral McCain had made this eminently clear.[16]

Kissinger understood, but the advantage of hitting Haiphong and Hanoi was primarily "psychological." By bombing these two cities they were letting the North Vietnamese government and the Russians know how tough and determined the administration was. And, most important, how willing it would be to raise the level of violence if it were necessary. This would hopefully inspire the Russians to pressure Hanoi into a more forthcoming approach to the peace negotiations.

Yet, presidents had been raising the level of violence in Vietnam for years to no salutary effect. And there was no reason to think this would prove more effective now. As national security advisor, Kissinger had the responsibility of clarifying options for the president. But when it came to bombing, his critical faculties seemed no sharper than Nixon's. "We will keep our chins up and keep kicking them in the balls," exhorted Nixon.[17] That angry stance was not easily altered, even if Kissinger had been so inclined. Yet the crude language employed by the president was the sign of his emotional state, which Kissinger had learned to indulge. Furious at the North Vietnamese, Nixon's stated attitude was to "kick the shit out of them no matter what the cost."

However, some costs mattered to others. For Secretary of Defense Laird, it was worry about the loss of public support, and of pilots, who could be shot down over Hanoi and killed or made prisoner.[18] For the US military leadership in Saigon, it was the diversion of planes that were desperately needed elsewhere. Indeed, 24 hours before the scheduled attacks on Hanoi and Haiphong, General Abrams cabled Washington with an urgent request, endorsed by Admiral McCain and Ambassador Bunker, asking for a postponement. The enemy was stepping up its activity in the Central Highlands and around An Loc. Should An Loc fall, the road to Saigon would be dangerously open. To meet these emergencies MACV was ratcheting up the bombing and needed to commandeer every available plane.

Hearing these recommendations, Nixon exploded. Despite the unanimity of his top military and political officials in Saigon, who had never been reluctant to express opinions at odds with the defense secretary, he was convinced that Laird had secretly sabotaged his plan. Overriding the objections of Abrams, McCain, and Bunker, Nixon ordered that the attacks on Hanoi and Haiphong, designated as Operation Freedom Porch Bravo, proceed on the weekend of April 15–16.

As instructed, the attacks began that Saturday night, with hundreds of fighter-bombers and B-52s striking targets in and around Haiphong—fuel dumps, railroads, and truck parks, as well as residential neighborhoods. The B-52s alone dropped 1,200 bombs, raining destruction over a wide area and killing many civilians. Nixon had anticipated the possible harm to local residents but regarded this as the inevitable cost of war: "[W]e don't deliberately aim for civilians but if a few slop over, that's just too bad."

The following morning a larger contingent of planes struck both Hanoi and Haiphong. Flying over the port city, fighter-bombers attacked warehouses, a naval base, two airfields, and a shipyard. Some came close enough to the docks to kill four port workers and inadvertently damage two Soviet merchant ships. Back in Washington, the president waited for news of the attacks in a state of high excitement. On Sunday morning he went to church, explaining to Haldeman that "It's always good for the soul to take an hour off once in a while."[19]

While his soul was resting, the two Vietnamese cities were still under bombardment. Nixon did not learn of the two damaged Soviet ships until later that day. However, early reports were impressive. The B-52s had been effective, he assured Haldeman, "the best ever in the war." People in the Pentagon were "jumping up and down" with delight. One thing was for sure: "We really left a good calling card."

The reaction from North Vietnam was blistering. The central committee of the Vietnam Workers Party claimed that during the past 24 hours, American warplanes had "indiscriminately bombed and strafed heavily populated areas in Haiphong and Hanoi."[20] The goal of the "Nixon clique" was to secure a position of strength while North Vietnamese were suffering heavy setbacks on the battlefield, forcing them to negotiate on US terms. But this would never happen. All previous American efforts had backfired, said the central committee, and this latest outrage would be no exception." As Ho Chi Minh had famously taught, Hanoi, Haiphong, and other cities could be destroyed "but the Vietnamese people will not be intimidated."

Deaf to Hanoi's words, the White House was keenly attuned to domestic rumblings. Since the onset of the Easter offensive, Nixon and his publicists had carefully packaged it as a clear-cut case of communist aggression in which the country of North Vietnam had invaded the different country of South Vietnam, endangering 60,000 American soldiers along with the POWS. Yet many politicians were extremely critical, especially the Democratic contestants for their party's presidential nomination.[21] Most predictable was Senator George McGovern, who denounced the raids as "a desperate gamble" designed to save the South Vietnamese government and Nixon's ill-conceived war policy. It was notable that McGovern's chief rivals for the Democratic nomination, Senators Hubert Humphrey and Edmund Muskie, were less timid than in 1968, arguing that the bombing of Hanoi and Haiphong "represents an escalation that is not in our national interest," with potentially "horrible" results.

How the broader public would react to the bombing was not yet clear. The earliest response was on college campuses, with the National Student Association calling for a country-wide strike. The presidents of the eight Ivy League colleges issued a statement deploring the bombing of North Vietnam and its civilian population and calling for American disengagement from the war.[22] Soon classrooms, churches, meeting halls, and newsrooms across the country were erupting in outrage over the horrors perpetrated on innocent civilians.

New York Times columnist Anthony Lewis wrote that confidence in the "fundamental decency and humanity in our country" had been "sorely tested" in recent years. The bombing of Hanoi and Haiphong had revealed an inescapable truth: "The United States is the most dangerous and destructive power in the world. And its political leadership seems virtually immune to persuasion by reason and experience." It had been seven years since President Johnson had first started bombing the North. "Only a fool or a madman could believe now that more bombing will bring peace." As for why this escalation was really happening, the correct answer was presidential "pique."[23]

Though Nixon's wrath was a factor, his avowed purpose was to signal to adversaries that they needed to reverse course, or else. Five days later, Kissinger was scheduled to meet Le Duc Tho in Paris and would be going on to Moscow for discussions there. Perhaps this violent warning would induce a reconsideration.

Also weighing on the president was the unreliability of his own military. His conflicts with Secretary Laird and others on civilian side of the Defense Department had been manifest almost from the beginning. However, both he and Kissinger had maintained greater confidence in the Joint Chiefs of Staff and the leadership of MACV and had been disposed to trust their advice. But during the intervening years, the connection to Abrams headquarters had frayed, and Nixon partly blamed the debacle of Lam Son 719 on MACV.

At this moment of crisis, neither he nor Kissinger trusted the reporting from Saigon. To gather more accurate information and to articulate White House priorities, Nixon sent Haig back to South Vietnam. Haig filled a vacuum created by the president's distrust of the CIA, the State Department, the Office of the Secretary of Defense, and General Abrams and his fellow officers. With these new developments Haig's sense of his own importance grew, as expressed in a memo to Kissinger: "From this point on, the game is ours, as are the problems. They are not Abrams', they are not Laird's, but rather yours and mine, as well as the President's."[24]

Nixon and Kissinger were counting on Haig to give them the real facts about how well their policy was working. However, because he was a military man, the general's primary source of information remained American and South Vietnamese officers, which limited from the outset what he could learn or would likely recommend.

On his first day in Vietnam, Haig visited MR III, where the fierce fighting in and around An Loc was continuing. The situation there was worse than he expected, with three enemy main force units, reinforced by tanks and artillery, deployed against one of ARVN's weakest divisions. There could be some "tough days" ahead, he warned, but he remained confident that with the support of American air power, the South Vietnamese would ultimately "hold" and drive the enemy out of the area. As he traveled through the other three military regions, he concluded that the North Vietnamese military was "stalled," giving the South Vietnamese government the possibility of "a major military and political victory."[25]

In accounting for this promising situation, Haig emphasized the role of American air support in both North and South Vietnam, which he termed "the psychological core" of ARVN's performance. Most exciting was the recent bombing of Hanoi and Haiphong, "an electrifying shot in the arm of military and civilian morale." Yet even where this air support was lacking, as in MR-1, the South Vietnamese army had held its own, aided in some places by the local militias. Through it all, President Thieu had demonstrated political strength and was likely to "improve his position as a successful national leader."

They were admittedly "not out of the woods" yet. During the summer there would be military tests and likely enemy attacks on population centers, which would require continuing American air strikes and funding. But fortunately, the South Vietnamese army was better equipped, better trained, and better led than before, and morale was high despite their losses.[26] Furthermore, the political situation in South Vietnam was also looking up. Among the populace there was a new unity and pride in the ability of their government to withstand the powerful enemy attack. This included students in Saigon and Hue, some of whom were previously anti-Thieu but were pitching in to assist the relief effort. Fortunately, people were greatly encouraged by US bombing of North Vietnam.

This was the kind of report that Nixon liked to hear. Upon his return, Haig joined the president for dinner on the *Sequoia* and reaffirmed his main findings—that the war was going well, and that the president's courageous bombing decisions had been "tremendous morale boosters" for both the South Vietnamese and American soldiers. Nixon wondered about the use of the B-52s, which had not been previously employed against northern cities. They were a "game-changer," Haig declared. "It's just a frightening weapon when you're on the ground. You just see these shockwaves. The whole ground trembles and you get no warning . . . You just hear, all of a sudden, this whistling, an eerie whistle." And did the ground shake, the president wanted to know. "The whole ground shakes," the general assured him.

Haig's findings were of a piece with countless official fact-finding missions over the years. And whether cautiously optimistic or mildly critical, these emissaries always shared a dependence on military officers and political leaders for their information. Yet for years, there had been alternate sets of facts about the war from non-official people—journalists, congressional staffers, visiting students, disaffected veterans, humanitarian workers—that were always disregarded. The early months of 1972 were not unusual. There were Americans on the ground in Southeast Asia who were seeing a different reality from that conveyed by Kissinger's deputy, and arguably they knew more.

Among them were people under the auspices of the American Friends Service Committee, some on short-term missions, others present for years. Their reports were regularly communicated to the American Friends Service Committee in Philadelphia, and reproduced in various newsletters circulating in the peace community. A few testified before Edward Kennedy's Sub-Committee on Refugees, and others submitted articles to mainstream publications. Yet their alternative facts made no impression on official circles. On select occasions, President Nixon liked to refer to his Quaker background, but the idea of consulting this batch of sentimental do-gooders would be as alien to him as poet Allen Ginsberg's proposal to Kissinger that everyone "get naked" and discuss American policy.

A potentially useful source of information was the American Friends Rehabilitation Center, which since 1967 had been treating Vietnamese civilians who had lost limbs during the war. The center was attached to the provincial hospital in Quang Ngai province, which over the years had been one of the most embattled places in South Vietnam. The village of My Lai was located here, and North Vietnamese doctor Dang Thuy Tram had opened her makeshift clinic here and was killed.

For the American Friends staff who worked at the center, the most relevant facts often concerned specific people whom they had helped and befriended. One heartbreaking example was Pham-thi-Toi, a young woman who had survived the My Lai massacre, which had killed six of her relatives. In its aftermath, the South Vietnamese army had compelled the remaining inhabitants to construct a new Tu Cong ("return to village") refugee camp elsewhere.[27] As the reluctant civilians warned, there were mines in the area, one of which exploded, severing Pham's arms and legs.[28] Over a period of 10 months she was treated in the rehab center, which fitted her with prostheses for her limbs and trained her in their use.

Returning to the refugee camp with a small stipend from the Quakers, she and her sister opened a small shop selling foodstuffs and supplies. They were both still there in April 1972, when South Vietnamese soldiers carelessly fired into the camp. Her sister died instantly. Severely wounded in her stomach and the stump of her arm, Pham was sent back to the Quaker Center but, before doctors could operate, she died—a triple victim of an endless war.

To the Americans working in the Quang Ngai Rehab Center, Pham-thi-Toi's death was not an incidental story. It exemplified the routine suffering of innocent people: the loss of beloved relatives, of ancestral land, of a home, of arms or legs—or in Pham Ba Toi's case, all four of her limbs and then her life. They also grasped something that escaped General Haig and the multiple "fact-finders" before him: the South Vietnamese Army and police, being propped up by the US government, were a brutal force in the countryside and loathed by many.

In Washington, what happened in places like the Tu Cung Refugee Camp was irrelevant except insofar as these "villages" could be rated as "secure" or not. Yet this moral indifference clouded their assessments. While Nixon and his advisors remained focused on the number of planes and bombs they could muster, most of Quang Ngai province was quietly returning to the control of the National Liberation Front. To Jane Barton, who had served for years as co-director of the Friends' center, this obtuseness was remarkable: "The Front has almost taken over the province and no one even knows it. What a crazy war."[29]

This divergence of perception was operative across a wide spectrum of subjects. From his conversations with South Vietnamese officials, General Haig had been impressed by the spirit of cooperation and pride to be found in the cities, including opposition-minded students helping with relief work in Hue and elsewhere. He had similarly concluded that the Thieu regime had gained new legitimacy with the public.

Yet for resident Quakers and other independent observers, political repression and mass incarceration were issues of foremost importance. For almost two years, Jane Barton had served as translator for female political prisoners in a special ward in the Quang Ngai hospital. The women were in a small dark room, chained to their beds and to each other in pairs. Most had been tortured during interrogations.[30] Their physical symptoms were manifold: seizures of varied intensity, cracked ribs, bruises, paralysis of limbs, profound emotional disturbance. Though all were categorized as political prisoners, some were clear supporters of the NLF while others were not. Nobody had been formally charged or brought to trial. Appalled by their excruciating stories, she and fellow staff members had tried to engage the attention of a nearby American advisor, to no avail.

The situation of student dissenters was less encouraging than Haig described. Even before the spring offensive, the Saigon government was swooping up young critics, some of whom had campaigned against General Thieu in South Vietnam's rigged election. Back in January the authorities had arrested Huynh Tan Mam, chairman of the Saigon Student Association, and scores of others. The arrest of one of the most influential university students in the city set off ripples of protest, which were immediately quelled by the police. According to subsequent reports, Mam had been severely beaten, was struggling to walk, and his face was swollen and peeling from hours of close exposure to a 200-watt bulb. Through another arrestee, he passed a note hidden in a cigarette package with a list of other students who were also in prison.[31]

In April, with North Vietnamese troops flooding into the South, the government struck again at dissident youth. In Hue, where university students were initially helping with the refugee crisis, the situation took an ugly turn. With city government overwhelmed by the hordes of people fleeing south, the students had set up five refugee centers at public schools, which ultimately housed 15,000 people.[32] When the authorities insisted that they all be moved to government camps, the refugees resisted and the students stood by them. Ten of their leaders were quickly arrested. While no specific reasons were provided, it was believed their support for the refugees and their vocal opposition to allied bombing in civilian areas were the explanation.

This realm of Vietnamese experience was light years away from the world of Washington policymakers. Not since 1963, when Buddhist monks had set themselves on fire, had political repression figured prominently in any of their "fact-finding" reports. But the brutal practices were described by the Quakers and a handful of journalists. The refugee camps that people were forced into, the destruction of their rice fields, the bombing of civilians, the arbitrary arrests and torture of prisoners, the persecution of students—all made the regime far more vulnerable than administration officials understood.

As Haig flew back to Washington, his optimistic report in hand, Henry Kissinger was on his way to Moscow. His mission was to plan the summit, complicated by the fact that American bombers had accidentally struck Soviet merchant ships in Haiphong harbor and that the North Vietnamese had abruptly cancelled his upcoming meeting with Le Duc Tho. In advance of his arrival, Ambassador Dobrynin alerted the foreign ministry he would likely put "his main emphasis" on Vietnam, since this was now Nixon's major preoccupation."[33] The president had previously thought his trips to Beijing and Moscow would enable him to win reelection even if the Vietnam War was unresolved. But the spring offensive had altered that perspective, and Nixon was "jumping back and forth" between appeals for a diplomatic solution and more daring military actions.

Despite the damage to their ships, the Russian government was extremely eager for the summit to occur and went out of their way to accommodate Kissinger. They readily acquiesced in his unusual demands for secrecy and security, which included concealing his presence in Moscow from the US Ambassador Jacob Beam.[34] As a sign of their seriousness, both Leonid Brezhnev and Andrei Gromyko allocated many hours over a three-day period to their discussions with him.

As anticipated, Kissinger dangled the many benefits a successful summit could produce: an arms control agreement, progress on European security issues, an expansion of trade and credits, cooperation on science and the environment, and other advantages. All that stood in the way of these immense achievements was the Vietnam War.[35] And yet the conflict was so unnecessary. The United States had no desire for permanent bases there, and its objectives were limited—an honorable removal of its troops and "a time interval between our withdrawal and the political process which would then start." If this occurred, then the US government was prepared "to allow the real balance of forces in Vietnam to determine the future."

By framing the situation in this manner, Kissinger was clearly implying that if enough time elapsed after the removal of troops, the United States was prepared to accept a communist takeover in the South. Brezhnev seemed a bit surprised: Were the North Vietnamese aware of this offer? Yes, said Kissinger, but they had rejected it, because "what we will not do under any circumstances . . . is to meet their demand . . . to install their government in Saigon." Although this had never been Hanoi's demand, Kissinger had the habit of describing it this way. He did acknowledge that given the tensions of the present, "a final settlement of the war . . . is probably not possible" In the short term, what they could achieve is "a definite reduction in the violence which will be guaranteed at least for a substantial period of time—say through the period of this year." If the North Vietnamese were amenable to this, then the United States would be prepared to reduce its own activities and to pull back the planes and ships Nixon had recently sent.

However, he went on to add that if the fighting in Vietnam continued in its present form, it could negatively affect the summit by making it impossible for Nixon to attend or by limiting the kind of compromises he was able to make. How foolish it would be to be so thwarted by "a little country whose heroism derives from a monomaniacal obsession with local problems." Three and a half years of experience had not dislodged Kissinger's idea that a Vietnamese desire for self-determination was somehow perverse and selfish. And how absurd it would be, he continued, for the United States and the Soviet Union "to run the risk of a conflict in an area where neither of us has any vital interests."

Clearly irked, Brezhnev observed that it was not Russia that started the war but the United States, and it was indeed absurd:

> The war has been going on eight years but for what sake? For what sake is money being squandered, for what sake are so many Americans being killed and thousands of Vietnamese? Has the war brought the United States anything positive? Surely nothing. For eight years this shameful war

> brought on the United States nothing but the wrath of the peoples. We did not engineer it.

Especially at this moment, when the entire world was looking for a dramatic change to come out of their historic meeting, why was the United States continuing? Bombing never solved anything, and Brezhnev doubted it would help President Nixon get reelected either. The Soviet Union was not responsible for Hanoi's spring offensive. There had been no agreement for additional supplies, nor did his government have any input on North Vietnamese planning. They made their own decisions, something the Americans ought to have realized by now.

The Soviet leader was careful to end this first meeting on a positive note, emphasizing that the summit could be "not only historic but epoch-making." While this sentiment was nice to hear, Kissinger knew that Nixon would be intently scrutinizing the cables to see if any breakthrough on Vietnam had been offered. In his cable to Haig, who was with Nixon at Camp David, he distorted the conversation. Although they had not yet discussed specifics, "I was brutal in explaining that a guaranteed de-escalation for a year was the minimum we could settle for." Embroidering further, he quoted Brezhnev as saying that his government is "now doing everything to help the President get re-elected."[36]

Nixon was not so easily fooled, and when he considered the cable he could readily see that Kissinger was not getting much help from Brezhnev. And as often happened, his chief advisor was being seduced by flattery. Lest there be any doubt, Kissinger reiterated that from the president's perspective, "the settlement of Vietnam is in order of magnitude ten times more important than the Soviet summit and he is fully prepared to sacrifice the summit if need be."[37]

Day two opened on a genial note, with Brezhnev, who was acutely aware of Kissinger's rivalry with the State Department, assuring him that "you and I can accomplish much together between us" so perhaps "we should just abolish our Foreign Offices."[38] On "our side we have already taken steps in that direction," Kissinger wittily replied, but perhaps "a reduction of Gromyko" might follow. The national security advisor presented an interim proposal for Vietnam. If the North Vietnamese would commit to private negotiation on May 2, during the interim the United States would suspend its military activities in the Hanoi–Haiphong area. Once the two sides met, he would propose that they all return to the conditions that existed on March 29. Hanoi, for its part, must pull back all the divisions that had most recently entered South Vietnam, and the United States would remove its reinforcements and cease all bombing of the North. The two parties should then agree to "an immediate reduction of the violence . . . guaranteed to last a reasonable period, for example, a year," while they each evaluated the other's peace offers.

It was a nonsensical proposal, which Kissinger must have known would have no chance of acceptance. In effect, the United States would be asking North Vietnam to give up all the territorial gains of the past month for the vague promise of some "generous" settlement down the road. Gromyko observed dryly that the withdrawal of North Vietnamese troops and the cessation of the bombing were not equivalent, because "you cannot return what has been destroyed." As a candidate for reelection, Nixon would obviously prefer an eight-month stretch of diminished violence. But why would North Vietnam go along?

On a happier note, conversation shifted to the arms control talks, where there was hope for an agreement that could crown a successful summit. In the year since May 1971, when Kissinger and Dobrynin had reached a preliminary accord, negotiators in Helsinki had wrestled over a host of technical questions. Among the items not yet resolved was the precise balance of ABM installations on each side, and the question of whether and how many submarine-launched ballistic missiles (SLBMs) would be incorporated into the final deal. In his eagerness to outrun the American arms control team, Kissinger had forgotten to include SLBMs in the May agreement.

In Moscow, Brezhnev was willing to make a firm offer, endorsing a two-site arrangement for ABM installations and a freeze on SLBMs. This would leave the Russians with 62 submarines and 950 launchers, as contrasted with 41 US submarines and 656 launchers. The Russian leader justified the disparity by citing the missiles and planes possessed by American allies that were aimed at their territory. Despite the bothersome inequality, Kissinger eagerly snapped this up, regarding it as a major achievement for the White House. His underlying assumption, during this and his previous negotiations was that so long as the United States had the exclusive capability of placing multiple warheads on long-range missiles, inferiority in number of launchers was of slight concern.[39]

By the end of this second day, the national security advisor was flying high. Brezhnev and Gromyko had spent another five hours with him in mostly convivial conversation, he cabled Haig.[40] They had found common ground on a range of issues, of which arms control could be the most dramatic. Even on Vietnam, Brezhnev had opened a tiny door, telling Kissinger near the end of the session that they had agreed "to think things over and return to it." Meanwhile, the Russian leader had found the conversations so productive that he hoped Kissinger could extend his visit by an additional day so that they could cover the outstanding items.[41]

Back at Camp David, Nixon was fuming. Just as he feared, Kissinger's vanity had got the better of him and despite his clear instructions had gone ahead and discussed the agenda for the summit despite no real progress on Vietnam.[42] Alerted by Haig to Nixon's wrath, Kissinger wrote back that for the first time ever "we have them engaged in trying to help in Vietnam." As a result of these talks, the United States was positioned "to get the best of all worlds: 1/ inflicting maximum punishment on Hanoi, 2/appealing to hawks, 3/ appealing to doves, 4/ making historic progress on SALT, and 5 /getting a highly acceptable communiqué." Why at this promising moment would "we consider blowing it all?"[43]

Ostensibly loyal to Kissinger, Haig tactfully suggested they might be "bludgeoning" him too hard while he was engaged in difficult negotiations. Taking the hint, Nixon dictated a lengthy personal cable assuring Kissinger that there was no question "about the skill, resourcefulness and determination you have displayed in conducting your talks to date."[44] Everyone was "enormously impressed," and he could stay in Moscow the extra day if something could be gained on the Vietnam front.

While Brezhnev failed to alter his government's basic stance on this last day, he did agree to send a high-ranking delegation to Hanoi to present the latest US peace proposals. Kissinger judged this to be extremely important. At a time when American bombers were striking North Vietnam, the appearance of a Soviet messenger would be a sign that their most important ally was wavering in its loyalty. This interpretation was perhaps unduly optimistic but, unlike Nixon, Kissinger had convinced himself that the desire for improved relations with the United States might really prompt the Russians to help the United States extricate itself from the war.

As he closed out his meetings with Brezhnev, Kissinger emphasized that the president was greatly encouraged by their progress. This was hardly the case, since Kissinger had been bedeviled throughout his Moscow visit with Nixon-generated complaints.[45] Indeed, as he flew home he was understandably apprehensive about the likely reception. However, by the time he arrived at Camp David, Nixon had calmed down, recognizing that preservation of the summit had political value.[46]

As he listened to Kissinger's description of the Moscow proceedings, the president's confidence revived. Although initially adamant that his national security advisor be prevented from doing press and congressional briefings, he recognized their political usefulness to him. It was also true that these appearances fed a growing perception of Henry Kissinger as "the miracle man" in the administration who was moving toward peace. Even commentators who were deeply critical of the administration's handling of Vietnam perceived him as a positive force. Here was this energetic, erudite professor, traveling tens of thousands of miles, sometimes in secret, in almost continuous pursuit of diplomatic solutions.

High on the list of media fans was columnist James Reston of the *New York Times,* who saw Kissinger as a beacon of hope in a darkened sky. "To master the details and complexities of the President's agenda in Peking and Moscow, to keep the summit meetings alive while American troops are in Taiwan and American bombers are over North Vietnam, to keep the fundamental differences straight and still find areas for agreement and common interest" was a remarkable achievement.[47] How he performed "this delicate and dangerous role is a miracle which defies physical and intellectual endurance."

Then there was Governor Rockefeller, one of his most effusive supporters. After reading Reston's column, he phoned Kissinger to say that "all your friends are admiring." The Russians were "a rough bunch," the national security advisor asserted, but he had laid it on the line and "one of Brezhnev's closest confidants is on his way to Hanoi."[48] The Soviet leader was "a tough little bastard," but the trick was "to dangle enough positive things in front of him," something he had managed to do. Perhaps Rockefeller had seen "The Godfather." In that film "when the gangsters wanted something, they made a proposition that you wouldn't be able to refuse." This was exactly what he was doing with North Vietnam. When the Russian emissary arrived in Hanoi, they would all see the results. Rockefeller wondered if the Russians truly wanted the Vietnam War to end. Three weeks ago they might not have, Kissinger replied, but "they sure as hell do now."

While Kissinger was again looking for a negotiated breakthrough, Nixon assumed that months of warfare lay ahead, which would necessitate accelerated bombing of North Vietnam. But how to maintain domestic support after all these years? In preparation for another national speech scheduled for April 26, he asked General Abrams for a progress report that could be used for public consumption. Abrams was encouraged to use "colorful terminology" to highlight the accomplishments of ARVN.[49]

Heeding this cue, the general waxed enthusiastic about the American role and the virtues of the South Vietnamese. Though their soldiers "had been pushed back in some places" to this point, the enemy had been restricted to the jungle and to "sparsely populated spaces."[50] US advisors and airpower were of tremendous value, but they would not have succeeded "if the armed forces of South Vietnam had not stood and fought." In another series of exaggerations, General Abrams stressed the "sound advice" provided by South Vietnam's governmental and military leaders, the bravery of their air force and navy, the vital role of their people and militias "fighting for their homes and families." At present 33 of South Vietnam's 44 provinces were still operating normally and, while there would surely be more fighting and hardship over the next weeks, he was entirely confident that these allies "will continue to hold."

Drawing liberally from Abrams' report, Nixon explained to his audience that South Vietnam had become the victim "of naked and unprovoked aggression." Fortunately, their soldiers were digging in and fighting hard. For this reason, he was now able to bring another 20,000 American troops home. However, he would be continuing the air and naval attacks on North Vietnam until such time as Hanoi chose to halt its unjustified invasion.

In the days following this speech, the enemy continued to advance in the Central Highlands and inside Quang Tri province. The American media was reporting on the poor morale and faulty leadership in ARVN, but Nixon had come to believe his own public relations and viewed these accounts as another instance of media bias.[51] As informed by General Haig and other military sources, he was confident that South Vietnamese troops supported by American airpower were inflicting massive casualties and halting the offensive.

It was therefore no small shock when word came on May 1 from General Abrams that the city of Quang Tri had fallen to the enemy.[52] Even worse, "I must report that as the pressure has mounted and the battle has become brutal the senior military leadership has begun to bend and, in some cases to break. In adversity it is losing its will and cannot be depended upon to stand and fight."

22

"Let Us Think of Tanya"

The fall of Quang Tri was itself alarming, but the character of the defeat was more ominous still. During the last days of April, the city had been subjected to a fierce barrage of artillery attacks by North Vietnamese soldiers who, with their Russian-made tanks, were slowly advancing into this provincial capital. On the outskirts of Quang Tri, South Vietnamese marines continued to fight on, though vastly outnumbered. Their zeal was atypical, however. As the North Vietnamese closed in, the approximately 10,000 infantrymen in ARVN's Third Division chose not to stand and fight, but to flee as fast as they could down Route 1 heading south toward Hue.

This exodus was made all the more traumatic because there were already thousands of civilians on the same road trying to escape the fighting. Armed with rifles, soldiers forced civilians to hand over their vehicles and in some cases their possessions, in one of the most shameful routs of the war.[1] Responsibility for this debacle went up the military ladder, as officers along with their subordinates sought escape. As described by *New York Times* reporter Sydney Schanberg:

> With horns blaring and headlights glowing in the midday sun, they raced down the center of the road, pushing other vehicles out of the way. They used trucks and tanks and they took over big buses and three-wheeled mini-buses. They stole motorcycles, riding as many as four to a bike. There were also many on foot, including the walking wounded.

For US advisors who had been assisting ARVN for months, the mass display of cowardice and disorganization was appalling. Nor was it confined to Quang Tri—elsewhere "Vietnamization" was revealing its limitations with large-scale desertions in Binh Dinh province on the coast of South Vietnam, and Kontum in the central Highlands. Back in Washington, General Abrams' report came as a shock: Saigon's military leadership might have lost its will to fight. Since Lam Son 719 the previous spring, Kissinger and Nixon had managed to convince themselves that the reports of ARVN's weakness had been exaggerated by the media. But reality was closing in on them. In his diary, Bob Haldeman wrote, "the P . . . is obviously facing the very real possibility now that we have had it in Vietnam."[2]

In these inauspicious circumstances, Henry Kissinger was preparing to depart for Paris where he was scheduled to meet Le Duc Tho on May 2. While Nixon was willing to humor his national security advisor on the remote chance that his diplomatic hopes were warranted, he was personally skeptical and had given him restrictive instructions that made progress unlikely.[3] Kissinger must be "brutally frank," he instructed, and leave no doubt that by stepping up the war and violating previous agreements, the North Vietnamese had pushed the president to the breaking point. Their choice was simple: "Settle or else."

There must be no delay, Nixon warned. "The tactics of your host will be to try desperately to give us some hope that we are going to get a settlement" to forestall an American air attack on Hanoi and Haiphong. Timing was crucial, however. If Hanoi dragged out discussions, the administration would "lose the best chance we will ever have to give them a very damaging blow, where it hurts not just now but in the future." Once the national conventions were underway, domestic opposition to vigorous action would grow and make it harder to act. Indeed, given "the viciously distorted" press coverage of the battlefield, the Congress might finally choose to tie their hands by cutting off war funding.

Meanwhile, one development materialized that Kissinger had been counting on. As promised, the Russians had sent an envoy to Hanoi to convey the substance of the American negotiating position, perhaps implying that it should be taken seriously. Yet the effort had backfired. North Vietnamese Prime Minister Pham Van Dong had responded angrily:

> Who allows them to threaten us? Who allows them to order us to do this and not to do that? What allows them to tell us that the White House does not tolerate dragging on the negotiations in an election year in the US?[4]

When the envoy raised the question of how their ongoing offensive in the South might fit with the Paris peace talks, the North Vietnamese leader maintained, "If we have no strong military activity, they will not talk to us. We have to act to let them understand that Vietnamization will surely fail, that the puppets will undoubtedly be swept away, that there is no way to revive them."

Although unaware of this specific interaction, by the time Kissinger boarded the plane to Paris his own hopefulness had dissipated. Indeed, the fall of Quang Tri had clearly emboldened Le Duc Tho, who readily dismissed the American's offer to stop the bombing of the North and pull back the US ships near its borders if Hanoi withdrew its troops from the South. His government had already devoted vast resources and sustained large casualties in pursuit of victory. With their soldiers making gains on the ground, there was no prospect they would turn around and go home.

Nevertheless, Kissinger could see nothing odd about demanding their removal as a prerequisite for peace. Neither he nor Nixon had ever accepted the idea that Vietnam was one country, not two. In their fourth year in office, they still thought of the DMZ as an international border to be respected rather than an arbitrary line imposed from the outside. From this perspective, the North Vietnamese were truly "invaders" who had no legitimate presence in the country.

To Le Duc Tho, their view made no sense:

> Now you affirm we are making an invasion of South Vietnam. This is absurd. We have not sent our troops to the United States. We are not bombing the United States. We have no ships in U.S. territorial waters. You sent one-half million troops to Vietnam and thousands of planes to bomb North Vietnam. So who is making aggression?[5]

To strengthen his position, he quoted some remarks from Senator Fulbright—a move that infuriated Kissinger: "I won't listen to statements by American domestic figures. Our domestic discussions are of no concern of yours." This was hardly the first time that the sentiments of America's dissenters would be raised, nor would it be the last. Both the North Vietnamese and the PRG negotiators were acutely aware of America's internal dissent and viewed it as a powerful lever to impact US policy.

When Le Duc Tho and Kissinger finally got down to the specifics of what would be needed for the war to end, it was again apparent there were still no grounds for a settlement. So long as the Thieu government remained in power, neither the North Vietnamese nor the PRG were willing to stop fighting—although the North Vietnamese had altered their position somewhat and were demanding only the removal of President Thieu himself. The others could remain in power temporarily, provided they altered the "repressive policies" of the existing government.[6]

Yet, getting rid of the "repressive policies" would be no small thing. As explained by the North Vietnamese negotiators, that would include such items as dismantling the existing concentration camps, freeing all political prisoners, and removing the ban on dissident newspapers. Unless these and other changes were put in place, any prospect for a free election would disappear.

Clearly these negotiations were going nowhere. With Hanoi clearly bent on continuing its offensive, Kissinger proposed an adjournment. In an indirect reference to the Soviets, Le Duc Tho suggested that, if in the future the Americans wanted to communicate something new about peace proposals, it was best "to tell it to us directly."[7] There was no need to go through third parties.

Deeply disappointed but hardly surprised, Kissinger flew immediately back to Washington, cabling the president that the meeting had been "thoroughly unproductive."[8] In light of North Vietnamese "intransigence," which seemed clearly "keyed to the military situation," he had broken off the talks for the time being. Nixon's expectations had been low from the beginning and, in a quick post-mortem with Haldeman, he observed that "on this whole business of negotiating with North Vietnam, Henry has never been right."

With no immediate prospect for a diplomatic solution, the president faced two major decisions: whether to continue attacking Hanoi and Haiphong, and whether to cancel the Moscow summit. In his frustration and fear, he was eager to bomb North Vietnam and to mine its harbors. He saw abundant rationales for attacking:

> What the hell else do you do? You've got to do it for American public opinion. You've got to do it for the South Vietnamese, keep their morale from dropping. And you've got to do it in order to have some bargaining position with the enemy.[9]

The complication was the forthcoming summit. If the United States launched an all-out attack on the North, including Haiphong where Russian ships were moored, Moscow might feel impelled to cancel the meetings. This could hurt domestically. People might say "peace has suffered a great blow because of the president's failure and smallness." If he himself took the initiative and cancelled the meeting out of concern that he should not be consorting with the leaders of a country that was arming North Vietnam, this could also disappoint Americans, who viewed the summit as an opportunity for peace.

Was it then worth jeopardizing the Moscow meeting by escalating US military activity over North Vietnam? For Nixon this was never really in question. Along with his emotional desire to retaliate harshly was a political conviction that he could not afford "to lose South Vietnam." Nor could he take the chance that intense fighting would still be occurring prior to election day. In this respect, his problem was more daunting than Lyndon Johnson's in the aftermath of Tet. The former president had backed into a Vietnam bog with insufficient awareness of the potential perils. But Nixon took office with those dangers graphically displayed, and a public somewhat amenable to withdrawal. Having opted to continue the war, he needed something positive to show for all the attendant pain and sacrifice, or his prospects for a second term could disappear.

Over the next five days, he and Kissinger debated whether to preemptively cancel the summit. The "hope thing" was the problem, Nixon lamented. As illustrated by the China visit, despite the lack of specific accomplishment it had given Americans hope. And that is what they liked: "getting to know you—all that bullshit." In reality, "the American people are suckers" who were captured by these sentimental events.

Nixon ultimately decided to follow the advice of Treasury Secretary Connally, who thought he could do both: take escalatory steps in North Vietnam while proceeding with plans for the summit. Meanwhile Kissinger was having conversations with Dobrynin designed to advance the Moscow meeting. A Soviet trade delegation was already being received by the US Commerce Department, and plans were afoot for the two leaders to exchange generous gifts—a hydrofoil for Nixon from the Russians, and a new car for Brezhnev. Although the president had specifically instructed Kissinger to avoid substantive discussion—"I don't give a damn about SALT, I just couldn't care less about it"—the national security advisor privately dismissed this.

Inside South Vietnam, the situation seemed to grow worse from day to day. As NVA troops continued their slow advance, tens of thousands of civilians fled the combat areas, producing chaos on the roads and fresh demands for humanitarian relief. With the fall of Quang Tri, the most immediate threat was to the city of Hue, a startling throwback to the 1968 Tet offensive, which had also occurred in an election year and provided the death warrant to the Johnson presidency.

Hue faced multiple threats: from North Vietnamese soldiers approaching from the southwest and west, from the 150,000 refugees jammed into the city, and most immediately from ARVN deserters, who were pumped up and furious. As the remnants of the disgraced Third Division arrived in the city, its soldiers were roaming the streets, looting stores, and firing on anyone who got in their way.[10] Outgunned law enforcement personnel remained passive, and as government functions ground to a halt, the disorder spread.

On the evening of May 3, groups of deserters from the ARVN Third Division "set fire to the city's sprawling central marketplace during a wild and drunken gunfight." It was unclear at whom their anger was directed. Some told friends that they had set the fire to express their rage at the officers who had abandoned them in Quang Tri. The fire "burned spectacularly all night—lighting both the sky and the adjacent Huong River as it gutted acres of small shops and buckled the main steel and concrete market building."

The marketplace had been a food distribution center in Hue. However, the impact of food shortages was less severe than might be expected, if only because by May 4 much of the population was in flight to Danang 50 miles to the south. Like the road leading out of Quang Tri, the road between Hue and Danang was clogged with people frantically seeking safety in vehicles laden with furniture and animals. For the wounded and injured who were unable to leave, the medical situation was disastrous, with most hospital staff having abandoned their posts.

Within two days the situation inside Danang also became untenable. Refugees had been flooding into the area for weeks. However, the fall of Quang Tri, along with the mounting threat to Hue, brought in 300,000 extra people seeking shelter in the city, according to the mayor.[11] Many were crowded into schools, churches, and pagodas—all located in an urban center which, under the best of circumstances, had limited running water, electricity, sanitary sewers, or garbage collection.

Problems were cropping up in other places, too—in Tay Ninh province near the Cambodian border, and in the continuing siege of An Loc.[12] General Abrams was also expressing worry about South Vietnam's central region should the city of Kontum fall to the enemy. In that event, North Vietnamese soldiers and their Viet Cong allies would try to link up with the three districts already under their control in Binh Dinh province. This would effectively cut South Vietnam in two, in a line extending from the Central Highlands to the South China Sea.[13]

During this first week of May, General Abrams's own attitude fluctuated wildly, alternately lamenting the failures of the South Vietnamese military while still asserting hope for the future. Ever since the inception of the Easter offensive in early April, he and the White House had been in dispute over the use of airpower. In the immediate aftermath of Kissinger's failed negotiations, the president was eager to make a point by launching another two-day strike on Hanoi and Haiphong. Abrams cabled his strenuous objection on the grounds that there were more immediate needs: two additional enemy divisions were poised to cross the DMZ into MR-1; the city of Kontum might be struck at any moment; and the assault on Hue was imminent.[14]

Although Abrams was fully supported by Admiral McCain in his assessment of the danger, Kissinger's wrath was directed at the general. In his view, this latest intervention was another illustration of Abrams' narrow viewpoint and failure to grasp that the White House was playing "the most complex game with the Soviets involving matters which extend far beyond the battle in Vietnam, as crucial as it is." That was why General Haig had been dispatched to Saigon a few weeks earlier, to make clear the larger geopolitical context in which the White House was operating. Evidently this communication had not sunk in. Perhaps the malevolent hand of Secretary Laird was playing a role.

Nixon's patience with Abrams had also run out.: "We have suffered with this son of a bitch on everything," he told Kissinger, "I don't want him to short-change our efforts to destroy North Vietnam in order for a half-assed effort to do something in South Vietnam."[15] This was a telling sentence, since the American public had always been told that the purpose of the US involvement in the war was to preserve the independence of South Vietnam. However, in the aftermath of Lam Son 719, there had been a subtle shift in Nixon's attitude from an emphasis on protecting the South to a determination to devastate the North.

Even if the resulting destruction did not cause Hanoi to settle the war, massive bombing and mining of the ports would be an impressive demonstration of American power and a lesson to others. Whatever practical reasoning underpinned Nixon's evolving outlook, an important determinant was his riled-up emotional state. During these challenging days, the president was furious at the Hanoi "bastards" whose resistance was jeopardizing his election prospects, at Democratic politicians whose criticisms had undermined the US negotiating stance in Paris, and at the disloyal saboteurs within his own administration who were failing to carry out his clear instructions.

Of the latter, Melvin Laird retained pride of place because of his relentless pressure to curtail the American involvement in Vietnam. Until Lam Son 719, the secretary had justified cutbacks of the US effort by claiming that

ARVN was up to the job. However, as evidence accumulated of their incapacity, Laird's position was unaltered. In his view, the Nixon administration had given South Vietnam ample tools to survive, and if its soldiers could not function competently there was no obligation for the United States to escalate its efforts. Moreover, he failed to see how a sustained bombing campaign over North Vietnam, accompanied by the mining of Haiphong harbor, was going to significantly improve the situation.[16]

Nevertheless, Nixon's attitude was hardening. "South Vietnam may lose," he asserted, "but the United States cannot lose . . . I have made the decision that whatever happens in South Vietnam, we are going to cream North Vietnam."[17] Outside the small circle of men whose primary loyalty was to him personally—Henry Kissinger, Bob Haldeman, John Mitchell, John Connally, and Al Haig—there was little enthusiasm for the escalation he had in mind. The list of skeptics included not only Laird and Abrams, but also CIA Director Helms and Secretary of State Rogers.

How then to move forward? It was here that Admiral Moorer, chairman of the Joint Chiefs of Staff, proved his value. Ever since December, when the White House discovered that the Joint Chiefs of Staff had been pilfering classified documents from the NSC with his knowledge, Moorer had become uniquely susceptible to presidential direction. On May 4, Nixon ordered him to circumvent the chain of command, including General Abrams:

> Admiral, what I am going to say to you now is in total confidence of the relationship with the commander in chief and the Chairman of the Joint Chiefs of Staff. *Nothing is to go to the secretary. Nothing is to go to Vietnam. Is that clear?*[18]

He had decided to mine North Vietnamese harbors and to launch a major bombing campaign inside North Vietnam, which he intended to announce publicly on May 8. In the interim, he instructed Moorer to secretly assemble a working group of the best people to work on implementation. His intention was to strike targets of military value, some of which were close to civilian populations. "You are not to be too concerned if it slops over," he admonished.

With a major presidential speech planned for May 8, the secret could not be kept for long. But the president wished to avoid a situation where Laird and Rogers would "come in here and piss all over me." His instinct was to have Kissinger break the news to them and others that decisions were already made, and "we're gonna go balls out front." Yet on reflection, he chose to schedule a National Security Council meeting for the morning of May 8, leaving little time for complaints.[19]

Added to the group was Secretary of the Treasury John Connally, whom Nixon counted on to advance his agenda, although national security was not his field. The president had already set his course, but pretended the choices were still open. A centerpiece was Moorer's detailed report on the specific arrangements for mining the ports and intensifying the bombing. During this recitation, he glibly dispensed with the most obvious objection to the plans: namely, the diversion of American resources away from the southern battlefield. General Abrams would be left "with what he needs," Moorer assured the group.

He explained to the group that the goal was to halt the supplies coming into North Vietnam and thus the flow of material into the South. However, it was general knowledge that the 12 North Vietnamese divisions inside South Vietnam already possessed sufficient resources for their offensive, with enough supplies on hand to last for several months. The simple fact was that nobody, not even Nixon, was able to explain how these impending actions would improve the chance of success. Yet there were no direct objections. Secretary Laird asked a handful of probing questions, while Secretary Rogers speculated about alternative outcomes. The most enthusiastic participants were Vice President Agnew and John Connally, who offered Cold War bromides about the importance of stopping communist aggression. As this bogus deliberation ended, the president got to the real point of the session: "Everyone must support the decision. I don't want to see columns appearing in the papers saying who agreed and who didn't agree."

Yet Nixon remained uneasy. What if South Vietnam collapsed suddenly? Would these actions have proved helpful or detrimental? The answer was elusive, but his propensity for violent solutions prevailed. Two PM was the time Admiral Moorer had given for the "execute" order for the mines to be laid. "It's a go," Nixon announced.

Once this operation was underway, the president needed to again rally the American public with a speech. His early drafts were too "truculent" even for Kissinger. By the time he went before the television cameras on the evening of May 8, the belligerent rhetoric had been toned down and he had reassumed his statesmanlike demeanor. The recent crisis, he explained, was caused by "a massive invasion" of South Vietnam by the North, made possible "by tanks, artillery and other advanced offensive weapons supplied to

Hanoi by the Soviet Union and other Communist nations."[20] Despite countless American efforts to settle the war, the North Vietnamese had met these overtures with aggression, creating the real danger that a Communist regime could be imposed" on the 17 million freedom-loving South Vietnamese. .

Until now, "the United States has exercised a degree of restraint unprecedented in the annals of war." But with 60,000 Americans troops in danger, the president had ordered the mining of all North Vietnamese ports and the continuation of air and naval strikes against military targets in North Vietnam, to cut off railroad and other means of transportation. Such actions would continue until there was an internationally supervised ceasefire in South Vietnam, and all of the American POWs had been returned.

Recognizing that these actions were certain to outrage the communist world and jeopardize the summit, Nixon heeded Kissinger's advice and addressed the Russians directly during the speech:

> We respect the Soviet Union as a great power. We recognize the right of the Soviet Union to defend its interests when they are threatened. The Soviet Union in turn must recognize our right to defend our interests. No Soviet soldiers are threatened in Vietnam. Sixty thousand Americans are threatened. Our two nations have made significant progress in our negotiations in recent months. We are near major agreements on nuclear arms limitation, trade, and a host of other issues. Let us not slide back toward the dark shadows of a previous age.

Nixon's final appeal was to the American public, for unity and resolve in the face of a contemptuous enemy that was propelling armed confrontation. As always, his goal was "end this war and to win the kind of peace that will last."

The following morning, Nixon ordered fresh airstrikes in the North. It was "imperative . . . that they be at the highest limit that Abrams can spare from the battle area."[21] Their greatest failure "would be to do too little too late." The public might be temporarily quiescent, but this would soon erode, so speed was of the essence. "What all of us must have in mind is that we must *punish* the enemy in ways that he will really hurt this time. Now that I have made this very tough, watershed decision, I intend to stop at nothing to bring the enemy to his knees."

His predecessor might have been squeamish about bombings that could result in civilian deaths, but with Operation Linebacker his administration was going to a new level of violence:

> The enemy has gone over the brink *and so have we.* We have the power to destroy his war making capacity. The only question is whether we have the *will* to use[22] that power. What distinguishes me from Johnson is that I have the *will* in spades. . . .

Despite widespread skepticism in the CIA, the State Department, and the Office of the Secretary of Defense, few people in the administration raised serious objections to the ferocious assault once it was underway.

As cabinet officers, both Laird and Rogers were expected to actively defend the administration positions before Congress and elsewhere, and despite their personal reservations about Linebacker they were willing to do so."[23] This was consistent with their previous behavior, as they repeatedly put their reputations on the line for decisions they had not supported, notably the bombing and subsequent invasion of Cambodia and the launching of Lam Son 719. Their public stamp of approval was of incalculable value to the administration, demonstrating that sober, responsible men such as themselves were comfortable with the president's choices.

With Linebacker under way, bombs were falling across Vietnam, with at least 200 strikes a day on the North. In theory, civilian damage was to be avoided, but newsmen from the United States and elsewhere who toured two provinces in the central region of North Vietnam found the 600-bed Thanh Hoah Provincial Hospital in ruins, with the wreckage of operating tables and X-ray equipment still visible inside the large craters.[24]

A few miles south in the village of Dongyen, reporters found a bombed out primary school which, according to inhabitants, had been attacked during morning classes. Local people told reporters that more than 20 children were dead, another 25 wounded. Days later, in the wake of the president's instruction to "punish the enemy in ways that really hurt this time," bombing raids in the center of Hanoi had struck the Soviet–Vietnamese Friendship Hospital.[25] Most staff members and patients had been evacuated to an underground shelter, but some surgeons stayed above to perform urgent surgery. While the building itself was still standing, reporters entering the operating room found blown out windows "and blood spattered on the walls."

For most Americans, the civilian damage inside North Vietnam was a non-event. Coverage in the United States was sparse: some scattered articles in newspapers, almost none on television. For many, Nixon's formulation—that a foreign invasion had taken place, with a requisite need for American help—could still seem persuasive. Insofar as these new measures did not involve US ground troops, they were less controversial than earlier ones.[26] These factors notwithstanding, opposition to Nixon's decisions had already emerged from a significant sector of the population. From the time American bombs started falling on North Vietnam in mid-April, national and local antiwar organizations had been calling for peaceful mass marches.[27] Over the next month, thousands of people poured into the streets—20,000 in Los Angeles, 30,000 in San Francisco, 50,000 in both New York and Washington.[28]

Impressive as these gatherings might be, they were also smaller than on previous occasions, leading activists to seek alternative approaches. For some young people this meant joining the presidential campaign of Senator George McGovern. More striking were the dramatic acts of civil disobedience spreading across the country: 12 nuns lying down in Saint Patrick's Cathedral in New York, wearing white sheets with the message "one more person dead in Indochina"; a canoe and rowboat blockade of a ship carrying weapons for Vietnam as it entered the Atlantic Ocean; hundreds of people sitting in at Westover Air Force Base in Western Massachusetts; 121 members of the clergy occupying the rotunda of the Capitol building.[29] In many small towns and cities, groups of protestors staged their own "blockades," stopping traffic, draft buses, and even trains, demanding an immediate end to the bombing and mining of North Vietnam.[30]

For those committing conscious acts of civil disobedience, there was a clear intention to remain nonviolent and to comply with arresting officers. However, on and near college campuses, ostensibly peaceful events could quickly turn violent, whether because of the actions of the police, the students, or some combination of the two.[31] In Boulder, Colorado, police fought with 1,000 demonstrators who were blocking traffic in a main thoroughfare. The Maryland governor declared a "state of emergency" in College Park, summoning the National Guard in response to the 3,000 students who were blocking a highway. There were also violent clashes at the University of Florida in Gainesville when police attacked demonstrators with tear gas and water hoses, sparking days of pitched battles and disrupted classes. The list of places where young people were battling the authorities continued to grow: Minneapolis, Madison, Ann Arbor, Ithaca, Palo Alto, Cambridge, and Princeton.[32]

Since the time of the Cambodian invasion, the antiwar issue had evolved. The threat of the draft had receded, and the face of the war was no longer that of US soldiers fighting an elusive foe in a foreign land, but of American bombs pummeling a peasant nation and shattering the lives of ordinary people. By

1972 the notion of "disillusioned youth" may have become a cliché, but it signified something of consequence: millions of young people had lost confidence in the essential goodness and virtue of their own country.

This disaffection was especially acute at the elite colleges. From the earliest months of Nixon's administration, the Ivy League universities had been the site of strong antiwar protests, which had reached a boiling point.[33] On April 20, all eight of their presidents, plus the president of MIT, wrote a collective letter to Nixon expressing their personal opposition to a national policy that prioritized winning over all other costs. The consequences of the bombing for Vietnamese civilians "are appalling and unjustified."[34] With several of their campuses on strike or otherwise disrupted, they requested a meeting with Nixon to outline their concerns.

This was a chore that Nixon was more than happy to delegate to Kissinger. Acting as group spokesman, Harvard president Derek Bok made it clear they had not come to discuss American foreign policy but to talk about "what the prolongation of the war was doing to our young people."[35] This was not just the protest activities on their campuses, but rather "the slow erosion of enthusiasm and confidence that this important group has with respect to their country." Although Bok and the others had tried to sidestep the policy issue, Kissinger insisted on its centrality, emphasizing the important strategic reasons why the Nixon administration had accelerated the bombing of North Vietnam regardless of their students' distress.

Arguably more productive was the effort by these university presidents to lobby members of Congress about the urgency of stopping the war. By so doing they were adding their voice to the thousands of people, from an array of organizations, stepping up pressure on their elected officials with visits to Capitol Hill and local offices.[36] A particular focus on the Senate side was the bipartisan Case–Church amendment, which would stop all appropriations for the war after December 31 subject to Hanoi's agreement to release the American POWs and to account for those missing in action. Among the Senate opponents of the most recent escalation were three presidential candidates: Senators Ed Muskie, Hubert Humphrey, and George McGovern, a sign to the White House of political danger ahead.

Congressional advocacy was most often the work of older activists. For many youthful radicals in the antiwar movement, such efforts seemed futile. Year after year, legislators had taken to the floor of the Senate or House to make eloquent speeches against the war. They had forced 80 roll calls on resolutions and amendments designed to stop the war through funding cutoffs or other mechanisms. Yet, apart from the Cooper–Church resolution on Cambodia, nothing with enforcement power ever seemed to pass. Though unappreciated at the time, the growing opposition in Congress had played a major role in administration thinking.

From the very beginning the prospect that Congress might act had underpinned the Vietnamization policy of both Nixon and Laird. Among other factors, this had necessitated the ongoing withdrawal of American troops, in the president's words "staying one step ahead of the sheriff." Out of fear of congressional intervention, Nixon carefully announced that another 20,000 soldiers would be leaving by July 1, despite the 12 North Vietnamese divisions advancing in the South and pressure from MACV for more manpower.

At this juncture the cross-pressures on Nixon were intense. The fate of Lyndon Johnson loomed large. He had been a strong, seemingly impregnable leader, suddenly done in by battlefield developments. Here again, despite Nixon's careful efforts, the enemy offensive had placed his political future in jeopardy. Meanwhile his circle of trusted advisors had shrunk, meaning fewer constraints on his angry decisions.

The clearest expression of his wrath was the preoccupation with bombing the North. It was unremarkable that he was reliant upon airpower, given ARVN's inability to stop the enemy on the ground. But until early 1972 these airstrikes were mainly conducted in support of American or South Vietnamese troops. Nixon's most recent conflict with General Abrams had signaled a shift in priorities—a new willingness to withhold planes needed on the battlefield in the service of punishing the North.

Typically, when bombing North Vietnam, Air Force policy was to first take out the nearby anti-aircraft sites to reduce the danger to the pilots, whose aircraft would follow. However, for Nixon these were "secondary targets" and, as Kissinger made clear in his orders to Moorer, the president did not want them to "fritter away" air strikes on air defense "except minimum necessary."[37] Though intimidated by the White House, Moorer was not quite ready to play dead. As he relayed these new orders to Air Force General Vogt, he acknowledged that he had failed to educate Kissinger on the importance of taking out air defense first. Therefore, when Vogt wrote his reports, "just talk about what you have hit with your air strike aircraft" and, other than saying we shot down some MIGs, "leave defenses out of it."

By the second week of May, the president had reverted to his long-standing grievance about military commanders blaming the difficult weather conditions for interfering with their mission. The Air Force leaders must be informed that he was "thoroughly disgusted with their performance in North Vietnam."[38] Their "refusal to fly unless the ceiling is 4,000 feet or more is . . . one of the most pusillanimous attitudes we have ever had in the whole fine history of the U.S. military." This was not the pilots' fault, but the commanders "who have been playing 'how not to lose' so long, now can't bring themselves to start playing 'how to win.' " He ordered Kissinger to convey his "utter disgust" to Admiral Moorer and, through him, to General Abrams. These Air Force leaders needed "to shape up or get out."

During this period, Nixon convinced himself that destruction in the North rather than military advances in the South was the real key to victory. By breaking Hanoi's spirit, they could obtain a favorable settlement in Paris.[39] But that would necessitate taking steps that would shock "the little scaredy cats in the State Department" as well as Pentagon personnel, who were just "a bunch of spineless bastards." Henry Kissinger was more than happy to fan these flames, which diminished his rivals. But there was nothing new or even rational about the president's excitement about bombing.

Nixon also wanted the CIA to implement a program of "dirty tricks," officially labeled as "psywar." The aim was to convince North Vietnamese troops in the South, as well as the inhabitants of North Vietnam, that there was "massive public support" in the United States for the president's policy. For this purpose they would need to disseminate misinformation. Yet specific ideas for how to accomplish this were slow in coming. Responding to his impatience, the CIA conducted a rapid "brainstorming session" and produced 21 new tricks for demoralizing the enemy, many of them ludicrous. Among their suggestions:

c. Spread the rumor that General Giap is dead and that a double is now acting in his place . . .

e. Spread the rumor that Le Duan is acting strangely these days: accordingly, he is never alone / he is always alone . . .

j. Drop leaflets entitled 'How to Find Out Where Your Soldier Son is Today?'. . .

k. Disseminate outdated or otherwise troublesome quotations from Ho Chi Minh (in his own voice if possible) . . .

s. Write new lyrics to North Vietnamese political songs to ridicule the leadership . . .

T. Cannibalize old speech tapes of Ho Chi Minh and provide daily advice from the grave to the populace . . .[40]

On a different front, the CIA had already set in motion another "psywar" effort aimed specifically at the leadership in Hanoi, to convince them that the US government was in contact with a dissident faction inside their own hierarchy. One recommendation that especially appealed to Nixon was to spread the word that members of this fictitious dissident faction had proposed the mining of Haiphong "as the only tangible way to break the power of the hardliners in Hanoi." Such disturbing news would presumably create serious tension and suspicion among the already "paranoiac" leadership group.[41]

There were also plans for printing and disseminating 144 million propaganda leaflets, some to be dropped over North Vietnam by B-52s.[42] This idea infuriated General Abrams, who was already battling another administration attempt to send more planes north. In a blistering cable back to Washington, he could think of "no diversion of assets from the battle for South Vietnam that would be as damaging to the outcome of the war" than this plan to drop leaflets.[43] There should be no illusions. The only reason that South Vietnam was still in this war was because of air strikes in support of their troops, which remained vitally important.

Given this ongoing conflict over military resources, the idea of using B-52s to drop millions of flyers seemed ridiculous. Absurd or not, Admiral Moorer recognized that it was dangerous to cross the president on this matter, and he urged McCain "to build a fire" under Abrams and "get it done." While the general's reasoning made good sense given the military crisis in the South, Kissinger reported this to Nixon as another case of hostile "collusion" between Abrams and Laird. For the president, the weakness of the "psywar" and the failures of implementation were not simply a sign of competing priorities but an expression of disloyalty throughout the Pentagon and CIA.

The president's investment in "dirty tricks" such as dropping leaflets was peculiar in the context of a shooting war, where hundreds of people were dying every day.[44] By mid-May, the most intense fighting was centered on the provincial capital of An Loc, 60 miles northwest of Saigon, which Haig had previously identified as the one "dark spot" in an otherwise encouraging picture. Encountering light resistance, the enemy's Fifth Division had established control in the town of Loc Ninh, directly north of An Loc, and within days had moved to surround the capital. The seriousness of this development was quickly apparent to President Thieu, who ordered his soldiers to fight "to the death" to hold the town, lest the enemy move on to Saigon. Yet during the early fighting, the South Vietnamese troops were ineffective, enabling the communists to take over the northern half of An Loc.

To break the siege, on April 9 President Thieu had ordered the 21st ARVN Division from the Mekong Delta, together with his own 400-man Palace Guard, to march into the area. However, these soldiers showed little appetite for the fight, and one month into their mission, South Vietnamese troops remained stalled 12 miles from the town, along Highway 13. American air strikes were unable to dislodge the enemy as the Fifth Division continued to ring An Loc in a standoff that persisted into mid-May. The result was that unlike Quang Tri, where South Vietnamese soldiers had fled in the face of enemy tanks and artillery, in this location there was no possibility of escape.[45]

Inside the garrison the mood was increasingly grim as the number of able-bodied fighters kept shrinking in size, from the original 6,500 to 3,100 men, many of them wounded.[46] ARVN's weakness on the ground was paralleled by their failure in the sky, as their Air Force pilots showed themselves reluctant to fly into heavy anti-aircraft fire to evacuate the wounded and resupply the trapped people.[47] Here as well, the Americans took the lead, dropping food and weapons to the beleaguered garrison while raining bombs on enemy soldiers, both within and outside An Loc, in one of the most ferocious air assaults of the war.

At the onset of the spring offensive, there were 30,000 people living in or around An Loc, considered to be one of the most beautiful towns in the region.[48] However, the combined firepower of North Vietnamese mortars and artillery, plus American airstrikes, had taken a huge toll. By mid-May, an estimated 15,000 to 20,000 inhabitants were still living there, picking their way through a landscape filled with garbage, the rubble of homes, and the corpses of domestic animals. Despite US efforts to supply the populace there was a lack of food, water, and medicine. Under these desperate conditions, cholera and other diseases were spreading, and hundreds of dead were buried quickly in mass graves.

ARVN's lackluster performance in An Loc seemed of a piece with its conduct in Quang Tri and elsewhere. Meanwhile, their more determined enemy pressed forward despite their staggering losses. Discussing the situation with Nixon, Kissinger said it was likely that An Loc would fall.[49] "So they get An Loc? What's the difference?" the president inquired. On second thought, "maybe they will not take it, but either way it is not a big thing," the national security advisor reflected. And should they lose An Loc, "it will be the incompetence of the God damn South Vietnamese, who have three divisions none of which is moving out of its area."

By this time Nixon and Kissinger were focusing on something bigger: the upcoming Moscow summit. They had initially worried that Nixon's decision to escalate would precipitate a Soviet cancellation. Indeed, one important factor in the president's decision to mine North Vietnamese harbors rather than blockade them was to avoid a situation where American vessels would be confronting Soviets on the high seas. But would that precaution suffice? By May 12 Kissinger had the answer, when Ambassador Dobrynin informed him that his government would shortly be forwarding texts of agreements to be considered at the Moscow summit.

Despite the bitter fighting in South Vietnam and the bombs raining down on Hanoi, it was clear that the superpowers would have their meeting after all.[50] Once again, Nixon's political fortunes were on the rise. The trip to China had dealt a powerful blow to his opponents, and a successful summit in Moscow could be a knockout. For that to happen, however, it was important to demonstrate concrete achievements. During the past months, Kissinger and Dobrynin had prepared a set of agreements on trade, the environment, science and technology, incidents at sea, and cooperation on space. A likely centerpiece would be a deal on arms control.

How then to approach the Vietnam question? On May 14, a note arrived from the Soviets proposing the resumption of negotiations with Hanoi, which sent Kissinger into the stratosphere.[51] It was "inconceivable," he assured Nixon, that the Russians would have done this without the consent of the Vietnamese. It was all because of Nixon's moves, he went on to say. "If anyone had said a week ago when you had the enormous courage" to make these military moves "in the face of all these odds that the summit would be preserved and that the North Vietnamese would ask for negotiations through the Russians within a week, they would have taken us away."

With no further disruptions, on May 22 the president and the US delegation arrived in Moscow, accompanied by an enlarged press corps and a multitude of television cameras. This marked the beginning of a weeklong pageant of peace, as night after night Americans were treated to footage of banquets, friendly toasts, signing ceremonies, and impressive cultural events honoring the historic first visit to Moscow by a sitting US president.[52] The cameras followed a smiling Pat Nixon as she toured Russian department stores, bought presents for her daughters, and examined the artwork of friendly school children.[53] Watching this news coverage, a war-weary

American public could begin to imagine the end, or at least diminution, of the world-threatening Cold War that had terrified people for decades.

Within hours of his arrival in Moscow, Nixon was whisked away to meet General Secretary Leonid Brezhnev. In this initial encounter, the Soviet leader looked back at what the grand alliance between their two countries had accomplished during the Second World War and looked forward to what the summit could accomplish for the future. Beyond the specific agreements they would be signing at this meeting, the two powers must take further steps to "lessen the danger of an outbreak of nuclear war." Toward that end, they needed a "no first use" of nuclear weapons agreement, one which could put them on the "epoch-making" path of eliminating all nuclear weapons.

Nixon had no such grand plan in mind.[54] After the obligatory rhetoric about his hopes for their new relationship, he wished to address a few mundane details about summit procedure. One major agreement that was awaiting their signature was the "Declaration of Principles to Govern Relations between the US and the USSR." Since the US State Department was unaware that this document already existed, he therefore hoped the Soviets could help them with a little ploy. Instead of acknowledging the existence of this paper, "let us make it appear as if the question arose and was settled in the course of discussions during this week."

It was an odd request for a president focused on demonstrating US credibility to its chief adversary. Yet this habit was already known to Brezhnev, who had encountered similar requests during Kissinger's recent visit to Moscow. By now, both the Soviets and Chinese were well aware of the White House practice of tricking their own State Department. Although Kissinger may have imagined that such maneuvers strengthened the bonds with foreign officials, it put him and Nixon the position of asking for special favors at a time when more substantive matters were being transacted. The other consequence of these childish methods was that Kissinger and Nixon forfeited the assistance of government experts in technical fields such as arms control, where mistakes could do long-term damage.

In Helsinki US negotiators were being kept busy with minor issues, while Kissinger and Dobrynin negotiated the limits on offensive nuclear weapons. By the time of the summit, the Russians had agreed to put SLBMs into the Interim Agreement. However, the agreed-upon numbers were unequal—41 submarines with 656 launchers for the United States as compared to 62 submarines with 950 launchers for the Soviets. For land-based ICBMs, a freeze on construction left the United States with 1,064 launchers as compared with 1,697 launchers for the Russians. On their face, these numbers appeared to register a substantial Russian advantage.

However, as Kissinger and others would repeatedly point out, these totals were misleading. Unlike the Russians, the Americans had European allies who possessed their own arsenal of nuclear weapons, which were not being counted in this tally. Moreover, the United States had mastered MIRV technology—namely the ability to place multiple warheads on an individual launcher—so if the official count was of warheads rather than launchers, the United States had a substantial advantage.

The clear danger, however, was that once the Soviet Union had acquired this technology, the balance would shift in their favor. Yet early on, Kissinger had yielded to the Joint Chiefs of Staff, who were unwilling to contemplate a MIRV ban. For the present, the United States was far ahead in warheads, paving the way for a dramatic arms control breakthrough at the summit. The professional arms controllers might carp, but the president considered the impending accord too important to let "Rogers and his people get a chance to piss on it."

The Interim Accord was already close to completion by the opening of the summit. However, Kissinger had wanted to leave some issues unsettled so that he and Nixon could garner credit for high-stakes diplomacy in Moscow. Compared to previous decisions, the items in dispute were relatively minor and technical, but nevertheless there was unexpected pressure from the home front to hold the line on these lesser matters, including how to calculate the number of sea-launched missiles on each side and the type of missile modernization and replacement that would be acceptable during the five-year period of the freeze.[55]

By Friday May 26, the Interim Agreement was finally completed, with Kissinger claiming credit for significant Soviet concessions.[56] He had in fact achieved some small victories on the rules for counting and replacing existing launchers. But the murky provisions on silo size and the uncertain distinction between "heavy" and "light" missiles opened the door to future difficulties.[57] Less controversial was the text of an ABM treaty, which limited each side to two sites—one for the defense of their capitols and the other for defending an ICBM missile field.

The most bizarre aspect of the arms control proceedings was Kissinger's insistence on keeping the US and Soviet delegations in Helsinki until the last minute, finishing up details and polishing the final document. Even then, Kissinger continued his disdainful treatment.[58] With just hours to spare before the signing ceremony, he invited only three of the US members to join. Upon arrival in the Moscow airport there were no embassy cars to meet them, which had them hustling for their own transportation. Paul Nitze, a senior member of the delegation, got separated from the group and was inadvertently excluded from the celebratory banquet. For Gerard Smith, who had labored at this project for years, this humiliation was the final straw. After years of technical work, he felt "like an alley cat looking for a scrap to eat."[59]

Apart from frayed feelings, Henry Kissinger's outsized influence in this field, from his control of the Verification Panel to his back-channel negotiations during the previous year, had yielded a flawed agreement that would complicate future arms control efforts. Yet none of these substantive dangers received consideration. For the present, a celebratory mood was building in Moscow as the two sides toasted one another and signed agreements every night.

The darkest cloud on the horizon remained the Vietnam War, a subject not fully engaged until midway through the conference. After a breakneck drive from the Kremlin to Brezhnev's rustic dacha overlooking the Moscow River, followed by a scenic water cruise in the general secretary's hydrofoil, the talk began. As on previous occasions, the Russian rhetoric was fierce. "Your war . . . is quite rightly called a shameful and aggressive war not only by us, but also by most countries in the world," said Brezhnev. And it is poisoning "the entire international situation." Nixon might claim that the US bombing campaign was to protect the 60,000 US soldiers still there, but nobody had asked them to come, and they could readily be sent home. "You say you want to end the war, and you calmly put forward this idea, while cruelly bombing not only military targets but also the civilian population. And you call this a method of ending the war? This is a method of destroying a country."[60]

Speaking as someone who had just been in Hanoi, chairman of the Presidium Nikolai Podgorny insisted that the North Vietnamese were open to a negotiated solution. Contrary to what Kissinger asserted, Hanoi was not insisting on replacing the Saigon regime with its own puppets. What they had proposed was sensible, a three-part interim government to conduct national business on a short-term basis until elections took place.

Despite some sharp exchanges, Nixon's overall response to the Soviet indictment was restrained. His chief argument, long repeated, was that he had inherited a war with 550,000 Americans under arms. During the past four years he had drastically reduced that number, while offering countless peace proposals to the inflexible men in Hanoi, which they had consistently rejected, instead requiring the overthrow of the Thieu government. So long as they were immoveable on this matter he had no choice but to use America's military might to bring this sorry chapter to a conclusion.

This Vietnam exchange took approximately three hours, sandwiched between the boat ride and a late-night dinner. When it was over, both Nixon and Brezhnev congratulated one another on their candor. On this pleasant note, the dignitaries repaired to yet another feast. In truth, both parties to the exchange had been proceeding almost by rote. By having agreed to the summit despite the intensified fighting and bombing inside Vietnam, the Soviets had signaled the limit of their commitment to a communist ally, while for their part the Americans had conveyed a surprising complacency about the Russian role in arming and supplying their enemy.

It was left to Kissinger and Gromyko to get beyond rote communications to the practical matters of how the war might be ended and, specifically, whether the Soviets could somehow assist in the suspended peace negotiations.[61] Gromyko seemed willing to dispatch yet another Soviet emissary to Hanoi, but he wanted some indication that the United States was going to be more flexible about the composition of an interim Saigon government following a ceasefire. This difference was not easily resolved.

As in previous exchanges with Zhou Enlai and with Brezhnev, Kissinger attempted to bridge the distance by implying that the United States might ultimately accede to a communist government in South Vietnam if their enemy was patient. If they were wise, "they would make an agreement with us now and not haggle about every detail, because one year after the agreement, there would be a new condition, a new reality." The Nixon administration was prepared to commit itself to a neutral South Vietnam, but because Hanoi was so determined "to get everything at once," the practical result was that they were getting nothing.

What was intolerable, the national security advisor continued, was North Vietnam's "entire policy" being directed "against the domestic structure of the United States." This peculiar complaint echoed previous suggestions that the North Vietnamese offensive was designed to "humiliate" Nixon in an election year. To outsiders this might be nonsense. However, for the president and his chief advisor it contained a psychological truth: for them the war in Vietnam had ceased to be a Cold War contest, if indeed it ever was, and had become instead a domestic challenge.

Five months away from election day, Nixon could not afford "to lose" South Vietnam in the immediate future. If in the process he needed the help of the communist superpowers, or needed to signal an eventual acceptance of a communist takeover, this was a price he was willing to pay. The American public might believe that its soldiers were still dying to defeat an enemy or to warn off powerful adversaries, but the only objective was to boost Nixon's credibility.

For the president, the overriding purpose of the Moscow summit was to burnish his credentials as a "peace-maker" that would strengthen his political position back home.[62] The important thing was to show an overall reduction of a military threat, regardless of the particulars of the SALT numbers.[63] If the fine print of these arms control documents contained less than met the eye, there were few in the American public who would understand that. Soviet premier Kosygin had declared that SALT was "a victory for all peace-loving people," and Nixon eloquently concurred.[64]

Also invaluable was the spectacle—the opportunity to appear before the cameras daily at 5:00 PM to sign yet another new accord. There were agreements not just on arms control but on space, the environment, the economy, and science. Nixon would be coming home with a raft of these agreements, including a Joint Communiqué and a "Declaration of Principles" affirming the right of all nations to conduct their internal affairs without interference by foreign powers.[65] From this standpoint, the week of the summit was arguably the most triumphant of his entire tenure in office. Even more than the China trip, it appeared to herald a new direction in international politics.

Not all of this was show. Throughout his week in Russia Nixon viewed himself as the heir to Franklin Roosevelt, picking up the threads of a World War II friendship. In that context it was particularly meaningful to visit the historic city of Leningrad, where President Podgorny took him to the Piskarevka Cemetery. Buried there were half a million Russians, the victims of the 900-day siege of Leningrad, one of the war's most iconic battles against Germany.[66] After placing a wreath on the Tomb of the Unknown Soldier, Nixon returned to the cemetery entrance where he saw the picture and diary of 12-year-old Tanya, whose entire family perished in the siege. In her last entry Tanya had written, "All are dead. Only Tanya is left." One year later the child was evacuated from the city, but she subsequently died of dysentery. Moved by this saga, the president wrote in the guestbook: "To Tanya and all the heroes of Leningrad, I hope it will never be repeated in all the world."

During his last night in Moscow, the president made a 30-minute speech on these themes, directly to the Soviet people. It had been one of his "principal aims," he declared, to improve the relations between their country and his.[67] The two nations had much in common. Indeed, "the memory of your soldiers and ours embracing at the Elbe as allies in 1945 remains strong in millions of hearts." "Let us think of Tanya," he intoned and related her story. As we move toward the future, "let us do all that we can to ensure that no children will have to endure what Tanya did and that your children and ours and all the children of the world can live their full lives together in friendship and peace."

It was a stellar performance, carried live on Russian television and by the three major American networks. There sat the old "Cold Warrior" Richard Nixon in the capital of the enemy—articulate, dignified, and expansive—offering a vision of international cooperation that all people of good will could embrace. For Nixon this had been a grueling week with long hours of detailed negotiations, but also an exhilarating one. The emotional peak had been Leningrad, where the diary of a little girl in a besieged city captured his imagination.

While Nixon was in the Soviet Union, the bombing of North Vietnam that he had ordered was continuing.[68] Before his departure he had instructed Alexander Haig that there must be no abatement of American air and naval strikes, which should remain at a minimum of 1,200 sorties a day.[69] Except for the area around Hanoi and close to the Chinese border, he urged "relentless" strikes on North Vietnamese targets, especially those "which will have major impact on civilian morale."

New York Times columnist Anthony Lewis, who was on the ground in North Vietnam during the week that overlapped the summit, observed some results.[70] In the village of Phuloc, five miles north of Haiphong, American B-52s had destroyed scores of houses and killed 63 people. The columnist summoned his readers to imagine the experience of Mrs. Pham Thi Viet, aged 38. She had been away the night of the bombing, and when she returned home, four of her six children were dead, as were her father, uncle, sister-in-law, niece, and nephew. "Why does Nixon send B-52s to kill our children while they are asleep?" she beseeched Lewis.

Vietnamese children were also dying every day in South Vietnam, including An Loc, enduring its seventh week under siege. Although the outcome of the fighting would not be "a big thing," either way, as Kissinger put it, enemy soldiers were continuing to pound An Loc with mortar and artillery fire, while air strikes by US gunship, tactical aircraft, and B-52s reached the 10,000 mark. By June there were only a handful of buildings still standing, with no running water or electricity. Almost all the civilians were gone, many of them dead, the survivors having sought refuge in nearby villages. With medical care almost nonexistent in these areas, those most at risk were the elderly and, of course, the children.

23

"Four More Years"

In June, Richard Nixon returned from Moscow in triumph. Millions of Americans had watched the televised broadcasts of their dignified, peace-seeking president being greeted with respect and honor in yet another communist capital. The enthusiastic response from the public, the press, and members of Congress in both parties exceeded Nixon and Kissinger's expectations. Former national security advisor McGeorge Bundy, who had become an establishment critic, lavishly praised both men for their "fantastic performance."[1] If there was any way he could help, they should let him know. Senate majority leader Mike Mansfield was also effusive, praising Nixon for leading America "out of the murky detours of the Cold War." History might "well record 1972 as the year in which a corner was turned for peace."[2] He gave Nixon much of the credit for "leading the world a long way towards sanity."

Over the next weeks, the plaudits continued. In conversation with Nixon, Kissinger observed that the public reaction "continues to be absolutely astounding." He had spoken with some Democratic friends on the West Coast who were switching their vote to Nixon.[3] The "tremendous transformation in the public attitude" exceeded the reaction to the China trip. Before going to Moscow, they had assumed they could not duplicate the excitement of the Beijing visit and that "this would be a dull working trip with its pluses," but nothing dramatic. However, the American people had been galvanized.

In the aftermath of the summit, Ambassador Dobrynin was equally enthused.[4] He carried a message from Brezhnev, who had been greatly impressed by Nixon. The Russian leader was pleased by their many breakthroughs, but he considered the "greatest success was the personal relationship" established between himself and the American president. Not since World War II had there been such cordial interactions. And of course, the national security advisor had made "a major contribution" to the accomplishments at the summit, in contrast to the Secretary of State, who seemed in the dark on most issues.

Buoyed by this and other communications, Kissinger was convinced that the Russian leaders were committed to pressuring Hanoi on a settlement. With Chinese officials also backing away from Hanoi, he believed "we are going to win in Vietnam," because with these defections the North Vietnamese would have no place to turn and would have to compromise at the peace table. Intelligence reports showed that they "were in deep trouble" and that their Politburo was sharply divided. Under brutal assault by American airpower, it was doubtful they could hold out. Though usually skeptical of Kissinger's upbeat predictions, Nixon was buoyant. "These people are not supermen"; they would have a breaking point.[5]

With so much accomplished in the international field, Nixon had renewed optimism about his prospects for reelection in November. He was at the pinnacle of his career, with his polls soaring and his reputation as an international statesman at an all-time high. But suddenly he encountered an unexpected threat. On June 17, 1972, the Washington DC police had arrested five burglars who had broken into Democratic National Committee headquarters in the Watergate apartments. Four of the burglars were Cubans; the fifth man was James McCord, a former CIA employee. While Nixon barely noticed the story when it appeared in the *Washington Post,* Haldeman and Ehrlichman were immediately alarmed because they knew the burglars were directly linked to the Committee to Re-Elect the President (CREEP) through McCord, who oversaw its security. Moreover, the break-in had been monitored and directed by Howard Hunt, who had previously worked for Chuck Colson in the White House, and G. Gordon Liddy, general counsel for CREEP. Alerted to these connections, the FBI had assumed jurisdiction over the investigation.

It was unclear to both Nixon and Haldeman the reasons why the Democratic National headquarters had been the target of the burglary and intended bugging.[6] But as the story continued to unfold in the press, both men began to fear the political implications. In a strategy session on June 20, Haldeman, Ehrlichman, and Mitchell met with White House counsel John Dean, and all agreed they needed "to keep the lid on" the FBI investigation.[7] The risk of a deeper probe was not only that it would implicate higher-level people but that it would cast light on the "plumbers" unit, which among other ventures had broken into the office of Daniel Ellsberg's psychiatrist seeking damaging information.

Nixon's first instinct had been that the American public "doesn't give a shit" about such shenanigans, because they would expect political campaigns to spy on each other. But as Haldeman carefully explained, they would face a serious problem if Hunt and Libby were traced to John Ehrlichman because of their questionable "process" in probing the Pentagon Papers case. That was why it was "so important to stay one jump ahead . . . and hopefully cut the whole thing off." However, to accomplish this they needed someone who would take the rap, someone who was important enough to seem responsible but not so prominent that he would bring down others.[8]

The logical candidate for this role was Gordon Liddy, a right-wing zealot who had reportedly offered to stand in front of a "firing squad" if need be to protect the president. If Liddy claimed sole responsibility for the plan to bug the DNC and for the recruitment of the Cubans, then perhaps further inquiry could be halted. While this might land him in jail, Haldeman thought the White House could make a strong case for compassion, describing him as "a poor misguided kid who read too many spy stories and was a little bit nutty."[9]

Yet there was one obvious glitch: how to account for the substantial cash payment that had been issued to the burglars? As Haldeman quickly learned, that money had been funneled from CREEP through a Mexican bank.[10] To keep that secret, Liddy would need to show some alternative source of funds. As they struggled for a solution, Nixon was insistent that they go on a counter-offensive. Every time there was a leak, Republicans should "charge that we're being bugged," even if they had to "plant one to discover it."

Of course, nothing would work if the FBI continued to pursue the matter aggressively. Unfortunately the FBI was a "problem area" because the agents of the new FBI director, Patrick Gray, were actively following the money trail, and Gray "doesn't exactly know how to control them."[11] Both Mitchell and John Dean thought the "only way to solve this" was to have the CIA instruct Gray that this was a matter of national security, and the FBI should stay out. For this purpose, Nixon suggested they work through CIA director Richard Helms. For obvious reasons, the president did not wish to be directly involved. "You call them in . . . . Play it tough," Nixon directed Haldeman.

In the ensuing days, Nixon became increasingly alarmed about the vulnerability of John Mitchell, who had hired Hunt and Liddy to gather intelligence on their political opponents and presumably to engage in other "dirty tricks." The former attorney general was himself a stony-faced man, given to silence. But his wife Martha was deeply upset by his work for CREEP. Although an emotionally volatile alcoholic, she was sharp enough to realize that Watergate was not a stand-alone crime but an outgrowth of other sleazy practices in that organization. Unfortunately for the White House, Martha was given to late night revelations to sympathetic reporters.[12]

Nixon reluctantly concluded that his old friend and law partner would have to resign from the campaign and his loquacious spouse be somehow discredited. In Haldeman's view, this was a "beautiful opportunity" to kill two birds with one stone. Mitchell could explain his departure by the need to care for his ailing spouse.[13] "He'll gain great sympathy. The Martha fans will think isn't that a wonderful thing . . . you know it's kind of like the Duke of Windsor giving up the throne for the woman he loves. The poor woman hasn't been well."

Despite White House machinations, the Watergate story was not going away. As intended, deputy CIA chief Vernon Walter was dispatched to the FBI to get the investigation shut down, but neither Gray nor Attorney General Kleindienst seemed either able or willing to cooperate. Haldeman was furious at their incompetence. It was up to John Mitchell to call Gray and Kleindienst and tell them, "Your people are investigating stuff that must not be investigated . . . that's the signal you've gotten from the CIA. For Christ's sake smarten up . . . and turn this off."[14]

Nixon's participation in a cover-up, in which he tried to coopt both the CIA and the FBI, occurred less than three weeks after his triumphant return from Moscow. The proximity of these events would later be viewed as a tragic accident: a masterful actor on the international stage undone by petty domestic machinations. Yet the two fields of activity were closely intertwined. It was Nixon's pursuit of antiwar dissenters, begun with illegal wiretaps in the spring of 1969 and embodied in the "plumbers" crusade against Ellsberg, which put him at risk.

Furthermore, in sabotaging the legitimate functions of governance the president was continuing a pattern in which he and Kissinger had run roughshod over institutional practices. In their conduct of relations with the Soviet Union and China, as well as the management of the Vietnam War, the two had normalized the habit of deceiving members of Congress, the secretaries of State and Defense, the Foreign Service, and the civilian leadership in the Pentagon.

There was some precedent for this. In past administrations, presidents had relied on favored advisors, privileged one federal bureaucracy over another, and played tricks on members of Congress. But never had the disrespect of established institutions and of duly selected high officials been so extreme. Indeed, the transgressions went beyond mere deception. The two had repeatedly undermined the functioning of government colleagues. With Nixon's approval, Kissinger had enlisted ostensible adversaries Zhou Enlai, Andre Gromyko, and even Leonid Brezhnev in scheming against other US officials. During a time of war, they had repeatedly deceived the Secretary of Defense, who was accountable to Congress, by issuing secret instructions to the Joint Chiefs of Staff and MACV in Saigon.

Yet nobody had quit over these irregularities, nor had anyone blown the whistle. By the summer of 1972, Nixon and Kissinger felt vindicated in their unorthodox methods. Had they let themselves be constrained by the fearful, unimaginative members of the cabinet or the lesser people in the bureaucracies, or even General Abrams, their great achievements would have eluded them. Against this backdrop a White House request to the CIA to shut down an FBI investigation was a small deviation from established practice.

It briefly appeared as though the Vietnam War might be under control as well. By late June, the North Vietnamese Army had stalled. Despite vigorous efforts and a huge loss of life, they had been unable to take Hue, Kontum, or An Loc, which Nixon and Kissinger attributed to American airpower. By moving all available airplanes into the region, they were able to inflict substantial damage in both North and South Vietnam. During a brief stopover at the American air base in Thailand, Kissinger was thrilled by the sight of all the B-52s stacked together. It was "absolutely awe inspiring," he cabled Nixon. "This is really punishing these people, believe me."

Whatever military targets they were hitting, this phase of the American air war was hurting civilians in the South, tens of thousands of whom had been left newly homeless—some for the second time—by the combination of American bombs and North Vietnamese shelling. The Senate Judiciary Sub-Committee on Refugees estimated that South Vietnam alone had as many as six million refugees.[15] And these were the lucky ones. During this latest escalation of the war, the estimates of civilian deaths ranged from 5,000–15,000, with another 20,000 to 50,000 wounded.

After so many years, the sheer number of people who were suffering—whether jailed, tortured, displaced, maimed, or killed—had become mind-numbing even for those outsiders who were paying attention. Yet, on June 8, there appeared a photo of one act of wartime violence that was so horrifying that it galvanized attention across the globe. Enemy forces had entered the town of Tra Bang, 40 miles northwest of Saigon. To drive them out, South Vietnamese Skyraiders had mistakenly targeted an area next to a pagoda where civilians had taken shelter. Frightened by the roar of incoming planes, several ran into the road. Suddenly canisters of napalm came hurtling down—terrifying balls of flame that landed directly on women and children, killing some instantly.

Nearby reporters watched the scene in shock.[16] One nine-year-old girl, Kim Phuc, was screaming in pain as the clothes burned off her back and her skin melted away. An Associated Press reporter, "Nick" Ut, was standing nearby and took a photo just before grabbing the burning girl and dousing her in water in a futile effort to end her pain. He then rushed her to the nearest medical facility, where nurses doubted that she would survive. Although unclear at the time, after a year of surgical interventions Kim would live.

Ut's picture of Kim and the panicked children running alongside of her was picked up by hundreds of national and international publications. Some, including the *New York Times*, hesitated to run it because of the little girl's nudity. However, the image of Kim Phuc's burnt body was too powerful a symbol of the war's inhumanity to ignore.[17] Back in Washington Nixon cynically wondered if this photo was "a fix."[18] Haldeman thought it possible. The picture of "the little girl without any clothes" had certainly given opponents "a hell of a bounce," he remarked.

There was no doubt, however, that this attack had taken place or that the South Vietnamese pilots had erred. But how the South Vietnamese people were affected by the actions of their own government was never of much interest in the Nixon White House. That indifference persisted into the summer despite growing repression by the Thieu regime. In response to the enemy offensive, on May 19 the Saigon government had declared martial law and arrested thousands of people whom they accused of communist sympathies.[19] Many of those jailed were known members of student, religious, or civil rights organizations opposed to the policies of the regime, but no clear evidence connected them to communists. This new wave of arrestees joined the many prisoners incarcerated following the sham October election.

Interrogations were known to be brutal. For years this had been a widely publicized in antiwar circles. The American Friends Service Committee and other humanitarian activists had repeatedly raised the issue, although this rarely appeared in mainstream media.[20] In August the *New York Times* published an unusually graphic story by veteran correspondent Sydney Schanberg detailing the torture being inflicted inside the South Vietnamese "interrogation centers."[21] Because journalists were prohibited from entering these facilities, Schanberg acknowledged that he was basing his story on descriptions by recently released prisoners and the smuggled accounts from inmates and even some jailers.[22] However, based on the available evidence, it seemed clear these abuses were widespread.

For many antiwar activists, revelations of this sort had underscored a moral question: why should the United States be sacrificing blood and treasure to prop up a government that treated its own people in a cruel and undemocratic fashion? But there was also a practical question, which rarely entered administration calculations: at what point did the Saigon government's mistreatment of its own people undermine its ability to survive once American troops were no longer present?

During the previous three years, it was the civilian population of South Vietnam who had paid the highest price for the war. Once the president lifted the restrictions on the bombing of North Vietnam, however, this began to change.[23] US military officials insisted that they were engaged in precision bombing and were not striking civilians. Kissinger himself knew better. When asked by McGeorge Bundy whether such claims were accurate, the national security advisor reminded him of "how it is in this job." Of course he had received "every assurance" that civilians were being spared, "but I don't believe a word of it."[24] One North Vietnamese official commented wryly, "Vietnam has many Tanyas"—a not-so-subtle jab at Nixon's peace-loving posture in Leningrad.

The summer of 1972 was rich in paradox. On the one hand President Nixon was issuing a dramatic call for international peace, reaching out to Moscow and Beijing and in July announcing the withdrawal of another 10,000 US troops from Vietnam, leaving only 39,000 noncombat soldiers in the country.[25] On the other hand American air attacks in North and South Vietnam were at their peak. The reason for their continuance was simple: while the enemy offensive had been halted, the Saigon regime seemed more vulnerable than ever, and despite exceptions, the overall military performance of the South Vietnamese continued to be disappointing.

Although US officials in Saigon were emphasizing the valor of the South Vietnamese troops fighting at An Loc, Kissinger laughingly acknowledged that the only reason they hadn't fled was that the North Vietnamese had them encircled. Indeed as of late June, two months after being dispatched to secure the road between Saigon and An Loc, thousands of South Vietnamese troops were stretched along Highway13, mission unaccomplished. These soldiers were making themselves "the laughingstock" of the war theater, Kissinger lamented.

Meanwhile the North Vietnamese had made significant territorial gains despite major losses in manpower and equipment. In the Mekong Delta, where American pacification efforts had appeared to eliminate most of the Viet Cong infrastructure, the insurgents had returned.[26] Most alarming, with thousands of their troops embedded in the South, the North Vietnamese were assuming control of new places along the border with Cambodia to the west, and in the northern sectors of Quang Tri province.

In calling for Operation Linebacker, Nixon and Kissinger had framed it as a strategy for disrupting North Vietnamese supply lines and dampening enemy morale. Yet according to an August 1972 study by the CIA, "a lack of supplies will not materially diminish the capabilities of enemy main force combat units." While the flow of goods to combat troops in the South had indeed been reduced, it was not enough to force their retreat. The CIA was also skeptical of results in the North. The US attacks on North Vietnam had created shortages of food and petroleum, but so far "the general population is sufficiently patient and resilient" to withstand its effects.

As they assessed the incoming intelligence, Nixon and Kissinger swung back and forth between euphoria over their own toughness under fire and cynicism about ARVN and its long-term prospects. They found some reassurance in the number of South Vietnamese troop casualties. "Whenever I see low ARVN casualties, I know they're sitting in their foxholes," the president observed, "but when I see them high, they must be out killing somebody."[27] Kissinger was also comforted by the enemy death toll, observing, "We've killed 70,000 people, not even counting the B-52s."

The domestic political landscape also looked promising, since it was virtually certain that George McGovern, whom Nixon and Kissinger considered the weakest of their possible opponents, would be the Democratic nominee. However, when it came to Vietnam Nixon was acutely aware of how quickly the tides could shift. Although the Easter offensive had been halted, he recognized that as they approached election day, a sudden flare-up of enemy activity could sink him. He also recognized that the American public was still in need of reassurance that the Vietnam War was essentially over.

These considerations dictated a return to the negotiating table. To achieve a satisfactory settlement, Kissinger continued to hope that the administration's new friendships with the Chinese and the Soviets would convince one or both of Hanoi's allies to pressure them into an agreement. In late June Kissinger travelled back to Beijing, fulfilling his promise to the Chinese that he would return after the Moscow summit. He once again assured Zhou that the United States had no desire for permanent military bases in Indochina and was eager to end the war.[28] A peace agreement was within reach if Hanoi would stop insisting on the replacement of the Thieu government as a condition of a ceasefire. They ought to be a little smarter about things, since once the American troops left, they would be 12,000 miles away, whereas the DRV would be 300 miles from Saigon.

For Zhou this was not so reassuring, because the Americans intended to maintain their military base in Thailand with hundreds of planes and thousands of men. If combat resumed, wouldn't these men and planes be used? Zhou asked. That would depend on the timing, Kissinger explained. If fighting started up immediately, it would be impossible for Washington to remain aloof. But "if after a longer period it starts again . . . my personal judgment is that it is much less likely." After all, "if we can live with a communist government in China, we ought to be able to accept it in Indochina," he observed amiably.

A more immediate grievance was the continued American bombing and blockade of North Vietnam, which meant that all supplies from outside had to go through China. And there was also a humanitarian issue. "Do you think we can watch people dying, without trying to save them?"[29] Zhou asked. Suppose matters were reversed and China was attacking Canada or Mexico. "Would you be able to sit there with your hands folded and refuse to try to save them?" Furthermore, some of these American bombs were falling on Chinese territory.

Kissinger was at pains to assure Zhou that these were all military accidents and that such attacks would not happen again. As for Zhou's worry that the United States could reenter the war, he reiterated that there was no cause for concern:

> Mr. Prime Minister, you have more experience in international affairs than I so you know there are certain situations in which it is very difficult to give a formal answer because one does not want to create a legal obligation for what may be taken care of by reality. I believe if a sufficient interval is placed between our withdrawal and what happens afterward that the issue can almost certainly be confined to an Indochina affair. From your own analysis of the American situation, it should be self-evident that in a second term we would not be looking for excuses to re-enter Indochina.

This might seem plausible in Beijing, Zhou said. But, given their previous history, the North Vietnamese were understandably skeptical.

Undeterred, Kissinger pressed the point. It would make a great difference, he maintained, if the Chinese could encourage their ally to look at the overall context and not just the words. In 1954 what had really mattered was not the text of the Geneva Accords but the negative attitude of President Eisenhower's Secretary of State, John Foster Dulles, toward Ho Chi Minh. The situation was different in 1972. But having given Ho Chi Minh flawed advice in the past, Zhou explained, "This time we are showing complete respect for the sovereignty of Vietnam, whether it be on their positions on the battlefield or toward their positions at the negotiating table."[30]

Moreover, the American reasons for protecting the Thieu government lacked validity. Kissinger had revealed that it was about saving face, but if "these face worries are to be maintained then the war will not be able to stop," the prime minister observed, and the chief beneficiaries will be "certain persons"—meaning the Russians. In reality the war could be halted immediately with "a turn of one's hand," because the government the United States was protecting was not some independent entity but instead a product of "its own creation."

Zhou also questioned why the idea of an interim coalition government was so disturbing to the United States. Kissinger's claim that this would inevitably lead to a DRV takeover seemed groundless. The North Vietnamese proposal was for a tripartite interim government, with representatives from the Saigon regime, the PRG, and mutually determined "neutralists." This hardly seemed so dangerous or unreasonable.

Despite the disagreements, this was the lengthiest and most substantive discussion of the Vietnam negotiation that Kissinger and Zhou had conducted. Kissinger seemed impressed by Zhou's willingness to listen and to understand both points of view.[31] Such intelligence was all too rare, he claimed, and for this reason, "your views are always taken seriously by us, more seriously than that of almost any other leader." He therefore promised to carefully review any new proposals coming from the leadership in Hanoi.

After five days in Beijing, Kissinger was euphoric. The warmth of his greeting in China exceeded what he had experienced previously. In addition to the 14 hours of official conversation with Zhou Enlai, there had been more relaxed encounters during a picnic and boat cruise at the Summer Palace. As he reported to Nixon, it was remarkable how far the Chinese had moved in the past year from an adversary posture to one which could only be described as "a tacit ally."[32] Although Zhou had said they would not try to impose America's terms on the North Vietnamese, he might decide to exert some pressure.

Most striking to Kissinger were Chinese apprehensions about the Soviet Union. Viewing the United States in a more positive light, they hoped its government would maintain a military advantage over the USSR. Zhou was therefore gratified to learn that Secretary Laird was seeking an increase in the military budget and that the SALT agreement did not preclude ongoing competition for a nuclear advantage. The important takeaway from the visit was that "the Chinese clearly put a higher priority on their national concerns, especially over the Soviet Union . . . than their ideological brotherhood with Hanoi."

Transcending the specifics of policy was the remarkable atmosphere of good will and friendship. At the final banquet, Vice Chairman Yeh Chien had asked him to convey their appreciation to President Nixon and "congratulate him in advance on his victory in the election because that also involves the world."[33] For Kissinger this experience fortified his conviction that thanks to Nixon's visit, "we have established a unique bond between ourselves and the Chinese which both sides highly regard and want to strengthen further." On the front of Kissinger's memorandum, Nixon scrawled a note: "an excellent account—In long run this is more important than day-to-day substance."

On the surface Nixon's foreign policy was a stunning success, confounding those who considered him a dyed-in-the-wool Cold Warrior. Only one urgent task remained: reaching an acceptable peace agreement with Hanoi. In the aftermath of the Moscow summit, Russian president Podgorny had visited North Vietnam, bringing with him the text of the most recent American peace proposal.[34] In this version there was reference to a tripartite electoral commission to oversee the balloting in South Vietnam. Perhaps Hanoi's negotiators could build on this to get closer to the coalition government they preferred. The Russian leader emphasized that based on their long discussions with Nixon and Kissinger, it was apparent that the Americans were desperately seeking an exit from Vietnam and were unlikely to return once they had gone.

Dependent on the Russians for economic and military aid, the North Vietnamese were not prepared to defy their benefactors outright. However, as Podgorny was leaving the capital they made their displeasure clear.[35] The leadership's anger at both the Russians and Chinese was less about their advice on negotiations than about the political cover they were giving to Richard

Nixon.[36] In a period when the US bombing of the North was reaching unparalleled levels of destructiveness, the two summit meetings had allowed the American president to position himself as an "international peace-maker." Unlike their superpower allies, they retained hope for a McGovern victory—an outcome the two summits had undercut.

No matter how unwelcome, Podgorny's advice about modifying their negotiating position had intersected a growing concern within the Politburo. By summer, their offensive had ground to a halt, while the ferocity of the American's attack on the North had taken them by surprise.[37] Despite their bravado, the bombing was causing immense and unceasing suffering to their people. Moreover, the mining of the harbors was creating mounting difficulties in supply.

As realists, the Hanoi leadership could not entirely ignore the changes in international relations.[38] In the aftermath of the Moscow summit it was becoming evident that the apparent rapprochement between the United States and the Soviet Union was more than a one-night affair. Nixon had returned from Russia with a raft of signed agreements—some prosaic sounding, others high profile, and all betokening a new degree of cooperation. If this pattern continued there were reasons to worry that Moscow might become less supportive.

The Chinese attitude was also of concern. Already Beijing was making life difficult by its refusal to permit Russian ships to use their ports for transshipment to Vietnam, although Haiphong harbor was effectively shut down. On a stopover in China on his way back to Paris, Le Duc Tho received some pointed advice from Zhou Enlai, which amplified the message Podgorny had offered. While praising the North Vietnamese government for its decision to fight and negotiate simultaneously, Zhou encouraged them to be more flexible in considering the future role of General Thieu. As "a puppet of the US" he could of course not be retained as permanent head of the South Vietnamese government. But, like him or not, Thieu was the relevant "chieftain." If Hanoi could "recognize him as a representative of one of the three forces in a coalition government," this might satisfy the Americans. Like Podgorny, Zhou was impressed by the desperation of American officials to exit the war, and he urged Le Duc Tho to prioritize that outcome. For obvious reasons, the North Vietnamese diplomat had less confidence in those assurances.

When the secret Paris negotiations resumed on July 18, the atmosphere had changed since the last session. Both Kissinger and Le Duc Tho had a heightened interest in a settlement, but neither party had decided what new concessions they were prepared to offer. Invoking his high-stakes diplomacy in Moscow and Beijing, Kissinger clumsily asserted, "we have settled with many other countries—with some of which we have had hostility for many decades, and which are of more concern to us than Vietnam could possibly be."[39] This was meant to be encouraging, but the suggestion that Vietnam was of secondary importance to the American government resonated poorly. "The United States is the biggest power in the world," replied Le Duc Tho, "has poured millions of tons of bombs and shells to devastate our country—a small country with an undeveloped economy. We can say no inch, no acre of our country can be spared U.S. shells. In every inch there is Vietnamese blood poured." Kissinger's analogy to the Soviet Union and China made no sense. In Vietnam, unlike these other places, "you have carried out an aggression very deep and very long."

Yet as fierce as the Vietnamese people could be in defending their independence from foreign rule, they were also a "peace-loving nation," Tho declared, and they had come to Paris with a sincere desire to end the war. When it came down to specifics, however, neither side had budged. The sticking point continued to be whether or not the Saigon government would be replaced with an interim coalition, before or after a ceasefire was in effect. After six and a half hours, the Paris meeting closed without a resolution. However, the overall mood was friendlier than usual, with an expectation on both sides that more serious bargaining would begin shortly.

Whatever the appearance, the underlying contradictions in the "national security" policy of the Nixon administration were more extreme than ever. On the one hand, immense violence aimed at North and South Vietnam (along with locations in Laos and Cambodia) and on the other, great cordiality directed toward the communist superpowers that remained Hanoi's allies and chief suppliers. Cold War logic had been turned on its head, and the exaggerated fears of communist expansionism that might once have underpinned the military project in Southeast Asia had ceased to apply.

In the week prior to the Paris meeting, Nixon had learned that Ambassador Dobrynin would be coming to the West Coast to confer with personnel in their San Francisco consulate. He had taken the opportunity to invite the ambassador and his wife to stay in the Western White House for a few days. As he explained to Kissinger, "The thing we want to remember about our communist friends—we have no illusion about their philosophies, but they are people."[40] And as it happened, Mrs. Nixon was especially fond of Mrs. Dobrynin.

Kissinger needed no prompting to join. Since he was intending to be on the West Coast that same week, he invited Dobrynin to tour Universal Studios with him, followed by lunch with film director Alfred Hitchcock and dinner with several other Hollywood personalities. So relaxed were the two men in each other's company after several years of intensive conversations that they spent an afternoon lying on a California beach with only one security guard to watch over them.[41] Of course all this socializing had a serious intent: to maximize US–Soviet cooperation across a spectrum of issues, especially the Vietnam War.

By early August Nixon and Kissinger were riding a new wave of confidence. The polls were showing the president to be 20% ahead of George McGovern, who had secured the Democratic ticket. Nixon had always viewed him as the preferred rival because the radical positions the senator had taken on an array of issues would likely alienate much of the party base. Even McGovern's strength—the energetic grassroots movement that had enabled him to achieve a streak of primary victories—was almost certain to marginalize and therefore antagonize the traditional party leadership.

Though tranquil in comparison to the 1968 convention in Chicago, the Democrats emerged from their conclave in Miami a divided party, just as Nixon expected.[42] McGovern's broader critique of an interventionist foreign policy and a defense budget of $78 billion dollars remained controversial for some. Also problematic was his liberal stance on domestic matters, including his advocacy of increased taxes on the wealthy, a $1,000 federal stipend for the poor, affirmative action, and busing to achieve desegregation of schools. Centrist voters were going to find one or more items in this package hard to swallow.

On top of this, the campaign had made an enormous political mistake. An exhausted staff with insufficient time for vetting made a last-minute decision to select Missouri senator Thomas Eagleton to be McGovern's running mate. Within days of the convention, rumors were circulating about the senator's alcoholism and repeated hospitalizations for mental problems. The facts of the case did not emerge clearly for over a week, during which time McGovern said he was "one thousand percent" behind Eagleton, but was then compelled to repudiate that position once more information became available. McGovern's waffling, coupled with his embarrassing hunt for a substitute, conveyed an impression of indecisiveness.

None of this might have mattered had the Vietnam War evolved differently. It was passionate opposition to this conflict that had created the

McGovern insurgency in the first place. To his most dedicated supporters, the ongoing war in Vietnam remained a source of anguish. That Nixon had needlessly extended the conflict for four years, expanded it to Cambodia and Laos, and was still bombing both North and South Vietnam constituted a searing indictment. What kind of leader would do this? And what kind of fanaticism could explain the fact that under Richard Nixon more than 20,000 Americans had perished in the service of this pointless enterprise, not to mention hundreds of thousands, perhaps millions of Asian casualties, most of them civilians?

But for most Americans the overriding fact was that by late summer, Nixon had brought all US combat troops home, which was no doubt why a Gallup poll found that only 25% of people considered the war to be of major importance. It was Senator McGovern and his antiwar colleagues in both houses of Congress who had forced Nixon to ultimately end American ground combat in Vietnam. Though almost none of the dozens of initiatives they drafted to end the war had passed, they had put so much pressure on the White House that his administration had been compelled to keep withdrawing troops.[43] Few people outside the government recognized how effective these pressures had been. Thus, ironically it was Nixon, not McGovern, who was likely to reap the political benefit of the winding down of the war.

Not everyone was susceptible to this erasure of the war's costs or to its continuance. Among those Americans least likely to succumb were the antiwar veterans. Most were convinced that so long as Richard Nixon remained president of the United States, peace would never come to Southeast Asia. Therefore, a large contingent of them was planning to go to the Republican convention, scheduled for late August in Miami, where they hoped to make a strong moral statement against the war.

From the outset, however, their mobilization was undermined by the infiltration of FBI spies and provocateurs, whose goal was to penetrate the ranks of Vietnam Veterans Against the War and incriminate the members of the organization.[44] One outgrowth of these and related FBI efforts was the July indictment of those who would subsequently be known as "the Gainesville 8," for "conspiring to promote, incite and participate in a riot" at the Republican convention.[45] Among those accused was Scott Camil, who had provided such excruciating testimony at the Winter Soldier hearings in Detroit. Paradoxically, at the very time White House lawyer John Dean was successfully delaying federal indictment of the Watergate burglars, the

Justice Department accelerated the indictment of VVAW members for a crime that had not yet occurred.

The arrests made the Vietnam Veterans Against the War especially determined to conduct their protest in a peaceful fashion. Calling themselves "The Last Patrol," three large caravans of former soldiers from different parts of the country streamed into Miami. They anticipated the presence of thousands of other young people who had come to protest. But they intended to separate themselves, hoping their service in Vietnam would give the antiwar message credibility.

Yet the circumstances in Flamingo Park, where they were encamped, were not favorable. Also gathered there were the "zippies," an array of alienated antiwar young people who, unlike the VVAW, had no interest in communicating with mainstream Americans.[46] While they greeted the arriving soldiers with enthusiasm, the "zippies," many of them stoned and eager to thumb their noses at anything that was part of the "square" world, were engaged in a festival of music, drugs, and guerilla theater that the vets had no desire to engage. For these men, this atmosphere of frivolity was unwelcome because it threatened to undercut the gravity of their own experience.[47]

While occupying a space on the perimeter of the park and creating their distinctive protest activities, the VVAW members were inevitably linked with the other dissenters because of their own scruffy appearance. For some that physical transition had begun in Vietnam, where military discipline had broken down. Wherever it started, these young veterans who had emerged from the "middle America" Richard Nixon had so assiduously cultivated resembled the bearded protesters more than their families back home. Moreover, their experiences in the war and its aftermath had for many of the vets created pools of pain and anger, which set them apart from their countrymen.

As a triumphant President Nixon arrived in Miami in preparation for his re-nomination, 1,200 of these veterans, arranged in platoons and organized by state, marched in silent protest across central Miami and then down Collins Avenue in Miami Beach to the Fontainebleau Hotel, the headquarters for the Republican convention.[48] At the head of the line were Bill Wyman, Bobby Muller, and Ron Kovic, crippled by the war and wheelchair-bound.[49]

Outside the hotel, the marchers were met by 1,000 Florida state troopers and Miami police, decked out in their own battle gear. Unable to proceed, the veterans sat down in a semicircle, blocking the flow of traffic. The soldiers demanded to meet with President Nixon. With the group refusing to move, a possibly explosive confrontation was averted when antiwar congressman Paul McCloskey arranged for Kovic, Wyman, and Muller to enter the Fontainebleau and speak with the Republican liaison to the hotel. It was a symbolic but meaningless gesture. The veterans' real intention had been to provoke a conversation with some Republican delegates that might be filmed by journalists. Yet the heavy police presence made that impossible.

The main event would come the next day, Wednesday August 23, when the president would give his acceptance speech. For the past week, tension had been mounting in Flamingo Park between the civilian protesters and the Miami police. Sometime that afternoon, the policemen guarding the area began shooting off canisters of tear gas. It was unclear whether that was provoked by violence from the group or for some other reason.[50] In what became a prolonged battle, the authorities clubbed and arrested demonstrators, many of whom fought back using their fists or makeshift weapons. Some of the Vietnam veterans were scattered throughout the crowd, and in the melee some tried to shield civilian protesters from police nightsticks. The overall scene, with clouds of gas, helicopters hovering overhead, and people fleeing, was eerily reminiscent of the war they had left.

Meanwhile inside the Fontainebleau, Nixon was beginning his acceptance speech. With help from Congressman McCloskey, Ron Kovic, Bill Wyman, and Bobby Muller had gained entrance into the hall. As Ron Kovic pushed his wheelchair toward the front, he began screaming at the audience: "Do you hear me people? Can you hear me when I say this war is a crime?" Next to him, Muller and Wyman began shouting "Stop killing women and children!" And then, repeatedly, "Stop the Bombing! Stop the Bombing."

For a moment, people were stunned, but some surrounding delegates began cursing, and one spat at the three men as security guards ejected them from the floor. As they were being removed, there were shouts of "Four more years! Four more years!" At the podium was the president of the United States, dignified and calm—unmoved by the brief tumult in the crowd. Kovic would later reflect, "This was the moment I had come three thousand miles for, this was it, all the pain and rage, all the trials and death of the war and what had been done to me and a generation of Americans, by the man who stood before us in the convention hall that night."[51]

From the stage, Richard Nixon was continuing with his prepared remarks, which included the incongruous admonition:

> I say to you tonight, in these times when there is so much of a tendency to run down those who have served America in the past and who serve it today, let us give those who serve in our Armed Forces and those who have served in Vietnam the honor and respect that they deserve and that they have earned.

Ron Kovic and his fellow antiwar veterans might be all-American youngsters, scarred by a national tragedy, but for the Republicans in the hall there was no "honor and respect" for these men. Their message was too discordant, and their memories of the war were best muffled.

Despite the protests in Miami, the media covered almost none of it. To those watching at home, the Republican convention appeared to be a unified, orderly gathering in celebration of a great president who had never been more popular or widely acclaimed than he was at that moment. With his extraordinary successes in Moscow and Beijing, large-scale withdrawals from Vietnam, and brilliant use of media, Nixon had made himself the mainstream candidate, far more in tune with the American public than either Senator McGovern or the haunted VVAW protesters.

As always, Nixon's message spoke to the idealism of the nation: We have the opportunity in our time to be the peacemakers of the world, because the world trusts and respects us and because the world knows that we shall only use our power to defend freedom, never to destroy it; to keep the peace, never to break it.[52]

By Labor Day, Richard Nixon seemed headed for a mammoth electoral victory. But this required that certain secrets be kept: the transactions surrounding Watergate, the real character of his diplomacy with the Soviet Union and China, and the disasters that were still brewing in Vietnam, Cambodia, and Laos.

24

"You're Three for Three, Mr. President!"

For George McGovern, the dynamics of the presidential contest were radically transformed once his opponent was Richard Nixon rather than a field of Democrats. Prior to his nomination, McGovern's unequivocal antiwar stand had been a clear asset, attracting thousands of volunteers across the country and winning millions of primary voters who enabled him to surge ahead of Hubert Humphrey and Edmund Muskie, despite their support from the party "establishment."

However, in a country that was still sharply divided on the war, McGovern's strong stance could easily be reframed as disrespect for the troops or even disloyalty to the United States. As a decorated veteran of World War II, McGovern might seem immune to such charges, but in the polarized atmosphere of that time he was not, especially since he had included amnesty for draft resisters in his platform. This call for amnesty touched powerful emotions on both sides. For most antiwar people, the refusal to fight in Vietnam—with an associated willingness to risk prison or flee to Canada—was a profoundly moral, patriotic decision. By contrast there were many people, including some families of servicemen, who viewed that decision as an act of cowardice that placed an extra burden on other young men.

In late September while on the campaign trail in Columbus, Ohio, McGovern was walking through the Western Electric plant shaking hands when he was stopped by factory worker Dan Gischler, who demanded: "How come you want amnesty for traitors?" Pointing to a bracelet inscribed with the name of a prisoner of war, the man denounced people "who won't fight for Vietnam and for America." McGovern replied that Nixon was actually "keeping him in jail by keeping this war going."[1]

Gischler seemed unconvinced, countering that the president was "trying to get him out." "How," retorted McGovern, "by bombing the hell out of people?" Gishler insisted that Nixon would get the prisoners out, "every last one of them." He only wished the president had "bombed a hell of a lot more of them," because it was necessary to show people that we're "not just a flunky second-rate country." While McGovern searched for a reply, another worker chimed in: "We don't believe in surrendering," which was why he planned to vote for Nixon. Did either man really think Richard Nixon would end the war? the candidate queried. Gischler retorted that it was Lyndon Johnson who had put 500,000 soldiers into Vietnam, while Nixon was "taking people out."

McGovern had been followed into the factory by a flock of reporters as well as a CBS camera crew who filmed this confrontation, which was aired on TV and widely covered in the press. It made McGovern look undignified, querulous, and weak, while reinforcing the impression that red-blooded, patriotic working people were rallying to the president. This was precisely what Chuck Colson, the White House operative who had in fact stage-managed this seemingly spontaneous exchange, had intended. Describing the episode to Nixon, Colson reflected that the three minutes on CBS news was "the finest television commercial I have seen in my life."[2]

Colson's staging of the factory scene was but one of the stunts deployed during the presidential campaign. Throughout his political career, Nixon had had a proclivity for "dirty tricks" like these, preferably outsourced to others. During the primaries and even before, such tricks had been deployed to advance the McGovern candidacy because Nixon and his team believed that McGovern would be the easiest candidate to beat.

The "dirty tricks" were being orchestrated by 31-year-old lawyer Donald Segretti.[3] Segretti presided over a group of young operatives calling themselves the "rat-fuckers," whose mission was to create confusion and ill will among the Democrats. Operating with funding provided by the Committee for the Re-election of the President (CREEP), they conducted a sabotage campaign that featured tactics such as forging letters on candidates' stationery or circulating false rumors about their sexuality.[4]

Most likely George McGovern would have obtained the Democrat nomination even without this White House mischief, because antiwar sentiment within the party was at such a peak. However, by the time of his campaign stop at the Western Electric plant, the war was disappearing from the front pages of most newspapers and receiving scant coverage on television news. Nixon had already announced that by December, American troop levels would be down to 27,000. He had also declared that by mid-1973 the United States would move to an all-volunteer army, thus ending the draft, which had been a rallying point for dissent among young people.

For McGovern, whose opposition to the Vietnam War was the centerpiece of his candidacy, these developments weakened his arguments. Nonetheless, he continued to remind audiences that the war was still ongoing, the United States was pounding Vietnam from the air, American pilots were still being shot out of the sky, American prisoners were languishing in North Vietnamese jails, that Nixon's claims about South Vietnamese capabilities were untrue, and above all that the president's promise to end the conflict should not be trusted.

Increasingly these claims were falling on deaf ears. Public opinion polls in September showed that the war had ceased to be a matter of major concern to voters. Insofar as it did still matter to them, it was Richard Nixon and not George McGovern who was benefiting. According to a *New York Times* / Yankelovich survey, nearly two-thirds of all voters and almost half of all Democrats believed that President Nixon was "doing all he can to end the war." Outside of the Northeast, the majority of voters considered the president to be "the real peace candidate." In a similar vein, the Lou Harris poll found that by a margin of 51% to 33%, responders preferred Richard Nixon's approach to McGovern's as a way of getting the troops home.[5]

Though it was invisible to most Americans, the Vietnam War was continuing at a high level of intensity in particular locations. One tragic development was the rapid disintegration of Cambodia, where in September residents of Phnom Penh rioted over rice, breaking into stores, assaulting the merchants, and looting the central market.[6] Two years earlier this had been a country with a rice surplus, but a recent drought, the breakdown of internal governance, and communist success in closing the roads to the capital had combined to bring people to the edge of starvation.

American bombing of Cambodia (still unknown to Americans) and the subsequent invasion had set in motion catastrophic events. Since the overthrow of Prince Sihanouk, two million Cambodians had become refugees while more than half of Cambodian territory was in enemy hands. When the United States first sent troops into the country, the number of Khmer Rouge insurgents had been estimated at 3,000. But intervening events—the shocking depredations of South Vietnamese soldiers in Cambodian villages, the relentless B-52 bombings in the eastern portion of the country—had multiplied their numbers. By the fall of 1972, estimates of the communist-led Khmer Rouge hovered between 30,000 and 40,000 men.[7]

While the original purpose of the American invasion of Cambodia had been to eliminate or reduce the North Vietnamese presence, four full North Vietnamese divisions were inside the country, and the entire length of the border between Cambodia and South Vietnam had become permeable, with

Hanoi freely moving troops back and forth across it in response to changing conditions.[8] US military officials feared that a sudden surge could threaten Saigon, or more likely Phnom Penh.[9]

Whatever hopes the Americans might once have placed in Lon Nol as a wartime leader had dissipated.[10] With American dollars, the size of the Cambodian army had grown from approximately 37,000 to 200,000 in the space of two years, but despite its size, it was inept and was steadily losing ground to the Khmer Rouge.[11] Moreover, its ranks were riddled with corruption, including the pervasive practice of "ghost counting"—Cambodian officers listing fictitious fighters on their rolls so they could pocket the wages.[12]

Politically, Lon Nol was doing no better. In the two years since the coup he had suspended the constitution and dissolved parliament. By fall 1972, there was a new constitution and a new national assembly, both approved in rigged elections.[13] Despite repeated shakeups in the cabinet, his immediate circle of supporters had continued to shrink. For the majority of Cambodian peasants who had formed the backbone of Prince Sihanouk's regime, the events since 1970 had proved to be an accelerating disaster. Many yearned for a return of the monarchy and the time when their country had been at peace.[14]

Lon Nol's weakness was no secret in Washington.[15] Yet whatever his shortcomings, neither Nixon nor Kissinger could think of a viable alternative. One risk of a regime change was that a successor might seek an accommodation with Hanoi and opt out of the war completely. That concern obviously applied to Sihanouk, who was still cooling his heels in Beijing. Although he was the one political figure who retained a significant base of support within the country and could potentially stabilize it, the White House considered his return too dangerous.

Despite all these grim realities, Nixon and Kissinger continued to assure one another that their move into Cambodia had been a bold stroke. Hoping that more foreign assistance could ameliorate the government's shortcomings, in October they asked Congress for an additional $209 million in economic and military aid to Cambodia, which included payment for emergency supplies of rice being flown in from Thailand. The White House also escalated the number of B-52 bombing raids along the Cambodian side of the border to ensure the safety of Saigon. To Nixon the ability to launch these flights was further proof that his incursion into Cambodia "had won the war."

The president was retreating further into self-deception and denial. It was not just Cambodia in severe straits; the situation in South Vietnam had also deteriorated. After the initial euphoria about stopping the communist advance into Hue and Kontum, by fall, plans to retake the conquered areas had faltered, and the army of South Vietnam was showing a limited offensive capacity. There was a moment of triumph in mid-September when South Vietnamese marines retook the citadel in Quang Tri City—a place of symbolic importance to the regime.[16] That achievement had come at a steep price. Months of artillery bombardment and hundreds of American B-52 air strikes had preceded the marines, and in the wake of the assault the city had been reduced to rubble.[17]

The problems on the battlefront were, if anything, dwarfed by the immense amounts of suffering experienced by civilians, unbeknownst to most Americans. For years some of the greatest hardships were borne by the residents of Quang Ngai province. It was never entirely clear if pacification had really taken hold there. Many of the people in the countryside had been pressed into government camps, where loyalty to the Saigon regime was dubious. Even in the towns where Saigon exercised official control, its grip remained tenuous. As the spring offensive gathered steam, leadership in some places quietly passed to the National Liberation Front.

Inside these swirling currents was the staff of the Quaker-supported Quang Ngai Rehab Center, who were committed to political neutrality and the provision of medical assistance for noncombatants. To carry out their mission, they refrained from questioning any of their local employees or patients too closely, while maintaining cooperative but distant relations with the American advisors in the area. Yet as the violence increased during the late summer and early fall, the functioning of the Center as a refuge was even more precarious.

Reflecting their situation, co-director David Barton wrote the home office that because of the fighting, their patient load was now higher than ever and they were "plagued with other problems: the threat of many of our workers being drafted, friends being thrown in jail and interrogated, patients losing their homes to artillery fire and bombing."[18] The danger he perceived was that there would soon be "massive retaliation" in the province, with a concomitant rise in civilian casualties.

Barton's concern was not misplaced. Not long after he wrote, fighting broke out between government troops and insurgents in the nearby town of Mo Duc. The B-52s were summoned into action. So severe was the bombardment that the normally intrepid Americans at the Rehab Center were badly frightened. As described by Caroline Elliot, a new arrival, "the sky seemed to be on fire," first a flash, then vibrations "which you could feel all the way down to your gut, where it makes you want to vomit and scream."[19]

Elliot likely knew nothing about Dang Thuy Tram, the young North Vietnamese physician who had been killed in Quang Ngai province two years before. Yet her diary expressed the same mixture of personal fear, anger, and concern for the civilians that Thuy's had:

> ". . . please make them stop. The ones driving the planes—they don't understand what they are doing—they can't—they don't know Mr. Bich and his wife who is nine months pregnant (he was planning to go home this weekend and take a long deserved rest and await the arrival of his baby). They don't know Canh and his family—his father who is just now beginning to recover from a rocket injury. If they could know them—play with them, eat in their huts, talk to them—they wouldn't, they couldn't. . . .

The next morning the Quaker team learned that both Mo Duc and the town of Duc Tho had been "flattened" by the overwhelming fire power of the B-52s, the Cobra gunships, and the rockets fired from offshore battleships. The roads leading to their facility were cut off by the fighting, and as they dreaded, several of their patients and local staff were directly affected.[20] Mr. Bich was unable to join his pregnant wife, who had been severely injured when a bomb exploded in a bunker. He learned from someone who had made it out that one of his older children had also been hurt.

Others were receiving awful news as well. A paralyzed patient learned that her entire family had been killed, others that cousins or siblings were missing, homes destroyed. Not all this damage could be attributed to American air power or to ARVN. The Viet Cong were also contributing to the suffering. According to Elliot, the local cadre had enlisted boys 10 to 12 years of age who, clad in their black pajamas, were "terrifying the villagers." With so many civilians caught in the middle, there was not much gain for "hearts and minds," she reflected. "Nobody is winning any popularity contests at this point."

Reports put the number of refugees in the province at somewhere between 70,000 and 140,000.[21] "We've heard many, many tales of the people trying to flee the bombing, running and hiding, moving from place to place, living underground for 40 days," David Barton wrote. "A few of the people never left the area and continue to live in holes and bunkers in the ground. When it rains, they sleep in the mud." There were mixed accounts about the behavior of the newly recruited members of the Viet Cong. "But nobody seemed to have a good word to say for ARVN," whose reputation for looting was once again confirmed.

From the perspective of the American advisors, the net result of these military operations was that by September the South Vietnamese government had regained the upper hand. However, in the view of the Rehab staff, this was illusory. The Saigon regime might have recouped "symbolic control," but the NLF had gained personnel and territory that ARVN was unlikely to retrieve.

The volatility in Quang Ngai province, with its long history of insurgency, was perhaps to be expected. But the Americans had developed greater confidence about the Mekong Delta, which they viewed as pacified. Once the spring offensive was underway, the Thieu government withdrew its main-force units from the area to join the battles at An Loc and elsewhere. Very quickly, Viet Cong cadres returned to the Delta and began mobilizing support, while thousands of North Vietnamese troops previously based in Cambodia moved over as well.[22] As in the years before the Tet Offensive, it was difficult for an outsider to know who was in charge.[23] By day it might appear that the Saigon government held the reins, whereas at night the Viet Cong might wield authority.

Yet throughout this period the Nixon White House radiated confidence. By September, its communications to the public stressed the effectiveness of ARVN in repelling what they described as a failed enemy offensive. Were these assertions true? Kissinger wanted greater clarity before heading into a new round of negotiations. During an August visit to Saigon, he had been treated to the familiar stream of good tidings.

After three years of illusory good news provided by the military, he listened skeptically to these accounts.[24] A less cheery outlook was coming from the State Department's bureau of intelligence and research (INR). Their report noted that one result of the enemy offensive was that communist main-force units had "returned in strength to base areas deep inside South Vietnam" and had "significantly expanded" their influence in rural areas.[25] The INR estimated that the percentage of the rural population under Saigon's firm control had dropped from 74.4% to 58.9% during the previous six months, with some of the more dramatic reductions occurring in the five northern provinces of MR-1 and the Mekong Delta. Even in the provinces surrounding Saigon, the communists had an increased ability to harass government operations.

The State Department analysts were mindful of the severe losses sustained by the enemy's main-force units and the continuing fragility of the Viet Cong infrastructure in most locations. However, their overall conclusion was that the enemy was emerging from its spring offensive with more territory and an enhanced ability to oversee the population. Whether these developments would be permanent would partly depend on the fighting capacity of ARVN, which remained in doubt.

In early October a team of National Security Council staffers conducted their own inquiry, with similarly mixed results. The good news was that the South Vietnamese marines and local militias had performed better than expected. Unfortunately, the same could not be said for the regular ARVN divisions, which had displayed serious weakness. While managing to defend most of the major targets, their offensive ability was dismal. The result was that even those enemy units that had been badly hurt were able to rebuild in their traditional base areas close to population centers.

For the time being, the North Vietnamese offensive had been stopped, and perhaps as many as 100,000 of their soldiers and southern allies had been killed or seriously wounded.[26] How much of that result was the consequence of American bombing was an open question. The intensity of US bombing over North and South Vietnam was extraordinary. According to the Pentagon's own statistics, the United States had dropped more bombs in Indochina during the previous 21 months than the total allied tonnage released over Germany during the period 1940–1945. Given this massive effort, perhaps the more noteworthy consequence was the equivocal military outcome.

While the suffering of people throughout Indochina was perhaps at its peak, news coverage of the war had greatly diminished. American soldiers were largely absent from ground combat, which meant dramatically reduced casualties. With domestic public interest drifting elsewhere, George McGovern's electoral prospects continued to sink. With only a month to go before election day, his campaign bought 30 minutes of television time for a major speech to the nation. The senator somberly observed that since January 1969, "20,000 young Americans have come home, not in glory to the cheers of a grateful nation—but in death to the bitter tears of their families." The president's "secret plan for peace will forever be a secret to them." And sadly "the war goes on for the people of Indochina," who were "literally being crushed under the weight of the heaviest aerial bombardment the world has ever known."[27]

Addressing one of the central contradictions in Nixon's policy, McGovern reminded the audience that the official reason for fighting in Vietnam had been "to stop Communist China or to stop Communist Russia." But once Nixon had been wined and dined in Beijing and Moscow, this rationale had evaporated. How could anyone reasonably argue "that it is good to accommodate ourselves to a billion Russian and Chinese communists, but we must somehow fight to the bitter end against a tiny band of peasant guerillas in the jungles of little Vietnam?"

McGovern's speech was his most eloquent of the campaign and drew favorable comments and a surge of donations. Yet once again, his presentation was overshadowed by events orchestrated from the White House. For after several months during which prospects for the peace negotiations in Paris had seemed uncertain at best, it suddenly appeared that Kissinger's efforts to secure an agreement with Hanoi might be coming to fruition.

During his unsuccessful August meeting with the North Vietnamese, Kissinger had noted Le Duc Tho's sudden desire for more frequent sessions. There were also hints that Hanoi might be moving away from its insistence on the removal of the South Vietnamese government prior to a ceasefire. In anticipation of a possible breakthrough, Ambassador Bunker was instructed to show President Thieu the most recent US proposal. The South Vietnam leader was upset by the contents. Not only had the United States stopped insisting on mutual troop withdrawals, a concession Kissinger had made two years earlier, but troublingly had introduced a new entity—a tripartite Council of National Reconciliation (CNR)—which could be established quickly.

On the US side, this was a switch from its call for a tripartite electoral commission, which would have as its exclusive responsibility the conduct of South Vietnamese elections. The mandate of the CNR was less precise. Although it was not intended to be a governmental structure, it would be given more extensive, albeit diffuse, responsibilities including implementation of the signed peace agreements and the achievement of national concord.[28] From Kissinger's perspective the vagueness was not a problem. As a tripartite body with representatives from the Saigon government, the PRG, and some agreed-upon neutral entity, it would be effectively paralyzed by a requirement of unanimity. The advantage was that it provided an ambiguous compromise if Hanoi retreated from its demand for an interim coalition government. However, Thieu considered this dangerous. With an ambiguous mandate, the CNR could too readily morph into a real government, Kissinger's assurances notwithstanding.[29]

This divergence precipitated a flurry of meetings and memos between Washington and Saigon. In trying to quell Thieu's objections, Kissinger resorted to a tactic he had used sporadically during the previous year—assuring the South Vietnamese leader that Hanoi was unlikely to accept the US proposal.[30] The purpose of this offer was to demonstrate flexibility to the American public, given the approaching election.[31]

Nixon also had his doubts about this tripartite CNR, since, as he told Haig, he thought that most Americans "want to see the United States prevail after all these years." Nonetheless he gave Kissinger the negotiating latitude he was seeking. At the September 15 meeting, Le Duc Tho proposed the idea of two temporary administrations in the South, which would reflect the existing military situation. In this formulation, the Saigon government would continue to administer all the South Vietnamese territory it presently controlled, while the PRG would administer the places where its troops held sway.[32] Instead of calling for a coalition government, he suggested that until elections could be held, both these administrative entities would be under the authority of a tripartite superstructure that would have limited responsibilities.[33]

A settlement was clearly within reach. Yet, having spent 18 months trying to dissuade the North Vietnamese from their insistence on a coalition government, Kissinger felt triumphant. Also exciting was that Le Duc Tho seemed willing to settle on a peace agreement by October 15—almost a month before election day in the United States.[34] Returning to Washington, Kissinger emphasized the desperation of the North Vietnamese: "They're in a panic" about what might happen in a Nixon second term."[35]

In his report to Nixon, Kissinger glossed over President Thieu's strong objection to a tripartite Council of National Reconciliation. Indeed, as more details of Kissinger's diplomacy with North Vietnam emerged, Thieu and his colleagues were increasingly outraged.[36] On September 26, Ambassador Bunker was handed a memo outlining their objections. Chief among them was the negotiating process itself. If Hanoi wished to discuss the political future of South Vietnam, they should be negotiating with the Saigon regime, not Washington.

Nevertheless, Kissinger was determined to forge ahead. With a peace agreement close to fruition, somebody was needed to enlist the Thieu government's cooperation. Once again, Alexander Haig was entrusted with a delicate task. On September 29 he sat down with Nixon and Kissinger to prepare for this trip. The easy part was to clarify the US proposal by making it clear that the Council of National Reconciliation was intended as a fig leaf to cover North Vietnam's retreat on a key issue.

The deeper problem was that Saigon might prefer to avoid a peace agreement and to continue fighting indefinitely. But that was unacceptable to Nixon:

> This war has got to stop. I mean, that's all there is to it . . . . We cannot go along with this sort of dreary business of hanging on for another four years. It's been too long. It's been too long. I mean it.[37]

Moreover, Thieu had to realize that the US president was not omnipotent. American engagement of any kind had to be approved and funded by Congress. During the last round of budget decisions, the administration had barely scraped through by a margin of two senators. If Hanoi's most recent peace proposals were reasonable, which they appeared to be, they could not be safely ignored without forfeiting congressional appropriations.

Nixon's instructions were clear, but useless. When Haig and Bunker met with Thieu and several of his high-ranking officials in Saigon, they found them united in outrage.[38] Thieu's special assistant Huong Doc Nha was standing in front of a blackboard, with an outline of their objections written in Vietnamese. The medium was the message: by what right did Americans presume to make decisions for South Vietnam?

Running through the particulars, Nha described the communist proposals as more "vicious than ever" and claimed the American proposals were no improvement. With so much anger in the room, the counter-arguments Nixon and Kissinger had provided to Haig fell on deaf ears. Especially lame was his suggestion that Hanoi might be changing its tactics and offering meaningful concessions. According to Thieu, the alleged concessions were imaginary and the future grim. "We are on the edge of catastrophe, on the brink of the abyss," he tearfully told the Americans.

Both Haig and Bunker had anticipated some pushback from the South Vietnamese, but the intensity of their anger was startling. Heading home, Haig cabled Kissinger that "there has been a collapse of confidence" so severe that the administration was faced with a fundamental choice—"withdraw support from Thieu or repair the breach" by addressing his concerns.[39] Haig favored the latter course, which would minimally require that negotiations with North Vietnam be slowed down.

Kissinger thought a delay at this point would be a mistake, but he also recognized a genuine dilemma. A public blowup with Thieu just before the election could prove politically dangerous. On the other hand, he also believed Hanoi was ready for compromise, an opportunity that should not be forfeited. And there were the Soviets and Chinese, who had been promised some US flexibility if Hanoi was more forthcoming.[40] How might they react if the Nixon administration turned down a fair offer?

The president was also of two minds. Given the resistance in Saigon, the idea of postponing matters until election day, to be followed by a draconian strike on North Vietnam prior to a new peace settlement, held definite appeal. At the same time Nixon shared Kissinger's frustration with Thieu for being so stubborn "with our Air Force and our prisoners." The lack of gratitude was shocking. "When you stop to think what we've done for him on Cambodia, what we've done on Laos, what we've done on May 8—Jesus Christ he owes us one now and he owes it damn fast."[41]

He decided to send Kissinger back to Paris on October 8, bringing with him a slightly modified political plan that fell short of the North Vietnamese desire for the NCR to possess more governmental power. Kissinger speculated that by following this course they would "come out with a great public record and no settlement and a free hand after the election." If, by some chance, Hanoi accepted the revised American offer? Then Kissinger should meet with Thieu and "cram it down his throat," Nixon opined.

At this juncture, neither man was fully aware of how far Hanoi was willing to go in accommodating some American concerns. By late September, the Politburo had made a definite decision to use the opportunity afforded by the US election to reach a rapid agreement. In the interests of speed, they had authorized Le Duc Tho to offer significant political concessions:

> Our primary requirement at present is to end the US war in SVN. The US should withdraw all of its forces, end its military involvement in SVN and stop its air and naval war and its mining in NVN. The end of the US military involvement and the cease-fire in SVN will lead to the *de facto* recognition of the existence of two administrations, two armies and two areas.[42]

Once the Americans departed, they said, this would "create a new balance of forces to our advantage" and open the door to a subsequent victory.

For years Hanoi had insisted on the necessity for a coalition government in the South. But with an estimated 140,000 troops in South Vietnam and a resurgent National Liberation Front in some locations, the situation looked different. By not insisting on their removal, Kissinger had implicitly accepted the idea of dual administrations. This made the composition of the interim South Vietnamese government less crucial. If the tripartite Council of National Reconciliation had fewer powers than the Politburo wished, this was unfortunate but not dire. The urgent task of the moment was to get the American military out of the country.

As he headed off to Paris on October 8 accompanied by Haig, Kissinger was acutely aware of Nixon's ambivalence about a preelection agreement.[43] He hoped that Hanoi's eagerness to settle would yield a deal so attractive that the skeptics in both Washington and Saigon would be mollified. For once, Kissinger's optimistic expectations were exceeded. With a few words, Le Duc Tho swept away his government's longest lasting impediment: "We do not want to let the political issues of SVN, which are the most difficult, to prolong our negotiations." Differences over the composition and function of the proposed CNR need not prevent a peace settlement. In fact, Hanoi was prepared to observe a ceasefire even before a tripartite council was put in place.

Hearing Le Duc Tho offer this concession on the very first day of the negotiations, Kissinger and his staff anticipated a great victory.[44] As explained by Tho, North Vietnam was adopting the core American position: ceasefire, return of the POWS, and complete withdrawal of US troops. A political settlement was effectively put on hold, to be resolved (if ever) by the two South Vietnamese parties, the Saigon government and the PRG. Under this new formulation it appeared as though President Thieu might remain in office for some unspecified amount of time. For Kissinger, this was an emotional high point: "We stood on the threshold of what we had so long sought, a peace compatible with our honor and our international responsibilities."

Over the remaining two days, a host of practical issues had to be resolved, including the future of Laos and Cambodia, the fate of civilian prisoners, the prospect of reparations payments, and the resupply of ARVN over the next months. For the most part Le Duc Tho took pains to address American concerns. What he was seeking in return was speed. After settling most of the substantive matters, they shifted their attention to the calendar, drawing up an itinerary for Kissinger—first to Washington, then Saigon, then Hanoi, where the actual signing would take place at the end of October.

For Kissinger and his team, there was a heady sense of achievement accompanied by genuine excitement at the prospect that the war might finally end. Though apprehensive about how Saigon would react, even Haig was pleasantly surprised by what they had accomplished at the peace table. For Kissinger personally, it seemed like a vindication of the policies he had so vigorously promoted. Some combination of US military power, which had been brutally employed during the previous months, plus Soviet and Chinese pressure had compelled Hanoi to abruptly change course. Or so it seemed.

During the three days of Paris negotiations, his communication with the White House had been sparse, irritating Nixon. Nevertheless, he was returning to the Capitol with excellent news: "You've got three for three, Mr. President," referring to the Beijing and Moscow visits, plus sudden progress in the Vietnam negotiations. "The deal we got Mr. President, is so far better than anything we dreamt of, I mean it was absolutely, totally hardline with them."[45] Kissinger was eager to review the details, but Nixon was focused on the likely response in Saigon. Would President Thieu go along? Kissinger wasn't sure, but he emphasized that all of his substantive concerns had been met.

Throughout the conversation, Nixon was in a strange mood, going off on angry tangents:

> Henry let me tell you this; it has to be with honor. But also, it has to be in terms of getting out. We cannot continue to have this cancer eating at us at home, eating at us abroad . . . . I'm not going to let the United States be destroyed in this thing. . . . Those little assholes are not going to do it to us.

So disjointed was his response that it was difficult to discern which "little assholes" he had in mind—members of the South Vietnamese government, or the NLF? Kissinger was able to convey the point that under this new bargain, the ceasefire and return of the US POWs would go into effect starting October 30, with work on the CNR to follow. For weeks Kissinger and his staff had focused on ways to make this body as toothless as possible. And the good news, he explained to Nixon, was this Council might never even be formed if Thieu and the PRG were unable to agree on its membership or functions. Given these alterations in the North Vietnamese position, Nixon thought there was no valid reason for Thieu to turn the accord down. If he did, they would have "to flush him."

Suddenly elated, the president ordered a bottle of his special wine, a '57 Lafite-Rothschild, to celebrate the day's events.[46] It was an "historic night," Haldeman wrote, with Nixon all "cranked up" and toasting them all.

Ending the Vietnam War was certainly "historic." But could this agreement serve that purpose? For more than a year, American decision-making on the war had been concentrated in fewer and fewer hands: Nixon, Kissinger, Haig. With fewer independent eyes on the problem, a certain myopia had crept in. For Kissinger, getting rid of the enemy's governmental demands had been uppermost. Seemingly this had been achieved. But essentially ignored was the new reality resulting from the spring offensive: the thousands of enemy troops in the South exercising political control. Given that condition, there was reason to doubt that the Saigon government would ever agree.

October 12 was a night to celebrate, not a time for hard questions or consideration of impending problems. Apart from Vietnam, there were other troubles brewing.

Unhappily for the president, Watergate—or at least one of its many tentacles, the "rat-fuckers"—made a return appearance on the front page of the *Washington Post.* The subject had never really gone away, but despite repeated efforts by George McGovern to bring it up, the story had been sidelined. During an August press conference, President Nixon informed reporters that because of the White House internal investigation of the break-in, he could "say categorically . . . that no one in the White House staff, no one in the administration, presently employed was involved in this bizarre incident." This was untrue. During this period, Haldeman and White House Counsel John Dean had been busily suppressing information that could lead to identifying those people in the administration and CREEP who were involved.

By mid-September the two men were confident that they had contained the damage, at least until election day. To their relief, the grand jury limited its indictment to those already named, the five actual burglars, plus Gordon Liddy and Howard Hunt. Attorney General Richard Kleindienst indicated that the Justice Department would be halting its probe. Hopefully, the burglars would plead guilty and remain silent about who had ordered the break-in.

Luckily for Nixon, the Cuban operatives seemed eager to comply. When interviewed on television they merely affirmed their anticommunist convictions. Having seen the news summary, Nixon told Haldeman, "I thought I'd die, it's so funny."[47] Haldeman shared his amusement: the men were such "simpleminded, totally sincere Cuban types," so earnest in their explanation that "they've seen communism and they're worried about it infiltrating into this country." The best part was that this truly was their motivation for acting against McGovern. The president thought these men perfectly cast for the role. "They have that intensity and the accent, they're worried, sincere and emotional."

However on October 10, Bob Woodward and Carl Bernstein, the two young *Washington Post* reporters who had been working story, had produced a shocking article that made it clear that the Watergate break-in was not a standalone event. It was merely one episode in "a massive campaign of political spying and sabotage conducted on behalf of President Nixon's re-election and directed by officials of the White House and the Committee for the Re-election of the President (CREEP)."[48] For this purpose, hundreds of thousands of dollars had been allocated to discredit Democratic candidates—through such activities as forging documents, stealing confidential files, manufacturing false items for the press, investigating the personal lives of campaign workers, and planting provocateurs at Democratic events. As described in the *Post,* the money for this project had been under the control of John Mitchell while he was still serving as Attorney General. It was later stored in the office safe of Maurice Stans, former Secretary of Commerce who had stepped down to serve as the chief fundraiser for CREEP, and dispensed by the president's personal attorney, Herbert Kalmbach.[49]

Woodward and Bernstein identified Donald Segretti as a central figure in the operation. A college friend of White House Appointments Secretary Dwight Chapin, Segretti had been flying around the country recruiting people to work on this dark underside of the Nixon campaign. From Segretti's experience in student government elections had come the picturesque term "rat-fuckers" to describe those who engaged in campaign-related dirty tricks. According to Woodward and Bernstein, Segretti's team had "rat-fucked" Ed Muskie by harassing his campaign. By identifying the adolescent-sounding Segretti, the *Washington Post* reporters were getting closer to the highest levels of the Nixon administration, possibly endangering the president.

As election day approached, the desirability of a Vietnam peace agreement was clear. In the light of Kissinger's favorable report, Nixon authorized him to fly back to Paris and nail down the deal. There was one caveat: the end product of his efforts could not be "a blowup" with President Thieu before election day. If the final terms of Kissinger's agreement with Le Duc Tho proved unacceptable to Saigon, then he was to walk away.[50]

Before departing, Kissinger drafted a letter to Thieu, signed by the president, which highlighted his administration's generosity toward South Vietnam over several difficult years:

> The military measures we have taken and the Vietnamization program, the dramatic steps that we took in 1970 against the Cambodian sanctuaries, the operations in Laos in 1971 and the measures against North Vietnam just this past May have fully attested to the steadfastness of our support. I need not emphasize that many of these measures were as unpopular to many in the U.S. as they were necessary.[51]

Throughout this ordeal, Nixon had stood firm against any effort to superimpose a new government on South Vietnam. Because of "the perseverance and heroism of your government," and American firmness at the negotiating table, there had been "a fundamental shift" in Hanoi's position. Its negotiators were willing to accept a standstill ceasefire in advance of any political change in the South. This would leave Thieu's government intact—a major accomplishment. In the president's view, "we have no reasonable alternative but to accept this agreement."

But would Thieu cooperate? In assessing the likely reaction, both Kissinger and Nixon were handicapped by their unwillingness to acknowledge, even to themselves, how damaging the spring offensive had been. The official line was that North Vietnam had just sustained a devastating defeat. However, two timely reports from the CIA's George Carver called attention to the "extreme concentrations of communist units" in numerous locations all across South Vietnam.[52] Most immediately disturbing was the situation west and south of the capital, "with the enemy inching closer to Saigon than at any time since the spring of 1968." Should there be a ceasefire in place, there is "a current communist 'presence' on at least three sides of the capital, with some enemy units located less than twenty-odd miles from the presidential palace."[53] Under these circumstances, Carver warned that Thieu would appraise whatever proposal Kissinger brought "in the spirit of a flint-eyed mortgage banker, coldly scrutinizing a complex loan application from a known poor credit risk."[54] There was "no chance whatsoever" he would make a favorable decision on Kissinger's proposed timetable.

Kissinger's first stop was Paris, where there were two unresolved questions: the release of civilian prisoners in South Vietnamese jails, and the replacement of weapons for both armies.[55] The North Vietnamese were insisting that under international law, once a war ended all sides were expected to return prisoners. Recognizing that in the case of South Vietnam this could involve the release of 30,000 civilians, Kissinger maintained that the United States could not decide this unilaterally, although it would use its influence in Saigon.

As for the replacement of weapons, the United States had proposed that both sides be permitted to replace damaged or used-up weapons "on a piece-to-piece basis," whereas the North Vietnamese argued there should be equal amounts permitted for each side. Concerned about speed, within 24 hours the North Vietnamese declared that "to show its serious attitude and good will" and to maintain the agreed schedule, they acquiesced to the American position on both issues.[56] With respect to the civilian detainees, this was a major concession because they were overriding the fervent wish of the PRG delegation whose members, including Madame Binh herself, had family and friends languishing in South Vietnamese jails.[57]

Filled with hope, on October 18 Kissinger flew to Saigon where first encounters seemed benign. Perhaps all the pieces would fall into place, he imagined.[58] He was mistaken. South Vietnam's highest ranking general, Cao Van Vien, chairman of the Joint General Staff, was blunt: the continued presence of North Vietnamese troops in the South posed a grave threat to the regime.[59] Back in March, "the relationship between the communists and South Vietnamese forces . . . had been favorable to us," but that was before the spring offensive. Now there were "four or five more divisions present," which posed a serious challenge. "Our soldiers are very tired," he continued, "and we do not have the strength to hold the line on all military fronts."

Efforts to persuade the South Vietnamese officials that Hanoi had "collapsed," and that ARVN was a vigorous fighting force, fell on deaf ears. As if to emphasize the point, during these sessions there were repeated enemy attacks on the outskirts of Saigon. Though Kissinger promised a massive delivery of military equipment and economic aid prior to the implementation of a ceasefire, such assurances were unpersuasive.

On the evening of October 21 came a new blow. In an interview with a *Newsweek* reporter, North Vietnamese President Pham Van Dong had shared details of the prospective agreement, conveying his government's enthusiasm and referring to a "three-sided coalition of transition" that was part of the arrangement.[60] This appeared to confirm the South Vietnamese suspicion that Kissinger's much-vaunted CNR was nothing more than a disguised "coalition government." Although Dong had not exactly said this, the phrase "coalition of transition" did the damage.

In a fury, Thieu charged that the "disguised coalition embodied in the agreement will lead to the collapse of the GVN." It was now perfectly clear that the United States had "connived with the Soviets and China" to sell out his government.[61] By granting legitimacy to the PRG, agreeing to the tripartite CNR, and allowing the North Vietnamese divisions to remain in the South, America had completely undermined his government's position.

Kissinger was livid. In a private session he warned Thieu that he was on a "suicidal course." The United States had "fought for four years . . . mortgaged our whole foreign policy to the defense of one country. What you have said is a very bitter thing to hear." Why had Thieu wasted his time? Kissinger had stayed four days in Saigon only to return home empty-handed. The South Vietnamese leader was unabashed. Four days was not too much time for his government to study an agreement that affected its entire future.

In responding to Thieu, Kissinger reiterated an essential point he had been making for the past four days: the Nixon administration was unable to continue the war. There was no longer any base of support in the United States or in Congress for its prolongation. In terms of expenditures, they were already $4 billion in the hole for the next fiscal year, and there was absolutely no way that Congress would continue appropriating funds if the South Vietnamese sabotaged the Paris Agreement. This was not a bluff. But Thieu was unmoved. Unlike Nixon and Kissinger, he could not ignore the strong possibility that, with thousands of North Vietnamese soldiers in the South and their own military exhausted, his government might not survive.

Kissinger was briefly tempted to fly to Hanoi and sign the peace agreement anyway, but quickly realized this approach was unsustainable. Any hope of a peace agreement before the election was dashed. Instead, it was decided to sweep the failed negotiations under the rug. Unfortunately for the White House, this rug was getting bigger with so many secrets to cover.

Watergate remained a growing problem. The seven defendants who were pleading guilty were blackmailing the White House for compensation, with more people involved in arranging the payments. Woodward and Bernstein were unrelenting. On October 25, the same day as Kissinger's negotiations collapsed, their *Washington Post* story revealed that Bob Haldeman was one of the five people who controlled a $700,000 Republican fund used to finance the "dirty tricks" against political opponents.

Nixon could not believe the boldness of the paper. Very soon, he assured Chuck Colson, "We're going to screw them."[62] Those people "don't realize how rough I can play." He could be a nice guy at times. "But when I start, I will kill them, there's no question about it." People at the *Washington Post* "should give some thought to taking on the guy that went into Cambodia and Laos, ran the Cambodia bombing campaign. What the hell do they think they're doing there?" The linkage (if not the logic) was clear: if you can blow up opponents abroad with impunity, you can do the same at home.

With two weeks left before the election, George McGovern was continuing to decry the administration's conduct of the Vietnam War and its handling of internal opposition. In a final telecast broadcast from Detroit, McGovern maintained that the United States faced a "moral and a constitutional crisis of unprecedented dimensions" because of the abuses of power occurring in the White House.[63] "Ambitious men come and go, but a free society might never recover from a sustained assault on its most basic institutions," he intoned. The senator from South Dakota seemed headed for ignominious defeat, making it easy to ignore his words.

25

"Miserable, Filthy People"

On November 7, President Nixon fulfilled expectations, overwhelming his political opponent 61% to 38% and carrying every state in the union but Massachusetts. George McGovern's defeat had multiple causes, but none so surprising as the president's emergence as "the peace candidate" in the 1972 election. Nixon's dramatic visits to Moscow and Beijing, plus the undeniable fact that his administration had withdrawn 500,000 US soldiers from Vietnam, all contributed to this impression and his landslide victory.

An ongoing public concern was the fate of the POWs, whose freedom was dependent on a peace agreement. On election eve, Nixon gave a televised speech announcing "a breakthrough in the negotiations which will lead to peace in Vietnam." All major issues had been resolved, he explained, except for "some details" that would be "nailed down." Fortunately, he could now say "with complete confidence . . . that we will soon reach agreement on all the issues and bring this long and difficult war to an end."

For George McGovern and his followers, these assurances carried little weight. Given past deceptions it was easy to imagine that the president's remarks were an electoral ploy.[1] In truth more than "details" stood in the way of a final settlement. But after four years, Nixon was fully determined to terminate American participation in the Vietnam War. With no US combat troops on the ground, a continuation could only mean endless bombing, which was unsustainable. Moreover, he was personally sick of the war, convinced that his entire first term had been blighted by this conflict, and was eager for a clean slate.

As the dismal election returns poured in, a deep sense of failure and shock pervaded McGovern headquarters. Nevertheless, in his concession speech the senator uttered words that were perhaps more apt than he realized. "There can be no question at all that we have pushed this country in the direction of peace." And if they had shortened the Vietnam War even by days, "then every minute and every hour and every bone-crushing effort in this campaign" was worth it.[2]

Although obscured by the lopsided vote, McGovern's candidacy had indeed given a hefty push toward the attainment of peace. In the months prior to his nomination, the senator had pulled his rivals to the left and consolidated the Democratic Party as a steady source of antiwar pressure.[3] That ongoing political challenge, underpinned by a still formidable antiwar movement, had accelerated Nixon's acceptance of Secretary Melvin Laird's schedule of troop removals, despite many unfavorable events on the ground.

Furthermore, as a proactive member of the Senate, McGovern had continually pushed for legislation that would set a time limit for the war by cutting off appropriations beyond that date. Although these bills failed to achieve majorities, the growing support for these measures sent a clear message to the White House: keep withdrawing troops, or Congress will force an end.

While Nixon genuinely desired a rapid peace agreement, prospects had dimmed during the two weeks before election day. Less than 24 hours after Kissinger's departure from Saigon, President Thieu had thrown a public monkey wrench into the proceedings. In deference to the Americans he did not reveal the existence of a specific document, but he made it clear that the proposal under discussion was unacceptable. A rapid ceasefire could only occur if all enemy troops were removed from the South. Any tripartite political arrangement, such as the hypothetical Council of National Reconciliation, would amount in practice to a new "coalition government" with the communists, which could result in "the massacre of as many as five million people in the South."[4]

To avoid a blowup before election day, Nixon scrapped the timetable Kissinger had agreed upon with Le Duc Tho. North Vietnamese officials were predictably incensed. From their perspective they had offered significant concessions, which had earned the ire of the PRG. In particular, their abandonment of the demand for the release of the approximately 30,000 political prisoners being held in South Vietnamese jails had upset their Southern allies, who had relatives and friends languishing there—among them Madame Binh's brother.

On the surface, the US request was minimal: a brief delay and another quick round of negotiations. But to the North Vietnamese that alteration suggested a reversal in the American position once the presidential election was over. To avoid that outcome, in a radio broadcast on October 26 they released the exact terms of the peace agreement they had reached with Kissinger, including the letters from Nixon indicating his satisfaction with the deal. Unfortunately, the Americans had chosen to renege on a clear commitment, they angrily charged.

The complaints emanating from Saigon and Hanoi were precisely the outcome Nixon had hoped to avoid. With Haig back in Washington whispering maliciously about "Henry's up-and-down emotional state," it was easy to blame Kissinger for the mess.[5] While Nixon had authorized his national security advisor to obtain Thieu's support for the agreement, he had also warned against excessive pressure. Yet according to Haig, in his zeal to get a settlement before election day Kissinger had put intense pressure on the South Vietnamese leadership, which had created the unfortunate backlash.[6] But would a gentler approach have made a difference? What Nixon was unwilling to admit, even to himself, was that the proposed agreement posed grave problems for their South Vietnamese ally.

In the wake of a landslide election outcome, Nixon was in a surprisingly black mood. One immediate problem was that his victory had not translated into comparable gains for his party. In the House of Representatives, Republicans gained only 12 seats—leaving the Democrats with a substantial majority of 243–192. The more dangerous situation was in the Senate, where the Democrats gained two additional seats with a new party breakdown of 57–43. Given the personnel involved, according to the White House count, there was a majority in the Senate for the antiwar legislation that had repeatedly failed in the past. To Nixon this was an additional motivation for moving quickly on a peace agreement.

Kissinger was seething over Thieu's obstructionism. After years of negotiating, his proudest achievement was that "we have destroyed the coalition government" idea so important to Hanoi.[7] The bargain he had struck was "a spectacular thing," he confided to Nelson Rockefeller, which "the maniacs" in South Vietnam were jeopardizing. He hoped this was merely a tactic designed to wrest a better deal. Yet by stalling in this fashion, President Thieu was forfeiting whatever good will remained in Congress. Such behavior was typical of Vietnamese actors, whether from North or South, "because you can never be sure that one of them won't do something suicidal."[8]

The irrationality of both ally and adversary was an old theme for Kissinger. Yet in the present circumstance this race-infused notion loomed larger. The lost opportunity was "murderous," he told *National Review* editor William Buckley.[9] "Like all Vietnamese he's incapable of understanding the requirements of others and what he claims domestically, he's going to lose here." Thieu could have "sent me back, putting his arm around me and saying

America has saved us and thank you very much," instead of this rather unnecessary diplomatic impasse.

For all his intellect, Kissinger's own inability to comprehend "the requirements of others" was handicapping his understanding of Saigon's reaction. In his excitement over torpedoing the North's demand for a coalition government, he failed to appreciate how the retention of thousands of North Vietnamese troops in the South constituted a lethal threat to the Thieu regime. In this regard, Haig had a better grasp of the problem. Perhaps "we are focusing too intensely on the achievements we have made at the negotiating table," the general suggested, while ignoring the political dangers surrounding President Thieu.

Contributing to Kissinger's myopia was his soaring reputation in Washington, New York, Hollywood, and elsewhere. Since the India–Pakistan fiasco, he had racked up a string of apparent achievements: the opening to China, the successful summit in Moscow, and the difficult negotiations with Hanoi, which seemed close to fruition. He was treated like a celebrity, his brilliance broadly acclaimed. Between the rude encounters in Saigon and the undiminished flattery on the home front, Kissinger was in a state of volatile grandiosity not conducive to critical reflection.

It was during these tumultuous weeks that he agreed to an interview with Oriana Fallaci, an Italian journalist who shrewdly ensnared him: "Dr. Kissinger how do you explain the incredible movie-star status you enjoy? How do you explain the fact that you are almost more famous and popular than a president?"[10] He initially demurred but could not resist the temptation to preen: "Americans like the cowboy who leads the wagon train by riding alone ahead on his horse, who rides all alone into the town with his horse and nothing else. Maybe even without a pistol since he doesn't shoot." It was a ridiculous analogy, but one guaranteed to infuriate Nixon, who most certainly did not regard Kissinger as a lone actor.

Under the best conditions, Nixon found his national security advisor hard to take, with his distinctive combination of pedantry and high-strung emotion. That Kissinger had largely orchestrated his greatest triumphs in China and the Soviet Union did not inspire gratitude. Moreover, the massive publicity surrounding Kissinger meant that achievements that might have been exclusively credited to Nixon were too often attributed to his brilliant Harvard subordinate. For the time being, the president was utterly dependent on Kissinger to end the Vietnam War in a fashion that would appear successful. But once this was accomplished, Nixon confided to others, he intended to replace him.[11]

Meanwhile, weapons were pouring into Vietnam from all directions. While a ceasefire seemed likely, nobody expected it to be more than temporary. For the Nixon administration, this seemed a last chance to provide the South Vietnamese government with a vastly increased arsenal of planes, tanks, artillery, and ammunition.[12] Under the rubric of Enhance Plus, with November 15 as a new endpoint, the Americans exhausted their own available supplies and called upon allies—Iran, South Korea, and even Taiwan—to donate their American-provided military goods with the promise of rapid replacement.

On a smaller scale, Hanoi was speeding up the supply of both men and material into South Vietnam.[13] From the Soviet Union and China, military aid was still flowing, enabling the North Vietnamese to provide vehicles, weapons, oil, and food to their southern soldiers. Despite years of American efforts to block this traffic it was coming through familiar routes: the Parrot's Beak in Cambodia, the Ho Chi Minh Trail in southern Laos, and even across the DMZ.

Despite the peace talks, fighting was intense as both sides sought to maximize their territorial advantage. North Vietnamese and NLF units might be depleted, but they were still managing to attack government forces in disparate locations.[14] While the Americans were no longer fielding combat troops, their bombers were striking hundreds of sites inside North and South Vietnam, Cambodia, and Laos.

This was a disheartening endgame, and Nixon was anxious to be free of it. On his next trip to Saigon, Haig carried a presidential letter to Thieu, expressing his "deep disappointment" over recent events.[15] "Your continuing distortions of the agreement and attacks upon it are unfair and self-defeating," with complaints that were "highly embarrassing to me." Going forward, his administration would suggest changes to the text, but Thieu should harbor "no illusion" that the United States would go beyond that.

Haig was under firm instruction to nail down Saigon's position. Mindful that Kissinger would be scrutinizing the transcripts from these conversations, Haig was at pains to praise his boss. The South Vietnamese ought to appreciate his contributions to their cause. During the past four years, there were only three men "responsible for mastering and preserving the assets needed for you to do your job" —namely Nixon, Kissinger, and Ambassador

Bunker.[16] "For you to single out Dr. Kissinger and portray him in any other context is self-defeating in the extreme."

Privately, Haig sympathized with the Joint Chiefs of Staff and General Westmoreland, who saw no reason to rush. From their perspective, finalizing the military arrangements was a priority, while giving ARVN more time to prepare for a US withdrawal. There was also more acceptance of Thieu's fears about the enemy troops scattered throughout the four military regions of South Vietnam. While the official line in MACV was that the South Vietnamese military had become a mighty force, its weakness was hardly a secret.

According to the *New York Times,* as of late October American army instructors were putting the "entire" South Vietnamese army through an intensive training program. Remarkably, more than 10 years after US military "advisors" had begun assisting Diem's army, the instructors had identified major shortcomings:

- The troops do not know how to shoot accurately, and they drain off ammunition at a dangerously high rate.
- They seem to have virtually no concept of even the simplest infantry tactics.
- They do not know how to use their mortars and recoilless rifles.
- They cannot maintain their relatively simple machine guns.[17]

As Kissinger's deputy, Haig could not openly express his personal worries about the military balance in the South. But after meeting with President Thieu, he found the latter flexible "on every issue, except his request that we explore the troop issue with Hanoi." Without some movement on this item, Haig deemed it unlikely that Thieu would ever agree to a ceasefire.[18]

Arriving in Paris on November 20, Kissinger was faced with three South Vietnamese ambassadors, summoned from other capitals to monitor his negotiations. In an accommodating gesture, he used the first meeting with Le Duc Tho to propose 69 changes to the agreement that Thieu had wanted.[19] While expecting their rejection, he hoped that the North Vietnamese would be flexible on a few points, which could hopefully appease Saigon. As he recognized, by so doing he was reneging on his commitment to the North Vietnamese that the United States would not try to alter the October 8 accord. Any hope he might have entertained was quickly shattered as Le Duc Tho furiously denounced the US retreat from their October agreement. "We have been deceived by the French, the Japanese and the Americans, but the deception has never been so flagrant as now."[20]

Le Duc Tho saw no reason to depart from the original text. But if the Americans insisted, they would make certain concessions provided they were matched by comparably important concessions on the US side. Among these was Le Duc Tho's demand that *all* American technicians assisting the South Vietnamese military be required to leave along with the troops. He also returned to a previous demand that the Saigon government release the tens of thousands of political prisoners still incarcerated in its jails.[21]

Kissinger had arrived in Paris anxious to settle, and it was difficult to assess how seriously he should take Le Duc Tho's vitriol. Perhaps this was merely a tactical ploy, which would be adjusted as the talks progressed?[22] The national security advisor quickly dropped most of the 69 points. But some of the remaining items were substantive, including significant reduction of North Vietnamese troops in the South, elimination of all references to the PRG in the text, and an effort to define the DMZ as a functioning border between North and South Vietnam. Taken together they significantly altered the peace agreement Kissinger had made in October. Predictably, Le Duc Tho turned him down.

In Washington, Nixon pored over his fluctuating reports from Paris, uncertain of his next move.[23] For months he had been clear about one thing: he would not begin his second term in office with Americans still fighting in Vietnam. More ambiguous was the route through which this would be accomplished. Could he rely exclusively on Kissinger's diplomacy to determine the outcome, or would he need a massive program of violence to achieve his purpose?[24]

Arguably, Operation Linebacker I had fit that description. Yet there was always the possibility of greater destruction. At present the American bombing of North Vietnam was ongoing, although in the aftermath of the October agreement Nixon had cancelled attacks north of the 20th parallel.[25] Did it make sense to maintain that limitation while waiting to see if Hanoi would move closer to South Vietnamese requirements? Or was it time to intensify the air war by wreaking havoc on North Vietnamese cities?

With so many lives hanging in the balance, the circle of "deciders" was even more constricted than usual. During this transition period before Nixon's second inauguration, some key figures in the administration were preparing to leave, among them Secretary of Defense Laird and CIA Director Richard Helms.[26] Secretary of State William Rogers was also on his way out, although the president had agreed that he could remain in place until the Vietnam War was over.[27] Even the once-powerful Joint Chiefs of Staff had been pushed to the sidelines.

This left three men responsible for ending the war—Nixon, Kissinger, and Haig, whose rivalries with one another complicated the task.[28] All were caught in a bind that had been years in the making. On the one hand was the domestic demand for peace, embodied in a newly elected Congress likely to cut off funds if the administration failed to achieve an agreement.[29] On the other hand was an entitled leadership in South Vietnam, bitterly opposed to any settlement with Hanoi that allowed North Vietnamese troops or PRG political structures to remain in the South.

Accompanying Kissinger on his flight back to Washington was Nguyen Phu Duc, a foreign affairs assistant to Thieu, who was scheduled to discuss the outstanding issues with Nixon. These conversations proved unproductive, as Duc merely reiterated the grievances previously expressed by the South Vietnamese leadership. Kissinger was especially infuriated by the complaints that the proposed agreement had left enemy troops in the South. After all, whose fault was it that the enemy controlled so much southern territory? The Americans had repeatedly urged the South Vietnamese military to be more proactive:

> There are divisions in MR-3 that haven't fought during the whole offensive. There are some in MR-4 that haven't fought since March 30. How many times has Ambassador Bunker mentioned General Minh? If the North Vietnamese had been pushed out, there would be no problem now.[30]

The situation on the ground might not be ideal, but to Kissinger the impending agreement would be of benefit to Saigon, or so he insisted.

Why were North and South Vietnamese so obtuse about their own self-interest? For both Nixon and Kissinger, this was a never-ending mystery. After four years, the two still had difficulty grasping the diverging motivations of either side in the Vietnamese conflict. In Kissinger's case, his heightened feelings of insecurity were distorting his judgment even more than usual. In the inner sanctum of the White House and elsewhere, there were rumors that he had mishandled the Vietnam negotiations by creating false expectations with his "peace is at hand" remarks.[31] Aware of these mutterings, Kissinger assumed the source was the State Department, where Rogers' loyalists were malevolently undercutting him.[32] The net effect was to make him even more defensive about the deal he had managed to negotiate.

Although assured by Haldeman that he had the president's confidence, there was a certain amount of fire underneath the smoke. Prompted by Haig, whose duplicity was steadily growing, Nixon had retroactively decided to blame Kissinger for his October efforts to nail down a deal with Hanoi.[33] He also worried about Kissinger's mental state, since his memoranda from Paris had veered to extremes, and his mood upon his return was explosive. However erratic his behavior, Nixon still considered him irreplaceable when it came to the Vietnam negotiations.

Yet as of late November, the negotiations seemed stalemated. Le Duc Tho had assented to some of the minor changes the Americans had asked for, but held firm on the chief issues in dispute.[34] Kissinger sought other options. Within a select circle of Washington officials, he claimed a hidden advantage. "We have almost made an arrangement with the Soviets and have some understanding with Peking with respect to their support for Hanoi," he asserted.[35] Indeed for many months, Kissinger had been in regular communication with Ambassador Dobrynin about the talks, providing him with more information than he had given the Secretary of State. During these conversations, Dobrynin had repeatedly assured him that the Soviets desired an end to the Vietnam War and that they were pressuring Hanoi to make a deal.[36] Of course, there was no way of gauging the seriousness of that pressure or the degree which it was affecting the North Vietnamese, since the level of Soviet aid was undiminished.

As for China, the cooperation was somewhat less than described. Just before leaving for Paris, Kissinger met with Ambassador Huong Chen, who had previously served as a useful channel of communication. "I'm caught between two groups of Vietnamese fighting each other. It is a terrible fate," Kissinger quipped.[37] The two sides were close to an accord, but the principal obstacle was the presence of so many North Vietnamese troops in South Vietnam. If "the North Vietnamese outside of the agreement would withdraw some troops or make some gesture that indicated they understood the problem," a settlement could occur more rapidly.

The Chinese ambassador rejected this overture. It was unfortunate that the Americans had not signed the agreement back in October. It was "very clear that you acted that way in order to suit your own unilateral needs." According to his information, over the past five days "the Vietnamese side has been carrying on the talks with great flexibility" and had "made all the concessions they can make." Now everything was up to the Americans. While his government was eager for the Vietnam War to be over, they would not involve themselves with the specific items in the peace talks, nor would they halt economic and military aid.[38]

Upon his return home, Le Duc Tho was rebuked by the Politburo. While still desirous of an agreement, it instructed him to firmly resist additional changes and to be "well prepared for coping with the US rashness in resuming the bombing of North Vietnam as a whole."[39] Reflecting these fresh guidelines, Le Duc Tho greeted Kissinger angrily when negotiations with the Americans resumed on December 4: "In the past ten years of war, we have known all the atrocities of war," he observed. And his government recognized that without a settlement "the war will be merciless." But they accepted that risk:

> You may bring B-52s to raze Hanoi and Haiphong. You say your President is determined; we know that he is determined to invade and devastate our country . . . We have undergone tens of millions of tons of bombs and shells equaling 500 to 600 atomic bombs, but we are not afraid.[40]

In a peroration that harked back to their earliest, bitter meetings, Le Duc added, "We will not submit; we cannot accept being slaves."

For weeks Kissinger had touted the virtues of the October agreement. But in a sudden reversal, he decided that to sign it would be "tantamount to overthrowing Thieu," who could not survive "this demonstration of his and our impotence." He was therefore recommending that the United States reject Le Duc Tho's most recent position and be prepared for a breakdown in the negotiations. Under that circumstance, the president would need to go on national television both to explain the impasse and justify expanded bombing.

This was the kind of emotional zigzag that Nixon detested. He was reluctant in any case to give up on the peace negotiations, recognizing the public's antiwar sentiment and eagerness for the rapid return of the POWs. However, he also wished to avoid a blowup with Saigon, which might underscore the futility of the war.[41] Faced with this dilemma, Nixon instructed Kissinger to keep pressing for changes and insisted that the talks must continue. As for the proposed bombing, he was prepared to give the order if negotiations stalled, but he had no intention of giving a dramatic speech to the American public justifying that decision.[42]

Once again Kissinger turned to the Chinese and the Soviets for assistance. Seeking out the Chinese ambassador Huang Chen, he outlined an urgent situation in the peace talks.[43] Despite the stream of complaints coming from Saigon, he explained, the United States had pared down the list of proposed changes to the October accord from 69 to four. Yet Le Duc Tho had seemed immoveable. If the situation did not change, the United States would have no choice but to cancel the talks and take "whatever action is necessary," with potentially "disastrous" results. Kissinger hoped that after consultation, "the friends of Hanoi" would communicate "the peaceful intention of the United States to their ally" and, by implication, encourage flexibility.

Kissinger also reached out to the Russians for rescue. In a worried message to Dobrynin on December 4, he complained inaccurately that Le Duc Tho's behavior was "completely inconsistent" with what the Soviet ambassador had led him to expect, creating a crisis akin to that of the spring. "If Moscow has any influence on Hanoi's attitude, it must act . . . preferably before tomorrow since talks may well break off at the next session."[44] Without their intervention, the situation will become "completely out of control."

In reality, the only emergency on the horizon was the potential damage to Kissinger's reputation if he failed to achieve an agreement in Paris, having previously announced that "peace is at hand." Dobrynin was evasive. His understanding was that Hanoi was truly desirous of a deal, and it was the United States that had demanded changes in the October agreement.[45] Without knowing the precise nature of the dispute, it was difficult for his government to intercede meaningfully. To clear up their confusion, Kissinger arranged for the Russian ambassador to be provided with secret notes of the Paris meetings, notes that other US officials had been denied.[46]

Nixon's insistence that Kissinger keep negotiating reflected the intense pressures in Washington.[47] His key congressional allies—Stennis, Goldwater, and Ford—were warning that without a rapid agreement, the new Congress was going to cut off the funds for the war. Military officials were also pushing back. Diehards like General Westmoreland might be willing to keep fighting, but in the absence of a coherent objective, others in the Pentagon were troubled by the sacrifice of men and planes.[48]

By December 8 it was beginning to appear as though an accord might be reached. Together, Kissinger and Le Duc Tho identified trade-offs that each side might accept.[49] The major sticking point was the provision concerning the definition of the DMZ, reflecting disagreement over whether South Vietnam should be considered a separate, sovereign country.[50] His hopes revived, Kissinger sent Haig back to Washington with instructions to meet with Dobrynin in order "to elicit their maximum help" on the DMZ issue.[51]

Unfortunately, back in Hanoi the mood was swinging in the other direction, as the Politburo had become angrier and more rigid—incensed by the continued American bombing south of the 20th parallel and by the flood of new American weapons, tanks, planes, and trucks flowing into South Vietnam since October 8.[52] While North Vietnam was also sending men and supplies into the South, the scale of this activity was small by comparison to the American program ("Enhance Plus"), which totaled more than one billion dollars. For whatever the precise reasons, the Politburo rejected any further concession on the status of the DMZ.[53]

Unaware of this rejection and the freshly aggrieved mood of the North Vietnamese Politburo, Nixon viewed the dispute over the DMZ as just another bothersome snag that could be overcome with Russian assistance. Haig explained the issue to Dobrynin, and Nixon followed up with a personal call emphasizing that their two nations had "bigger fish to fry." Dobrynin seemed sympathetic but asked for time to facilitate communications between his government and Hanoi.[54] Haig was hopeful this intervention might work, cabling Kissinger that it appeared as though "Moscow would go to bat for us rather strenuously."

It was a telling, if laughable, metaphor—the Russians "going to bat" for the United States. For most Americans, the Vietnam War had only made sense as a major front of the Cold War. Nobody had seriously suggested that Vietnam, Laos, or Cambodia posed a threat to US national security. It was the connection to the communist "superpowers" that made their internal governance a matter of overriding importance to the United States. There were variations in how officials had presented this item to the public: was it Russia or China that was the greater menace? And was the relevant danger a potential loss of territory, or a loss of credibility?

Over the years, different versions of the Cold War theme had emanated from Washington, but each contributed to the maintenance of domestic consent for the war. By December 1972 it was clear that the American relationship with the Soviet Union and the People's Republic of China had significantly improved, which for some critics rendered the Vietnam War superfluous. If Nixon was toasting the communists in Moscow, what sense did it make to be killing them in Vietnam? The paradox existed in plain sight.

What remained a Nixon–Kissinger secret was their continued reliance on Moscow and (to a lesser degree) Beijing to obtain a favorable settlement of the war. During the past 18 months, Kissinger had been offering concessions to the Russians and Chinese, in part to obtain this help. This was one reason that he had used Soviet and Chinese translators for important conversations, without American interpreters in the room. It was not simply his personal rivalry with Rogers, but an awareness that his approach to the USSR and China would be sharply questioned by State Department professionals if they knew.

Of the two, the Russians remained the more significant actor as the largest contributor of economic and military aid to Hanoi. In recent months, the United States and the Soviet Union had nailed down a host of agreements—academic and scientific exchange, the settlement of Lend-Lease and the US extension of credit, the opening of trade opportunities that were mutually beneficial. However, it was in the field of arms control that the hidden "linkage" with Vietnam had been the most consequential.

From early on, Kissinger had wrested control over these negotiations from the designated arms control specialists—overtly through the Verification Panel, and secretly through private discussions with Soviet officials.[55] As the war dragged on, his need for a public relations coup and a Moscow summit led him to a flawed agreement with negative implications for the future. On the one hand, the opportunity to promote real disarmament by supporting an ABM or MIRV ban was discarded. On the other hand, by freezing a Soviet numerical advantage in both land-based and sea-based nuclear missiles, he provided arms control opponents with grounds to object. Kissinger might minimize this symbolic inequality, yet this fit uncomfortably with the rationale for US military operations in Southeast Asia, where the need to appear strong was deemed essential for "national security."

Fortunately for Nixon, in the later months of 1972 the number of American casualties was declining precipitously. However, in other places the war was exacting a heavy toll on soldiers and civilians alike. Suffering was especially acute in Cambodia and Laos, though often left out in the media. In Cambodia, the spillover from the Vietnamese conflict was continuing to ravage the countryside, swelling Phnom Penh and other towns with refugees. The combination of American bombing, an inept Cambodian military, and a rising Khmer Rouge was making normal life impossible for millions of previously apolitical farmers.

For rural Laotians, 1972 had been another nightmare year as the continued strife between the Americans and North Vietnamese obstructed a resolution of their own civil war.[56] The US role in the ground war remained clandestine. In 1970 the Senate had prohibited the use of American soldiers, as well as assistance to third-party nations that might send troops. Yet under the rubric of the American International Development mission, US advisors were still involved in military action. Through a clever ruse, the Nixon administration was paying thousands of Thai troops, who were enlisting as "volunteers" under the nominal authority of the Laotian government.[57] Meanwhile American bombing was continuing, as was the accelerated use of cluster bombs, large canisters containing dozens of small explosives that could scatter over a wide area and be activated at any time. By the end of 1972, at least one-third of the Laotian population of three million had become refugees.[58]

While a constellation of forces had created the human tragedy in these places, the sheer destructive power of the American military was most consequential. On December 11, Henry Kissinger returned to Paris hoping to finally reach a settlement. He was emotionally spent, fearful and angry about the hostile rumors in the White House, and flummoxed by what he perceived as the obstinacy of the two Vietnamese principals.

As the negotiating session commenced, there were two remaining items to be resolved: the wording on the DMZ, and the question of whether the Saigon government and the PRG would be expected to sign the agreement. Le Duc Tho apologetically explained that he was without clear instructions on the DMZ but expected them to arrive the next morning. Irritated by this delay, Kissinger took offense at a new North Vietnamese demand that American technicians, who were aiding the South Vietnamese military, should be required to leave within six months.

The latter request was a direct response to a recent article in the *New York Times* stating that "American officials are secretly planning a major postwar presence of United States civilians . . . with many of them doing jobs formerly done by the military." The figure cited was 10,000 civilian advisors and technicians, who would work under Defense Department contract. When that story appeared, Kissinger had immediately recognized that it would likely affect the North Vietnamese negotiating position, leading him to complain to Laird, "if people do not shut up we'll lose everything we've ever achieved."[59] Whether the leak was from the State Department, the Pentagon, or Saigon, when "every goddamn second-rater talks his goddamn head off," it leads the North Vietnamese to "raise the ante."[60]

It was therefore understandable that Le Duc Tho had raised this issue. But Kissinger had no tolerance for anything new and was worried by Hanoi's stalling.[61] Meanwhile, outside pressure was mounting. Assuming that a peace agreement was imminent, journalists and photographers jostled for chances to catch American and North Vietnamese negotiators as they completed the last stages of their work. In the United States there was still talk of POWs coming home for Christmas.

Then came the rude awakening. On December 12, in a scalding address to the South Vietnamese people, President Thieu denounced the impending accord as a "cunning, crafty trick."[62] If the proposed agreement went into effect, he warned, "the annexation of South Vietnam through military means will only be a question of time."

It was no secret that the government of South Vietnam had been critical of the emerging deal. But after numerous conversations with US officials, there was reason to think it would unhappily acquiesce in a last version. Moreover, Kissinger's labors in Paris were aimed at making the accord more palatable to Saigon. Yet, Thieu was not about to yield gracefully despite the vast quantities of new weaponry the Americans had provided to his million-man military.

In Washington, Haig alerted Nixon to this ominous news, together with Kissinger's warning that they could have "a very, very tough problem" on their hands if he extracted a favorable agreement from Hanoi.[63] In that event, they might need "to push Thieu into acceptance," recognizing "there's some risk that we'll have to crush him." They might be reaching "the point of no return" with Thieu, the president mused. The United States had "nursed him along" for years and "stood by him when nobody else in the world" would do so. But he could no longer tell the American people that to satisfy Thieu "we're going to continue the war . . . there's no way I could."

In Paris, Kissinger was poised for word from Hanoi about the language on the DMZ. He had somehow decided that if this wording implicitly acknowledged the sovereignty of the South Vietnamese government, this would be meaningful to Saigon. Unfortunately, Le Duc Tho's new instructions did not meet this requirement. As specified by the Politburo, "South and North Vietnam shall respect the demilitarized zone on either side of the Provisional Military Demarcation Line," with the "modalities of movement" across that line to be negotiated in the future.[64] This was clever drafting, but Kissinger concluded that absent the word "civil" before "modalities," this could mean that additional North Vietnamese troops would be permitted into the South.

There were other points of friction. On December 12–13, the "experts" from both countries had been hammering out the associated "Understandings" and "Protocols" for implementing the proposed agreement. However when it came to the specific language, there were significant differences that in

Kissinger's view would alter the meaning of the main text: "What you are convincing us of, Mr. Special Advisor, is that no agreement with you is worth making, because either you will break it two days later or your experts will point out to you some way of evading it."[65] Le Duc Tho demurred, claiming that the differences were matters of detail, the inevitable snags in a negotiation when "experts" reviewed the documents.

Yet Kissinger was right about one thing: the North Vietnamese were not ready to settle. On December 13, Le Duc Tho informed Kissinger there were differences of opinion between his delegation in Paris and the Politburo. To clear them up, they needed to return to Hanoi for conversations. In the interim, their experts could continue their work in Paris and the two sides could communicate by message. He assured Kissinger that a final peace agreement was within reach.

While this high-stakes Paris diplomacy was underway, Nixon was faced with another alarming Watergate development. He had received word of an airplane crash near Chicago's Midway Airport killing Dorothy Hunt, the wife of defendant Howard Hunt.[66] In her suitcase was $10,000 in neatly piled one-hundred-dollar bills. Fearing this must be the "hush money" paid to the Watergate burglars, the president realized that news of this cash might deepen suspicions that the defendants were being bribed to keep their silence, thus triggering a new round of public inquiries.[67]

There was a small circle of people assisting Nixon on Watergate, but when it came to Vietnam, the circle was even smaller. While Kissinger was negotiating in Paris, Nixon was relying almost exclusively on Al Haig. As the general reviewed the negotiating reports from Paris, he took the opportunity to dispense hardline advice. In truth, he had never been a great enthusiast of Kissinger's October deal, recognizing the danger it posed to South Vietnam. With progress stalled, he openly urged Nixon to take strong military action.

On December 14, Kissinger returned from Paris in a furious state. Knowing that the president had expected him to nail down a deal, he was appropriately worried about his personal future. He was in a rage at the North Vietnamese for unexpectedly slowing down the negotiations. Perhaps this was a plot to widen the breach between the United States and Saigon. Or perhaps simply a desire to embarrass him and, by extension, the Nixon administration. Whatever the reason, it was malicious. Excluded from his reflections was the thought that the intense opposition from Saigon might be generating new doubts in the Politburo. Nor did he give any credence to the idea that Le

Duc Tho was returning to Hanoi to persuade his government colleagues to accept the existing deal.

In a long meeting with Nixon and Haig, Kissinger provided a grim and somewhat distorted account of this negotiating round, highlighting the way in which the North Vietnamese made concessions and then withdrew them. "What we are seeing now is their normal negotiating habit. They're shits . . . they are tawdry, miserable, filthy people. They make the Russians look good," he declaimed.[68]

He joined Haig in urging the president to take strong military action against the North. Kissinger's preference was for a time-limited approach, with perhaps seven days of airstrikes with B-52s and then a pause. Haig went further, insisting that the moment had arrived to implement a full-scale bombing campaign against Northern targets, unrestricted by location or duration.[69]

Nixon was uncharacteristically ambivalent. He was drawn to stronger action, but also apprehensive that this time the American people would not understand an escalation because in reality "it was the U.S. and not Hanoi that was backing away from the agreement," while the "other culpable party was Saigon and not Hanoi." Such action would negatively impact Congress. The previous week he had met with Admiral Moorer and Deputy Defense Secretary Kenneth Rush, both of whom had emphasized that any acceleration of the war would invite a congressional cutoff of funds. In a follow-up memo, Secretary Laird had written, "Ken Rush, Tom Moorer, and I jointly believe that you have only one realistic choice," which is "to sign the agreement now."[70] The North Vietnamese proposal of early October had met all the American criteria presented to Congress months earlier, making it difficult to understand "why the return of the POWs was being postponed."

Nixon reminded Kissinger and Haig that their domestic critics remained. "The election didn't change it. The only friends we've got . . . are a few people of rather moderate education out in this country and thank God they're about sixty-one percent of the people." The unstated implication was that more knowledgeable people would disapprove of their action, because after all this really was Thieu's fault. If that "son of a bitch" hadn't insisted on "total victory," they could have made the deal months before.

Or could they? Did the North Vietnamese really wish to settle, Nixon wondered. Both Kissinger and Haig were sure they did:

KISSINGER: They're scared shit out of their minds that you'll resume bombing. They have taken shit from me that you wouldn't believe . . . here is Le Duc Tho, the number three man in his country and the things I have said to him. In front of his people, you would not believe.

NIXON: Like what?

KISSINGER: . . . about his tawdry performance; about his extraordinary trickery. And then just making fun of him . . .[71]

What they needed, Haig suggested, was "a good kick in the ass" to compel them to stop stalling. Kissinger thought there was "a fifty-fifty chance if we gave them a tremendous wallop . . . not the sort of shit the Air Force likes to do," that could do the job. Such action could be helpful with the South Vietnamese, who might feel reassured by the American willingness to bomb North Vietnamese cities.

For once, Nixon was cornered by his own hawkish advisors. Left to his own devices, he might have pushed ahead with negotiations and compelled the Saigon regime to accept the peace agreement or forfeit all American aid. However, Kissinger was his negotiator, and at this late date there was nobody to replace him. Furthermore, on matters of Vietnam policy the president had come to rely almost exclusively on these two men. Others like Laird and Moorer might proffer opinions, but they were not part of any formal process. After four years, the president had eliminated the State Department, the National Security Council, and the Cabinet as arenas for serious discussion and debate.[72]

He therefore decided that, beginning on December 18, American bombing of Hanoi and Haiphong would continue for the remainder of the month, excluding Christmas Day. In a nod to political reality, he also determined that these attacks would end by January 3. Nixon insisted upon this date because the new Congress would be coming to Washington and would terminate the war if an alternative were not in place. There would be the inevitable handwringing in the media, Nixon observed. "Severeid and Rather and all those jackasses. Cronkite will cry all those buckets of tears." So the three of them needed to rest and be prepared, always keeping in mind "that when it's toughest we're the best."[73]

Their justification was simple: North Vietnam was unwilling to make peace and was instead building up its forces, which it was again infiltrating into the South. This was false, as was Kissinger's briefing to the press:

> It is clear that the interplay between Saigon and Hanoi is one of the complicating features of the negotiation. But the basic point we want to make clear is this: We have had our difficulties in Saigon. But the obstacle to an agreement at this moment is not Saigon, because we do not as yet have an agreement that we can present to them.[74]

In defending their actions, both he and the president conveyed the idea that North Vietnam had broken off negotiations, which was not the case. They also sought to conceal the fact that it was the United States that had backed away from a clear agreement, insisting on substantive concessions and then complaining when Le Duc Tho proposed changes.

In ordering this new military effort, to be known as Linebacker II, Nixon and Kissinger were still nursing grievances with the Air Force that had been building since Lam Son 719. They considered its previous behavior to be dishonest, unimaginative, and weak. In a preemptive message to Admiral Moorer, the president warned. "I don't want any more of this crap about we couldn't hit this target or that one. This is your chance to use military power effectively to win this war and if you don't, I'll consider you responsible."[75]

Unfortunately for the White House, safety had become a more salient issue. During the previous six months, the North Vietnamese had placed a high priority on improving their anti-aircraft capability and had made significant advances. At a time when the Vietnam War was clearly ending, military officials were concerned that American pilots and their airplanes might be placed at unnecessary risk. Laird had predicted that once the bombing commenced, for every hundred B-52 strikes over the northern cities, three US planes would be downed. Almost immediately this warning was borne out.

From the inception of Linebacker II, criticism of the administration was sharp and quick. However, Kissinger remained adamant that "having crossed the Rubicon . . . the only thing we can do is total brutality."[76] Nixon concurred. Although they had chosen to bomb North Vietnam, both men privately understood that the real culprit was Thieu. "What's killing us now," Kissinger lamented, "is that we have neither a settlement with Hanoi, nor a settlement with Thieu." This was happening because the South Vietnamese president was "an unmitigated, selfish, psychopathic person, son-of-a-bitch." And since the "bastard can't figure out how he's going to stay in office in a free political contest," he had effectively undermined the American position.

An insider might wonder how exactly this new bombing campaign was going to improve the situation. In public, the rationale for Linebacker II kept changing: forcing the North Vietnamese back to the negotiating table; encouraging Thieu to sign the peace accord; demonstrating the administration's commitment to "peace with honor." Underneath these shifting explanations was a deeper truth: America's Vietnam War was a failure.

26
"A Terrific Letdown"

When the bombs began falling on North Vietnamese cities on December 18, few Americans were present in those locations. US journalists covering the war were mainly in Saigon or Washington, where they were relying on second-hand descriptions. Any direct accounts came from foreign embassy or consular staff based in Hanoi, along with a handful of reporters from other nations.

One exception was a four-person group of Americans who had arrived in Hanoi as emissaries from the Committee of Liaison with Families of Servicemen Detained in North Vietnam. This organization was led by antiwar activists, whose more cordial relationship with the North Vietnamese had previously enabled them to obtain the release of three prisoners and to transmit news between some families and men still in custody.[1] This new delegation consisted of Columbia Law Professor Telford Taylor, who had previously served as Chief Counsel at the Nuremberg war crimes trial; folksinger Joan Baez; Reverend Michael Allen, associate dean of the Yale Divinity School; and Lieutenant Barry Romo of Vietnam Veterans Against the War. They were bringing with them hundreds of Christmas cards, letters, and presents for distribution to the American prisoners.[2]

All were under the impression that a peace agreement was imminent, and nobody expected to be bombed. Indeed, during their first two days the delegation encountered relative calm as they met with their Vietnamese hosts and were accompanied to various sites outside Hanoi.[3] In one village, they observed that a railroad yard had been destroyed but the nearby school, where they were greeted by singing children, had been left intact. Telford Taylor considered this noteworthy because it suggested a serious American effort to differentiate military targets from civilian facilities.

The group arrived in Hanoi on December 18, just hours before American planes began striking the city. From evening until the early morning, hundreds of F-111 fighter jets and B-52s flew over overhead, dropping their lethal loads. The most terrifying planes were the B-52s, which both Nixon and Kissinger were increasingly inclined to use because of their psychological impact. Flying in groups of three, they rained destruction across a wide area in the city, while the sound of these explosions reverberated far beyond the initial hit.

The humanitarian emissaries were staying at the Hoa Binh Hotel, blocks away from where the first bombs struck. Crammed into the underground shelter with other foreign guests and hotel workers, Joan Baez suddenly realized she might never see her three-year-old son again. Veteran Barry Romo tried to assuage her fear, promising they would all survive the assault.[4] By the second evening, Baez was sufficiently calm to take out her guitar and sing, with others in the shelter joining in. Since it was easy to learn, an early favorite with the polyglot group was the civil rights song, "Don't Let Nobody Turn You Around."

Thus began a five-day regimen for the Americans of nights huddled in the shelter and days spent touring the areas their government had recently bombed. One of the hardest days was a trip to Kham Tiem Street in downtown Hanoi.[5] Following in a caravan with what remained of the international press, they came upon large piles of rubble, all that was left of people's small houses. Joan Baez was struck by the sight of a woman standing amidst the ruins and "sobbing hysterically," clenching and unclenching her fists. The singer took the woman's hand, as did a girl, who was also weeping. Behind them was a North Vietnamese official running down the numbers "215 killed, 257 wounded." Close by were the ruins of a shelter that had taken a direct hit. Another anguished woman was picking up bricks and putting them down, chanting "Where are you now my sons, where are you now?" As explained by an interpreter, "both of her sons were buried under the bricks and there was no chance she would ever see them again." Weeks later when the singer returned to the United States, "Where are you now, my son?" became the refrain of a new song.

For the four Americans, these daily excursions were almost unbearable, but they did not feel entitled to look away. On the morning of December 23, the North Vietnamese government announced that Bach Mai hospital, North Vietnam's largest and most modern facility, had been destroyed by two separate B-52 raids. In Washington, the Pentagon was refusing to acknowledge that these attacks had occurred. When foreign observers got to the site, any doubt was removed. Everything was smashed.[6] According to Baez, "there were people racing all around carrying bleeding patients piggyback out of the debris."[7] Using cranes, bulldozers, and in some cases their own hands, rescue workers were combing the rubble for victims.

Despite the devastation, the original purpose of the humanitarians' journey remained to deliver holiday items to the POWs and gather news for their worried families. The prison camp that housed some captives (sarcastically called the "Hanoi Hilton") was located near a bomb site. Of the 13 men whom the delegation was permitted to meet, several seemed frightened by the air blitz. Damage to their quarters was plainly visible, although nobody had been hurt.

One POW expressed surprise that this American bombing was continuing. "Kissinger said peace was at hand, isn't that what he said?" Exhausted and furious at the suffering she had seen, Baez replied, "That's what he said. . . . Maybe he didn't mean it. They lie a lot." In a more positive spirit, she and Reverend Allen conducted a brief Christmas service, took everyone's name, and promised to call family members back in the United States.[8]

The hosts from the Vietnam–American Friendship Society insisted on hosting a farewell party, somehow even producing a cake for them.[9] For Lieutenant Barry Romo, a decorated combat veteran, the disturbing memories and feelings elicited by the trip became overwhelming. Observing his tears, Mr. Quat from the Friendship Society responded, "You can't blame yourself for what happened in southern Vietnam. . . . I know you don't believe me, but the war is going to end. . . ."

In this time and place, it was difficult for these Americans to envision that the Vietnam War would ever end. It was not even clear that they could leave North Vietnam, given the bombing of the railroad system and airports. However, after a short delay it was arranged for them to fly out on a Chinese plane. Driving along the road they had initially traveled to Hanoi, they passed the village they had seen on their way to the to the city; the school they had visited had been leveled.[10] Throughout the trip Telford Taylor had been the quietest, but seeing the decimated schoolhouse, he broke down and wept.

Around the world, people were learning about the Christmas bombings from their diplomats in Hanoi or those few journalists who were there. It did not improve the international atmosphere that American bombers had accidentally struck the embassies of Egypt, Cuba, and India, along with two foreign ships in Haiphong harbor. There were official complaints from West European governments, and numerous denunciations in the foreign press. The French newspaper *Le Monde* compared the American action to the German bombing of Guernica during the Spanish Civil War; the British *Manchester Guardian* called it "the action of a man, blinded by fury and incapable of seeing the consequences of what he is doing." In Germany, *Die Zeit* claimed that this Christmas bombing was "nothing but terror and torture. Even allies must call this a crime against humanity."

Back in the United States the reaction from the mainstream media and from politicians in both parties was equally sharp. Linebacker I had been controversial, but with a North Vietnamese offensive underway, the reasons for undertaking it were clear. By contrast, these airstrikes had no comprehensible purpose, despite the shifting explanations from the White House. To many it looked like policy by temper tantrum. For antiwar critics it seemed proof, lest any still be needed, that a penchant for mindless violence had engulfed the Nixon administration.

For this brief interval, the calendar was giving the White House room to maneuver. With Congress out of session, college students on winter break, and millions of Americans preparing for the holidays, Nixon had ordered *Linebacker II* acutely aware that time was short. Kissinger imagined they had another six months of bombing if the North Vietnamese proved stubborn, but Nixon knew better. Whatever happened in Hanoi or Saigon, he was determined to reach a peace agreement by early January. If this meant going back to Kissinger's October deal, he was fully prepared to do this. And if President Thieu withheld his consent, Nixon would proceed bilaterally.

However, knowing the time was limited, he was determined to inflict as much devastation on North Vietnam as possible. In this determination both he and Kissinger were closely aligned. In theory, their intended targets were military. Yet it was apparent from the outset that they wished to destroy what remained of Hanoi's economic infrastructure and if, as a result, civilian casualties ran high, this was no deterrent. The demoralization of the populace was a long-standing goal, and if people were terrorized, this contributed to their purpose.

Inevitably they were running afoul of Secretary of Defense Laird, who kept raising concerns about the cost to the airmen, as almost every day the B-52s were being shot out of the sky with pilots and crews either captured or dead,[11] Faced with these casualties, Laird attempted to shorten the time for *Linebacker II* or modify the plan. Kissinger alerted Admiral Moorer to Laird's approach. "I don't want to pick the targets for you," he explained, but "we want to make damn sure we don't get into the same syndrome we got into this summer."[12] Having crossed a bridge, "let's brutalize them." The military's job was "to have a maximum impact on the North," and if it failed to carry this out, they would have "massive problems with the president."

There was increasing urgency to this task because by the third day of the air attacks, the negative reporting was exploding. Journalists from *Agence France-Presse* were moving around Hanoi observing the damage to various neighborhoods, including the wreckage of Bach Mai hospital. Their articles and photos were being picked up by various wire services, including in the United States. The spectacle of what appeared to be a deliberate attack on civilian facilities and on ordinary people going about their lives was producing outrage in many quarters, including American newsrooms.

In its editorial ("Terror from the Skies"), the *New York Times* excoriated the administration, observing that "the big B-52 bombers that are being used for the first time over heavily populated Hanoi–Haiphong are not precision weapons."[13] Dropping 20,000 tons in the first few days, "the equivalent of a Hiroshima bomb," must have created immense human suffering. What would happen in New York or some other city "if a comparable enemy force were unleashed to attack such targets . . . as railroads, shipyards, command and control facilities, warehouses and transshipment areas, communications facilities, vehicle repair facilities" and so forth? It was horrifying to imagine.

Perhaps this display of military force was intended to rebuke Hanoi for intransigence at the negotiating table, the editorial continued. However, this "indiscriminate use" of American air power to impose its will on a foreign nation was "terrorism on an unprecedented scale." If another nation had behaved in this fashion, the United States would be first to condemn it. That same moral standard should apply here.

On a strategic level, the Christmas bombings showed no immediate sign of affecting the leadership of either North or South Vietnam. On a quick visit to Saigon, Haig found President Thieu to be immoveable, still insisting this his "country's survival is at stake." In North Vietnam, the immediate result of the bombing was to make its government less tractable. The White House was promoting the falsehood that Hanoi had broken off the Paris talks, thus necessitating the air strikes. In truth, Le Duc Tho had been clear that he was returning home to obtain more flexible instructions and was leaving his technical advisors in Paris to continue work on the protocols. Ironically, on the day that American bombs started to fall, the Politburo had acceded to his recommendation.

But now the North Vietnamese were enraged. At the next technical experts meeting in Paris, their representative Nguyen Co Thach complained that the Americans had violated their agreement to refrain from bombing north of the 20th parallel while peace negotiations were ongoing.[14] Such behavior was certain to drive the peace talks into deadlock, because "the Vietnamese people will never submit to force and will fight to the end in defense of their national rights." The North Vietnamese government had decided to postpone the meeting of the technical experts until at least December 23.

While determined to continue the air assault until December 31, Nixon and Kissinger had no intention of scrapping the peace negotiations. On December 22, as US bombs slammed into Bach Mai hospital, came their renewed offer: the Americans would stop the bombing as of midnight December 31 if a private meeting between Le Duc Tho, Xuan Thuy, and Henry Kissinger was arranged for January 3, 1973.[15] This was Nixon's secret schedule from the outset: bomb until the end of the year, and then negotiate before Congress ended the war.

The North Vietnamese had a different timetable: the United States needed to put "an immediate end to its acts of war escalation." If the situation was returned to what it had been as of December 18 then the technical talks could resume, along with the negotiations of Kissinger and Le Duc Tho. In other words, they would resume discussions at any time once the bombing stopped. This might have surprised some Americans, who had been given the impression that Hanoi had ended the talks—although Kissinger and the president knew better.

With each passing day the human cost of Linebacker II grew higher, as domestic and international audiences looked on in shocked disbelief. Religious leaders from diverse backgrounds issued a pastoral letter calling for a halt to the air strikes. Such pleas were echoed widely, from Cardinal Krol, the president of the National Conference of Catholic Bishops to Pope Paul.[16] In one of the harshest statements, Swedish premier Olaf Palme compared the American campaign to the behavior of the Nazis. Among the denouncers was First Secretary Leonid Brezhnev, speaking at the 50th anniversary of the founding of the Soviet Union, who described this as "the dirtiest of all the wars known in American history."[17] It was apparent to everyone "that the United States military adventure in Vietnam has failed. And no new outrages can break the will of the heroic people of Vietnam or shake the determination of their friends to give them every support."

For all their shrewdness, Nixon and Kissinger had placed themselves in an absurd position. The South Vietnamese government had rejected the peace agreement because they correctly assessed the danger to their regime. With an estimated 140,000 North Vietnamese troops in the South and the Provisional Revolutionary Government (PRG) exercising temporary authority in the areas they controlled, the prospects were grim. That this situation was largely the product of Saigon's incompetence and corruption did not alter the fact that Kissinger's October peace deal posed a genuine problem for them. If they were blocking a settlement, this was not because they were "psychopaths" but because they would not put a positive gloss on a perilous arrangement.

In previous years, Nixon and Kissinger had reinforced each other's illusions, convincing themselves and others that the Saigon government and its military were an ever-improving force. Lam Son 719 had punctured that picture. But it was not until the Easter offensive that the inability of the South Vietnamese army to defend itself in the absence of US airpower was driven home. Richard Nixon was up against the same harsh reality that had destroyed his predecessor: thousands of Americans soldiers had died on his watch, with no perceptible gain.

Neither man had reached this precipice on his own. In their initial decision-making, both Lyndon Johnson and Richard Nixon had been following the conventional wisdom of the national security bureaucracies, which strongly advocated pursuit of the war. Yet having brought home half a million troops—against military advice—Nixon and Kissinger were now dangerously exposed to public criticism.

From its inception it was far from clear what this "Christmas bombing" was supposed to achieve. At best, it would open the door to a peace agreement that would look meaningful on the surface. Of one thing President Nixon was certain: he could not continue the Vietnam War past his inauguration. His strongest allies in Congress had told him they no longer had the votes to fund the war, and there was simply no public support for its continuation. Nixon's poll numbers were plummeting and would likely sink further if the brewing Watergate crisis finally burst through.

The question remained: what could the administration do if South Vietnam refused to sign the peace agreement? Under that circumstance, Nixon was prepared to make a bilateral deal with the North. The administration would offer to stop the bombing and withdraw the remaining US troops in exchange for the POWs. But this was a galling prospect. The danger, said Nixon, was that people like George McGovern and Mike Mansfield would say, "Well look, we could have had our withdrawal for prisoners long ago when these insane people wouldn't do it."[18] And "that's the thing that really sticks in my craw," Nixon observed. Yet this scenario was itself optimistic because the North Vietnamese might find a bilateral deal unacceptable. At a bare minimum, they might insist that as part of the price for returning prisoners, the United States must halt all military aid to South Vietnam.

Once underway, it remained unclear how Linebacker II was going to solve these problems. But at least it would impress both Vietnamese parties with American determination and power. Whatever damage the airstrikes managed to inflict on North Vietnam would postpone the date when its military could launch the inevitable offensive. Kissinger had come to loathe the Vietnamese, both North and South, and his resentment was like kindling to the president's firewood. Upon learning that US planes had hit Bach Mai hospital twice, along with the Bulgarian embassy, Kissinger entertained the "happy thought" that "in Hanoi you can only hit unpleasant bastards."[19] In light of this attitude, the president was aggravated by press reports, perhaps inspired by the national security advisor himself, that Kissinger had opposed the bombing on humanitarian grounds.

For Nixon, the six weeks following his reelection had been an emotional maelstrom. Despite his smashing electoral victory, he was enough of a realist to recognize, as many liberals did not, that this victory had been an endorsement of his peace initiatives. But the difficulties of the Paris negotiations had taken a toll. Having tethered American "honor" to a corrupt, authoritarian regime lacking firm support from its people, it had become clear that to never lose, the United States could never leave. Yet remaining in Vietnam was no longer an option. In the early hours of December 24, the president tried to cheer himself up, writing in his diary:

> I must get away from the thought of considering the office at any time a burden.... As a matter of fact, I think the term glorious burden is the best description... On this day before Christmas it is God's great gift to me to have the opportunity to exert leadership, not only for America but on the world scene... From this day forward, I am going to look upon it that way and rise to the challenge with as much excitement, energy, enthusiasm, and wherever possible, real joy that I can muster.[20]

Yet there was not much to celebrate. According to his own schedule, there were only five days left to punish North Vietnam before resigning himself to a flawed peace agreement.

On December 26, as bombs fell on Hanoi, Kissinger called the president with an exciting update. The North Vietnamese were agreeing to resume negotiations on January 8—it was "a terrific cave," he exclaimed.[21] One little item: "they want us to stop the bombing immediately." Of course he and Nixon had planned to keep on bombing until the end of the year, but they "could exchange a few more messages with them to run it up to the 31st." As had frequently occurred, Kissinger was apt to discern "a terrific cave" where none existed. Despite returning to Hanoi for new instructions, Le Duc Tho had always said negotiations would continue.

The unspoken alternative was to take the North Vietnamese communication as a reason to stop the bombing immediately. Among its advantages, this would lighten the burden on American airmen, at least 55 of whom were dead or imprisoned. Nixon was aware that US forces were losing an average of three planes per day, but he had no appreciation of the poor morale among the airmen, who in order to fulfill his exacting requirements were losing rest periods and were flying perilous missions subject to attack by Hanoi's arsenal of surface-to-air missiles.[22] On Guam, men were calling themselves "POGS" (Prisoners on Guam). At the base there was heavy drinking and rowdiness. Some men were calling in sick, or in other cases refusing to fly. It was difficult to see the purpose of the mission with peace so close at hand.

For Nixon, the remarkable fact was that after years of American military and economic aid, totaling billions of dollars, the government of South Vietnam was so reluctant to stand on their own feet. It had taken him four turbulent years to reach a conclusion that so many former US officials had reached much earlier, "that we have tended to erode their will by making them too dependent upon us." Somehow or other, the Russians and the Chinese had avoided this trap:

> They have built up the will of the North Vietnamese. They have helped them . . . with moral support and just enough material support, but they haven't sent in the men and the advisers. They've made the North do it themselves. . . . I think that's one of the great lessons out of this war, looking to the future, is that Americans are basically paternalistic in our attitude toward all countries we've helped, and we weaken them.[23]

So, the imperative was clear: "we've got to get out of South Vietnam, and . . . go home." Unless the North Vietnamese came back "with ridiculously unacceptable demands," it was time for the United States to settle. Nixon had no further patience with Saigon's complaints. "Now we go in and make the deal with the North and tell the South to either stick it or stuff it."

With the American pledge to stop bombing by the end of December, the North Vietnamese had resumed work on the protocols and agreed that Le Duc Tho would meet with Kissinger on January 8. Nixon and Kissinger had somehow convinced themselves of a false narrative that Hanoi had abandoned negotiations and was being forced back to the table by the force of American air strikes. This was because "we gave them a hell of a good bang," Nixon observed. It was really "another spectacular for you," said Kissinger. "And it took terrific courage to do it."[24]

The president thought that maybe now "our brethren in the press" might give them a break. But this was not the case for the *Washington Post,* which issued a withering critique of Linebacker II:

> To pretend . . . that we are making 'enduring peace' by carpet-bombing our way across downtown Hanoi with B-52s . . . is to practice yet one more cruel deception upon an American public, already cruelly deceived. It is to compound what is perhaps the real immorality of this administration's policy—the continuing readiness to dissemble; to talk of 'military targets' when what we are hitting are residential centers and hospitals and commercial airports; to speak of our dedication to the return of our POWs and our missing in action, even while we add more than seventy to their number in little more than a week.[25]

"They're done," the president proclaimed. "The main thing now . . . is that we have to pull this off, and it's going to be tough titty."

The public announcement of the forthcoming peace negotiations occurred on December 30. It came none too soon.[26] On December 31 the House Democratic caucus voted 154–76 to cut off all funds for the Vietnam War if Hanoi agreed to release the POWs. On that same day, the Senate Democratic caucus voted by 36–12 on a similar measure. But it was not only the Democrats who were throwing up obstacles. Republican loyalist Senator William Saxbe of Ohio, whose son had served in Vietnam, stated, "I have followed President Nixon through all of his convulsions and specious arguments, but he appears to have lost his senses on this."[27]

Meanwhile Watergate woes were mounting. The plane crash that killed Dorothy Hunt had created greater restlessness among the Watergate defendants, whose trial was about to begin in federal court. Hunt himself seemed on the verge of a breakdown and through his lawyer was upping his demand for money and reassurance. John Dean, the president's lawyer, was continuing his effort to insure the defendants' silence. But there were no guarantees his arrangements would hold.

On January 3, Haldeman explained to Nixon that there was more to Special Counsel Chuck Colson's involvement in Watergate than he had previously realized. Along with John Mitchell, chairman of the Committee to Re-elect the President, and his deputy John Stuart Magruder, Colson had falsely claimed to the FBI under oath that they were ignorant of the plan to bug the Democratic headquarters. By so doing they had opened up the possibility of perjury charges.[28]

Thus, in the days leading up to Kissinger's climactic negotiations in Paris, Nixon was distracted by the drama unfolding in Judge Sirica's courtroom. At first glance the contrast could not have been more extreme: the settlement of a war that had disrupted the lives of millions of people, and the criminal disposition of a failed burglary carried out by seven inept men. Yet it was the latter that posed the greatest threat to Nixon's presidency.[29]

Many of these Watergate troubles were linked to the Vietnam War. The creation of "the plumbers" had been largely inspired by the desire to suppress antiwar criticism. Yet apart from the particulars, there was something deeper at work because the secretiveness and lies, which had been a feature of previous administrations, had assumed epic proportions. To a degree that the American public or members of Congress could scarcely imagine, the ordinary processes of national security decision-making had been torn loose from any institutional moorings.

Richard Nixon's White House had become a claustrophobic place in which illusions flourished and moral boundaries disappeared. The "old Nixon" might well have approved the "dirty tricks" of the plumbers, but the cover-up of Watergate —the suborning of perjury, the bribery of witnesses, the money laundering, the intimidation of the FBI and CIA—together signified a different level of criminality.

Despite his expressed excitement about "a cave," Kissinger en route to Paris was unsure what he might encounter. One source of uncertainty was the role of the Russians and Chinese. For more than a year he had been counting on these communist superpowers to help the United States extricate itself from an embarrassing conflict. In the service of that end, Kissinger had been surprisingly forthcoming on a range of other contested issues, but in the process he had sacrificed the "credibility" of the United States and revealed American weakness.

To bring the Russians and Chinese onboard, Kissinger repeatedly hinted that all he was seeking was a "decent interval." Once the United

States withdrew from Vietnam, if sufficient time passed, Washington would not intervene if the communists took over South Vietnam. As he assured Zhou Enlai in June 1972, when fighting in the South was near its peak:

> . . . from the time we came into office, we have attempted to end the war. And we have understood . . . that the Democratic Republic of Vietnam is a permanent factor on the Indochinese peninsula and probably the strongest entity. And we have had no interest in destroying it or even defeating it. After the end of the war, we will have withdrawn 12,000 miles. The Democratic Republic will still be 300 miles from Saigon. That is a reality which they don't seem to understand.[30]

Whether or not this reassurance was convincing, Moscow and Beijing were disposed to assist the United States in its quandary. Both eagerly sought improved relations with Washington and considered the ongoing Vietnam War to be an impediment to significant progress. However, their rivalry with each other for leadership in the communist world constrained both.[31] The practical result was that while officials from both nations increasingly counseled the North Vietnamese leadership to make a peace agreement, they notably refrained from using their most effective tool: the withdrawal of aid. Indeed, throughout 1972 the stream of economic and military assistance from the Soviet Union and China increased.[32]

The shocking commencement of Linebacker II altered the rhetoric from the communist superpowers. With B-52s filling the skies over Hanoi and Haiphong, the Chinese and Soviet governments could hardly avoid denouncing the Americans. From the Chinese Foreign Ministry came an angry statement:

> This act of aggression on the part of the United States is not only a new barbarous crime against the Vietnamese people but also a provocation to the American people and to the people of the whole world. Now the whole world can see clearly that it is the United States and not the Vietnamese side that has gone back on its commitment. . . .[33]

The Chinese people, it affirmed, "will . . . resolutely perform their internationalist duty and give all out support and assistance to the Vietnamese people in their war against US aggression."

Speaking in Moscow on the 50th anniversary of the Russian revolution, Leonid Brezhnev issued a similar condemnation:

> It is clear to everyone by now that the United States military adventure in Vietnam has failed. And no new outrages can break the will of the heroic people of Vietnam or shake the determination of their friends to give them every possible support and aid in their just struggle of liberation.[34]

Yet these remarks were coming in the wake of a cordial Nixon letter, expressing enthusiasm for a future "high point" in the coming year when the Russian leader would be paying a visit to the United States.[35]

Despite their blistering critique, neither the Soviets nor the Chinese were prepared to scrap their improved relationship with the Nixon administration, regardless of events in Vietnam.[36] Nor would they alter their advice to the North Vietnamese. On December 29 Madame Binh passed through Beijing on her way to Hanoi, as she had done on many previous occasions. This time she was honored with a tumultuous rally in Tiananmen Square and a banquet the following evening attended by Zhou Enlai and other top officials.[37]However, during this visit the "venerated" and "beloved" Chairman Mao also urged a rapid negotiated settlement. They might all be "the same family," but if there was success in Paris, the North's relation to the Americans could be "normalized."[38] In a similar vein, Zhou Enlai recommended to Le Duc Tho that he make a deal and "let the Americans leave." In six months or a year, the situation would change.

Behind a cordial veneer, the North Vietnamese bitterly resented the willingness of China and the Soviet Union to play into Nixon's hands. However, irrespective of this outside pressure, the previous summer the leadership of North Vietnam seemed to have concluded on its own that it was time to make peace. The Easter offensive had produced mixed results, with significant gains of territory but immense losses in personnel and weaponry. Once it was clear that a peace agreement with the Americans would allow thousands of their soldiers to remain in the South with cadres administering these areas, the case for settling had tipped. This did not mean they would accept any language the Americans put forward, as they had demonstrated when Kissinger seemed to set aside the October agreement.

As intended, the Christmas bombing had exacted a steep price. By December 29 when the American attack ceased, its planes had flown 3,420 bombing and support sorties over North Vietnamese cities, of which 795 were strikes by B-52 bombers.[39] Though described as an attack on military targets, by bombing industrial plants, railroad yards, electrical power stations, bridges, and radio facilities in heavily populated cities, Linebacker II had inevitably harmed civilians. The estimated death toll was 2,196 civilians killed and perhaps another 1,557 wounded. These numbers would have been even greater had the North Vietnamese authorities not ordered an evacuation of hundreds of thousands of children and adults just prior to the attack.

However, the viciousness of Linebacker II had also increased domestic pressure for a rapid peace settlement and a complete US withdrawal.[40] Once again the challenge for Kissinger in Paris was twofold: could he coax the North Vietnamese to provide language that would enable him to claim that South Vietnamese security concerns had been met? And would Saigon embrace whatever changes he was able to accomplish, enabling him to declare "peace with honor"?

The signals from Saigon were unfavorable. Prior to his departure, Kissinger had received word that the Thieu government intended to dispatch legislators to Washington to rally members of Congress against the impending deal. This had resulted in an explosive encounter with the South Vietnamese ambassador, Tran Kim Phuong:[41] this news "had managed to enrage the President almost beyond belief," Kissinger claimed. Wasn't it clear that the only reason congressional funds for South Vietnam had not been cut was "because of White House efforts"? The administration had been trying "to build up President Thieu, not take him down." These disastrous leaks about himself and others were intolerable. "If there are more stories—no matter who inspires them—against the White House, we will start attacking. The party is over. We have taken everything we are going to take."

Ambassador Phuong responded lamely that he personally felt "the presence of North Vietnamese troops is very important." Kissinger replied that he raised this subject in the negotiations for three months, forgoing the opportunity for a much earlier settlement. But this was where they had ended up. He shared Saigon's hostility and distrust of Hanoi: "They are a bunch of SOBS. They are the worst I have ever met. It is a pleasure to bomb them." But right now, South Vietnam's fate rested on a continuation of American economic and military aid. The ambassador should take a hard look at the sentiments of the American press and members of Congress. If the Nixon administration failed to reach a deal, or South Vietnam refused to sign, the promised American aid would go up in smoke.

Against this tense backdrop, Kissinger arrived in Paris on January 8. During the first session, Le Duc Tho launched the expected critique:

> Under the pretext of interrupted negotiations, you resumed the bombing of North Vietnam, just at the moment that I reached home. . . . Your action I can say is flagrant and gross. You thought that by doing so, you could submit us. You were mistaken . . . . You and no one else stained the honor of the United States.[42]

In this setting, Kissinger could not claim, as he did back home, that the North Vietnamese had walked out on the negotiations. In justifying the Christmas bombing, he replied more accurately that their December behavior in the peace talks had led Washington to believe that they were deliberately delaying a settlement.

With recriminations out of the way, the two sides readily agreed that the peace agreement was almost finished, and all that remained were two contentious issues: the status of the DMZ and the procedure for signing the completed document. With both Kissinger and Le Duc Tho driving for an agreement, these items were resolved within a day. On the DMZ, the relevant provision now read: "North and South Vietnam shall respect the Demilitarized Zone on either side of the Provisional Military Demarcation Line. Among the questions to be negotiated are the modalities of civilian movement across the Provisional Military Demarcation Line." On the surface, this wording came closer to South Vietnamese concerns by seeming to exclude the possibility of military crossings of the DMZ. Yet as a practical matter, the North Vietnamese military controlled much of the area south of the line in Quang Tri province, which made the provision less meaningful than it appeared.

As for the signing procedure, the contested point was that the South Vietnamese did not want to approve a peace agreement that specifically mentioned the PRG. To circumvent this problem, Kissinger and Le Duc Tho dropped specific references in the text to the PRG, substituting the phrase "the two Vietnamese parties." This would enable all four entities to sign the main document, while the preamble, which mentioned the Provisional Revolutionary Government, would be approved by the United States and North Vietnam exclusively.

By January 9, the main outlines of the agreement had been settled. Its chief features resembled the October deal: a ceasefire in place to be monitored by an international control commission; the United States to stop all bombing and mining of territorial waters; the withdrawal of all foreign troops from South Vietnam; the return of all foreign military prisoners of war; and the establishment of the (now officially named) National Council of National Reconciliation and Concord to organize the election of a new South Vietnamese government and implement the peace agreement.

By that evening, Kissinger felt sufficiently confident of their progress to cable Nixon. "We celebrated the President's birthday today, by making a major breakthrough in the negotiations."[43] All outstanding questions in the text had been "settled," plus "a constructive beginning on the associated understandings." It was "the President's firmness" he explained, that had brought them to this promising place, and the North Vietnamese awareness that he would "not be affected by congressional or public pressure." In fact, the opposite was true. The North Vietnamese diplomat had often invoked the congressional and political pressure on the White House as a way of highlighting the weakness of its position. But Nixon always liked to hear that his "tough" stance had cowed an adversary.

With the end nearly in sight, on January 12 Kissinger was visited by the South Vietnamese foreign minister Tran Van Lam, and two former officials, Bui Diem and Tran Van Do, who were most recently in Washington. While acknowledging the pressure for peace in the United States, they contended that as a defender of the "free world," South Vietnam deserved Kissinger's help in obtaining some North Vietnamese concession on troop withdrawal.

Not possible, Kissinger replied:

> We can't play games with you. We have to decide . . . We have come here three times under difficult circumstances—bombed Hanoi—and made an effort to get the maximum concessions. My sincere conviction is that we can't get more within the time frame.

There was going to be an agreement. And sometime in the coming days, President Thieu would have to make his decision. Once the document was complete, the official announcement would be briefly delayed to allow for consultation. But if in the end Saigon chose to withhold its signature, the congressional "doves" would feel vindicated and the chances for ongoing assistance would evaporate.

The next day, Kissinger flew from Paris to Nixon's holiday location in Key Biscayne, stopping in Washington to pick up Haig. He was bringing with him the details of the peace agreement he had finally reached with the North Vietnamese. The two sides had also hammered out a tentative schedule for an announcement of the accord, the implementation of a country-wide bombing halt, and the official signing ceremony in Paris. If this schedule proved viable, it would allow Nixon to proclaim peace in Vietnam on the eve of his January 20 inauguration.

Despite the uncertainty surrounding South Vietnam, both Nixon and Kissinger recognized that they had reached a milestone. It had taken the entire four years, but American troops and prisoners of war would be coming home. And they could now assure the public that they had brought peace to Vietnam. In a rare emotional exchange, described by Nixon:

> I walked out to the car with him and I told him that the country was indebted to him for what he had done. It is not really a comfortable feeling for me to praise people so openly. I prefer to do it a little more discreetly. On the other hand, Henry expects it, and it is good that I did so. He in turn responded that without me having the, as he put it, courage to make the difficult decision of December 18, we would not be where we are today.[44]

Kissinger also experienced the weight of this moment: "I felt that night an odd tenderness toward him. He had seen our country through perilous times. He had reached his decisions by arcane processes. But he had honored me by his trust and at the end of the day he had sought to sustain our country's strength and dignity as he saw it."[45]

Such sentiments reflected their joint sense of embattlement, even victimhood—as well as their emotional disconnection from the multiple tragedies their policy choices had created. For Nixon and Kissinger, the "Christmas bombing" had been a heroic ordeal displaying their willingness to sustain 10 days of intense national and international criticism in pursuit of a national goal. Missing from their reflections was concern for the pilots or for terrified people who were experiencing the impact of this fleet of B-52s. What mattered was the demonstration of American power and the appearance of victory regardless of the situation on the ground. And in the end, through their own willful blindness, they chose to ignore something they had known since Lam Son 719: absent American support, the South Vietnamese army was incapable of fighting effectively against their Northern enemy.

Meanwhile they were relying on Haig, who was again dispatched to Saigon to sell the peace agreement to the South Vietnamese. Claiming that Kissinger had negotiated important changes to the October accord, Haig made it plain that this time President Nixon was determined to sign it with no changes.[46] It was hoped that President Thieu would be willing to agree, in which case the administration would respond "violently" should the enemy violate its terms. But if the South Vietnamese government refused, then the United States would sign a separate accord with Hanoi and cease all military and economic assistance to Saigon.

As he listened to Haig's presentation, Thieu was "emotional and extremely despondent." He offered a host of objections, including the most troubling item: "the agreement provides for no more than a ceasefire and leaves unanswered provisions for the withdrawal of 300,000 enemy troops in the South. As long as troops are in South Vietnam, it is impossible to implement the political formula." Over the course of two long meetings, the displeasure of the South Vietnamese officials was plainly manifest and could not be assuaged by Haig's rationalizations.[47] Thieu handed the General a letter for President Nixon that reiterated his disapproval, citing the failure to address "basic vital issues," namely the continued presence of North Vietnamese troops after the ceasefire and "the pretentions of the Communists to establish a government parallel to the GVN in SVN."

Despite these complaints, Haig thought the South Vietnamese government was getting ready to sign. The cost of refusal was simply too high. If that was the case, then Nixon wondered why Thieu had written the letter. Kissinger claimed it was predictable:

> This son of a bitch is now building a record to prove that he was raped. So that when his own domestic opposition afterwards accuses him of selling out, which they will those irresponsible guys, he will then be able to say he fought until the last minute . . . .

Following Haig, Kissinger was confident that by inauguration day the South Vietnamese government would opt for peace. However, Nixon was anxious about appearances. "If he pulls back now, it's going to make us look so goddamned dumb," he fretted.

Kissinger insisted they had no reason for alarm. Thieu was going to accept, but he was doing so "in his tortuous, crooked, complicated, devious way." With his inauguration day looming, Nixon was compulsively monitoring the news from Saigon, distressed by reports that Thieu was trying to delay the signing of the peace agreement for three or four days.[48] Why? "I'm afraid he can't face it because he can't face peace," Kissinger replied. "I think the problem is that none of these military guys there can really face the problem of any free electoral process." After four years of public claims that the United States was defending democracy in South Vietnam, it was a revealing observation.

In the lead-up to his inauguration there was no mistaking Nixon's uncharacteristic edginess and fear of calamity. Some of his agitation was likely driven by the other unfolding drama: the Watergate trial. By now the story had become front page news, with increasing questions being loudly posed: Why were five Watergate defendants pleading guilty? Who had sent them on their mission? What was the source of the money paying for their lawyers and other expenses? These inquiries were coming ever closer to Nixon's personal circle.

Growing tighter as well were the linkages between "national security" matters and electoral skullduggery. Underneath the particulars was the toxic atmosphere of the White House and its autocratic habits. The concentration of decision-making in the hands of a few, the demonization of alternative voices inside and outside the administration, the blanket of secrecy and the normalization of lying—each contributed to the simmering scandal of Watergate. At the commencement of a second term, Nixon faced a double exposure of his domestic crimes and the poor results of his Vietnam policy.

As for the latter, both he and Kissinger fluctuated between realism and self-deception, alternately aware of the fragility of the peace agreement and in denial about its pitfalls. Unfortunately for Nixon, the delays in Saigon limited his ability to claim diplomatic success on his second inauguration day. In advance of his speech, Kissinger had also cautioned Nixon to limit his claims.[49] If he referred to the Paris negotiations, he should not "nail" himself to the phrase "lasting peace . . . because this thing is almost certain to blow up sooner or later." This was no hindrance. Throughout his four years, the president had been a master of inspirational messages regardless of circumstance.

On a gray, blustery morning, Nixon placed his hand on the Bible, opened to a passage in Isaiah: "They shall beat their swords into plowshares, and their spears into pruning hooks; nation shall not lift up sword against nation, neither shall they learn war anymore." And then, his uplifting rhetoric: "We stand on the threshold of a new era of peace in the world." In harmony with others, "let us continue to bring down the walls of hostility which have divided the world for too long, and to build in their place bridges of understanding." It was his earnest hope that "despite profound differences between systems of government, the people of the world can be friends."

Away from the Capital steps where Nixon was taking his oath, the streets of Washington were filled with thousands of antiwar protestors, far more than had appeared four years earlier. Whatever was occurring in Paris, this outpouring of people, estimated by Park police at 60,000, reflected the moral shock created by the Christmas bombing along with years of disappointed hopes.[50] "Richard Nixon's secret plan for peace killed my son and 25,300 GIs in Vietnam," read one sign. Unappreciated by many demonstrators was the fact that years of antiwar activity, public disillusion, and congressional resistance had forced the steady removal of American troops from Vietnam and was compelling the president to promote a peace agreement deemed lethal by his South Vietnamese ally.

Henry Kissinger arrived in Paris on January 21, planning to initial the peace agreement with or without Saigon's consent. Thieu had slight room for maneuver. Nixon had made it clear that if by noon of that day the South Vietnamese government had not signaled its concurrence, he would drop any request to Congress for additional aid. Faced with this threat, the South Vietnamese leader had no choice but to go along.[51] However, in meeting with his cabinet, his presentation was bleak:

> The United States leaves us without any alternative. . . . Kissinger treats both Vietnams as adversaries. He considers himself an outsider in these negotiations and does not distinguish between South Vietnam, as an ally, and North Vietnam, as an enemy. The Americans let the war become their war; when they liked the war, they carried it forward. When they want to stop it, they impose on both sides to stop it . . . .[52]

As a description of Kissinger's attitude, Thieu was not wide of the mark. Since Lam Son 719, Kissinger's contempt for the Saigon regime was never far from the surface. His hostility had only increased after its government blew up his October deal. Underpinning this mutual ill will was the "original sin" of the war itself—an American decision to bring into existence a South Vietnamese country where none existed, and to prop it up with vast infusions of military power when it was unable to stand by itself.

After draconian negotiations, Henry Kissinger and Le Duc Tho met on January 23 to initial the "Agreement on Ending the War and Restoring Peace in Vietnam," A four-power signing was scheduled for the 27th.[53]

As prearranged, official announcements of the accord were issued in Washington and Hanoi. President Nixon requested time on national radio and television to bring the news to the American public. For the United States, there was much to celebrate. Sixty days after the ceasefire would go into effect, all American forces would be removed from South Vietnam, and within this same period the POWS would be coming home.

But what did this agreement portend for their Vietnamese ally? In his televised remarks, President Nixon falsely claimed that the settlement "meets the goals and has the full support of President Thieu and the government of the Republic of Vietnam." To their citizens, he extended his warm congratulations: "By your courage, by your sacrifice you have won the precious right to determine your own future and you have developed the strength to defend that right."[54]

To his own countrymen: "Your steadfastness in supporting our insistence on peace with honor has made peace with honor possible." He hoped everyone would understand that his reticence during the past weeks was in the service of attaining that goal. "Let us be proud that America did not settle for a peace that would have betrayed our allies, that would have abandoned our prisoners of war or that would have ended the war for us but continued the war for the 50 million people of Indochina." American soldiers had "served with honor and distinction in one of the most selfless enterprises in the history of nations." In a faint echo of the Gettysburg Address, Nixon called upon the public "to consecrate this moment by resolving . . . to make the peace we have achieved a peace that will last."

As Kissinger would later recall, at midnight "Nixon called from the Lincoln Sitting Room, where he was brooding alone. He knew that every success brings a terrific letdown. I should not let it get to me. I should not be discouraged. There were many battles yet to fight."[55] There would be such battles. But for Richard Nixon, this was his last unalloyed moment of triumph, as the daily drip of Watergate was slowly eroding his presidency.

Adding to his consternation was the fact that Henry Kissinger was emerging as the hero of the hour. Kissinger had returned from Paris to the accolades of the Washington elite and his admirers around the country. With his instinct for self-promotion, he had conveyed the impression of an agonized, reluctant warrior, creatively seeking peaceful solutions, a mission that had now come to fruition with the ending of America's longest war.

It was maddening, this public adulation of his national security advisor. At his briefings with the press and subsequent testimony before both houses of Congress, Kissinger was being greeted with standing ovations. Yet for all Nixon's grumbling about his subordinate's glory-seeking, he was nevertheless doing essential work for the president, which was to disseminate in a convincing manner the false account of what had transpired in Paris.

The most preposterous "cover-up" was the claim that this peace agreement had been done in harmony with the government of South Vietnam. Also fake was the contention by Nixon and Kissinger that the Paris agreement was a bona fide plan for peace and reconciliation. Neither man believed that the fighting between North and South was permanently ended. There was no prospect that the South Vietnamese government would coexist peacefully with the North Vietnamese army and a PRG administration inside their territory. Nor did Nixon or Kissinger think that Hanoi would passively await the result of elections under the auspices of the Thieu government.

Although reluctant to admit it, even to themselves, for Nixon and Kissinger the Paris Peace Agreement was never about "peace." It was about getting US prisoners home, withdrawing the troops, and establishing interim processes that could persuade domestic adversaries that their pursuit of the war, with its attendant sacrifice of blood and treasure, had yielded something positive. In Hanoi, people were dancing in the streets,[56] believing their excruciating ordeal might be finally over. In Saigon the mood was somber.[57] On Kissinger's staff, the head of his Vietnam team John Negroponte was sure this peace agreement was a sham.[58] From the other side of the political spectrum, many cynical peace activists refused to believe that the American Vietnam War was truly over.

27

"Let the Americans See Me"

America's Indochina war did not end on January 27, 1973. Once a bombing halt was instituted for Vietnam itself, the White House directed that the B-52s and fighter jets be instructed to strike targets in Laos and Cambodia. Bombing of these places had been ongoing, but during 1972 the priority had been North Vietnam. With the cessation of bombing there, hundreds of planes became available for this purpose. Border areas were the natural targets, but given the surplus of planes available, locations in the interior were also fair game—provided "we can shut up the military briefing officers out there," said Kissinger.[1]

Although on his way out as Secretary of Defense, Laird tried to limit the number of planes that could be used in Laos and Cambodia and to maintain restrictions on target selection so as to minimize the danger to civilians. This was consistent with the extraordinary role he had played during the previous four years. Whether Laird believed in the necessity of the American war in Vietnam was unclear, but he had relentlessly sought to limit its scope. His commitment to reducing the American troop presence was unwavering.[2] For most of the contemplated escalations, he attempted to apply the brakes. On some of these—notably Linebacker I and II—his advice had been ignored. But his constant pressure for troop reductions had yielded a more satisfactory result. With each increment of troop withdrawals the American ability to wage an effective war was reduced.

Yet through it all, Secretary Laird remained a consummate insider. He never went public with his objections, nor did he accurately inform Congress of his point of view. When required to speak with the press or congressional committees, he was stalwart in defense of administration policy. As an exercise in morality it was a fateful choice. His intervention had saved hundreds, perhaps thousands of American lives.[3] Yet, given the reservoir of respect and goodwill he enjoyed on Capitol Hill, a more candid statement of his objections might have affected decisions there.

But this was not his way. Laird remained to the last a "team player," perhaps the only dissenter to have remained on amicable terms with both Nixon and Kissinger. Before leaving, he warned Kissinger about the danger of overselling the peace agreement. It was possible that fighting would cease for the next six to ten months; however, "they'll be fighting again" and the administration should not pretend otherwise. Kissinger understood this.

Despite fulsome praise of Laird's patriotism and loyalty, Nixon and Kissinger moved swiftly to eliminate his influence and avoid future problems. Laird's successor was Elliot Richardson, who seemed more pliable. But just to be sure, they reduced the high-ranking personnel in his office, and instructed him to coordinate more closely with NSC staff and "meet frequently with Henry." On Vietnam matters, he was encouraged to rely on General Haig, the newly appointed Deputy Chief of Staff of the Army, instead of his boss Creighton Abrams, who was "no good at Army." He was also informed that the president would be meeting periodically with the chairman of the Joint Chiefs of Staff without Richardson present.[4]

The goal was to centralize even more power in the White House. Even without these changes, the internal practices of the Nixon administration had become twisted and dangerous. As the Pentagon Papers had made clear, the habit of misleading the American public and lying to Congress was hardly a new development. Indeed, secrecy and deception had been the hallmark of US policy in Vietnam for more than a decade before Richard Nixon took office. However, the newer development in his administration was the warping of the internal institutions responsible for "national security," with the accompanying degradation of individuals charged with the task. Whether it was the Secretary of State, a bevy of ambassadors, CIA area specialists, American military officers, or arms controllers, Nixon and Kissinger bypassed and deceived them all. For that small circle of people surrounding the president, the breach of procedural norms had become a way of life. As the cover-up of Watergate slowly peeled away, there was a tendency among observers to differentiate this sordid tale of domestic misdeeds from the more prestigious management of "national security." Yet when it came to internal processes, it was a distinction without a difference.

Among the negative consequences of Nixon's and Kissinger's deceptiveness was the forfeit of specialized knowledge as well as necessary information. The less recognized effect was to twist policy priorities in an irrational direction. "Credibility" had been the magic word that made local interventions seem essential and that quieted the moral reservations of those employed by the "national security state." Yet, as their wooing of China and Russia intensified, that rationale for killing people in Vietnam, Cambodia, and Laos was ever more tenuous. And under that rubric, Nixon and Kissinger had quietly inverted means and ends. To establish their personal "credibility" with the American public, they had chosen to woo the communist superpowers while seeking a freer hand in Indochina and elsewhere.

Nixon's opening to China had proved unexpectedly popular with the American public. After years of war, any measure that seemed to reduce the prospect of violence in the world was inherently attractive. Added to this was the excitement of something genuinely new—through the medium of television, people were gaining their first look at a society that to an American audience had been invisible for two decades. The narrower aims of Kissinger and Nixon were scarcely visible.

With the signing of the Paris peace agreement, Kissinger was eager to return to China. He had found the interactions with Zhou Enlai personally exciting in contrast to the more prosaic individuals surrounding the president, or the didactic toughness of the North Vietnamese. Here at last was an intellectual peer, a witty, knowledgeable person who might fare well at Harvard and whose revolutionary background added drama to their interaction.

Kissinger also had serious business to transact. Although Hanoi had finally signed a peace agreement and seemed likely to release the POWs on schedule, there was no guarantee that it would observe the ceasefire beyond the period when all US troops withdrew. Also in limbo was the situation in Laos and Cambodia, places where Chinese cooperation could be helpful. And there was one other incentive: President Nixon wanted to visit China one more time.[5] The trip had been a high point of his embattled first term, and he was eager to repeat it.

As Kissinger prepared for his own trip, Nixon perceived a potential snag: "what the hell we do on Taiwan . . . they might call in our bargaining chip on that." The "bargaining chip" he had in mind was Kissinger's repeated suggestion to Zhou Enlai that once the Vietnam War was over, the United States would begin a process of withdrawing all its military forces from Taiwan. Not the least of the ironies here was Kissinger's repeated insistence in various contexts that because the United States could not afford to "betray an ally," it needed to keep fighting in Vietnam. Yet the more serious act of betrayal was this promise to Beijing. For the immediate future, Kissinger thought the matter could be finessed with the removal of half of the approximately 9,000 US military personnel from Taiwan, citing the end of the Vietnam War.

This left unsettled the question of "normalizing" relations between the United States and the People's Republic. To Kissinger's happy surprise, his

Chinese hosts were flexible on this matter. In advance of US recognition, they were willing to open liaison offices, one in Washington DC and the other in Beijing, to facilitate more regular communication. For the Chinese the greater concern was American relations with the Soviet Union. Aware that another US–Soviet summit was scheduled for later that spring, their priority was to enlist the Nixon administration for their anti-Russian ("anti-hegemonic") agenda. It was perhaps for this purpose that Kissinger was treated to a rare two-hour interview with Chairman Mao.

"I don't look bad, but God has sent me an invitation," the Chinese leader began disarmingly."[6] So we are two enemies," he continued. "Two former enemies," Kissinger corrected. "I have told the Prime Minister that we speak to no other country as frankly and as openly as we do to you." Alluding to Vietnam, Mao extended a compliment: "Your business was done well. You've been flying everywhere. Are you a swallow or a pigeon? And the Vietnamese issue can be counted as basically settled." Kissinger concurred, while emphasizing the necessity for a "transitional period toward tranquility."

Fortunately, he added, the United States and China both faced "the same danger," and while their methods might differ from time to time, it was "for the same objectives." That was the important thing, Mao reflected: "We would not harm you nor would you harm us and we can work together to commonly deal with a bastard." Sometimes they would have to criticize each other for ideological reasons: "You say, away with your communists. We say, away with you imperialists. Sometimes we say things like that." But this was no obstacle to cooperation.

Halfway into their meeting, Mao observed that Kissinger's voice was very hoarse. "Why do you want to continue to talk so much?" In a stunningly sycophantic answer, the American replied:

> Because it is very important that you and we understand what we are going to do and to coordinate our actions, and therefore we always tell the Prime Minister what our plans are in various areas of the world so that you can understand the individual moves when they are made.

Given this abject stance, Mao offered some friendly advice on dealings with the Japanese. On this Asian tour, Kissinger had only scheduled one day in Tokyo, which perhaps caused them to lose face. For the future, the American should be more solicitous of their feelings "and talk a bit more with them."

Seemingly oblivious to this paternalistic tone, Kissinger was anxious to demonstrate American reliability. He sought to clarify for Mao that while the Nixon administration at times used "complicated methods because of our domestic situation," with regard to "our fundamental objectives we will act very decisively and without regard to public opinion." If any "hegemonial intentions became active," the United States would be firm in response. Perhaps the Americans and Europeans would be happy to see the Soviets and Chinese fighting one another, Mao speculated. "What Europe thinks, I am not able to judge," replied Kissinger. "They cannot do anything anyway. They are basically irrelevant." But Washington was clear-sighted enough to recognize that if the Russians managed to "overrun China," it would negatively affect the security of all other countries.

But what action would the US government undertake in that eventuality? After all, Mao laughingly asked, "since being bogged down in Vietnam you met so many difficulties, do you think they (American people) would feel good if they were bogged down in China?" With this sardonic inquiry, Mao was reflecting the absurdity of the Nixon administration's claim that by showing strength in Vietnam they were demonstrating American "credibility" to the rest of the world. It did not require the shrewdness of Mao for outside observers to reach the opposite conclusion—that the Vietnam War had revealed the weakness and limitations of American power.

For most of his time in China, Kissinger was primarily engaged in talks with Zhou, whom he was eager to convince of his anti-Soviet convictions. It might appear that the Americans had been taken in by the Russians and were genuinely committed to détente. But as Zhou surely knew, the Nixon administration "had a very difficult period domestically" because of the Vietnam War. It therefore needed "to rally our own people by some conspicuous successes in foreign policy, to establish a reputation for thoughtful action." And they had also needed to end the war under conditions that did not appear as "an American disgrace." However, assuming the situation in Indochina did not become "a constant source of conflict" and that the Paris agreement was sustained, the administration could turn back to "the more fundamental problems" of US foreign policy—namely resistance to Soviet "hegemonic" schemes.

Much depended on the behavior of North Vietnam, he continued. In his estimation, the DRV had two choices: "It can either use the agreement as an offensive weapon in the short term and constantly use it to undermine the existing structure, or it can use it in the long-term . . . in which the situation is tranquil for a period." If Hanoi chose the second route, "we will cooperate with them," but if they took the first then the United States must resist. "So they have to be patient." Implicit in these remarks was Kissinger's questionable assumption that the Chinese government could play a significant role in determining Hanoi's decision.

On his return to Washington, Kissinger gave Nixon an exuberant report of his experience. During this Chinese visit he found himself "in the extraordinary situation that with the exception of the United Kingdom, the PRC might well be closest to us in its global perceptions."[7] Most remarkable were its leaders Mao and Zhou. "No other world leaders have the sweep and imagination" of these two men, "nor the capacity and will to pursue long-range policy." Despite differences in ideology between the United States and China, "the objective factors induce tacit cooperation for at least several years."

"Peking has chosen normalization because of our strength," Kissinger claimed. It was because Nixon had insisted on "a responsible world role" and displayed a willingness to take strong measures that the Chinese leadership perceived the United States as a "useful counter-weight" to the Soviet threat. "We have come a long way," Kissinger claimed. Paying his usual homage to Nixon, he thought the "watershed" was the president's talks with Mao and Zhou "when you stamped your personal imprint on our course." By sharing his worldview, Nixon had made a deep impression on the two men.

Of course, Vietnam had prevented the relationship from coming to full fruition. "But on this trip the floodgates opened." The two Chinese leaders felt free to share their profound concern about Soviet intentions, and "rather than being scolded for our global presence" the United States was being faulted for doing too little. Whether it was arming other countries, maintaining its own superior military, or strengthening ties with allies, the Chinese were encouraging American assertiveness.

In a separate memorandum Kissinger was at pains to describe his extraordinary interview with Mao. The Chairman seemed in better health than previously. He spoke with great animation and coherence, "while demonstrating a quick and earthy sense of humor." He remained a physically impressive person:

> "One thinks of him as being large rather than fat. He radiates authority and deep wisdom, and Zhou—as in your meeting—was deferential. There is no question who is boss."[8]

Of course part of that wisdom, as rendered by Kissinger, was that Mao placed their conversation "in the framework of his talk with you." Indeed, on several occasions, "he referred specifically to points you had made." As for Vietnam, Mao thought that the Nixon administration had done "good work" by ending it, and he agreed with Kissinger's observation that "We needed now a transitional period of tranquility." And as it turned out the PRC "only goes through the motions of ideology." Mao liked us, and not our communist party; and he also liked Pompidou, and not the French communist party. Kissinger had left the session "even more impressed by the grandeur of the Chairman this time than last." One could easily imagine "the power and intelligence of this man in his prime."

As a matter of personal psychology, Kissinger's sophomoric response to the Chinese leadership could be viewed as humorous if people were not dying in the name of anticommunism. By 1972 the Cold War orthodoxy, which had initially secured public consent for the Vietnam War, had ceased to preoccupy the White House. While there was ongoing competition with the Soviet Union for military and geopolitical advantage, this was at a great remove from an earlier time when fears of an international communist conspiracy bent on world conquest had dominated foreign policy discussion.

As of February 1973, the president and his national security advisor were in a relatively benign period with regard to both the Russians and the Chinese, believing they had been moderately helpful in their negotiations with Hanoi. During these amiable weeks, Kissinger had taken Ambassador Dobrynin to dinner with Frank Sinatra. Tricia Nixon and her husband Edward Cox had been treated warmly on their recent trip to the Soviet Union. And most important, Nixon and Kissinger were anticipating a productive summit conference when Leonid Brezhnev visited in the spring. Already in process were new agreements to be signed.

Given these conditions and the recent conclusion of the Paris peace agreement, the opportunity for the United States to stop the killing was ripe. But instead, the killing continued thanks to the president's decision to redirect planes that had been used against North Vietnam to Laos and Cambodia, where they continued to do great damage.

Among its weaknesses, the Paris agreement was ambiguous in relation to both Laos and Cambodia. Under Article 20, the signers had recognized the "independence, sovereignty, unity, and territorial integrity" of these nations and the obligation to "totally withdraw" their troops, military advisors, armaments, and other war material. However, no specific timeline had been prescribed, nor was there provision of any enforcement machinery. Through that loophole, the war was continuing.

During the negotiations Le Duc Tho had indicated that within 15 days of the signing the fighting in Laos would be stopped and a peace accord reached.[9] However, the task of peace-making between the Pathet Lao and the Royal Laotian Government proved more complicated than anticipated, exceeding the 15 days suggested by Le Duc Tho. Although the bargain was clearly imminent, the Nixon administration used the delay to increase the bombing along the Ho Chi Minh Trail and in northern Laos. For the interval between January 27 and February 22 when an agreement was reached, the American air strikes totaled 8,900 sorties or 350 strikes a day. By this time, Laos had the distinction of making it per capita the most heavily bombed nation in history.[10] One-tenth of the population had already died, hundreds of thousands had become refugees, entire villages had disappeared—but for the Nixon administration, the opportunity to use this period for additional air strikes had been irresistible.

In Cambodia, the already tragic situation was about to become much worse. In his talks with the Cabinet and members of Congress, Kissinger had acknowledged that the situation there was more difficult to resolve because of the fragmented nature of the opposition. Nevertheless, there were "understandings" with Hanoi, which led him to expect that a de facto ceasefire "will come into being over a period of time relevant to the execution of this agreement."

Before taking further action, Kissinger urged Lon Nol to demonstrate good faith by declaring a three-day cessation of hostilities with an offer to continue it if the enemy would make peace. However, fighting quickly resumed with no resolution in sight. It was not even clear who the negotiating partner should be. One possibility was to engage Prince Sihanouk, who as leader of the Royal Khmer National Union remained the nominal head of the opposition forces. Yet so toxic was his relationship with Lon Nol that neither man seemed open to discussion. Nor did Kissinger favor this option.[11]

The most relevant adversary was the Khmer Rouge. As they had promised Kissinger, the North Vietnamese had tried to pressure its leaders to attempt a deal. However, during the previous two years the organization had grown larger (from 3,000 to perhaps 50,000) and more militant.[12] To some of their leaders, Hanoi's willingness to bargain with the Americans was a sign of weakness or even treachery, a manifestation of Vietnamese chauvinism.[13]

While both US and Cambodian officials chose to emphasize the North Vietnamese troops as the source of their problem, by 1973 it was the Khmer Rouge that had become the main enemy of the regime.[14] That posed a legal problem for the Nixon administration. As prescribed by Congress in the Cooper–Church amendment, the US military was prohibited from bombing in support of the Cabodian government except in response to a North Vietnamese aggressor. Yet that line had already been breached and by February, American air power was striking both local insurgents and the foreign troops.

The result was a six-month period mor hellish than its predecessor.[15] Under loosened American rules, much of the countryside became a virtual "free-fire zone." Caught between the advancing Khmer Rouge on the one hand and American bombers on the other, normal life for millions of Cambodians had become unsustainable.

Even before the Paris peace agreement, the situation in the Cambodia had been spiraling downward. By early 1973, the Lon Nol government had abandoned any pretense of democratic functioning and was mired in corruption. As reported by *New York Times* reporter Sydney Schanberg, a handful of people were buying fancy villas and cars, using money obtained selling weapons and drugs or by siphoning payments for "ghost soldiers" in the Cambodian army. Meanwhile "hundreds of thousands of Cambodian refugees, uprooted by the fighting and jammed into Phnom Penh often cannot afford to buy rice." Tragically, these people "live in new shantytowns, in empty railroad cars and with relatives in houses with wall-to-wall people."[16] A city that until recently had a population of 600,000 was suddenly home to 1.2 million people.

Into this troubled land came an expanded American air war. Whereas previously most US bombing occurred in the eastern zone of Cambodia adjacent to the South Vietnamese border, American planes were striking targets across the country. Outside Phnom Penh, there were reports that "no fewer than 3,000 civilians" were killed during the last three weeks of March.[17] According to United Press International, "Refugees swarming into the capital from the target areas report dozens of villages, both east and southeast of Phnom Penh, have been destroyed and as much as half their population killed or maimed in the current bombing raids."[18]

While the Americans had no monopoly on the violence in Cambodia, by 1973 there was clear evidence that the ferocity of their air war was generating new recruits for the Khmer Rouge.

This dynamic was hardly new, even if the location had changed. Ever since the United States had expanded the Vietnam War in the mid-1960s it had become evident that many civilians were terrorized by American firepower. Less visible to outsiders was the nature of the developing insurgency, with the rising influence of the most ideologically rigid and ruthless people.

Nixon and Kissinger were determined to continue, even if this involved deceiving both Congress and the American public. In April, the Senate Foreign Relations Committee dispatched two veteran observers, James Lowenstein and Richard Moose, on a fact-finding trip to Southeast Asia.[19] Their briefing by Air Force personnel in Thailand conveyed the impression of carefully selected attacks, primarily designed to halt "the movement of North Vietnamese personnel, tanks, artillery and supplies towards South Vietnam."

When they arrived in Phnom Penh, the American Embassy, under instruction from Washington, attempted to conceal the fact that it was actively coordinating the air strikes in Cambodia. Following a series of complaints, Lowenstein and Moose discovered that the embassy was not only directing the bombing but, contrary to Cooper–Church, at least 80% of these raids were in direct support of Lon Nol in his battle with the Khmer Rouge, with perhaps 20% involved in interdiction activities.

When they had left Washington Moose and Loewenstein had been under the impression that the purpose of US policy was to advance a ceasefire between the Cambodian government and its opponents. Upon arrival, however, they realized this was not the objective—if indeed it ever was. Informed observers emphasized the political and military weakness of Lon Nol's regime and the efforts by American operatives "to insure the government's survival."

This left a question: why was Lon Nol's survival an American priority? Insofar as there was a reason, according to the White House, it was to bring about a stable settlement that could strengthen such trends in the neighboring countries, presumably South Vietnam. For members of Congress, who had never signed on to a Cambodian war, the official case made little sense.

Even some airmen responsible for the bombing were expressing their distress in letters to elected officials. These messages were so poignant and powerful that they were placed in the Congressional Record by Senator Fulbright and given to the *New York Times* by Senator Kennedy, with the men's names redacted.[20]

To Fulbright:

> I write to you today with much despair in my heart. I had mulled over these words in my mind many a time but now I must sit down and bear my conscience.
>
> I am an AC-130 gunship navigator fighting the war in Cambodia on a day to day basis. I come as close as one can get to observe the conflict at hand. What I see is an absurd effort by my Commander in Chief to preserve an unpopular, corrupt, dictatorial government at any expense. We have become once again involved in a civil conflict and as a result of our involvement have escalated the death and destruction on a massive scale.
>
> I love my country and have served it faithfully for five years, but I fear my conscience can no long endure this senseless, indiscriminate bombing by B-52s and F-111s that kill and injure thousands of civilians and create hundreds of thousands of refugees. As a crew member in an AC-130 gunship I feel a terrible sense of guilt. We do not use bombs—only artillery shells over a battlefield, but we contribute to the prolongation of this meaningless, unconstitutional war. (May 4, 1973).

And to Kennedy:

> Please do not misjudge this letter as the ravings of a wild-eyed radical. I am, as my father before me, an officer of the United States Air Force.[21]
>
> Ostensibly there are no American ground troops in Cambodia and yet the bombing continues 'at the request of the Cambodian Government.' What about the American Government? Where are the American people? Where is the Congress? Congress may offer token protests but we are the ones who must subjugate our conscience and carry out the day by day business of preparing and flying the aircraft. Sixty sorties each day, over 600 tons of high explosives. Congress debates, we destroy. The American people wonder, we kill . . . (April 15, 1973)[22]

* * *

By the spring, there was a strong impetus to call a halt to this and other military involvement in Indochina, absent specific congressional approval. By an overwhelming 67–15 roll call vote on June 14, the US Senate added such an amendment to a State Department authorization bill, with over half of the Republicans voting "Aye." The following week, the House of Representatives—historically reluctant to challenge the White

House—passed their own anti-bombing measure by voice vote. After subsequent efforts to reconcile the House and Senate amendments, the House approved a final version by 240–72, the largest vote ever registered for an antiwar measure.[23]

Two days later President Nixon vetoed the appropriations bill on the grounds that the enactment of the Cambodia rider "would cripple or destroy the chances of an effective negotiated settlement in Cambodia and the withdrawal of all North Vietnamese troops."[24] The president's objections bore no relation to the realities on the ground. By now it was clear to most members of Congress that in Cambodia there was "no negotiated settlement" in sight. The regime and its military had proven to be inept, and since the Americans had deepened their involvement the internal communist danger had increased, not diminished. In making his case the president argued, as he had done so many times in the past, that a cessation of the bombing would be "a serious blow to America's international credibility . . . a blow that would be felt far beyond Indochina." Yet there were finally limits to how many times this rationale could be successfully invoked.

Nixon's objection to the "rider" notwithstanding, he still needed passage of the appropriations bill. This time Congress extracted a clear commitment, specifying that after August 15 no funds previously appropriated or provided under the continuing resolution could be used "to finance directly or indirectly combat activities" by American forces in or over Cambodia, Laos, North Vietnam, or South Vietnam.[25] This war-ending measure was long overdue, and not coincidentally it came at a point when all American ground troops were already removed. Yet it was nevertheless a significant assertion of congressional power.

Meanwhile the Nixon administration had been given six weeks' leeway for the ostensible purpose of enabling Henry Kissinger to effect a ceasefire. Yet this complex project, which might have necessitated a belated collaboration with the Chinese to bring back Sihanouk, had no prospect of success.[26]

As for these six weeks, Senator Fulbright had warned that this interval should "not be an occasion for an escalation of the bombing" and that every effort be made "to minimize damage to civilian property in Cambodia."[27] Preoccupied with Watergate matters, Nixon had left this situation to his national security advisor. While Kissinger did not encourage an escalation, neither was he inclined "to minimize" the damage. From his perspective, military activity that delayed the fall of Cambodia for even a few weeks was contributing to the stability of South Vietnam.

It was perhaps no surprise that on August 6, nine days prior to the suspension of all American air strikes, a terrible accident occurred. Because of a mishap in targeting, an American B-52 bomber dropped its payload along a one-mile strip in the center of Neak Luong, a ferry and garrison town.[28] It had struck most heavily near barracks where pro-government soldiers resided with their wives and children. In the uncanny way in which US planes seemed to hit hospitals, the local facility was badly damaged, and large sections of the town were demolished.

Sydney Schanberg, the *New York Times* reporter, encountered the victims as they were carried to the Preah Ket Mealea hospital in Phnom Penh. As he described it, "there were scenes of blood and weeping. Infants, shattered by shrapnel, lay unconscious on stretchers." Whole families had been affected. One marine corporal's five-year-old son had been killed and the rest wounded. The man was seated on the floor, holding his stomach and moaning. "I don't have anything anymore. I am finished."[29]

At the American Embassy, Colonel David Opfer was briefing the press. "The destruction was minimal," he said. As was so often the case throughout the war—whether in South Vietnam, Laos, or Cambodia, the instinct of US government officials was to downplay the destruction. Colonel Opfer suggested that Neak Luong was "essentially a small village," although 10,000 people lived in or around the town.

Making his way there, Schanberg encountered a different reality:

> A large part of the market area in the center of town is smashed flat and many of the two-story concrete shops and apartment buildings on either side are shattered and uninhabitable, with walls and roofs reduced to rubble.
>
> A third of the hospital is demolished, with the rest damaged and unusable until major repairs are made. Several patients were wounded, and some are believed killed. A bomb fell on the northeast corner of the hospital, blowing some walls down and scattering concrete, beds and cabinets.[30]

As he walked along the riverbank, the American reporter came upon a soldier "sobbing uncontrollably." Spotting Schanberg, he cried, "All my family is dead. . . . All my family is dead! Take my picture, take my picture! Let the Americans see me."

When the official count was taken, there were 400 casualties in Neak Luong: 137 killed and 268 wounded. There were nine days left to go on the

Nixon administration's request. When the time was up, Henry Kissinger had not achieved a ceasefire, nor was there any indication of an impending settlement.

* * *

While these events were transpiring, members of Congress had discovered something even more alarming than the destruction of yet another town. For 14 months, beginning in March 1969, the Nixon administration had been secretly bombing Cambodia while publicly professing neutrality in its internal conflicts.

The Armed Services Committee was shocked by the July 15 testimony of former Air Force Major Hal Knight, who as operations officer for the Strategic Air Command radar site in South Vietnam "was responsible for electronically guiding the B-52s to their targets."[31] The officer described in some detail how he had repeatedly falsified flight records to show that attacks in Cambodia had occurred in South Vietnam. Under orders from his superiors, he had burned any documents that might have contradicted this account. According to Knight, one of those officers had provided as a reason the need to keep these facts away from Senator Fulbright, a strong critic of the Vietnam War.

This was by no means a rogue operation. The bombings of Cambodia and the associated deception had been coordinated with the Eighth Air Force on Guam and with high-ranking officials connected to MACV. Although the Major could not testify to the extent of this practice, he had learned from colleagues that similar falsifications were being carried out by officers at other Strategic Air Command sites.[32] On further investigation, the Armed Services Committee had quickly ascertained that over this 14-month period there had been 3,630 unannounced bombing raids inside Cambodia.

These revelations raised a host of questions: which officials had given the order to falsify military records? And who was responsible for a policy of secret bombing raids in a neutral country without the consent of Congress or the knowledge of the American people? Ultimately those decisions rested with the president. As General Wheeler, former chairman of the Joint Chiefs of Staff subsequently testified, Nixon had repeatedly instructed him that the bombing be conducted with the tightest security measures possible.[33]

As Secretary of Defense at the time, Laird was aware of the decision to bomb Cambodia, as were Secretary of State Rogers, Director of the CIA Richard Helms, and several others. Yet none of them had chosen to make their dissent public, and nobody had encouraged the president to inform the public about extending the war to another country. To members of the Armed Services Committee, it was clear that the main culprit was Richard Nixon, who had violated the Constitution by failing to consult Congress on the question of war and peace.

It was summer in Washington, and government officials were in an angry mood. Following the damning testimony of the president's lawyer John Dean, the Watergate scandal was consuming the Capitol. There was mounting evidence that Nixon had broken several laws in orchestrating a "cover-up," and a major constitutional fight was looming over access to executive tapes and documents.[34]

For some members of Congress the newly revealed secret bombing of Cambodia loomed as large and was inextricably connected to the crimes of Watergate. The devastation of that country, the thousands of people who had died there unnecessarily, the senseless prolonging of the Vietnam War itself, were worthy of national attention. On July 31, 1973, Representative Robert Drinan, Democrat of Massachusetts, introduced a resolution calling for the impeachment of President Nixon for "high crimes and misdemeanors" based initially on these Cambodia revelations. For many of his colleagues this seemed premature, and to others less consequential than the Watergate transgressions, which were still unfolding. Yet, emerging on Capitol Hill was the slowly dawning realization that how this litany of misdeeds was remembered, or perhaps forgotten, would become the legacy for future generations.

Epilogue

"We Were Serious People!"

"Is there anything you would like to apologize for?" Brian Williams, the panel moderator posed the question to Henry Kissinger. There was a packed audience at the Kennedy Library, attending its 2006 Conference on "Vietnam and the Presidency."[1] Under the sponsorship of the National Archives, the program had been structured to minimize acrimony, with historians and policymakers scheduled for different days. However, audience members had been invited to submit questions on index cards, and some of their wartime anger seeped through.

Kissinger deemed the query "highly inappropriate" to the occasion. This had nothing to do with his "personal feelings," he explained, but with "how as a country, we look at ourselves. That serious people make serious decisions ought to be taken for granted." During the Kennedy years, he said, Harvard colleagues engaged in debate about "what was doable, what was not doable," which he had viewed as constructive. Unfortunately, subsequent discussions about Vietnam "had become about the moral quality of American leadership," which even now "is a way of dividing us, torturing ourselves." All the presidents who made decisions about Vietnam had been animated by a "noble motive."

Kissinger reminded the audience that the Nixon administration had not chosen to send 500,000 soldiers to Vietnam—that was already done. So they faced a different problem: "How do you extricate when you are the country on which the security of the world depends?" Plus, there was the practical difficulty involved "when you are surrounded by a million North Vietnamese and a million South Vietnamese, who could turn on you if you suddenly pulled the plug." The administration had done what it could to avert "catastrophe," and if in the end the war was lost, this was because of the "divisions" in the United States. As a country, it was time to face "the fact that we defeated ourselves."

The claim that the Vietnam War was lost because of domestic dissent was a familiar one, which also contained an element of truth. From the time Richard Nixon assumed the presidency, there were significant constraints on his decision-making, created by a vigorous antiwar movement, a restless Congress, and an impatient public. Their most profound effect was to force the ongoing removal of large numbers of US troops, with the result that by late 1972 there were no US combat troops left in Vietnam. For Kissinger, this policy—spearheaded by Defense Secretary Melvyn Laird under the rubric of Vietnamization—had been constantly frustrating because it reduced the incentive for the North Vietnamese to make concessions at the negotiating table.

Without this domestic opposition, it is probable that the Nixon administration would have pursued the war longer and more vigorously than it did, with even higher casualties and greater destruction. However, the dissent does not explain why the Vietnam War was lost. That outcome was rooted in factors that preceded Nixon's election: the unpopularity, weakness, and corruption of the Saigon government; the poor morale of the South Vietnamese military; the discipline and dedication of the adversary; and the indigenous nature of the insurgency. By 1969 there was little reason to believe that as a foreign power, the United States could successfully impose its ideological preferences on a people who resided 10,000 miles away.

The perplexing question is why the Nixon administration continued this endeavor for four years in the face of these negative elements? In this regard, they were continuing the puzzling pattern of the Kennedy and Johnson administrations, which had stubbornly forged ahead despite the many premonitions of failure.[2] However, in the aftermath of the 1968 Tet Offensive, the new administration had the option of terminating the war quickly and blaming the failure on its predecessors. Yet this course of action was never earnestly considered.

The ostensible motivation for these ongoing policy choices was US "credibility"—the need to demonstrate to friend and foe alike the overwhelming power and resolve of the United States. Yet by the time of Tet, if not earlier, the escalating American involvement in Southeast Asia was less a demonstration of strength than a sign to much of the world of American weakness and cruelty. This pattern did not change once Nixon assumed the office. Most remarkable in this regard was Nixon's and Kissinger's secret diplomacy with the Soviet Union and the People's Republic of China to gain their assistance in obtaining a face-saving agreement with Hanoi.

At the president's behest, Kissinger had lost no time informing the Russian ambassador of the administration's indifference to the future of Eastern Europe.[3] Any rhetoric to the contrary, he suggested, was merely a sop to certain segments of the electorate and could be safely ignored. Enticements were ongoing and varied, including concessions on arms control with Moscow and secret assurances about the future of Taiwan with Beijing. While improved relations with the Soviet Union and China was desirable for many reasons, neither Brezhnev nor Zhou Enlai could fail to see the Americans' desperation on Vietnam.

In reality, "credibility" in its various formulations was less an explanation for the administration's decisions than an excuse. Allowing for a certain dollop of self-deception, Nixon and Kissinger prolonged the war as long they did because it served their own needs and met other institutional requirements. Had it initially been possible to obtain a negotiated settlement in which all North Vietnamese troops left the South, with the Thieu government in firm control, they would have happily agreed and declared success. Since this outcome was unachievable, they continued the fighting. After one year, 10,000 US soldiers had died, narrowing their options and creating a need to justify the sacrifice.

The unwillingness to stop a futile war was partly a result of Nixon's and Kissinger's character and outlook. By temperament both men were drawn to military solutions and had reached a pinnacle of power by virtue of their "hawkish" credentials. Frustrated by what they viewed as North Vietnamese recalcitrance, they readily embraced violent initiatives. Nevertheless, from the outset their decision-making was operating within the framework of the "national security" bureaucracies they had inherited. Inside these bodies, successful careers were built on a willingness to deploy, threaten, or use the instruments of war. Although there were disagreements about the merits of specific policies, the people working within these organizations shared a reluctance to accept an American defeat, given their prior role in expanding the US military commitment.

At the end of four years, Kissinger was compelled to sign a peace agreement far different from what he and his colleagues would have preferred. As was often the case, Richard Nixon's announcement to the American people was eloquent, high-minded, and deceptive:

> Now that we have achieved an honorable agreement, let us be proud that Americans did not settle for a peace that would have betrayed our allies,

> that would have abandoned our prisoners of war, or that would have ended the war for us but would have continued the war for 50 million people of Indochina. Let us be proud of the 2 ½ million young Americans who served in Vietnam, who served with honor and distinction in one of the most selfless enterprises in the history of nations.[4]

As the president and his national security advisor recognized, the Paris Agreement was merely cover for the United States to exit the conflict, bringing its remaining troops and POWs safely home. There was no possibility of peace for the people of South Vietnam, Laos, and Cambodia.

The two also understood that the chances that the Saigon government could ultimately survive were slim. As General Thieu and his cabinet had repeatedly emphasized, the presence of approximately 140,000 North Vietnamese troops in the South exercising sovereign power in the occupied area was a dagger at the throat of the regime. In terms of sheer numbers, it might have seemed otherwise. With American assistance, the South Vietnamese military had been built up to one million men with the most modern equipment. However, as the 1972 spring offensive demonstrated, none of this was sufficient to halt major territorial gains by the enemy. In the end that offensive was stopped, but this was largely because of the massive engagement of US airpower. North Vietnamese forces had been significantly damaged ss a result, but once those air strikes were not forthcoming it was difficult to see how long the South Vietnamese government could survive.

The regime held power for the following two years and three months. The collapse, when it finally came on April 30, 1975, was even faster than Hanoi had anticipated. President Thieu had been openly contemptuous of the Paris Agreement from the beginning. In the spirit of the "Four Nos"—no recognition of the enemy, no coalition government, no neutralization of South Vietnam, no concession of territory—Thieu had moved swiftly to regain captured territory.[5] Hanoi had been more cautious at first, worrying about a possible US return and needing time to recover from its losses during the 1972 spring offensive.[6] Meanwhile they secretly infiltrated additional troops and weapons into the South. By October 1973, the North Vietnamese Politburo had reversed course and called for "continuous revolutionary violence" to overthrow the regime.

With the two sides plainly at war, the Nixon administration had pressed Congress tor additional aid, but the mood on Capitol Hill was decidedly unpropitious. On August 15, 1973, in reaction to the revelations about the continued bombing of Cambodia, Congress cut off funding for all US military operations in Indochina. One year later, as the South Vietnamese military situation deteriorated and in the face of Kissinger's warnings that the US abandonment of South Vietnam "would have a corrosive effect on our interests beyond Vietnam," Congress halved the administration's request for $1.5 billion in military and economic aid to Saigon.

The resignation of Richard Nixon in August 1974 did not alter the trajectory of failure. With his economy in shambles and his military disintegrating, President Thieu had no strategy for halting the enemy advance. In March 1975, as North Vietnamese troops moved into the Central Highlands, General Thieu ordered a retreat. As described by *Baltimore Sun* reporter Arnold Isaacs, that directive "led to a sudden catastrophic release of all the deep social and moral flaws of the regime." As had previously occurred:

> From the corps level down, few commanders bothered to assemble and organize their troops. They just collected their families and possessions and fled. Those officers who did try to lead were helpless in the breakdown of military order. The every-man-for-himself morality that had pervaded the system for years was now in command, turning the withdrawal into a desperate, doomed race for survival.[7]

In short order, the failure in the Central Highlands was replicated in Quang Tri, Hue, Danang, Quang Ngai, and elsewhere, as panicking South Vietnamese soldiers abandoned their posts, discarding heavy weapons and equipment, clogging roads, and in some cases turning their fear and fury on civilians.

With Saigon dangerously exposed, President Ford went before a joint session of Congress on April 10, calling for an emergency military appropriation of $722 million plus another $250 million in humanitarian aid. Echoing Kissinger, Ford sought to shift responsibility for the debacle to America's domestic actors.[8] "A vast human tragedy has befallen our friends in Vietnam and Cambodia," he pronounced. In the face of egregious North Vietnamese violations of the Paris Peace Agreement, "We deprived ourselves by law of the ability to uphold it." Recognizing the rapidly deteriorating situation in South Vietnam, President Ford contended that

"Fundamental decency requires that we do everything in our power to ease the misery and the pain of the monumental human crisis which has fallen the people of Vietnam."

Congress had no further interest in subsidiziing a lost cause. The prevailing attitude was bluntly expressed by Republican Senator William Lloyd Scott of Virginia: "Given the situation in Vietnam, I think we would just be wasting the money."[9] Additional funding would be for the purpose of evacuating the 6,000 Americans still in the South, along with some fraction of the Vietnamese who had worked closely with the United States. Inside Saigon, President Thieu had nurtured the illusion, almost to the end, that somehow the Americans would rescue his tottering regime. With no such assistance forthcoming, and thousands of enemy soldiers approaching the city, Thieu angrily resigned on April 21. He blamed the United States.[10] High among his grievances was the Paris Peace Agreement of 1973, which he had been compelled to sign despite his warnings to Kissinger that it would augur communist victory.

At the Kennedy Presidential Library, the former Secretary of State and National Security Advisor was unrepentant: "We have to start with the assumption that serious people were making serious decisions with the national interest and the world interest at heart." In offering this defense so many years later, Kissinger was remaining loyal to a particular conception of "serious"—one that was largely shared by his colleagues in the Nixon administration as well as many who worked for Presidents Johnson and Kennedy. As practical men of affairs, their overwhelming preoccupation was with the "doable." Regarding the nations of Indochina, that meant the deployment of military power. Largely excluded were the human costs for the people of Vietnam, Laos, and Cambodia, or for their own countrymen in uniform.

Yet, this exclusion of moral concerns inhibited wise decision-making. Rarely acknowledged by US officials at the time were the ways in which the unrestrained use of American firepower had multiplied enemies and discredited friends. By the end of 1975, all three Washington-supported governments had been overthrown. At the time, it was widely recognized that the Nixon administration's policy in Southeast Asia had been disastrous.. Lamentably, the self-serving belief that the freedom and security of people around the world depended on US military might, somehow survived.

Notes

Introduction

1. Full Text of Articles of Impeachment, July 27,1974, https://watergate.info/impeachment/articles-of-impeachment
2. William Shawcross, *Sideshow: Kissinger, Nixon and the Destruction of Cambodia* (New York: Simon and Schuster, 1979), 19–35; Seymour Hersh, "Secret Raids on Cambodia Before '70 Totaled 3500," *New York Times*, July 18,1973.
3. "US Admits Secret Cambodia Bombing," *Washington Post*, August 13, 1973; "Secret Bombing of Cambodia: ABC's of a Growing Dispute," *US News and World Report*, August 13, 1974.
4. "AF Secretary Not Told of Bombings," *Washington Post*, July 26, 1973.
5. Statement of Hon. John Conyers Jr. A Representative in Congress from the First Congressional District of the State of Michigan, Hearings of the Committee on the Judiciary House of Representatives, Ninety-Third Congress, Second Session, Pursuant to H. Res. 803, July 24–30, 1974, 492.
6. William Beecher, "Raids in Cambodia by U.S. Unprotested," *New York Times*, May 9, 1969.
7. At that time, they also filed a resolution of impeachment in the House of Representatives. This measure was never brought to the floor. In addition to John Conyers, co-sponsors included William Ryan, Bella Abzug, Shirley Chisholm, Ron Dellums, Charles Rangel, Louis Stokes, and Parren Mitchell.
8. Supplemental Views of Mr. Drinan, in Impeachment of Richard M. Nixon, Final Report of the Committee on the Judiciary House of Representatives, 421–429.
9. Statement of Mr. Latta, Hearings of the Committee on the Judiciary House of Representatives, Ninety-Third Congress, 493.
10. Statement of Mr. Flowers, Hearings of the Committee on the Judiciary House of Representatives, Ninety-Third Congress 507–508.
11. Author's Interview with Elizabeth Holtzman: Supplemental Views of Mr. Drinan, 421–423.
12. Statement of Mr. Seiberling, Hearings of the Committee on the Judiciary House of Representatives, Ninety-Third Congress, 511–512.
13. An additional consideration was General Wheeler's testimony that some members of Congress had been notified about the secret bombing. This included Senators Richard Russell, John Stennis, and Everett Dirkson.
14. Statement of Mr. Owens, Hearings of the Committee on the Judiciary House of Representatives, Ninety-Third Congress, 512–513.

15. Sydney Schanberg, "Town is Devastated in Cambodian 'Victory,'" *New York Times*, July 28, 1974.
16. "Schanberg, "Phnom Penh Streets Home for Thousands," *New York Times*, July 29, 1974.
17. Henry Steele Commager, "Five Grounds for Impeaching the President," *New York Review of Books*, June 28, 1974.
18. Cited in Seymour M. Hersh, *The Price of Power: Kissinger in the Nixon White House* (New York: Summit Books, 2012).
19. For important books on the Vietnam War, see especially. Pierre Asselin, *A Bitter Peace: Washington, Hanoi and the Making of the Paris Agreement* (Chapel Hill: University of North Carolina Press, 2002); Larry Berman, *No Peace, No Honor: Nixon, Kissinger and Betrayal in Vietnam.* (New York: Free Press, 2001); Robert K. Brigham, *Reckless: Henry Kissinger and the Tragedy of Vietnam* (New York: Public Affairs, 2018); William Burr and Jeffrey P. Kimball, *Nixon's Nuclear Specter: The Secret Alert of 1969 Madman Diplomacy and the Vietnam War* (Lawrence: University of Kansas Press, 2015); Greg Daddis, *Withdrawal: Reassessing America's Final Years in Vietnam* (New York: Oxford University Press, 2017); David W. P. Elliott, *The Vietnamese War: Revolution and Social Change in the Mekong Delta, 1930–75.* (Armonk, NY: M. E. Sharpe, 2007); Greg Grandin, *Kissinger's Shadow* (New York: Metropolitan Books, 2015); Kenneth Hughes, *Fatal Politics: The Nixon Tapes, the Vietnam Wars and the Casualties of Re-Election* (Charlottesville: University of Virginia Press, 2015); Kenneth Hughes, *Chasing Shadows: The Nixon Tapes, the Chennault Affair, and the Origins of Watergate* (Charlottesville: University of Virginia Press, 2015); Arnold R. Isaacs, *Without Honor: Defeat in Vietnam and Cambodia* (Baltimore: Johns Hopkins University Press, 1983); Jeffrey Kimball, *Nixon's Vietnam War* (Lawrence: University of Kansas Press, 1998); Joshua Kurlantzick, *A Great Place to Have a War: America in Laos and the Birth of a Military CIA* (New York: Simon and Schuster, 2016); Lien-Hang T. Nguyen, *Hanoi's War: An International History of the War for Peace in Vietnam* (Chapel Hill: University of North Carolina Press, 2012); John Prados, *Vietnam: the History of an Unwinnable War, 1945–75* (Lawrence: University of Kansas Press, 2009); David Schmitz, *Richard Nixon and the Vietnam War* (Lanham, MD: Rowman and Littlefield, 2014); Lewis Sorley, *A Better War: The Unexamined Victories and Final Tragedy of America's Last Year in Vietnam* (New York: Harcourt Brace, 1999); Tim Weiner, *One Man Against the World: The Tragedy of Richard Nixon* (New York: Henry Holt & Company, 2015).

    Important works discussing Nixon's and Kissinger's diplomacy with the Soviet Union and China: Robert Dallek, *Nixon and Kissinger: Partners in Power* (New York: Harper Collins 2007); Mario del Pero, *The Eccentric Realist: Henry Kissinger and the Shaping of American Foreign Policy* (Ithaca: Cornell University Press, 2010); Ilya Gaiduk, *The Soviet Union and the Vietnam War* (Chicago: Ivan R. Dee, 1996); Raymond L Garthoff, *Détente and Confrontation: American-Soviet Relations from Nixon to Reagan* (Washington, DC: Brookings Institution, 1994); Jussi Hanhimaki, *The Flawed Architect: Henry Kissinger and American Foreign Policy.*(New York: Oxford University Press, 2004); Jussi Hanhimaki, *The Rise and Fall of Détente: American Foreign Policy and the Transformation of the Cold War* (Washington, DC: Potomac Books, 2013); Seymour M. Hersh, *The Price of Power: Kissinger in the Nixon White House.* (New York: Summit Books, 1983); Joan Hoff, *Nixon Reconsidered* (New York: Basic Books, 1994); Margaret MacMillan, *Nixon and Mao: The Week that Changed the World* (New York: Random House, 2007); Richard A. Moss, *Nixon's Back Channel to Moscow: Confidential Diplomacy and Détente* (Lexington: University Press of Kentucky, 2017); Keith L. Nelson, *The Making of Détente* (Baltimore: Johns Hopkins Press, 1995); Franz Schurmann, *The Logic of World Power: An Inquiry into the Origins, Currents, and Contradictions of World Politics* (New York: Pantheon, 1974); Thomas A. Schwartz, *Henry Kissinger and American Power* (New York: Hill and Wang, 2020); Robert A. Schulzinger, *Henry Kissinger: Doctor of Diplomacy* (New York: Columbia University Press, 1989); Tad Szulc, *The Illusion of Peace: Foreign Policy in the Nixon Years* (New York: Viking Press, 1978); Chris Tudda, *A Cold War Turning Point: Nixon and China, 1969–72* (Baton Rouge: University of Louisiana Press, 2012).

20. Richard M. Nixon Speech, April 30, 1970. https://millercenter.org/the-presidency/presidential-speeches/april-30-1970-address-nation-situation-southeast-asia.
21. Jason von Meding, "Fifty Years Later, Agent Orange Still Kills in Vietnam," https://nationalinterest.org/blog/reboot/fifty-years-later-agent-orange-still-kills-vietnam-173463;

    Tuan V. Nguyen, "Agent Orange in Vietnam," in Mark Pavlick and Caroline Luft, (eds.), *The United States, Southeast Asia and Historical Memory* (Chicago: Haymarket Books, 1969), 53–74; Channapha Khamvongasa and Elaine Russell, "Legacies of War: Cluster Bombs in Laos," in Pavlick and Luft, *The United States*, 23–52; "Manmade Wasteland in Vietnam," *New York Times*, January 2, 1971.
22. Classic example is David Halberstam, *The Best and the Brightest* (New York: Ballantine Books, 1969).
23. You "might as well not," Secretary Laird replied. "They're pretty terrible." Telcon, Kissinger and Laird, November 21, 1969, Box 3, Nixon Presidential Materials and Records (PNMR), National Archives and Records (NARA).

Chapter 1

1. Tom Wells, *The War Within: America's Battle Over Vietnam* (Berkeley: University of California Press, 1994), 222.
2. Stanley Karnow, *Vietnam A History* (New York: Viking, 1983), 541.
3. South Vietnam 1960s film, Huntley film archives. https://www.youtube.com/watch?v=S5T4pcALoog
4. Transcript, Walter Cronkite, We Are Mired in Stalemate Broadcast, February 27, 1968. https://www.humanitiestexas.org/sites/default/files/teacher-institute/suri_cronkite_nixon.pdf

5. "War Doubts in Senate," *New York Times*, February 12, 1968.
6. Lewis Chester, Godfrey Hodgson, and Bruce Page, *An American Melodrama: The Presidential Campaign of 1968* (New York: Viking Press, 1969), 78–79
7. E. W. Kentworthy, "College Students Drum Up Support for McCarthy," *New York Times*, March 4, 1968; Ward Just, "Student Power Boosts McCarthy," *Washington Post*, March 12, 1968; Samuel Winfred Brown Jr., "A Student for McCarthy," *New York Times*, March 14, 1968.
8. Chester, Hodgson, and Page, *Melodrama*, 119–126.
9. Evan Thomas and Walter Isaacson, *The Wise Men: Six Friends and the World They Made* (New York: Simon and Schuster, 2013), 695.
10. Among the "wise men" were McGeorge Bundy, Dean Acheson, Douglas Dillon. Cyrus Vance, Arthur Goldberg, George Ball, Robert Murphy, Arthur Dean, Maxwell Taylor, Abraham Fortas, Henry Cabot Lodge, John McCloy, General Matthew Ridgeway, and General Omar Bradley.
11. Notes of Meeting, March 26, 1968. Foreign Relations of the United States (hereafter FRUS), *Lyndon B. Johnson Administration, 1964–68, Vol. VI Vietnam, January–August 1968*, ed. Kent Sieg (Washington DC: Government Printing Office, 2002), Document 158.
12. Theodore H. White, *The Making of the President*, 1968 (New York: Harper Perennial, 1969), 138–141.
13. "McCarthy Favored Over Johnson in Wisconsin Vote Tuesday," *New York Times*, March 31, 1968; Conversation with Larry O'Brien, cited by Lloyd C. Gardner, *Pay Any Price: Lyndon Johnson and the War for Vietnam* (Chicago: Ivan R. Dee, 1995), 456.
14. Transcript of Lyndon Johnson, March 31, 1968, Speech. https://millercenter.org/the-presidency/presidential-speeches/march-31-1968-remarks-decision-not-seek-re-election
15. "Impact on McCarthy," *New York Times*, April 4, 1968.
16. "McCarthy Vote Exceeds 400,000," *New York Times*, April 4, 1968
17. Luu Van Loi and Nguyen Anh Vu, *Le Duc Tho–Kissinger Negotiations in Paris* (Hanoi: The Gioi Publishers, 1995), 16–17.
18. Jules Witcover, *The Resurrection of Richard Nixon*, (New York: G. P. Putnam's Sons, 1970), 258.
19. "Nixon Vows Vietnam Silence to Aid Peace Move," *New York Times*, April 20, 1968..
20. McCarthy Presses U.S. on War Stand," *New York Times*, April 17, 1968; "Kennedy Calling U.S. Power Obsessed, Appeals for New Policy," *New York Times*, April 18, 1968; "Kennedy is Critical of Delay on Vietnam Talks," *New York Times*, April 19, 1968.
21. "Party Chiefs Say Humphrey has Strong Support," April 28, 1968; "Humphrey Gains in Johnson Camp," *New York Times*, April 13, 1968.
22. "Kennedy is Critical of Delay on Vietnam Talks," *New York Times*, April 19, 1968.
23. Jules Witcover, *The Year the Dream Died: Revisiting 1968 in America* (New York: Time-Warner, 1997), 301.
24. *Ibid.*, 265

25. Richard Nixon, Remarks on Accepting the Presidential Nomination of the Republican National Convention, August 23, 1968. https://millercenter.org/the-presidency/presidential-speeches/march-31-1968-remarks-decision-not-seek-re-election
26. "Chicago: An Armed Camp for Democratic Convention," *US News and World Report*, August 26, 1969.
27. Witcover, *The Year the Dream Died*, 320–332.
28. Chester, Hodgson, and Page, *Melodrama*, 531–537; "How President Forced A Tough Plank on Vietnam Through the Platform," *New York Times*, August 28, 1968. See as well Arnold Offner, *Hubert Humphrey: The Conscience of the Country* (New Haven: Yale University Press, 2018), Chapter 8.
29. Tom Hayden, *Reunion: A Memoir* (New York: Random House, 1988), 311.
30. Norman Mailer, *Miami and the Siege of Chicago* (New York: New York Review of Books, 1968) 168–170.
31. Todd Gitlin, *The Sixties: Years of Hope, Years of Rage* (New York: Bantam, 1993), 333; "Police Battle Demonstrators in Streets," *New York Times*, August 29, 1968.
32. By then, Hubert Humphrey obtained the nomination by a healthy margin with 1761 3/4 votes compared to 601 for McCarthy and 146 1/2 for George McGovern.
33. Nancy Zaroulis and Gerard Sullivan, *Who Spoke Up? American Protest Against the War in Vietnam, 1963–1975* (New York: Holt Rinehart and Winston, 1984),195–196.
34. "Even before the Democratic convention, Richard Nixon enjoyed a healthy lead in the polls with a 45% to 29% advantage over Humphrey. "Nixon Increases Gallup Poll Lead," *New York Times*, August 21, 1968; "Poll Rates Nixon Best at Handling War," *New York Times*, August 25, 1968.
35. Eric Sevareid: "Obviously there's a new Nixon, a phrase we've often heard. . . . There's an air of solidity about this man that wasn't there some years ago. A great air of a kind of natural authority about him, much different from '52 when he was a 39-year-old man at the time, not sure of his footing." (August 8, 1972); CBS News, Republican National Convention, Museum of Television, Broadcasting Archive, NYC; James Reston, "A Remarkable Comeback for Nixon," *New York Times*, August 8, 1972.
36. "Transcript of Speech by the Vice President on Foreign Policy," *New York Times*, October 1, 1968.
37. Offner, *Hubert Humphrey*, 318–319.
38. As Mrs. Chennault remembered "Anna, I am speaking to you on behalf of Mr. Nixon. It is very important that our Vietnamese friends understand our Republican position and I hope you have made that clear to them." Cited in Larry Berman, *No Peace, No Honor: Nixon, Kissinger and Betrayal in Vietnam*, (New York: Free Press, 2001), 133.
39. Witcover, *The Year the Dream Died*, 417–418
40. Stephen Ambrose, *Nixon: The Triumph of a Politician*, 1962–72 (New York: Simon and Schuster, 1989), 212
41. Kenneth Hughes, *Shadows, the Nixon Tapes, the Chennault Affair, and the Origins of Watergate* (Charlottesville: University of Virginia Press, 2015), 35.
42. John A. Farrell, *Richard Nixon* (New York: Harper Collins, 2007), 343.
43. Hughes, *Shadows*, 50–51.

44. See persuasive discussion of this issue in Offner, *Hubert Humphrey*, 322–326.
45. Hughes, *Shadows*, 44–45.
46. Jules Witcover, *Resurrection of Richard Nixon*, 447.
47. "GOP TV Commercial Evokes Protests on Image of Humphrey," *New York Times*, October 29, 1968.

Chapter 2

1. Richard Nixon, Inaugural Address, January 20, 1968. https://www.presidency.ucsb.edu/documents/inaugural-address-1
2. Henry A. Kissinger, *Nuclear Weapons and Foreign Policy* (New York: Norton, 1957).
3. Dale Van Atta, *With Honor: Melvin Laird in War, Peace, and Politics*, (Madison: University of Wisconsin Press, 2008) 156–157.
4. Laird to Kissinger, RE: Your Memorandum dated January 3, 1969, Concerning a New NSC System, January 9, 1969, NSC Henry A. Kissinger Office File (hereafter HAK), Box 1, Sec. Laird Folder, Nixon Presidential Records and Materials (hereafter NPRM), National Archives Records Administration (hereafter NARA).
5. Van Atta,, *With Honor*, 157.
6. Henry Kissinger, "The Vietnam Negotiations," *Foreign Affairs* 45, no. 2 (January 1969): 38–50.
7. Jeffrey Kimball, *Nixon's Vietnam War* (Lawrence: University of Kansas Press, 2014), 91–92.
8. Daniel Ellsberg, *Secrets: A Memoir of Vietnam and the Pentagon Papers* (New York: Viking, 2002), 236–238.
9. Lewis Sorley, (ed.) *The Abrams Tapes, 1968–1972.*(Lubbock, TX: Texas Tech University Press, 2004), 94–95,135–136; Gregory A. Daddis, *Withdrawal: Reassessing America's Final Years in Vietnam* (New York: Oxford University Press, 2017), 54–55.
10. Van Atta, *With Honor*, 158; Philip B. Davidson, *Vietnam at War: The History 1946–75* (New York: Oxford University Press, 1988), 601–602.
11. Few Americans had ever heard of Lieutenant General Robert Pursley, who was Laird's most trusted advisor on Vietnam matters. Pursley previously served as military assistant to Defense Secretary Robert McNamara in his last years, and to his successor Secretary of Defense Clark Clifford. When Clifford handed the reins of office to Laird, he advised him that this Air Force veteran was one of the "smartest guys around," who if retained would prove invaluable—an assessment that Laird came to share. (Author's phone Interview with Melvin Laird, July 2002).
12. Sorley, *Abrams Tapes*, 138–139.
13. William J. Webb, *The History of the Joint Chiefs of Staff, The Joint Chiefs of Staff and the War in Vietnam, 1971–1973, Part I*. Historical Division, Joint Secretariat Joint Chiefs of Staff (document generously provided by historian John Prados),14.
14. Telcon, Kissinger and Nixon, March 8, 1969, Box 1, NSC, NPRM, NARA.
15. Van Atta, *With Honor*, 179.

16. Shawcross, *Sideshow*, 31.
17. Hersh, *Price of Power*, 63–64.
18. Summary of Interagency Responses to NSSM-1, March 22,1969, US Department of State, *FRUS, 1969–76, Vietnam, Vol. VI*, eds. Edward C. Keefer and Carolyn Yee (Washington: Government Printing Office, 2006), Doc. 4.
19. Webb, *History of the Joint Chiefs of Staff, Part I*, 12–13.
20. Ibid., 130.
21. Ibid., 141.
22. Webb, *History of the Joint Chiefs of Staff, Part I*, 17.
23. Minutes of National Security Council Meeting, March 25, *FRUS, 1969–76, Vol VI:* 164–176.
24. Note from the Soviet Leadership to President Nixon, Undated, US Department of State, David C. David C.Geyer and Douglas Selvage (eds.) *Soviet-American Relations: The Détente Years 1969–72* (Washington: Government Printing Office, *2007)*, 11–13.
25. Memorandum of Conversation (US) RE: Ambassador Dobrynin's Initial Call on the President, February 17, 1969, NSC, President's Trip Files, Box 489, Folder 1, NPRM, NARA.
26. Memorandum of Conversation (USSR), February 14, 1969, in Geyer and Selvage (eds.), *Soviet-American Relations*, 4–6.
27. Meeting Between Presidential Assistant Kissinger and Ambassador Dobrynin, February 21, Ibid., 20–21.
28. Memorandum of Conversation (USSR), February 17, 1969, Ibid., 17.
29. Telegram from Ambassador Dobrynin to the Soviet Foreign Ministry, April 15, 1969, Ibid., 52–53.
30. Telcon, The President and Kissinger, April 17, 1969, Kissinger Telephone Conversation Transcripts, Box 1, NPRM, NARA.
31. "Death in a Quiet Week," *Newsweek*, April 28, 1969.

Chapter 3

1. "Raids in Cambodia by U.S. Unprotested," *New York Times*, May 9,1969.
2. Hersh, *Price of Power*, 86–87.
3. "Ohio Town of 450 Bitter Over Six Lost in Vietnam," *New York Times*, April 30,1969.
4. See important discussion by military historian Greg Daddis, *Withdrawal*, 35–44.
5. Webb, Joint Chiefs of Staff, *History of Vietnam War, Part I*, 83.
6. "Criticism and Evasion of the Draft Grow with the Unpopularity of the Vietnam War," *New York Times*, May 14,1969.
7. "Javits Warns Nixon to End A Sterile Policy on Peace," *New York Times*, May 9, 1969.
8. "Vietnam Pullout Urged as Senate Resumes Debate," *New York Times*, May 1, 1969.
9. "Scott Joins Aiken in Urging Pullout," *New York Times*, May 2, 1969,

10. Address to the Nation on Vietnam, May 14, 1969. https://www.nixonfoundation.org/2017/09/address-nation-vietnam-may-14-1969/
11. Telcon, Kissinger and Nixon 9:35 PM May 14, 1969. Box 1, NSC, NPRM, NARA.
12. Telcon, Nixon and Kissinger, 10:50 PM May 14, 1969, NSC, NPRM, NARA.
13. H.R. Haldeman, *The Haldeman Diaries: Inside the Nixon White House* (New York: Putnam, 1994), May 18, 1969
14. Samuel Zaffiri, *Hamburger Hill, the Brutal Battle for Dong Ap Bia, May 1–20, 1969* (New York: Presidio Press, 1988), 66.
15. A spider hole was a camouflaged one-man foxhole from which a hidden soldier could stand and fire a weapon. A punji stick is a type of booby trap, sharpened, heated, and set in a hole.
16. James Wright, *Enduring Vietnam: An American Generation and Its War* (New York: St. Martin's Press, 2017), 55.
17. Zaffiri, *Hamburger Hill,* 87.
18. Ibid., 90–93.
19. Ibid, 136.
20. Ibid, 218.
21. Ibid. 228–229.
22. Ibid., 271.
23. David Hackworth, "About Hamburger Hill," *Military Times*, March 1990.
24. "Woe to the Victors," *Newsweek*, June 2, 1969.
25. "The Battle for Hamburger Hill," *Time*, May 30, 1969.
26. "Edward Kennedy's Challenge to President Nixon," *New York Times*, May 21, 1969.
27. "Dirksen Denounces Criticism by Kennedy on War," *New York Times*, June 3, 1969.
28. "Kennedy Rebuts Nixon on Critics: Attack on U.S. Policy Gets Applause at Fordham," *New York Times,* June 8, 1969.
29. "45 in Congress Seek Rein on Military," *New York Times*, June 2, 1969.
30. "Question Over Military," *New York Times*, May 25, 1969; Statement by Senator Stephen Young *Congressional Record–Senate*, May 29, 1969, 14530; "Mansfield Urges Dialogue on War," *New York Times*, May 29, 1969; "President's Speech Stirs Resentment in Congress," *New York Times*, June 4,1969.
31. Military Commentary by Chueb Binh, "Ap Bia—A Heavy Defeat for the Americans," Hanoi, *Quan Doi Nhan Dan*, May 27, 1969, in Douglas Pike Collection, Vietnam Center and Sam Johnson Vietnam Archive, Texas Tech University (Lubbock, TX).
32. "69 War Woe Told at Yale Exercises," *New York Times*, June 10,1969.
33. "Antiwar Protesters Burn Draft Records in Chicago," *New York Times*, May 26, 1969.
34. "The Faces of the American Dead in Vietnam: One Week's Toll," *Life*, June 27, 1969.
35. Alexander Butterfield to Honorable Melvin Laird and Dr. Henry Kissinger, Subj: Comment by the President (Information only), June 11, 1969, NSC Vietnam Country File, Box 67, Folder 5, NPRM, NARA.

Chapter 4

1. For valuable discussion of Secretary Laird's evolving position, see: Richard A. Hunt, Melvin Laird and the Foundation of the Post-Vietnam Military, 1969–73 (Washington, DC: Historical Office of thc Secretary of Defense, 2015); Laird, *With Honor*; David Prentice, "Choosing the Long Road: Henry Kissinger, Melvin Laird, Vietnamization and the War Over Nixon's Vietnam Strategy," *Diplomatic History* 3, no. 3(June 2016): 445–447.
2. William J. Webb, *The History of the Joint Chiefs of Staff, The Joint Chiefs of Staff and the War in Vietnam, 1969 –1970, Part I,* 107–110.
3. Bunker to Secretary of State, May 26, 1969, NSC Vietnam Subject File, Box 62, NPRM, NARA.
4. Richardson to Bunker and Burger, May 26, 1969, NSC Vietnam Subject File, Box 73, NPRM, NARA.
5. Memorandum from the President's Assistant for National Security Affairs (Kissinger) to President Nixon, Your Meeting with President Thieu at Midway, June 3, 1969, and Memorandum of Conversation, President Nixon, President Thieu, Henry Kissinger, Ngiyen Phu Suc, June 8, 1969, FRUS, Vol. VI, *Vietnam, January 1969–July 1970*, eds. Edward C. Keefer and Carolyn Yee (Washington: Government Printing Office, 2006).;
6. Al Haig to Kissinger, Joint Statement and Bunker Resume of Meeting with Theiu, June 5,1969, NSC Lake Chron Files, Box 1048; Haig to Kissinger, June 6, 1969, NSC Haig Special File, Box 1008, NPRM.
7. "Saigon Closes 3 Papers; Total for the Year is Now 30," *New York Times*, May 2, 1969.
8. US Study Team on Religious and Political Freedom in Vietnam, Congressional Record–US Senate, July 2, 1969, 18216–18222.
9. Hunt, *Melvin Laird,* 134–137.
10. Clark Clifford, "Vietnam Reappraisal: The Personal History of One Man's View and How it Evolved," *Foreign Affairs* 47, no. 4 (July–August 1969):601–622.
11. "Vance Backs Call for Cease-Fire by all Sides in Vietnam," *New York Times*, June 14, 1969.
12. Telcon, Secretary Rusk and Henry Kissinger, June 8, 1969; Telcon, Tom Johnson and Kissinger, June 18, 1969. Box 2 NSC, NPRM, NARA.
13. "Transcript of the President's News Conference on Foreign and Domestic Matters," *New York Times*, June 20, 1969.
14. Haldeman Diary, June 19 and June 20, 1969.
15. Memorandum of Conversation (USSR), US Department of State, *Soviet-American Relations: the Détente Years, 1969–70*, eds. David C. Geyer and Douglas Selvage. Quotations are from Dobrynin's detailed description of this meeting to his superiors in Moscow. Kissinger's description of the exchange to the president is much briefer and does not contain this material. See Memorandum from Presidential Assistant (Kissinger) to President Nixon, June 11, 1969, *Ibid.*, 62–64.
16. See discussion in Robert K. Brigham, *Guerilla Diplomacy: The NLF's Foreign Relations and the Vietnam War* (Ithaca: Cornell University Press,1999), 84–90.

17. David Chanoff and Doan Van Toai, *A Vietcong Memoir: An Insider Account of the Vietnam War and Its Aftermath* (New York: Vintage,1985), 145–156.
18. Author's interview with Madame Nguyen Thi Binh, Hanoi, March 4, 2009As discussed in her memoir, the creation of the Provisional Revolutionary Government was a major strategic move by the insurgents, designed among other things to garner significant international support. Unpublished English version of her autobiography by Nguyen Thi Binh, *Family, Friends and Country,* 126–130.
19. David Chanoff and Doan Van Toai,, A *Viet Cong Memoir* (New York: Vintage Books, 1985), 156–175.
20. Brigham, *Guerilla Diplomacy*, 88–90; Nguyen, Lien Hang T., *Hanoi's War: An International History of the War for Peace in Vietnam* (Chapel Hill: University of North Carolina Press, 2012), 140–141.
21. Bunker to Secretary of State, July 2–3, 1969, NSC Vietnam Subject Files, Box 74, NPRM, NARA.
22. "Text of Thieu's Address on Elections in Vietnam," *New York Times,* July 11, 1969.
23. Hanoi Radio on Thieu Proposal, "Another Bluff of the US Lackeys in Saigon," July 13, 1969, Pike Collection, Texas Tech Virtual Archive.
24. "US War Deaths in Week 3 at Lowest Point Since January," *New York Times,* July 10, 1969.
25. George McGovern Speech, "Vietnam and the Declaration of Independence," Congressional Record–Senate, July 2,1969, 18216–18220.
26. Thomas Eagleton, Speech, Congressional Record Senate–July 2, 1969, 18205–18206.
27. Sorley (ed.), *Abrams Tapes*, 228.
28. Ibid., 236–237.
29. "Gallup Poll Finds 53% Approve Nixon's Policy on Vietnam War, *New York Times*, July 31, 1969.
30. Melvin Laird, Memo for the President, Statement of Mission of US Forces in Southeast Asia, August 7, 1969, NSC Subject File, Vietnam /Southeast Asia Folder, Box 76, NPMR, NARA; Webb, *History of the Joint Chiefs of Staff,* 90–99.
31. "A Joyful Confirmation That Good Things Can Happen Here," *New York Times*, August 24,1969; "The Message of History's Biggest Happening," *Time*, August 29, 1969.
32. Lyrics sourced at: https://www.songfacts.com/lyrics/country-joe-the-fish/i-feel-like-im-fixin-to-die-rag
33. Quoted in *Time* magazine, "Incident in Song Chang Valley," September 5, 1969.
34. James Reston, "A Whiff of Mutiny," *New York Times*, August 27, 1969.

Chapter 5

1. Jeffrey Kimball, *The Vietnam War Files Uncovering the Secret History of Nixon-Era Strategy* (Lawrence: University of Kansas Press, 2004), 21–24; William Burr and Jeffrey P. Kimball, *Nixon's Nuclear Specter: The Secret Alert of 1969, Madman Diplomacy and the Vietnam War* (Lawrence: University of Kansas Press, 2015), 202–230.

2. Memorandum, Alexander Haig to Henry Kissinger, RE: Items to Discuss with the President, September 9, 1969, included in Kimball, *Vietnam War Files*, 101.
3. Burr and Kimball, *Nixon's Nuclear Specter*, 244–252.
4. Thomas Wells, *The War Within: America's Battle Over Vietnam* (Berkeley: University of California Press, 1994), 328–331.
5. Todd Gitlin, *The Sixties: Years of Hope, Years of Rage* (New York: Bantam, 1987), 380–388.
6. Ibid., 266–267.
7. Ibid., 376–379.
8. Hunt, *Laird and Foundations of Post-Vietnam*, 371–374.
9. Admiral Moorer, Memorandum for the Record, Joint Chiefs of Staff Meeting with the President, October 11, 1969, NSC Alexander M. Haig's Special File, Box 1008, Folder: Haig's Vietnam File, NPRM, NARA.
10. Patrick Buchanan to the President, Notes from Republican Leadership Meeting, September 30, 1972, President's Office File (POF) Box 79, Folder September 20, NPRM. NARA.
11. "Give Nixon Time on War, Aiken Asks," *New York Times*, October 12, 1972
12. "Premier Welcomes US Antiwar 'Offensive,'" Hanoi, VNA International Service, October 14, 1969, Virtual Archive, Texas Tech University.
13. Nguyen Thi Binh, *Family Friends and Country* ,136–143.
14. Among them, Sinclair Armstrong, vice president of the Sinclair Trust Company and former chair of the Securities and Exchange Commission; Benjamin Buttenweiser, a partner in Kuhn, Loeb & Company; Michael Burke, president of the New York Yankees; Andre Meyer, senior partner of Lazard Freres & Company; and many other recent converts.
15. "October 15: A Day to Remember," *Newsweek*, October 27,1969.
16. "Massive Protest on Vietnam War Expected Today," *New York Times*, October 15, 1969.
17. "Work for Peace—a Rising Scale of Protest," *US News and World Report*, October 20, 1969.
18. "October 15, 1969, A Day to Remember," *Newsweek*, October 20, 1969.
19. John Prados, *Vietnam: The History of an Unwinnable War, 1945–75.* (Lawrence, KS: University of Kansas Press, 2009) 309–311; Henry Kissinger, *Ending the Vietnam War: A History of America's Involvement and Extrication from the Vietnam War* (New York: Simon and Schuster, 2003) 92–93.
20. Melvin Laird to Kissinger, October 23, 1969, NSC Vietnam Subject Files, Box 76, NPRM, NARA.
21. See especially, Burr and Kimball, *Nixon's Nuclear Specter. 231–264.*
22. Memorandum of Conversation (USSR), October 20, 1969, in Geyer and Selvage, *Soviet-American Relations*, 92–93.
23. Memorandum of Conversation, President Nixon and Ambassador Dobrynin, October 20, 1969, in Geyer and Selvage, *Soviet-American Relations*, 86–87.
24. Ibid., 95.

25. For General Haig, Master Copy Game Plan for the President's November 3rd Speech on Vietnam, NSC Vietnam Subject Files, Box 73, Folder 2, NPRM, NARA.
26. Meeting of Kissinger with Carl Albert and John McCormack, November 3, 1969, NSC Vietnam Subject Files, Box 73, Folder 2, NPRM, NARA.
27. At the end of September, he had announced an additional 30,000 troop withdrawals.
28. *Haldeman Diary,* November 2, 1969.
29. Telcon, President and Kissinger, November 3, 11:33 pm., Box 3, NSC, NPRM, NARA.
30. Telcon, President and Kissinger, Nov 3–4 Midnight., Box 3, NSC, NPRM, NARA.
31. "Congress Doves Unhappy," *New York Times*, November 4, 1969.
32. Chapin to Haldeman, RE Gallup Telephone Poll—The President's Speech, NSC, Vietnam Subject file, Box 78, Folder 5, NPRM, NARA.
33. "The Critics: It Is Not a Plan to End US Involvement," *New York Times*, November 9, 1969.
34. "Nixon, in Visit, Thanks Congress for War Support," and "Transcript of the President's Remarks," *New York Times,* November 14, 1969.
35. "Burch Calls Networks on Nixon's Speech," *New York Times*, November 14, 1969.
36. Cited in Pearlstein, *Nixonland*, 431.
37. *Haldeman Diary,* November 14, 1969.
38. "3 Networks Reply to Agnew Attack," *New York Times*, November 14, 1969.
39. *Haldeman Diary,* October 21, 1969.
40. David Mixner, *Stranger Among Friends* (New York: Bantam Books, 1996), 104–111.
41. Zaroulis and Sullivan, *Who Spoke Up*, 287–289.
42. Ibid., 283.
43. "A War Critic in Vietnam," *New York Times*, November 13, 1969.
44. *Haldeman Diary,* November 13 &14.
45. Wells, *War Within,* 395; Zaroulis and Sullivan, *Who Spoke Up,* 291–293.

Chapter 6

1. Seymour Hersh, "Lieutenant Accused of Murdering 109 Civilians," *St. Louis Post-Dispatch,* November 13, 1969.
2. Seymour Hersh, "Hamlet Attack Called 'Point-Blank Murder.'" *St. Louis Dispatch,* November 20, 1969.
3. "GI Says He Saw Vietnam Massacre," *New York Times,* November 20, 1969.
4. Henry Kamm, "Vietnamese Say GI's Slew 567 in Town," *New York Times*, November 17, 1969; "Song My: A US Atrocity," *Newsweek*, December 1, 1969.
5. Alexander Butterfield to the President, December 17, 1969, RE: Ronald Ridenhour, White House Special Files (WHSF) President's Office File (POF) Box 4, Folder 3, NPRM, NARA.
6. Telcon, Kissinger and Laird, November 21, 1969, Box 3, NSC, NPRM, NARA.
7. "Transcript of Interview of Vietnam War Veteran on His Role in Alleged Massacre," *New York Times*, November 25,1969.

8. "Meadlo's Hometown Regards Him as Blameless," *New York Times*, November 25, 1969.
9. "Most Back Calley in Poll," *New York Times*, January 1, 1970.
10. "Pinkville Gadfly," *New York Times*, November 29, 1969.
11. Cited by Michael Bilton and Kevin Sim, *Four Hours in My Lai* (New York: Penguin, 1992), 219.
12. Ibid., 196
13. Ibid., 220.
14. Seymour Hersh, "My Lai 4," *Harper's Magazine*, May 1970.
15. Statements by Ziegler, Resor, and Stennis. *New York Times*, November 27, 1969.
16. "NBC Report Says 100 Murdered Nearby," *Washington Post*, February 19, 1970; "Another Vietnam Atrocity Reported," February 20, 1970, United Press International; Seymour Hersh, "Coverup," *New Yorker*, January 15, 1972.
17. "New Atrocity Photos Allegedly Show Viet Thrown from Copter," *Reuters*, December 1969; "Pictures Studied by Army," *Washington Post*, November 30, 1969.
18. Quoted in Bilton and Sim, *Four Hours*, 266.
19. "Two In Congress Ask Study of Massacre Report," *New York Times*, November 21, 1969.
20. Daddis, *Withdrawal*, 78–105.
21. Ronald H. Spector, *After Tet: The Bloodiest Year in Vietnam* (New York: Free Press, 1993), 288.
22. Sorley, *Abrams Tapes*, 308–309.
23. Telcon Kissinger and Nixon, December 19, 1969, Box 3, NSC, NPRM, NARA.
24. Keith Walker, *A Piece of My Heart: The Stories of 26 American Women Who Served in Vietnam* (Novato, CA: Presidio Press, 1985), 77.
25. *Ibid*, 80-81.
26. Dang Thuy Tram, *Last Night I Dreamed of Peace* (New York: Three Rivers Press, 2017), 125.
27. Ibid., 142.
28. Ibid., 164.
29. David W. P. Elliot, *The Vietnamese War, Revolution and Social Change in the Mekong Delta, 1930–75* (Armonk, New York: M. E. Sharpe, 2007), 230–232.
30. David W. P. Elliot, *The Vietnamese War*, Revolution and Social Change in the Mekong Delta, 1930-75 (Armonk, New York: M. E. Sharpe, 2007), 301–302.
31. Nick Turse, *Kill Everything That Moves: The Real American War in Vietnam* (New York: Picador, 2013), 192–221.
32. Kevin Buckley "Pacification's Deadly Price," *Newsweek*, June 19, 1972.
33. According to Buckley, the effort to drive out the Viet Cong had ripped apart the entire fabric of the society: "People were driven off their productive land into refugee centers. Farm animals were killed and schools and hospitals destroyed." As devastating as Buckley's story remained, it had been significantly censored by *Newsweek* editors; see Nick Turse, "The Vietnam Expose that Wasn't," *The Nation*, November 13, 2008; Author interview with Kevin Buckley, Spring 2009.

34. David Hackworth and Eilhys England, *Steel my Soldier's Hearts*, (New York: Simon and Schuster, 2002), 368–371.
35. Christian Appy, *The Reckoning: the Vietnam War and Our National Identity* (New York: Viking Press, 2015). 179.
36. In the Mekong Delta, because of its extensive waterways, the Navy SEALS played a major role in targeting the VCI, sometimes leading and at other times conducting the actual mission. Mistakes were common, although as with My Lai, they could be covered up. One such operation, led by 25-year-old Lieutenant Robert Kerrey, came to light decades later, by which time Kerrey was serving in the US Senate representing his home state of Nebraska. His seven-man SEAL team was instructed to "take out" the NLF district secretary, but while this person was never found, their operation resulted in the deaths of 21 Vietnamese inhabitants including 13 women and children. Although these appeared to be civilians, this did not deter Lieutenant Kerrey from reporting to headquarters that his men had killed Viet Cong. For this achievement, he was awarded a Bronze Star. When these events were brought to light, Kerrey was accused by some of his men of responsibility for a massacre. See George Vistica, "One Awful Night in Thanh Phong, *New York Times*, April 21, 2001; Meryl Gordon, "Bob Kerrey's New War," *New York*, April 21, 2003; Tony Karon, "Bob Kerrey's Mission Impossible," *Time*, April 27, 2001.
37. Citizens Commission of Inquiry, *The Dellums Committee Hearings on War Crimes in Vietnam* (New York: Vintage, 1972), statement of Michael Uhl, 91–105.
38. Committee on Foreign Relations, U.S. Senate, "Vietnam: December 1969: A Staff Report," p. 6. (Washington DC: Government Printing Office, 1970).
39. Peter Kann, "The Hidden War," *Wall Street Journal*, March 26, 1969; also "The Invisible Foe: New Intelligence Push Attempt to Wipe Out Vietcong Underground," *Wall Street Journal*, September 5,1969.

Chapter 7

1. "US Foreign Policy for the 1970s: a New Strategy for Peace," Report by President Nixon to the Congress, February 18, 1970, US State Department, FRUS, Richard M. Nixon and Gerald Ford Administrations, 1969–76, *Foundations of Foreign Policy, 1969-1972*, Vol.1, eds. Louis J. Smith and David Herschler (Washington: Government Printing Office, 2003), 95–206.
2. "New Support for Nixon," *Time*, January 13, 1970.
3. Gen Haig's Trip to Vietnam in Jan 1970, Talking Points. NSC Alexander M. Haig Special File, Box 1007, Folder 2, NPRM, NARA.
4. 9 Feb 1970: Practice for SecDef/CJCS Given to General Abrams and Staff, Sorley, *Abrams Tapes*, 362–363.
5. 11 Feb 1970 SecDef Laird and CJCS Wheeler Brief, *Abrams Tapes*, 371.
6. Memorandum from Secretary of Defense Laird to the President, February 17, 1970. FRUS, *Vietnam: VI*: 590–592.

7. Haig to National Security Advisor (Kissinger), February 24, 1970, NSC, Alexander M. Haig Special File, Box 1008, Vol. IV, NPRM, NARA.
8. Loi and Vu, *Le Duc Tho-Kissinger Negotiations,* 108–109.
9. *Haldeman Diary,* February 17 and 20, 1970.
10. Loi and Vu, *Le Duc Tho-Kissinger Negotiations* 118–121.
11. *Haldeman Diary.* March 17, 1970.
12. Joshua Kurlantzick, *A Great Place to Have a War: America in Laos and the Birth of the Military CIA* (New York: Simon and Schuster, 2016) 154–155.
13. "Laos Will Evacuate Civilians from Plaines des Jarres," *New York Times*, February 5, 1970.
14. USIS report, "200 Interviewees from Plain of Jars.78% say homes damaged," contained in the Douglas Pike Collection, Box 13, (TT).
15. Henry Kamm, "Laotian Refugees Tell of Life Under Bombing" *New York Times,* October 11, 1969.
16. Kurlantzick, *Laos,* 130–131.
17. Van Atta, *With Honor*, 340.
18. Fred Branfman, *Voices from the Plain of Jars,* (Madison, WI: University of Wisconsin Press, 2013), 10–13.
19. Fred Branfman, Unpublished memoir (Branfman Collection shared with the author).
20. "Study of US Combat Role in Laotian War is Demanded by Senator Cooper," *New York Times* September 18,1969; "Senators Survey Depth of US Role in Laos Struggle," *New York Times*, September 18,19,1969.
21. William B. Macomber Jr. to Robert F. Mayo, September 22, 1960. NSC Vietnam Subject files, Box 75, Folder 7, NPRM, NARA.
22. "Laos: The Unseen Presence," *Time* October 17, 1969.
23. "Senate Opposes a GI role in Laos," *New York Times*, December 16,1969.
24. From Kissinger to Nixon (undated), FRUS, *1969–76 Vietnam, Vol. VI*, 570–572.
25. "B-52's Seek to Block Heavy Traffic Along the Ho Chi Minh Trail," *New York Times*, February 24, 1970.
26. "Secret US-Run Base Deep in Laos Seems Placid," *New York Times*, March 5, 1970; visit described in author interview with T. J. Allman.
27. "Senators Assail Policy of Nixon on War in Laos," *New York Times*, February 25, 1970; "Laos 2: Fear Test of the Nixon Doctrine," *New York Times*, March 1,1970; "US Will Release Information on Laos," *New York Times*, Mar 6,1970; "Senators Voice Concern," *New York Times*. March. 2, 1970.
28. "About the Situation in Laos," Editorial Note, FRUS, *Vietnam, Vol. VI:* Doc. 197.
29. "Deaths of 27 Americans in Laos Disclosed by US," *New York Times,* March 6, 1970.
30. *Haldeman Diary,* March 11, 1970.
31. And as Nixon emphasized to Kissinger, "we want to make it clear we have no combat forces in Laos. No one cares about B-52s in Laos. But people worry about our boys." Editorial Note, FRUS, 1969–76, Vol. VI: Doc. 197.
32. Sorley, *Abrams Tapes*, 393.
33. Minutes of Washington Special Action Group, March 19, 1970, 10: 08–11:55 AM Subject Laos and Cambodia, FRUS, 1969–76, Vol. VI: Doc. 203.

34. Minutes of Washington Special Actions Group Meeting, March 19, 1970 1:00–2:20 PM FRUS, 1969-76, Vol.VI: Doc. 204.
35. "Mansfield is Told that B-52s Won't Bomb North Laos Again," *New York Times*, March 15, 1970.
36. Kissinger to the President, B-52s in Laos, March 21, 1970, NSC Vietnam Subject Files, Box 64, 5-E Laos, PNRM, NARA.
37. Minutes of Washington Special Actions, Group Meeting, March 26, 1970, FRUS, *Vietnam*, Vol VI: Doc. 212.

Chapter 8

1. William P. Bundy, *Tangled Web: The Making of Foreign Policy in the Nixon Presidency* (New York: I. B. Tauris, 1998), 116–117.
2. Although as Bundy points out, "Lon Nol and his associates were confident they would have US support if they took power." The "clincher," he observes, was the American use of B-52s, which demonstrated to Lon Nol where US sympathies would lie if there was a concerted campaign to get rid of them. Bundy, *Tangled Web*, 49–150
3. Shawcross, *Sideshow*, 129–130.
4. William J. Webb, *The History of the Joint Chiefs of Staff; The Joint Chiefs of Staff and the War in Vietnam, 1971–1973, Part I*, Historical Division, Joint Secretariat Joint Chiefs of Staff, 127–129.
5. Secretary of Defense to the President, April 17, 1970, NSC Vietnam Country Files, Box 145, NPRM, NARA.
6. Al Haig to Henry Kissinger, April 8, 1970, NSC Alexander M. Haig Chronological File, Box 964, Folder 6, NPRM, NARA.
7. Memorandum of Conversation, April 4, 1970, FRUS, *1969–76, Vol VI*: 768–792.
8. Kissinger to Nixon, My Meeting with Le Duc Tho and XuanThuy, April 6, 1970, FRUS, *1969–76, Vol. VI*: Doc. 223.
9. *Haldeman Diaries* April 13, 1970.
10. Telcons, Kissinger and Nixon, March 20, 1970; Kissinger and Wheeler, March 20, 1970, Box 4 NPRM, NARA.
11. Kissinger to Nixon, March 27, 1970 RE: B-52 Operations in Cambodia, FRUS, *1969–76, Vol. VI:* Doc. 47.
12. "Saigon's Raid in Cambodia Stir US Aides' Concern," *New York Times*, April 1, 1970.
13. Kissinger to Nixon, March 19, 1970, FRUS, *Vietnam, Vol. VI*: Document 20, ftn. 1.
14. Shawcross, *Sideshow*, 132–133.
15. Henry Kamm, "89 Civilians Slain in Cambodia Fight, *New York Times*, April 10, 1970.
16. "Indochina's Crumbling Frontiers," *Time*, April 20, 1970.
17. T. D. Allman, "Massacre at Takeo," in *Reporting Vietnam: American Journalism, 1959–75*, ed. Milton J. Bates (New York: Library of America, 1998), 428–434.
18. "A Night of Death in Takeo," *Time*, April 27, 1970.

19. Memorandum from Director of Central Intelligence Helms to the President's Assistant for National Security Affairs (Kissinger), March 23, 1970, FRUS, *1969–76,* Vol. VI: Doc. 208.
20. Telcon, Kissinger and Ziegler April 15, 1970, Box 4, *NPRM, NARA.*
21. Telcon, Kissinger and Laird, April 20, 1970, Box 4, *NPRM, NARA.*
22. Richard M. Nixon, Address to the Nation on Progress Toward Peace in Vietnam, April 20, 1970. https://www.nixonfoundation.org/2017/09/address-nation-progress-toward-peace-vietnam-april-20-1970/
23. Prados, *Vietnam: an Unwinnable War,* 360.
24. Editorial Note, FRUS, *1969-76,* Vol. VI: Doc. 239; Webb, *The History of the Joint Chiefs of Staff, 1969–1970,* 247–248.
25. Memorandum from President Nixon to his Assistant for National Security Affairs, April 22, 1970; FRUS, *January 1969–July 1970, Vietnam, Vol. VI:* Doc. 245.
26. Memorandum from the Acting Chairman of the Joint Chiefs of Staff (Westmoreland) to Secretary of Defense (Laird), April 21, 1970, FRUS, *Vietnam, Vol. VI:* Doc. 244.
27. National Security Council Decision Memorandum 56, Actions in Support of the Cambodian Government, April 22, 1970, FRUS, *Vietnam VI:* Doc. 249.
28. Telcon, Kissinger and Rogers, April 22, 1970, Box 5, NPRM, NARA.
29. Memorandum from Roger Morris, Winston Lord and Anthony Lake to the President's Assistant for National Security Affairs (Henry Kissinger) April 22, 1970, NSC Country Files, Far East, Cambodia, Box 506, Folder: Volume III, NPRM, NARA; Tony Lake and Roger Morris, April 29, 1972, NSC Lake file, Box 1047, Folder 3, NPRM, NARA.
30. Telcons, Henry Kissinger and William Rogers 9:50 and 12:30 PM April 23, 1970, Box 5 NPRM, NARA.
31. Telcon, Henry Kissinger and Senator Mike Mansfield, April 23, 1970, Box 5, NPMR, NARA.
32. Alexander M. Haig Jr., *Inner Circles: How America Changed the World: A Memoir* (New York: Grand Central Publishers, 1992), 236–237.
33. There were no notes from this meeting, in which according to Kissinger, Moorer and Helms favored the use of American troops in Fishhook. Editorial note, FRUS, *Vietnam, VI:* Doc. 254.
34. For deception of Laird, see Hunt, *Melvin Laird,* 158–160.
35. Memorandum of Conversation, WSAG Meeting, April 24, 1970, FRUS, *Vietnam, VI:* Doc. 257.
36. Walter Isaacson, *Kissinger* (New York: Simon and Schuster, 1992), 263.
37. Roger Morris, *Uncertain Greatness,* (New York: Harper and Row, 1977), 174–175.
38. Transcript of Telephone Conversation between President Nixon, his Assistant for National Security Affairs (Kissinger) and the Chairman of the Armed Services Committee (Stennis), April 24, 1970, FRUS, *Vietnam, VI:* 876–878.
39. Transcript of Telephone Conversation Between President Nixon and his Assistant for National Security Affairs (Henry Kissinger), April 24, 1970. FRUS, *Vietnam, VI:* Doc. 258.
40. Webb, *Joint Chiefs of Staff History,* 253–254.

41. Memorandum from the President's Assistant for National Security Affairs (Kissinger), April 26, 1970, FRUS, *Vietnam, VI*: 885–886, ftn. 2.
42. Richard Nixon, National Security Decision Memorandum, April 26, 1970, FRUS, *Vietnam, VI*: 889.
43. Memorandum from Secretary of Defense Laird to President Nixon, April 27, 1970. FRUS, *Vietnam, VI*: 893, Ftn.1.
44. *Haldeman Diary,* April 27, 1970.
45. Laird, *With Honor,* 263–264.
46. Hersh, *Price of Power,* 190–191.
47. Isaacson, *Kissinger,* 276–277.
48. Stanley Karnow, "Cambodia's New Government Blundered into Predicament," *Washington Post,* April 27, 1970.
49. Alexis Johnson to Michael Rives, April 27, 1970. NSC Country File Far East Cambodia, Box 84, NPRM, NARA.
50. Michael Rives to Secretary of State William Rogers, April 28, 1970. NSC Country Files Far East Cambodia, Box 84, Vol. IV, NPRM, NARA.
51. Marshall Green to American Embassy, Phnom Penh, April 28, 1970, and Alexis Johnson to Ambassador Bunker, April 28, 1970, Box 84, Vol. IV, NPRM, NARA.
52. Telcon Kissinger and Rogers, April 23, 1970, Box 5, NPRM, NARA.
53. Telcon Kissinger and Governor Rockefeller, April 30, 1970, Box 5, NPRM, NARA.
54. Telcon Kissinger and Governor Reagan, April 3, 1970, Box 5, NPRM, NARA.
55. Comments of Madame Nguyen Thi Binh, April 21, 1970, Vietnam Information Group: Intelligence and Other Reports, Gerald R. Ford Presidential Library, (GRFL)
56. Memorandum from John Holdridge of the Operations Staff of the National Security Council to the President's Assistant for National Security Affairs (Henry Kissinger), April 28, 1970, FRUS, *Vietnam, VI*: Doc. 268.

Chapter 9

1. Shawcross, *Sideshow,* 150–151
2. https://millercenter.org/the-presidency/presidential-speeches/april-30-1970-address-nation-situation-southeast-asia
3. "Klein Reports Heavy Support for Nixon on Cambodia," *New York Times,* May 3,1970.
4. Webb, *The Joint Chiefs of Staff and the War in Vietnam, 1971–1973,* Part I, 265–266.
5. "Excerpts from Mansfield Speech on the War," *New York Times,* May 2, 1970.
6. Thomas M. Grace, *Kent State: Death and Dissent in the Long Sixties* (Amherst: University of Massachusetts Press, 2016), 13–14.
7. "Military Hallucination—Again," *New York Times,* May 1, 1970.
8. "Few Reds Found in Cambodia Drive," *Washington Post,* May 2, 1970.
9. Telcon, Kissinger and the President, May 2, 1970, Box 5, NSC, NPMR, NARA.
10. "128 US Planes Carry Out Attack in North Vietnam; Supply Lines are Targets," *New York Times.* May 3, 1970.

11. Cited in Melvin Small, *The Antiwarriors: The Vietnam War and the Battle for America's Hearts and Minds* (Lanham, MD: Scholarly Resources, 2004), 122.
12. "Nixon Put Bums Label on Some College Radicals," *New York Times*, May 2, 1970.
13. Grace, *Kent State: Death and Dissent*, 13–14.
14. Ibid., 122–123; Author interview with Howie Emmer, March 2011.
15. Grace, *Kent State: Death and Dissent*, 199.
16. "Kent State: Martyrdom That Shook the Country, *Time*, May 18,1970.
17. Kent State, Description of Events May 1-May 4. Written by May 4 Task Force of Kent State Students, March 23, 2006. Kent State University Records (KSUA).
18. Cited in Grace, *Kent State: Death and Dissent,* 208–209.
19. Among those who were joining the crowd was Alan Canfora, who had brought along some black flags in memory of his hometown friend Sergeant Bill Caldwell, which he had planned to fly once the demonstration was underway. (Author interview with Alan Canfora, March 2011.) Grace, *Kent State: Death and Dissent,* 193.
20. James A. Michener, *Kent State: What Happened and Why* (New York: Random House, 1971), 259.
21. Ibid., 199.
22. Carol Mirman, "This is Not What It Sounds Like on TV," May 4 Collection, KSUA.
23. Michener, *Kent State: What Happened,* 281–284.
24. Ibid., 282.
25. Cited in Ibid., 362.
26. *Haldeman Diary,* May 4, 1970.
27. "Houses in Snoul Burn as GIs Battle Hanoi Troops," *New York Times*, May 6, 1970; "Operation Successful: Outcome Uncertain," *Newsweek*, May 18,1970; "Two Kinds of War," Peter Kann, *Wall Street Journal*, May 11, 1970; Gloria Emerson, "Ruined Cambodian Town Can't Understand Why," *New York Times*, May 23, 1970. Journalist Peter Arnett thought the sacking of Snoul was an important story, but when he submitted it, his managing editor killed it, telling him there was a "highly charged situation in the United States" and that they "must guard our copy and see that it is down the middle and subdues emotion." Peter Arnett, *Live from the Battlefield* (New York: Simon &Schuster, 1994) 266–267.
28. "Marcher Felt She Had to Do Something," *New York Times,* May 8, 1970; "Spock Delivers Eulogy," *New York Times,* May 8, 1970.
29. Ibid.
30. Wells, *War Within,* 420–437; Zaroulis and Sullivan, *Who Spoke Up,* 318–320.
31. "South Carolina Students Clash with the Guard Again," *New York Times,* May 13, 1970; "Students Step Up Protests on War: Assail 4 Deaths," *New York Times*, May 6, 1970; "College Strife Spreads," *New York Times*, May 8,1970.
32. "Athletes Joining Campus Protest," *New York Times,* May 7, 1970.
33. Veterans had played a significant role at Kent State, among them Peter Winnen, who fought at Khe Sahn. Addressing a rally in Cleveland, Winnen explained, "I saw enough violence, blood and death and I vowed 'never again, never again' . . . I'm not a leftist, but . . . I'll do damn near anything to stop the war now." Quoted in "At War with War," Time, May.

34. Ron Kovic, *Born on the Fourth of July, 40h Anniversary edition* (New York: Akashic Books, 2016), 135.
35. "37 College Chiefs Urge Nixon Move for Prompt Peace," *New York Times*. May 5, 1970.
36. Wells, *War Within*, 433–434.
37. Edward Morgan for the President's File, Mid-day meeting in the President's office with eight university presidents, May 7, 1970, White House Special File (WHSF), President's Office File (POF), Box 80, Folder May 3, 1970, NPRM, NARA.
38. "Nixon Will Bar Hostile Comments on Students by Agnew and Others; Summons 50 Governors to Meeting," *New York Times*, May 8, 1970.
39. Telcon, Kissinger and Nathan Pusey, May 7, 1970, Box 5, NPRM, NARA.
40. Telcon, Kissinger and Haldeman May 8, 1970. Box 5, NPRM, NARA.
41. Telcon, Kissinger and President, May 8, 1970, Box 5, NPRM, NARA.
42. William Safire, *Before the Fall: An Inside View of the Pre-Watergate White House* (New York: Belmont Towers Books, 1975), 202–212.
43. Richard Nixon, *RN: The Memoir of Richard Nixon* (New York: Viking Press, 1979), 461–465.
44. "Nixon in Pre-Dawn Tour Talks to War Protestors," *New York Times*, May 10, 1970.
45. Haldeman Diary, May 9, 1970.
46. Ibid., May 11, 1970.
47. Nixon, *RN*, 460–462.
48. Walter J. Hickel to the president, May 6, 1970. Cited in Zaroulis and Sullivan, *Who Spoke Up?* 321–322.
49. Haldeman Diary, May 7, 1970.
50. "Collegians Warn Congress on War, *New York Times*, May 11, 1970; "Heavy Mail to Congress Opposes Cambodia War, *New York Times*, May 16, 1970.
51. "1000 Establishment Lawyers Join War Protest," *New York Times*, May 15, 1970; "Warren Praises Lobby for Peace," *New York Times*, May 20,1970.
52. Cited by Richard Reeves, *President Nixon Alone in the White House* (New York: Simon and Schuster, 2001), 215.
53. "Former Secretary of Commerce Scores Move into Cambodia," *New York Times*, May 9, 1970.
54. Telcon, Kissinger and David Rockefeller, May 6, 1970, Box 5, NSC, NPRM, NARA.
55. Correspondence of Elaine Miller with the author, July 12, 2011.
56. "Nixon Explains Cambodia Policy to 45 Governors," *New York Times*, May 12, 1970.

Chapter 10

1. Letters cited in Michener, *Kent State*, 391–396.
2. Kent State University Libraries, May 4 Special Collections and Archives, Box 99, Folder 17, (KSUA).
3. "Gallup Poll Finds 57% Support the President on Cambodian Policy," *New York Times*, May 10, 1970.

4. "War Foes Here Attacked by Construction Workers," *New York Times*, May 9, 1970.
5. "After Bloody Friday, New York Wonders if Wall Street Is Becoming a Battleground," *Wall Street Journal*, May 11, 1970; "War Foes Here Attacked by Construction Workers," *New York Times*, May 9, 1969; Richard Rogin "Joe Kelly Has Reached His Boiling Point," *New York Times Magazine*, June 28, 1970.
6. "Unions Differ on Indochina War," *New York Times*, May 13, 1970.
7. Memorandum to Bob Haldeman from the President, May 14, 1970. President's Personal File, Box 2, NPRM, NARA.
8. "For the Flag and For Country, They March," *New York Times*. May 21, 1970.
9. Memcon, Dr. Kissinger w/Mr. Robert McNamara, May 10, 1970, Box 5, NPRM, NARA.
10. Telcon, Kissinger and Otis Chandler, May 6, 1970, Box 5, NSC, NPRM, NARA.
11. Shawcross, *Sideshow*, 156.
12. Kissinger, *White House Years*, 514–515.
13. Telcon Kissinger and the President, May 7, 1970, Box 5, NSC, NPRM, NARA.
14. Telcon Kissinger and General Wheeler, May 5, 1970, Box 5, NSC, NPRM, NARA.
15. Telcon Nixon and Kissinger, May 5, 1970, Box 5, NSC, NPRM, NARA.
16. Press conference of the president of the United States, May 8,1970, NSC Cambodia Operations, Box 585, folder 2, NPRM, NARA.
17. 9 May 1970, WIEU (Weekly Intelligence Estimate Update) Sorley, *Abrams Tapes*, 413
18. 16 May 1970, *Ibid.*, 415.
19. Embassy Saigon to SecState, May 7, 1970, Record Group (RG) 59 VIET, NPRM, NARA.
20. "Cambodian Coast Under Blockade by Allied Fleet," *New York Times*, May 13, 1970; "World: Now It's Operation Buy Time," *Time*, May 25, 1970.
21. "Saigon's Zeal Raises Eyebrows," *Washington Post*, May 1970.
22. "Cambodia Seeking Help on Refuges," *New York Times*, May 9, 1970.
23. This entire experience is described in Richard Dudman, *40 Days with the Enemy* (New York: Liveright,1971).
24. "Nixon Popularity Increases in Poll," *New York Times*, June 7,1970.
25. Cited in Philip B. Davidson, *Vietnam at War: The History, 1946–1975* (New York: Oxford University Press, 1988), 282.
26. Hunt, *Melvin Laird*, 164; Van Atta, *With Honor*, 264–270.
27. Laird, Memorandum for the President RE: Cambodian Operations, May 7, 1970. NSC Subject Files Box 318, Folder 2, NPRM, NARA.
28. Telegram from the Department of State to the Embassy in Cambodia, May 21, 1970, FRUS, *1969–76*, Vol VI: Doc. 301; Memorandum from the President's Assistant for National Security Affairs (Kissinger) to President Nixon, undated, FRUS, *1969–76, Vol VI:*, Doc. 302.
29. Dick Kennedy to Gen Haig, May 20, 1970 NSC Haig Special File, Box 1011, Folder 1, NPRM, NARA.
30. 21 May 1970 Brigadier General Haig, Sorley, *Abrams Tapes*, 421–422.
31. Brigadier General Haig and Lon Nol, Prime Minister of Cambodia, May 23, 1970. NSC, Country Files, Far East Cambodia, Box 509, NPRM, NARA.

32. To Dr. Kissinger from Brigadier General Haig, undated, Haig Special File, Box 1011, NPRM, NARA.
33. Haig to Kissinger, May 26, 1970, NSC Haig Country Files, Far East, Cambodia, Box 509, Vol. VI, May 23,1970–June 1970, May 1970, NPRM, NARA.
34. Memorandum of Conversation, May 31, 1970, San Clemente, FRUS, *Vietnam, Vol VI:* Doc. 313.
35. *Ibid.*
36. "Nixon Encouraged by Briefing on War," *New York Times,* May 31, 1970.
37. https://www.nixonfoundation.org/2017/09/address-nation-cambodian-sanctuary-operation-june-3-1970/
38. As for making a real estimate of the impact of recent operations: "It's really very sickening to sit around here and contemplate the fact that we've been . . . talking about a basket full of fog." June 6, 1970: WIEU, Sorley, *Abrams Tapes*: 427–432.
39. Shawcross, *Sideshow*, 73.
40. Arnold R. Isaacs, *Without Honor: Defeat in Vietnam and Cambodia* (Baltimore, MD: Johns Hopkins University Press, 1997) 206; Merle Pribbenow (trans.), *Victory in Vietnam: Official History of the People's Army of Vietnam, 1954–1975* (Lawrence: University of Kansas Press, 2002) 257–257; "Hanoi Sees All Indochina as an Arena," *New York Times*, June 17, 1970; "Cambodia Incursions by US Appears to Unite Foe," *New York Times,* June 29, 1970.
41. Sydney Schanberg, "Problems of Cambodia," *New York Times*, June 8, 1970; "Airstrip Lost in Cambodia," *Washington Post*, June 8, 1970.
42. "Some Aids Doubt US Can Stop Reds in Cambodia," *New York Times*, June 14, 1970.
43. "Enemy Strength Evaluated," June 9, 1970; "Laotians Reported Joining Forces in Cambodia," *New York Times*, June 11, 1970; Joint State-Defense Message to Secretary of State, June 9, 1970, US Department of State (Central Files) Record Group 59. POL 27 CAMB/KHMER, NARA.
44. "Foe Still Holds Cambodian City, Despite Attacks," *New York Times*, June 16, 1970; Telcon, The Kissinger and the President, June 6, 1970, Box 5, NPRM, NARA.
45. Telcon, Kissinger and Packer, June 16, 1970, Box 5, NPRM, NARA.
46. "Cambodian City Retaken but Enemy Troops Escape," *New York Times*, June 17, 1970; "S Viets Help Take Cambodian Town," *Washington Post*, June 17, 1970; "Cambodians Complain Bitterly of Looting by Saigon's Troops," *New York Times*, June 26, 1970.
47. "Cambodia: Agony of a Nation Caught in the Middle," *New York Times*, June 28, 1970.
48. "Enemy in Cambodia Cuts Last Operating Line," *New York* Times, June 18, 1970; "Road to Saigon Severed," *New York Times*, June 19, 1970.
49. James Lowenstein and Richard M. Moose, *Cambodia: May 1970*. Senate Foreign Relations Committee Staff Report, June 7, 1970.
50. Bryce Harlow, Memo for the President, June 9, 1970, RE: Meeting with Vietnam Fact-Finding Trip, POF Box 81, NPRM, NARA.
51. "Fire Base Spruced Up for a Visit," *New York Times*, June 8, 1970.
52. Cited by Kissinger in phone conversation with Packard, June 9, 1970, Box 5, NPRM, NARA.

53. Bryce Harlow, Memo for the President, June 9, 1970, RE: Meeting with Vietnam Fact-Finding Trip, POF Box 81. NPRM, NARA.
54. Diary of White House Leadership Meetings, 91st Congress, June 9, 1971, Gerald R. Ford Library.
55. "Nation: No Confidence on Cambodia," *New York Times*, June 22, 1970.
56. Professions Join Lobby for Peace, *New York Times* June 11, 1970.
57. "Agnew Finds Senate Indecisive in Crisis" *New York Times*, June 25,1970.
58. "Lieut. Saxbe Tells Senator Saxbe He is Wrong," *New York Times*, June 25, 1970.
59. Richard Dudman, "In Flight with Guerillas in Cambodia," *New York Times*, June 24, 1970.
60. Sydney Schanberg "In a Cambodian Town, War and Terror," *New York Times*, June 17, 1970; Gloria Emerson, "Highway Incident Reflects Hostility of Indochina Allies," *New York Times*, July 6, 1970.
61. Webb, *Joint Chiefs of Staff History, Vol I*: 317; Sydney Schanberg, "Cambodian Economy is Badly Hurt by the War." *New York Times,* July 6, 1970.
62. Henry Kamm, "Cambodian Town is Just a Ruin," *New York Times*, July 8, 1970.
63. "In Cambodia, Gloom Returns After US Pullout," *New York Times*, July 2,1970.
64. Dudman, *40 Days with the Enemy*, 67; Interview with author.
65. Webb, *Joint Chiefs of Staff History, Vol. I*, 317.
66. CBS News Poll, June 30, 1970; Robert T. Hartman Papers, Box 38, House of Representatives file, Gerald R. Ford Library.

Chapter 11

1. Meeting Between President Nixon and Ambassador Dobrynin, Memorandum of Conversation (US) June 10, 1970, Geyer and Selvage (eds.) *Soviet-American Relations,* 148.
2. Memorandum from Presidential Assistant Kissinger to President Nixon, June 10, 1970, Ibid., 153–154.
3. See both Kissinger Memorandum of Conversation, June 10, 1970, Ibid.,154–159 and Dobrynin Memorandum of Conversation, June 10, 1970, Ibid. 159–165.
4. Kissinger Memorandum of Conversation, June 10, 1970, Ibid., 158.
5. Ibid., 159.
6. Raymond Garthoff, *Détente and Confrontation: American–Soviet Relations from Nixon to Reagan* (Washington DC: Brookings Institution, 1994), 36–38.
7. Garthoff, *Détente and Confrontation*, 128.
8. In July 1969 Gerard Smith, the newly appointed chief US negotiator for the Strategic Arms Limitation Talks estimated that if another year passed without a halt, "under present rates of construction the USSR will have about 1300 ICBMs with some 300 more under construction and about 300 SLBMs with another 300 under construction. Smith to Nixon, July 21 1969, NSC, Alexander M. Haig Chronological File, Box 959, Folder 3, NPRM, NARA.

9. The most helpful discussion of the arms control negotiations is Gerard Smith, *Doubletalk: The Story of the first Strategic Arms Limitation Talks* (New York: Doubleday,1980). Also illuminating is Garthoff, *Détente and Confrontation,* 146–223.
10. Ibid., 154.
11. Ibid., 136–140. An additional asymmetry was that the US was calling for a ban on testing and deployment but not the actual production. Since the USSR had not tested or deployed MIRV, as the United States had done, this would lock in their permanent position of inferiority. When negotiations resumed in Vienna, the USSR put forward a skewed proposal of their own—which would have banned the production and deployment of MIRV missiles, but not testing.
12. Ibid., 136–140. An additional asymmetry was that the US was calling for a ban on testing and deployment but not the actual production. Since the USSR had not tested or deployed MIRV, as the United States had done, this would lock in their permanent position of inferiority. When negotiations resumed in Vienna, the USSR put forward a skewed proposal of their own—which would have banned the production and deployment of MIRV missiles, but not testing.
13. This posed a particular problem for Dobrynin because the head of the Soviet delegation, Vladamir Semenov, was a deputy foreign minister and therefore Dobrynin's superior. See Richard A Moss, *Backchannels to Moscow*, 75–77.
14. Telcon, Kissinger and Rogers, May 15, 1970, Box 5, NSC, NPRM, NARA.
15. Memorandum of Conversation (USSR), July 7, 1970, *Soviet–American Relations,* 170.
16. Kissinger, *White House Years*, 551–554
17. Telegram from Ambassador Dobrynin to the Soviet Foreign Ministry, July 20, 1970, *Soviet–American, Relations,*181–182.
18. Telcon, Kissinger and Dobrynin, July 28, 1970, Box 6, NSC, NPRM, NARA.
19. Telcon, Kissinger and Nixon, July 8, 1970, Box 6. NSC, NPRM, NARA.
20. Typewritten note handed to John Ehrlichman. Discussed in Hersh, *Price of Power*, 227.
21. *Haldeman Diary,* July 13, 1970.
22. Memorandum of Conversation, NSC Meeting: Vietnam Ceasefire and Possible Diplomatic Initiatives, July 21, 1970, FRUS, *1969-76, Vol. VI:* Doc. 348.
23. Memorandum of Conversation, Xuan Thuy, Henry Kissinger et al, September 7, 1970, FRUS, *1969–76, Vietnam VII:* Document 34.
24. Memorandum from the President's Assistant for National Security Affairs (Kissinger) to President Nixon, September 7, 1970, Ibid., Doc. 35.
25. Webb, *Joint Chiefs of Staff History*, Vol I: 494–496.
26. "Senate Defeats 'End War' Move by Vote of 55–39," *New York Times,* September 2, 1970..
27. Kissinger to Nixon, September 7, 1970, *Soviet–American Relations,* 91–96.
28. Telcon, Kissinger and Joseph Alsop, Box 7, NSC, NPRM, NARA.
29. "Nixon Will Offer "Major" Proposal on War Tonight," *New York Times,* October 7, 1970.
30. "Transcript of President's Address Offering New Proposals for Indochina Peace," *New York Times,* October 8,1970.

31. Richard Nixon, Address to the Nation October 7, 1970. https://www.youtube.com/watch?v=-
32. Editorial note, *Foreign Relations of the United States* (FRUS) *1969–1976,* Volume VII, *Vietnam,* eds. David Goldman and Erin Mahan (Washington DC: Government Printing Office, 2010), Doc. t 46.
33. Telcon, Kissinger and Safire, October 6, 1970, Box 7, NSC, NPRM, NARA.
34. "A Plan to End to End the War," *New York Times*, October 18, 1970.
35. *Refugee and Civilian War Casualty Problems in Indochina*, Staff Report for Subcommittee to Investigate Problems connected with refugees and escapees, Committee on the Judiciary, US Senate, September 28, 1970.
36. Ibid.
37. The "standstill ceasefire" was proposed at a time when most of the North Vietnamese army was no longer in South Vietnam but in Cambodia, Laos, and just over the Demilitarized Zone in North Vietnam. With over 300,000 US troops in South Vietnam and close to a million men under Saigon's authority, a ceasefire would clearly disadvantage the enemy. For candid discussion with the cabinet, see Memorandum for the President's File, Cabinet meeting October 7, 1970 (document provided by John Prados).
38. Cold War History Project, "77 Conversations Between Chinese and Foreign Leaders, Zhou Enlai and Pham Van Dam," 174–175.
39. In an interview with the author in March 2009, Madame Binh explained that an important function in Paris was to provide a link to antiwar groups in the United States and around the world. See as well, Loi and Vu, *Le Duc Tho–Kissinger Negotiations,* 153–155.
40. Memorandum of Conversation (US) September 25,1970, 10 AM, *US-Soviet Relations,* 191–192; Memorandum of Conversation (US), September 25, 1970, 5:30 PM, 193–194; Memorandum of Conversation (USSR), September 25, 1970, 194–197.
41. Telcon Kissinger and Nixon, October 12, 1970, Box 7, NSC, NPRM, NARA.
42. Memorandum of Conversation (USSR), October 9, 1970, *US-Soviet Relations,* 206–207.
43. Memorandum of Conversation (US), October 22,1970, Ibid., 217–225.
44. Ibid., 224.

Chapter 12

1. Gerald Nicosia, *Home to War: A History of a Vietnam Veterans Protest Movement* (New York: Crown, 2001), 56–57.
2. "Veterans for Peace Simulate the War," *New York Times*, September 8, 1970.
3. Flyer, Vietnam Veterans Against the War, "A US Infantry Company Just came Through Here!!" http://www.wintersoldier.com/graphics/VVAW06.jpg
4. Nicosia, *Home to War*, 61; Flyer, "Operation Turning the Guns Around," Terry J. Dubose Collection Box 2, Posters and flyers from Vietnam Veterans Against the Warm (TTU).

5. Vietnam Veterans Against the War, Operation RAW schedule, Terry J. Dubose Collection, Box 2, Texas Tech Virtual Archive (TTU).
6. Cited in Nicosia, *Home to War*, 72–73.
7. Andrew E. Hunt, *The Turning: A History of Vietnam Veterans Against the War*, (New York: New York University Press, 1999), 54–55.
8. Nicosia, *Home to War*, 5–6.
9. Hunt, *The Turning*: 41–42.
10. Ibid.
11. "The floor of the small hut was covered with them, screaming and thrashing their arms back and forth, lying in pools of blood, crying wildly, screaming again and again. They were shot in the face, in the chest, in the legs, moaning and crying." Kovic, *Born on the Fourth of July*, 200.
12. "Our Wounded Warriors," *Life Magazine*, May 22, 1970.
13. Ibid.
14. *Haldeman Diary*, September 22, 1970
15. Safire, *Before the Fall*, 318–322.
16. Richard Reeves, *President Nixon Alone in the White House* (New York: Simon and Schuster, 2001) 264–265.
17. "Agnew is Heckled at Campaign Stop," *New York Times*, September 17, 1970.
18. Nixon, *RN*, 492–493.
19. "Bringing the Boys Home," *New York Times*, October 17, 1970.
20. "Nixon in New Jersey Bids Voters Help Silence Radicals," *New York Times*, October 18,1970; "President Scores Tide of Terrorism," *New York Times*, October 20,1970.
21. Wells, *The War Within*, 465.
22. *Haldeman Diary*, October 29, 1970.
23. "Eggs and Rocks Thrown at Nixon After Coast Talk," *New York Times*, October 30,1970.
24. "Nixon Sharpens Drive on Thugs," *New York Times*, October 31, 1970.
25. Terry H. Anderson, "The GI Movement and the Response from the Brass," in Melvin Small and William D. Hoover (eds.), *Give Peace a Chance: Exploring the Antiwar Movement* (Syracuse: NY: Syracuse University Press, 1992), 105..
26. For a superb account of the coffee house movement, see David L. Parsons, *Dangerous Grounds: Antiwar Coffee Houses and Military Dissent in the Vietnam Era* (Chapel Hill: University of North Carolina, 2017).
27. David Cortwright, *Soldiers in Revolt: The American Military Today* (New York: Doubleday, 1975), 53–54.
28. Larry G. Waterhouse and Marianne G. Wizard, *Turning the Guns Around: Notes on the GI Movement* (New York: Delta, 1972), 79–82.
29. "Antiwar Officers See Retaliation," *New York Times*, October 23, 1970.
30. List provided in Waterhouse and Wizard, *Turning the Guns*, 128–30.
31. Gloria Emerson, "GI's Now Wear A Lot the Army Didn't Issue," *New York Times*, August 28, 1970.
32. Kyle Longley, *Grunts: The American Combat Soldiers in Vietnam* (Armonk, New York: M. E. Sharpe, 1984),139.

33. Shelby S. Stanton, *The Rise and Fall of the American Army: US Ground Forces in Vietnam* (Novato, CA: Presidio Press 1985), 363.
34. Longley, *Grunts,* 136.
35. *Newsweek* cited the example of 22-year-old Sergeant Ralph Mitchell, who stated bluntly: "If I think a mission will be too costly, I weigh the value of it and my men come first." And if the mission seemed too costly, he wouldn't do it. *Newsweek*, "The Troubled Army in Vietnam," January 11, 1971.
36. "The Troubled US Army in Vietnam," *Newsweek.* January 11, 1970; MACV, Military Police, "Drug Abuse Suppression Program," December 16, 1970, NSC Haig Special File, Box 1011, Folder 4, NPRM, NARA.
37. Col. Robert D. Heinl, "The Collapse of the Armed Forces," *Armed Forces Journal,* June 7, 1970.
38. Drew Middleton, "Morale Sag Afflicts Career Servicemen." *New York Times*, October 26, 1970.
39. Cited in Richard Moser, *The New Winter Soldiers: GI and Veteran Dissent During the Vietnam Era* (New Brunswick, NJ: Rutgers University Press, 1996), 48.
40. "American Atrocity: Remembering My Lai," *Life*, December 5, 1969.
41. Printed Pamphlet, "The Winter Soldier Investigation," Terry J. Dubose Collection, (TTU)
42. Vietnam Veterans Against the War, *The Winter Soldier Investigation: An Inquiry into American War Crimes* (Boston: Beacon Press, 1972), 1–4.
43. Testimony of Ted Eckert, Ibid., 99.
44. Testimony of Sergeant Joe Bangert, Ibid, 72–74.
45. Testimony of Fred Nienke, *Ibid.*, 81–82
46. Testimony of Scott Camil, Ibid. 12–15. On napalm, "many times, we've called in air before we'd go into a village, or if we had a village where we'd lost people because of booby traps, we'd call in napalm and it just burns down the village and the people."
47. Testimony of Robert Craig, Ibid., 18–19.
48. Testimony of Ernie Sachs, Ibid., 17.
49. Testimony of Michael Erard, Ibid., 89.
50. Testimony of Ernie Sachs, Ibid., 17.
51. Testimony of Joe Bangert, Ibid., 72.
52. Testimony of Robert Clark Ibid., 91–93.
53. Sgt. Don Duncan, Closing Statement, Ibid., 165–172.

Chapter 13

1. "Jets Give Direct Support to Cambodian Troops," *New York Times*, August 6, 1970; "Laird Denies US Orders Air Raids to Aid Cambodians," *New York Times*, August 7, 1970.
2. "Air War in Indochina is Vastly Changed," *New York Times*, December 14, 1970.
3. "An awful lot of Americans just can't believe that one of these runts, wearing shower shoes and so on, could just be that goddamn smart," he told his generals." So, "people

got hung up, calling them 'slopes' and 'dinks' and that sort of thing, unable to believe that these little bastards are that clever." Sorley, *Abrams Tapes*, 470–471.

4. *Haldeman Diar*, December 3, 1970.
5. JCS to CINCPAC. July 6, 1970, State Department, RG 59 Pol 27 VIET 5, NPRM, NARA; JCS Recommendation, Operating Authorities, October 21, 1970, Ibid; "Air War in Indochina Is Vastly Changed," *New York Times*, December 4,1970.
6. Editorial Note, November 18, 1970, FRUS, *Vietnam, Vol. VII:* Doc. 70.
7. Memorandum from the President's Assistant for National Security Affairs (Kissinger) to President Nixon, RE: The Military Situation in Cambodia, December 9, 1970, FRUS, *Vietnam, Vol VII*: Doc. 85.
8. Diary entry by the Chairman of the Joint Chiefs of Staff (Moorer), December 10, 1970, FRUS, *Vietnam, Vol VII:*, Doc. 86.
9. Telcon, Nixon and Kissinger, December 9, 1970, Box 8, 8:45 PM, NSC NPRM, NARA.
10. Earlier, Nixon had sent a message to General Abrams expressing his fear that in the coming months, the situation in Cambodia would so deteriorate that enemy forces might reoccupy the areas bordering on South Vietnam. Transcript of Telephone Conversation between President Nixon and his assistant for National Security affairs (Kissinger), December 9, 1970, FRUS, *Vietnam, Vol VII:* Doc.83, ftn 6.
11. Diary entry by the Chairman of the Joint Chiefs of Staff, December 10, 1970, FRUS, *Vietnam VII*: Document 86.
12. Telcon, Nixon and Kissinger, December 9, 1971, 8:45 PM. NSC Box 8, NPRM, NARA.
13. Transcript of a Telephone Conversation between President Nixon and his Assistant for National Security affairs (Kissinger). December 12, 1970. FRUS, *Vietnam, Vol VII:* Doc. 88.
14. Kimball, *Nixon's Vietnam War* 239–240.
15. Haig to Dr. Kissinger, December 16, 1970, NSC, Haig Special File, Box 1011, Folder 6, NPRM, NARA.
16. Memorandum of Conversation, RE: Meeting between President Thieu, Ambassador Bunker and General Haig, December 17, 1970, FRUS, *Vietnam, Vol. VII*: Doc. 91.
17. "Vietnam Riot: Anti-GI Feelings Boil Over," *New York Times*, December 14, 1970.
18. Memorandum of Conversation, RE: Meeting between President Thieu, Ambassador Bunker and General Haig, December 17, 1970, FRUS, *Vietnam, Vol. VII*: Doc. 91, NPRM, NARA.
19. Pressed by Winston Lord, a junior member of his team, he included a proviso that "every effort be made" to avoid hitting non-combatants and to stick to the enemy. Winston Lord to Kissinger, RE: Cambodia/Vietnam Trip. NSC Haig Special Files Box 1011, Folder 3, NPRM, NARA.
20. Hunt, *Melvin Laird*, 176–177.
21. Memorandum Prepared by Admiral R. C. Robinson of Office of the Chairman of the Joint Chiefs of Staff, December 22, 1970, FRUS, *Vietnam, VII*: Doc. 93.
22. Admiral Moorer, Memorandum for the Record, December 23, 1970, FRUS, *Vietnam, Vol. VII:* Doc. 96.
23. "Attack by Saigon Against Chup Plantation Reported," *New York Times*, December 13, 1970.

24. See discussion, Richard A. Hunt, *Melvin Laird, and the Foundation of the Post Vietnam Military,* 177–178; Memorandum for the Record, Conference with President Nixon, December 23, 1970, FRUS, *Vietnam, Vol VII,* Doc. 96.
25. Melvin Laird to President Nixon, January 23, 1971, NSC, Vietnam Subject Files, Box 81, Operations in Laos, and Cambodia, NPRM.
26. Memorandum for the President's File, January 18, 1971, White House Special Files (WHSF), President's Office File (POF) Box 88, NPRM, NARA.
27. Ibid.
28. Minutes of Washington Special Action Group, January 2, 1971. FRUS, *Vietnam VII*: 296–304; General Bruce Palmer, "US Intelligence and Vietnam," in *Studies in Intelligence,* 88. (Document provided by John Prados).
29. Minutes of a Meeting of the Washington Special Action Group, January 21, 1971 FRUS. *Vietnam VII*: Doc. 108.
30. William P, Rogers to President Nixon, January 2, 1971, Record Group (Record Group) 59 POL 27 Viets, NPRM, NARA.
31. Ambassador Godley to Henry Kissinger, January 25, 1971, FRUS, *Vietnam, Vol. VII*: Doc. 109, ftn. 3.
32. *Haldeman Diary,* January 25, 1971.
33. Memorandum for the President's files. Deputy Assistant for National Security Affairs (Haig) January 26, 1971, FRUS, *Vietnam,* Vol. VII: Doc. 109.
34. Minutes of a meeting of the Senior Washington Special Actions Group, January 16, 1971, FRUS, *Vietnam, Vol. VII*: Doc.110, ftn. 10.
35. Bundy, *A Tangled Web,* 214.
36. Memorandum for the President's File by the Deputy Assistant for National Security Affairs (Haig), January 27, 1971. FRUS, *Vietnam, Vol. VII*: Doc. 112.
37. Ibid. The president also claimed that the important part of his promise was that he would not use ground troops in Cambodia—a commitment he had kept.
38. Ambassador Godley to General Haig, January 27, 1971, NSC, Vietnam Subject Files, Special Ops. in Laos and Cambodia, Box 83, Vol. 1, NPRM, NARA.
39. Derek Shearer, "An Evening with Henry," *The Nation,* March 8, 1971.
40. For descriptions of the event there are three accounts with diverging perspectives that oddly dovetail on the facts: Ellsberg, *Secrets,* 351–354; Henry Kissinger, Memorandum for the Record, Meeting with Project Runnymeade Conference, January 29, 1971, NPMR; Derek Shearer, "An Evening with Henry," *The Nation,* March 8, 1970.
41. American Embassy Ambassador Godley Vientiane to Secretary of State, January 29, 1971, 1971, US Dept of State, RG 59 Pol 27, Viets, NARA.

Chapter 14

1. "US News Blackout in Saigon Tried to Keep Even its Existence Secret," *New York Times,* February 5, 1971.
2. "Hanoi Expects Big Drive," *New York Times,* February 2, 1971.

3. "Vietnam: The Communication Breakdown," *Washington Post,* February 5, 1971.
4. This ended in tragedy for four photographers who perished during the first week when their helicopter was shot down over enemy held territory in Laos. "This Strange War Fascinates Me," *Time,* February 22, 1971.
5. James Reston, "Don't Ask, Just Listen," *New York Times,* February 12, 1971.
6. Minutes of a Meeting of the Washington Special Action Group, February 9, 1971, FRUS, *Vietnam VII:* 375–386.
7. "Rain, Fog and Mud Slow Drive into Laos," *New York Times,* February 10, 1970; Minutes of the Washington Special Actions Group, February 10, 1971 FRUS, *Vietnam: VII:* 387–397.
8. Not only Helms, Dick Smyser on Kissinger's staff raised similar concerns. James H. Willbanks, *A Raid Too Far: Operation Lam Son 719 and Vietnamization in Laos* (College Station: Williams-Ford Texas A&M University, 2014), 74.
9. Diary Entry by the Chairman of the Joint Chiefs of Staff, February 12, 1971, FRUS, *Vietnam VII:* 395, Doc. 127.
10. "Big Gap at the Briefings on Laos," *New York Times,* February 13, 1970; ."US Copter Pilot Taking Some of the Worst Fire of War," *New York Times,* February 12, 1971: "Two More Copters of US Downed in Drive on Laos," *New York Times,* February 13, 1971.
11. Memorandum for the President from Henry Kissinger, (with attachment), February 1, 1971, NSC Files, Vietnam Subject File, Vietnam Operations in Laos and Cambodia, Box 81 NPRM, NARA.
12. "30 Reported Dead at CIA Base in Laos," *Washington Post,* February 16, 1971l; "U.S Accidentally Bombs Laos Allies at C.I.A Base," *New York Times,* February 15, 1971.
13. "200 Laos Civilians Wounded in Bombing Error Are Moved," *New York Times,* February 18, 1971.
14. "Bomb Error Kills 6 S. Viets Massed at Laotian Border," *Washington Post,* February 8, 1971.
15. The indiscriminate character of such assaults is well illustrated by the disclosure that an American plane accidentally dropped bombs on a friendly unit near a CIA base in Laos. "Air War in Laos," *New York Times,* February 15, 1971.
16. Richard Helms to Henry Kissinger, April 9, 1971, Allegations of Intelligence Failures in Connection with Lam Son 719, April 9, 1971, attachment Sanitized, Memo for the CIA Director, RE: An Assessment of Allegations Regarding an Intelligence Failure in Connection with Lam Son 719, March 30, 1971; A Defense Department estimate of enemy strength cited 25,000 enemy troops in the Tchepone area, with an additional 40,000 troops in other parts of the Panhandle. Bob Houdek for Henry Kissinger, February 10, 1971. NSC Vietnam Subject, Box 84, Vol V, NPRM, NARA.
17. "Fierce Battle in Laos Slows S. Viet Drive," *Washington Post,* February 20, 1970.
18. "Allied Incursion in Laos Stalled for Second Day," *New York Times,* February 20, 1971.
19. Transcript of Telephone Conversation Between President Nixon and the Chairman of the Joint Chiefs of Staff (Moorer) February 22, 1971, FRUS, *Vietnam VII*: Doc. 134.
20. "Troops Retreat in Big Setback; Losses Heavy," *Washington Post,* February 22, 1971; "Indochina: the Soft-Sell Invasion," *Newsweek,* February 22, 1971.

21. Henry Kamm, "On Ho Chi Minh Trail," *New York Times*, February 22, 1971; "Reds Move More Supplies on Trail Since Offensive," *Washington Post*, February 22, 1971.
22. Telcon, Kissinger and Laird, February 23, 1971, 8:10 AM, Box 8, NSC. NPRM, NARA.
23. Telcon, Kissinger and Laird, February 23, 1971, 8:55 AM, Box 8, NSC, NPRM, NARA.
24. Telcon Kissinger and James Reston, February 23, 1971, Box 8, NSC, NPMR, NARA.
25. Summary of Conclusions of a Meeting of the Washington Special Actions Group, February 23, 1971, FRUS, *Vietnam: Vol. VII*: Doc. 136.
26. "South Vietnamese Battered by Foe at A Base in Laos," *New York Times*, February 27, 1971.
27. Conversation among President Nixon, Secretary of State Rogers, Secretary of Defense Laird, and the President's Assistant for National Security Affairs (Kissinger) and the Chairman of the Joint Chiefs of Staff (Moorer), February 27, 1971, FRUS, *Vietnam, Vol VII*: Doc. 140.
28. Ibid.
29. Gloria Emerson, "Copters Return from Laos with the Dead," *New York Times*, March 3, 1971.
30. Telcon, Kissinger and Reston, March 1, 1971, Box 8 NSC, NPRM, NARA.
31. Backchannel Message for the Presidents Assistant for National Security Affairs (Kissinger) to the Ambassador to Vietnam (Bunker), March 1, 1971. FRUS, *Vietnam, Vol. VII*: Doc 142.
32. Memorandum from the President's Assistant for National Security Affairs (Kissinger) to President (Undated) Tab A Assessment of the Laotian Operation. FRUS, *Vietnam, Vol. VII:* Doc. 142.
33. Telcon, Kissinger and Admiral Moorer, March 4, 1971, 1 1:40 pm; Telcon Kissinger and President, mid-afternoon March 4, 1971, Box 8, NSC, NPRM, NARA.
34. "Saigon's Forces Enter Tchepone Key Goal in Laos," *New York Times,* March 7, 1971.
35. Davidson, *Vietnam at War*, 648–649.
36. "Shift of Best Troops to Cambodia and Laos Worries Saigon Area," *New York Times*, March 9, 1971.
37. Backchannel Message from the President's Assistant for National Security Affairs (Kissinger) to the Ambassador to Vietnam (Bunker), March 9, 1971, FRUS, *Vietnam,* Vol. VII: Doc. 147.
38. Telcon, Kissinger and Moorer, March 9, 1971, Box 8, NSC, NPRM, NARA.
39. "Saigon's Forces in Laos Pull Back: Quit Hill Positions Near the Town of Tchepone," *New York Times*, March 13, 1971.
40. *Haldeman Diary*, March 11, 1971.
41. Oval Office Conversation, no. 466-23, 4 PM March 11, 1971 White House Tapes, in Kimball, *Vietnam War Files,* March 13, 1971, 144–146.
42. "Saigon's Forces Said to Establish New Battle Bases," *New York Times*, March 14, 1971.
43. "Saigon Sees Laos Invasion as Success," *Washington Post*, March 13, 1971; "Saigon's Forces Quit Fourth Base in Laos Fighting," *New York Times*, March 18, 1971; "ls Laos Drive Successful," *Washington Post,* March 14, 1971..
44. Telcon Kissinger and Moorer, March 13, 1971, Box 8, NSC, NPMR. NARA.

45. Memorandum from the President's Assistant for National Security Affairs (Kissinger) to President Nixon, South Vietnamese Operations in Laos and Cambodia, March 15, 1971; FRUS, *Vietnam, Vol. VII*: Doc. 150.
46. Dick Kennedy to General Haig, March 17, 1971, NSC, Vietnam Subject File, Box 84, Special Operations, NPRM, NARA.
47. "According to Plan, US Says," *New York Times*, March 18, 1971.
48. Telcon Kissinger and Admiral Moorer, March 18, 1971, Box 8, NSC, NPRM, NARA.
49. Henry Kissinger to Ambassador Bunker, March 18, 1971, NSC, Vietnam Subject Files, Box 84, NPRM.
50. General Haig to Dr. Kissinger, March 18, 1971, NSC Alexander Haig Special Files, 1013, Folder 1, NPRM, NARA.
51. Telcon, Kissinger and Moorer, March 19, 1971, Box 8, 1971, NSC, NPRM, NARA.
52. Oval Office Conversation, no. 471–2, March 19, 1971 in Kimball, *Vietnam War Files*, 146–150.
53. "Laos: the Bloody Battle to Get Out," *Newsweek*,, March 29, 1970..
54. Kissinger to Nixon, RE: General Abrams Remarks to the Press on Lam Son 719. Questions and Answers Following Background Briefing in Saigon, March 21, 1971, NSC, Vietnam Subject, Box 82, NPRM, NARA.
55. Telcon, Kissinger and Ziegler, March 17, 1971, Box 8, NSC. NPRM, NARA.
56. Dick Kennedy to General Haig, March 28, 1971, RE: Talking Points on Lam Son 719, NSC, Vietnam Subject File, Box 85 Special Operations Folder, NPMR, NARA.
57. Gloria Emerson, *Winners and Losers*, 114–118.
58. "GI Mood at Battered Khe Sanh: We Don't Want to be Relieved—We Want to Get Out," *New York Times*, March 26, 1971.
59. Ibid.

Chapter 15

1. For valuable overview of the military consequences of Lam Son 719, see Willbanks, *A Raid Too Far*, 158–179.
2. "Slugging it Out, *Newsweek*, March 29, 1971.
3. "Indochina The Invasion Ends," *Time Magazine*, April 5, 1971.
4. "The Helicopter War," *Newsweek*, March 15, 1971.
5. "Calley: Symbol of a Divided and Bitter Nation," *New York Times*, April 4, 1971.
6. *Haldeman Diary*, April 2, 1971.
7. "Calley Verdict Brings Home the Anguish of War to Public," *New York Times*, April 4, 1971; "The Wound Reopened," *Time Magazine*, April 12, 1971.
8. "Many in Nation Perturbed by Conviction of Calley," *New York Times*, March 31, 1971.
9. A resolution passed by the Kansas House of Representatives called for the release of Calley, claiming that if he was guilty, so was the country in a war "that has rotted and decayed our nation deeply." "Calley: Symbol of a Divided and Bitter Nation," *New York Times*, April 4, 1971.

10. The nine Senators were Jacob Javits, Hugh Schott, George Aikin, John Cooper, Charles Matthias, Charles Percy, Richard Schweiker, Lowell Weicker, and Ted Stevens. "President Prodded on War," *Washington Post*, April 7, 1971.
11. "More of the Same," *Time Magazine*, April 19, 1970.
12. Nixon and Kissinger, April 6, 1971, Conversation White House Tapes 001-004, White House Tapes, NARA.
13. Text of the Address by President Nixon, *New York Times*, April 8, 1971.
14. Telcon, Kissinger and Nixon, April 7, 1971, 9:30 PM; Telephone Tape 001-010, White House Tapes.
15. Telephone Tape, Conversation with William Rogers, April 7, 1971, 001-016, White House Tapes.
16. Telephone Tape, April 7, 1971, Conversation with Rebozo, 001-027; Conversation with Colson 00 1-031; Conversation with Ziegler 001-032, White House Tapes.
17. Telcon, Henry Kissinger and Nelson Rockefeller, April 7, 1971, 1:50 PM, Box 9, NSC, NPRM, NARA.
18. Telephone Tape, Conversation with Haldeman, April 7, 1971. 001-017. White House Tapes, NARA.
19. Telephone tape, Conversation with Haldeman, April 7, 1971, 001-039, White House Tapes, NARA.
20. Telephone Tape, Conversation with Kissinger, April 7,1971, 001-023 White House Tapes, NARA.
21. Telephone Tape, Conversation with Kissinger 001-041, April 7, 1971, White House Tapes, NARA.
22. Telcon Kissinger and Mrs. Carl Taylor, 11:28 pm, April 7, 1971, Box 9, NSC, NPRM, NARA.
23. "Nixon on Vietnam: More of the Same," *New York Times*, April 8, 1971.
24. Anthony Lewis, "The Conscience of the King," *New York Times*, April 10, 1971.
25. "Reaction to Talk Mixed in Capitol," *New York Times*, April 19, 1971.
26. "Nixon Suddenly Seems Like a Man under Siege," *New York Times* April 14, 1971; "Nixon: More of the Same," *New York Times*, April 18, 1971.
27. Richard Nixon, "Asia After Vietnam," *Foreign Affairs*, October 1967.
28. For a valuable discussion of the Nixon Administration's approach to "triangular diplomacy," see Garthoff, *Détente and Confrontation*, 227–295.
29. Memorandum of Conversation, Ambassador Corneliu Bogdan and Henry Kissinger, January 20, 1971. Presidential/HAK Memcons, NSC, Box 1025, Folder 3, NPRM, NARA.
30. Telcon, Kissinger and Nixon, April 12, 1971, Box 9, NSC, NPRM, NARA.
31. National Security Decision Memorandum 105, Steps Towards Augmentation of Travel and Trade Between the People's Republic of China and the United States, April 13, 1971, FRUS, *China, Vol. XVII*: Doc. 116.
32. Cited in Kenneth Hughes, *Fatal Politics: the Nixon Tapes, the Vietnam War, and the Casualties of Re-election* (Charlottesville: University of Virginia Press, 2015), 24–25.
33. Telephone Tape. Conversations with Kissinger, April 16, 001–104, 1–108, White House Tapes, NARA.

34. Telcon Kissinger and Nixon, April 15, 1971, Box 9, NSC, NPRM, NARA.
35. Nixon with Colson Conversation, 001–078 April 13, 197, White House Tapes, NARA.
36. "Build-up at the DMZ reported," *New York Times*, April 4, 1971.
37. Telephone Tape, Conversation with Kissinger, April 18, 1971, 001–145, White House Tapes. NARA.
38. "McCloskey Says US Hid Extent of Laos Bombing," *New York Times*, April 21, 1971.
39. Memo from Rosemary Woods to Haldeman, with attachment. Presidents (PPF) Personal Files, Memo-Feb 1971, NPRM, NARA.
40. Conversation between President Nixon and his Assistant for National Security Affairs (Kissinger), FRUS, *1969–76, VII*: Doc. 188.
41. Conversation between President Nixon and his Assistant for National Security Affairs, April 26, 1971. FRUS, *1969–76, VII*: Doc. 191.
42. Telcon Kissinger and Nixon April 12, 1971, Box 9, NSC, NPRM, NARA.
43. Cited in Kissinger *White House Years,* 714.
44. Telcon Nixon and Kissinger April 27, 1971, Box 9, NSC, NPRM, NARA.
45. Cited in Kimball, *Vietnam War Files*, Oval Office Conversation 488–15, Nixon and Kissinger, April 27, 1971, 158–159.

Chapter 16

1. Nixon, Kissinger Conversation, June 21, 1971, White House Tapes, NPRM, NARA
2. Nicosia, *Home to War*. 108–109.
3. Memorial Service, Conducted April 19, 1971, Vietnam Veterans against the War, Terry J. Dubose file, the Vietnam Center and Sam Johnson Vietnam Archive, Texas Tech University (hereafter TTU).
4. "Court Declines to Overrule Burger's Order on Mall 'Sleep-in'" *New York Times*, April 21, 1971.
5. "Objectives of Vietnam Veterans Against the War, DuBose Collection, TTU.
6. Andrew Stapp, *Up Against the Brass*: *Epilogue with Terry DuBose*, (New York: Simon and Schuster, 1970)196.
7. *Haldeman Diary* April 23, 1971.
8. "A Garbage Heap of Honor," *Newsday*, April 25, 1971.
9. Hunt, *The Turning,* 112–113.
10. Conversations with Charles Colson, April 20, 1971 (002–021) and April 22, 1971 (002–030), White House Tapes, NPRM.
11. "Men of Conscience," *Akron Beacon Journal*, April 26,1971; "Two Faces of Patriotism," *The Boston Globe*, April 20, 1971; "Voices of Authority," *Philadelphia Daily News*, April 22, 1971; William Raspberry, "Some Good Things About War Protest," *Washington Post*, April 27, 1971.
12. Jan Barry, "Why Veterans March Against the War," *New York Times*, April 23, 1971.
13. Conversation Between President Nixon and his Assistant for National Security Affairs (Kissinger), April 23, 1971, FRUS, *1969-76, Vol. VII*: Doc. 190.

14. Melvin Small, *Johnson, Nixon, and the Doves,* (New Brunswick, NJ: Rutgers University Press, 1988), 143.
15. On the dais were Senators Mike Gravel (D-Alaska) and Vance Hartke (D-Indiana), along with Congressional Representatives Herman Badillo, Bella Abzug, and many others. Prominent among the speakers were Coretta Scott King, the Reverend William Sloane Coffin, and VVAW spokesman John Kerry. See Tom Wells, *The War Within*, 498–500.
16. Conversation between President Nixon and his Assistant for National Security Affairs (Kissinger), April 21, 1971, FRUS, *1969-76, Vietnam, Vol. VII*: Doc. 188,
17. All Sides Applaud Peaceful Protest in Washington, *New York Times,* April 26, 1971.
18. "New Wave of War Protests-With a Difference." *US News and World Report*, May 10, 1971.
19. "The Mayday Tribe: Creativeness, Joy and Life against Bureaucracy and Grim Death," *New York Times*, May 3, 1971.
20. Wells, *War Within,* 500–502.
21. Ibid., 504–505.
22. "3 Representatives Decry Arrests on Capitol Steps," May 6, 1971; Nixon-Kleindienst Conversation. May 4,1971, Conversation (002–074) White House Tapes; Conversation with Haldeman, May 4, 1971 (002–080), White House Tapes, NARA. John Dean, Memoranda for the Presidents Files, May 7 and May 8, 1971, America Since Hoover File, Box 9, Folder 2, Gerald Ford Presidential Library,
23. "War Rally Here Attracts 10,000," *New York Times*, May 6, 1971.
24. Zaroulis and Sullivan, *Who Spoke Up,* 364–365.
25. Ellsberg, *Secrets,* 376–381.
26. Neil Sheehan, *A Bright Shining Lie: John Paul Vann and America in Vietnam* (New York: Random House, 1988), 592–598.
27. Ellsberg, *Secrets.* 127–132.
28. David Rudenstine, *The Day the Presses Stopped: A History of the Pentagon Papers Case* (Berkeley: University of California Press, 1996), 40; Ellsberg, *Secrets*, 188–191.
29. Ibid., 257–261.
30. "Laird Refused 69 Fulbright Request for the Pentagon Study on Vietnam," *New York Times*, June 17, 1971.
31. Daniel Ellsberg, "Laos: What Is Nixon Up To?" *New York Review of Books*, March 11, 1971.
32. "The Covert War," *New York Times*, June 13, 1971.
33. Conversation with Kissinger, June 13, 1971 (005–059), White House Tapes, NARA.
34. Conversations with John Mitchell, June 14, 1971 (005–068 and 005–070). White House Tapes, NARA.
35. *Haldeman Diary.* June 17, 1971; Wells, *War Within,* 517
36. Conversation with Kissinger, June 17, 1971 (001–525) White House Tapes, NARA.
37. Cited in Pearlstein, *Nixonland,* 581.
38. "Mansfield Offers Amendment for a Pullout within 9 Months," *New York Times*, June 22, 1971.
39. "House Votes on Withdrawal," *New York Times*, June 27, 1971.

40. "Senate on War: A Message to Nixon—Speed up Withdrawal," *New York Times*, June 27, 1971.
41. See useful discussion of Nixon's suspicions of Morton Halperin and Leslie Gelb, by Kenneth Hughes, *Chasing Shadows*, 94–99.
42. President, Haldeman, Mitchell, Kissinger, Ziegler and Laird, June 30, 1971, in Stanley Kutler, (ed.), *Abuse of Power: The New Nixon Tapes* (New York: Simon & Schuster, 1997), 6–7.

Chapter 17

1. Oval Office Conversation no. 527-16, Nixon, Haldeman, Kissinger and John Ehrlichman, June 23, 1971, Jeffrey Kimball, *Vietnam War Files*, 170.
2. Oval office conversation no. 534-2, Nixon, Kissinger and Haig, July 1, 1971, Ibid. 175–181.
3. Oval office conversation no. 634-3, Nixon, Kissinger, and Haig, July 1, 1971, Ibid. 184–185.
4. Gary J. Bass, *The Blood Telegram* (New York: Alfred A. Knopf, 2018), xi–xxiv.
5. Memorandum of Conversation, Chou En-lai, Henry Kissinger et al., July 9, 1951, FRUS,*1969–76, Volume XVII, China, 1969–72.* (Washington DC: Government Printing Office, 2006), Doc. 139.
6. Kimball, *Vietnam War Files*, 190–191.
7. "Word for Word—Kissinger in China: Beijing, 1971: Oh to Be a Fly on the Great Wall." *New York Times*, March 3, 2002.
8. Kissinger, *White House Years*, 756–757.
9. Hersh, *Price of Power*, 372.
10. "Congress Chiefs Pleased," *New York Times*, July 16, 1971.
11. Telcon, July 17, 1971, Henry Kissinger and Nelson Rockefeller, Box 6, NSC, NPRM, NARA.
12. Telegram from the Department of State to the Embassy in the Republic of China, July 16, 1971, FRUS, *Richard M. Nixon and Gerald R. Ford Administrations (1969–1976)*, Volume XVII: Doc. 145.
13. Memorandum to the President RE: Dr. Kissinger's Discussion with Ambassador Shen on the President's Visit to Peking," July 27, 1971, FRUS, *1969–76, Vol, XVII*: Doc. 152.
14. Telcon Reagan and Kissinger August 8, 1971, Box 6, NSC. NPRM, NARA.
15. "Three Democrats, Nixon Run Close in a Poll," *New York Times*, June 4,1971; "Poll Shows Nixon Tops 3 Democrats," *New York Times*, September 5, 1971.
16. Nixon Tape, Nixon and Haldeman, July 20, 1971, Conversation 540-1, White House Tapes, NARA.
17. Memorandum of Conversation, Kissinger and Henry Grunwald, Hugh Sidey, Jerry Schechter, August 13, 1971, NSC, HAK Memcons, Box 1025, Folder 3, NPRM, NARA.

18. Chinese Representation in the United Nations, Statement by William P. Rogers, August 2, 1971: "Text of Two U.S. Resolutions on China," *New York Times*, August 5, 1972.
19. Foreign Service officers were dismayed that neither government had been adequately prepared for news of Kissinger's July visit to China. The Japanese government had been notified a mere hour before Nixon's dramatic announcement to the entire world. Bundy, *Tangled Web*, 238.
20. As Kissinger had warned Zhou, there were rogue elements in the American "bureaucracy" who would create difficulties for their rapprochement. With his statements on dual representation, Rogers was unknowingly fulfilling Kissinger's warning. Nixon-Kissinger, Telcon, August 4, 1971, Box 6, NSC, NPRM, NARA; "A Sharp Turn on the Road to Peking: China Vote," *New York Times*, August 8, 1970.
21. "Bush Insists US Will Press 'Two China' Policy in the UN," *New York Times*, August 12, 1971.
22. Conversation between President Nixon and National Security Advisor Kissinger, September 30, 1971, transcript reprinted by National Security Archive, https://nsarchive2.gwu.edu/NSAEBB/NSAEBB70/doc6.pdf
23. Telcon President/Kissinger, October 2, 1971, Box 7, NSC, NPRM, NARA.
24. *Newsweek*, October 18, 1971.
25. Henry Kissinger to the President, My October Visit: The Atmospherics, October 29, 1971, FRUS, *1969–76, China, 1969–1972*, Vol: XVII: Doc. 163.
26. Memorandum of Conversation, Prime Minister Chou-en-lai and Dr. Henry Kissinger, October 21, 1971, 10:30–:45 PM, FRUS, *1969-76, China:* Vol XVII: Doc. 162.
27. Memorandum of Conversation, Beijing, October 21, 1971, 4:42–7:17, Prime Minister Chou En-lai, Henry Kissinger et al., FRUS, *1969–76, Vol .E-13,* Documents on China 1969–1972, Doc. 41.
28. Memorandum of Conversation, Prime Minister Chou Enlai and Dr. Henry Kissinger, October 21, 10:30 PM, FRUS, *1969–76, Vol. E-13, Documents on China 1969–1972,* ed. Steven Philips, Doc. 39.
29. Memorandum of Conversation, Prime Minister Chou-en-lai and Dr. Henry Kissinger, October 21, 1971, 10:30-1:45 PM, FRUS, *China,* Vol XVII: Doc. 162.
30. Memcon Prime Minister Chou-en-lai and Dr. Henry Kissinger, October 21, 1971, afternoon, NSC China/ Vietnam Negotiations, Box 1034, NPRM, NARA.
31. Memorandum of Conversation, Beijing, October 21, 1971, 4:42–7:17, FRUS, Volume E-13, *Documents on China*, Doc.41
32. Ibid.
33. Henry Kissinger to Haig, October 21, 1971, NSC Files, Box 1034, NPRM, NARA.
34. Messages from the President's Deputy Assistant for National Security Affairs (Haig) to the President's Assistant for National Security Affairs (Kissinger) Washington, October 22, 1971, FRUS, *1969–76,* Vol.E-13, Doc. 42
35. Memcon, Chou EnLai and Henry Kissinger, October 26, 1971, 5:30 -8:10 PM, FRUS, *1969–1976, E-13, Documents on China,* Doc. 55.

36. Quang Zhai, *China and the Vietnam Wars, 1950–75* (Chapel Hill: University of North Carolina Press, 2000), 137; "Hanoi and Peking Strengthen Ties," *New York Times*, September 29, 1971.

Chapter 18

1. *Haldeman Diary*, May 26, 1971.
2. Bundy, *Tangled Web*, 90–91.
3. Soviet Note, handed to Kissinger, April 23, 1971, and Memorandum of Conversation Kissinger and Dobrynin, April 23, 1971, NSC President's Trip Files, Box 491, Folder 1, NPRM, NARA.
4. Smith, *Double Talk*, 231–236.
5. *Haldeman Diary*, May 19, 1971.
6. Van Atta and Laird, *With Honor*, 196–197.
7. Garthoff, *Détente and Confrontation*, 147–148; Smith, *Double Talk*, 222–233.
8. Memorandum for the President from Henry Kissinger, May 1971, White House Special File, President's Office File, Box 84; Memorandum for the President's File NSC by Clarke McGregor, May 20, 1971, White House Special File President's Office File, Box 84, NPRM, NARA.
9. Telcon, Kissinger and Haldeman, May 12, 1971, Box 14, NSC, NPRM, NARA.
10. "Remarks by the President on National Radio and Television in the Briefing Room," *New York Times*, May 20, 1971.
11. Smith, *Double Talk*, 225.
12. Telcon, Kissinger and Smith, June 30, 1971, Box 14, NSC, NPRM, NARA.
13. James Reston, Washington, *New York Times*, May 21, 1971.
14. Anatoly Dobrynin, *In Confidence: Moscow's Ambassador to America's Six Presidents* (New York: Times Books, 1995), 223–224; Memorandum of Conversation (USSR), US Department of State, Geyer and Selvage, *Soviet--US Relations*, 337–338.
15. Discussed in Carolyn Eisenberg, *Drawing the Line: The American Decision to Divide Germany* (New York: Cambridge University Press, 1996), 12–71, 363–410.
16. Keith Nelson, *The Making of Détente* (Baltimore: Johns Hopkins Press,1995), 59–63:;Garthoff, *Détente and Confrontation*, 125–127.
17. Telegram from Ambassador Dobrynin to the Soviet Foreign Ministry US, June 10, 1971, Geyer and Selvage, *Soviet–US Relations*, 375–376; and Meeting Between Presidential Assistant Kissinger and Soviet Ambassador Dobrynin (US), June 8, 1972, 368–371.
18. Conversation Nixon, Kissinger, and Alexander Haig, June 29, 1971, in Douglas Brinkley and Luke A. Nichter (eds.), *The Nixon Tapes, 1971–72* (New York, Houghton Mifflin, 2014). 185–186.
19. Transcript of Telephone Conversation, Kissinger and Dobrynin, July 15, 1971, *Soviet–US Relations*, 399.
20. Nelson, *Détente*, 99.

21. *Haldeman Diary,* July 23, 1971.
22. Loi and Vu, *Le Duc Tho–Kissinger Negotiations,* 181–183.
23. Ibid., 196-197.
24. Ibid., 191–193; Lien-Hang-Nguyen, *Hanoi's War,* 210–212.
25. Jeffrey Kimball, *Nixon's Vietnam War,* 270–276.
26. "Minh Quits Vietnam Race Saying Thieu Rigs the Election," *New York Times,* August 20, 1971.
27. "Ky Leaves Race Despite US Pleas" and "Withdrawal Regretted by US," *New York Times,* August 24, 1971.
28. Memorandum of Conversation Henry Kissinger, Xuan Thuy et al., September 1971, FRUS, *1969–76, Vol. VII:* Doc. 254.
29. "McGovern Begins a Fact-finding Tour of Vietnam," *New York Times,* September 14, 1971. For critical discussion of the McGovern trip, see Larry Berman, *No Peace, No Honor,* 91–97.
30. Kimball, *Nixon's Vietnam War,* 166–169.
31. Telcon, Kissinger and Ziegler, September 2, 1971, Box 11, NSC, NPRM, NARA.
32. *Haldeman Diary,* September 8, 1971,
33. Telcon, Kissinger and Laird, September 20, 1971, Box 11, NSC, NPTM, NARA.
34. Memorandum from President's Assistance for National Security (Kissinger) to the President (Nixon), September 18, 1971, FRUS, *1969–76, Vol VII:* Doc. 257.
35. Memorandum for the President from Henry Kissinger, Highlights of My Talk with Dobrynin, September 20, 1971, *Soviet–US Relations,* 444–445.
36. Meeting Presidential Assistant Kissinger and Foreign Minister Gromyko, September 29, 1971, *Soviet–US Relations,* 478–479.
37. Ibid., 479.

Chapter 19

1. Meeting Between Presidential Assistant Kissinger and Ambassador Dobrynin, October 30, 1971. Geyer and Selvage, *Soviet-American Relations,* 504–505.
2. Editorial Note, Department of State, FRUS, *Vietnam July 1970–January 1972,* VII: 986.
3. Hanhamaki, *The Flawed Architect,* 159–151: Nguyen, *Hanoi's War,* 226–227.
4. Memorandum of Conversation (US), November 18, 1971, Geyer and Selvage, *Soviet-American Relations,* 520–521, and Memorandum of Conversation (USSR) November 18, 1971, 525–526.
5. Editorial Note, October 25, 1971, FRUS, *1969-76, Vol. VII:* Doc .272.
6. Conversation Between President Nixon and his Assistant for National Security Affairs (Kissinger), November 20, 1971, FRUS. *Vietnam, VII:* 1001–1006.
7. Transcript, Conversation of Nixon and Kissinger, November 20, 1971, Brinkley and Nichter, *Nixon Tapes,* 324–327.
8. Ibid.

9. Bass, *Blood Telegram*, 60–61.
10. Ibid., 231–232.
11. Robert J. McMahon, "The Danger of Geopolitical Political Fantasies: Nixon, Kissinger and the South Asia Crisis of 1971," in Fredrik Logevall and Andrew Preston (eds.), *Nixon in the World*, 261–263; Bundy, *Tangled Web*, 274–275.
12. Transcript, Conversation of Nixon, Kissinger, Haldeman, November 5, 1971, Brinkley and Nichter, *Nixon Tapes*, 312–315.
13. Resolutions Submitted to UN Council, *New York Times*, December 6, 1971.
14. See important discussion in Garthoff, *Détente and Confrontation*, 299–322.
15. Bass, *Blood Telegram*, 272–273.
16. Telcon, Kissinger and Sisco, November 22, 1971, Box 12, NSC, NPRM, NARA.
17. *Haldeman Diary*, December 6, 7, and 9.
18. Bass, *Blood Telegram*, 301–303.
19. Dallek, *Partners in Power*, 343–347.
20. Quoted in Bass, *Blood Telegram*, 322.
21. McMahon, "The Danger of Geopolitical Political Fantasies," 264.
22. Anthony Lewis, "Tilt: the Machine Stops," *New York Times*, January 10, 1972; Tom Wicker "The Anderson Papers," *New York Times*, January 4, 1971.
23. Thomas and Isaacson. *Kissinger*, 380–385.
24. Reeves, *Nixon Alone in the White House*, 411–413.
25. *Haldeman Diary*, January 5, 1972.
26. Robert Dallek, *Partners in Power*, 349–351.
27. Richard A. Moss, *Nixon's Backchannel to Moscow: Confidential Diplomacy and Détente* (Lexington: University of Kentucky Press, 2017) 194–195.
28. Message from the Commander, Military Assistance Command, Vietnam (Abrams) to the Commander in Chief, Pacific (McCain), January 20, 1972, FRUS, *Vietnam, Vol. VIII*: Doc. 1.
29. John Ehrlichman, *Witness to Power: the Nixon Years* (New York: Simon and Schuster,1982), 279.
30. Kissinger, *White House Years*, 918.

Chapter 20

1. Talking Points—Opening Session, Undated, NSC Files, China/Vietnam Negotiations Box 1037, Folder 1, NPRM, NARA.
2. Memorandum of Conversation, Prime Minister Chou En-lai, General Haig et al., January 3, 1972, NSC Files, China/Vietnam Negotiations, Box 1036, Folder 3, NPRM, NARA.
3. National Military Command Center, Memorandum for the Record, Subject: Proud Deep, December 30, 1971, NSC Vietnam Subject File, Box 123, Folder 5, NPRM, NARA; "Heavy American Bombing of North Goes Into 3rd Day," *New York Times*,

December 28, 1971; Editorial, "Limited Air War," *New York Times,* December 28, 1971.

4. Cited in Margaret MacMillan, *Nixon and Mao: The Week That Changed the World* (New York: Random House, 2007), 227.
5. Haig to Kissinger, January 8, 1972, NSC China/Vietnam Negotiations, Box 1037, Folder 1, NPRM, NARA.
6. Memorandum of Conversation, Minister Chou En-lai, General Haig et al., January 3, 1972, NSC China/Vietnam Negotiations, Box 1036, Folder 3, NPRM, NARA.
7. Haig to Kissinger, January 6, 1972, NSC China/Vietnam Negotiations, Box 1037, Folder 1, NPRM, NARA.
8. Hersh, *Price of Power,* 482–484; "Poll Finds 4-point Gain in Nixon Support," *New York Times,* February 17, 1972.
9. "Transcript of the President's Address to the Nation on U.S. Policy in Vietnam," *New York Times,* January 26, 1972.
10. Hersh, *Price of Power,* 484–485.
11. Telcon, Governor Rockefeller/ Mr. Kissinger, January 25, 1972, Box 12, NSC, NPMR, NARA.
12. Sorley, *Abrams Tapes,* 1968–1972, Southeast Asia Assessment, January 4, 1972, 740–742.
13. Ibid., Transcript Weekly Intelligence Estimate Update, January 15, 1972, 749–753.
14. Transcript, Richard Nixon and National Security Council, February 2, 1972, Brinkley and Nichter, *Nixon Tapes,* 362–363.
15. Ibid., 379.
16. Ibid., 382–383.
17. National Security Council Decision Memorandum 149, to the Secretary of Defense, Additional Authorities for Southeast Asia, February 4, 1972, FRUS, *1969–1976, Vol. VIII:* Doc. 15.
18. *Haldeman Diary,* February 14, 1972.
19. Transcript, Richard Nixon and Henry Kissinger in the Oval Office, February 14, 1972, in Brinkley and Nichter, *Nixon Tapes,* 394–396.
20. Henry Kissinger, Memorandum for the President's File, February 14, 1972, Meeting with Mr. Andre Malraux, February 14, 1972, NSC, HAK/President's Memcons, Box 1026, Folder 1, NPRM, NARA.
21. Henry Kissinger, Memorandum for the President's File, February 14, 1972, Dinner in Honor of M. Andre Malraux, the White House, NSC, HAK/President's Memcons, Box 1026, Folder 1, NPRM, NARA.
22. Henry Kissinger, Memo for the President, RE: Mao, Chou and the Chinese Litmus Test," NSC February 19, 1972.
23. President Nixon to William P. Rogers, Henry A. Kissinger, January 19, 1972, PPF, Box 2, NPRM, NARA; John H. Holdridge to Henry Kissinger, Papers Under Preparation for the President's Trip to the PRC, January 18, 1972, NPRM, NARA.
24. Anthony Lewis, "China and Vietnam," *New York Times,* February 21, 1972.
25. Tad Szulc, *The Illusion of Peace: Foreign Policy in the Nixon Years* (New York: Viking, 1978), 516

26. Memorandum of Conversation, Dr. Henry Kissinger, and Prime Minister Zhou Enlai, February 21, 1972, FRUS, *1969–76, Vol. E-11*: Doc. 89.
27. Memorandum of Conversation Chairman Mao-Tse-Tung, President Nixon et al., February 21, 1972, FRUS, *China*, Vol. XVIII: Doc. 194.
28. Memorandum of Conversation, February 21, 1972, 2:50–3:55 PM, President Nixon, Chairman Mao Tse Tung et. al, FRUS, *China*, Vol. XVIII: Doc. 194.
29. MacMillan, *Nixon and Mao*, 74–75.
30. Interview With Ambassador Winston Lord, Episode 15 China, https://nsarchive2.gwu.edu/coldwar/interviews/episode-15/lord1.html.
31. MacMillan, *Nixon and Mao*, 146–148.
32. "Transcript of the Toasts by Premier Chou and President Nixon," *New York Times*, February 22, 1972.
33. Memorandum of Conversation, Beijing, February 21, 1972. Kissinger/Zhou En Lai et al., FRUS, *Volume E-13: Documents on China 1969–1972*, Doc. 89.
34. Mike Chino, "The Biggest Story I Ever Covered," *China-US Focus*, February 12, 1972,
35. Hugh Sidey, "A President Wrapped in an Enigma," *Life Magazine*, March 3, 1972.
36. "Mrs. Nixon's Shopping Day: Pajamas, China," *New York Times*, February 26, 1972.
37. "Nixon and Chou Stroll and Go Boating in Hangchow," *New York Times*, February 27, 1972.
38. MacMillan, *Nixon and Mao*, 274; Hersh, *Price of Power*, 498–499.
39. Ibid., 264.
40. Memorandum of Conversation, The President, Chou Enlai et al. Tuesday February 22, 1972, 2:10-6:00 PM, FRUS, *Documents on China, 1969–76, Volume XVII*, Doc. 196.
41. Memorandum of Conversation, The President, Dr. Kissinger, Chou Enlai, February 24, 1972, 5:15- 8:05 PM, FRUS, *1969–76, Volume XVII, China:* Doc. 199.
42. Memorandum of Conversation, Beijing, February 25, 1972, 4:50–5:25, FRUS, *1969–1976, Vol. E-13, Documents on China*, 1969–1972: 100.
43. *Haldeman Diary*, February 23, 1972.
44. Memorandum of Conversation, Hangchow, February 26–27, 1972, FRUS, *1969-1976, Vol. E-13, Documents on China, 1969–1972*: Doc. 104.
45. Macmillan, *Nixon and Mao*, 311–312
46. Memorandum of Conversation, February 27–28, 11:05 PM-12:05 AM, FRUS, *China 1969–73, Vol. XIII:* Doc. 202.
47. Nixon, *RN*, 572.
48. "Transcript of President's Speech on His Return Home," *New York Times*, February 19, 1972.
49. Telcon, Kissinger and Goldwater, February 28, 1972, Box 13, NSC, NPRM, NARA.
50. Telcon, Kissinger and Reagan, February 28, 1972.10:30 PM, Box 13, NSC, NPRM, NARA.
51. In preparing for a final press conference in Beijing, Kissinger alerted the Chinese that in order to cement "the bureaucracy" to their new approach, "I will therefore claim a greater degree of participation for the bureaucracy in the process than you might remember." FRUS, *1969–76*, E–11: Doc. 106.

52. Memorandum for the President's File, Meeting with Bipartisan Leadership, Tuesday, February 29, 1972, President's Office File, Box 88, NPRM, NARA.
53. Notes for the President's File—RK Price, Meeting of the Cabinet, Tuesday, February 29, 1972, President's Office File, Box 88, NPRM, NARA.

Chapter 21

1. Message from the Commander Military Assistance Command, Vietnam (Abrams) to the Chairman of the Joint Chiefs of Staff (Moorer) and the commander in Chief, Pacific (McCain). March 8, 1972. FRUS, *1969–76, Vol. VIII*: Doc. 35.
2. Willard Webb, *The Joint Chiefs of Staff and the War in Vietnam, 1971–73 Part II*: 283–288; 290–292. (Document shared by historian John Prados).
3. Telcon, Kissinger and Nixon, March 27, 1972, Box 13, NSC, NPRM, NARA.
4. "Advisors Uneasy," *New York Times,* April 2, 1971.
5. "Half of Province in South Vietnam Lost to Invaders," *New York Times*, April 2, 1972.
6. Conversation Between President Nixon and the President's Assistant for National Security (Kissinger), April 3, 1972, in Brinkley and Nichter, *Nixon Tapes*, 436–437.
7. Hunt, *Melvin Laird,* 218; Joint Chiefs of Staff, Memorandum for the Secretary of Defense, Subj: Urgent Request for Air Authorities, March 9, 1972, NSC Haig Special File, Box 1016, Folder 1, NPRM, NARA; Telcon, Kissinger and the President, March 11, 1972, Box 13, NSC, NPRM. NARA.
8. Telcon, Nixon and Kissinger April 12, 1972, Box 13, NSC, NPRM, NARA.
9. Conversation among President Nixon, the President's Assistant for National Security Affairs (Kissinger) and the Chairman of the Joint Chiefs of Staff (Moorer), April 3,1972, FRUS, *Vietnam Vol. VIII*: Doc. 54; Hunt, *Melvin Laird,* 224–225.
10. Webb, *History of the Joint Chiefs of Staff, Vol. II*: 224–225, 355–360.
11. Meeting Between Presidential Assistant (Kissinger) and Ambassador Dobrynin, April 3, 1972, David C. Geyer and Douglas Selvage (eds.), *Soviet-American Relations,* 638–641.
12. Ibid., ftn. 2, 638.
13. Memorandum of Conversation, Nixon and Dobrynin, April 10, 1972, Geyer and Selvage, *Soviet-American Relations,* 653–654.
14. Memorandum of Conversation between Presidential Assistant Kissinger and Ambassador Dobrynin, April 8, 1972, Geyer and Selvage, *Soviet-American Relations,* 641–642.
15. Telcon, Nixon and Kissinger, April 12, 1972, Box 13, NSC, NPRM, NARA,
16. Telcon, Secretary Laird and Kissinger, April 11, 1972, NSC, NPRM, NARA.
17. Telcon, Nixon and Kissinger, April 9, 1972, Box 13, NSC, NPMR, NARA.
18. Hunt, *Melvin Laird,* 229–231.
19. *Haldeman Diary,* April 16, 1972.

20. Vietnam Workers Party Central Committee, "Lets Shatter All Military Adventures of the US Aggressors and Their Henchmen," April 6, 1972, Pike Collection, Texas Tech Archive (TTU).
21. "Candidates Score Nixon on Bombing," *New York Times,* April 17,1972; "Humphrey, Muskie and Kennedy Assail Bombing," *New York Times,* April 16,1972.
22. "9 College Heads Deplore Bombing," *New York Times,* September 20, 1972.
23. Anthony Lewis, "At Home Abroad," *New York Times,* April 17, 1972.
24. Stephen Randolph, *Powerful and Brutal Weapons* (Cambridge: Harvard University Press, 2017), 90.
25. Al Haig, Memorandum for Henry Kissinger, April 19, 1972, NSC, Alexander M. Haig Special Files, Box 1014, Folder 3, NPRM, NARA.
26. Alexander Haig, South Vietnam Trip Report (April 16–18). NSC, Alexander M. Haig Special Files, Box 1014, NPRN, NARA.
27. The Tu Cong ("Return to Village") camp was one of many constructed by the South Vietnamese military during the previous years as a prong of the government's pacification program. As described by Marin Teitel, director of the American Friends Overseas Refugee program, these facilities were "more like concentration camps" than a functioning village. See Martin Teitel testimony, prepared for Senator Edward Kennedy's subcommittee on Refugees, May 8, 1972 (AFSC Archive).
28. Martin Teitel, "Again the Suffering of Mylai," *New York Times,* June 7, 1972.
29. Jane Barton to Friends Headquarters, April 1972, American Friends Service Committee Archive.
30. Jane Barton, "Female POWs," 1972, Report to the American Friends Service Committee, American Friends Service Committee Archive
31. Diane Jones to Martin Teitel, January 17,1972, attachments, Arrest of Saigon Student Leader Huynh Tan Mam and Statement of South Vietnam Students Concerning the Policy of Continuation of the War of the Nixon Administration (AFSC Archive); Statement of the Executive Bodies of Student Associations at Saigon, Van Hanh, Can Tho, and Hue Universities and of the Saigon High School Student Association; Diane Jones to Beth Burbank, June 10, 1972; (Unsigned) Report on Student Repression in South Vietnam, April 26, 1972 (AFSC Archive).
32. "Refugees Flocking into the Hue Area," *New York Times,* April 5, 1972.
33. Telegram From Ambassador Dobrynin to the Soviet Foreign Ministry, April 19, 1972, *Soviet-American Relations,* 675-679.
34. Szulc, *Illusion of Peace,* 543–544.
35. Memorandum of Conversation Leonid Brezhnev, Henry Kissinger et al., (US) April 21, 1972, Selvage and Geyer, *Soviet-American Relations,* see especially, 686–595; Memorandum of Conversation, Leonid Brezhnev, and Henry Kissinger et al. (USSR), April 21, 1972, see especially 701–708.
36. Kissinger to Haig. April 21, 1972, NSC, HAK Trip File, Box 32, Folder 1, NPRM, NARA.
37. Cited in Moss, *Nixon's Back Channel,* 259.
38. Meetings Between Presidential Assistant Kissinger and General Secretary Brezhnev, April 22, 1972, *Soviet-American Relations,* 712–716.

39. To be sure that final credit for this deal would go to himself and to the White House, not to the US arms control delegation, Kissinger urged Brezhnev to temporarily withhold information from Helsinki and to leave certain items unsettled, which Nixon could sign at the summit. Agreement could be reached with Nixon at the summit. Geyer and Selvage, *Soviet-American Relations,* 719–720.
40. Henry Kissinger to General Haig, April 22, 1972, NSC, HAK Trip Files, Box 21, HAK's Secret Moscow Trip, NPRM, NARA.
41. Ibid. Reporting to Haig, Kissinger described the "deadly serious," substantive character of the talks, his own firmness on Vietnam issues, and Brezhnev's insistence that his government had not stepped up weapons deliveries to Hanoi.
42. *Haldeman Diary,* April 23, 1972.
43. Kissinger to Haig, April 23, 1972, NSC, HAK Trip Files, Box 21, Folder 1, NPRM, NARA.
44. From: President to Henry Kissinger, April 23, 1972. NSC HAK Trip Files, Box 21, Folder 1, NPRM, NARA.
45. Kissinger to General Haig, April 22, 1972, NSC HAK Trip Files, Box 21, Folder 1, NPRM, NARA.
46. *Haldeman Diary,* April 24, 1972.
47. James Reston, "The Kissinger Story," *New York Times,* April 26, 1972.
48. Telcon Kissinger and Rockefeller, April 26,1972, Box 13, NSC, NPNR.
49. Memorandum, General Haig to Ambassador Bunker, April 23, 1972, NSC Convenience File, Embassy Saigon series, Washington to Saigon 2/21/72–7/23/72, Gerald Ford Presidential Library.
50. Text cited in Bunker to Kissinger, April 26, 1972, Ibid., Gerald Ford Presidential Library.
51. "Enemy Overruns Donha in Drive on Quang Tri City," *New York Times,* April 28, 1972; "American Officer Says Saigon Troops, Defeated Near Kontum, Fought Poorly," *New York Times,* April 29, 1972; "Convoys to Quang Tri Blocked: Refugees Crowd Hue," *New York Times,* April 30, 1972; "As Town Falls, American Sees Valor and Cowardice," *New York Times,* April 30, 1972; "Base Near Quang Tri Vacated, *New York Times,* May 1, 1972; "US General Says Situation at Quangtri is Tenuous," *New York Times,* May 1, 1972.
52. Memorandum from the President's Assistant for National Security Affairs (Kissinger) to President Nixon, General Abrams Assessment of the Situation in Vietnam, May 1, 1972, FRUS, *Vietnam, Vol IX:* Doc. 105.

Chapter 22

1. "Retreat Leaves Small Unit of Marines Facing Enemy," *New York Times,* May 3, 1972.
2. *Haldeman Diary,* May 1, 1972.
3. Henry Kissinger to President Nixon, April 30, 1972, FRUS, *1969-76,* Vol. VIII: Doc. 103.

4. Van Loi and Anh Vu, *Le Duc Tho–Kissinger Negotiations,* 225.
5. Ibid., 370–371.
6. Ibid., 230–232.
7. Ibid., 385.
8. Memorandum from the President's Assistant for National Security Affairs (Kissinger) to President Nixon, May 2, 1972, FRUS, *1969-76, Vol. VIII:* Doc. 110.
9. Transcript, Nixon and Haldeman, May 2, 1972, Brinkley and Nichter, *Nixon Tapes,* 523.
10. "It's Everyone for Himself, As Troops Rampage in Hue," *New York Times,* May 4, 1972.
11. "300,000 Refugees from North Jam into Danang as Mayor Appeals to Saigon for Help," *New York Times,* May 7, 1972.
12. Intelligence Report, INR East Asia and the Pacific, "South Vietnam: The decisive battle at Hue," May 5, 1972, NSC, Vietnam Info Group Intelligence and Other reports, Box 9, Subject file: North Vietnamese Military, Gerald Ford Presidential Library.
13. "Abrams Report on Danger Area," *New York Times,* May 3, 1972.
14. Message from the Commander, Military Assistance Command, Vietnam (Abrams) to the Chairman of the Joint Chiefs of Staff (Moorer) and the Commander in Chief, Pacific (McCain), May 4, 1972. FRUS, *1969–76, Vietnam VIII*: Doc. 118.
15. Telcon, Nixon and Kissinger, May 6, 1972, Box 14, NPRM, NARA.
16. Hunt, *Melvin Laird,* 240–242; Paper Prepared by the Department of Defense, May 1,1972, FRUS, 1969-1976, *Vietnam, Vol.VIII,* Doc.108.
17. Transcript Nixon, Kissinger, Connally and Moorer, May 4, 1972. Brinkley and Nichter, *Nixon Tapes,* 537.
18. Ibid, 537; Transcript Nixon and Moorer, May 4, 1972, FRUS, *1969-76, VIII:* Doc. 121.
19. Telcon, Nixon and Kissinger, May 6, 1972, Box 14, NSC, NPRM, NARA.
20. Transcript of President Nixon's Address to the Nation on his Policy in Vietnam War, *New York Times,* May 9, 1972.
21. Memorandum from President Nixon to the President's Assistant for National Security Affairs, May 9, 1972, FRUS, *Vietnam, VIII:* Doc. 139.
22. Ibid.
23. "Laird Says Raids Can Go On if Foe Keeps Up Invasion," *New York Times,* April 19, 1972; Van Atta, *With Honor,* 404–410.
24. "Bombing Damage Shown in North," *New York Times,* May 9, 1972.
25. "Hospital in Hanoi Bears Scars from the Air War," *New York Times,* May 12, 1973.
26. Telcon, Connally and Kissinger, May 10, 1972, Box 14, NSC, NPRM, NARA.
27. "Peaceful Antiwar Protests Held Here and in Other Cities Across the Nation," *New York Times,* May 14, 1972.
28. Zaroulis and Sullivan, *Who Spoke Up?* 382–385.
29. "133 Arrested in Capitol War Protest," *Washington Post,* May 17, 1972.
30. "Violent Actions Reported Rising," *New York Times,* May 12, 1972.
31. "Antiwar Protests Erupt Across US," *New York Times,* May 10, 1972.
32. "Columbia Protestors Stone Bank and Are Dispersed by the Police," *New York Times,* May 9, 1972.

33. "Campus Outbreaks Spread: Harvard Center is Stormed," *New York Times*, April 19, 1972.
34. "9 College Heads Deplore Bombing," *New York Times*, April 20, 1972.
35. Memorandum of Conversation, Participants: Ivy League President and Henry Kissinger, May 17, 1972. NSC, Presidential/HAK Memcons, Box 1025, Folder 4, NPRM, NARA.
36. Among the many organizations that organized congressional lobbying activities against the war were the Friends Committee on National Legislation, Americans for Democratic Action, National Committee for a Sane Nuclear Policy, the Women's International League for Peace and Freedom, and Women's Strike for Peace. See Charles De Benedetti with Charles Chatfield, *An American Ordeal: The Antiwar Movement of the Vietnam Era* (Syracuse, NY: Syracuse University Press,1990), 328.
37. Transcript of a Telephone Conversation between the Chairman of the Joint Chiefs of Staff (Moorer) and the President's Assistant for National Security Affairs (Kissinger), May 8, 1972. FRUS, *1969–76, VIII*: Doc. 133.
38. Nixon, Memorandum for Kissinger and Haig, May 19, 1972. NSC, Haig Special File, Box 1007, Folder 5, NPRM, NARA.
39. Conversation among President Nixon, the President's Assistant for National Security Affairs (Kissinger) and the head of the US Delegation to the Paris Peace Talks (Porter), May 19, 1972, FRUS, *1969–76, VIII:* Doc. 164.
40. Memorandum from the Special Assistant for Vietnamese Affairs, Central Intelligence Agency (Carver) to John H. Holdridge of the National Security Council Staff, May 18, 1972, FRUS, *1969-76, VIII*: Doc. 161.
41. President marked this sentence as "good." FRUS, *1969–76,* Doc. 162, ftn. 9.
42. Memorandum from the President's Assistant for National Security Affairs (Kissinger) to President Nixon, May 18.1972. FRUS, *Vietnam, VIII*: Doc. 164.
43. Message from the Commander, Military Assistance Command, Vietnam (Abrams) to the Commander in Chief, Pacific (McCain), May 18, 1972. FRUS, *1969–76, VIII*: Doc. 157.
44. At a meeting of the Washington Special Action Group on Vietnam, General Haig explained that the president's concern about "psychological operations" was because his real goal was to bring about a change in the North Vietnamese leadership. It was now *"essential that the leadership be changed. That's his target."* Minutes of Washington Special Action Group, May 22, 1972, FRUS, *1969–76, Vietnam VIII*, 632.
45. "Focus at An Loc Shifts to Relief Column," *New York Times*, May 27, 1972; "Rating the ARVN—Some Lessons from An Loc," *Christian Science Monitor,* May 22,1972.
46. Randolph, *Powerful and Brutal Weapons,* 241.
47. "Saigon Pilots Shun Dangers of Anloc," *New York Times,* June 24, 1972.
48. "A Record of Sheer Endurance," *Time Magazine*, June 26, 1972.
49. Telcon, Nixon and Kissinger, May 12, 1972, Box 14, NSC, NPRM, NARA.
50. Meeting Between Presidential Assistant Kissinger and Ambassador Dobrynin, May 12, 1972, *Soviet-American Relations, 813.*
51. Telcon, President/Kissinger, May 14, 1972, Box 14, NSC, NPRM, NARA.
52. Isaacson and Thomas, *Kissinger*, 436-437.

53. "What Nixon Brought Home from Moscow," *Time Magazine*, June 5, 1972.
54. Editorial Note, FRUS, *1969-76 Volume XXXII,* SALT I, 1969–1972 (Washington DC: Government Printing Office, 2010) 969–972.
55. As reported by Haig, there could be a "massive revolt"" from the Joint Chiefs of Staff and certain influential senators if SALT seemed too favorable to the USSR. See Memorandum from President Nixon to the President's Deputy Assistant for National Security Affairs (Haig), May 20, 1972; FRUS, *1969-76, Vol. XXXII,* SALT I: Doc. 286; Backchannel Message from the President's Deputy Assistant for National Security Affairs (Haig) to the President's Assistant for National Security Affairs, (Kissinger), May 25,1972, FRUS, *1969-76, Vol. XXXII,* SALT I: Doc. 310,
56. Safire, *Before the Fall,* 453–454.
57. Szulc, *The Illusion of Peace,* 568–569.
58. Hersh, *Price of Power,* 555–556; Smith, *Doubletalk,* 437–438; Garthoff, *Détente and Confrontation,* 255–269.
59. Smith, *Doubletalk,* 436.
60. Memorandum of Conversation, May 24,1972, *Soviet-American Relations,* 886–895
61. Memorandum of Conversation, Kissinger, Gromyko et al. Subject Vietnam, May 27, 1972. *Soviet-American Relations,* 958–965.
62. "He Hopes to Celebrate a Double Triumph," *New York Times* May 21, 1972.
63. Nelson, *The Making of Détente,* 146.
64. "Ceilings Are Set," *New York Times,* May 28, 1972.
65. "Texts of Nixon-Brezhnev Declaration and of Joint Communique at End of Visit," *New York Times,* May 30, 1972
66. "President Honors Leningrad Dead: Calls for Peace," *New York Times,* May 28, 1972.
67. "Transcript of Nixon's Television Address to the Soviet People from the Great Kremlin Palace," *New York Times,* May 29, 1972.
68. "Bombing of North Termed Highly Effective by the US," *New York Times,* May 24, 1972; "US Planes Strike at Power Plants in the Hanoi Area," *New York Times,* May 25, 1972.
69. Memorandum from President Nixon to the President's Deputy Assistant for National Security Affairs (Haig), May 20, 1972. FRUS, *1969–1976, VIII:* Doc. 172.
70. Anthony Lewis, "Missiles and Pigs Coexist in North Vietnamese Countryside," *New York Times,* May 26, 1972; "The Graduates," *New York Times,* May 27, 1972; "The Turn of the Screw," *New York Times,* May 29, 1972.

Chapter 23

1. Telcon, Kissinger and McGeorge Bundy, June 2,1971, Box 14, NSC, NPRM, NARA.
2. "Mansfield Praises the President's Efforts towards World Peace." *New York Times,* June 10, 1972.
3. Telcon, Kissinger and Nixon, June 23, 1972, Box 14, NSC, NPRM, NARA.

4. Memorandum of Conversation, Anatoli Dobrynin and Dr. Henry Kissinger, June 8, 1972. FRUS, *1969-76, Vol. XV,* Soviet Union, 368–370.
5. Telcon, Nixon and Kissinger, June 8, 197, Box 14, NSC, NPRM, NARA.
6. *Haldeman Diary,* June 19–20, 1972.
7. President and Haldeman, June 20, 1972, 4:35–5:25, Kutler, *Abuse of Power*, 47–49.
8. President, Haldeman and Colson, June 21, 1972, 9:30–10:38 AM, 51.
9. Ibid., 54–55.
10. *Haldeman Diary,* June 23, 1972.
11. The President and Haldeman, June 23, 1972, 10:04–11:39, Kutler, *Abuse of Power,* 67–69.
12. Including one to White House correspondent Helen Thomas, which was suddenly interrupted when Martha's assigned bodyguard pulled the telephone cord out of the wall. Helen Thomas, *In Front Row at the White House* (New York: Simon and Schuster, 1999), 210–211.
13. The President and Haldeman, 11:16 AM–1:55, June 28, 1972, Kutler, *Abuse of Power,* 74–75.
14. The President and Haldeman, 3:38–4:22, June 30, 1972, Kutler, *Abuse of Power*, 78–80.
15. "Indochina: A Generation of Refugees," *Time,* May 10, 1971; "Again, the Refugees Are on the Road," *New York Times,* June 4, 1972.
16. Denise Chong, *The Girl in the Picture* (New York: Simon and Schuster, 1999), 60–69.
17. "South Vietnamese Drop Napalm on Own Troops," *New York Times*, June 9, 1972; "The Fire This Time," *New York Times*, June 11, 1972.
18. http://www.cbsnews.com/news/nixon-the-a-bomb-and-napalm-28-02-2002
19. "Thousands Arrested by Saigon for Suspected Vietcong Links," *New York Times*, June 23, 1972; "20 Innocent in Jail, Saigon Senators Say," *New York Times*, August 16, 1972.
20. Jane Barton Griffith, "Prison Conditions: Quang Ngai Province," Report from the Field Co-Director, Quaker Service, Quang Ngai, July 20, 1972 (AFSC).
21. Sydney Schanberg, "Saigon Torture in jails Reported," *New York Times*, August 14, 1972.
22. Sydney Schanberg, "He Calls it Closing the Gates to Communism," *New York Times*, August 13, 1972.
23. Although it was not US policy to bomb North Vietnamese dikes, Nixon and Kissinger were aware of incidents in which American planes had accidentally hit them. Infuriated that UN Secretary-General Kurt Waldheim had raised the issue, Kissinger asked Nelson Rockefeller to contact him "on a personal basis . . . warn him against getting himself involved in Vietnam because we'll just have to smash him if he keeps this up." Telcon, Kissinger and Nelson Rockefeller, July 25, 1972, Box 15, NSC, NPRM, NARA.
24. Telcon, Kissinger and McGeorge Bundy, June 2, 1972, Box 15, NSC, NPRM, NARA.
25. https://www.nytimes.com/1972/07/01/archives/u-s-soldiers-in-vietnam-an-army-of-noncombatants.html
26. "Once Again the Battle was not Decisive," *New York Times*, June 18, 1972; "Control of Mekong Delta, A Matter of Perspective," *New York Times*, August 25, 1972.

27. Conversation between President Nixon and the President's Assistant for National Security Affairs (Kissinger), August 2, 1972, FRUS, *Vietnam, Vol. VIII*: Doc. 224.
28. Memorandum of Conversation, June 20, 1971, China, FRUS *Vol XVII:* Doc. 231.
29. Memorandum of Conversation, Prime Minister Chou En-lai, Dr. Kissinger et al., June 21, 1972, NSC, Vietnam Subject Files, Box 97, Folder 4, NPRM, NARA.
30. Ibid.
31. Memorandum of Conversation, Kissinger, Zhou Enlai et al. June 22, 1972, NSC, Vietnam Subject Files, Box 97, Folder 4, NPRM, NARA.
32. Henry Kissinger to the President, June 27, 1972. NSC, HAK Office Files, Box 97, Folder 4, NPRM, NARA.
33. To Nixon from HAK, June 27, 1972, RE: Atmospherics of My Visit to Peking, NSC, HAK Office Files, Box 97, Folder 4, NPRM, NARA.
34. Loi and Vu, *Le Duc Tho-Kissinger Negotiations*, 236–237.
35. Report, American Embassy Saigon to Secretary of State, June 1972, NSC Information Group, Box 12. Gerald Ford Presidential Library.
36. Intelligence Reports, US Embassy Saigon to Secretary of State, June 1972 DRV/USSR Relations, Security Advisor NSC Vietnam Information Group, Intelligence, and other Reports, Box 12, Gerald Ford Presidential Library.
37. Loi and Vu, *Le-Duc Tho-Kissinger Negotiations*, 239–241.
38. Nguyen, *Hanoi's War*, 260–261.
39. Loi and Vu, *Le Duc Tho-Kissinger Negotiations*, 246–247.
40. Telcon, Kissinger and Nixon, July 9, 1972, Box 15, NSC, NPRM, NARA.
41. Anatol Dobrynin, *In Confidence*, 264–265.
42. Bruce Miroff, *The Liberal Moment* (Lawrence: University Press of Kansas, 2007), 72–97.
43. Julian Zelizer, "How Congress Got Us Out of Vietnam," *The American Prospect*, February 19, 2007.
44. Hunt, *The Turning*, 148–149.
45. Ibid.,154–155.
46. "Miami Beach Tent City A Carnival of Protestors," *New York Times*, August 21,1972.
47. Nicosia, *Home to War*, 237.
48. Hunt, *The Turning*, 158–159.
49. Kovic, *Born on the Fourth*, 169–173.
50. Nicosia, *Home to War*, 244–245.
51. Kovic, *Born on the Fourth*, 189.
52. Transcript of Richard Nixon's Acceptance Address, August 24, 1972, https://www.nytimes.com/1972/08/24/archives/transcript-of-nixons-acceptance-address-and-excerpts-from-agnews.html

Chapter 24

1. "Factory Workers Argue with McGovern on War," *New York Times*, September 21, 1971.
2. Kutler, *Abuse of Power Tapes*, President and Colson, September 16, 1972, 152–153.
3. "Segretti is Linked to Calls to White House in Spring," *New York Times*, October 18, 1972; "Republican Agent with Friends in High Places," *New York Times*, October 16, 1972; "New Account of Sabotage," *New York Times*, October 26,1972.
4. Stephen Ambrose, *Nixon, Volume II* (New York: Simon and Schuster,1989), 638–641.
5. From Haig to Lord/Howe for Dr. Kissinger, Washington Post, "Swelling Majority Supports President's Stand on War," September 11, 1972, NSC, HAK Trip Files, Box 24, Folder 6, NPRM, NARA.
6. "Phnom Penh Residents Riot, Looting Markets for Rice," *New York Times*, September 8, 1972; "Aliens in Cambodia Fear New Purge, *New York Times*, September 11,1972; "US Will Airlift Rice to Cambodia, *New York Times*, September 10, 1972,
7. "Cambodia Seems Adrift After 2 Years as a Republic," *New York Times*, June 6,1972.
8. "Cambodia: Fear of Forces Beyond Control," *New York Times*, October 10, 1972.
9. "Phnom Penh Raided by Enemy Force," *New York Times*, October 7, 1972.
10. Memorandum from Phillip Odeen of the National Security Staff to the President's Assistant for National Security Affairs (Kissinger) RE: Cambodia, October 16, 1972, FRUS, *1969–76, Vol IX*: Doc. 21.
11. Minute of Washington Special Actions Group Meeting, September 28, 1972, FRUS, *Vietnam, VIII*: Doc. 268.
12. Shawcross, *Sideshow*, 202–204, 228–229.
13. "Cambodian Election Won by Pro Government Party," *New York Times*, September 29, 1972.
14. Malcolm Brown, "Troubled Cambodians Miss the Monarchy," *New York Times*, September 11,1972.
15. NSSM-152, "Cambodia Political Stability and Prospects for Change and Implications for the Military Situation, April 24, 1972 (document shared by John Prados).
16. John Prados, *Vietnam*, 487.
17. Isaacs, *Without Honor*, 25–26.
18. Letter from David Paul Barton to Home Office, August 29, 1972 (AFSC).
19. Diary entry of Caroline Elliot, September 20, 1972.; Elliot Letter to Peter, Jane Dean and Other Friends, September 24, 1972; Peggy to Friends, Undated (AFSC).
20. David L to Irene, Dean and Peter, September 21, 1972 (AFSC).
21. David Barton, Dear Folks, October 7, 1972 (AFSC).
22. Craig Whitney, "Giap Teaches us a Lesson: It's Over Our Heads," *New York Times*, September 24, 1972.
23. "Elliot, *Vietnamese War*, 400–498; Sydney Schanberg, "Control of Mekong Delta A Matter of Perspective," *New York Times*, August 25, 1972.
24. "The plain fact is that there are only three divisions in South Vietnam that are worth a damn," Kissinger contended. To pretend otherwise was "to mislead ourselves."

Minutes of a Washington Special Actions Group Meeting, September 28, 1972, FRUS, *1969–76, VIII*: Doc. 268.

25. Intelligence Report, US Department of State, "South Vietnam: The Communists Strengthen the Base for Political or for Protracted War, October 6, 1972, NSC, Vietnam Information Group, Box 9, Folder 3, Gerald Ford Presidential Library.
26. Minutes of a Washington Special Actions Group Meeting, September 28, 1972, FRUS, *1969–76, Vietnam, Vol. VIII*: Doc. 268.
27. "Transcript of McGovern's Speech Offering a Plan for Peace in Vietnam," *New York Times*, October 11, 1972.
28. Kimball, *Nixon's Vietnam War*, 338–339.
29. Memorandum from the President's Deputy Assistant for National Security Affairs (Haig) to President Nixon, September 14, 1972; FRUS, *Vietnam, 1969–76, Vol. VIII*: 259; Bunker for Kissinger, GVN Reaction to our Response to their Memoranda on Our Peace Proposals, NSC, Lord Files, China Trip, Box 862, Folder 1, NPRM, NARA.
30. Berman, *No Peace*, 142–143.
31. Memorandum of Conversation President Thieu, Henry Kissinger et.al. August 17 &18, 1972, NSC, For the President's Files (Winston Lord) China Trip/Vietnam, Box 864, Folder 4, NPRM, NARA; Kissinger to Nixon, Your Meeting with Ambassador Bunker, August 30, 1972, NSC, Lord Files, China Trip/Vietnam, Box 862, Folder 2, NPRM, NARA.
32. Memorandum RE: Communist Proposals and US Memorandum of September 19, 1972, sent September 27, 1972, NSC, Convention Files for the US Embassy, Saigon Box 9, Folder 3, Gerald Ford Presidential Library.
33. Loi and Vu, *Negotiations*, 286–297.
34. Kissinger to Bunker, September 15, 1972, HAK Trip Files, Box 24, Folder 3, NPRM, NARA.
35. Transcript, Nixon and Kissinger September 15, 1972, Nichter and Brinkley, *Nixon Tapes*, 615–619.
36. Bureau of Intelligence and Research, "Vietnam: Thieu's Rhetoric Hardens," October 2, 1972, National Security Advisor, NSC, Vietnam Information Group 1967–75, Box 12. Gerald Ford Presidential Library.
37. Nichter and Brinkley, *Nixon Tapes*, 622–623.
38. Memorandum of Conversation General Alexander Haig, Ambassador Bunker, President Nguyen Van Thieu et al., October 2 and October 4, 1972, NSC, Lord Files, China Trip/Vietnam, Box 864, Folder 2, NPRM, NARA.
39. Editorial Note, FRUS, *Vietnam, Vol VIII*: Doc. 294.
40. Kimball, *Nixon's War*, 318–319.
41. Transcript of a Telephone Conversation Between President Nixon and the President's Assistant for National Security Affairs (Kissinger), FRUS, *Vietnam, Vol VIII:* Doc. 10.
42. Loi and Vu, *Negotiations*, 303.
43. See discussion of this subtle issue in Kimball, *Nixon's War*, 328–329.
44. Henry Kissinger, *Ending the Vietnam War*, 327–330.

45. Transcript, Nixon, Kissinger and Haig, October 12, 1972, Nichter and Brinkley, *Nixon Tapes*, 628–634.
46. *Haldeman Diary*, October 12, 1972.
47. Kutler, *Nixon Tapes*, President and Haldeman, September 15, 1972, 144–145.
48. "FBI Finds Nixon Aides Sabotaged Democrats," *Washington Post*, October 10, 1972.
49. Ibid.
50. Telephone Conversation between President Nixon and the President's Assistant for National Security Affairs (Kissinger), October 15, 1972. FRUS, *1969–76: Volume IX*: Doc. 16.
51. Letter from President Nixon to South Vietnamese President Thieu, October 16, 1972. FRUS, *1969–76, Vol. IX*: Doc. 20.
52. Including Quang Tri province, west of Hue, southwest of Danang, west of Tam Ky and in the southern Quang Ngai-Binh Dinh areas. Haig to Winston Lord for Mr. Kissinger, October 16, 1972, NSC, HAK Trip Files, Box 25, Folder 2, NPRM, NARA.
53. "An Increase in B-52 Raids around Saigon is Reported," *New York Times*, October 5, 1972; "Enemy Reported Moving on Saigon by a River Route," *New York Times*, October 9, 1972.
54. Carver Memo, October 16, 1972, forwarded by Haig to Kissinger, NSC HAK trip files, Box 25, Folder 2, NPRM, NARA.
55. Loi and Vu, *Negotiations*, 336–341.
56. Haig to Kissinger, October 19, 1972, forwarded message from Vo Van Sung, NSC HAK Trip files, Box 25 Folder 2, NPRM, NARA.
57. Brigham, *Guerilla Diplomacy*, 106–197.
58. Major General Haig to the President, October 19, 1972, NSC, HAK Trip File, Box 25, Folder 4, NPRM, NARA.
59. Memorandum of Conversation, General Thieu, Henry Kissinger, et al. October 20, 1972. NSC, For the President's Files (Winston Lord)-China/Vietnam Box 864, Camp David, Folder 2, NPRM, NARA.
60. Kissinger, *Ending the Vietnamese War*, 360.
61. Backchannel message from the Ambassador to Vietnam (Bunker) to the President, US Deputy Assistant for National Security Affairs (Haig), October 22, 1972, FRUS, *1969–76, Vol. IX*: Doc. 49.
62. The President and Colson, 12:29–1:10. October 25, 1972, Kutler, *Abuse of Power*, 173.
63. "McGovern Charges Abuse of Power," *New York Times*, October 25, 1972.

Chapter 25

1. "McGovern Asserts Nixon Pretended to be Near Peace," *New York Times*, November 4, 1972.
2. Miroff, *Liberal Moment*, 247.
3. Pearlstein, *Nixonland*, 745–746.

4. American Embassy Saigon to Sec State, October 24, 1972, Gerald Ford Presidential Library; Excerpts from "Thieu's Address to the Nation on the New Proposal for Peace," *New York Times,* October 25, 1972.
5. Hersh, *Price of Power,* 600–604.
6. Kissinger, *White House Years,* 1395.
7. Telcon, Kissinger and Alex Johnson, October 24, 1972, Box 16, NSC, NPRM, NARA.
8. Telcon Kissinger and Nelson Rockefeller, October 25,1972, Box 16, NSC, NPRM, NARA.
9. Telcon, Kissinger and William Buckley, October 25, 1972, Box 16, NSC, NPRM, NARA.
10. Isaacson and Thomas, *Kissinger,* 477–479.
11. *Haldeman Diary,* November 17, 1972; Dallek, *Nixon and Kissinger,* 437–438.
12. Memorandum of Secretary of Defense Laird to President Nixon, RE: Expedited Delivery of Material to the RVNAF (Project Enhance Plus,) November 17, 1972, FRUS, *1969–1976, Vol. IX*: Doc. 111; Kimball, *Nixon's Vietnam War,* 347.
13. "Hanoi Said to Speed War Supplies into South," *New York Times*, November 1, 1972; "Hanoi is Reported Moving 100 Tanks into the South," *New York Times*, November 4, 1972.
14. "US Planes Bomb Heavily in North and Near Saigon," *New York Times*, October 23, 1972; "Ground Fighting Widens in South," *New York Times*, October 25, 1972.
15. President Nixon to President Thieu, November 8, 1972, NSC, Convenience File, US Embassy Saigon, Box 9, Gerald Ford Presidential Library.
16. Memorandum of Conversation, Meeting Between President Nguyen Van Thieu, General Alexander Haig et.al, November 10, 1972, FRUS, *1969–76,* Vol IX: Doc. 99.
17. "US Pushing Retraining of Saigon's Entire Army," *New York Times*, October 25, 1972.
18. Message from the President's Deputy Assistant for National Security Affairs (Haig) to the President's Assistant for National Security Affairs (Kissinger), November 13, 1972, *FRUS, 1969–76, Vol. IX*: Doc. 103.
19. Kissinger, *Ending the Vietnam War*, 389.
20. Loi and Vu, *Negotiations*, 357.
21. According to estimates of Amnesty International, there were as many as 200,000 civilians held in South Vietnamese jails. "Amnesty Unit Makes Appeal on 200,000 Held by Saigon," *New York Times*, December 3, 1972.
22. "As for timing, we were not in such a hurry as in October," Loi and Vu, *Negotiations,* 355.
23. *Haldeman Diary*, November 21, 1971.
24. *Haldeman Diary,* November 23, 1971.
25. "Heavy B-52 Raids Continue in North," New York Times, November 24, 1972.
26. See for example, the cautiously dissenting critique of CIA analyst George Carver, Memorandum from the Special Assistant for Vietnamese Affairs, Central Intelligence Agency (Carver) to the President's Assistant for National Security Affairs (Kissinger,) October 30, 1972, *FRUS, 1969-76,* IX: Doc. 84.
27. *HD,* November 18, 1972,
28. *HD,* November 19, 1972
29. Kissinger, *Ending the Vietnam War*, 388-389

30. *Ibid.*
31. See for example, column by James Reston, "And What Now About Henry?" New York Times, December 1, 1972.
32. Telcon, Haldeman and Kissinger, November 28, 1972, Box 17, NSC, NPRM, NARA.
33. *HD,* November 29, 1972.
34. Kissinger to Kennedy (for the President), November 24,1972, NSC HAK Trip Files, Box 26, Folder 1, NPRM, NARA; Kissinger to Kennedy (for the President), November 25, 1972, *Ibid.;* Kissinger to the President, RE Changes Obtained in the Draft Agreement, November 25, 1972, NSC HAK Trip Files, Box 36, Folder 1, NPRM, NARA,
35. Alexander Haig, Memorandum for the President's Files, RE: The President's Meeting with the Joint Chiefs of Staff, November 30, 1972, *FRUS,1969-76,* IX: Doc.132.
36. Telcon, Kissinger and Nixon. November 20, 1972, Box 17, 1972; Telcon, Kissinger and Haldeman, Box 17, NPRM.
37. Memorandum of Conversation Ambassador Huang Chen, Henry Kissinger, November 25, 1972; *FRUS 1969-76 Volume E-13 Documents on China, 1969-1972*: Doc.196
38. Memorandum of Conversation, Ch'iao Kuan-hua, Vice Minister of Foreign Affairs, Henry Kissinger, et. al., November 13, 1972 *Ibid.;* 146. Memorandum of Conversation Chou-En-lai, Henry Kissinger et. al. June 22-June 23, 1972, *Ibid;* 147; Memorandum from the President' Assistant for National Security (Kissinger) to President Nixon, June 27, 1972, *Ibid.*
39. Loi and Vu, *Negotiations,* 387.
40. *Ibid.,* 355.
41. Kennedy to General Haig (for Kissinger), December 6,1972, NSC HAK Trip files, Box 27, Folder 1 NPRM, NARA.
42. Nixon, *RN, 726-732.*
43. 269. Memorandum of Conversation Henry Kissinger, Ambassador Huang Chen et.al. December 7-8. *FRUS, 1969-1976, Vol. VIII, China, 1969-1972:* 269.
44. General Haig for Richard T. Kennedy, December 4, 1972, NSC HAK Trip File, Box 27, Folder 6, NPRM, NARA.
45. Col. Kennedy to Guay (for Mr. Kissinger), December 5, 1972, NSC. HAK Trip File, Box 27, Folder 1, NPRM, NARA; From Col. Kennedy to General Haig, December 6, 1972, NSC, AK Trip File, Box 27, Folder 1, NPRM, NARA; Kennedy to Haig, December 7, 1972, NSC HAK Trip, Box 27, Folder 1, NPM, NARA.
46. Dobrynin, *In Confidence,* 267.
47. Nixon, *RN,* 723.
48. Haig, *Inner Circle,* 306; Kennedy to Haig, December 7, 1972, NSC HAK Trip File, Box 27 Folder 1, NPRM, NARA
49. Kissinger to Kennedy, December 9, 1972; NSC HAK Trip, Box 27, Folder 6, NPRM, NARA, Kissinger to Bunker, December 8, 1972, *Ibid.*
50. Kissinger to Nixon, December 9, 1972 Memorandum of Conversation, *FRUS Vietnam, Vol. IX*: Doc.152.

51. Kissinger to Kennedy, December 9, 1972, NSC HAK Trip Files, Box 27, Folder 6. NPRM, NARA
52. "US Reports Heavy Raids to Cut Enemy's Supplies," New York Times, December 5, 1972. "Bombing is Heavy Over Saigon Area," New York Times, December 12, 1972.
53. Loi and Vu, *Le Duc Tho-Kissinger Negotiations, 406*-411; "The two zones will agree on the status of the DMZ and lay down the regulations on movement across the provisional demarcation line."
54. Haig to Kissinger, December 11, 1972, NSC HAK Trip Box 27, folder 4, NPRM, NARA.
55. Garthoff, *Détente or Confrontation*, 185.
56. "3 Top Pathet Lao Negotiators Leave Peace Talks in Vientiane," New York Times, December 12, 1972: Joseph Zasloff, "Laos 1972: The War, Politics and Peace Negotiations," Asian Survey, Vol.13, No.1 (January 1973), 69–71.
57. As of early 1972, American estimates of Thai fighters were 6000, with many additional people still coming in. *Thailand, Laos and Cambodia: January 1972.* Staff Report prepared for the use of subcommittee on US Security Agreements and Commitments Abroad. (to be referred to as Moose-Lowenstein report, May 8, 1972.)
58. "Secret Air Raids Extended to Laos, Senators Believe," New York Times, July 29, 1973.
59. Telcon Melvin Laird and Kissinger, November 11,1972, Box17, NSC, NPRM, NARA.
60. Memorandum of Conversation, December 11, 1972*; FRUS, 1969-76,* Kissinger-Le Duc Tho Negotiations, *Vol. XLII:* Doc. 38.
61. 156. Message from the President's Assistant for National Security (Kissinger) to the President's Deputy Assistant for National Security (Haig), December 11,1972 *FRUS Vietnam. IX*: Doc. 156.
62. "Thieu's Speech is Viewed as Bid for Better Terms," New York Times, December 12, 1972.
63. Conversation Between President Nixon and the President's Deputy Assistant for National Security Affairs (Haig), December 12, 1972, *FRUS, 1969-76,* Vol. IX: Doc. 156
64. 40. Memorandum of Conversation Henry Kissinger, Le Duc Tho et.al. December 12, 197213:07-7:35 PM. *FRUS, 1969-76, Vol XLII*: Doc.40
65. Memorandum of Conversation, December 13, 1972, 10:30 am-4:24 pm, FRUS, Vol/ XLII, Vietnam: The Kissinger-Le Duc Tho Negotiations, No. 41.
66. "Watergate Figure's Dead Wife Had $10,000 to Invest, He Says," *New York Times*, December 11,1972; John Dean, *The Nixon Defense* (New York: Penguin, 2014) 185–189.
67. December 11, 1972, "The President, Haldeman, and Ehrlichman," Stanley Kutler, *Abuse of Power, The New Nixon Tapes* (New York: Simon and Schuster, 1997), 180–184.
68. Transcript of Conversation, Nixon, Haig, Kissinger, December 14, 1972, Brinkley and Nichter, *Nixon Tapes*, 677.
69. Message from the President's Deputy Assistant for National Security Affairs (Haig) to the President's Assistant for National Security Affairs (Kissinger), December 13, 1972, *FRUS, 1969-76,* Vol. IX: Doc. 172.

70. Memorandum from Secretary of Defense Laird to President Nixon, December 12, 1972. RE: Ceasefire Agreement, *FRUS Vietnam., Vol VIII:*166.
71. Transcript of Conversation, Nixon, Haig, Kissinger, December 14, 1972, Brinkley and Nichter, *Nixon Tapes,* 684.
72. Telcon, Nixon and Kissinger, December17, 1972 10:45., Box 17, NSC. NPRM, NARA.
73. *New York Times* December 14, *1972;* Nichter and Brinkley, *Nixon Tapes,* 1971-72, 702–703.
74. Kissinger's Statement at News Conference and Question-and-Answer excerpts. *New York Times,* December 17, 1972.
75. Nixon, *RN,* 734.
76. Kissinger and Nixon, Telephone, December 19, 1972, Brinkley and Nichter, *Nixon Tapes,* 707-708.

Chapter 26

1. "Hanoi Frees 3 POW's; Wife and Mother Greet 2," *New York Times,* September 18, 1972.
2. Joan Baez, *And a Voice to Sing With* (New York: Simon and Schuster, 1987), 103–194.
3. Michael Allen, "And a Hazard to an Unwelcoming People," *Washington Post,* December 30, 1972.
4. Baez, *And a Voice to Sing With,* 208.
5. "4 Who Visited Hanoi Tell of Destruction," *New York Times,* January 2, 1973; "Newsmen in Hanoi Visit Street of Ruins," *New York Times,* December 29, 1972.
6. Telford Taylor, "Hanoi is Reported Scarred But Key Services Continue," *New York Times,* December 25, 1972.
7. Baez, *And a Voice to Sing With,* 209–210.
8. "Joan Baez Performs at a Service in Hanoi," *New York Times,* December 21, 1972; Baez, *And a Voice to Sing With,* 212–213; Tim Cahill, "Joan Baez in Hanoi: Twelve Days Under the Bomb," February 1, 1973.
9. Michael Allen, ". . . and a Hazard to an Unweakening People," *Washington Post,* December 30, 1972.
10. Interview with Barry Romo, "Remembering the Christmas Bombing," Spring 2013, http://www.vvaw.org/veteran/article/?id=2204
11. Transcript of Telephone Conversation between Secretary of Defense Laird and the President's Assistant for National Security Affairs (Kissinger), December 19,1972, FRUS, *1969–76,* Vol. IX: Doc. 200.
12. Telcon, Kissinger and Moorer, December 19, 1972, Box 17, NSC, NPRM, NARA.
13. "Terror from the Skies," *New York Times,* December 22, 1972.
14. Colonel Guay to General Haig, December 20, 1972, NSC, China Trip/Vietnam Negotiations, Box 865, NPRM, NARA.

15. Message from the Air Attaché at the Embassy in France (Guay) to the President's Deputy Assistant for National Security Affairs, December 26, 1972 (Haig), FRUS, *Vietnam, IX*: Doc. 224.
16. "US Clerics Decry the Bombing and Urge End to Vietnam War," *New York Times*, December 23, 1972; "Pope Questions Painful Delay," *New York Times*, December 23, 1972; "Europe Reacts to Bombing with Increasing Protests," *New York Times*, December 24, 1972.
17. "Excerpts from the Kremlin Address of Soviet Leader," *New York Times*, December 22, 1972.
18. Telcon President Nixon and Henry Kissinger, December 17, 1972, Box 17, NSC, NPRM, NARA.
19. Telcon, Ambassador Sullivan and Henry Kissinger, December 23, 1972, Box 17, NSC, NPRM, NARA.
20. Nixon, *RN*, 739; Kissinger, *White House Years*, 1462.
21. Telcon, Nixon and Kissinger, December 26, 1972, Box 17, NSC, NPRM, NARA.
22. Max Hastings, *Vietnam: An Epic* Tragedy (New York: Harper-Collins, 2018) 659–665.
23. Conversation between President Nixon and Richard T. Kennedy, December 27, 1972, FRUS, *Vietnam, October 1972–January 1974*, Vol IX: Doc. 227.
24. Transcript, Nixon and Kissinger, December 28, 1972, in Nichter and Brinkley, *Nixon Tapes*, 719–730.
25. "Terror Bombing in the Name of Peace," *Washington Post*, December 28, 1972.
26. Message from Richard T. Kennedy of the National Security Staff, December 29, 1972, FRUS, *Vietnam IX*: Doc. 236.
27. "More in Congress Decry the Raids," *New York Times*, December 30, 1972; "Congress Critics of War Threaten to Fight Funding," *New York Times*, January 3, 1973.
28. Nixon, *RN*, 745; Tim Weiner, *One Man Against the World: The Tragedy of Richard Nixon* (New York: Henry Holt, 2015), 226–227.
29. On January 8, Nixon sat down with Colson to discuss strategy. This Watergate matter has been "tough for all of you," the president reflected—not only Colson, but Haldeman and Ehrlichman as well. But "we're just not going to let it get us down. This is a battle. It's a fight. It's war . . . remember we'll cut them down one of these days. Don't you agree?" Douglas Brinkley and Luke Nichter, *The Nixon Tapes: 1973* (New York: Mariner Books, 2015), 8–9.
30. Kissinger and Zhou Enlai, June 20, 1972, FRUS, *1969–1976, China*, Vol. XVII: Doc. 231.
31. Nguyen Co Thach, Interview with Jeffrey Kimball, 9/24/94 in Kimball, *Uncovering the Secret History*, 235–236; Nguyen Thi Binh, *Family Friends and Country*, 138 (American translation, unpublished).
32. American Embassy to Secretary of State, RE: DRV/PRC Relations, October 1972, NSC, Vietnam Information Group, Intelligence and other reports, Box 10, Folder 3, Gerald Ford Presidential Library; American Consul (Hong Kong) to Secretary of State, November 1972 RE: PRC Aid to Vietnam, Ibid.; "Peking-Hanoi Pact Signed," *New York Times*, November 27, 1972.
33. Foreign Ministry Statement Condemns Renewed U.S. Bombing, December 20, 1972.

34. "Excerpts from the Kremlin Address of Soviet Leader," *New York Times*, December 22, 1972.
35. 71. Letter from President Nixon to Soviet General-Secretary Brezhnev, December 18, 1972. FRUS, *1969–1976*, Vol XV: Doc. 71.
36. Report, American Consul (Hong Kong) to Secretary of State, PRC-Vietnam, December 20, 22 and 27, NSC Vietnam Information Group, Box 10, Folder 3, Gerald Ford Presidential Library; Report, American Embassy (Moscow) to Secretary of State, RE: Brezhnev December 21 Speech, NSC Vietnam Information group, Intelligence and Other Reports, Box 12, Gerald Ford Presidential Library.
37. Thanking the Chinese people for their generous support of the Vietnamese struggle, she took an obvious jab at Nixon's diplomacy, observing that one of "the most vicious designs" of imperialism was "to drive wedges between the Vietnamese people and the people of China and other countries." See American Consul (Hong Kong) to Secretary of State, PRC-Vietnam, December 28, 1972, NSC, Vietnam Information, Box 10, Folder 4, Gerald Ford Presidential Library; "Madame Binh Speaks in Peking," *New York Times*, December 29, 1972.
38. Discussion between Mao Zedong and Nguyen Thi Binh, December 29, 1972, and Discussion between Zhou Enlai and Le Duc Tho, January 3, 1973, Wilson Center Digital Archive.
39. Prados, *Vietnam*, 510–511; Kimball, *Nixon's Vietnam War*, 364–365.
40. Author's interview with John Negroponte, January 5, 2018.
41. Memorandum of Conversation, Henry Kissinger, Ambassador Tran Kim Phoung et al., January 3, 1973, FRUS, *1969-76, Vietnam, Vol. IX:* Doc. 243.
42. Loi and Vu, *Negotiations*, 424–425.
43. Memorandum, Richard Kennedy to the President, Attached Letter from Kissinger, January 9, 1973, America Since Hoover,1929–1980, Box 7, Folder 1, Gerald Ford Presidential Library.
44. Nixon, *RN*, 747–748.
45. Kissinger, *White House Years*, 1468–1469.
46. Isaacs, *Without Honor*, 58–61.
47. Backchannel message from the Vice Chief of Staff of the Army (Haig) to the President's Assistant for National Security Affairs (Kissinger), January 17, 1973. FRUS, *1969-76*, Vol IX: Doc. 285.
48.. Transcript of a Telephone Conversation between President Nixon and the President's Assistant for National Security Affairs (Kissinger), January 17, 1973, 4–5 PM. *FRUS, 1969-1976, Vol IX*: Doc. 289.
49. Backchannel Message From the Vice Chief of Staff of the Army (Haig) to the President's Assistant for National Security Affairs (Kissinger)· January 20, 1973, Ibid., Doc. 311.
50. "War Scored by Thousands in Protests in the Capital," *New York Times*, January 20. 1973.
51. Letter from South Vietnamese President Thieu to President Nixon, January 21, 1973, FRUS, *1969-76, Vol. IX:* Doc. 320.

52. Cited in Nguyen Tien Hung and Jerrold L. Schecter, *The Puzzle Palace: Vietnam Secret Documents* (New York: Harper-Collins, 1989), 145.
53. Kissinger, *White House Years*, 1472. In this final meeting, Le Duc Tho expressed the hope that when Kissinger made his expected visit to Hanoi that he could make an offer of $4.5 billion in money and commodities. Kissinger demurred, citing concerns about an adverse congressional reaction. Privately, Kissinger found this pressure "obnoxious"—fussing about money on this special day. Kissinger, *White House Years*, 1472.
54. Richard Nixon, Address to the Nation Announcing an agreement on Ending the war in Vietnam, January 23, 1973, https://www.nixonfoundation.org/2017/08/address-nation-announcing-conclusion-agreement-ending-war-restoring-peace-
55. Kissinger, *White House Years*,1474.
56. "Hanoi Celebrates Truce Accord on the Streets and in the Palace," *New York Times*, January 24, 1972.
57. "Saigonese React with Relief, Skepticism and Fear," *New York Times*, January 25, 1973.
58. So disgusted was he that he refused to attend the official signing ceremony, held on January 27. Impervious to the domestic pressures, his preference was for the United States to continue the war in South Vietnam. Negroponte, *State Department Autobiography*, 54; Interview with author, January 2018.

Chapter 27

1. Telcon, Kissinger and Moorer, January 16, 1972, Box 18, NSC, NPRM, NARA.
2. Hunt, *Melvin Laird*, 555.
3. Author's interview with Melvin Laird, August 21, 2007.
4. Memorandum for the President's file, Meeting with the President and Secretary of Defense Designate, January 4, 1973, NSC, Presidential Memcons, Box 1025, Folder19, NPRM, NARA.
5. Telephone Conversation between President Nixon and the President's Assistant for National Security Affairs (Kissinger), February 1, 1973, FRUS, *1969-1976, China, 1973–76*, ed. David P. Nickles (Washington: Government Printing Office, 2007), Vol. XVIII: Doc. 22.
6. Memorandum of Conversation, Henry Kissinger, Mao-Tse-tung et.al., February 17–18, FRUS, *1969–1976, China*, Vol. XVIII: Doc. 12.
7. From Henry Kissinger to the President, February 27, 1973, NSC, Kissinger Office Files, Country Files, Far East, Box 98, NPRM, NARA.
8. Memorandum for the President from Henry Kissinger, My Meeting with Chairman Mao, February 24, 1973, Ibid.
9. Isaacs, *Without Honor*, 171.
10. Fredrik Logevoll, "Laos: America's Lesser Known Human and Political Disaster in Southeast Asia," *Washington Post*, February 2, 2017.

11. 16. Message from the President's Assistant for National Security (Kissinger) to the President's Deputy Assistant for National Security Affairs (Scowcroft), February 12, 1973, FRUS, *Vietnam,* Vol. X: Doc. 16.
12. Shawcross, *Sideshow,* 248.
13. Isaacs, *Without Honor,* 188.
14. Henry Kamm, *Cambodia: Report from a Stricken Land* (New York: Arcade Publishing, (1975), 114–115.
15. Nearly half of the bombing tonnage was dropped during this six-month period. See Ben Kiernan, "The American Bombardment of Kampuchea, 1969–73," in *Vietnam Generation: Vol I: No.1, Article 3.*
16. "Cambodian War Enriches the Corrupt, Debases the Poor," *New York Times,* November 30, 1972; Isaacs, *Without Honor,* 209.
17. Kiernan, *Stricken Land,* 11.
18. Ibid.
19. Subcommittee on U.S. Security Agreements and Commitments Abroad, Committee on Foreign Relations, US Senate, and Staff Report, "US Air Operations in Cambodia: August 1973, 1–6.
20. J. William Fulbright, Additional Letters from U.S. Airmen Involved in Cambodian Operations, *Congressional Record–Senate,* 15969–15970.
21. "Dear Senator: Letters from U.S. Flyers," *New York Times,* June 10, 1973.
22. Ibid.
23. "House Approves Cutoff of Funds to Bomb Cambodia," *New York Times,* June 25, 1973; "House Again Acts to Curb Bombing," *New York Times,* June 26, 1973.
24. Text of Nixon's Veto on Money Bill and "Cambodia Bill," *New York Times,* June 28, 1973.
25. "Nixon Agrees to Stop Bombing by U.S. in Cambodia by August 15, with New Raids Up to Congress," *New York Times,* June 30, 1973.
26. See Kissinger, *Ending the Vietnam War,* 480–488; and Minutes of Washington Special Action Group, July 10, 1973, FRUS, *1969–76,* Vol X: Doc. 92.
27. "Nixon agrees to Stop Bombing by U.S. in Cambodia by Aug. 15 with New Raids Up to Congress," *New York Times,* June 30, 1973.
28. Isaacs, *Without Honor,* 228.
29. Sydney Schanberg, "US Planes Bomb Cambodia Town in Error," *New York Times,* August, 1973.
30. Sydney Schanberg, "Bomb Error Leaves Havoc in Neak Luong," *New York Times,* August 9, 1973.
31. Seymour Hersh, "US Confirms Pre-1970 Raids on Cambodia," *New York Times,* July 17, 1973.
32. "Cambodian Raids Reported Hidden Before '70," *New York Times,* July 15, 1973.
33. "Wheeler Asserts Bombing Secrecy Was Nixon's Wish," *New York Times,* July 31, 1973.
34. "Text of Letters and Orders on Nixon Refusal to Respond to Subpoenas on Tapes," *New York Times,* July 26, 1973.

Chapter 28

1. https://www.archives.gov/files/presidential-libraries/events/vietnam/pdf/transcript-05.pdf
2. Ample evidence of this emerged in the Pentagon Papers. See *New York Times Complete and Unabridged Pentagon Papers* (New York: Bantom Books, 1971).
3. Meeting Between Presidential Assistant Kissinger and Ambassador Dobrynin, February 21, 1969 (USSR), Geyer and Selvage, *Soviet-American Relations,* 21.
4. "Transcript of the Speech by the President on Vietnam," *New York Times,* January 24, 1973.
5. "His Answer is Still Four 'No's'" *New York Times,* October 22, 1972; "Thrusts by Saigon Troops to Gain Ground Recorded," *New York Times.* January 21, 1973.
6. George Herring, *America's Longest War: The United States and Vietnam, 1950–1975* (New York: McGraw Hill, 2001), 325.
7. Isaacs, *Without Honor,* 350.
8. "Transcript of President's Address Before Congress on the State of the World," *New York Times,* April 11, 1975.
9. "Defeat For Ford," *New York Times,* April 18, 1975.
10. "Excerpts from Thieu's Address on Resignation," *New York Times,* April 22, 1975.

Bibliography

Archives

Gerald R. Ford Presidential Library, Ann Arbor, Michigan
- General Subject File, Vietnam
- National Security Adviser File
  - NSC Planning and Coordination Staff Files, 1972–73
  - Memoranda of Private Conversations
  - NSC Convenience Files, US Embassy Saigon 1963–75
  - Vietnam Information Group: Intelligence and Other Reports

- Gerald Ford, Vice Presidential Papers, HIT Notes
- Robert T. Hartman Papers
- Kissinger-Scowcroft West Wing Office Files
- Legislative Interdepartmental Group Files
- Memoranda of Conversations, 1973–77
- NSC East Asian and Pacific Staff Files
- Saigon Embassy Files, Kept by Ambassador Graham Martin

National Archives and Records Administration, College Park, Maryland. Nixon Presidential Materials Project

White House Files

President's Office Files
- President's Handwriting File

White House Special File: Staff Members and Office Files

Charles W. Colson

John W. Dean

H. R. Haldeman

Alexander Haig

President's Personal Files

Vietnam Subject Files

White House Special Files: Subject Files

Presidential Tapes

NSC Files
- Presidential Daily Briefings
- Paris Talks/Meetings

Cambodian Operations
Convenience Files
Country Files–Europe
Country Files–Vietnam/Cambodia
Institutional Files
Presidential Correspondence
President's Trip Files
President's Handwriting File
For the President's Files–China Trip/Vietnam Negotiations (Lord)
Presidential/HAK Memcons
Lake Chron Files

Henry A. Kissinger (HAK) Office Files
Administrative and Staff Files
Henry A. Kissinger, Trip Files
Henry Kissinger, Country Files Eur-USSR
President's Trip File, Dobrynin/Kissinger
Henry A. Kissinger Country Files.-Far East-Vietnam Negotiations
Alexander M. Haig Special and Chronological Files
President's Trip Files
Vietnam Subject Files:
Memcon Dobrynin
Memcon Kissinger/President
Haig Trip to Vietnam
Lord Vietnam Negotiations
Institutional File
Alexander M. Haig Special Files
Alexander Haig Telcons
Kissinger Telcons, 1969–1973

National Archives and Records Administration, College Park, Maryland. Modern Military Branch
RG 218 Chairman of the Joint Chiefs of Staff
RG 330 Office of the Secretary of Decense

State Department , RG 59 (Central Files)
POL 27 CAMBODIA
POL 27 LAOS
POL 27 VIETS

American Friends Service Committee (AFSC), Archive, Philadelphia PA
Records from Quang Ngai Rehabilitation Center

Fred Branfman Collection Private Archive (shared with author)
Kent State University Libraries (KSUA)
Special Collections and Archives, May 4 Collection

National Security Archive, Washington DC
Vietnam Series, 1969–74.

Vietnam Center and Sam Johnson Vietnam Archive, Texas Tech University (TTU), Lubbock Texas

Terry J. Dubose Collection
John Kniffin Collection
My Lai Collection
Douglas Pike Collection

Printed Government Documents

Congressional

Senate Committee on Foreign Relations, Staff Report by James Lowenstein and Richard M. Moose, Cambodia: May 1970.

Senate Committee on Foreign Relations, Staff Report by James Lowenstein and Richard M. Moose, Cambodia: December 1970. Report of Senate Foreign Relations Committee staff members on a visit of November–December 1970.

Senate Committee on Foreign Relations, Staff Report by James Lowenstein and Richard M. Moose, Laos: April 1971.

Senate Committee on the Judiciary, Subcommittee on Refugees and Escapees, *War-Related Civilian Problems in Indochina*, Part II: *Laos and Cambodia*. Hearings, April 21–22, 1971.

Senate Committee on the Judiciary, Subcommittee on Refugees and Escapees, Staff Report, September 28, 1970.

Senate Committee on Foreign Relations, Staff Report by James G. Lowenstein and Richard M. Moose, *Thailand, Laos, and Cambodia: January 1972*, May 8, 1972.

Senate Committee on the Judiciary, Hearings of the Subcommittee on Refugees and Escapees, Part I: *Problems of War Victims in Indochina*, Part II: *Cambodia and Laos*, May 9, 1972.

US Committee on Foreign Relations, US Senate, "Vietnam: December 1969: A Staff Report."

House of Representatives: Committee on the Judiciary, Final Report on the Impeachment of Richard M. Nixon, August 20, 1974 (

Executive Branch

US Department of Defense

Richard A. Hunt, *Melvin Laird and the Foundation of the Post-Vietnam Military, 1969–73*. Secretaries of Defense Historical Series, Washington DC, 2015.

Willard J. Webb, *The History of the Joint Chiefs of Staff, The Joint Chiefs of Staff and the War in Vietnam, 1969-1970,, Part I*. Historical Division, Joint Secretariat Joint Chiefs of Staff, 2002

Willard. 2007J. Webb, *The History of the Joint Chiefs of Staff, The Joint Chiefs of Staff and the War in Vietnam, 1971–1973, Part II*. Historical Division, Joint Secretariat Joint Chiefs of Staff, 2007.

US Department of State, Office of the Historian

US Department of State, *Foreign Relations of the United States* (FRUS). Washington DC: Government Printing Office. Can also be accessed electronically at https://history.state.gov/historicaldocuments/nixon-ford:

Foundations of Foreign Policy, Volume 1 1969–72
Vietnam, Volume 6 January 1969–July 1970
Vietnam, Volume 7 July 1970–January 1972
Vietnam, Volume 8 January–October 1972
Vietnam, Volume 9 October 1972–January 1973
South Asia Crisis, 1971 Volume 11
China, 1969–1972 Volume 17
China, 1973–1976 Volume 18
Documents on South Asia, 1969–1972, E-7
US Department of State (ed. David C. Geyer and Douglas Selvage), *Soviet-American Relations: The Détente Years,* Washington DC: Government Printing Office, 2007.

Periodicals

Foreign Affairs
Life Magazine
Newsweek
The Nation
New York Review of Books
New York Times
St. Louis Post-Dispatch
Time
Washington Post
Wall Street Journal

Memoirs, Diaries, Published Documents

Christian Appy (ed.), *Patriots: The Vietnam War Remembered From All Sides* (New York: Penguin Books, 2004).
Peter Arnett, *Live From the Battlefield* (New York: Simon & Schuster,1994).
Dale Van Atta with Melvin Laird, *With Honor* (Madison: University of Wisconsin Press, 2008).
Joan Baez, *Joan Baez: A Memoir and a Voice to Sing With* (New York: Simon and Schuster, 1987).
Milton J. Bates and Lawrence Lichty (eds.), *Reporting Vietnam: American Journalism, 1959–1975* (New York: Library of America, 1998)
Nguyen Thi Binh, *Family, Friends, and Country Autobiography* (Unpublished English translation shared with the author).
Fred Branfman, *Voices from the Plain of Jars* (New York: Harper Colophon, 1972).
Douglas Brinkley and Luke A. Nichter (eds.), *The Nixon Tapes. 1971–72* (Boston: Houghton Mifflin, 2014).
Douglas Brinkley and Luke A. Nichter (eds.), *The Nixon Tapes, 1973* (Boston: Houghton Mifflin, 2015).
Patrick Buchanan, *Nixon's White House Wars* (New York: Crown, 2017).
William P. Bundy, *Tangled Web: the Making of Foreign Policy in the Nixon Presidency* (New York: I. B. Tauris, 1998).

William Burr (ed.), *The Kissinger Transcripts: the Top Secret Talks With Beijing and Moscow* (New York: New Press,1998).

Citizens Commission of Inquiry, *The Dellums Committee Hearings on War Crimes in Vietnam: An Inquiry into Command Responsibility in Southeast Asia* (New York: Vantage, 1972).

Clark Clifford and Richard Holbrooke, *Counsel to the President: A Memoir* (New York: Random House, 1991)

John Dean, *The Nixon Defense* (New York: Penguin, 2014).

Anatoly Dobrynin, *In Confidence: Moscow's Ambassador to America's Six Presidents* (New York: Times Books, 1995.)

Richard Dudman, *40 Days with the Enemy* (New York Liveright, 1971).

Bernard Edelman (ed.), *Dear America: Letters Home From Vietnam* (New York: W. W. Norton, 1985).

W. D. Ehrhart, *Passing Time: Memoir of a Vietnam Veteran Against the War* (Boston: University of Massachusetts, 1986).

John Ehrlichman, *Witness to Power: The Nixon Years* (New York: Simon and Schuster, 1982).

Duong Mai Elliot, *The Sacred Willow: Four Generations in the Life of a Vietnamese Family* (New York: Oxford University Press, 1999).

Daniel Ellsberg, *Secrets: A Memoir of Vietnam and the Pentagon Papers* (New York: Viking. 2002).

Robert M. Gates, *From the Shadows: The Insider's Story of Five Presidents and How They Won in the Cold War* (New York: Simon and Schuster, 1996).

David H. Hackworth and Eilhys England, *Steel My Soldiers' Hearts* (New York: Touchstone, 2003).

Alexander Haig, *Inner Circles: How America Changed the World: A Memoir* (New York: Grand Central Publishers, 1992).

H. R. Haldeman, *The Haldeman Diaries: Inside the Nixon White House* (New York: Putnam, 1994).

H. R. Haldeman with Joseph DiMona, *The Ends of Power* (London: WH. Allen, 1973).

Tom Hayden, *Reunion: A Memoir* (New York: Random House, 1988).

Richard Helms with William Hood, *A Look Over My Shoulder: A Life in the Central Intelligence Agency* (New York: Random House, 2003).

Michael Herr, *Dispatches* (New York: Vintage 1991).

Seymour M. Hersh, *Reporter: A Memoir* (New York: Alfred F.Knopf, 2018).

U. Alexis Johnson with Jeff Olivarious Oliver, *The Right-Hand of Power: The Memoirs of an American Diplomat* (Englewood Cliffs, NJ: Prentice-Hall, 1984).

John Kerry and the Vietnam Veterans Against the War, *The New Soldier* (New York: Collier Books, 1971).

Jeffrey Kimball, *The Vietnam War Files: Uncovering the Secret History of Nixon-Era Strategy* (Lawrence: University Press of Kansas, 2004).

Henry Kissinger, *Ending the Vietnam War: A History of America's Involvement and Extrication from the Vietnam War* (New York: Simon & Schuster, 2003).

Henry Kissinger, *White House Years* (Boston: Little Brown, 1979).

Ron Kovic, *Born on the Fourth of July* (New York: Akashic Books, 1976).

Stanley Kutler (ed.), *Abuse of Power: The New Nixon Tapes* (New York: Simon and Schuster, 1997).

Luu Van Loi and Nguyen Anh Vu, *Le Duc Tho–Kissinger Negotiations in Paris* (Hanoi: The Gioi Publishers, 1995).

George McGovern, *Grassroots: The Autobiography of George McGovern* (New York: Random House, 1977).

Richard Nixon, *RN: The Memoirs of Richard Nixon* (New York: Viking, 1979).

William Safire, *Before the Fall: An Inside View of the Pre-Watergate White House* (New York: Belmont Towers Books, 1975).

Al Santoli, *Everything We Had: An Oral History of the Vietnam War by 33 American Soldiers Who Fought It* (New York: Random House, 1993).

Lewis Sorley (ed.), *The Abrams Tapes, 1968–1972.* (Lubbock: Texas Tech University Press, 2004).

Gerard Smith, *Double-Talk: The Story of the First Strategic Arms Limitation Talks.* (Garden City: Doubleday, 1980).

Richard Stacewicz, *Winter Soldiers: An Oral History of Vietnam Veterans Against the War* (New York: Twayne, 1997).

Truong Nhu Tang, David Chanoff, and Doan Van Toai, *A Viet Cong Memoir: An Inside Account of the Vietnam War and its Aftermath* (New York: Vintage, 1985).

Dang Thuy Tram, *Last Night I Dreamed of Peace* (New York: Three Rivers Press, 2017).

Michael Uhl, *Vietnam Awakening* (North Carolina: McFarland, 2007).

Vietnam Veterans Against the War, *Winter Soldier Investigation* (Boston: Beacon Press, 1971).

Keuth Walker, *A Piece of My Heart: The Stories of 26 American Women Who Served in Vietnam* (Novato, CA, Presidio Press, 1985).

Roger Warner, *Backfire: The CIA's Secret War in Laos and Its Link to the War in Vietnam* (New York: Simon and Schuster,1995).

Odd Arne Westad et.al. (eds.), *77 Conversations Between Chinese and Foreign Leaders on the Wars in Indochina, 1964–1977,* Cold War International History Project, Working Paper No. 22 (Washington DC: Woodrow Wilson Center for International Scholars, 1998).

Ron Young, *Crossing Boundaries in the Americas, Vietnam and the Middle East* (Eugene, OR: Resource Publications, 2014).

Elmo R, Zumwalt, *On Watch: A Memoir* (Chicago: Quadrangle, 1976).

Books

Stephen E. Ambrose, *Nixon: The Triumph of a Politician, 1962–1972* (New York: Simon and Schuster, 1989).

Terry H. Anderson, *The Movement and the Sixties: Protest in America from Greensboro to Wounded Knee* (New York: Oxford University Press, 1995).

Dale Andrade, *Ashes to Ashes: the Phoenix Program and the Vietnam War* (Lexington, MA: Lexington Books,1990).

Christian Appy, *Working Class War: American Combat Soldiers in Vietnam* (Chapel Hill: University of North Carolina Press, 1993).

Christian Appy, *The Reckoning: the Vietnam War and Our National Identity* (New York: Viking Press, 2015).

Pierre Asselin, *A Bitter Peace: Washington, Hanoi and the Making of the Paris Agreement* (Chapel Hill: University of North Carolina Press, 2002).

Pierre Asselin, *Vietnam's American War: A History* (New York: Cambridge University Press, 2018).

Richard Barnet, *The Roots of War.* (Baltimore: Penguin,1971).

Gary J. Bass, *The Blood Telegram* (New York: Alfred A. Knopf, 2018).

Larry Berman, *No Peace,vNo Honor: Nixon, Kissinger and Betrayal in Vietnam* (New York: Free Press, 2001.)

Larry Berman, *The Perfect Spy: The Incredible Double Life of Pham Xuan An* (New York: Smithsonian Books/Collins, 2007).

Michael Bilton and Kevin Sim, *Four Hours in My Lai* (New York: Penguin, 1992).

Robert K. Brigham, *Reckless: Henry Kissinger and the Tragedy of Vietnam* (New York: Public Affairs, 2018).

Robert K. Brigham, *Guerilla Diplomacy: The NLF's Foreign Relations and the Vietnam War* (Ithaca: Cornell University Press, 1999).

Patrick J. Buchanan, *The Greatest Comeback* (New York: Crown Forum, 2013).

William Burr and Jeffrey P. Kimball, *Nixon's Nuclear Specter: The Secret Alert of 1969, Madman Diplomacy and the Vietnam War* (Lawrence: University Press of Kansas, 2015).

David Callahan, *Dangerous Capabilities: Paul Nitze and the Cold War* (New York: Harper Collins, 1991).

Lewis Chester, Godfrey Hodgson, and Bruce Page, *An American Melodrama: The Presidential Campaign of 1968* (New York: Viking Press, 1969).

Denise Chong, *The Girl in the Picture* (New York: Simon and Schuster, 1999).

Mark Clodfelter, *The Limits of Air Power The American Bombing of North Vietnam* (New York: Free Press, 1969).

David Corn, *Blond Ghost: Ted Shackley and the CIA's Crusades* (New York: Simon and Schuster, 1994).

David Cortright, *Soldiers in Revolt: The American Military Today* (Garden City: Doubleday, 1975).

Cecil Barr Currey, *Long Binh Jail: An Oral History of Vietnam's Notorious U.S. Military Prison*, (Washington DC: Brassy's, 1999).

Greg Daddis, *Withdrawal: Reassessing America's Final Years in Vietnam* (New York: Oxford University Press, 2017).

Charles DeBenedetti with Charles Chatfield, *An American Ordeal: The Antiwar Movement of the Vietnam Era* (Syracuse, NY: Syracus University Press: 1990).

Robert Dallek, *Nixon and Kissinger: Partners in Power* (New York: Harper Collins, 2007).

Philip B. Davidson, *Vietnam at War: The History 1946–75.* (New York: Oxford University Press, 1988).

Mario del Pero, *The Eccentric Realist: Henry Kissinger and the Shaping of American Foreign Policy* (Ithaca: Cornell University Press, 2010).

David W. P. Elliott, *The Vietnamese War: Revolution and Social Change in the Mekong Delta, 1930–75.* (Armonk, NY: M. E. Sharpe, 2007).

Gloria Emerson, *Winners and Losers* (New York: W. W. Norton, 1972).

Fred Emery, *Watergate* (New York: Times Books, 2006).

David Farber, *Chicago '68* (Chicago: University of Chicago Press, 1988).

John A. Farrell, *Richard Nixon* (New York: Harper Collins, 2007).

Ilya Gaiduk, *The Soviet Union and the Vietnam War* (Chicago: Ivan R. Dee, 1996).

Lloyd C. Gardner, *The Great Nixon Turnabout* (New York: New Viewpoints, 1973).

Lloyd C. Gardner, *Pay Any Price: Lyndon Johnson and the Wars for Vietnam* (Chicago: Ivan R. Dee, 1995).

Raymond L. Garthoff, *Détente and Confrontation: American–Soviet Relations from Nixon to Reagan,* Rev. ed. (Washington DC: Brookings Institution, 1994).
William Gibson, *The Perfect War: the War We Couldn't Lose and How We Did* (NY: Vintage Books, 1986). xxx
Todd Gitlin, *The Sixties: Years of Protest, Days of Rage* (New York: Bantam, 1987).
Greg Grandin, *Kissinger's Shadow* (New York: Metropolitan Books, 2015).
David Greenberg, *Nixon's Shadow: The History of an Image* (New York: W. W. Norton, 2003).
David Halberstam, *The Best and the Brightest* (New York: Random House, 1972).
Jussi Hanhimaki, *The Flawed Architect: Henry Kissinger and American Foreign Policy.* (New York: Oxford University Press, 2004).
Jussi Hanhimaki, *The Rise and Fall of Détente, American Foreign Policy and the Transformation of the Cold War* (Washington DC: Potomac Books, 2013).
Daniel Hallin, *The "Uncensored War": The Media and Vietnam* (New York: Oxford University Press, 1986).
Max Hastings, *Vietnam: An Epic Tragedy, 1945–1975* (New York: Harper-Collins, 2018).
Tom Hayden, *Hell No! The Forgotten Power of the Vietnam Peace Movement* (New Haven: Yale University Press, 2017).
Kenneth J. Heineman, *Campus Wars: The Peace Movement at American State Universities in the Vietnam Era* (New York: New York University Press, 1993).
Mary Hershberger, *Traveling to Vietnam: American Peace Activists and the War* (Syracuse, NY: Syracuse University Press, 1998).
George C. Herring, *America's Longest War: The United States and Vietnam, 1950–75* (New York: Alfred A. Knopf, 1979).
Seymour M. Hersh, *The Price of Power: Kissinger in the Nixon White House.* (New York: Summit Books, 1983).
Gary R. Hess, *Vietnam: Explaining America's Lost War* (Malden, Ma: Blackwell, 2009).
Christopher Hitchens, *The Trial of Henry Kissinger* (New York: Verso Press, 2001).
Joan Hoff, *Nixon Reconsidered* (New York: Basic Books, 2006).
Kenneth Hughes, *Chasing Shadows: The Nixon Tapes, the Chennault Affair, and the Origins of Watergate* (Charlottesville: University of Virginia Press, 2015).
Kenneth Hughes, *Fatal Politics: The Nixon Tapes, the Vietnam Wars and the Casualties of Re-Election* (Charlottesville: University of Virginia Press, 2015).
Andrew E. Hunt, *The Turning: A History of Vietnam Veterans Against the War* (New York: New York University Press, 1999).
Nguyen Tien Hung and Jerrold L. Schecter, *The Palace File: The Remarkable Story of the Secret Letters from Nixon and Ford to the President of South Vietnam* (New York: Harper and Row, 1986).
Arnold R. Issacs, *Without Honor: Defeat in Vietnam and Cambodia* (Baltimore: Johns Hopkins University Press, 1983).
Arnold R. Isaacs, *Vietnam Shadows The War, Its Ghosts, and its Legacy* (Baltimore: Johns Hopkins Press, 1997).
Walter Isaacson, *Kissinger* (New York: Simon and Schuster, 1972).
Walter Isaacson and Evan Thomas, *The Wise Men: Six Friends and the World They Made* (New York: Simon and Schuster, 2013).
Maurice Isserman and Michael Kazin, *America Divided: The Civil War of the 1960s* (New York: Oxford University Press, 2015).

Chen Jian, *Mao's China and the Cold War* (Chapel Hill: University of North Carolina Press, 2001)

Andrew L. Johns, *Vietnam's Second Front: Domestic Politics, the Republican Party and the War* (Lexington: The University Press of Kentucky, 2010).

Greg Jones, *Last Stand at Khe Sanh,* (Boston: DeCapo Press, 2014).

Marvin and Bernard Kalb, *Kissinger* (New York: Dell, 1975).

Henry Kamm, *Cambodia: Report from a Stricken Land* (New York: Arcade Publishing, 1998).

Stanley Karnow, *Vietnam: A History* (New York: Viking, 1983).

Jeffrey Kimball, *Nixon's Vietnam War* (Lawrence: University of Kansas Press, 1998).

Henry Kissinger, *Nuclear Weapons and Foreign Policy* (New York: Harper Bros., 1957).

Gabriel Kolko, *Anatomy of a War: Vietnam, the United States and the Modern Historical Experience* (New York: Pantheon Books 1985).

James Simon Kunen, *Standard Operating Procedure: Notes of a Draft Age American* (New York: Avon, 1973).

Mark Kurlansky, *1968: The Year That Rocked the World* (New York: Penguin Random House, 2005).

Joshua Kurlantzick, *A Great Place to Have a War* (New York: Simon & Schuster, 2016).

Stanley I. Kutler, *The Wars of Watergate* (New York: W. W. Norton,1990).

Penny Lewis, *Hardhats, Hippies and Hawks: the Vietnam Antiwar Movement as Myth and Memory* (Ithaca, NY: Cornell University Press 2013).

Michael Lind, *Vietnam, the Necessary War: A Reinterpretation of America's Most Disastrous Military Conflict* (New York: Free Press, 1999).

Frederik Logevall, *Choosing War: The Last Chance for Peace and the Escalation of War in Vietnam* (Berkeley: University of California Press, 1999).

Frederik Logevall and Andrew Preston (eds.), *Nixon in the World: American Foreign Relations, 1969–1977* (New York: Oxford University Press, 2008).

Kyle Longley, *Grunts: The American Combat Soldiers in Vietnam* (Armonk, NY: M. E. Sharpe, 1984).

Margaret MacMillan, *Nixon and Mao: The Week That Changed the World* (New York: Random House, 2007).

Norman Mailer, *Armies of the Night* (New York: New American Library, 1968).

Norman Mailer, *Miami and the Siege of Chicago* (New York: New York Review of Books, 1968).

James Mann, *About Face* (New York: Vintage Books, 1998).

James A. Michener, *Kent State: What Happened and Why* (New York: Random House 1971).

Robert Miraldi, *Seymour Hersh, Scoop Artist* (Nebraska: Potomac Books, 2013).

Roger Morris, *Haig: The General's Progress* (Playboy Press, 1982).

Roger Morris, *Uncertain Greatness* (New York: Harper & Row, 1977)

Roger Morris, *Haig: The General's Progress* (New York: Playboy Press, 1982)

Bruce Miroff, *The Liberal Moment* (Lawrence: University Press of Kansas, 2007)

Richard A. Moss, *Nixon's Back Channel to Moscow, Confidential Diplomacy and Détente* (Lexington: University Press of Kentucky, 2017).

Richard Moser, *The New Winter Soldiers: GI and Veteran Dissent During the Vietnam Era* (New Brunswick, NJ: Rutgers University Press, 1996).

Mark Moyar, *Triumph Forsaken: The Vietnam War,* (Cambridge: Cambridge University Press, 2006).

Deborah Nelson, *The War Behind Me* (New York: Basic Books, 2008).
Keith L. Nelson, *The Making of Détente* (Baltimore: Johns Hopkins Press, 1995).
Gerald Nicosia, *Home to War: A History of a Vietnam Veterans Protest Movement* (New York: Crown 2001).
Lien-Hang T. Nguyen, *Hanoi's War: An International History of the War for Peace in Vietnam* (Chapel Hill: University of North Caroline Press, 2012).
Bao Ninh, *The Sorrow of War: A Novel of South Vietnam* (New York: Riverhead Books, 1991).
Keith Nolan, *Battle for Hue: Tet 1968* (Novato, CA: Presidio Press, 1996).
Arnold A. Offner, *Hubert Humphrey: The Conscience of the Country* (New Haven: Yale University Press, 2018).
James S. Olson and Randy Roberts, *Where the Domino Fell: America and Vietnam, 1945–2004* (NY: Brandywine Press, 2004).
Stewart O'Nan (ed.), *The Vietnam Reader* (New York: Anchor Books, 1998).
Bruce Palmer Jr., *The 25-Year War: America's Military Role in Vietnam* (Lexington: University Press of Kentucky, 1984).
Laura Palmer, *Shrapnel in the Heart: Letters and Remembrances from the Vietnam Veterans Memorial* (New York: Vintage, 1987).
David L. Parsons, *Dangerous Grounds: Antiwar Coffee Houses and Military Dissent in the Vietnam Era* (Chapel Hill: University of North Carolina Press, 2017).
James Patterson, *Grand Expectations* (New York: Oxford University Press, 1996).
Mark Pavlick with Caroline Luft (eds.), *The United States, Southeast Asia, and Historical Memory* (Chicago: Haymarket Books, 2019).
Rick Pearlstein, *Nixonland: The Rise of a President and the Fracturing of America* (New York: Simon and Schuster, 2010).
Gareth Porter, *A Peace Denied: The United States, Vietnam and the Paris Peace Agreement* (Bloomington: Indiana University Press, 1975).
John Prados, *Lost Crusader: The Secret Wars of CIA Director William Colby* (New York: Oxford University Press, 2003).
John Prados, *President's Secret Wars* (Chicago: Ivan R. Dee, 1996).
John Prados, *Vietnam: The History of an Unwinnable War, 1945–75* (Lawrence: University of Kansas Press, 2009).
Merle Pribbenow, *Victory in Vietnam: The Official History of the People's Army of Vietnam, 1954–75* (Lawrence: University Press of Kansas, 2002).
Stephen Randolph, *Powerful and Brutal Weapons: Nixon, Kissinger and the Easter Offensive* (Cambridge: Harvard University Press, 2007).
Richard Reeves, *President Nixon Alone in the White House* (New York: Simon and Schuster, 2001).
James Rosen, *The Strong Man: John Mitchell and the Secrets of Watergate* (New York: Random House, 2008).
David Rudenstein, *The Day the Presses Stopped: A History of the Pentagon Papers Case* (Berkeley: University of California Press, 1996).
Kirkpatrick Sale, *SDS* (New York: Vintage, 1974).
Harrison E. Salisbury, *Without Fear or Favor: An Uncompromising Look at the New York Times* (New York: Random House, 1980).
David Schmitz, *Richard Nixon and the Vietnam War* (Lanham, MD: Rowman and Littlefield, 2014).

Jonathan Schell, *The Real War: The Classic Reporting on the Vietnam War* (New York: Pantheon, 1988).

Robert D. Schulzinger, *A Time for War: The United States and Vietnam, 1941–1975* (New York: Oxford University Press, 1997).

Robert D. Schulzinger, *Henry Kissinger: Doctor of Diplomacy* (New York: Columbia University Press, 1989).

Franz Schurmann, *The Logic of World Power* (New York: Pantheon, 1974).

William Shawcross, *Sideshow: Kissinger, Nixon and the Destruction of Cambodia* (New York: Simon and Schuster, 1979).

Neil Sheehan, *A Bright Shining Lie: John Paul Vann and America in Vietnam* (New York: Random House, 1988).

Michael S. Sherry, *In the Shadow of War: The United States Since the 1930s* (New Haven: Yale University Press, 1995)

Wiliam J. Shkurti, *Soldiering on in a Dying War: The True Story of Firebase Pace Incidents and the Vietnam Drawdown* (Lawrence: University of Kansas Press, 2011).

Asaf Siniver, *Nixon, Kissinger, and U.S. Foreign Policy Making: The Machinery of Crisis* (New York: Cambridge University Press, 2008).

Melvin Small, *The Antiwarriors: The Vietnam War and the Battle for America's Hearts and Minds* (Maryland: Scholarly Resources Inc., 2004).

Melvin Small and William D, Hoover (eds.), *Give Peace a Chance: Exploring the Antiwar Movement* (Syracuse, NY: Syracuse University Press, 1992).

Melvin Small, *Johnson, Nixon and the Doves* (New Brunswick, NJ: Rutgers University Press, 1988).

Melvin Small, *The Presidency of Richard Nixon* (Lawrence: University Press of Kansas, 1999).

Lewis Sorley, *A Better War: The Unexamined Victories and Final Tragedy of America's Last Year in Vietnam* (New York: Harcourt Brace, 1999).

Ronald H. Spector, *After Tet: the Bloodiest Year in Vietnam* (New York, The Free Press, 1993)

Shelby S. Stanton, *The Rise and Fall of an American Army: U.S. Ground Forces in Vietnam, 1954–73* (Novato, California: Presidio Press, 1985).

Jeremy Suri, *Henry Kissinger and the American Century* (Cambridge: Harvard University Press, 2007).

Evan Thomas, *Being Nixon: A Man Divided* (New York: Random House, 2015).

Nancy Bernkopf Tucker, *Taiwan, Hong Kong, and the United States, 1945–1992* (New York: Twayne Publishers, 1995).

Chris Tudda, *A Cold War Turning Point: Nixon and China, 1969–72* (Baton Rouge: University of Louisiana Press, 2012).

William A. Turley, *The Second Indochina War: A Concise Political and Military History* (Lanham, MD: Rowman and Littlefield, 2009).

Nick Turse, *Kill Anything that Moves: The Real American War in Vietnam* (New York: Picador, 2013).

Douglas Valentine, *The Phoenix Program* (New York: Avon, 1990).

Gregory L. Vistica, *The Education of Lieutenant Kerrey* (New York: Thomas Dunne Books, 2003).

Tuong Vu, *Vietnam's Communist Revolution: The Power and Limits of Ideology* (New York: Cambridge University Press, 2017).

Larry G. Waterhouse and Marianne G. Wizard, *Turning the Guns Around: Notes on the GI Movement* (New York: Delta, 1972).

Tim Weiner, *One Man Against the World: The Tragedy of Richard Nixon* (New York: Henry Holt, 2015).

Tom Wells, *The War Within: America's Battle Over Vietnam* (Berkeley: University of California Press, 1994).

Odd Arne Westad, *The Global Cold War* (Cambridge: Cambridge University Press, 2007).

Theodore H. White, *Breach of Faith: The Fall of Richard Nixon* (New York: Atheneum Publishing, 1975).

Theodore H. White, *The Making of the President, 1968* (New York: Harper Perennial, 1969).

Theodore H. White, *The Making of the President, 1972* (New York: New American Library, 1973).

Tom Wicker, *One of US: Richard Nixon and the American Dream* (New York: Random House, 1991).

Jules Witcover, *The Resurrection of Richard Nixon* (New York: G. P. Putnam, 1970).

Jules Witcover, *The Year the Dream Died: Revisitng1968 in America,* (New York: Time-Warner, 1997).

Randall B. Woods (ed.), *Vietnam and the American Political Tradition: The Politics of Dissent* (NewYork: Cambridge University Press, 2003).

Bob Woodward and Carl Bernstein, *All the President's Men* (New York: Simon and Schuster, 1974).

James Wright, *Enduring Vietnam: An American Generation and Its War* (New York: St. Martin's Press, 2017).

Marilyn B. Young and Robert Buzzanco (eds.), *A Companion to the Vietnam War* (Malden, MA: Blackwell Publishers, 2002).

Marilyn B. Young, *The Vietnam Wars* (New York: Harper Collins, 1991).

Samuel Zaffiri, *Hamburger Hill: The Brutal Battle for Dong Ap Bia, May 1–20*, 1969 (New York: Presidio Press, 1988).

Nancy Zaroulis and Gerald Sullivan, *Who Spoke Up? American Protest Against the War in Vietnam, 1963–1975* (*New York:* Holt, Rinehart and Winston,1984).

Quang, *China and the Vietnam War, 1950–1975* (*Chapel Hill: University of North Carolina Press*, 2000).

Articles

Fred Branfman, "My Experience with Laos and the Indochina War," unpublished memoir. https://fredbranfman.wordpress.com/laos-automated-war-archive/

Fred Branfman, "A Visit to a Refugee Camp" *Liberation News Service,* July 3, 1970.

William Burr and Jeffrey Kimball "Nixon's Secret Nuclear Alert: Vietnam War Diplomacy and the Joint Chiefs of Staff Readiness Test," *Cold War History* 3, no.3 (2003): 113–156.

Clark Clifford, "Vietnam Reappraisal: The Personal History of One Man's View and How it Evolved," *Foreign Affairs* 47, no. 4 (July–August 1969): 601–622.

Henry Steele Commager, "Five Grounds for Impeaching the President," *New York Times,* June 28, 1974.

Jussi Hanhimaki, "Some More Smoking Guns: The Vietnam War and Kissinger's Summitry with Moscow and Beijing, 1971–73," *SHAFR Newsletter* 32, no. 4 (2001): 40–45.

Robert D. Heinl Jr., "The Collapse of the Armed Forces," *Armed Forces Journal,* (June 1971)

Ken Hughes, "Fatal Politics: Nixon's Political Timetable for Withdrawing From Vietnam," *Diplomatic History* 34, no. 3 (2010): 497–506.

Jeffrey Kimball, "Kissinger Gets It Wrong Again," http://www.niemanwatchdog.org/index.cfm?fuseaction=background.view&backgroundid=00189 (2012)

Jeffrey Kimball, "The Case of the 'Decent Interval': Do We Now Have a Smoking Gun?" *SHAFR Newsletter* 32, no. 3 (September 2001): 35–39.

Alfred W. McCoy, "America's Secret War in Laos," in Robert Buzzanco and Marilyn B. Young (eds.), *A Companion to the Vietnam War,* (Malden: Blackwell Publishers, 1988), 286–290.

David L. Prentice, "Choosing the Long Road: Henry Kissinger, Melvin Laird, Vietnamization and the War over Nixon's Vietnam Strategy," *Diplomatic History* 3, no.3 (June 2016): 445–447.

Interviews

United States (by phone and in person)

T. D. Allman, Journalist (September 2015)
Kevin Buckley, Journalist (July 2009)
Ron Canfora, Kent State student (March 2011)
Richard Dudman, Journalist (February 2012)
Howard Emmer, Kent State student (April 2010)
Jane Barton Griffith, co-director of Quang Ngai Province Rehabilitation Center (October 6, 2016)
Elizabeth Holtzman, Congresswoman, House Judiciary Committee\
John Isaacs, former Foreign Service
Melvin Laird, Secretary of Defense (August 20 and August 21, 2007)
John Negroponte, head of Vietnam Affairs, National Security Council (January 2018)
Chuck Paturick, Veteran, Hue (February 2016)
Elizabeth Pond, Journalist (February 23, 2012)
Donald Shanley, Veteran, Khe Sanh (January 2016)

Vietnam (partial list, in person)

In Hanoi (March 2009)

Pham Khac Lam—journalist during the war, editor of *Viet-My*
Trinh Ngoc Thai—member of DRV delegation in Paris Peace Talks
Mr.Ha Dang—PRG assistant to Xuan Thuy
Madame Nguyen Thi Binh—head of the PRG delegation in Paris Peace Talks, subsequently vice president of the government of Vietnam
Mr. Nguyen Dinh Uoc—former Director of Military Historical Academy
Mr. Ho Khang—Vietnamese Academy for Military History; Deputy Director of Institute of Military History
Lt. General Vu Xuan Vinh—former director of international relations department, Ministry of Defense; in charge of anti-aircraft defense of Hanoi 1972
Lt. Gen. Tran Hahn—former Chief of General Staff of Vietnamese People's Army and formerpPresident of Vietnam Veterans Association

In Quang Tri (March 2009)

Hoang Dang Mai—director of Department of Foreign Affairs, Vice President of Friendship Association

Troung Hong Tan—standing member of Quangtri Union of Friendship Organizations, former fighter for National Liberation Front

Mr. Hoang Anh Tuan—Deputy Foreign Minister of the PRG

Thai Huu Lieu—International Cooperation Section, Department of Foreign Affairs, Quang Tri

In Danang (March 2009)

Ha Phouc Mai—Museum of Danang

Nguyen Dinh An—chairman, Danang Union of Friendship Organizations

Nguyen Huu Son—Vice Director of VAVN Office

Truong Minh Tri—Director VAVN Office

Index

For the benefit of digital users, indexed terms that span two pages (e.g., 52–53) may, on occasion, appear on only one of those pages.